Oct -- 2020

Rick

CROATIA
& SLOVENIA

Rick Steves & Cameron Hewitt

CONTENTS

Croatia and Slovenia

To Budapest

HUNGARY

egerszeg · Keszthely · Lake Balaton · Kalocsa

M-7

ykanizsa · Letenye · Csurgó · Nagyatád · Kaposvár · MECSEK HILLS · Komló · Szekszárd · Baja · Subotica

rivnica · Gyékényes · Szigetvár · Pécs · Mohács

Bjelovar · Barcs · Sombor

Vicovitica · Drava R. · Osijek · **SERBIA**

CROATIA

SLAVONIA · Našice · Đakovo · Vukovar · Novi Sad

70 · Kutina · Vinkovci

ik · Požega · Nova Gradiška · Slavonski Brod · Žid

CONCENTRATION CAMP MEMORIAL · Jasenovac · Novska · Županja · To Belgrade

Brčko

Novi Grad · Prijedor · Banja Luka · Doboj · Bijelina · **SERBIA**

Tuzla

BOSNIA-HERZEGOVINA · Zavidovići · Zvornik

Drvar · Jajce · Travnik · Zenica · Srebrenica

DINARIC MTNS. · Visoko · Sarajevo

Knin · Livno · ▲Ivan Planina · Goražde

Perković · Konjic · Srbinje

DIOCLETIAN'S PALACE · Jablanica

gir✈ · Split · Neretva R. · Mostar

iovo · Omiš · Makarska · MEĐUGORJE✈ · Buna · Nevesinje

Solta · Brač · BOL · Drvenik · Počitelj · Gacko · **MONTE-NEGRO**

Stari Grad · Vrgorac · Čaplinja · Stolac

Hvar · Hvar · Ploče · Metković · Neum · Ljubinje · Bileća

is · Vis · Orebić · Pelješac Peninsula · Trebinje

iža · Vela Luka · Korčula · Korčula · Ston · Dubrovnik · Perast · Podgorica

Polače · Elaphite Islands · Herceg Novi · Kotor · Cetinje

Pomena · Sobra · Mljet · Lokrum · Cavtat · Čilipi · Bay of Kotor

Lastovo · To Bari, Italy · Budva · Sveti Stefan

DALMATIAN COAST

Dubrovnik

SIGHTS

1. Bell Tower
2. Buža Gate
3. Cable Car
4. Cathedral
5. Church of St. Savior
6. City Wall Entrances (3)
7. Dominican Monastery Museum & Church
8. Fort of St. Lawrence
9. Foundry Museum
10. Franciscan Monastery Museum & Church
11. Jesuit St. Ignatius' Church
12. Lazareti (Old Quarantine Building)
13. Luža Square & Orlando's Column
14. Maritime Museum & Aquarium
15. Minčeta Tower
16. Old Port
17. Pile Gate
18. Ploče Gate
19. Rector's Palace
20. To Red History Muse
21. Rupe Granary & Ethnographic Museu
22. Serbian Orthodox Church & Icon Museu
23. Sponza Palace & Memorial Room of Dubrovnik Defenders
24. St. Blaise's Church
25. Stradun (a.k.a. Placa
26. Synagogue Museum
27. War Photo Limited

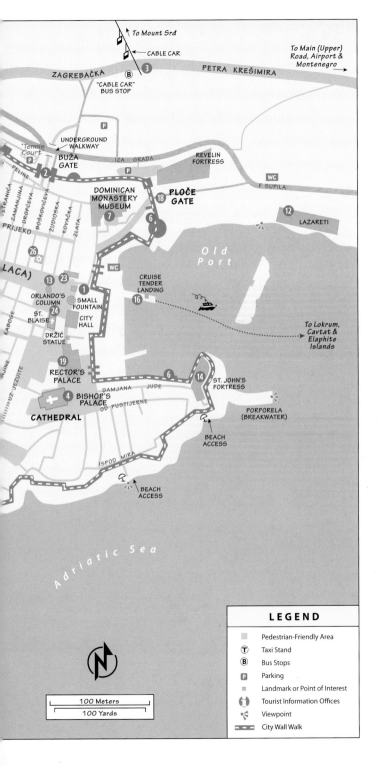

To Mount Srd

CABLE CAR

To Main (Upper)
Road, Airport &
Montenegro

ZAGREBAČKA   **B**   **3**   PETRA KREŠIMIRA

"CABLE CAR"
BUS STOP

P

UNDERGROUND
WALKWAY

IZA GRADA   REVELIN
FORTRESS

"Tennis
Court"

P   PELINE

BUŽA GATE

P

WC

STRANIĆA
ZAMANJINA
DROPČEVA
BOŠKOVIĆEVA
ŽUDIOSKA
KOVAČKA
ZLATA

DOMINICAN
MONASTERY
MUSEUM
7

18 PLOČE GATE

F. SUPILA

PRIJEKO

6

12

LAZARETI

26

Old
Port

LACA)

13   **23**

WC

CRUISE
TENDER
LANDING

1

ORLANDO'S
COLUMN

SMALL
FOUNTAIN

16

ST. BLAISE
24

CITY
HALL

To Lokrum,
Cavtat &
Elaphite
Islands

DRŽIĆ
STATUE

KABOGE

19

RECTOR'S
PALACE

DAMJANA JUDE

6

14

ST. JOHN'S
FORTRESS

UZ JEZUITE

4

BISHOP'S
PALACE

OD PUSTIJERNE

PORPORELA
(BREAKWATER)

UNJINE

CATHEDRAL

BEACH
ACCESS

ISPOD MIRA

BEACH
ACCESS

Adriatic Sea

N

100 Meters

100 Yards

LEGEND

-   Pedestrian-Friendly Area
- **T**   Taxi Stand
- **B**   Bus Stops
- **P**   Parking
-   Landmark or Point of Interest
- **†**   Tourist Information Offices
-   Viewpoint
-   City Wall Walk

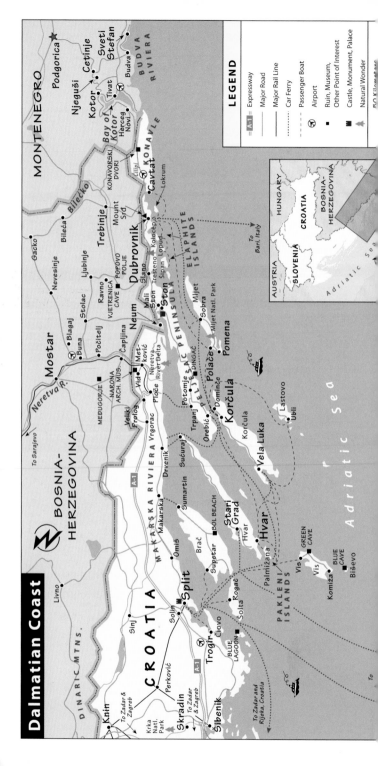

Dalmatian Coast

Rick Steves.

CROATIA
& SLOVENIA

Welcome to Rick Steves' Europe

Travel is intensified living—maximum thrills per minute and one of the last great sources of legal adventure. Travel is freedom. It's recess, and we need it.

I discovered a passion for European travel as a teen and have been sharing it ever since—through my tours, public television and radio shows, and travel guidebooks. Over the years, I've taught millions of travelers how to best enjoy Europe's blockbuster sights—and experience "Back Door" discoveries that most tourists miss.

Written with my talented co-author, Cameron Hewitt, this book offers you a balanced mix of Croatia and Slovenia's lively cities and cozy towns, from mountaintop hikes and Adriatic cruises to thought-provoking museums and sky-high driving tours. It's selective: Rather than listing dozens of island getaways, we recommend only the best ones. And it's in-depth: Our self-guided museum tours and city walks provide insight into the region's vibrant history and today's living, breathing culture.

We advocate traveling simply and smartly. Take advantage of our money- and time-saving tips on sightseeing, transportation, and more. Try local, characteristic alternatives to expensive hotels and restaurants. In many ways, spending more money only builds a thicker wall between you and what you traveled so far to see.

We visit Croatia and Slovenia to experience it—to become temporary locals. Thoughtful travel engages us with the world, as we learn to appreciate other cultures and new ways to measure quality of life.

Judging by the positive feedback we receive from our readers, this book will help you enjoy a fun, affordable, and rewarding vacation—whether it's your first trip or your tenth.

Sretan put! Happy travels!

Rick Steves

INTRODUCTION

Set sail on the shimmering Adriatic for a remote island whose name you can't pronounce but whose wonders you'll never forget. Corkscrew your way up impossibly twisty mountain roads to panoramic vistas of cut-glass peaks. Lie on a beach in the hot sun, listening to the lapping waves as a Venetian-style bell tower clangs out the hour. Ponder the fading scars of the Yugoslav Wars, and admire how skillfully the locals have revitalized their once-troubled region. Dine on a seafood feast and sip a glass of local wine as you watch the sunset dip into the watery horizon. Unfamiliar as they might seem, Croatia and Slovenia have what you've been looking for: some of Europe's most spectacular natural wonders, a fascinating recent history, and a spirit of adventure.

Here in the land where the Adriatic meets the Alps, there are countless ways to have fun. Begin your adventure by flipping through this book, which covers Croatia's and Slovenia's best big-city, small-town, and back-to-nature destinations. You'll get all the specifics and opinions necessary to wring the maximum value out of your limited time and money. If you're planning a trip of a month or less, this book is all you need.

Croatia and Slovenia were once part of the union called Yugoslavia. But today, that feels like ancient history, as each country is proudly independent. Carefree Croatia, with its long and enticing coastline, beckons vacationers with dramatically scenic terrain, romantic old towns, sunshine-bathed pebbly beaches, and an irrepressible seafaring spirit. Perky Slovenia surprises travelers with its tidy quaintness, breathtaking mountainscapes, colorful towns, and exceptionally friendly natives. And for good measure, I've also included detours into two other parts of the former Yugoslavia, each one offering a striking contrast to Croatia or Slovenia: the craggy

INTRODUCTION

Top Destinations in Croatia & Slovenia

coast of Montenegro, and a pair of diverse and fascinating Bosnian cities—bite-sized Mostar and bustling Sarajevo.

Experiencing Europe's culture, people, and natural wonders economically and hassle-free has been my goal for much of my life of traveling, tour guiding, and writing. With this book, I pass on to you all the lessons I've learned, painstakingly updated—in person—for this edition.

Rick Steves Croatia & Slovenia covers the predictable biggies and adds a healthy dose of "Back Door" intimacy. Along with strolling the walls around Dubrovnik's peerless Old Town, you'll poke your way into a hidden little tavern clinging like a barnacle over the sea. I've been selective, including only the top destinations and sights. For example, Croatia has over a thousand islands. But why not focus on the very best? That's Korčula, Hvar, and Mljet.

The best is, of course, only my opinion. But after spending my adult life researching Europe, I've developed a sixth sense for what travelers enjoy. Just thinking about the places featured in this book makes me want to sing *klapa* music.

Planning Your Trip

This section will help you get started planning your trip—with advice on trip costs, when to go, and what you should know before you take off.

TRIP COSTS

Traveling in Croatia and Slovenia costs about on par with the European average, or perhaps a bit cheaper. If you're careful to avoid inflated tourist-trap prices (by following my tips on where to stay and where to eat), a trip to this region can be a great value. If you detour into Bosnia-Herzegovina, you'll find prices substantially lower (though Montenegro is, if anything, pricier than Croatia and Slovenia).

Five components make up your trip costs: airfare to Europe, transportation in Europe, room and board, sightseeing and entertainment, and shopping and miscellany.

Airfare to Europe: A basic round-trip flight from the US to Ljubljana or Dubrovnik can cost $900-1,500, depending on where you fly from and when (cheaper in winter). Consider saving time and money in Europe by flying into one city and out of another; for instance, flying into Ljubljana and out of Dubrovnik often saves the extra cost (not to mention wasted time) of a 12-hour overland return trip to Ljubljana.

Transportation in Europe: For the two-week whirlwind trip described in this chapter, allow $150 per person for public transportation (train, bus, and boat tickets). Train travelers will probably save money by simply buying tickets along the way, rather than purchasing a rail pass (see "Transportation," in the Practicalities chapter). If you plan to rent a car, allow at least $250 per week, not including tolls, gas, and supplemental insurance. If you need the car for three weeks or more, leasing can save you money on insurance and taxes. Exorbitant fees for dropping off in a different country can make renting a car prohibitively expensive if you're going to both Croatia and Slovenia (for strategies to avoid this headache, see "Renting a Car," in the Practicalities chapter). A short flight can be cheaper than the train (check Skyscanner.com for intra-European flights).

Room and Board: You can thrive in Croatia and Slovenia on $100 a day per person for room and board (much less in Bosnia-Herzegovina). This allows $15 for lunch, $25 for dinner, and $60 for lodging (based on two people splitting the cost of a $120 double room that includes breakfast). Students and tightwads can eat and sleep for as little as $50 a day ($30 per hostel bed, $20 for groceries and snacks).

Sightseeing and Entertainment: Sightseeing is cheap here.

Croatia & Slovenia at a Glance

Croatia

▲▲**Zagreb** Croatia's underrated capital city, with interesting museums (the best feature Naive Art and broken relationships), lush parks, and a lively urban bustle.

▲▲▲**Plitvice Lakes National Park** Arguably Europe's most breathtaking natural wonder: a forested canyon filled with crystal-clear lakes, stunning waterfalls, and easy-to-hike boardwalks and trails.

▲▲**Istria** Croatia's most Italian-feeling corner, with the romantic, Venetian-flavored coastal town of Rovinj; top Roman ruins in the city of Pula; and a rolling interior of vineyards and picturesque hill towns (including Motovun). Nearby are the genteel Habsburg resort of Opatija and the port city of Rijeka.

▲▲**Split** Unofficial capital city and transit hub of the Dalmatian Coast, with a bustling urban vibe, people-filled seaside promenade, and lived-in warren of twisting lanes sprouting out of a massive Roman palace, plus the nearby town of Trogir and the waterfalls of Krka National Park.

▲▲**Hvar** Ritzy island and Old Town known for its jet-set appeal, high prices, rugged interior, seductively relaxing beaches, and easy escapes to nearby islets.

▲▲**Korčula** Low-key island and walled peninsular Old Town with a fjord-like backdrop, a lush islandscape, a fish-skeleton street plan, and quirky, offbeat museums.

▲▲▲**Dubrovnik** The "Pearl of the Adriatic": a giant walled Old Town with a scenic wall walk, tons of crowds, great beaches, modest but engaging museums, a stunning mountaintop viewpoint, an epic past and difficult but inspiring recent history, and a well-earned reputation as Croatia's single best destination.

Near Dubrovnik Boat excursions from Dubrovnik's Old Port, the art-packed resort village of Cavtat, the nearby Trsteno Arboretum, the walled town of Ston, the vineyard-draped Pelješac Peninsula, and the giant national park at Mljet Island.

Bosnia-Herzegovina

▲▲**Mostar** An easy taste of Bosnia-Herzegovina, with a striking setting, vivid Muslim culture, old Turkish architecture, evocative war damage, and an inspiring, rebuilt Old Bridge; plus nearby sights: scenic gorge house at Blagaj, hill town of Počitelj, Roman ruins near Metković, workaday burg of Stolac, and Catholic pilgrimage site of Međugorje.

▲▲▲**Sarajevo** Formerly war-torn, now rejuvenated Bosnian capital, with a fascinating layered history and a spectacular mountain-valley setting.

Montenegro
▲▲**The Bay of Kotor** Steep bay with fjord-like inlets, visit-worthy towns and sights, and the remarkably fortified Old Town of Kotor.

The Montenegrin Interior Rugged mountain road leading up the cliffs into the Montenegrin heartland, ending at the historic capital of Cetinje.

The Budva Riviera Glitzy, emerging beach-resort zone with a mix of cheap and luxury resort hotels.

Slovenia
▲▲**Ljubljana** Slovenia's vibrant yet relaxing capital, with a fun-to-browse riverside market, scintillating architecture, and inviting riverside promenade.

▲▲▲**Lake Bled** Photogenic lake resort huddled in the foothills of the Julian Alps, with a church-topped island, cliff-hanging castle, lakefront walkway, tasty desserts, and appealing side-trips.

▲▲**The Julian Alps** Cut-glass peaks easily conquered by a twisty and scenic mountain road over the Vršič Pass, ending in the tranquil Soča River Valley, with the fine WWI museum in Kobarid.

▲**Logarska Dolina and the Northern Valleys** Remote mountain valleys with grand vistas and traditional farming lifestyles.

Ptuj and Maribor In Ptuj, a charming-if-sleepy historic town topped by a castle; and Maribor, Slovenia's "second city."

▲**The Karst** Windblown limestone plateau with world-class caves (Škocjan and Postojna), the Lipizzaner Stallion stud farm at Lipica, and the dramatically situated Predjama Castle.

▲**Piran** Slovenia's adorable Adriatic resort town—a Back Door gem.

Top 10 Small Coastal Towns

1. Rovinj (Croatia)
2. Korčula (Croatia)
3. Hvar (Croatia)
4. Piran (Slovenia)
5. Kotor (Montenegro)
6. Opatija (Croatia)
7. Cavtat (Croatia)
8. Perast (Montenegro)
9. Trogir (Croatia)
10. Poreč (Croatia)

Figure about $3-6 per major sight (museums), and $10-25 for splurge experiences (e.g., watching the *Moreška* sword dance in Korčula, or seeing Slovenia's Lipizzaner stallions). You can hire your own private guide for three or four hours for about $100-150—a good value when divided among two or more people. An overall average of $20 a day works for most people. Don't skimp here. After all, this category is the driving force behind your trip—you came to sightsee, enjoy, and experience Croatia and Slovenia. Fortunately, the region's best attractions—the sea, mountains, and sunshine—are free.

Shopping and Miscellany: Figure $2-3 per postcard, coffee, beer, and ice-cream cone. Shopping can vary in cost from nearly nothing to a small fortune. Good budget travelers find that this category has little to do with assembling a trip full of lifelong memories.

SIGHTSEEING PRIORITIES

So much to see, so little time. How to choose? Depending on the length of your trip, and taking geographic proximity into account, here are my recommended priorities:

3 days:	Dubrovnik
5 days, add:	Mostar, Split
7 days, add:	Korčula or Hvar (for a relaxing island experience); Montenegro's Bay of Kotor (for dramatic scenery); or Sarajevo (for a more in-depth look at Bosnia)
8 days, add:	Plitvice Lakes
10 days, add:	Lake Bled and the Julian Alps
12 days, add:	Ljubljana, more time for Dalmatian islands
14 days, add:	Istria
16 days, add:	Whatever you skipped on day 7 (Korčula/Hvar, Montenegro, or Sarajevo)
18 days, add:	The Karst, Zagreb
21 days, add:	More mountains (Logarska Dolina) or coastal villages (Piran, Mljet)

More time, add: Ptuj, Opatija, and even more islands and coastal villages

The map and the two-week itinerary on the next page include all of the stops in the first 14 days.

As you plan your trip, don't underestimate the long distances. (For example, Lake Bled and Dubrovnik are a full day's drive apart.) If you have a week or less, focus on either the south (Dalmatian Coast—Dubrovnik, Split, and the islands—plus Mostar and Montenegro) or the north (Slovenia, Istria, and Zagreb). The worth-a-detour Plitvice Lakes are midway between these two areas, but reachable from either one (easiest by car, possible by bus). Sarajevo also requires a detour (2 hours beyond Mostar)—but those who make the trek won't regret it. (Frequent, affordable flights between Sarajevo and Zagreb make it more convenient than it seems.)

Where Should I Go?

The perfect Croatian vacation is like a carefully refined recipe—a dash of this, a pinch of that, a slow simmer...and before long, you've got a delicious feast. Here's my tried-and-true recipe for how to prioritize your time:

Begin with the biggies. Dubrovnik is a must, period. If you like big cities, Split is entertaining. Plitvice Lakes National Park, while difficult to reach, rarely disappoints. The bustling capital city, Zagreb—while far from Croatia's famed beaches—is vastly underrated, and much appreciated by urbanites.

Fold in one or two seafront villages. Adriatic coastal towns are all variations on the same theme: A warm stone Old Town with a Venetian bell tower, a tidy boat-speckled harbor, ample seafood restaurants, a few hulking communist-era resort hotels on the edge of town, and *sobe* and *apartman* signs by every other doorbell. Of course, each town has its own personality and claims to fame (for a quick run-down, see the "Croatia & Slovenia at a Glance" sidebar). Beach bums, sightseers, yachters, historians, partiers—everyone you'll talk to has their own favorite town. Don't trust this advice blindly, and don't sweat the decision too much. If a beach vacation is your goal, you can hardly go wrong.

Sprinkle liberally with Slovenia. You won't regret splicing Slovenia into your itinerary. Its spectacular mountain scenery, colorful capital (Ljubljana), Germanic efficiency, and extremely friendly natives are a pleasant contrast to Croatia. In hindsight, most travelers cite Slovenia as the biggest pleasant surprise of their itinerary—and wish they'd budgeted more time there.

Add some spice. This is my secret ingredient. After you've been to one or two of the coastal resorts, you could head for another one...or you could use that time for something completely different. Some of these options are easy and convenient: the Roman ruins

Croatia and Slovenia: Best Two-Week Trip by Car

Day	Plan	Sleep in
1	Arrive at Ljubljana's airport, go to Lake Bled	Lake Bled
2	Relax at Lake Bled	Lake Bled
3	Pick up car, drive through Julian Alps, end in Ljubljana	Ljubljana
4	Ljubljana	Ljubljana
5	Drive through the Karst and Piran to Rovinj*	Rovinj
6	Tour Istria	Rovinj
7	Drive to Plitvice Lakes via Istria's hill towns	Plitvice
8	Hike the lakes, then drive to Split and drop car	Split
9	Split	Split
10	To Hvar or Korčula	Hvar/Korčula
11	Relax on Hvar or Korčula	Hvar/Korčula
12	To Dubrovnik	Dubrovnik
13	Dubrovnik	Dubrovnik
14	Rent a car or hire a driver to day-trip to Mostar or to Montenegro's Bay of Kotor	Dubrovnik

* To save the substantial extra cost of picking up your car in one country and then dropping it off in another (see page 796), come up with a strategy for turning in your rental car in Slovenia and then taking public transportation to Croatia, where you can pick up a different rental car for your time there. For example, you could take the bus from Ljubljana to Rovinj, then pick up a rental car in nearby Pula or Poreč; or take the train from Ljubljana to Zagreb or Rijeka, then pick up your rental car in one of those cities.

of Pula, the hilltop hamlets of the Istrian interior, the imported-Austrian-resort feel of Opatija. But my favorites involve crossing borders and broadening horizons: the cities of Mostar and Sarajevo, in Bosnia-Herzegovina; and Montenegro's spectacular Bay of Kotor. A year from now, you'll barely remember the difference between all those little seaside towns you toured. But you'll never forget the mosques of Mostar.

By Public Transportation

This itinerary can be done entirely by public transportation, with a few modifications. Skip (or hire a driver for) the Julian Alps, and take the bus from Lake Bled to Ljubljana. Skip Istria; instead, take the train from Ljubljana to Zagreb, see that city, then take a bus to Plitvice. The bus connects Plitvice to Split, and from there, you'll continue down the Dalmatian Coast by boat or bus.

Even if you're using public transportation, seriously consider periodically renting a car for the day; this is most useful to reach the Julian Alps, Istria, Mostar, and Montenegro's Bay of Kotor.

WHEN TO GO

For the best mix of good weather and fewer crowds, I'd focus on shoulder season: mid-May through June, or September through early October. Here's why.

Tourist traffic in this part of Europe (especially the coastal towns) is extremely seasonal. The peak season hits suddenly and floods the towns like a tidal wave, only to recede a couple months later—leaving empty streets and dazed locals. In general, the tourist season runs roughly from mid-May through early October, peaking in early August. (If you're staying in bigger cities or land-

INTRODUCTION

locked towns, the seasonal influence is much less pronounced.) You may find the climate chart in the appendix helpful.

Peak Season: July and especially August are top-of-top season—boats, buses, and budget accommodations are packed to the gills with mostly European vacationers. Visiting Croatia in July or August is like spending spring break in Florida—fun, but miserably crowded and hot. Hotels charge top dollar, and you'll miss out on the "undiscovered" quality that pervades most of the region the rest of the year.

Shoulder Season: Mid-May through June, and September through early October are shoulder seasons—and the time when most of my readers are visiting. Within these time spans, late June and early September are nearly as crowded as peak season (particularly on weekends at seaside towns), but the rush subsides substantially in May and October; by the second week of October, restaurants are already starting to close down for the winter. Shoulder season is my favorite time to visit—I enjoy the smaller crowds, milder weather, and less-frenzied locals.

Off-Season: Mid-October through mid-May, small towns are dead as a doornail. Many resorts close down entirely, with only one hotel and one restaurant remaining open during the lean winter months; many residents move to the interior to hibernate. Anything that's open keeps very limited hours (weekday mornings only). Boat and bus schedules can be dramatically reduced, and some boat connections or mountain roads (such as Slovenia's Vršič Pass) are simply closed. The weather can be cool and dreary, and night will draw the shades on your sightseeing before dinnertime. If traveling in the winter, skip the coast (or limit yourself to bigger towns like Split and Dubrovnik), and focus on the cities and the interior.

Seasonal Changes: Because of this region's extreme seasonality, opening times and prices are especially flexible. It's not unusual for a hotel to charge six different rates for the same room, depending on the time of year. (A hotel receptionist once showed me a binder with hundreds of potential rates they could charge, based on room size, type, views, season, and length of stay.) And museum admission prices can jump dramatically, overnight, without notice. With every visit, I dutifully hike around these towns trying to pin down hours for tourist offices, travel agencies, and museums. And every time, they change. It's always smart to call ahead to double-check opening times.

Rick's Free Video Clips and Audio Tours

Travel smarter with these free, fun resources:

 Rick Steves Classroom Europe, a powerful tool for teachers, is also useful for travelers. This video library contains over 400 short clips excerpted from my public television series. Enjoy these videos as you sort through options for your trip and to better understand what you'll see in Europe. Check it out at Classroom.RickSteves.com (just enter a topic in the search bar to find everything I've filmed on a subject).

The **Rick Steves Audio Europe app** makes it easy to download audio content to enhance your trip. Use the app to listen to audio tours of Europe's top sights, plus interviews from my public radio show with experts from Europe and around the globe. Find it in your app store or at RickSteves.com/AudioEurope.

Before You Go

You'll have a smoother trip if you tackle a few things ahead of time. For more information on these topics, see the Practicalities chapter (and RickSteves.com for helpful travel tips and talks).

Make sure your travel documents are valid. If your passport is due to expire within six months of your ticketed date of return, you need to renew it. Allow up to six weeks to renew or get a passport (www.travel.state.gov). Beginning in 2021, you may also need to register with the European Travel Information and Authorization System (ETIAS). A useful private website with more details is www.schengenvisainfo.com/etias.

Arrange your transportation. Book your international flights. Figure out transportation options within the region: It's worth thinking about buying train, bus, or boat tickets online in advance, getting a rail pass, renting a car, or booking cheap European flights. (You can wing it once you're there, but it may cost more.) Drivers: Consider bringing an International Driving Permit—sold at AAA offices in the US—along with your license.

Book rooms well in advance, especially if your trip falls during peak season (July and August) or any major holidays or festivals. Booking ahead during shoulder season is also advisable if you want the best range of choices. Many of my favorite accommodations are quite small, with only a few rooms, so they fill up early.

Consider travel insurance. Compare the cost of the insurance to the cost of your potential loss. Check whether your existing insurance (health, homeowners, or renters) covers you and your possessions overseas.

Call your bank. Alert your bank that you'll be using your debit and credit cards in Europe. Ask about transaction fees, and get the PIN number for your credit card. You don't need to bring euros or kunas for your trip; you can withdraw the local currency from cash machines in Europe.

Use your smartphone smartly. Sign up for an international service plan to reduce your costs, or rely on Wi-Fi in Europe instead. Download any apps you'll want on the road, such as maps, translators, transit schedules, and Rick Steves Audio Europe (see sidebar).

Rip up this book! Turn chapters into mini guidebooks: Break the book's spine and use a utility knife to slice apart chapters, keeping gummy edges intact. Reinforce the chapter spines with clear wide tape; use a heavy-duty stapler; or make or buy a cheap cover (see Travel Store at www.ricksteves.com), swapping out chapters as you travel.

Pack light. You'll walk with your luggage more than you think. I travel for weeks with a single carry-on bag and a daypack. Use the packing checklist in the appendix as a guide.

Travel Smart

If you have a positive attitude, equip yourself with good information (this book), and expect to travel smart, you will.

Read—and reread—this book. To have an "A" trip, be an "A" student. Note opening hours of sights, closed days, crowd-beating tips, and whether reservations are required or advisable. Check the latest at www.ricksteves.com/update.

Be your own tour guide. As you travel, get up-to-date info on sights, reserve tickets and tours, reconfirm hotels and travel arrangements, and check transit connections. Visit local tourist information offices (TIs). Upon arrival in a new town, lay the groundwork for a smooth departure; confirm the train, bus, or road you'll take when you leave.

Outsmart thieves. Pickpockets abound in crowded places where tourists congregate. Treat commotions as smokescreens for theft. Keep your cash, credit cards, and passport secure in a money belt tucked under your clothes; carry only a day's spending money in your front pocket. Don't set valuable items down on counters or café tabletops, where they can be quickly stolen or easily forgotten.

Minimize potential loss. Keep expensive gear to a minimum. Bring photocopies or take photos of important documents (passport and cards) to aid in replacement if they're lost or stolen. Back up photos and files frequently.

Beat the summer heat. If you wilt easily, choose accommodations with air-conditioning, start your day early, take a midday siesta at your hotel, and resume your sightseeing later. Churches offer a cool haven. Take frequent ice cream breaks.

Guard your time and energy. Taking a taxi can be a good value if it saves you a long wait for a cheap bus or an exhausting walk across town. To avoid long lines, follow my crowd-beating tips, such as making advance reservations, or sightseeing early or late.

Be flexible. Even if you have a well-planned itinerary, expect changes, strikes, closures, sore feet, bad weather, and so on. Your Plan B could turn out to be even better.

Attempt the language. Many Croatians and Slovenes—especially in the tourist trade and in cities—speak English, but if you learn some Croatian and Slovenian, even just a few phrases, you'll get more smiles and make more friends. Practice the survival phrases at the end of the Croatia and Slovenia chapters, and even better, bring a phrase book.

Connect with the culture. Interacting with locals carbonates your experience. Enjoy the friendliness of the Croatian and Slo-

venian people. Ask questions; most locals are happy to point you in their idea of the right direction. Set up your own quest for the best bell tower, mountain vista, or scenic seafront perch. When an opportunity pops up, make it a habit to say "yes."

Croatia and Slovenia...here you come!

CROATIA

Hrvatska

CROATIA

With thousands of miles of seafront and more than a thousand islands, Croatia's coastline is Central Europe's Riviera. Holiday-makers love its pebbly beaches, balmy summer weather, and dramatic mountains. Croatia is also historic. From ruined Roman arenas and Byzantine mosaics to Venetian bell towers, Habsburg villas, and even communist concrete, past rulers have left their mark.

Especially along its coast, Croatia feels more Mediterranean than "Eastern European." Historically, the Croatia that most tourists visit has more in common with Venice and Rome than Vienna or Budapest. If you've become accustomed to the Germanic efficiency of Slovenia, Croatia's relaxed and unpredictable style can come as a shock.

Despite its fun-in-the-sun status, around 25 years ago Croatia was one of the battlegrounds of the most violent European conflict since World War II. While we refer to "the Yugoslav Wars," locals call it "The Homeland War" or "The Last War" (though it's unclear whether they mean "final" or "most recent"). Thankfully, the bloodshed is now a generation in the past— a distant memory even to those who actively participated. But trying to understand the war, its causes, and its effects provides thoughtful travelers with a perspective-broadening and poignant dimension to their trip.

Adding to the country's fame are high-profile media appearances—from serving as a major location for *Game of Thrones*, to a wildly popular South Korean dating/reality show. Croatia is ready for its close-up.

Croatia's 3,600 miles of coastline—its main draw for tourists—is loosely divided into three regions. Most people flock to the Dalmatian Coast, in the south, where dramatic limestone cliffs rise from the watery deep and islands are scattered just offshore (the most appealing are Hvar and Korčula). Here you'll find Croatia's top tourist town, Dubrovnik, and the big city of Split, with its impressive Roman ruins. Up in the northern corner of the country is the flatter, wedge-shaped, Italian-flavored peninsula called Istria, with a rolling interior blanketed with vineyards and topped with hill towns, Roman ruins in the city of Pula, and my favorite seaside town between Dubrovnik and Venice—Rovinj. Wedged between Dalmatia and Istria is the Kvarner Gulf, a windy, arid no-man's-land that has few worthwhile attractions, but ample rugged scenery and a few fine islands offshore.

Enjoy the coast, but don't ignore the interior. The bustling capital of Zagreb is urban, engaging, and full of great museums and foodie restaurants. And Croatia's single best natural wonder (in this country that's so full of them) are the stunning waterfalls at Plitvice Lakes National Park.

It's possible to blow a lot of money here. Croatian hotels, especially on the coast, are priced at a premium, and the many touristy restaurants consider overcharging tourists a good day's work. But

CROATIA

if you know where to look, you can find some wonderful budget alternatives—particularly *sobe* (rooms in private homes). *Sobe* are a comfortable compromise: fresh, hotelesque doubles with a private bathroom and air-conditioning for a fraction of the cost of an anonymous hotel room (for details, see page 773).

Europeans are reverent sun-worshippers, and on clear days, it seems every square inch of coastal Croatia—beaches, rocks, and even promenades—is occupied by a sunbather on a beach towel. Nude beaches are a big deal, especially for vacationing Germans and Austrians. If you want to work on an all-around tan, seek out a beach marked *FKK* (from the German *Freikörper Kultur*, or "free body culture"). First-timers get comfortable in a hurry, finding they're not the only novices on the rocks.

Perhaps because sunshine and fishing are so important to the economy, Croatians are particularly affected by the weather. They complain that the once-predictable climate has become erratic, with surprise rainy spells or heat waves in the once perfectly consistent summer months. Locals—and, often, tourists—find that their mood can be noticeably affected by which way the wind is blowing (for more, see page 164). The Croatian weather report includes a *biometeorološka prognoza* that indicates how the day's weather will affect your mood. Weather maps come with smiley or frowny faces, and forecasts predict, "People will be tired in the afternoon and not feel like working."

Every Croatian coastal town has two parts: The time-warp old town, and the obnoxious resort sprawl. Main drags are clogged with gift shops selling shell sculptures and tasteless T-shirts. Fortunately, it's relatively easy to ignore the touristy scene and instead poke your way into twisty old medieval lanes, draped with drying laundry and populated by gossiping neighbors, humble fishermen's taverns, and soccer-playing kids.

Croatian popular music, the mariachi music of Europe, is the ever-present soundtrack of a Dalmatian vacation. The late Oliver Dragojević—who sang soulful Mediterranean ballads with a gravelly, passionate voice—was the Croatian Tom Jones. Known simply as "Oliver," this beloved crooner still gets airplay across Europe and has spawned many imitators (such as the almost-as-popular Gibonni).

More traditional is the hauntingly beautiful *klapa* music—men's voices harmonizing a cappella, like a barbershop quartet with a soothing Adriatic flavor. Typically the leader begins the song, and the rest of the ensemble (usually 3 to 12 singers) follows behind him with a slight delay. You'll see mariachi-style *klapa* groups performing in touristy areas; a CD of one of these performances is a fun souvenir.

Many Croatians place a lot of importance on their Catholic faith. Under communism, religion was de-emphasized, and many people gave up the habit of attending Mass regularly. But as the wars raged in the early 1990s, many Croatians rediscovered religion (which also became tied to surging nationalism). Today, you may be surprised by how many people you see worshipping in the churches of this recently communist country.

In the Yugoslav era, Croatia was a vacation hotspot for both Europeans and Americans; at its peak, Croatia hosted about 10 million visitors a year, who provided the country with about a third of its income. Of course, the war decimated tourism, and recovery was gradual. But these days there's no question that Croatia has rebounded, becoming more popular than ever on the world tourism scene. About 15 million visitors flock here each year, to the tune of more than $10 billion. In fact, some worldly Croatians are now pursuing a more sustainable approach to tourism—a concern that will certainly grow alongside the number of visitors.

Some of those many visitors find that service in Croatia can be...relaxed. Maybe *too* relaxed. This is partly thanks to the local philosophy of *malo po malo*, "little by little"—the easygoing, no-worries, *mañana* Dalmatian lifestyle. While you'll meet plenty of wonderfully big-hearted Croatians, some of my readers characterize Croatian waiters or hotel receptionists as "gruff" or even "rude." Be prepared for what I call the "Croatian Shrug"—a simple gesture meaning, "Don't know, don't care."

Today's Croatia is crawling with a Babel of international guests speaking German, French, Italian, every accent of English...and a smattering of Croatian. And yet, despite the tourists, this place remains distinctly and stubbornly Croatian. You'd have to search pretty hard to find a McDonald's.

CROATIA

Croatia Almanac

Official Name: Republika Hrvatska, or just Hrvatska for short.

Size: 22,000 square miles (similar to West Virginia). Of the country's 4.5 million people, 90 percent are ethnic Croats (Catholic) and 4.5 percent are Serbs (Orthodox). (The Serb population was more than double that before the ethnic cleansing of the 1991-1995 war.) The population also includes ethnic Bosniaks (Muslims), Hungarians, and Slovenes. "Croatians" are citizens of Croatia; "Croats" are a distinct ethnic group made up of Catholic South Slavs. So Orthodox Serbs living in Croatia are Croatians (specifically "Croatian Serbs")...but they aren't Croats.

Geography: This boomerang-shaped country has two terrains: Stretching north to south is the long, rugged Mediterranean coastline (3,600 miles of beach, including more than 1,100 offshore islands), which is warm and dry. Rising up from the sea are the rocky Dinaric Mountains. To the northeast, beginning at about Zagreb, Croatia's flat, inland "panhandle" (called Slavonia) is an extension of the Great Hungarian Plain, with hot summers and cold winters.

Latitude and Longitude: 45°N and 15°E (similar latitude to Venice, Italy or Portland, Oregon).

Biggest Cities: The capital, Zagreb (in the northern interior), has 790,000 people; Split (along the Dalmatian Coast) has 178,000; and Rijeka (on the northern coast) has 129,000.

Snapshot History: After losing their independence to Hungary in 1102, the Croats watched as most of their coastline became Venetian and their interior was conquered by Ottomans. Croatia was "rescued" by the Habsburgs (eventually becoming part of Austria-Hungary). After World War I, it became part of Yugoslavia, which splintered apart in the early 1990s when Croatia fought a bitter war to become a modern, independent state.

Economy: Much of the country's wealth (about $95 billion GDP, or $24,700 GDP per capita) comes from tourism, banking, and trade with Italy.

Currency: 1 kuna (kn, or HRK) = about 17 cents, and 6 kunas = about $1. One kuna is broken down into 100 lipas. *Kuna* is Croatian for "marten" (an animal in the same family as weasels and ferrets), recalling a time when fur pelts were used as currency. A *lipa* is a linden tree.

HELPFUL HINTS

Telephones: For details on how to dial to, from, and within Croatia, see page 784.

Addresses: Addresses listed with a street name and followed by "b.b." have no street number. In most small towns, locals ignore not only street numbers but also street names—navigate with a map or by asking for directions.

Government: The single-house assembly (Sabor) of 151 legislators is elected by popular vote. The country's prime minister (the head of the majority party in parliament, the center-right HDZ party) is currently Andrej Plenković; the directly elected (but more figurehead) president Zoran Milanović, from the center-left Social Democratic Party (SDP).

Flag: The flag has three horizontal bands (red on top, white, and blue) with a traditional red-and-white checkerboard shield in the center.

The Average Croatian: The average Croatian will live to age 76 and have 1.4 children. He or she absolutely adores the soccer team Dinamo Zagreb and absolutely despises Hajduk Split...or vice versa.

Notable Croatians: A pair of big-league historical figures were born in Croatia: Roman Emperor **Diocletian** (AD 245-313) and—supposedly (though unlikely)—explorer **Marco Polo** (1254?-1324). More recently, many Americans whose names end in "-ich" have Croatian roots, including actor **John Malkovich** and Ohio politicians **Dennis Kucinich** and **John Kasich,** not to mention baseball legend **Roger** Marich...I mean, **Maris.** More Croatian athletes abound: tennis star **Goran Ivanišević** is internationally known; NBA fans might recognize **Toni Kukoč** or **Gordan Giricek;** and at the 2002 and 2006 Winter Olympic Games, the women's downhill skiing events were dominated by **Janica Kostelić** (her brother **Ivica Kostelić** medaled in 2006, 2010, and 2014). Actor **Goran Višnjić** (from TV's *ER*) was born and raised in Croatia, and served in the army as a paratrooper. You may not yet know the beloved Croatian sculptor **Ivan Meštrović**...but you will soon, as his expressive works are all over the country (as well as in the United States). Inventor **Nikola Tesla** (1856-1943)—who, as a rival of Thomas Edison's, invented alternating current (AC)—was a Croatian-born Serb. And a band of well-dressed 17th-century Croatian soldiers stationed in France gave the Western world a new fashion accessory—the cravat, or necktie (for the full story, see page 189).

Hotel Prices: Most hotels quote prices in euros for the convenience of their international guests, but they'll convert the bill to kunas to determine your final payment.

Slick Pavement: Old towns, with their well-polished pavement stones and many slick stairs, can be quite treacherous, especially after a rainstorm. (On a recent trip, one of your co-authors nearly broke his arm slipping down a flight of stairs.) Tread with care.

Siesta: Croatians eat their big meal at lunch, then take a traditional Mediterranean siesta. This means that many stores, museums, and churches are closed in the mid-afternoon, especially in smaller towns.

Pack Smart: Croatia is known for its glimmering beaches. However, most are pebbly or rocky rather than sandy—and spiny sea urchins are not uncommon. In addition to your swimsuit, pack (or buy in Europe) a pair of water shoes for wading, as well as a beach towel (many of my recommended accommodations don't provide these). Good sunscreen, a sun hat, and bug spray can also be handy. And if you'll be hiking on Croatia's many scenic coastal trails, which can be rugged, pack sturdy shoes.

Landmine Warning: Certain parts of the Croatian interior were once full of landmines. Most of these mines have been removed, and fields that may still be dangerous are usually clearly marked. As a precaution, if you're in a former war zone, stay on roads and paths, and don't go wandering through overgrown fields and deserted villages.

CROATIAN HISTORY

For nearly a millennium, bits and pieces of what we today call "Croatia" were batted back and forth between foreign powers: Hungarians, Venetians, Ottomans, Habsburgs, and Yugoslavs. Only in 1991 did Croatia (violently) regain its independence.

Early History

Croatia's first inhabitants were the mysterious Illyrians. While they left behind a few scant artifacts, little is known about this group, who were likely the ancestors of today's Albanians.

During antiquity, the Greeks and Romans sailed ships up and down the strategic Dalmatian Coast. They founded many towns that still exist today, introduced winemaking and other agriculture, and littered the Adriatic seabed with shipwrecks. Romans built larger settlements on the Dalmatian Coast as early as 229 BC, and in the fourth century AD, Emperor Diocletian—who was born in what's now Croatia and rose through the military ranks to become the most powerful man on earth—built his retirement palace in the coastal town of Split.

As Rome fell in the fifth century, many different peoples migrated across Europe—including the Slavs (the ancestors of today's Croatians). They moved into deserted Roman settlements (Diocletian's Palace, in Split, is a prime example) and made them their own. The northern part of Croatia's coast fell briefly under the Byzantines, who slathered churches with shimmering mosaics (the best are in the Euphrasian Basilica in Poreč, Istria).

Beginning in the seventh century, Slavic Croats began to control most of the land that is today's Croatia. In AD 925, the Dalmatian Duke Tomislav united the disparate Croat tribes into a single kingdom. By consolidating and extending Croat-held territory and centralizing power, Tomislav created what many consider to be the first "Croatia."

Loss of Independence

By the early 12th century, the Croatian kings had died out, and neighboring powers (Hungary, Venice, and Byzantium) threatened the Croats. For the sake of self-preservation, Croatia entered into an alliance with the Hungarians in 1102—and for the next 900 years, the Croats were ruled by foreign states. The Hungarians gradually took more and more power from the Croats, exerting control over the majority of inland Croatia. Meanwhile, the Venetian Republic conquered most of the coast and peppered the Croatian Adriatic with bell towers and the winged lion of St. Mark.

The Ottomans (from today's Turkey) conquered most of inland Croatia by the 15th century and challenged the Venetians—unsuccessfully—for control of the coastline. Most of the stout walls, fortresses, and other fortifications you'll see all along the Croatian coast date from this time, built by the Venetians to defend against Ottoman attack.

Through it all, the tiny Republic of Dubrovnik flourished—paying off whomever necessary to maintain its independence and becoming one of Europe's most important shipbuilding and maritime powers. Although it was surrounded by the Ottoman threat, Dubrovnik persisted as a plucky rival to powerful Venice.

In the 17th century, the Habsburgs forced the Ottomans out of inland Croatia. Then, after Venice and Dubrovnik fell to Napoleon in the early 19th century, the coast also went to the Habsburgs—beginning a long tradition of Austrians basking on Croatian beaches.

The Yugoslav Era, World War II, and the Ustaše

When the Austro-Hungarian Empire broke up at the end of World War I and the map of Europe was redrawn, the Croats banded together with the Serbs, Slovenes, and Bosnians in the union that would become Yugoslavia. But virtually as soon as the Kingdom of Yugoslavia was formed, many Croats began to fear that the Serbs would steer Yugoslavia to their own purposes.

The parliamentarian Stjepan Radić spoke out passionately for Croat rights within the kingdom—until he was assassinated by a Serb on the morning of June 20, 1928, during a parliamentary session. This outbreak of violence alarmed Yugoslavia's Serb king, Alexander Karađorđević, who abolished the parliament and declared himself absolute ruler of the kingdom—squelching the Croats' fervently desired autonomy.

It was in this political climate, during the 1930s, that the Ustaše ("Uprisers")—a nationalistic, fascist movement bent on creating an ethnically pure "Greater Croatia"—gained popularity among a small but dangerous fringe of Croats. On September 9, 1934, Ustaše operatives assassinated King Alexander. The Kingdom of Yugoslavia—so young and fragile—was already unraveling.

But even larger concerns loomed on the horizon. On April 6, 1941, Hitler's Luftwaffe began aerial bombardment of Belgrade; less than two weeks later, Nazi Germany controlled Yugoslavia. Hitler divvied up the territory among his Italian, Hungarian, and Bulgarian allies. He created the misnamed "Independent State of Croatia"—encompassing much of today's Croatia and Bosnia-Herzegovina, and parts of Serbia—to be led by Ante Pavelić and the Croatian Ustaše Party. The Ustaše operated one of the most brutal Nazi puppet states during World War II. Ustaše concentration camps—including the notorious Jasenovac extermination camp—were used to murder tens of thousands of Jews and Roma (Gypsies), as well as hundreds of thousands of Serbs.

The Croatian Catholic leader Cardinal Alojzije Stepinac was one Croat who made the mistake of backing the Ustaše. By most accounts, Stepinac was a mild-mannered, extremely devout man who didn't agree with the extremism of the Ustaše...but also did little to fight it. Following the war, Stepinac was arrested, tried, and imprisoned, dying under house arrest in 1960. In the years since, Stepinac has become a martyr both for Catholics and for Croat nationalists.

At the end of World War II, the Ustaše and the Nazis were forced out by Yugoslavia's homegrown Partisan Army, led by a charismatic war hero named Josip Broz, who went by the nickname "Tito." Tito became "president for life," and Croatia once again became part of a united Yugoslavia. This union would hold together for more than 40 years, until it broke apart amid attempts by Serbian President Slobodan Milošević and Croatian President Franjo Tuđman to redraw boundaries.

For more details on Yugoslavia and its breakup, see the Understanding Yugoslavia chapter.

Independence Regained

Croatia's declaration of independence from Yugoslavia in 1991 was met with fear and anger by many of its more than half-million Serb residents. Even before independence, the first volleys of a bloody war had been fired. The conflict had two phases: First, in

1991, Croatian Serbs declared independence from the new nation of Croatia, forming their own state and forcing out or murdering any Croats in their newly claimed territory (with thinly disguised military support from Slobodan Milošević). Then a tense cease-fire fell over the region until 1995, when the second phase of the war ignited: Croatia pushed back through the Serb-dominated territory, reclaiming it for Croatia and forcing out or murdering Serbs living there.

Imagine becoming an independent nation after nine centuries of foreign domination. Croatians seized their hard-earned freedom with a nationalist fervor that bordered on fascism. It was a heady and absurd time, which today's Croatians recall with a mix of excitement, regret, and nostalgia.

In the Croatia of the early 1990s, even the most bizarre notions seemed possible. Croatia's first post-Yugoslav president, the nationalist Franjo Tuđman (see sidebar), proposed bold directives for the new nation—such as privatizing all of the nation's resources and handing them over to 200 super-elite oligarchs. While this never quite happened, privatization relied heavily on nepotism, and Tuđman's highly placed allies enjoyed a windfall.

The government rechristened the language "Croatian" (to distinguish it from "Serbo-Croatian") and created new words from Croat roots. Some outside-the-box thinkers even briefly considered replacing the Roman alphabet with the ninth-century Glagolitic script to invoke Croat culture and further differentiate Croatian from Serbia's Cyrillic alphabet. (Fortunately for tourists, this plan didn't take off.)

After Tuđman's death in 1999, Croatia began the new millennium with a more truly democratic leader, Stipe Mesić. The popular Mesić, who was once aligned with Tuđman, had split off and formed his own political party when Tuđman's politics grew too extreme. Tuđman spent years amending the constitution to give himself more and more power, but when Mesić took over, he reversed those changes and handed more authority back to the parliament.

After a successful decade as president, the term-limited Stipe Mesić stepped down in 2010. Ivo Josipović, running on a strong anti-corruption platform, won by a landslide.

Croatia Today

In 2013, Croatia joined the European Union—a benchmark of the progress the nation has made since Tuđman. But the road to EU membership has been a rocky one, and several thorny issues face contemporary Croatians.

The legacy of the Yugoslav Wars has yet to fully resolve itself in Croatia. The then-popular president, Franjo Tuđman, is now

CROATIA

Franjo Tuđman (1922-1999)

Independent Croatia's first president was the controversial Franjo Tuđman (FRAHN-yoh TOOJ-mahn). Tuđman began his career fighting for Tito on the left, but later made a dramatic ideological swing to the far right. His anticommunist, highly nationalistic HDZ party was the driving force for Croatian statehood, making him the young nation's first standard-bearer. But even as he fought for independence from Yugoslavia, his own ruling style grew more and more authoritarian. Today, years after his death, Tuđman remains a divisive figure.

Before entering politics, Tuđman was a military officer. He fought for Tito's Partisans in World War II, and was the youngest general in the Yugoslav People's Army. But later in life, Tuđman—now a professional historian—came to revere the Ustaše, Croatia's Nazi-puppet government during World War II. Because the Ustaše governed the first "independent" Croatian state since the 12th century, Tuđman considered them Croatian "freedom fighters." But that same state had murdered hundreds of thousands of Serbs in its concentration camps. (In a history book he authored, Tuđman controversially deflated this death toll to between 30,000 and 60,000—a figure no legitimate historian accepts.)

In the 1980s—following Tito's death, and as Yugoslavia began to unravel—Tuđman gained support for his nationalistic, anticommunist political party, the Croatian Democratic Union (Hrvatska Demokratska Zajednica, HDZ). In 1990, during Croatia's first free elections of the post-Tito era, voters decisively supported Tuđman and the HDZ—effectively voting out the communists. In 1992, Tuđman was formally elected president.

As Tuđman took power, he wasted no time in reintroducing many Ustaše symbols, including their currency (the kuna, still used today). These provocative actions raised eyebrows worldwide, and raised alarms in Croatia's Serb communities.

Tuđman espoused many of the same single-minded attitudes about ethnic divisions as the ruthless Serbian leader Slobodan Milošević. Croat forces—which may or may not have been acting

viewed with regret and suspicion by a significant segment of Croatian society (see sidebar). Others feel shame about reports that have emerged about Croatian soldiers' ethnic-cleansing activities during the war. Several Croatian officers were indicted for war crimes by the International Criminal Tribunal for the Former Yugoslavia (ICTY) in The Hague, Netherlands. The highest-profile of these—Lieutenant General Ante Gotovina—was discovered hiding in Spain in 2005, arrested, extradited, tried, convicted...and then acquitted on appeal in 2012. To this day, many Croatians feel that the soldiers branded as "war criminals" by The Hague are instead heroes of their war of independence.

under Tuđman's orders—carried out wide-scale ethnic cleansing, targeting Serb and Muslim minorities. Tuđman and Milošević had secret, Hitler- and Stalin-esque negotiations even as they were ripping into each other rhetorically. According to some reports, at one meeting they divvied up a map of Bosnia-Herzegovina on a cocktail napkin. Their so-called "Karađorđevo Agreement" completely left out the Bosniaks, who constituted the largest ethnic group within the nation whose fate was being decided.

To ensure that he stayed in power, Tuđman played fast and loose with his new nation's laws. He was notorious for changing the constitution as it suited him. By the late 1990s, when his popularity was slipping, Tuđman extended Croatian citizenship to anyone in the world who had Croatian heritage—a ploy aimed at gathering votes from Croats living in Bosnia-Herzegovina, who were sure to line up with him on the far right.

Tuđman kept a tight grip on the media, making it illegal to report anything that would disturb the public—even if true. When Croatians turned on their TV sets and saw the flag flapping in the breeze to the strains of the national anthem, they knew something was up...and switched to CNN to get the real story. In this oppressive environment, many bright, young Croatians fled the country, causing a "brain drain" that hampered the postwar recovery.

Tuđman died of cancer at the end of 1999. While history will probably judge him harshly, the opinion in today's Croatia is qualified. Most agree that Tuđman was an important and even admirable figure in the struggle for Croatian statehood, but he ultimately went too far. The most elaborate tomb in Zagreb's national cemetery (Mirogoj) honors this "Croatian founding father," and Zagreb's international airport is named after him. However, prosecutors at the International Criminal Tribunal in The Hague have said that if Tuđman were alive, he would be standing trial for war crimes.

Croatia's relations with its neighbors—many of whom were involved in the Yugoslav Wars—remain problematic. While Croatia and Slovenia shared the same goal (separating from Yugoslavia), many Croatians resent Slovenia's lack of military support for Croatian independence. Decades later, tensions still persist. Slovenia briefly blocked Croatia's EU membership bid in an effort to resolve a longstanding border dispute (described on page 752). Ironically, even many Croatians who were vehemently opposed to EU membership were outraged that Slovenia tried to prevent it. On recent trips to this region, when I show people the cover of this book,

CROATIA

people in both countries express displeasure about being grouped together.

Another vexing issue in today's Croatia is government corruption—perhaps best embodied by one of the country's previous prime ministers, Ivo Sanader, who abruptly resigned in 2009, and soon after was arrested, convicted, and sent to prison.

Croatians—and especially expats living here—report that the country is excessively bureaucratic, and can be a tough place to do business. Laws tend to be implemented, then quickly overturned. In the last few years, a ban on shops being open on Sundays, a smoking ban, and a zero blood-alcohol limit for drivers have all come and gone.

In 2012, two-thirds of Croatians voted in favor of joining the EU. But the reality of EU membership rocked Croatia in the fall of 2015, when a wave of immigrants from war-torn Syria (as well as many other Middle Eastern and Balkan nations) began to flood into Europe. When neighboring Hungary closed its borders to refugees, many began to spill into northern Croatia. While refugees camped out at the borders, Croatian government agencies and NGOs alike scrambled to deal with simultaneous humanitarian and diplomatic crises.

Despite such geopolitical challenges, Croatia continues to emerge as a red-hot destination for holiday-makers, and with some of the growing pains of new nationhood behind it, seems poised for an ever-brighter future.

CROATIAN FOOD

While Croatia is not quite the foodie destination that the tourist board likes to promote, visitors can eat well here. Until quite recently, local cuisine was just functional and filling. But a new generation of chefs is introducing new techniques and a more cosmopolitan sensibility to Croatian cooking. Even so, it's easy to fall into a predictable rut of pizza, pasta, and no-frills seafood (especially along the coast). This is just fine for many travelers, but if you care about good food, it's worth seeking out more interesting alternatives. These can be rare in smaller tourist towns, but cities have a better variety. (My restaurant listings highlight the best of both functional and memorable eateries.)

Two staples in Croatia, as in most Mediterranean lands, are wine and olive oil. You'll see vineyards and olive groves blanketing the Croatian countryside and islands. Another major part of the local diet is the air-dried ham called *pršut* (a.k.a. prosciutto—see sidebar on page 537).

While you'll find places called *restaurant*, you'll more often see the name *konoba*—which means an unpretentious tradition-al restaurant, like an inn. To request a menu, say, *"Meni, molim"* (MEH-nee, MOH-leem; "Menu, please"). To get the attention of your waiter, say *"Konobar"* (KOH-noh-bahr; "Waiter"). When the waiter's ready to take your order, they'll say, *"Izvolite."* When they bring your food, they'll likely say, *"Dobar tek!"* ("Enjoy your meal!"). When you're ready for the bill, ask for the *račun* (RAH-choon).

Main Dishes

On the coast, seafood is a specialty, and the Italian influence is ob-vious. According to Dalmatians, "Eating meat is food; eating fish is pleasure." They also say that a fish should swim three times: first in the sea, then in olive oil, and finally in wine—when you eat it.

You can get all kinds of seafood: fish, scampi, mussels, squid, octopus, you name it. Keep in mind that prices for fish dishes are listed either by the kilogram (1,000 grams) or by the 100-gram unit (figure about a half-kilo, or 500 grams—that's about one pound—for a large portion). Frozen fish is not uncommon—if you want something fresh from the market, ask. If you get a whole fish, you can usually ask the server to delicately separate its fillets from its backbone (a difficult task if you've never done it).

Interpreting menus can be tricky. For example, *škampi* (shrimp) often come still in their shells (sometimes with crayfish-like claws), which can be messy and time-consuming to eat. Before you order shrimp, ask if it's shelled. The menu item called "small fried fish" is generally a plate of deep-fried minnows. If you see something described as "Dalmatian-style," it usually means with lots of olive oil, parsley, and garlic.

Don't shy away from unusual menu items—they can be surprisingly deli-cious. Jump at the chance to sample a good, fresh an-chovy—which, when done right, has a pleasant flavor and a melt-in-your-mouth texture that's a world away from the salty, withered little fish you might find topping a pizza back home. Those not accustomed to eating octopus might want to try octopus salad: a flavorful mix of octopus, tomatoes, onions, capers, and spices. In the interior, trout is popular.

Croatian Wine

For gourmands, one of the most pleasant surprises about a trip to Croatia is the quality of the wines. While much of the industry was state-run and focused on mass production during communist times, today vintner families are returning to their roots—literally—and taking a renewed pride in Croatian wines. Thanks partly to the interest and investment of American vintners, Croatian wines are gaining respect worldwide. Because very few Croatian wines are exported, a visit here

is a good chance to sample some new tastes.

The northern part of the country primarily produces whites (*bijelo vino,* bee-YEH-loh VEE-noh), usually dry (*suho,* SOO-hoh) but sometimes semi-dry (*polusuho,* POHL-soo-hoh) or sweet (*slatko,* SLAHT-koh). The sunny mountains just north of Zagreb are covered with vineyards producing whites. From Slavonia (Croatia's inland panhandle), you'll find *graševina*—crisp, dry, and acidic (like a dry Riesling). Well-respected brands include Krauthaker and Enjingi (whose prizewinning Venje wine is a blend of five white grape varieties). Istria corks up some good whites, including *malvazija,* a very popular, light, mid-range wine. (Muscat is also popular.) The best reds from this region are made from the *teran* grape, though you'll find some cabernet sauvignon and merlot as well. Top producers here include Degrassi (try their Terre Bianche white and red blends), Kabola, Kozlović, and Matošević (all of these can be visited for a tasting).

As you move south, along the Dalmatian Coast, the wines turn red—which Croatians call "black wine" (*crno vino,* TSUR-noh VEE-noh). The dominant grape here is *plavac mali* ("little blue")—a distant relative of Californian zinfandel. Many of the best coastal reds are produced on the long Pelješac Peninsula, across from Korčula (the most well-respected regions are Dingač and Postup). But each island also produces its own good wines. Korčula (especially near the villages of Čara and Smokvica) makes excellent white wine from *pošip* grapes (which are high alcohol and low acidity—locals like to cut this with carbonated water), as well as *grk* ("Greek") grapes that grow only around Lumbarda—try it at the Bire winery) and *korčulanka.* Hvar's wines tend to be fruitier and less tannic; they specialize in *pošip,* as well as *bogdanuša* ("from the gods")—which has low alcohol and high acidity. On Hvar, good places to try wines include the Tomić winery, in the village of Jelsa, and at Vina Pinjata in Vrboska.

Other wines to look for include the heavenly, sweet dessert wine called *prošek* (similar to port wine or Italian vin santo). While rosés aren't a big business here, some producers make them to keep up with winemaking trends; you may see them called Opolo (*pol* means "half").

When looking at wine labels, watch for these three official classifications: *stolno* ("table," the lowest grade), *kvalitento* ("quality"—actually mid-range), and *vrhunsko* (top-quality). In general, if only the grape is listed (e.g., *mali plavac*), the quality isn't as good as when the region is prominently noted (e.g., Dingač or Postup). You may also see the words *vinogorje* (vineyard), *položaj* (location), and *barrique* (barrel-aged).

The big name in Croatian wines is Miljenko Grgić. Born in Croatia in 1923, Grgić emigrated from communist Yugoslavia to the US and—as "Mike Grgich"—worked at the Chateau Montelena Winery in Napa Valley. In the famous "Judgment of Paris" in

1976, Grgić's 1973 chardonnay beat out several well-respected French wines in a blind taste test. Considered a turning point in the winemaking world, this event brought new respect to American winemakers and put Napa on the mapa.

Having revolutionized American winemaking, Grgić turned his sights on his Croatian homeland. He imported California know-how to the slopes of the Pelješac Peninsula, where he set about making some of Croatia's first truly well-respected wines. Grgić grows his red *plavac mali* on the Pelješac Peninsula (at Dingač and nearby, at Trstanik), and his white *pošip* wine on Korčula Island.

The prices for Grgić's wines match his reputation; for producers that are comparable but a bit more affordable, look for these red-wine alternatives: Madirazza (they make a great Postup), Frano Miloš (try the full-bodied Stagnum), and Matuško and Skaramuća (good Dingač). Philipp, by a famously meticulous Swiss-Croatian vintner, produces a good Postup, as well as a fine summer white that blends *rukatac* and chardonnay.

While Croatian wines are impressive, don't overlook their neighbors' vintages as well. Slovenia corks up some excellent bottles (especially in the western and eastern reaches of the country), and Montenegro has some of the best wines in the region.

Croatia also has plenty of meat options. A delicious Dalmatian specialty is *pašticada*—braised beef in a slightly sweet wine-and-herb sauce, usually served with gnocchi. Dalmatia is also known for its mutton. Since the lambs graze on salty seaside herbs, the meat—often served on a spit—has a distinctive flavor. Throughout Croatia, look for the spicy, flavorful stewed pork-and-vegetables dish called *mućkalica*. The most widely available meat dish is the "mixed grill"—a combination of various Balkan grilled meats, best accompanied by the eggplant-and-red-pepper condiment *ajvar* (see the "Balkan Flavors" sidebar on page 425).

The best meat dish in Croatia is veal or lamb prepared under a *peka*—a metal baking lid that's covered with red-hot coals, to allow the meat to gradually cook to tender perfection. (*Ispod peka* means "under the bell.") Available only in traditional restaurants, this dish typically must be ordered in advance and for multiple people. You'll also find a break from seafood in the north (Zagreb) and east (Slavonia), where the food has more of a Hungarian flavor—heavy on meat served with cabbage, noodles, or potatoes.

Budget-conscious tourists reserve meat and fish for splurge dinners and mostly dine on cheaper and faster pastas and pizzas. You'll see familiar dishes, such as spaghetti Bolognese and spaghetti carbonara, gnocchi *(njoki)*, and lasagna. Risotto *(rižoto)* is popular here; most common is "black risotto," mixed with squid ink and various kinds of seafood.

Side Dishes

There are many good local varieties of cheese made with sheep's or goat's milk. Pag, an island in the Kvarner Gulf, produces a famous, very salty, fairly dry sheep's-milk cheese *(paški sir)*, which is said to be flavored by the herbs the sheep eat.

A common side dish is boiled potatoes and mangold *(bltiva)*; sometimes identified as "Dalmatian chard," this green is similar to Swiss chard. When ordering salad, choose between mixed (julienned cabbage, carrots, and turnips, often with some tomatoes or beets, and occasionally with a bit of lettuce) or green (mostly lettuce). Throughout Croatia, salad is typically served with the main dish unless you request that it be brought beforehand.

Dessert and Beverages

For dessert, look no further than the mountains of ice cream *(sladoled)* that line every street in coastal Croatia. While most *slad-*

oled isn't quite gourmet (don't expect the *artigianale* brilliance of Italian *gelaterias*), I've worked hard to sample and recommend the best ice-cream parlors in each town (someone has to do it). Dalmatia's typical dessert is a flan-like, crème caramel custard, called *rozata*.

Water is *voda*, and mineral water is *mineralna voda*. Jamnica is the main Croatian brand of bottled water, but you'll also see Bistra and Studenac. Many restaurants—especially fancier ones—might not want to bring you a glass of tap water, but you can try asking for *voda iz slavine*. For coffee *(kava)*, the easiest choice is *bijela kava* (BEE-yeh-lah KAH-vah)—"white coffee," or espresso with lots of milk (similar to a *caffè latte*). For black coffee, ask for *crna kava* (TSUR-nah KAH-vah).

The biggest brands of Croatian beer *(pivo)* are Ožujsko and Karlovačko, but you'll also see the Slovenian brand Laško (which is also brewed here in Croatia). Fans of dark beer *(crno pivo)* enjoy Tomislav. Most places also serve nonalcoholic beers *(bezalkoholno pivo)*; most common are Ožujsko Cool and Stella Artois NA.

Even more beloved in Croatia is wine *(vino; see "Croatian Wine" sidebar, earlier)*. Along the coast, locals find it refreshing to drink wine mixed with mineral water (called *špricer*—pronounced "spritzer"). When toasting with some new Croatian friends, raise your glass with a hearty *"Živjeli!"* (ZHEE-vyeh-lee).

CROATIAN LANGUAGE

Croatian was once known as "Serbo-Croatian," the official language of Yugoslavia. Most Yugoslav republics—including Croatia, Serbia, and Bosnia-Herzegovina—spoke this same language. And while each of these countries has tried to distance its language from that of its neighbors since the war, the languages spoken in all of these places are still very similar. The biggest difference is in the writing: Croatians and Bosniaks use our Roman alphabet, while Serbs use Cyrillic letters.

Since independence, Croatia has attempted to artificially make its vocabulary different from Serbian. In Yugoslav times, you'd catch a plane at the *aerodrom*. Today, you'll catch that same flight at the *zračna luka*—a new coinage that combines the old Croatian words for "air" and "port." These new words, once created, are actively injected into the lexicon. Croatians watching their favorite TV show will suddenly hear a character use a word they've never heard before...and think, "Oh, we have another new word." In this way, Croatian really is becoming quite different from Serbian (in much the same way Norwegian evolved apart from Swedish a century ago).

Remember, *c* is pronounced "ts" (as in "bats"). The letter *j* is pronounced as "y." The letters *č* and *ć* are slightly different, but they both sound more or less like "ch"; *š* sounds like "sh," and *ž* sounds like "zh" (as in "leisure"). One Croatian letter that you won't see in other languages is *đ*, which sounds like the "dj" sound in "jeans." In fact, this letter is often replaced with "dj" in English.

When attempting to pronounce an unfamiliar word, remember that the accent is usually on the first syllable (and never on the last). Confusingly, Croatian pronunciation—even of the same word—can vary in different parts of the country. This is because modern Croatian has three distinct dialects, called Kajkavian, Shtokavian, and Chakavian—based on how you say "what?" (*kaj?*, *što?*, and *ča?*, respectively). That's a lot of variety for a language with only five million speakers.

Attentive travelers will frequently hear two Croatian phrases that are used as enthusiastic affirmatives, like "sure" or "OK": *može* (MOH-zheh; can do) and *ajde* (EYE-deh; let's go).

For a smoother trip, take some time to learn a few key Croatian phrases (see the Croatian survival phrases on the next page).

Croatian Survival Phrases

In the phonetics, ī sounds like the long i in "light," and bolded syllables are stressed.

English	Croatian	Pronunciation
Hello. (formal)	Dobar dan.	**doh**-bahr dahn
Hi. / Bye. (informal)	Bok.	bohk
Do you speak English?	Govorite li engleski?	**goh**-voh-ree-teh lee **ehn**-glehs-kee
Yes. / No.	Da. / Ne.	dah / neh
I (don't) understand.	(Ne) razumijem.	(neh) rah-**zoo**-mee-yehm
Please. / You're welcome.	Molim.	**moh**-leem
Thank you (very much).	Hvala (ljepa).	**hvah**-lah (**lyeh**-pah)
Excuse me. / I'm sorry.	Oprostite.	oh-**proh**-stee-teh
problem	problem	proh-**blehm**
No problem.	Nema problema.	**neh**-mah proh-**bleh**-mah
Good.	Dobro.	**doh**-broh
Goodbye.	Do viđenija.	doh veed-**jay**-neeah
one / two	jedan / dva	**yeh**-dahn / dvah
three / four	tri / četiri	tree / **cheh**-teh-ree
five / six	pet / šest	peht / shehst
seven / eight	sedam / osam	**seh**-dahm / **oh**-sahm
nine / ten	devet / deset	**deh**-veht / **deh**-seht
hundred / thousand	sto / tisuća	stoh / **tee**-soo-chah
How much?	Koliko?	**koh**-lee-koh
local currency	kuna	**koo**-nah
Write it?	Napišite?	nah-**peesh**-ee-teh
Is it free?	Da li je besplatno?	dah lee yeh **beh**-splaht-noh
Is it included?	Da li je uključeno?	dah lee yeh **ook**-lyoo-cheh-noh
Where can I find / buy...?	Gdje mogu pronaći / kupiti...?	guh-**dyeh** moh-goo **proh**-nah-chee / **koo**-pee-tee
I'd like / We'd like...	Želio bih / Željeli bismo...	**zheh**-lee-oh bee / **zheh**-lyeh-lee **bees**-moh
...a room.	...sobu.	**soh**-boo
...a ticket to ___.	...kartu do ___.	**kar**-too doh ___
Is it possible?	Da li je moguće?	dah lee yeh **moh**-goo-cheh
Where is...?	Gdje je...?	guh-**dyeh** yeh
...the train station	...kolodvor	**koh**-loh-dvor
...the bus station	...autobusni kolodvor	**ow**-toh-boos-nee **koh**-loh-dvor
...the tourist information office	...turističko informativni centar	**too**-ree-steech-koh **een**-for-mah-teev-nee **tsehn**-tahr
...the toilet	...vece (WC)	**veht**-seh
men / women	muški / ženski	**moosh**-kee / **zhehn**-skee
left / right / straight	lijevo / desno / ravno	**lee**-yeh-voh / **dehs**-noh / **rahv**-noh
At what time...?	U koliko sati...?	oo **koh**-lee-koh **sah**-tee
...does this open / close	...otvara / zatvara	**oht**-vah-rah / **zaht**-vah-rah
(Just) a moment.	(Samo) trenutak.	(**sah**-moh) treh-**noo**-tahk
now / soon / later	sada / uskoro / kasnije	**sah**-dah / **oos**-koh-roh / **kahs**-nee-yeh
today / tomorrow	danas / sutra	**dah**-nahs / **soo**-trah

In a Croatian Restaurant

English	Croatian	Pronunciation
I'd like to reserve...	Rezervirao bih...	reh-zehr-**veer**-ow bee
We'd like to reserve...	Rezervirali bismo...	reh-zehr-**vee**-rah-lee **bees**-moh
...a table for one / two.	...stol za jednog / dva.	stohl zah **yehd**-nog / dvah
Is this table free?	Da li je ovaj stol slobodan?	dah lee yeh oh-vī stohl **sloh**-boh-dahn
Can I help you?	Izvolite?	eez-voh-lee-teh
The menu (in English), please.	Jelovnik (na engleskom), molim.	yeh-**lohv**-neek (nah **ehn**-glehs-kohm) **moh**-leem
service (not) included	posluga (nije) uključena	**poh**-sloo-gah (**nee**-yeh) **ook**-lyoo-cheh-nah
cover charge	couvert	**koo**-vehr
"to go"	za ponjeti	zah **pohn**-yeh-tee
with / without	sa / bez	sah / behz
and / or	i / ili	ee / **ee**-lee
fixed-price meal (of the day)	(dnevni) meni	(duh-**nehv**-nee) **meh**-nee
specialty of the house	specijalitet kuće	speht-see-yah-**lee**-teht **koo**-cheh
half portion	pola porcije	**poh**-lah **port**-see-yeh
daily special	jelo dana	**yeh**-loh **dah**-nah
fixed-price meal for tourists	turistički meni	**too**-ree-steech-kee **meh**-nee
appetizers	predjela	**prehd**-yeh-lah
bread	kruh	kroo
cheese	sir	seer
sandwich	sendvič	**send**-veech
soup	juha	**yoo**-hah
salad	salata	sah-**lah**-tah
meat / poultry	meso / perad	**may**-soh / **peh**-rahd
fish / seafood	riba / morska hrana	**ree**-bah **mor**-skah **hrah**-nah
fruit	voće	**voh**-cheh
vegetables	povrće	**poh**-vur-cheh
dessert	desert	deh-**sayrt**
(tap) water	voda (od slavine)	**voh**-dah (ohd **slah**-vee-neh)
mineral water	mineralna voda	**mee**-neh-rahl-nah **voh**-dah
milk	mlijeko	mlee-**yeh**-koh
(orange) juice	sok (od naranče)	sohk (ohd **nah**-rahn-cheh)
coffee	kava	**kah**-vah
tea	čaj	chī
wine	vino	**vee**-noh
red / white	crno / bijelo	**tsehr**-noh / bee-**yeh**-loh
sweet / dry / semi-dry	slatko / suho / polusuho	**slaht**-koh / **soo**-hoh / **poh**-loo-soo-hoh
glass / bottle	čaša / boca	**chah**-shah / **boht**-sah
beer	pivo	**pee**-voh
Cheers!	Živjeli!	**zhee**-vyeh-lee
More. / Another.	Još. / Još jedno.	yohsh / yohsh **yehd**-noh
The same.	Isto.	**ees**-toh
Bill, please.	Račun, molim.	**rah**-choon **moh**-leem
tip	napojnica	**nah**-poy-neet-sah
Delicious!	Izvrsno!	**eez**-vur-snoh

ZAGREB

Surprise: The landlocked Croatian capital is, quite possibly, the country's most underrated destination. In this land of time-passed coastal villages, Zagreb (ZAH-grehb) offers a welcome jolt of big-city sophistication. You can't get a complete picture of modern Croatia without a visit here—away from the touristy resorts, in the lively and livable city that is home to one out of every six Croatians (pop. 790,000). Think of it as a palate cleanser before or after your time on the coast. And, because things here are priced for locals rather than tourists, it's relatively affordable.

In Zagreb, you'll find historic neighborhoods, a thriving café culture, an impressive variety of good restaurants, my favorite urban people-watching in Croatia, an almost Prague-like Old World streetscape, and relatively few tourists. The city is also the country's best destination for museum going, with wonderful collections highlighting distinctively Croatian artists (the Naive Art movement and sculptor Ivan Meštrović), a quirky exhibit telling tales of fractured relationships, and a smattering of other fine options (modern art, city history, arts and crafts, and much more). Get your fill here before heading to smaller cities and towns, where worthwhile museums are in short supply.

Zagreb began as two walled medieval towns, Gradec and Kaptol, separated by a river. As Croatia fell under the control of various foreign powers—Budapest, Vienna, and Belgrade—the two hill towns that would become Zagreb gradually took on more religious and civic importance. Kaptol became a bishopric in 1094, and it's still home to Croatia's most important church. In the 16th century, the Ban (Croatia's governor) and the Sabor (parliament) called Gradec home. The two towns officially merged in 1850, and soon after, the railroad connecting Budapest with the Adriatic port city of Rijeka was built through the city. Zagreb prospered. After centuries of being the de facto religious, cultural, and political center of Croatia, Zagreb officially became a European capital when the country declared its independence in 1991.

Today, while tourism is on the rise, Zagreb may be the only destination in this book that still feels largely undiscovered. The city richly rewards those who choose to visit.

PLANNING YOUR TIME

If you can only spare a few hours as you pass through Zagreb, throw your bag in a locker at the train station and zip into the center for a quick visit. Better yet, spend the night. If you enjoy urban bustle and good museums, you won't regret investing some time here. One full day (with two nights) is plenty for a complete visit—but even with one overnight (and a half-day of sightseeing), you can get a good feel for the city.

If you're very tight on time, make a beeline for Jelačić Square to follow my self-guided walk. Take the funicular up to Gradec, visit the excellent Croatian Museum of Naive Art and the Museum of Broken Relationships, and stroll St. Mark's Square. Then wander down through the Stone Gate to the lively Tkalčićeva scene (good for a drink or meal), through the market (winds down around 14:00), and on to Kaptol and the cathedral. Depending on how much you linger, this loop can take anywhere from three hours to a full day.

With additional time, visit more of Zagreb's museums (the Meštrović Atelier and City Museum, both in the compact Gradec zone, are worthwhile), wander the series of parks called the "Green Horseshoe" (with even more museums), pay a visit to the beautiful Mirogoj Cemetery (one of Europe's finest final resting places), or head to the enjoyable nearby town of Samobor.

Orientation to Zagreb

Zagreb, just 30 minutes from the Slovenian border, stretches from the foothills of Medvednica ("Bear Mountain") to the Sava River. In the middle of the sprawl, you'll find the modern Lower Town (Donji Grad)—centered on Jelačić Square (YEH-lah-cheech)—and the two parts of the historic Upper Town (Gornji Grad): Gradec (GRAH-dehts) and Kaptol (KAHP-tohl). To the south is a U-shaped belt of parks, squares, and museums that make up the "Green Horseshoe." The east side of the U is a series of three parks, with the train station at the bottom (south) and Jelačić Square at the top (north).

Zagrebians have devised a brilliant scheme for confusing tourists: Street names can be given several different ways. For example, the street that is signed as ulica Kralja Držislava (King Držislav Street) is often called simply Držislavova (Držislav's) by locals. So if you're looking for a street, don't search for an exact match—be willing to settle for something that has a lot of the same letters.

TOURIST INFORMATION

Zagreb has Croatia's best-organized TI, right on Jelačić Square (Mon-Fri 8:30-21:00, Sat-Sun 9:00-18:00; Oct-May Mon-Fri 8:30-20:00, Sat 9:00-18:00, Sun 10:00-16:00; Trg bana Jelačića 11, tel. 01/481-4051, www.infozagreb.hr). Additional TI branches are at the train station and bus station (both open Mon-Fri 9:00-21:00, Sat-Sun 10:00-17:00); at the airport (daily 7:00-22:00); and in the Burglars' Tower at the top of the funicular in Gradec (daily 9:00-21:00 in summer, shorter hours off-season). Pick up the monthly events guide, the *Zagreb Times* newspaper, and the great *Step by Step* brochure (with a couple of good self-guided walking tours).

The **Zagreb Card** includes public transit and an odd assortment of museums (including the Zagreb 360° viewpoint, the Museum of Broken Relationships, and the City Museum), plus discounts on others. If you'll be sightseeing a lot, this could save you a bit (98 kn/24 hours, 135 kn/72 hours, sold inside main TI).

ARRIVAL IN ZAGREB

By Train: Zagreb's main train station (Glavni Kolodvor) is a few long blocks south of Jelačić Square, at the base of the Green Horseshoe. The straightforward arrivals hall has a train information desk, ticket windows, luggage lockers (lining the hallway to the left as you exit the platform), ATMs, pay WCs, a Konzum grocery store, and newsstands. To reach the city center, go straight out the front door. You'll run into a taxi stand and then the tracks for **tram** #6 (direction: Črnomerec zips you to Jelačić Square; direction: Sopot takes you to the bus station—the third stop, just after you turn right and go under the big overpass). You can also take tram #13 to Jelačić Square (direction: Žitnjak). For either tram, buy a 4-kn red ticket from any kiosk by the tram stop, and validate it when you board—use the yellow box nearest the driver. If you **walk** straight ahead through the long, lush park, you'll wind up at the bottom of Jelačić Square in 10 minutes.

By Bus: The user-friendly but inconveniently located bus station (Autobusni Kolodvor) is a few long blocks east of the main train station. Upstairs, you'll find ticket windows and access to the buses. Tram #6 (direction: Črnomerec) takes you to the main train station, then on to Jelačić Square. Walking from the bus station to Jelačić Square takes about 25 minutes.

By Plane: Zagreb's Franjo Tuđman Airport—which was completely redesigned in a bold, futuristic style in 2017—is 10 miles south of the center (code: ZAG, tel. 01/626-5222, www.zagreb-

Zagreb

<u>Accommodations</u>
1. Jägerhorn Hotel
2. Hotel Dubrovnik
3. Hotel Park 45
4. Hotel Astoria
5. 4 City Windows
6. Sobe Zagreb 17
7. To Hotel Ilica
8. Shappy Hostel & Green Point Eatery

<u>Eateries</u>
9. Pivnica Mali Medo
10. Agava
11. La Štruk
12. Plac
13. Cremme
14. Trilogija
15. Konoba Didov San
16. Heritage
17. Lari & Penati
18. Bistro Fotić
19. Vinodol
20. Kavkaz
21. Sandwich Bar Pingvin & Good Food
22. Good Food (2)
23. Cogito
24. Ginger Sushi & Chocolat 041
25. Zagreb Slastičarnica
26. Slastičarnica Vincek
27. Kraš Choco Bar

ZAGREB

airport.hr). A Croatia Airlines shuttle bus connects the airport to the bus station (30 kn, 2/hour, 30 minutes); from there, you can hop on a tram into town (see "By Bus," earlier). The public bus (#290) is cheaper (covered by 10-kn blue transit ticket), but it's less frequent and slower (drops you at Kvaternikov Trg, hop on tram #11 or #12 to the center). It can be worth the convenience to pay for a 30-minute taxi ride right to your hotel (the fair metered rate is around 200 kn, but crooked cabbies try to charge more—ask for an estimate before you get in). It's cheaper to take a taxi from the city to the airport—figure 100-150 kn.

By Car: Parking can be tricky in the town center. Get tips from your hotel, or if you're dropping in for the day, aim for one of two user-friendly, underground garages near the main sightseeing zone: The **Langov Trg garage** is slightly more convenient, just behind the cathedral, but can fill up at very busy times; the **Tuškanac garage** is on the opposite (west) end of the old town center, situated in the valley at the base of the Upper Town. The two have similar rates (around 7 kn/hour, cheaper after hours, 55 kn/24 hours). On-street parking in the center is generally limited to two hours, so a garage is more practical.

GETTING AROUND ZAGREB

The main mode of public transportation is the **tram,** operated by ZET (Zagreb Electrical Transport). Most rides in town are covered by a 30-minute red ticket for 4 kn; a longer ride—such as the public bus connection to/from the airport—is covered by a 1.5-hour blue ticket (10 kn). You can buy tickets from a kiosk near the tram stop (ask for *ZET karta*—zeht KAR-tah) or from the driver. When you board, punch your ticket in the yellow box nearest the front of the tram. A day ticket *(dnevna karta)* costs

30 kn. The most useful tram for tourists is #6, connecting Jelačić Square with the train and bus stations.

Taxis start at 10-15 kn, then run 5-7 kn per kilometer (exact rate depends on company, 3 kn extra for each piece of baggage). To avoid getting overcharged, call one of the main companies: Radio Taxi (tel. 1717), Cammeo (tel. 1212), or Ekotaxi (tel. 1414). If you hail a cab on the street, beware of corrupt cabbies; ask for an estimate up front. A typical ride within the city center shouldn't run more than about 30 kn.

Uber is active in Zagreb and typically charges lower rates than taxis. If you're comfortable using Uber back home, it works the same way here—take advantage of it.

HELPFUL HINTS

Sight Hours: Most of Zagreb's museums are closed on Sunday afternoon and all day Monday; most also close early Saturday afternoon. (Fortunately, one of the town's most important and worthwhile museums—Broken Relationships—is open daily.)

Some museums stay open late one night a week in summer (usually Thu). On Sunday morning, the city is very active—but by afternoon, it's extremely quiet. Sunday is also the day for a bustling antique/flea market at Britanski Trg (British Square), a 15-minute walk west of Jelačić Square (Sun 8:00-14:00, along busy Ilica street—hop on tram #1, #6, or #11 from Jelačić Square to Britanski Trg).

Festivals: Zagreb's **Christmas Market** is becoming known internationally and attracts visitors from the end of November through mid-January. The rest of the year features a regular parade of festivals, including ones for street performers (late May/early June), animated films (June), classical music (June/July), puppet theater (Sept), and food and film (Sept). Check the TI's website (www.infozagreb.hr) for what's going on when you're in town.

Changing of the Guard: Zagreb's touristy "Changing of the Guard" ceremony enlivens the city center on summer weekends. The 17th-century-costumed guards wear jaunty red scarves (an homage to the tale of how Croat soldiers "invented" the necktie) as they proceed through the center of town—passing landmarks such as St. Mark's Square, Tkalčićeva street, Jelačić Square, and the statue of Mary in front of the cathedral. On Saturdays it begins in front of the cathedral, while on Sundays it begins at St. Mark's Square up in Gradec (mid-April-Oct only, begins at 12:00, ask for complete schedule at TI). The Croatian government has also revived its own, more staid Changing of the Guard (June-Sept Saturdays at 12:00, St. Mark's Square).

Tours in Zagreb

Local Guides

While I've covered the basics in my self-guided walk, Zagreb gets even more interesting with a good tour guide. I recommend two sharp and talented guides who know their city well and enjoy sharing its charms with visitors. **Darija Gotić** (who also guides my tours in this part of Europe) offers a number of creative itineraries (550 kn for up to 2.5 hours, mobile 098-186-7719, darija@assistere.biz). **Neven Kamenski,** a marathon runner who's spent a lot of time in the US, is another good guide (520 kn/2 hours, mobile 091-343-4023, neven@kamenski.us).

Night Walks

After-hours walking tours are popular post-dinner infotainment. The **Mysterious Zagreb: Ghosts and Dragons Tour** focuses on spooky stories (75 kn, 2/week at 21:00, 2 hours, mobile 097-673-

8738, www.secret-zagreb.com), while the **Secrets of Grič Tour** ("Grič" is the nickname for Gradec) brings that historic quarter to life with a costumed guide imparting local legends (150 kn, June–mid-Sept Sat only at 21:00, one hour, mobile 091-461-5677, www.tajnegrica.hr). Both of these require reservations.

Bike Tours

Blue Bike runs a variety of bike-tour routes through the city, starting on Jelačić Square (330 kn, 2/day, reservations required, mobile 098-188-3344, www.zagrebbybike.com). They also rent bikes (75 kn/day; office is in the courtyard at Jelačić Square 15).

Zagreb Walk

The following self-guided orientation walk, rated ▲▲, begins and ends at Jelačić Square, linking almost everything that's worth seeing in this city, including the two hilltop towns that merged in 1850 to become Zagreb: Gradec and Kaptol. If you don't enter any of the sights, the entire route takes about 1.5 hours. But if you take your time, you can use it as a framework for a full day of sightseeing. The city's colorful food market—which is near the end of this walk—becomes quiet after about 14:00, so you may want to tour that first (just a block away from our starting point; see page 60 for tips).

▲▲Jelačić Square (Trg bana Jelačića)

The "Times Square" of Zagreb bustles with life. Watching the crowds pile in and out of trams and seeing the city buzz with activity, you'll feel the energy of an on-the-rise capital of a vibrant nation. This is also a popular place for any kind of special event in town—from concerts and sporting events to folk festivals, protests, and rallies. The city's busy pedestrian scene, sense of style, and healthy mix of tourists and locals make it arguably Croatia's best people-watching destination.

It's hard to believe that this Donji Grad (lower town)—now so frenetic—once held the townspeople's farm fields. Our walk takes you from here up to two towns—Gradec and Kaptol—that merged in 1850 to become the city of Zagreb. At that time, it was a small settlement of about 16,000 people. But under the auspices of the Habsburg monarchy, the newly united Zagreb began to industrialize and grow like mad. These former fields sprouted aristocratic villas as well as low-rent housing for factory workers.

Today, the square features a prominent equestrian statue of national hero **Josip Jelačić** (YOH-seep YEH-lah-cheech, 1801-1859), a 19th-century governor who extended citizens' rights and did much to unite the Croats within the Habsburg realm. In Jelačić's time, the Hungarians were exerting extensive control over Croatia, even trying to make Hungarian the official language. Meanwhile, Budapesters revolted against Habsburg rule in 1848. Jelačić, ever mindful of the need to protect Croatian cultural autonomy, knew that he'd have a better shot at getting his way from Austria than from Hungary. Jelačić chose the lesser of two evils and fought alongside the Habsburgs to put down the Hungarian uprising. A century later, in the Yugoslav era, Jelačić was considered a dangerously nationalistic symbol, and this statue was dismantled and stored away. But when Croatia broke away in 1991, Croatian patriotism was in the air, and Jelačić returned. Though Jelačić originally faced his Hungarian foes to the north, today he's staring down the Serbs to the south.

Get oriented. As you face Jelačić's statue, down a long block to your left is a funicular that takes you up to one of Zagreb's original villages, Gradec. Look for the TI to the right. If you exit the square ahead and to the right, you'll reach the city's other original village, Kaptol, and the cathedral (you can't miss its huge, pointy, Neo-Gothic spires—visible from virtually everywhere in Zagreb). And if you just need a break, several fine cafés ring the square. For the best view in town, ascend to the **Zagreb 360°** viewing platform at the top of the tallest glass skyscraper on the square (60 kn, daily 10:00-22:00, café, www.zagreb360.hr).

Taking the small street behind Jelačić (and a little to the left) would lead you to the market (best in the morning) and the enticing café-and-restaurant street, Tkalčićeva (lively any time of day or night; we'll circle back here later on the walk).

To see a unique bit of public art on this wide-but-short street, pause at the modern building with an arcade of blocky pillars, on the left. Look closely at the back of the first pillar (closest to Jelačić Square) and find the small silver plaque with a little ball labeled *Venus* (about eight feet up, facing the building). This is one piece of the 10-part work called **"Zagreb's Solar System."** Its center lies a short walk away, two blocks in front of Jelačić (on Bogovićeva street): a large spherical sculpture called *The Grounded Sun*. Scattered around the city are each of the nine planets, completely to scale—from the size of a marble to the size of a basketball—and each one at the appropriate distance from the "sun." The artist did the project in secret, so Zagrebians had to seek out each of the nine planets on their own, in a kind of citywide scavenger hunt.

But for now, head up to the hill called Gradec.

Walk from Jelačić Square to Gradec

Go a long block down busy Ilica street (to the left as you face Jelačić). Watch on your right for #8 (labeled *Tunnel Grič—Entrance*

4). This marks one of several entrance points to the **Tunnel Grič**, which burrows beneath Gradec. Townspeople used the tunnel as a shelter during World War II and again during the Yugoslav Wars of the 1990s. Now it's been renovated and, from time to time, serves as a venue for art installations and light shows. Ask around town whether there's anything going on in the tunnel during your visit...otherwise, there's nothing to see (though locals sometimes use it as a cool shortcut to escape the hot summer sun).

Across the street, and slightly to the left, look for the grand entryway marked *Privedna Banka Zagreb* (at #5). Cross over and pop inside the **Octagon shopping gallery.** This was the ultimate in iron-and-glass shopping elegance a century ago and still features a few of the city's top shops (including Croata, the tie store that loves to explain how Croatians invented the necktie; for the whole story, see page 189).

Walk all the way through the gallery, exiting into the inviting café-lined square called **Trg Petra Preradovića.** It hosts a flower market all day and inviting al fresco cafés throughout the day and into the night. Survey your options for a coffee break, then turn right and head back out to Ilica street, where you'll turn left and continue the way you were headed.

After another block, cross the tram tracks and turn right up Tomića, where you'll see a small **funicular** (ZET Uspinjača) crawling up the hill. Dating from the late 19th century, this funicular is looked upon fondly by Zagrebians—both as a bit of nostalgia and as a way to avoid some steps. You can walk up if you want, but the ride is more fun and takes only 55 seconds. Locals claim this is the "shortest funicular in the world" (5 kn, validate ticket in yellow box before you board, leaves every 10 minutes or with demand, daily 6:30-22:00).

Before boarding the funicular, take a short detour to an interesting little pocket of funky counterculture. Facing the bottom of the funicular, look left for the little passage at Tomićeva ulica 5, marked for the Basement bar. Go through this passage, passing the bar and the youth hostel beyond. You'll emerge into the fascinating **Art Park.** Once a notorious hangout for addicts, this has been transformed into a venue for local street artists, whose graffiti and other creations scamper up the steep slopes toward the Upper Town. There's even a playground and a little café—perfect for just hanging out in an overlooked corner of the city center.

When you're done here, head back out to the funicular and ride it up.

Gradec

From the top of the funicular, you'll enjoy a fine panorama over Zagreb. The tall tower on the left as you exit is one of Gradec's

ZAGREB

original watchtowers, the **Bur-glars' Tower** (Kula Lotrščak). After the Tatars ransacked Central Europe in the early 13th century, King Béla IV decreed that towns be fortified—so Gradec built a wall and guard towers (just like Kraków and Budapest did). Look for the little cannon in the top-floor window. Every
day at noon, this cannon fires a shot to commemorate a 15th-century victory over the besieging Ottomans.

The **Strossmayer Promenade** runs along the top of the hill, overlooking the city. The fenced section next to the funicular station is dubbed Strossmartre (a pun on "Montmartre"), which, in good summer weather, hosts a fun little outdoor café and often features works by local artists and live music. This fine promenade is just the start; along the outside of Gradec is a forested greenbelt that—while just a few minutes' walk away—feels miles from the city. It's a favorite place for locals to go for an urban hike, walk their dogs, or get away from the asphalt heat of summer.

Head up the street to the right of the tower, entering Gradec (often called "Grič" for short). Although this is one of the oldest parts of Zagreb, it lacks the cutesy cobbled charm you might expect. That's because little remains of medieval Gradec. When the Ottomans overran Europe, they never managed to take Zagreb, but the threat was enough to scare the nobility into the countryside. When the Ottomans left, the nobles came back, and they replaced the medieval buildings here with Baroque mansions.

At the first square, to the right, you'll see the Jesuit **Church of St. Catherine.** It's not much to look at from the outside, but the interior is intricately decorated—bubbly pink-and-white Baroque, dripping with stucco (only open to visitors during Mass). The same applies to several mansions on Gradec. This austere-outside, ornate-inside style is known as "Zagreb Baroque."

As you continue up the street, notice the old-timey **street signs,** holdovers from the Austro-Hungarian era: in both Croatian (Gospodzka ulicza) and German (Herren Gasse).

From here, you're a few steps from Zagreb's most interesting museums: On the right is the **Museum of Broken Relationships,** and if you turn right at the end of this block, head straight to reach the **Croatian Museum of Naive Art** in the Klovićevi Dvori Gallery (both listed later, under "Sights in Zagreb").

In the next block, on the left, is the yellow **"city parliament"** building (basically the Town Hall, and a popular place for weddings on summer Saturdays). To the left of the door, look for the plaque honoring **Nikola Tesla** (1856-1943), the prominent scientist who championed alternating current (AC) as a better electrical system than Thomas Edison's direct current (DC). Although Tesla was an ethnic Serb (his father was an Orthodox priest), he was born in a remote village in central Croatia, so both Serbs and Croats claim him. (Today, Tesla is a rare figure who is revered both in Zagreb and in Belgrade.) This plaque proudly trumpets that on May 24, 1892, Tesla came to this building and suggested that Zagreb become the first city in the world to build an AC power station. But the plaque fails to mention that the city parliament rejected this suggestion...so Tesla went to the US, where he successfully pitched the same idea to Buffalo, New York.

While Zagreb eventually did adopt AC, this part of town still clings to a much, much older form of lighting. Flanking the doors of the city parliament are two of the 217 old-fashioned **gaslights** that illuminate Gradec. These are lit and extinguished each day by two city employees. Notice that each lamp is numbered.

At the end of the block, you'll come to **St. Mark's Square** (Markov trg), centered on the **Church of St. Mark.** The original church here was from the 13th century, but only a few fragments remain. The present church's colorful tile roof, from 1880, depicts two coats of arms. On the left, the red-and-white checkerboard symbolizes north-central Croatia, the three lions' heads stand for the Dalmatian Coast, and the marten (*kuna*, like

the money) running between the two rivers (Sava and Drava) represents Slavonia—Croatia's northern, inland panhandle. On the right is the seal of Zagreb, featuring a walled city.

In the years since these tiles were laid, the **city seal** has changed in two ways (as you can see by comparing it to the city flag that flies from the city parliament building). First, while the castle doors are closed on the roof, today's seal shows wide-open doors—to demonstrate that Zagreb is strong, but still welcoming to visitors. Second, the city color has been changed from red to blue. If you pay attention around town, you'll notice the liberal use of Zagreb's distinctive hue of blue—for example, on city buses and trams. And devoted fans of the immensely popular local soccer team, Dinamo Zagreb, are called the "Bad Blue Boys."

While it would be nice to see the inside of St. Mark's Church, the priest doesn't appreciate tourists, so it's closed except during services. (If you manage to slip in, you'll see frescoes with Bible scenes, and sculptures by the talented 20th-century sculptor Ivan Meštrović: the crucifix over the main altar, a pietà on the left, and on the right, Madonna and Child sitting cross-legged, in a typical Meštrović pose. If you can't get in, you can still enjoy some Meštrović works at his nearby museum, described later.)

As you face the church, the long building on the right is the **Sabor,** or parliament. Since at least the 13th century, Croatian noblemen have met to make important decisions regarding their territories. This gradually evolved into today's modern parliament. While this square used to be a congested parking lot, Zagreb's mayor declared it a traffic-free zone; now members of parliament either have to be bused in from off-site parking lots (watch for the cute little blue bus that comes and goes periodically) or have their drivers sit tight nearby (look for unmarked black cars patiently waiting on the street in front of the city parliament).

Across the square from the Sabor (to your left as you face the church) is **Ban's Palace** (Banski Dvori), today the offices for the prime minister. This was one of the few buildings in central Zagreb damaged in the war following Croatia's independence. In October 1991, Yugoslav People's Army pilots targeted this building in an air strike. (Notice the different-colored tiles where the roof had to be patched.) They landed a direct hit on the room where Croatian president Franjo Tuđman and his right-hand man, Stipe Mesić (who would later succeed him as president), were scheduled to be meeting. But coincidentally, the meeting had been moved to another location at the last minute—so Croatia's first two presidents survived. (It's eerie to think what might have become of this fledgling nation if its leadership had been wiped out at this early stage.)

Before moving on, consider visiting two more excellent museums, which sit just a short walk away (both described in detail later, under "Sights in Zagreb"). The talented 20th-century sculptor **Ivan Meštrović's former home and studio** is now a museum of his works. It's about a block away: Go down the street behind the church on the left-hand side, and you'll see the museum on the right. And the extensive, well-presented **Zagreb City Museum** explains the story of this town from prehistoric times to the modern day. To reach it, walk along the front of the Sabor and continue straight ahead two blocks, watching for the museum on your right.

Walk from Gradec to Kaptol

For an interesting stroll from St. Mark's Square to the cathedral, head down the street (Kamenita ulica) to the right of the parliament building. Near the end of the street, on the right, you'll see the oldest **pharmacy** in town—recently restored and gleaming (c. 1355, marked *gradska ljekarna*). Across the street is **Lav Caffe**

Galerija, a fun, relaxing coffeehouse and art gallery; this is just one of many inviting coffee-break opportunities you'll see between here and the end of this walk.

Just beyond, you'll reach Gradec's only surviving town gate, the **Stone Gate** (Kamenita Vrata). Inside is an evocative chapel.

The focal point is a painting of Mary that miraculously survived a major fire in the house up above in 1731. When this medieval gate was reconstructed in the Baroque style, it was turned into a makeshift chapel. The candles (purchased in the little shop) represent Zagrebians' prayers. Notice the soot-blackened ceiling over the forest fire of blazing candles in the big metal bin. The stone plaques on the wall say "thank you" *(hvala ti)* for prayers that were answered. You may notice people making the sign of the cross as they walk through here, and often a crowd of worshippers gathers, gazing intently at the painting. Mary was made the official patron saint of Zagreb in 1990.

As you leave the Stone Gate and come to **Radićeva,** turn right and begin walking downhill. Looking down to the bottom of Radićeva, you'll see where this street is becoming a popular shopping zone, with local boutiques popping up all the time—a fun area to browse later.

But for now, head just a few steps down Radićeva, then watch for the orange building at **#30** on your left. Go through the big, arched entryway and bear right down the wooden steps. At the bottom of these stairs, you'll come to a little row of **old-time houses.** In times past, this was one of the most popular areas in town... as home of the red light district. While prostitution is illegal now, it was once allowed and carefully regulated, with routine medical examinations for the working girls. Legally, only a woman (over age 30) could own and operate a brothel. Locals note, with some irony, that the balconies on the opposite side of these houses of ill repute—which we'll see in a moment—face the stern spires of the cathedral.

Turn left, walking along the row of old houses (and noticing the remains of the old Gradec town wall on your left), then turn right down the stairs. You've just dropped down into the middle of Zagreb's most appealing street, **Tkalčićeva** (tuh-KAHL-chee-chay-vah). Do a slow spin to savor this in-love-with-life drag. This traffic-free street combines some of the most atmospheric old homes of Zagreb with some of its most enticing eateries and peo-

ZAGREB

ple-watching. (For starters, you're literally surrounded by tables for the recommended Pivnica Mali Medo brewpub.)

If you need a break from sightseeing, Tkalčićeva is just the ticket: Nurse a coffee, beer, or meal anywhere along this street (I've listed several recommendations under "Eating in Zagreb," later).

If you stood here 200 years ago, you'd be washed away by a rushing river that separated Gradec (behind you) and Kaptol (in front of you). In the Middle Ages, the two towns were at odds and sometimes fought. ("Downriver" from here is a cross street that's still called Krvavi Most—"Blood Bridge.") But in 1850, after the towns had long since set aside their differences, they merged to become Zagreb. The polluted, stinky river had become a nuisance, so they diverted its flow and covered over the valley to create Tkalčićeva.

Turn right and enjoy a stroll down Tkalčićeva (toward the onion-domed tower of Holy Mary Church). You'll pass (on the right) the balconies of the brothels we saw earlier, then a fine park on the right with a genteel lady prepared for rain. (The parasol is part of the official folk costume for Zagreb.) Just beyond the park, next to the door for the recommended Cremme dessert café, is the *Mars* plaque for the solar system sculpture. Directly across the street, walk up the hill toward the cathedral towers (on Skalinska, passing outdoor restaurant tables and the entrance to the recommended eatery La Štruk).

Kaptol

As you walk uphill, you're entering Kaptol, the second of medieval Zagreb's twin towns.

At the top of the street, turn right and go down the stairs to find Zagreb's lively-in-the-morning **market** *(dolac)*. If you're here at prime time, browse the market's double-decker delights (noticing that the meat and cheese halls are below your feet—use the stairs or elevator in the blocky white building to get there). For pointers on what to see at the market, see page 60.

When you're done at the market, go through the gap between the buildings toward the **cathedral** spires. Crossing the square, you can enter Croatia's most important house of worship (described later, under "Sights in Zagreb"). From here, you can head downhill one block to Jelačić Square—where our walk began.

Sights in Zagreb

MUSEUMS IN THE CENTER

Zagreb has more than its share of museums, and many of them are excellent—making up for the lack of great Croatian museums outside the capital. It would take you days to see all the city's museums; I've selected the most worthwhile (still enough to fill a couple of days—choose the ones that interest you the most).

▲▲▲Croatian Museum of Naive Art at the Klovićevi Dvori Gallery

This remarkable collection (the Hrvatski Muzej Naivne Umjetnosti), founded in 1952 as the "Peasant Art Gallery," is one of the most enjoyable exhibitions in Croatia. It features expressionistic paintings by untrained peasant artists, mostly Croatians, from the 1930s to the 1980s. A new museum building is in the works to showcase these paintings (at the far end of Gradac hill, at Demetrova 18; opens in 2024 at the earliest). In the meantime, many of the paintings are on display at Klovićevi Dvori Gallery, offering an easily digestible sampling of the top names from the Naive Art movement. Viewing these works, it's important to remember that this isn't considered "folk art" or "amateur art" but top-quality works by great artists who were, by fluke or fate, never formally trained.

Cost and Hours: 40 kn, Tue-Sun 11:00-19:00, closed Mon, Jezuitski trg 4, tel. 01/485-1926, www.gkd.hr, for new museum updates check www.hmnu.hr.

Visiting the Museum: Here's an overview of some of the big names of the Naive Art movement. As the collection in this gallery is temporary, not every painter or painting will be on display.

Ivan Generalić (1914-1992): Generalić is the founder and star of Croatian Naive Art. (Look for his self-portrait, with a blue background.) Generalić was discovered in the 1930s by a Paris-trained Croatian artist. Early paint-

ings show his evolution as an artist (and the evolution of Croatian Naive Art in general): While his early works come with a social or political agenda (such as *Requisition,* where two policemen repo a cow from an impoverished couple), he eventually mellows his focus to show simple, typical village scenes that gradually become more and more fantastical *(Harvesters),* and eventually strips away people entirely to focus on the land (1956's *Deer in the Forest* and 1959's *Flood*). In 1953, Generalić—still relatively unknown outside his homeland—did a show in Paris, sold everything, and came home rich. This put Croatian Naive Art on the international map and kick-started a new vigor in the movement.

Woodcutters, from 1959, shows the next phase, as Generalić's works became even more rich with fantasy—the peacock, the men clinging to treetops, and the trademark "coral trees." Instead of showing, Generalić is evoking; Naive Art strove to capture the spirit and emotion of peasant life. Paintings such as this one inspired Generalić's followers (called the "Hlebine School," for the village where Generalić lived). In *Solar Eclipse* (1961), villagers cower and roosters crow as the sun is mysteriously gobbled up by a black disc. People respond in different ways: some by staging impromptu religious processionals, others by clutching their belongings close and fleeing.

Next, look for works by the following two Naive Art painters, who were inspired (if not trained) by Generalić.

Ivan Večenaj (1920-2013): Večenaj focused on religious scenes (you may see his gruesome *Evangelists on Calvary* crucifix). His masterpiece is *Moses and the Red Sea* (1973), an expressionistic re-telling of the familiar biblical story. Moses, glowing against an inky black sky and with feet muddy from having just crossed the seabed, watches the sea—literally red with Egyptian blood—washing away his pursuers. The footprints emerging from the sea (at the bottom) suggest that the Israelites' exodus has been a successful one. On the left, see the pyramids (Egypt), and on the right, a cozy village (the Promised Land). Flying around Moses are 10 birds (representing the Commandments); he's equipped with some of his typical symbols, including the horn around his neck, a ram, and a snake (which, as the story goes, he conjured from a staff to convince the pharaoh to allow the Israelites to leave Egypt).

Mijo Kovačić (1935-): Kovačić specialized in peasant landscapes; you may see one of his most representative works, *Winter*

Landscape with Woman. Notice how Kovačić took a style of painting pioneered by Generalić and brought it to the next level. Winter scenes were most common, because the peasant artists were busy working the fields the rest of the year. (Early on, such artists were sometimes called "Sunday painters," because they had to work their "real" jobs from Monday to Saturday.) Kovačić also enjoyed winter scenes for the black-and-white contrast they allowed. Like Dalí, Magritte, and other Surrealists, Kovačić juxtaposed super-realism (look at each individual hair on the swine

Origins of Naive Art

Starting in the late 19th century, the art world began to broaden its definition of great art, seeking out important work originating outside the esteemed academies and salons of the day. The goal: to demonstrate that art was not simply a trained skill but an inborn talent. Intellectuals began to embrace an "anti-intellectual" approach to art. Interest grew in the indigenous art of Africa, Mesoamerica, and Polynesia (Picasso went through an African mask phase, and Gauguin went to live in Tahiti); composer Béla Bartók collected traditional folk melodies from the Hungarian countryside; the Art Brut movement preserved artwork by people deemed "insane" by mainstream society; the autodidactic (self-taught) painter Grandma Moses became well-known in the US and Europe; and art by children gained acclaim.

Here in Croatia in the 1930s, the focus was on art by untrained peasants. At that time, as in much of rural Europe, 85 percent of Croatians lived virtually medieval lifestyles—with no electricity or other modern conveniences—and the majority were illiterate and uneducated. These artists captured this humble reality, creating figurative works in an increasingly abstract age. By the 1950s and 1960s, Croatian Naive Art had emerged at the forefront of a Europe-wide phenomenon.

ZAGREB

in his painting *Swineherd*, pictured below) with fantastical, almost otherworldly settings.

More Naive Artists: As the movement grew, more and more artists adopted the Naive style and made it their own. Notice that they frequently painted on glass. It was cheaper and more readily available in rural areas than art canvases, and—because it required no special technique—was an easier medium for the untrained artists to work on.

Here are some artists to look for in the collection:

Dragan Gaži (1930-1983), a friend and neighbor of Generalić's, painted landscapes and portraits. His *The Wind in Winter* (1973) is an intoxicating landscape.

Martin Mehkek (1936-2014) painted evocative portraits of

Roma (Gypsy) people. For the one depicting his cross-eyed neighbor Steve, Mehkek mostly painted with his fingers, using brushes only for fine details (such as the Hitler-style moustache).

Josip Generalić (1936-2004), the movement founder's less-talented son, painted *Guiana '78*—showing the gruesome aftermath of the Jim Jones mass suicide, with a pair of monkeys surveying the smiling corpses. (While vivid, this painting doesn't reflect the Croatian peasant experience, and the curator admits it's not the best representative of Naive Art.)

Ivan Lacković Croata (1932-2004) painted works that focus on different seasons. In his paintings, watch for more of those distinctively spiny, bonsai-like trees that pervade Naive works.

Ivan Rabuzin (1921-2008), arguably the movement's second most important artist (after Ivan Generalić), painted lyrical landscapes. Like a visual haiku, Rabuzin's dreamlike world of hills, trees, and clouds is reminiscent of Marc Chagall.

Emerik Feješ (1904-1969) specialized in colorful scenes of famous monuments from around Europe—Paris, Venice, Vienna, and Milan. Feješ never traveled to any of these places—his paintings are based on romantic black-and-white postcards of the era, which Feješ "colorized" in his unique style.

Matija Skurjeni (1898-1990) painted the almost crayon-like *Animal World* (1961). While it looks like the roll call for Noah's ark, it's loaded with symbolism. The dinosaur is Skurjeni's self-portrait, the other large animals are his friends and artistic colleagues, the butterflies fluttering around represent spirituality (a new spin on the white dove of the Holy Spirit)...and the devil in the base of the tree, with wings and a crown, is one of Skurjeni's harshest critics—who also happened to be the curator of this museum at the time.

Drago Jurak (1911-1994) painted *Luxury Boat* (1974), which looks like a Bollywood Titanic.

Rounding out the collection are works by Naive artists from other countries (Russia, Japan, France, and Poland). You may also see pencil sketches used by Naive artists to create their works (including one for Generalić's *Solar Eclipse*). After the sketch was complete, the artist would put it against a pane of glass to paint the scene—small details first, gradually filling in more and more of the background. After being composed essentially "backward," the glass painting would be flipped over to be viewed. All of the works on glass you've seen in this collection were actually painted backward.

▲▲Museum of Broken Relationships

Opened in 2010 by a couple who had recently broken up, this extremely clever museum lives up to all the attention it's received in

the international press. The museum's mission is simple: collect true stories of failed couples from around the world, tell their story in their own words, and display the tale alongside an actual item that embodies the relationship. The items and stories provide insights into a shared human experience—we can all relate to the anger, sadness, and relief expressed in these poignant, at times hilarious, displays. In addition to the predictable "he cheated on me so I broke his favorite fill-in-the-blank" items, the ever-changing collection delves into other types of fractured connections: an unrequited childhood crush, the slow fade of lovers who

gradually grew apart, disappointment in a politician who failed to live up to lofty expectations, the premature end of a love cut short by death, and so on. You'll see discarded wedding albums, sex toys with stories about unreasonable requests for kinky acts, films that attempt to capture the essence of a relationship, children's playthings representing the innocence of young love (and, perhaps, the universality of stuffed animals), and plenty of items broken with vengeful wrath. The museum is small—just a few rooms—but rewards those who take the time to read each story. The collection has been such a hit, they've taken it on the road, garnering fans in cities worldwide. If you enjoy the collection, the 184-kn "museum book"—with the stories and photos—is a good souvenir.

Cost and Hours: 40 kn, daily 9:00-22:30, Oct-May until 21:00, café, Sv. Ćirila i Metoda 2, tel. 01/485-1021, https://brokenships.com.

▲Ivan Meštrović Atelier

Ivan Meštrović—Croatia's most famous artist—lived here from 1922 until 1942 (before he fled to the US after World War II). The house, carefully decorated by Meštrović himself, has been converted into a delightful gallery of the artist's works, displayed in two parts: residence and studio. Split's Meštrović Gallery (described on page 194) is the definitive museum of this 20th-century Croatian sculptor, but if you're not going there, Zagreb's gallery is a convenient place to gain an appreciation for this prolific, thoughtful artist. For more on Meštrović, see page 196.

Cost and Hours: 30 kn, Tue-Fri 10:00-18:00, Sat-Sun until 14:00, closed Mon, behind St. Mark's Square at Mletačka 8, tel. 01/485-1123, www.mestrovic.hr.

Visiting the Museum: When you buy your ticket, be sure to pick up the large floor plan—it's the only way to identify the pieces on display here (they're marked only by number; I've noted the numbers for important works in this description). Then enter the high-ceilinged dining room of Meštrović's **home.** He designed the crucifix on the wall (#83, Christ being supported by an angel), the wood-carved chandeliers, and the furniture, right down to the carvings on the backs of the chairs. Overlooking the table is a sculpture of his mother (#59), wearing the traditional headdress of her Dalmatian village homeland, legs crossed, hands clasped in intent prayer—a favorite pose of Meštrović's. At the other end of the table is a self-portrait bust of Meštrović, head cocked quizzically (#76). In the alcove at the bottom of the stairs, see the *Madonna and Baby,* tenderly kissing (#38).

Head **upstairs** to see sketches and plaster casts Meštrović did in preparation for some of his larger works. The rooms on this floor are filled with busts and small, characteristically elongated statues, all of them expressive. In the far room, appreciate his fine ceiling frescoes; in the adjoining room, find Meštrović's powerful sculpture depicting his mentor and friend, Auguste Rodin, furiously at work (#26).

Continue up to the **top floor,** where you'll find several evocative pieces: Meštrović's wife breastfeeding their son (#54); a portrait of Michelangelo, Meštrović's artistic ancestor, holding a chisel and hammer and portrayed with his trademark high forehead and smashed nose (#56); and a copy of the powerful pietà from St. Mark's Church (#89). The next room holds a cowering *Job* (#88), the head of an archangel (#97), a tender portrait of a mother teaching her child to pray (#55), and a small model of one of Meštrović's biggest and best-known works, *Bishop Gregory of Nin* (#61, in Split, described on page 187). In the small, final room is a praying woman with a beehive 'do (#33).

Back downstairs, cross through the **garden** to reach the studio. Outside are several more fine pieces, including another one of the museum's top works: *The History of the Croats* (#90), with a woman sitting cross-legged (remember this pose?) with a book resting on her lap. The top of the book has a unique Croatian spiral design, and along the front of it are the letters of Croatia's Glagolitic alphabet. Back against the wall, *John the Evangelist* studiously takes notes, looking up for divine inspiration (#71). And the small *Prince Marko on Šarac* (#16)— while clearly a Croatian theme— evokes two of Meštrović's most famous works, the giant Native Americans on horseback that stand in Chicago's Grant Park.

Those towering sculptures were created in this very studio and later transported (in pieces) to the United States. Originally, those sculptures were commissioned to be a cowboy and an Indian...but Meštrović said, "How about *two* Native Americans...?"

Go into Meštrović's **studio.** Next to the door to the inner courtyard is a skinny, Modigliani-esque sculpture of Meštrović's first wife, Ruža (#70). In the middle of the room are two sculptures modeled after his second wife, Olga: the unfinished, walnut-carved *Mother and Child* (#100), and the exquisite, white-marble *Woman Beside the Sea* (#58, one of the collection's highlights). Nearby is a sculpture of the *Evangelist Luke* (#72)—the twin of John out in the garden. Upstairs around the gallery are smaller pieces, including a study for the spiny-fingered hand of Split's *Bishop Gregory of Nin* (#62).

On your way back out, take a moment to linger in the **courtyard**—with the large *Woman in Agony* (#67) in the center and less-agonized women all around.

▲Zagreb City Museum (Muzej Grada Zagreba)

This collection, with a modern, well-presented exhibit that sprawls over two floors of an old convent, traces the history of the city through town models, paintings, furniture, clothing, and lots of fascinating artifacts.

Cost and Hours: 30 kn, Tue-Sat 10:00-19:00, Sun until 14:00, closed Mon, 20-kn audioguide nicely supplements the posted descriptions, at north end of Gradec at Opatička 20, tel. 01/485-1361, www.mgz.hr.

Visiting the Museum: After buying your ticket, head through the door and turn left, then work your way up through the ages. Each display has a fine English description. On the largely skippable ground floor, you'll loop through the prehistoric and Roman periods and the medieval growth of the twin towns of Gradec and Kaptol. You'll see city symbols and flags, a town model from 1795, statues from the main portal of the cathedral (17th-century Baroque) and other religious art, and a small collection of cleverly decorated 18th-century weathervanes.

Upstairs, the exhibit lingers on Zagreb's boom time in the 19th century, when it was an increasingly spruced-up and genteel outpost of the Austro-Hungarian Empire. The exhibits consider various facets of society during that era. You'll see more religious art, furniture, aristocratic portraits, another town model (from the 1860s), a life-size portrait of national hero Josip Jelačić (and his actual uniform), and colorfully painted shooting targets. One room has a giant city map on the floor, punctuated with models of key buildings. You'll also find models of old storefronts, theater costumes, and exhibits on public utilities and social life.

The coverage of the tumultuous 20th century is perhaps most engaging, though it has an understandably bad attitude about the Serb-dominated first Yugoslav period. Propaganda posters cheer on the communist period, while all of this historical heaviness is balanced by a lighthearted exhibit about Zagreb's popular cartoon industry. The finale is a room dedicated to the creation of independent Croatia, including an exhibit on damage sustained during the war and a film with clips from various landmarks in Croatian independence: a violent riot at a heated 1990 soccer match between Dinamo Zagreb and Belgrade's Crvena Zvezda (Red Star) team; the election and arrival in parliament of the pro-independence Franjo Tuđman; and the return of the statue of Jelačić to his namesake square.

OTHER SIGHTS IN THE CENTER
▲▲Market (Dolac)

In 1930, Zagreb tore down much of Kaptol's rickety, medieval Old Town to build this as-central-as-possible market. Today, it's jammed with producers from the surrounding countryside—and all over Croatia—selling all manner of fruits, vegetables, meats, cheeses, fish, and other foodstuffs. A stroll through the market offers insight into the colorful local culture and the chance to pick up a few picnic items. To reach the market easily from Jelačić Square, walk one block up the street to the left of the Jelačić statue, and climb up the stairs (open Mon-Sat 7:00-14:00, Sun until 13:00).

Visiting the Market: The market has two sections—indoor (with meat and cheese) and outdoor (produce, just above). Begin by exploring the outdoor section, then head inside. At the top of the stairs coming up from Jelačić Square, notice the statue of the *kumica*—a villager wearing a traditional dress (with a head scarf) and balancing a basket of produce on her head.

Filling the square is the **produce market,** with vendors from all around selling what's fresh. What you'll see changes with the season (for instance, in late summer, you'll see plums and grapes; in fall, look for nuts and mushrooms), but a few things are mainstays. The honey *(med)* is a reminder that the mountain behind Zagreb is called Medvednica. In Croatian, a bear is poetically called a *medved*—literally "honey-seer." So *Medvednica* means "place of the honey-seer." The big red umbrellas with white, yellow, and green stripes evoke the parasols that are part of the traditional costume for the region around Zagreb. The stalls behind the boxy white building (which is the entrance to the lower, indoor market) sell various components of that same costume (such as embroidered scarves); while tourists can buy them, most customers are locals. Nearby, the few "souvenir" stands (at the top part of the market, near the cathedral) show off colorful, traditional wooden toys, still made the way they have been for centuries (men do the carving, women do the painting); the wooden birds on sticks—which flap their wings when you roll them along the floor—are a favorite.

As you face the top of the market, to the left you'll see the fragrant **fish market** *(ribarnica)*. While Zagreb is far from the sea, the freshest catch is trucked in daily.

To get to the indoor market *(tržnica)*, enter the boxy white building and descend using the stairs or elevator. You'll pop out in the **meat market.** Stroll the stalls, noticing—in addition to the typical array of sausages, salamis, and *pršut* (cured ham)—the local affection for horsemeat (from a young horse—*ždrebetina*, or an adult—*konjetina*). Also watch for piles of a local delicacy called *čvarci*. Vaguely similar to pork rinds, these were created as a way to use up otherwise unused bits and pieces of pork; they'd press all of the fat out of them, creating a crispy snack. While this used to be simple peasant food, these days meat production is streamlined to process pork leftovers in other ways—and so *čvarci* are considered a rare and expensive delicacy (*prešani čvarci* are even more pressed—and more expensive).

From the meat market, look for the **dairy** section (marked *mlijenči proizvodi*, on the left from where you entered). Most cheese here is cow cheese *(kravlji)*, typically very fresh and soft, and sometimes with flavorings (such as paprika or chives) mixed in. Goat cheese *(kozji)* is more rare. In this area, you'll also see some local starches. The extremely skinny noodles called *rezanci* are used in soups; the big, flat squares that look like tortillas *(mlinci)* are served with poultry—they soak up drippings to become soft and delicious.

▲▲Cathedral (Katedrala)

The most important church in a very devoutly Catholic country, Zagreb's cathedral is worth a visit. The full name is the Cathedral of the Assumption of the Blessed Virgin Mary and the Saintly Kings Stephen and Ladislav (whew!)—but most locals just call it "the cathedral." Inside, you'll see monuments to many late, great Croatians and get a taste of the faith that pervades this country.

Cost and Hours: Free, Mon-Sat 10:00-17:00, Sun from 13:00.

Visiting the Cathedral: Before entering, stand in the **square** in front of the cathedral (near the gilded Madonna on a pillar—sculpted by the same artist who did the Jelačić statue on the main square) to ponder the history of this site. In 1094, when a diocese was established at Kaptol, this church quickly became a major center of high-ranking church officials. In the mid-13th century, the original cathedral was destroyed by invading Tatars, who used it as a stable. It was rebuilt and surrounded by a stout medieval wall—practically turning it into a castle to defend against potential Ottoman invasion. You can still see the pointy tops of the round guard towers on either side of the church; until a century ago, this wall ran along the road behind you, completely enclosing the building. (The St. Mary pillar stands upon the round footprint of another one of the towers.) The church was severely damaged again, this time by an earthquake, in 1880. The current version is Neo-Gothic (completed in 1902), incorporating a few original Gothic elements. Much of the wall was torn down to allow the town to grow.

Walking closer to the main door, look to the left to see the **two spires** displayed just inside the wall. The one on the left, eroded down to a pathetic nub, demonstrates what happens when you use abundant—but porous—limestone to build a church in a climate with cold, freezing winters. (They can get away with using limestone on the coast, but in chilly Zagreb, it's just not the right material.) Some part of the church will certainly be covered by scaffolding during your visit—as it has been for decades, as restorers have gradually been replacing worn elements with new ones...this time, using a more durable stone.

Just before entering the church, appreciate the modern tympanum (carved semicircular section over the door). Then step inside and wander down the nave, taking in the opulence of the church. When it was completed, Zagreb was a small city of about 70,000 people; the construction of a church this finely decorated hints at the wealth of the city during its boom time. (In later times, that money dried up; the big chandeliers hanging in the nave were reportedly imported from Las Vegas—the best source for affordable glitz—in the 1970s.)

First, head to the **main altar** and look closely at the silver relief: a whimsical scene of the Holy Family doing chores around the house (Mary sewing, Joseph and Jesus building a fence...and angels helping out).

From the altar, turn left, then head to the front of the church. In the front-left corner (on the wall, between the confessionals), find **Ivan Meštrović's monument to Alojzije Stepinac.** We'll learn more about Stepinac

in a moment, but for now pay attention to this beautifully carved piece of sculpture. Meštrović, the talented Croatian sculptor, worked in the early 20th century before fleeing communist Yugoslavia. Notice that this work was carved in "Detroit, Mich, USA," where Meštrović lived out his days in a self-imposed exile. Meštrović was a close friend of Stepinac and carved this monument from half a world away.

Facing the nearby altar, on the right look for the bronze monument to **Josip Jelačić,** the statesman whose statue adorns Zagreb's main square. Remember that Jelačić gained fame fighting against the Hungarians during the Habsburg era; the monument explains that his efforts allowed Zagreb to become an archbishopric, increasing its independence. But the large altar next to him celebrates three early Hungarian sainted kings, who (back when Croatia was part of Hungary, centuries before Jelačić) founded this church. You can imagine a Croat viewing this and thinking, "Those wonderful Hungarians, to whom we owe this church—thank God we defeated them."

Walk up the steps to the area behind the main altar. Here you'll find a glass case containing a waxy, eerily lifelike sculpture of **Alojzije Stepinac.** (His actual remains are below.) Stepinac was the archbishop of Zagreb during World War II, when he shortsightedly supported the fascist Ustaše movement, pledging his allegiance to Ante Pavelić's Nazi puppet government in Croatia. Like many Croatians, Stepinac believed that this was the ticket to greater independence from Serbia. When Tito came to power, he put Stepinac on trial and sent him to jail for five years, before he was banished to live out his life in the remote, poor village where he was born. But Stepinac never lost his faith, and many Croatian Catholics consider him something of a martyr—and arguably the most inspirational figure of their faith. He's also respected in the US, where some Catholic schools bear his name. But many Serbs still consider Stepinac a villain who cooperated with the genocidal activities of the brutal Ustaše.

Before leaving, pull up a pew and ponder the role of faith in contemporary Croatian life. By definition, Croats are Catholics. And, although religion was not encouraged in communist Yugoslavia, it was also not prohibited (as it was in most Warsaw Pact countries). Politicians, military officers, and civil servants (such as teachers) couldn't publicly profess their faith, but many were privately devout. And with the breakup of Yugoslavia and the ensuing wars, Catholicism has seen a huge boost. In this part of the world, where ethnicity is tied to faith, nationalism (which is also on the rise) hews closely to religion—too closely, many impartial observers fear. The increasing influence of the Catholic Church on Croatian politics will be a hot potato here for years to come.

As you leave the cathedral, look high on the wall to the left of the door. This strange script is the **Glagolitic alphabet** *(glagoljca)*, invented by Byzantine missionaries Cyril and Methodius in the ninth century to translate the Bible into Slavic languages. Though these missionaries worked mostly in Moravia (today's eastern Czech Republic), their alphabet caught on only here, in Croatia. (Glagolitic was later adapted to become the Cyrillic alphabet—still used in Serbia, Russia, and other parts east.) In 1991, when Croatia became its own country and nationalism surged, some Croats flirted with the idea of making this the official alphabet.

ELSEWHERE IN ZAGREB
▲Mirogoj Cemetery (Groblje Mirogoj)

Of Europe's many cemeteries, Mirogoj (MEE-roh-goy) is one of the finest, studded with great architecture and beautifully designed tombs. This peaceful spot, a short bus ride from the city center, memorializes many of the greats who built the Croatian nation. Anyone can enjoy a quiet walk here, but to provide context to your stroll, stop by the TI first for their free, thorough booklet of maps and descriptions identifying the most significant graves.

The cemetery was designed by Herman Bollé, an Austrian architect who lived and worked for most of his career in Zagreb, leaving his mark all over the city before becoming a permanent resident in this cemetery. From the stately, domed main mausoleum, a long arcade (with VIP tombs) stretches along the road in both directions, punctuated by smaller domes. Entering through the main gate, circle behind the mausoleum to find the biggest tomb here: Franjo Tuđman, the leader who spearheaded the creation of independent Croatia but left behind a questionable legacy (for more on Tuđman, see page 26). Continuing straight past Tuđman's grave, you'll reach the Central Cross, which usually has a field of flowers around it, and beyond that, a monument to the dead of World War I. In every direction, as far as the eye can see, are the final resting places of great Croatians.

Cost and Hours: Free, daily 6:00-20:00, Oct-March 7:30-18:00.

Getting There: Catch bus #106 from in front of the cathedral (3/hour) and ride six stops, or about 10 minutes, to the stop called simply "Mirogoj" (the one *after* the stop called "Mirogoj Arkada"). The return bus leaves from across the street.

Sights in and near the Green Horseshoe

With extra time, stroll around the Green Horseshoe (the U-shaped belt of parks and museums near the city center). The museums on and near this park aren't as interesting as those on Gradec but may be worth a peek on a rainy day. Like most museums in Zagreb, these close early on Sundays and all day Monday. The Modern Gallery, described later, is also in this area.

The **Arts and Crafts Museum** (Muzej za Umjetnost i Obrt) features furniture, ceramics, and fashion, all well-displayed chronologically (Trg Republike Hrvatske 10, www.muo.hr).

The **Mimara Museum** (Muzej Mimara) fills a grand, empty-feeling building with the eclectic art collection of a wealthy Dalmatian, ranging from ancient artifacts to paintings by European masters. While the names in the second-floor painting gallery are major—Rubens, Rembrandt, Velázquez, Renoir, Manet—the paintings themselves are minor. The first floor displays sculpture and applied arts, while the ground floor has vases, carpets, and objects from the Far East (Rooseveltov trg 5, www.mimara.hr).

The **Botanical Garden** (Botanički Vrt), run by the University of Zagreb, offers a back-to-nature change of pace from the urban bustle (free, closed Nov-March, at southwest corner of the Green 'Shoe, Marulicev trg 9A).

Other Museums

The **Zagreb 80's Museum** offers a look at an alternate universe of 1980s pop culture and consumer goods from behind the Iron Curtain. Between Gradec and Kaptol, the small collection of objects from the waning days of Yugoslavia is hands-on, so you can flip through old cookbooks, try on dated fashions, play antiquated video games, and sit behind the wheel of a vintage car. Though overpriced, there's nothing else quite like it in town (40 kn, daily 11:00-21:00, Radićeva 34, www.zagreb80.com).

The ingenious little **Museum of Illusions** is worth considering if you need to entertain the kids or need a rainy-day activity. The dozens of brain teasers and interactive, head-scratching illusions (along with explanations of how they work) don't have anything to do with Croatia, but they're fun. Infinity mirrors, off-kilter rooms, and optical puzzles provide some good photo ops, too (50 kn, daily 9:00-22:00, Ilica 72, tel. 01/799-9609, www.muzejiluzija.com).

In addition to the art gallery at the Mimara Museum (described earlier), art lovers may want to visit the following museums. Three different collections cover works from the 20th century through today: The **Modern Gallery** features art from the early 20th century, mostly focusing on artists from southeastern Europe (a few blocks south of Jelačić Square at Andrije Hebranga 1, www.moderna-galerija.hr); the **Museum of Contemporary Art** focuses on mid-century art (south of the river and not as convenient to visit, avenija Dubrovnik 17, www.msu.hr); and the innovative **Lauba,** with more cutting-edge works from the past few years, as well as frequent performances and shows (Baruna Filipovića 23A, www.lauba.hr). For details on any of these, check their websites or ask at the TI.

Sleeping in Zagreb

Zagreb is a convention and business town, so rates at business-oriented hotels are highest on weekdays mid-February through mid-July, then again from September through October. At other times of year, and weekends year-round, you'll generally enjoy lower rates. I've classified my listings based on rates in spring and fall.

$$$$ Jägerhorn Hotel enjoys an ideal location (one long block from Jelačić Square, along the busy Ilica boulevard but tucked back on a quieter courtyard). Its 18 rooms are small but well-appointed and provide a fine downtown refuge (air-con, free parking a few blocks away, Ilica 14, tel. 01/483-3877, www.hotel-jagerhorn.hr, info@hotel-jagerhorn.hr).

$$$$ Hotel Dubrovnik is a high-rise business-class hotel with 222 rooms. While lacking personality, it's comfortable and ideally located at the bottom of Jelačić Square (rooms overlooking the square don't cost extra but can come with some noise, air-con, elevator, Gajeva 1, tel. 01/486-3555, www.hotel-dubrovnik.hr, reservations@hotel-dubrovnik.hr).

$$$ Hotel Park 45 has no special design touches or atmosphere, but what it does, it does well: provide spiffy, well-located, high-standard rooms for a reasonable rate. Though it's right on busy Ilica, windows are soundproofed, and the pay parking in the adjacent courtyard is very convenient (air-con, elevator, Ilica 45, tel. 01/409-5999, www.hotelpark45.hr, info@hotelpark45.hr).

$$$ Hotel Astoria, a Best Western, offers 100 smallish but plush rooms and a high-class lobby. It feels professional and polished, but still friendly. It's on a humdrum street about a 10-minute walk from Jelačić Square—ideal if you want to sleep near the train station (air-con, elevator, limited free parking—first come, first served, Petrinjska 71, tel. 01/480-8900, www.hotelastoria.hr, sales@hotelastoria.hr).

$$ 4 City Windows is well-located just a few minutes' walk from Jelačić Square. The four rooms are bursting with creativity, each designed by owner Tanja, who also provides a warm welcome along with her husband, Ivo (Palmotićeva 13, tel. 01/889-7999, mobile 091-383-8110, www.4citywindows.com, tanja@4citywindows.com).

$$ Sobe Zagreb 17, run by Irena, rents seven cute and colorful rooms in a conveniently located old building—just steps from Gradec, the Tkalčićeva restaurant street, and Jelačić Square (no breakfast, cash only, reception open 8:00-20:00, air-con, laundry service, airport transfers, Radićeva 22, mobile 091-170-0000, www.sobezagreb17.com, info@sobezagreb17.com).

$ InZagreb, run by Ksandro and Ivana Kovačić, rents 10 one- and two-bedroom apartments scattered around the city. The units are nicely equipped and come with welcoming touches, including kitchens with basic supplies and fresh fruit. Find an apartment that appeals to you on their website, check its location—some are handier to downtown sightseeing than others—and make a reservation. Clearly communicate your arrival time; they can arrange transfers from the train or bus stations or the airport (two-night minimum, no breakfast, air-con, laundry machine, free loaner bikes, guiding services, mobile 091-652-3201, www.inzagreb.com, info@inzagreb.com).

¢ **Hotel Ilica** is a 15-minute walk or short tram ride from Jelačić Square. The hotel's idiosyncratic sense of style—with chandeliers and Roman busts that Liberace would find gaudy—helps compensate for its dull urban neighborhood. It's set back on its own courtyard with a garden behind it, making it an oasis of quiet in the heart of the city. Its 25 rooms and four apartments are quirky, but owner Branko is effusive, and the place is a fine value if you don't mind commuting to your sightseeing by tram (air-con, pay off-street courtyard parking, Ilica 102, two tram stops from Jelačić Square near Britanski trg stop, tel. 01/377-7522, www.hotel-ilica. hr, info@hotel-ilica.hr).

¢ **Shappy Hostel**—slick, shabby-chic, and modern—is the most appealing of Zagreb's many design hostels. Surrounding a courtyard in a very central, urban-feeling area, its sleek, stylish, hotelesque doubles are well worth considering, even for nonhostelers (no breakfast, air-con, limited free parking—ask when you book, Varšavska 8, tel. 01/483-0483, www.hostel-shappy.com, info@hostel-shappy.com).

Eating in Zagreb

As a cosmopolitan European capital, Zagreb enjoys a refreshingly varied restaurant scene. It's also a good value; while most of the touristy towns in this book have inflated-for-tourists prices, most diners here are natives, and competition to lure value-conscious local foodies keeps things refreshingly affordable. I rank eateries from $ budget to $$$$ splurge. For more advice on eating in Croatia, including ordering and tipping, see the "Eating" section of the Practicalities chapter.

Most restaurants focus on modern, international menus, but a few offer traditional Zagreb-area cuisine: hearty peasant grub—sausage, sauerkraut, potatoes, *sarma* (cabbage rolls)—that seems more "Eastern European" than the seafood, pizza, and pastas of the coast. Personally, I'd skip traditional Croatian food altogether here, since the capital has an appealing variety of cuisines you won't find elsewhere in Croatia.

Look beyond restaurants, too: Several enticing sandwich shops, chichi bakeries, burger joints, and gourmet coffee bars are scattered around the center, catering to businesspeople on their lunch breaks. Many newer places bill themselves as "bistros"—cafés serving a short menu of food.

Be warned that many of Zagreb's best eateries are closed on Sundays.

PEOPLE-WATCHING AND COFFEE-SIPPING

One of my favorite Zagreb pastimes is lingering over a drink or meal along its thriving people zones, watching an endless parade of fashionable locals saunter past, and wondering why they don't create such an inviting space in my hometown. The best place is on **Tkalčićeva street,** Zagreb's main café street and urban promenade rolled into one (starts a block behind Jelačić Square, next to the market; I've listed my favorite Tkalčićeva eateries next). Honorable mention goes to **Trg Petra Preradovića,** a pleasant square just steps from Jelačić Square (up Ilica street) that bustles with appealing outdoor cafés and bars.

It's generally fine to buy a pastry at one of Zagreb's many boutique bakeries and dessert shops, then eat it with coffee ordered at an outdoor café—provided that café doesn't serve food of its own.

ON OR NEAR TKALČIĆEVA STREET

Tkalčićeva has the highest concentration of inviting restaurants in town. Strolling its entire length (about a 10-minute walk), you'll pass plenty of drinks-only cafés, but also pizzerias, Turkish eateries, *ćevapi* (grilled meat) joints, burger places, cake and dessert shops, *fritule* (doughnut) windows, and the restaurants listed below. Keep an eye out for the drinks-only **Melin** bar, set just above

the bustle of the street; it's the hipster's choice, with mismatched secondhand furniture and a mellower vibe.

$ Pivnica Mali Medo ("Little Bear") is a rollicking brewpub serving seven beers—plus rotating seasonal taps—from the Medvedgrad brewery ("Bear Town"—named for a fortress near Zagreb). The heavy, stick-to-your-ribs pub grub feels closer to Prague than to Dubrovnik. The outdoor seating right on Tkalčićeva's most colorful stretch will seduce you into staying for another beer. The pubby interior is convivial, but less enticing (Mon-Sat 10:00-24:00, Sun from 12:00, food served until 22:00, evening live music from the little upstairs window, Tkalčićeva 36, tel. 01/492-9613).

$$$ Agava is classier than most places on this see-and-be-seen drag, with tables on a terrace from which you can survey the action at a civilized distance. Its menu leans Mediterranean, but with a variety of international and traditional Croatian dishes (daily 9:00-23:00, Tkalčićeva 39, tel. 01/482-9826).

Skalinska Street: This tight, steep lane connects Tkalčićeva to the market and cathedral. Tucked between the sprawling pizzerias is a gem: **$ La Štruk** is a great place to try several varieties of the local ravioli, called *štrukli*. A few are simply boiled, but most are served "gratinated"—baked in a small casserole and topped with gooey cheese and breadcrumbs. While most eateries along here have seating out on the street, this one has its own little oasis of a garden tucked way back inside the courtyard, through a maze of concrete corridors (Mon-Sat 11:00-23:00, Sun 11:30-22:00, at #5). Other handy places also line this lane.

At the Market: Zagreb's busy market offers plenty of options. Assemble a fresh picnic directly from the producers; for pointers on local ingredients to look for, see the market listing, earlier, under "Sights in Zagreb." Or, for something already prepared, duck into one of the many cheap restaurants and cafés on the streets around the market. The middle level of the market, facing Jelačić Square, is home to **$ Plac,** a great spot to try simple but tasty Croatian grilled-meat dishes (such as *ćevapčići*—the classic Balkan grilled-meat dish, described on page 425). You can squeeze into the tight but pretty tiled interior, or—better—sprawl out on the big terrace (Mon-Sat 9:00-23:00, Sun 11:00-18:00, up the stairs at the southeast corner of the market at Pod Zidom 1A, tel. 01/487-6761).

Dessert: Cremme has a wide array of delicious American-style cookies, brownies, cakes, and other goodies. Pull up a table for a brownie à la mode, or get a cookie sandwich to go. They have outdoor tables along a delightful stretch of Tkalčićeva (daily 9:00-23:00, Tkalčićeva 21, mobile 099-494-9400).

IN THE UPPER TOWN (GRADEC)

$$$ Trilogija, just above the Stone Gate, is a casual wine bar serving up delicious, well-presented, and affordable international dishes made with local ingredients. There's no printed menu because they cook what they find at the market—your server can explain the chalkboard menu. As this place is deservedly popular, reservations are smart (Mon-Sat 11:00-24:00, Sun until 16:00, Kamenita 5, tel. 01/485-1394, www.trilogija.com).

$$ Konoba Didov San ("Grandfather's Dream") offers a meat-heavy traditional menu from the Dalmatian hinterland (specifically the Neretva River Delta, near Metković). You'll find the normal Dalmatian specialties, plus eel, frog, and snail. Choose between the homey, traditional interior—which really does feel like a remote country *konoba*—and the outdoor tables. Reservations are smart on weekends (daily 10:00-24:00, a few steps up from the Ivan Meštrović Atelier at Mletačka 11, tel. 01/485-1154, www.konoba-didovsan.com).

IN THE LOWER TOWN, NEAR JELAČIĆ SQUARE

Most of these places are on fairly dreary urban streets, and many have outdoor seating. You're here not for the al fresco ambience (that's what Tkalčićeva is for) but for good, modern food at reasonable prices.

$ Heritage is an appealing, fresh-feeling little spot for sampling locally produced flavors. A tapas-style menu proudly invites you to explore a variety of cheeses, meats, and flatbreads. It's ideal for a light, local meal (daily 12:00-20:00, shorter hours off-season, Petrinjska 14, mobile 097-684-2306).

$$ Lari & Penati hides a couple of blocks from the train station, about a 10-minute walk from Jelačić Square. Trendy yet casual, they dish up eclectic and affordable meals. Choose between the clean-white interior and the woody outdoor tables on a nondescript street (Mon-Sat 12:00-22:30, closed Sun, Petrinjska 42A, tel. 01/465-5776).

$$ Bistro Fotić is another good foodie choice, with country-classy decor under little birdies and a few outdoor tables on a dull street. The menu (with a focus on Mediterranean fare) changes daily, based on what's fresh at the market. They share the space with a local photography club, whose members display their works on the walls (Mon-Sat 8:00-23:00, closed Sun, Ljudevita Gaja 25, tel. 01/481-0476).

$$$ Vinodol is a sprawling, white-tablecloth-classy dinner spot, with a peaceful covered terrace and a smartly appointed dining room under an impressive vaulted ceiling. The clientele is a mix of local old-timers and tourists. The good, reasonably priced cuisine includes lamb or veal prepared *peka*-style, under a baking lid covered with hot coals (*peka* served only at certain times—generally at 13:00 and 19:00; open daily 11:30-24:00, Teslina 10, tel. 01/481-1427).

$$$$ Kavkaz is short for "Kazališna Kavana" (Theater Café), and whether you choose the vaguely Art Deco interior or the tables out front, you'll have lovely views of the National Theater building. But the food equals the views here: The seafood, pastas, and meats are all done well, and the price isn't exorbitant for the quality. This is a bit of old Zagreb sparklingly refurbished and worth a splurge, whether for a nice breakfast, dinner, or just coffee and cake (Mon-Sat 7:30-23:00, Sun 9:00-22:00, Trg Republike Hrvatske 1, tel. 01/615-4868).

Light Bites: $ Sandwich Bar Pingvin, busy with locals dropping by for takeaway, is a favorite for quick, cheap, tasty sandwiches with chicken, turkey, steak, or fish. They'll wrap it all in a pita and top it with your choice of veggies and sauces to go—or, to eat here, sit at one of the few tiny tables or stools (Mon-Sat 10:00-late, Sun 18:00-late, about a block below Jelačić Square at Teslina 7). Next

ZAGREB

door to Pingvin, **$ Good Food** lives up to its name with healthy salads, soups, and sandwiches. Its three locations provide a quick, satisfying respite from Zagreb's carnivorous predilections (Mon-Sat 10:00-late, Sun 11:00-23:00; at Teslina 7, Palmotićeva 1, and the Importanne Center; reduced Sun hours at the latter two locations). **$ Green Point,** another convenient hole-in-the-wall, offers veggie- and vegan-friendly burgers and salads, as well as tasty smoothies and shakes (Mon-Sat 9:00-22:00, closed Sun, Varšavska 10).

Local Eats on Masarykova: This street, which angles from the café-jammed Trg Petra Preradovića out toward the National Theater, is a fun strip to explore. It's lined with some appealing shops, as well as a variety of eateries aimed at locals. Coffee aficionados won't find better gourmet coffee in Croatia than at **Cogito;** they have multiple locations, the most central of which hides on a passageway connecting Masarykova (enter at #18) and Varšavska (Mon-Fri 8:00-20:00, Sat 9:00-19:00, closed Sun, Varšavska 11). Farther along, you'll reach **$$ Ginger Sushi**—the best spot in town for affordable sushi (at #21)—with a nice little cheese shop next door, and just beyond, the **Chocolat 041** *gelateria* (see below).

Ice Cream: Several places in the center offer good *sladoled* (Italian gelato-style ice cream). Here are four favorites: The best may be at **Chocolat 041**—worth the extra couple of blocks' walk. Run by a Zagrebian who played professional soccer in Milan—where he learned how to make real, Italian-style gelato—it's a local favorite (daily, near the end of Masarykova—just before the National Theater—at #25). Three others are a bit more central and nearly as good: **Zagreb Slastičarnica,** which usually features some unusual flavors (hiding behind the statue of Tesla just past the bottom of the Trg Petra Preradovića café square at Masarykova 4); **Slastičarnica Vincek,** whose specialty is the chocolate-and-walnuts Vincek flavor (closed Sun, two blocks west of Jelačić Square on the busy tram-lined Ilica street at #18); and, across the street, **Kraš Choco Bar,** the flagship store of the Croatian candy empire, with ice-cream flavors that match its candies (closed Sun, Ilica 15).

Zagreb Connections

From Zagreb by Train to: Rijeka (2/day direct, 4-5 hours), **Split** (2-4/day, 6 hours, plus 1 direct night train, 8 hours), **Ptuj** (4-5/day, 3 hours, usually requires transfer in Pragersko and sometimes also Zidani Most), **Ljubljana** (4/day direct, 2.5 hours), **Vienna** (1/day direct, 7 hours; more with change in Villach, 9 hours), **Budapest** (1-2/day direct, 6-7 hours), **Lake Bled** (via Lesce-Bled, 4/day, 3-3.5 hours), **Munich** (4/day direct, including a night train,

9 hours; more with transfer in Villach or Graz). Train info: Tel. 060-333-444.

By Bus to: Samobor (about 2-3/hour, 30-50 minutes), **Plitvice Lakes National Park** (about hourly, 2.5 hours; the best choice is the express bus operated by Prijevoz Knežević, which runs 3/day in summer and 1-2/day in shoulder season—see page 78), **Rijeka** (hourly, 2-3.5 hours), **Rovinj** (nearly hourly, 3-6 hours), **Pula** (almost hourly, 4 hours), **Split** (at least hourly, 5-8 hours), **Mostar** (8/day, 9 hours, includes a night bus), **Sarajevo** (6/day, 8 hours, includes night bus), **Dubrovnik** (nearly hourly including some overnight options, 10 hours), **Korčula** (1/day, 9-13.5 hours depending on route), **Kotor** (2/day, overnight, 13-16 hours).

Bus schedules can be sporadic (for example, several departures clustered around the same time, then nothing for hours)—confirm your plans carefully (inquire locally, ask the TI to print schedules for you, or use the good online schedules at www.akz.hr). Popular buses, such as the afternoon express to Split, can fill up quickly in peak season. Book ahead online. While the official site (www.akz.hr) offers online booking, you may find it easier to book on www.getbybus.com or www.vollo.net. If you don't have a ticket, get to the station early (two hours in advance on summer days). For bus information, call 060-313-333 (from a US number, dial +385-1-611-2789).

Near Zagreb: Samobor

This charming little town, tucked in the hills between Zagreb and the Slovenian border, is where city dwellers head to unwind, get away from the clattering trams, and gorge themselves on sausages and cream cakes. While popular with Croatian and German tourists, Samobor is virtually undiscovered by Americans. Cuddled by hiker-friendly hills, bisected by a gurgling and

promenade-lined stream, favored by artists and poets, and proud of its tidy square, Samobor is made to order for a break from the big city. Samobor works as a small-town home base near Zagreb, but it's perhaps best suited for a low-impact lunch or dinner stop en route between Zagreb and points west or north.

Samobor (with 15,000 people, plus 20,000 more in the surrounding area) has a pleasantly compact tourist zone. Virtually anything you'd want to see or do is within sight of its centerpiece,

King Tomislav Square (Trg Kralja Tomislava). A stream called Gradna cuts through the middle of town. The **TI,** dead center on the main square, hands out town maps and is eager to offer hiking advice (Trg Kralja Tomislava 5, tel. 01/336-0044, www.samobor. hr/en/visit).

Getting There: You can reach Samobor by **bus** from Zagreb's main bus station (30 kn, 2-3/hour, 30-50 minutes—if possible, avoid slower buses that stop in smaller villages, such as Novaki and Rakitije). Samobor's bus station is about a 15-minute walk from the main square: Head left along the very busy road (Grada Wirgesa), cross straight ahead through the big intersection, then turn right onto the footpath just before the little river; you can follow this pleasantly all the way into town. By **car,** Samobor is just off the main Zagreb-Ljubljana expressway. Exit following signs for *Samobor,* then follow the bull's-eyes to the *Centar.* Head for the yellow steeple, then carry on past the steeple and the main square; just after the square, watch for the covered bridge on your left, which leads to a handy pay parking lot.

Visiting Samobor: Samobor is more about ambience than sightseeing. Its main square, **Trg Kralja Tomislava,** is cobbled, cutesy, and ringed by pretty Baroque architecture. The town's little river flows right past the square, covered by a variety of picturesque footbridges. It's a delight to simply sit at a café, gaze at the surrounding hills, and contemplate a hike.

For extra credit, drop into the sleepy **Samobor Museum,** an old mansion with miscellaneous bric-a-brac from the town's history (closed Mon, across the covered bridge from the main square at Livadićeva 7, tel. 01/336-1014, www.samobor.hr/muzej).

Those interested in **hiking** find Samobor a pleasant base for venturing into the hills that begin just west of town. One popular option is to drive up to the Šoićeva Kuća mountain lodge, then hike to a nearby peak (either Oštrc or Japetić). Another option is to walk from Samobor to Okić and back. You can get specifics and buy hiking maps at the TI.

Sleeping in Samobor: If you'd prefer a cheaper, small-town home base, Samobor is a decent alternative to Zagreb. Consider **$ Hotel Livadić** (21 faded-elegant rooms and a garden courtyard located over a classy café right on the main square, Trg Kralja Tomislava 1, tel. 01/336-5850, www.hotel-livadic.hr).

Eating in Samobor: Samobor is highly regarded among Zagrebians for its filling, rustic cuisine. First, an aperitif: Samobor's own Bermet is a sweet red wine made with fruits and grasses from the Samobor hills. As it's an acquired taste, start with just a sip. The local sausage, *češnjovke* (sometimes translated on menus as "garlic sausage"), is traditionally eaten with the town's own mustard, *Samoborska Muštarda* (Dijon-esque but without much kick, also sold around town in little ceramic pots). Round out your meal with a piece of *kremšnita* cream cake (curiously similar to Lake Bled's specialty).

$$ Gabreku 1929, every local's top recommendation for good Samobor cooking, serves the classics described above, a delicious mushroom soup, veal brains and liver, and plenty of other (mostly meat-centric) options (at far end of town, 15-minute walk from main square—head upriver on path after covered bridge then cross second bridge; free parking, Starogradska 46, tel. 01/336-0722).

$ Pri Staroj Vuri ("By the Old Clock"), with a similar menu of regional dishes, as well as homemade *štrukli* (cheese ravioli), has a traditional interior with a wall of namesake old clocks and a fine outdoor terrace in a tranquil garden (5-minute walk from square—from small fountain at intersection near end of church, head uphill for a couple of blocks, veering right at the fork; Giznik 2, tel. 01/336-0548).

$ Samoborska Klet ("Samobor Cellar") is the most convenient option, tucked in a courtyard on the main square, with a meaty menu, a modern dining room, and a more rustic tavern in the back, but no seating on the square itself (Trg Kralja Tomislava 7, tel. 01/332-6536).

ZAGREB

PLITVICE LAKES NATIONAL PARK

Nacionalni Park Plitvička Jezera

Plitvice (PLEET-veet-seh) is one of Europe's most spectacular natural wonders. Imagine Niagara Falls diced and sprinkled over a heavily forested Grand Canyon. There's nothing else like this lush valley of 16 terraced lakes, separated by natural travertine dams and laced together by waterfalls, boat rides, and miles of pleasant plank walks. Countless cascades and water that's both strangely clear and full of vibrant colors make this park a misty natural wonderland. Over time, the water has simultaneously carved out, and, with the help of mineral deposits, built up this fluid landscape. Decades ago, after eight or nine visits, I thought I really knew Europe. Then I discovered Plitvice and realized you can never exhaust Europe's surprises. Best of all, Plitvice is blessedly compact: You can enjoy the best of its scenery in just a few hours.

Plitvice became Croatia's first national park in 1949, and was a popular destination during the Yugoslav period. On Easter Sunday in 1991, the first shots of Croatia's war with Yugoslavia were fired right here—in fact, the war's first casualty was a park policeman, Josip Jović. The Serbs held Plitvice until 1995, and most of the Croats you'll meet here were evacuated and lived near the coast as refugees. During those five years, the park saw virtually no tourists, and was allowed to grow wild—allowing the ecosystem to recover from the impact of so many visitors. Today, the park is again a hugely popular tourist destination, with more than a million visitors each year (and yet, relatively few are from the US).

While Plitvice never fails to amaze visitors, a trip here brings you through one of the poorest, remotest areas of inland Croatia. You'll see physical evidence of the Yugoslav Wars: Some villages still have bombed-out churches and homes, most of which likely belonged to local Serbs who fled after the conflict. The national park represents the only real industry for miles around, which can make locals insular and a bit greedy. Prices here are much higher than they should be for such a remote area. But Plitvice is worth paying for. And although public transportation is workable, it requires some effort. This region is easiest by car.

PLANNING YOUR TIME

You can see all the best scenery at Plitvice in a three- to four-hour, mostly level hike. If your time or energy is short, you can see a lot even in just 90 minutes. While you can give yourself more time here, it's not necessary—the secondary trails pale in comparison to the convenient main route. Two nights and a full day at Plitvice is overkill.

Since it takes some time to get here (about two hours by car or bus from Zagreb), the most sensible plan is to spend one night in the area—either at one of the park's hotels, or at a guesthouse nearby. Arrive in the evening, get an early start in the park the next morning, and be underway after lunch (south to the coast, or north to Zagreb).

Crowd-Beating Tips: The reservation system (described next) helps mitigate Plitvice's ever-worsening crowd problems. However, it's still most enjoyable to hit the trails when the park is quieter, and that means before and after day-trippers show up from other parts of Croatia. If visiting in the morning, try to hit the trails by 8:30. If coming in the afternoon, aim for after about 15:00 (though off-season, check carefully when buses and boats stop running). This is even more important during the peak month of August. The Upper Lakes are often less crowded later in the day.

Reservations Strongly Recommended: Plitvice limits the number of daily visitors. Once your dates are set, book ahead on the park website (https://ticketing.np-plitvicka-jezera.hr). While reservations are not required (at least, not yet), tickets can sell out

PLITVICE LAKES

at busy times—particularly in summer and on weekends between 10:00 and 15:00. (In August, it's smart to book two to three weeks ahead.) Online tickets must be booked at least two day in advance and are good for a one-hour entry window at a specific entrance. (My recommended route begins at Entrance 1.) You can either print your ticket, or simply show it on your phone. If you don't book ahead, you can still try to buy a ticket on arrival—but come before the rush arrives.

GETTING TO PLITVICE

Plitvice Lakes National Park, a few miles from the Bosnian border, is located along the old highway between Zagreb and Split. Driving is the easiest option, but the park is also reachable by bus. The park's official bus stop is along the main road, about a 5- to 10-minute walk from the park's hotels. If taking a bus to Plitvice, check schedules and ideally book tickets in advance (websites listed later). If you catch a bus on the fly, confirm that it will actually stop at Plitvice.

From Zagreb and Points North

By **car,** Plitvice is two hours south of Zagreb on the old highway #1 (a.k.a. D-1). Leaving Zagreb, take the A-1 expressway south for about an hour, exiting at Karlovac (marked for *Plitvice*). From here, follow yellow signs toward *Split* to get through Karlovac. Once you pop out the other side, you'll track brown *Plitvice* signs along D-1. This takes you directly south about another hour to the park (for a description of what you'll pass on the way, see "En Route" below). If you're staying at the official park hotels, you can park for free at the hotel lot; to park at the lots at Entrance 1 or Entrance 2, you'll have to pay. For information about driving onward from Plitvice, see "Route Tips for Drivers" at the end of this chapter.

Buses leave from Zagreb's main bus station in the direction of Plitvice (trip takes 2-2.5 hours). Various bus companies handle the route; the best option is the **express bus** operated by a Plitvice-based company, Prijevoz Knežević (3/day in late June-early Sept, 1-2/day in shoulder season, first bus likely departing at 8:00, bus does not run late Oct-April; also see "Plitvice Connections," later). One evening departure leaving Zagreb lets you enjoy a full day of sightseeing in the capital, reach Plitvice just in time to get some sleep, and wake up early for your lake hike. Check schedules and book tickets for this bus at Knezevic.GetByBus.com. If you need more choices, consider the many other buses—operated by various companies—that run from Zagreb about hourly. Many of these buses are listed at GetByBus.com (the express departures explained above are labeled "PKN"); you may find additional buses listed at

AKZ.hr (look for "Plitvička Jezera"). I'd avoid the sporadic late-night buses, which don't get you to the park until after midnight.

En Route: By car or bus, you'll see some thought-provoking terrain between Zagreb and Plitvice. Exiting the expressway at Karlovac, then heading south on D-1, you'll pass through the village of **Turanj**—part of the war zone in the 1990s. Notice the military museum (on the right as you drive through), with tanks, heavy-artillery cannons, and other war machines that actually saw action. The destroyed, derelict houses belonged to Serbs who have not come back to reclaim and repair them. Farther along, about 25 miles before Plitvice, you'll pass through the striking village of **Slunj,** perched picturesquely on travertine formations (like Plitvice's) and surrounded by sparkling streams and waterfalls. The most traditional part of the town, perched just above the water, is called **Rastoke,** which has a memorable restaurant (see "Eating in and near Plitvice," later). If you're driving, this is worth a photo stop. This town, too, looks very different from how it did before the war—when it was 30 percent Serb. As in countless other villages in the Croatian interior, the Orthodox church has been destroyed.

From Split

Drivers head north on the A-1 expressway, exiting at Gornja Ploča; from here, follow road D-1 about an hour north (passing Udbina and Korenica) through desolate scenery to the park.

Various **buses** run from Split to Plitvice (up to 7/day in summer, 4-5/day in winter, 4-6 hours). The best option is the express bus operated by Plitvice-based Prijevoz Knežević (2-4/day May-Oct, no express buses off-season, 4 hours, check schedule and buy tickets at http://knezevic.getbybus.com). Additional, nonexpress buses are listed at GetByBus.com and at Autobusni-Kolodvor.com (at the latter website, click English, then the "Terminals" tab, and look for "Plitvička Jezera").

Orientation to Plitvice

Plitvice's 16 lakes are grouped into the Upper Lakes (Gornja Jezera) and the Lower Lakes (Donja Jezera). The park officially has two entrances *(ulaz),* each with ticket windows and snack and gift shops (see the sidebar and the map). There is no town at Plitvice. The nearest village, Mukinje, is a residential community mostly for park workers, with virtually no services for tourists; Rakovica, about a 10-minute drive north, has a grocery store.

Cost: In June-Sept, it's 250 kn (150 kn after 16:00). The price drops dramatically outside of peak season: 100 kn April-May and Oct, and 60 kn Nov-March. This price covers park entry, boats, and shuttle buses.

Plitvice Lakes National Park

Hours: Daily June-late Aug 7:00-20:00, late March-May and late Aug-Sept until 19:00, Oct 8:00-18:00, Nov-late March until 16:00. The last entrance to the park is two hours before closing time, and the last boats and shuttle buses depart 30-60 minutes before the park closes (if hiking late in the day, ask about this before you head out). The quick boat ride between P-1 (below the hotels) and P-2 (at the Upper Lakes) runs later.

Getting Tickets: To better manage the crowds, the park allows visitors to book an entry time at least two days in advance (https://ticketing.np-plitvicka-jezera.hr). While not required, reserving is smart (and may become obligatory in coming years). Tickets can sell out, especially in summer (August is busiest) or on weekends during the midday rush (10:00-15:00). For details, see "Planning Your Time," earlier.

Maps and Information: Big maps are posted all over the park. Unless you're planning a more ambitious hike than the typical circuit I describe, there's no need to buy a map or a guidebook. Park info: Np-Plitvicka-Jezera.hr.

Services: While you'll find WCs at both entrances, once you're on the trails, they're rare: The only convenient one is near the P-3 boat dock (the Kozjak Lake boat dock for the Lower Lakes).

LOWER LAKES

Kozjak

CONTINUE TOUR BY BOAT (P-3 to P-2)

P-3

WC

Gavanovac

Milanovac

B

ST-1

ŠUPLJARA CAVE

Kaluđerovac

BIG WATERFALL (Veliki Slap)

Korana River

D-1

7

TOUR BEGINS

ENTRANCE 1 (Rastovača)

WC

P

To Slunj, & Zagreb

4

MAIN ROAD

7

1

6

7

500 Meters

500 Yards

❶ Hotel Jezero
❷ Hotel Plitvice
❸ Hotel Bellevue & Restaurant Poljana
❹ To Hotel Degenija, Villa Plitvička Sedra & Slovin Unique Rastoke
❺ To Plitvice Mirić Inn
❻ Restaurant Lička Kuća
❼ Groceries (2)

There is no WC at the P-2 boat dock—the only WC at the Upper Lakes is at the ST-3 bus stop, at the very top of these lakes.

GETTING AROUND PLITVICE

Plitvice is designed for hikers. But the park has a few other ways (included in entry cost) to help you connect the best parts. Use this chapter's map and the "Park Signs and Symbols" sidebar to get oriented to your options.

By Shuttle Bus: These rubber-tired tourist trains are useful mostly for guests at the official park hotels, or for returning to your car at the end of the hike—saving you a 40-minute walk along a boring highway. Buses start running early and continue until late afternoon (frequency depends on demand—generally 3-4/hour; buses run from March until the first snow—often Dec).

By Boat: Low-impact electric boats ply the waters of the biggest lake,

PLITVICE LAKES

Park Signs and Symbols

While spectacular, Plitvice has a long history of poor management by government bureaucrats and could be more user-friendly. The trails can be confusingly marked. These symbols—which you'll see throughout the park—are explained on maps posted around the park.

There are two official **entrances** to the park:

Entrance 1 is a steep 10-minute hike above the Lower Lakes.

Entrance 2, about a mile and a half south, sits just below the park's three official hotels (Jezero, Plitvice, and Bellevue). It's about a 10-minute walk downhill to the dock, where you can take a quick boat ride to the Upper Lakes or a longer boat ride to the Lower Lakes.

Boat icons point you to one of the park's three boat docks:

P-1 is the dock that's a steep hike below Entrance 2.

P-2 is just across the water from the P-1 dock, at the bottom of the Upper Lakes.

P-3 is all the way across the biggest lake, at the top of the Lower Lakes.

Train icons direct you to one of the three stops for the shuttle buses (not actual trains) that move visitors around the park:

ST-1 is a 10-minute walk below Entrance 1 (Lower Lakes).

ST-2 is below Entrance 2 (a short boat ride from the Upper Lakes).

ST-3 is at the very top of the Upper Lakes.

Letters denote various recommended hiking routes. These are largely nonsensical; while I mention these letters occasionally to help you find your way, don't get too hung up on them.

Kozjak, with three stops: a steep hike below Entrance 2 and the park hotels (stop P-1), at the bottom of the Upper Lakes (P-2), and at the far end of Kozjak, at the top of the Lower Lakes (P-3). From Hotel Jezero to the Upper Lakes, it's a quick five-minute ride; the boat goes back and forth continuously. The trip from the Upper Lakes to the Lower Lakes takes about 20 minutes, and the boat goes roughly twice per hour—typically at the top and bottom of every hour. (In busy times, you may have to wait for a seat on this boat.)

Plitvice Lakes Hike

Plitvice's system of trails and boardwalks makes it easy for visitors to immerse themselves in nature. Hiking here is easily worth ▲▲▲. In some places, the path leads literally right up the middle of a waterfall. The official park map and signage recommend a variety of hikes, but there's no need to adhere strictly to these suggestions if you want to create your own route.

Planning Your Time: You can see everything—Upper Lakes and Lower Lakes—in a few hours. You can do these areas in either order. I prefer starting at Entrance 1 and doing the Lower Lakes first, which offers slightly better head-on views of the best scenery and saves the most picturesque stretch for last. (That's the route I've described here.) Figure about an hour for the Lower Lakes, about an hour for the Upper Lakes, and a half-hour to

connect them by boat—though it can take longer than this when the park is crowded, which it often is. Three to four hours total is a safe estimate.

LOWER LAKES (DONJA JEZERA)

From Entrance 1, you'll descend a steep path with lots of switch-backs, as well as thrilling postcard views over the canyon of the Lower Lakes. As you reach the lakes and begin to follow the boardwalks (use the route marked *B*), you'll have great up-close views of the travertine formations that make up Plitvice's many waterfalls. Count the trout. If you're tempted to throw in a line, don't. Fishing is strictly forbidden.

After you cross the path over the first lake, an optional 10-minute detour (to the right) takes you down to the **Big Water-**

fall (Veliki Slap). It's the biggest of Plitvice's waterfalls, where the Plitvica River plunges 250 feet over a cliff into the valley below. Depending on recent rainfall, the force of the Big Waterfall varies from a light mist to a thundering deluge.

If you're a hardy hiker, consider climbing the steep steps from the Big Waterfall up to a **viewpoint** at the top of the canyon (marked *Sightseeing Point/Vidikovac;* it's a strenuous 10-minute hike to the top). Take the stairs, bearing to the right at the top (near the shelter) to find a viewpoint overlooking the Big Waterfall. From here, you can carry on along the road that actually goes up over the top of the Big Waterfall, offering more views over the park. (Go as far as you like, then return the way you came.) The giant mill perched at the top of the Big Waterfall was used to grind grains.

The Science of Plitvice

Plitvice is a perfect storm of unique geological, climatic, and biological features found in very few places on earth. Plitvice's magic ingredient is calcium carbonate ($CaCO_3$), a mineral deposit from the limestone. It's the same thing that makes "hard water" hard, and leaves calcium deposits on your cold-water faucet. But these deposits build up only at the faucet, not inside the pipes. That's because when hard water is motionless (as it usually is in the pipes), it holds on to the calcium. But when the water is subjected to pressure and movement—as it pours out of the faucet—it releases the calcium.

Plitvice works the same way. As water flows over the park's limestone formations, it dissolves the rock, and the water becomes supersaturated with calcium carbonate. Then, when the water spills over the edges of the lakes, it deposits calcium carbonate on the lake bed and at the edges of the lakes. Eventually, these deposits build up to form a rock called travertine. As the travertine thickens, barriers—and eventually dams and new waterfalls—are formed. In some places, the stone hangs down like foliage, because moss and grass guide the growth of the stone. Because of this ongoing process, Plitvice's landscape is perpetually changing.

And why is the water so clear? For one thing, it comes directly from high-mountain runoff, unspoiled by impurities. And because the water calcifies everything it touches, it prevents the creation of mud—so the bottoms of the lakes are entirely stone. A different mineral in the water, magnesium carbonate, both gives the water its special color and makes it highly basic, preventing the growth of algae and other plant life that could cloud the water.

The park contains nearly 1,300 species of plants. Wildlife found in the park includes deer, wolves, wildcats, lynx, wild boar, voles, otters, snakes, 350 species of butterflies, 42 types of dragonflies, 21 species of bats, and more than 160 species of birds (including eagles, herons, owls, grouse, and storks). The lakes (and local menus) are full of trout, and you'll also see smaller, red-finned fish called *klen* (chub in English). Perhaps most importantly, Plitvice is home to about 40 or 50 brown bears—a species now extremely endangered in Europe. You'll see images of this park mascot plastered everywhere.

When you're done at the Big Waterfall, backtrack up to the main trail and continue along the boardwalks. You'll skirt the rim of Kaluđerovac Lake; then, after you pass another bank of waterfalls, a smaller trail branches off (on the left) toward **Šupljara Cave.** You can actually climb through this slippery cave—whose name means "bottomless"—all the way up to the trail overlooking the Lower Lakes (though it's not recommended). This unassuming cavern is a big draw. In the 1960s, several German and Italian "Spaghetti Westerns" were filmed at Plitvice and in other parts of Croatia (which, to European eyes, has terrain similar to the American West). The most famous, *Der Schatz im Silbersee (The Treasure in Silver Lake)*, was filmed here at Plitvice, and the treasure was hidden in this cave. The movie—complete with *Deutsch*-speaking "Native Americans"—is still a favorite in Germany, and popular theme trips bring German tourists to movie locations here in Croatia. (If you drive the roads near Plitvice, keep an eye out for strange, Native American-sounding names such as Winnetou—fictional characters from these beloved stories of the Old West, by the German writer Karl May.)

After Šupljara Cave, you'll stick to the east side of Gavanovac Lake, pass some picturesque terraces, then walk along the shore of Milanovac Lake, before crossing over one more time to the west, where you'll cut through a comparatively dull forest. You'll head up the paved road, branching off to the left (following the boat icon) to emerge at a pit-stop-perfect clearing with WCs, picnic tables, a souvenir shop, and a self-service restaurant.

From here you can catch the shuttle boat across **Lake Kozjak** (Jezero Kozjak) to the bottom of the Upper Lakes (usually every 30 minutes, 20-minute ride). The ride across Kozjak, the park's biggest lake, offers a great chance for a breather.

UPPER LAKES (GORNJA JEZERA)
Focus on the lower half of the Upper Lakes, where nearly all the exotic beauty is (between P-2 and Lake Galovac). You'll soon experience some of the most striking waterfalls in the whole park.

Climbing up steeply on stepped boardwalks from the boat dock (following signs for *C*), you'll pass deep pools with fallen trees stretching along the bottom, illustrating just how magnificently clear the water here is. Soon you'll curl along the waterline of Gradinsko Lake. At the end of the lake, you'll come to the park's finest cascades, which tumble dramatically from Galovac into Gradinsko. You'll hear the waterfalls, then you'll see them, and finally you'll feel them, as the spray pelts your face while you stroll the boardwalks. First you'll pass by thundering **Veliki (Big) Prštavac,** then hook up a tight-and-steep uphill bend—literally walking in the middle of a waterfall—to the nearly as spectacular **Mali (Small) Prštavac.** Then you'll stroll along a whole wall of other waterfalls. Continuing up, you'll weave through another grand set of pools and falls, with views down on the pond of **Galovački Buk.** Walk along here, enjoying more ponds and cascades. Eventually you'll emerge at a fork in the path. Here, you have two options:

1. Make your hike a loop by turning left (following signs for

the boat icon, *P-2,* and *E, H,* and *K*). This is the easiest and most enjoyable choice for most hikers. First, you'll walk down a stepped boardwalk with gurgling water underfoot. Then you'll circle back around the far (south) side of Gradinsko Lake and through a forest. Finally you'll pass a small picnic shelter, then walk down past one last set of falls to the P-2 boat dock, where you can take the boat back over to the hotels (P-1 stop). From here, hike up to Entrance 2; if you left your car back at Entrance 1, you can hop on the shuttle bus to get there.

2. Turn right (following the icon for the shuttle bus and *C*) to continue hiking up to the top of the Upper Lakes. I'd choose this option only if you have energy and time to burn. This route leads you along the top of the best waterfalls (heard, but not seen), then loops you the long way around Galovac Lake and eventually to the ST-3 bus stop. From here on up, the scenery is less stunning, and the waterfalls are fewer and farther between. At the top, you'll finish at shuttle bus stop ST-3 (with food stalls and a WC), where the bus zips you back to the entrances and hotels.

Nice work!

Sleeping in and near Plitvice

AT THE PARK

The most convenient place to sleep is at one of Plitvice's official park lodges, which are all run by the same office (reservation tel. 053/751-015, www.np-plitvicka-jezera.hr). It's best to book on their website (emails may go unanswered in busy times). These are all located a few minutes' walk apart, along the main highway and just above the park's Entrance 2. Note that none of these hotels has air-conditioning (which is rarely needed in this climate), and all of them include breakfast.

$$$ Hotel Jezero is big and modern, with all the comfort—and charm—of a Holiday Inn. It's well-situated right at the park entrance and offers 210 rooms; ones facing the park have big glass doors and balconies (elevator, reception tel. 053/751-500).

$$ Hotel Plitvice, a better value than Jezero, offers 51 rooms and mod, wide-open public spaces on two floors with no elevator. Choose between the fine, older-feeling economy rooms or a larger, more updated, and more expensive standard or superior rooms (reception tel. 053/751-200).

$ Hotel Bellevue, dated and faded, feels like a Tito-era leftover, with a musty orange-and-dark-brown color scheme in its 74 rooms. While not up to the standards of the other park hotels, it's cheap (no elevator, closed Nov-March, reception tel. 053/751-800).

OUTSIDE THE PARK

Drivers should consider sleeping at one of the many options near the park. Prices here are also high, but these choices have a bit more personality. Many countryside accommodations have a half-board option; ask about this when you book.

North of Plitvice

Dozens of midsize hotels and small *sobe* line the highway for about 10 miles north of the national park. Options are so abundant here that spontaneous travelers can show up without reservations and take their pick. I've listed some favorites below. To reach Villa Plitvička Sedra, turn left off the main road toward *Bihać,* after entering the town of Rakovica. Hotel Degenija is right along the main road, a bit closer to Plitvice.

$$$ Hotel Degenija offers all the big-hotel comforts in a homier package than the park lodges. Its 20 modern, stylish rooms are in a building behind the bustling roadside restaurant. They also have an outdoor pool with a poolside bistro (air-con, elevator, bikes available, Selište Drežničko 57a, tel. 047/782-143, www.hotel-degenija.com, info@hotel-degenija.com). The busy **$$** restaurant is justifiably popular with tour groups (pastas and pizzas, daily 7:00-23:00).

$ Villa Plitvička Sedra may be the best value around. It's a homey yet modern-feeling stone-and-wood complex that sits in a pleasant parklike setting, with tennis courts, a billiards pavilion, and an outdoor swimming pool. The 23 rooms have all the comforts you'll need for an overnight near the park (air-con, Irinovac 155, mobile 098-133-5305, www.restoran-sedra.hr, info@restoran-sedra.hr). The **$$** restaurant is also inviting (open long hours daily).

In Rastoke: Described later, under "Eating in and near Plitvice," **$ Slovin Unique Rastoke** rents two rooms above the restaurant, along with a cozy simple bungalow with air-conditioning, TV, and Wi-Fi.

A Few Minutes South of Plitvice

$$ Plitvice Mirić Inn offers the friendliest welcome in the region. The Mirić family (daughter Lili speaks great English) offers 13 smallish, modern-chalet rooms, lots of good travel advice, and a homemade breakfast (air-con, Jezerce 18/1, watch for it along the main road on the left as you head south from the park, mobile 098-930-6508, www.plitvice-croatia.com, info@plitvice-croatia.com). While better for drivers, this can work by bus: It's 300 yards from the nearest bus stop (Mukinje Village) and about a mile and a half from Entrance 2.

In Mukinje Village: Just south of the park is the village of Mukinje, which feels like a holdover from communist times: It's basically a planned workers' town, where crumbling concrete apartment blocks mingle with newer chalet-style homes renting rooms to travelers. Unfortunately, attitudes here seem trapped in communist times, too; most of the *sobe* I've inspected here are run by locals who are grouchy and indifferent, and the prices are too high. In a pinch, you could drive into town and check a few options.

Eating in and near Plitvice

Local cuisine is hearty countryside grub, offering a nice, landlocked change of pace from the seafood-heavy and Italian-flavored menus of most of Croatia's tourist towns. You'll see mushroom soups, soft spreadable cheeses, and grilled trout, with the fish pulled fresh from the lakes. Restaurants here are functional—don't expect high cuisine.

AT THE NATIONAL PARK

The park runs a variety of uninspired restaurants, with institutional food and ambience. If you're staying at the hotels, you have the option of paying for half-board with your room (lunch or dinner). The half-board option is worth doing if you're here for dinner, but don't lock yourself in for lunch—you'll want more flexibility as you explore Plitvice (memorable picnic spots and decent food stands abound inside the park). All of these eateries are open long hours daily.

Near Entrance 1, the rustic **$$$ Restaurant Lička Kuća** has more character than the other park eateries. It's across the highway from the entrance and gift shop.

Near Entrance 2, most people opting for half-board dine at the **$$** restaurants inside **Hotel Jezero** and **Hotel Plitvice,** but you can also use the voucher at other park eateries (you'll pay the difference if the bill is more). **Restaurant Poljana,** behind Hotel Bellevue, has the same park-lodge atmosphere in both of its sections: self-service **$** cafeteria or the sit-down **$$** "national restaurant" with open wood-fired grill; both parts have dreary communist decor.

A variety of other humble, park-run eateries—with similar menus—are located near the various shuttle bus stops and boat docks (but there's nothing at P-2, the boat dock at the bottom of the Upper Lakes).

For **picnic** fixings, there's a tiny grocery store at Entrance 1 and another one with a larger selection across road D-1 (use the pedestrian overpass). If you're driving in from the north, consider getting your provisions at the better-stocked grocery store in the village of Rakovica on your way through. Once inside the park, at the P-3 boat dock, you can buy grilled meat and drinks. Friendly old ladies sell homemade goodies (such as strudel and hunks of cheese) throughout the park, including at Entrance 1.

OUTSIDE THE PARK
Roadside Restaurants
Many truck stop-type restaurants line the highway for miles in both directions from Plitvice. These cater primarily to tour buses— and their drivers, who dine like kings in exchange for bringing in so much business. Most of these places are unexciting, but two good options are at the recommended **$$ Hotel Degenija** and **$$ Villa Plitvička Sedra** (for details, see listings earlier).

Eating in Bosnia
Adventurous drivers may want to make a short jaunt across the border for a bite in Bihać (BEE-hahch). This small Bosnian city is about a 30-minute drive southeast of the national park—be sure to bring your passport and "green card" proof of car insurance. If this is your only chance to dip into Bosnia, and you have an evening to kill, it can be a fun option. For more on Bosnian food, see page 424.

A Memorable Meal Amid Waterfalls
About 30 minutes north of Plitvice, on the main highway between Zagreb and Plitvice, you'll pass above, then through, the striking town of Slunj (pronounced "sloon"), which is surrounded by its own little "mini-Plitvice" ecosystem of waterfalls. This can be an enjoyable pit stop, whether or not you eat here.

The lower part of the town—buried deep amid all those cascades—is the village of Rastoke (meaning roughly "Beautiful Water"), which has its share of touristy restaurants. The most elaborate is the complex of **Slovin Unique Rastoke,** where you can explore a series of canals, waterfalls, canyons, and viewpoints. The grounds also have an old mill, a small collection of traditional local furniture, tools, and so on, and a trail down to the Korona River canyon. While you can pay a small fee to explore (they'll give you a map), it's free for those who dine at their restaurant, **$$ Pod Rastočkim Krovom** (Under Rastoke's Roof). They specialize in trout—you can see their ponds out back—and also have a wide range of other local dishes, including some prepared with grains ground by traditional mills (open long hours daily, Rastoke 25B, mobile 099-215-0907, www.slunj-rastoke.com). While a bit hokey and tour group-oriented, Rastoke gives you a chance to see some bonus waterfalls.

PLITVICE LAKES

Getting There: Approaching the town of Slunj from the north, you'll see Rastoke filling the valley below. After crossing the first bridge, turn right at the *Rastoke* sign, then park next to—and walk over—the dilapidated old concrete bridge; finally, turn right and walk down the hill to Slovin Unique Rastoke.

Plitvice Connections

To reach the park, see "Getting to Plitvice," earlier. Moving on from Plitvice is trickier.

BY BUS

Bus Schedules and Options: Buses pass by the park in each direction—northbound (to **Zagreb,** 2-2.5 hours) and southbound (to coastal destinations such as **Split,** 4-6 hours). In summer, the best choice is the **Prijevoz Knežević express bus,** designed to zip Plitvice hikers directly to major destinations. (The regular buses take longer, make several stops en route, and can fill up with passengers to other destinations.) The express bus connects the park to Zagreb in the north (2 hours) and to Split in the south (4 hours; connections to Zadar and Skradin at Krka National Park are also possible). Express buses run 3-4 times per day in summer (July-Aug), and 1-2 times per day in shoulder season (no buses off-season). You can check schedules and buy tickets at Knezevic.GetByBus. com. To research additional options, check out GetByBus.com (the express buses are marked as "PKN") or Autobusni-Kolodvor.com (look for "Plitvička Jezera" under the "Terminals" tab). Most buses can be booked online; for others, buy your ticket on board.

Catching the Bus: There is no bus station at the park—just a low-profile *Plitvice Centar* bus stop shelter near Entrance 2. To reach it from the park, go out to the main road from either Hotel Jezero or Hotel Plitvice, then turn right; the bus stops are just after the pedestrian overpass. The one on the hotel side of the road is for buses headed for the coast (southbound); the stop on the opposite side is for Zagreb (northbound). Confirm the bus schedule with the park or hotel staff, then head out to the bus stop and wave down the bus.

If you haven't booked a ticket online, and a bus is full when it passes by, it won't stop at Plitvice to pick you up. This is most common on days when the buses are jammed with people headed to or from the coast. For example, on Fridays—when everyone is going from Zagreb to Split—you're unlikely to have any luck catching a southbound bus at Plitvice after 12:00. Similarly, on Sunday afternoons, northbound buses are often full. In general, don't plan on taking the last bus of the day. This is why the Prijevoz Knežević express buses are a great option: They originate at Plitvice, and they can be purchased online.

ROUTE TIPS FOR DRIVERS

Plitvice is an hour away from the handy A-1 expressway that connects northern Croatia to the Dalmatian Coast. You have three ways to get from Plitvice to the expressway, depending on which direction you're heading.

Going North: If you're heading north (to Zagreb or Slovenia), drive about one hour north from Plitvice on D-1 to the town of **Karlovac,** where you can access the A-1 expressway northbound. Alternatively, you can take A-1 southbound to A-6, which leads west to Rijeka, Opatija, and Istria (though this route is more boring and only slightly faster than the route via Otočac, described below).

Going South: If you're heading south (to Split and the rest of Dalmatia), catch the expressway at **Gornja Ploča.** Drive south from Plitvice on D-1—through Korenica, Pećane, and Udbina— then follow signs for the A-1 expressway (and *Lovinac*) via Kurjak to the Gornja Ploča on-ramp. Once on A-1, you'll twist south through the giant Sveti Rok tunnel to Dalmatia.

Going to Central Croatia: If you're going to central destinations on the coast—such as Istria, Rijeka, or Opatija—get on the expressway at **Otočac.** From Plitvice, go south on D-1, then turn west on road #52 to the town of Otočac (about an hour through the mountains from Plitvice to Otočac). After Otočac, you can get on A-1 (north to Zagreb, south to the Dalmatian Coast) or continue west and twist down the mountain road to the seaside town of Senj, on the main coastal road of the Kvarner Gulf. From Senj, it's about an hour north along the coast to Rijeka, then on to Opatija or Istria.

During the Yugoslav Wars, the front line between the Croats and Serbs ran just east of **Otočac** (OH-toh-chawts), and a few bullet holes still mar the town's facades. Today Otočac is putting itself back together, and it's a fine place to drop into a café for a coffee or pick up some produce at the outdoor market. The Catholic church in the center of town, destroyed in the war but now rebuilt, displays its damaged church bells in a memorial out back. Notice that the crucifix nearby is made of old artillery shells. Also in the churchyard are big white blocks, each one honoring a Croatian hero; notice

[Side margin: PLITVICE LAKES]

that a character from Glagolitic script (the ancient Croatian alphabet) is carved in the top of each one.

Just up the main street, you'll come to a fine, manicured park, dominated by a huge monument honoring the lives lost in the fight to create a free Croatian nation. It reads: "In order to make real the vision of a Croatian homeland, they laid upon the altar their dreams, their hopes, and their lives." Noticing the giant block splintering into four pieces, it's easy to imagine how this might illustrate the splitting up of the Yugoslav state...and might make you wonder how local Serbs feel about this provocative monument.

At the far end of the park is the Orthodox church. Otočac used to be about one-third Serb, but the Serbs were forced out during the war, and this church fell into disrepair. But, as Otočac and Croatia show signs of healing, about two dozen Serbs have returned to town and reopened their church.

ISTRIA

Rovinj • Pula • The Brijuni Islands • Poreč • Hill Towns • Opatija and Rijeka

Idyllic Istria (EE-stree-ah; "Istra" in Croatian), at Croatia's northwest corner, reveals itself gradually and seductively. Pungent truffles, Roman ruins, striking hill towns, quaint coastal villages, carefully cultivated food and wine, and breezy Italianate culture all compete for your attention. The wedge-shaped Istrian Peninsula, while not as famous as its southern rival (the much-hyped Dalmatian Coast), gives Dalmatia a run for its money.

The Istrian coast, with gentle green slopes instead of the sheer limestone cliffs found along the rest of the Croatian shoreline, is more serene than sensational. It's lined with pretty, interchangeably tacky resort towns, such as the tourist mecca Poreč (worthwhile only for its mosaic-packed Byzantine basilica). But one seafront village reaches the ranks of greatness: romantically creaky Rovinj, my favorite little town on the Adriatic. Down at the tip of Istria is big, industrial Pula, offering a bustling urban contrast to the rest of the time-passed coastline, plus some impressive Roman ruins (including an amphitheater so remarkably intact, you'll marvel that you haven't heard of it before). Just offshore are the Brijuni Islands—once the stomping grounds of Marshal Tito, whose ghost still haunts a national park peppered with unexpected attractions.

But Croatia is more than the sea, and diverse Istria offers some of the country's most appealing reasons to head inland. In the Istrian interior, between humble concrete towns crying out for a paint job, you'll find vintners painstakingly reviving a delicate winemaking tradition, farmers pressing that last drop of oil out of their olives, trained dogs sniffing out truffles in primeval forests, and a smattering of fortified medieval hill towns with sweeping

Istria

To Venice · ITALY · A-3 · *To Ljubljana* · Pivka · Divača · Ilirska Bistrica

Trieste · SLOVENIA

A-1

Piran · Izola · Koper

SALT FIELDS · Portorož

C R O A T I A · A-7

Umag · Buje · Grožnjan · Buzet · Roč · Lupoglav · Opatija · Rijeka

Brtonigla · Oprtalj · 44 · Hum · UČKA TUNNEL · *To Zagreb*

Završje · Livade · Mirna River Valley

Motovun

Novigrad · A-8

See Hill Towns of the Istrian Interior map

Poreč · A-9 · Pazin

I S T R I A

Vrsar · Matošević · Žminj · Brestova

Limski Canal · BRITISH-AMERICAN TOBACCO FACTORY · Labin · Porozina

Rovinj · Cres

Bale · A-9

Adriatic Sea

Fažana · Vodnjan

Brijuni Islands

Pula

10 Kilometers
10 Miles

Medulin

	"Ipsilon" Highway
	Expressway
	Other Roads
	Rail Line
	Boat Route

ISTRIA

views over the surrounding terrain—including the justifiably popular village of Motovun.

PLANNING YOUR TIME

Istria offers an exciting variety of attractions compared to the relatively uniform, if beautiful, string of island towns farther south. While some travelers wouldn't trade a sunny island day for anything, I prefer to sacrifice a little time on the Dalmatian Coast for the diversity that comes with a day or two exploring Istria's hill towns and other unique sights.

Istria's main logistical advantage is that it's easy to reach and to

Istria at a Glance

▲▲▲**Rovinj** Extremely romantic, Venetian-style coastal town with an atmospheric Old Town and salty harbor. See page 97.

▲▲**Pula** Big, industrial port city with one of the world's best-preserved Roman amphitheaters. See page 123.

▲▲**Motovun** Touristy but enjoyable hill town with a fun rampart walk offering sweeping views over inland Istria. See page 144.

▲**Opatija** Former Austrian beach resort (just outside Istria) with sparkling beaches and a touch of classy Viennese-style architecture. See page 160.

▲**Brijuni Islands** Tito's former summer residence, now a national park with a Tito museum, mini safari, and other offbeat sights. See page 137.

▲**Grožnjan** Sleepy artists' colony hill town in the interior. See page 154.

Završje Picturesque, mostly deserted hill town overlooking Motovun and its valley. See page 155.

Buje Big hill town mingling charm with urban flair. See page 153.

Hum Minuscule, touristy town deep in the interior. See page 159.

Poreč Big coastal resort squeezed full of European holiday-makers, plus a church with remarkably intact Byzantine mosaics. See page 141.

Oprtalj Hill town that's striking from afar and small and quiet up close. See page 157.

Livade Modest valley village with some top-notch truffle eateries. See page 158.

Brtonigla Hill town worth visiting only for its great restaurants. See page 152.

Rijeka Hulking transit-hub metropolis sitting on a pretty bay just outside Istria. See page 167.

ISTRIA

explore by car. Just a quick hop from Venice or Slovenia, compact little Istria is made-to-order for a quick, efficient road trip.

With a car and two weeks to spend in Croatia and Slovenia, Istria deserves two days, divided between its two big attractions: the coastal town of Rovinj and the hill towns of the interior. Ideally, make your home base for two nights in Rovinj or in Motovun, and day-trip to the region's other attractions. To wring the most out of limited Istrian time, the city of Pula and its Roman amphitheater are worth a few hours. If you have a car, it's easy to joyride through the Istrian countryside, visiting a few hill towns and wineries en route. The town of Poreč and the fun but time-consuming Brijuni Islands merit the time only if you've got at least three days.

GETTING AROUND ISTRIA

Istria is a cinch for **drivers,** who find distances short and roads and attractions well-marked. Summer traffic, however, can be miserable (especially on weekends), and parking can be tricky—and expensive—in some towns. Istria is neatly connected by a speedy highway nicknamed the *ipsilon* (the Croatian word for the letter Y, which is what the highway is shaped like). One branch of the "Y" (A-9) runs roughly parallel to the coast from Slovenia to Pula, about six miles inland; the other branch (A-8) cuts diagonally northeast to the Učka Tunnel (leading to Rijeka). You'll periodically come to tollbooths, where you'll pay a modest fee for using the *ipsilon*. Following road signs here is easy (navigate by town names), but if you'll be driving a lot, pick up a good map to more easily navigate the back roads. As you drive, keep an eye out for characteristic stone igloos called *kažun* (a symbol of Istria). Formerly used as shelters by shepherds and farmers, now the few surviving structures—sometimes built right into a dry-stone wall—are mostly a symbol of local pride.

If you're relying on **public transportation,** Istria can be frustrating: The towns that are easiest to reach (Poreč and Pula) are less appealing than Istria's highlights (Rovinj and Motovun). Linking up the coastal towns by bus is doable if you're patient and check schedules carefully, but the hill towns probably aren't worth the hassle. Even if you're doing the rest of your trip by public transportation, consider renting a car for a day or two in Istria—or just focus on Rovinj.

Driving from Istria to Rijeka (and the Rest of Croatia): Istria meets the rest of Croatia at the big port city of Rijeka (described at the end of this chapter). There are two ways to get to Rijeka: The faster alternative is to take the *ipsilon* road via Pazin to the Učka Tunnel, which emerges just above Rijeka and Opatija (for Rijeka, you'll follow the road more or less straight on; for Opatija, you'll twist down to the right, backtracking slightly to the seashore below you). Or you can take the slower but more scenic **coastal road** from Pula via Labin. After going inland for about 25 miles, this road jogs to the east coast of Istria, which it hugs all the way into Opatija, then Rijeka.

From Rijeka, you can easily hook into Croatia's expressway network (for example, take A-6 east to A-1, which zips you north to Zagreb or south to the Dalmatian Coast). For more driving tips, see the end of this chapter.

By Boat to Venice, Piran, or Trieste: Various companies connect Venice daily in summer with Rovinj, Poreč, and Pula (about three hours). While designed for day-trippers from Istria to Venice, these services can be used for one-way travel. As the companies and specific routes change from year to year, check each of these websites to see what might work for your itinerary: **Venezia Lines** (www.venezialines.com), **Adriatic Lines** (www.adriatic-lines.com), and **Commodore Cruises** (http://commodore.fwd.hr). **Liberty Lines** (www.libertylines.it) connects Rovinj and Poreč to Piran (Slovenia), then Trieste (Italy).

Rovinj

ISTRIA

Rising dramatically from the Adriatic as though being pulled up to heaven by its grand bell tower, Rovinj (roh-VEEN; in Italian: Rovigno/roh-VEEN-yoh) is a welcoming Old World oasis. Among the villages of Croatia's coast, there's something particularly romantic about Rovinj—the most Italian town in Croatia's most Italian region. Rovinj's streets are delightfully twisty, its ancient houses are characteristically crumbling, and its harbor—lively with real-life fishermen—is as salty as they come. Like a little Venice on a hill, Rovinj is the atmospheric setting of your Croatian seaside dreams.

Rovinj was prosperous and well-fortified in the Middle Ages. It boomed in the 16th and 17th centuries, when it was flooded with

Istrian Food and Wine

Foodies consider Istria the best part of Croatia. Though much of the country's coastline is arid, Istria is noticeably greener—its fertile soil bursts with a cornucopia of ingredients. Like the Istrian people, Istrian cuisine is a mix of cultural influences, including Italian-style elements, farmer fare, game, and seafood. Truffles are used liberally, and are a big hit with the many tourists who come here for their pungent flavor (see page 151).

For pastas, you'll see familiar dishes such as gnocchi and risotto, but Istria also adds some unique noodles. *Fuži* are little pasta squares that are rolled up to create hollow noodles, roughly shaped like penne; *pljukanci* are short, thick, nearly transparent twists (similar to Italian *trofie*).

Pršut is the air-cured ham that is Istria's answer to prosciutto. You'll often find game on the menu, as well as *boškarin*—the meat of an indigenous Istrian longhorn cattle. *Ombolo* is pork loin.

Istria is also a major wine-growing region. And now that they've made progress repairing the damage done by communist-era winemaking cooperatives, Istrian wines are gaining international renown. Relatively few Istrian wines are exported (though the number is growing), so this region gives wine lovers a good opportunity to discover some new bouquets.

About 80 percent of Istrian wines are white, many made with the grape called *malvazija* (mahl-VAH-zee-yah; known to English-speakers as malvasia)—producing a delicious, light white wine that can be either sweet *(slatko)* or dry *(suho)*. *Malvazija* wines are produced throughout Europe, but Istria's *malvazija* is indigenous. *Malvazija* comes in several forms: "fresh" (table wine, aged in stainless steel) or aged in barrels (often in French oak or in local Istrian acacia; look for *barrique* on the label). White blends (usually including some *malvazija*) are also common.

Red wines are made from the *teran* grape, which produces a "big" wine that you can chew on. Because *teran* is full-bodied, it's often blended with merlot or other grapes, resulting in some softer, lovely flavors and a finer wine. *Teran* pairs well with *pršut*.

For more on Istrian wines—including wineries where drivers can stop off for a taste—see the sidebar on page 156. If you're carless, ask about local wines as you explore your nightlife and dining options in Rovinj.

refugees fleeing both the Ottoman invasions and the plague. Because the town was part of the Republic of Venice for five centuries (13th to 18th centuries), its architecture, culture, and even language are strongly Venetian. The local folk groups sing in a dialect that's considered more Venetian than what the Venetians themselves speak these days. (You can even see Venice from Rovinj's church bell tower on a very clear day.)

After Napoleon seized the region, then was defeated, Rovinj became part of the Habsburgs' domain. The Venetians had neglected Istria, but the Austrians invested in it, bringing the railroad, gas lights, and a huge Ronhill tobacco factory. (This factory—recently replaced by an enormous, state-of-the-art facility labeled "British-American Tobacco" that you'll pass on the highway farther inland—remains one of the town's most elegant structures.) The Habsburgs tapped Pula and Trieste to be the empire's major ports—cursing those cities with pollution and sprawl, while allowing Rovinj to linger in its trapped-in-the-past quaintness.

Tourism came to Rovinj in the late 1890s, when a powerful Austrian baron bought one of the remote, barren islands offshore and brought it back to life with gardens and a grand villa. Soon another baron bought another island...and a tourist boom was under way. In more recent times, Rovinj has become a top destination for nudists. The resort of Valalta, just to the north, is a popular spot for those seeking "southern exposure," as a very revealing brochure at the TI illustrates (www.valalta.hr). Whether you want to find PNBs (pudgy nude bodies) or avoid them, remember that *FKK* is international shorthand for nudism.

Rovinj is the most atmospheric of all of Croatia's small coastal towns. Maybe that's because it's always been a real town, where

poor people lived. You'll find no fancy old palaces here—just narrow streets lined with skinny houses that have sheltered humble families for generations. Rovinj retains the soul of a fishermen's village. It's rougher around the edges than Dubrovnik, and many people still live in cramped Old Town apartments. But things are beginning to change, and a snazzy new yacht harbor may attract a deep-pocketed new clientele to the town. Enjoy Rovinj now...before it changes too much. It will.

ISTRIA

PLANNING YOUR TIME

Give Rovinj the better part of a day. You can get the gist of the town in a one-hour wander. The rest of your time is for enjoying the ambience, savoring a slow meal, or pedaling a rental bike to a nearby beach. When you're ready to overcome your inertia, there's no shortage of day trips (the best—a half-day each in Pula and Motovun—are outlined in this chapter). Be aware that much of Rovinj (like other small Croatian coastal towns) closes down from mid-October through Easter.

Orientation to Rovinj

Rovinj's Old Town is divided in two parts: a particularly charismatic chunk on the oval-shaped peninsula, and the rest on the mainland (with similarly time-worn buildings but fewer tourists). The mainland meets the peninsula at the broad, bustling Tito Square (Trg Maršala Tita). The Old Town peninsula—traffic-free except for the occasional moped—is topped by the massive bell tower of the Church of St. Euphemia.

TOURIST INFORMATION

You'll find Rovinj's TI on the Square at the Bridge (May-Oct daily 8:00-20:00, July-Aug until 22:00; Nov-April Mon-Fri until 16:00, Sat until 13:00, closed Sun; Trg na Mostu 2, tel. 052/811-566, www.rovinj-tourism.com).

ARRIVAL IN ROVINJ

By Car: Only local cars are allowed to enter the Old Town area. To get as close as possible—whether you're staying in the Old Town or just visiting for the day—use the big waterfront Valdibora parking lots just north of the Old Town, which come with the classic Rovinj view (5 kn/hour, or 4 kn/hour overnight, cheaper off-season). As you drive in from the highway through the outskirts of Rovinj, the road forks, sending most hotel traffic to the left (turn off here if you're staying outside the Old Town); but if you want to reach the Old Town, go right instead, then follow *Centar* signs, which eventually lead you directly to the two Valdibora lots: Valdibora 2 (a.k.a. Little Valdibora, farther from the Old Town), then Valdibora 1 (a.k.a. Big Valdibora, closer to the Old Town). During busy times, the slightly closer Valdibora 1 is reserved for residents; in this case, signs will divert you into Valdibora 2.

If both Valdibora lots are full, you'll be pushed to another pay lot farther out, along the bay northwest of the Old Town (a scenic 15-minute walk from town, 5 kn/hour, free 23:00-6:00; cheaper mid-Oct-April). Yet another option is to use the free lot near the corner of ulica Stjepana Radića and ulica Stanke Pauletića,

Greater Rovinj

1. Arupinum Hotel
2. Vila Kristina
3. Villa Baron Gautsch
4. Hotel Vila Lili
5. Rooms Barbieri
6. Elda Markulin Rooms/Apartments
7. Grand Park Hotel
8. Hotel Lone
9. Hotel Monte Mulini
10. Hotel Eden
11. Island Hotel Katarina
12. Maestral Restaurant
13. Laundry

a 20-minute walk from the Old Town (see the "Greater Rovinj" map). Even if the Valdibora lots are available, budget-oriented drivers may prefer these cheaper outer lots—the cost adds up fast if you're parking over several nights. Accommodations outside the Old Town generally have on-site (or nearby streetside) parking, often free; a few places in the Old Town have parking available outside of town.

By Bus: The bus station is on the south side of the Old Town, close to the harbor. Leave the station to the left, then walk on the bustling, traffic-free Carera street directly into the center of town.

By Boat: The few boats connecting Rovinj to Venice, Piran, and Trieste may dock along the Valdibora parking lots, north of the Old Town, or at the long pier protruding from the south side Old Town peninsula. Either way, it's an easy stroll into town.

ISTRIA

HELPFUL HINTS

Laundry: Smack-dab in the center, the coin-op **Self-Service Laundry Rovinj** is at Zdenac 21 (daily 8:00-22:00, mobile 091-523-6788). A full-service launderette, **Galax,** hides up the street beyond the bus station. You can usually pick up your laundry after 24 hours, though same-day service might be possible if you drop it off early enough in the morning (in summer generally daily 6:00-20:00, or possibly later; shorter hours and closed Sun off-season; up Benussia street past the bus station, on the left after the post office, tel. 052/816-130).

Local Guide: Pula-based **Mariam Abdelghani** can come meet you for a tour in Rovinj (see listing in the Pula section later in this chapter).

Best Views: The town is full of breathtaking vistas. Shutterbugs are very busy in the magic hours of early morning and evening, and even by moonlight. The postcard view of Rovinj is from the parking lot embankment at the north end of the Old Town (at the start of the "Rovinj Ramble," next). For a different perspective on the Old Town, head for the far side of the harbor on the opposite (south) end of town. The church bell tower provides an almost aerial view of the town and a grand vista of the outlying islands.

Rovinj Ramble

This self-guided walk, rated ▲▲▲, introduces you to Rovinj in about an hour. Begin at the parking lot just north of the Old Town (Valdibora 1).

Old Town View

Many places offer fine views of Rovinj's Old Town, but this is the most striking. Boats bob in the harbor, and behind them Venetian-looking homes seem to rise from the deep.

The Old Town is topped by a church, whose bell tower is capped by a weathervane in the shape of Rovinj's patron saint, Euphemia. Local fishermen look to this saintly weathervane for direction: When Euphemia is looking out to sea, it means the stiff, fresh Bora wind is blowing, bringing dry air from the interior...a sailor's delight. But if she's facing the land, the humid Jugo wind will soon bring bad weather from the sea. After a day or so, even a tourist learns to look to St.

Euphemia for the weather forecast. (For more on Croatian winds and weather, see "The Bora" sidebar near the end of this chapter.)

As you soak in this scene, ponder how the town's history created its current shape. In the Middle Ages, Rovinj was an island surrounded by a double wall—a protective inner wall and an outer seawall. Because it was defended so well against pirates and other marauders (and carefully quarantined from the plague), it was extremely desirable real estate. And yet, it was easy to reach from the mainland, allowing it to thrive as a trading town. With more than 10,000 residents at its peak, Rovinj became immensely crowded, which explains today's pleasantly claustrophobic Old Town.

Over the centuries—as demand for living space trumped security concerns—the town walls were converted into houses, with windows grafted on to their imposing frame. Gaps in the wall, with steps that seem to end at the water, are where fishermen would pull in to unload their catch directly into the warehouses on the bottom level of the houses. (Later you can explore some of these lanes from inside the town.) Today, if you live in one of these houses, the Adriatic is your backyard.

• *Now head into town. In the little park near the sea, just beyond the end of the parking lot, look for the big, blocky...*

Yugoslav-Era Monument

Dating from the time of Tito, this celebrates the Partisan Army's victory over the Nazis in World War II and commemorates the

victims of fascism. The minimalist reliefs on the ceremonial tomb show a slow prisoners' parade, the victims prodded by a gun in the back from a figure with a Nazi-style helmet. Notice that one side of the monument is in Croatian, and the other is in Italian. With typical Yugoslav grace and subtlety, this jarring block shatters the otherwise harmonious time-warp vibe of Rovinj. Fortunately, it's the only modern structure near the Old Town.

• *Now walk a few more steps toward town and past the playground, stopping to explore the covered...*

Market

The front part of the market, near the water, is for souvenirs. But natives delve deeper, to the produce stands. In both areas, merchants aggressively push free samples. Everything is local and

ISTRIA

Rovinj Center

200 Meters
200 Yards

Adriatic

PILLBOX
BEACH

AMOLONGO

VLADIMIRA SVALBE

SALITA F. BODI

BREGOVITA

VLADIMIRA SVALBE

UPSON

WALK
ENDS

BELL
TOWER

CAENAZZA

4

CHINCA

**ST.
EUPHEMIA**

GRISIA

CASALE

8

BALOTA
BEACH

17

GRISIA

MONTALBANO

18

GARZOTTO

TREVISOL

16

SVETOGA

7

15

21

KRIZA

22

14

13

3

5

12

**HOUSE OF THE
BATANA BOAT**

LONG
PIER

To Boats to
Piran, Venice,
etc.

Accommodations
1 Hotel Adriatic & Café
2 Porta Antica Apartments
3 Casa Garzotto (Reception
   & Apartments)
4 Casa Garzotto (Rooms)
5 Villa Markiz & Villa Bianca
6 Villa Cissa
7 Hey Rovinj
8 Casa Casale
9 To Island Hotel Katarina

10 Direct Route to Maistra
   Hotels, Other
   Accommodations,
   Laundry & Free Parking
11 Scenic Route to Maistra
   Hotels & Other
   Accommodations

ISTRIA

mostly homemade. Consider this snack-time tactic: Loiter around, joking with the farmers while sampling their various tasty walnuts, figs, cherries, grapes, olive oils, honey, *rakija* (the powerful fruit brandy popular throughout the Balkans), and more. If the sample is good, buy some more for a picnic. In the center of the market, a delightful and practical fountain from 1908 reminds locals of the infrastructure brought in by their Habsburg rulers a century ago. The fish market labeled *Ribarnica/Pescheria* at the back of the market is where locals gather ingredients for their favorite dish, *brodet*—a stew of various kinds of seafood mixed with olive oil and wine. It's slowly simmered and generally served with polenta.

• *Continue up the broad street, named for Giuseppe Garibaldi—one of the major players in mid-19th-century Italian unification. Imagine: Even though you're in Croatia, Italian patriots are celebrated in this very Italian-feeling town (see the "Italo-Croatia" sidebar later in this chapter). After one long block, on your left, you'll come to the wide cross street called...*

Square at the Bridge (Trg na Mostu)

This marks the site of the medieval bridge that once connected the fortified island of Rovinj to the mainland (as illustrated in the small painting above the door of the Kavana al Ponto—"Bridge Café"—

on your left). Back then, the island was populated mostly by Italians, while the mainland was the territory of Slavic farmers. But as Rovinj's strategic importance waned and its trading status rose, the need for easy access became more important than the canal's protective purpose—so in 1763, it was filled in. The two populations integrated, creating the bicultural mix that survives today.

Notice the breeze? Via Garibaldi is nicknamed Val di Bora (Valley of the Bora Wind) for the constant cooling wind that blows here. On the left side of Trg na Mostu is the TI; on the right is the Rovinj Heritage Museum (described later, under "Sights in Rovinj"). Next door, the town's stately, yellow cultural center posts lovingly hand-lettered signs in Croatian and Italian announcing upcoming musical events (generally free, designed for locals, and worth noting and enjoying). Next to that is an outlet of Bonbonnière Kraš, Croatia's favorite chocolate company.

Nearby (just past Kavana al Ponto, on the left), the Viecia Batana Café—named for Rovinj's unique, flat-bottomed little fishing boats—has a retro interior with a circa-1960 fishermen's mural that evokes an earlier age. The café is popular for its desserts (the chocolate cake is tasty).

• Now proceed down Garibaldi to the little fountain in the middle of the square, facing the harbor.

Tito Square (Trg Maršala Tita)

This wide-open square at the entrance to the Old Town is the crossroads of Rovinj. The **fountain,** with a little boy playing a fish like a bagpipe, celebrates the government-funded water system that finally brought running water to the Old Town in 1959. Walk around the fountain, with your eyes on the relief, to see a successful socialist society at the inauguration of this new water system. Despite the happy occasion, the figures are pretty stiff, in accordance with the idealized aesthetic of Socialist Realism.

Now walk out along the concrete pier, called the **Mali Molo (Little Pier).** From here, you're surrounded by Rovinj's crowded harbor, with fishing vessels and excursion boats that shuttle tourists out to the offshore islands. If the weather's good, a **boat trip** can be a fun way to get out on the water for a different angle on Rovinj.

Scan the **harbor.** Look for the building marked *MMC,* the local meeting and concert hall. Along the waterfront to the right of the MMC, you'll see the Grand Park Hotel, with its glitzy yacht harbor. A recom-

Italo-Croatia

Apart from its tangible attractions, one of Istria's hallmarks is its biculturalism: It's an engaging hybrid of Croatia and Italy. Like most of the Croatian Coast, Istria has variously been controlled by Romans, Byzantines, Slavs, Venetians, and Austrians. After the Habsburgs lost World War I, most of today's Croatia joined Yugoslavia—but Istria became part of Italy. During this time, the Croatian vernacular was suppressed, while the Italian language and culture flourished. But this extra chapter of Italian rule was short-lived. After World War II, Istria joined Yugoslavia, and Croatian culture and language returned. What followed was a so-called Italian exodus, during which many Istrian Italians were forced to relocate to Italy—leaving behind hill towns, valley villages, and farm estates that are abandoned even to this day.

The Istrians who stayed behind were saddled with an identity crisis. Many people here found it difficult to abandon their ties to Italy, and continued to speak the language and embrace the culture. Today, depending on whom you ask, Istria is the most Italian part of Croatia...or the most Croatian part of Italy. Istria pops up on Italian weather reports. Former Italian Prime Minister Silvio Berlusconi once declared that he still considered Istria part of Italy—and he wanted it back. When I wrote an article about Istria for a newspaper, some Italian readers complained that I made it sound "too Croatian," while some Croatians claimed my depiction was "too Italian."

People who actually live here typically don't worry about the distinction. Locals insist that they're not Croatians and not Italians—they're Istrians. They don't mind straddling two cultures. Both languages are official (and often taught side-by-side in schools), street signs are bilingual, and most Istrians dabble in each tongue—often seeming to foreign ears as though they're mixing the two at once.

As a result of their tangled history, Istrians have learned how to be mellow and take things as they come. They tend to be gregarious, open-minded, and sometimes seem to thrive on chaos. A twentysomething local told me, "My ancestors lived in Venice. My great-grandfather lived in Austria. My grandfather lived in Italy. My father lived in Yugoslavia. I live in Croatia. My son will live in the European Union. And we've all lived in the same town."

mended bike path starts just past this area, leading into a nature preserve and the best nearby beaches, which you can see in the distance. For more on boat trips and bike rentals, see "Activities in Rovinj," later.

Now head back to the base of the pier. A short walk to the left are the **House of the Batana Boat** museum, and a delightful **restaurant row** with several tempting places for a drink or a meal. Fishermen pull their boats into this harbor and carry their catch across the street to a waiting restaurateur.

Next, walk straight past the fountain and face the Old Town entrance gate, called the **Balbi Arch.** On top, the winged lion of St. Mark is a reminder that this was Venetian territory for centuries.

• *Head through the gate into the Old Town. Inside and on the left is the red...*

Town Hall

On the old Town Hall, notice another Venetian lion, as well as other historic crests embedded in the wall. Along with flags for Rovinj, Croatia, and the EU, the Town Hall sports an Italian flag, and faces a square named for Giacomo Matteotti, a much-revered Italian patriot.

Continue a few more steps into town. You'll find another little square, which once functioned as a cistern (collecting rainwater, which was pulled from a subterranean reservoir through the well you see today). The orange-ish building on your left is the Italian Union—yet another reminder of how Istria has an important bond with Italy.

• *Now begin walking up the street past the Italian Union, bearing right, then left, up...*

Grisia Street

The main "street" (actually a tight lane) leading through the middle of the Old Town is choked with tourists during the midday rush and lined with art galleries and souvenir kitsch. This inspiring town has attracted many artists, some of whom display their works along this colorful stretch. See the rusty little nails speckling the walls? Each August, locals hang their best art on this street. With paintings lining the lane, the entire community comes out to enjoy each other's creations.

As you walk, keep your camera ready, as you can find delightful scenes down every side lane. Remember that, as crowded as it is today, little Rovinj was even more packed in the Middle Ages. Keep an eye out for arches that span narrow lanes (such as on the right, at Arsenale street). Many of these additions created hidden little courtyards, nooks, and crannies that make it easy to get away from the crowds and claim a corner of the town for yourself. The distinctive chimneys poking up above the rooftops are another sign of Rovinj's overcrowding. These chimneys, added long after the buildings were first constructed, made it possible to heat previously underutilized rooms...and squeeze in even more people.

• *Continue up to the top of Grisia. Capping the town is the can't-miss-it...*

▲Church of St. Euphemia (Sv. Eufemija)

Rovinj's landmark Baroque church dates from 1754. It's watched over by an enormous 190-foot-tall campanile, a replica of the famous bell tower on St.

Mark's Square in Venice. A copper weathervane with the weather-predicting St. Euphemia, the church's namesake, tops the tower.

Cost and Hours: Free, generally open May-Sept daily 10:00-18:00, April and Oct-Nov open only for Mass and with demand, generally closed Dec-Easter.

Visiting the Church: Enter the church through its right transept. The vast, somewhat gloomy interior boasts some fine altars of Carrara marble (a favorite medium of Michelangelo's). Services here are celebrated using a combination of Croatian and Italian, suiting the town's mixed population.

To the right of the main altar (follow *sarkofag* signs) is the church's highlight: the chapel containing the **relics of St. Euphemia.** Before stepping into the chapel, notice the altar featuring Euphemia—depicted, as she usually is, with her wheel (a reminder of her torture) and a palm frond (symbolic of her martyrdom), and holding the fortified town of Rovinj, of which she is the protector.

Now circle around behind this altar to find a gigantic tomb, and above, two large paintings that illustrate significant events from the life of this important local figure. Euphemia was the virtuous daughter of a prosperous early-fourth-century family in

Chalcedon (near today's Istanbul). She used her family's considerable wealth to help the poor. Unfortunately, her pious philanthropy happened to coincide with anti-Christian purges by the Roman Emperor Diocletian. When she was 15 years old, Euphemia was arrested for refusing to worship the local pagan idol. She was brutally tortured, her bones broken on a wheel. Finally she was thrown to the lions as a public spectacle. But, the story goes, the lions miraculously refused to attack her. You can see this moment depicted in one of the paintings above—as a bored-looking lion tenderly nibbles at her right bicep.

Flash forward to the year 800, when a gigantic marble sarcophagus containing St. Euphemia's relics somehow found its way into the Adriatic and floated all the way up to Istria, where Rovinj fishermen discovered it bobbing in the sea. They tugged it back to town, where a crowd gathered. The townspeople realized what it was and wanted to take it up to the hilltop church. But nobody could move it...until a young boy with two young calves showed up, and said he'd had a dream of St. Euphemia. Sure enough, he succeeded in dragging her relics to where they still lie. In the second painting, see the burly fishermen looking astonished as the boy succeeds in moving the giant sarcophagus. Note the depiction of Rovinj fortified by a double crenellated wall—looking more like a castle than like the creaky fishing village of today. At the top of the hill is an earlier version of today's church.

Now turn your attention to Euphemia's famous sarcophagus. The front panel (with the painting of Euphemia) is opened with much fanfare every September 16, St. Euphemia's feast day, to display the small, withered, waxen face of Rovinj's favorite saint.

• *If you have time and energy, consider climbing the...*

Bell Tower

Scaling the church bell tower's creaky wooden stairway requires an enduring faith in the reliability of wood. It rewards those who brave its 192 stairs with a commanding view of the town and surrounding islands. The climb doubles your altitude, and from this perch you can also look down—taking advantage of the quirky little round hole in the floor to photograph the memorable staircase you just climbed.

Cost and Hours: 20 kn, same hours as church, enter from inside church—to the left of the main altar.

• *Leave the church and head out to the plaza in front of the bell tower, overlooking the Adriatic. Your walk is over. A peaceful café on a park terrace (once a cemetery) is just ahead of and below you. Just to the right, a winding, cobbled lane leads past the café entrance and down toward the water, then forks. A left turn here zigzags you past a WWII pillbox and leads along the restaurant row, where you can survey your options for a drink or a meal (see "Eating in Rovinj," later). A right turn curls you down along the quieter northern side of the Old Town peninsula. Either way, Rovinj is yours to enjoy.*

Sights in Rovinj

▲House of the Batana Boat (Kuća o Batani)

Rovinj has a long, noble shipbuilding tradition, and this tiny but interesting museum gives you the story of the town's distinctive *batana* boats. The flat-bottomed vessels are favored by local fishermen for their ability to reach rocky areas close to shore that are rich with certain shellfish.

Cost and Hours: 20 kn; daily May-Sept 10:00-13:00 & 18:00-21:00, June-Aug until 23:00; Oct-Nov and March-April 10:00-16:00; closed Dec-Feb; Obala Pina Budicina 2, tel. 052/812-593, www.batana.org, Ornella.

Visiting the Museum: The state-of-the-art exhibit tells the story of the *batana* and the community it represents. Look for the entertaining time-lapse video showing a boat built from scratch in five minutes. You'll also have the opportunity to hear Rovinj sailors

talk in the local dialect, as well as some beautiful *bitinada*—local music with harmonizing voices that imitate instruments.

Activities: The museum, which serves as a sort of cultural heritage center for the town, also presents a variety of engaging *batana*-related activities. For details, see "Nightlife in Rovinj," later.

Rovinj Heritage Museum (Zavičajni Muzej Grada Rovinja)

This ho-hum museum in an old mansion combines art old (obscure classic painters) and new (obscure contemporary painters from Rovinj) with exhibits on local history. Explanations are often in Croatian and Italian only. Temporary exhibits during the busy season are a big draw; in recent years, these have showcased big-name modern artists, such as Dalí and Miró. Impressive as they are, they have nothing to do with local culture and drastically increase the price.

Cost and Hours: April-Aug—60 kn including special exhibits, off-season—15 kn; open April-Aug daily 10:00-22:00, shorter hours off-season and closed Sun-Mon; Trg Maršala Tita 11, tel. 052/816-720, www.muzej-rovinj.hr.

Activities in Rovinj

Boat Trips

For a different view of Rovinj, consider a boat trip. The scenery is pleasant rather than thrilling, but the craggy and tree-lined coastline and offshore islets are a lovely backdrop for an hour or two at sea. You'll see captains hawking boat excursions at little shacks all along Rovinj's harbor. The most common option is a loop around the Golden Cape (Zlatni Rt) and through Rovinj's own little **archipelago;** this is most popular at sunset (around 75 kn/1 hour). A two-hour "dolphin safari" costs around 100 kn. For a longer cruise, consider the four-hour, 150-200-kn sail north along the coast and into the underwhelming **Limski Canal** (a.k.a. Limski Fjord), where you'll have one to two hours of free time. Dolphin sightings are not unusual, and some outfits throw in a "fish picnic" en route for extra. Stroll the harbor and comparison-shop.

You can also take a boat to one of the larger offshore islands. This lets you get away from the crowds and explore some relatively untrampled beaches. These boats—run by the big hotel chain with branches on those islands—depart about hourly from the end of the concrete pier (known as the Mali Molo, or Little Pier) in the Old Town. The two choices are **St. Catherine** (Sv. Katarina—the lush, green island with a recommended hotel, just across the harbor, about a 5-minute trip, 35 kn) and **Red Island** (Crveni Otok—farther out, about a 15-minute trip, boats may be marked "Hotel Istra," 45 kn).

▲Swimming and Sunbathing

Rovinj doesn't have any sandy beaches—just rocky ones. (The nearest thing to a sandy beach is the small, finely pebbled beach on Red Island/Crveni Otok.) The most central spot to swim or sunbathe is at **Balota Beach,** on the rocks along the embankment on the south side of the Old Town peninsula, just past La Puntulina restaurant (no showers, but scenic and central). On nice days, Balota can get crowded; if you continue around Rovinj's peninsula to the tip, just before the old WWII pillbox, you'll find the more secluded **Pillbox Beach,** where steps lead steeply down to a cluster of more secluded rocks. For bigger beaches, go to the wooded **Golden Cape** (Zlatni Rt) south of the harbor (past the big, waterfront Grand Park Hotel). This cape is lined with walking paths and beaches, and shaded by a wide variety of trees and plants. For a scenic sunbathing spot, choose a perch facing Rovinj on the north side of the Golden Cape. Another beach, called **Kuvi,** is beyond the Golden Cape. To get away from it all, take a boat to an island on Rovinj's little archipelago (see previous listing).

▲Bike Ride

The TI's free, handy biking map suggests a variety of short and long bike rides. The easiest and most scenic is a quick loop around the Golden Cape (Zlatni Rt). You can do this circuit and return to the Old Town in about an hour (without stops). Start by biking south around the harbor and past the waterfront Grand Park Hotel, where you leave the cars behind and enter the wooded Golden Cape. Peaceful miniature beaches abound. The lane climbs to a quarry (much of Venice was paved with Istrian stone), where you're likely to see novice rock climbers inching their way up and down. Cycling down-

hill from the quarry and circling the peninsula, you hit the Lovor Grill (with drinks and light meals, open only in summer)—a cute little restaurant housed in the former stables of the Austrian countess who planted what today is called Wood Park. From there, you can continue farther along the coast or return to town (backtrack two minutes and take the right fork through the woods back to the waterfront path).

For a more ambitious, inland pedal, pick up the TI's free *Basilica* bike map, which narrates a 12-mile loop that connects several old churches.

Bike Rental: Bikes are rented at subsidized prices from the city parking lot kiosk (5 kn/hour, open 24 hours daily except no rentals in winter). Various travel agencies around town rent bikes for much more (around 20 kn/hour); look for signs—especially near the bus station—or ask around.

Nightlife in Rovinj

Rovinj is a delight after dark. Views that are great by day become magical in the moonlight and floodlight. The streets of the Old Town are particularly inviting when empty and starlit.

Concerts

Lots of low-key musical events take place right in town (ask at the TI, check the events calendar at www.rovinj-tourism. com, and look for handwritten signs in Croatian and Italian on Garibaldi Street near the Square at the Bridge, across from the TI). Groups perform at various venues around town: right along the harborfront (you'll see the bandstand set up); in the town's churches (especially St. Euphemia and the Franciscan church); in the old cinema/theater by the market; at the pier in front of the House of the Batana Boat (described earlier, under "Sights in Rovinj"); and at the Multi-Media Center (a.k.a. the MMC, which locals call Cinema Belgrade—its former name), in a cute little hall above a bank across the harbor from the Old Town.

Bars

Valentino Champagne and Cocktail Bar is a romantic, waterfront, painfully pretentious place to sip a very expensive drink at

sunset or late at night. Fish, attracted by its underwater lights, swim by from all over the bay...to the enjoyment of those nursing a cocktail on the rocks (literally—you'll be given a small seat cushion to plunk down in your own seaside niche). Or you can choose to sit on one of the terraces. Candelabras twinkle in the twilight, as couples cozy up to each other and the view. While the drinks are expensive (starting around 100 kn), this place is unforgettably cool (best at sunset, closed off-season, Via Santa Croce 28, tel. 052/830-683, Patricia cultivates a snobby atmosphere).

If Valentino is too pricey, too chichi, or too crowded for your tastes, a couple of alternatives are nearby. The **Mediterraneo** bar, along the same drag but a bit closer to the harbor, is fun-loving and serves much cheaper drinks (daily 9:00-late, closed Oct-Easter, mobile 091-532-8357). Or consider **La Puntulina**, beyond Valentino, with a similarly rocky ambience, prices somewhere in the middle, and a bit less panache than Valentino (listed later, under "Eating in Rovinj"). I'd scout all three and pick the ambience you prefer.

Batana Boat Activities

In summer, the House of the Batana Boat (described earlier, under "Sights in Rovinj") often hosts special events. On some summer evenings, you can take a boat trip on a *batana* from the pier near the museum. The trip, which is accompanied by traditional music, circles around the end of the Old Town peninsula and docks on the far side, where a traditional wine cellar has a fresh fish dinner ready, with local wine and more live music (June-mid-Sept, boat trip costs 70 kn and runs nightly around 19:30, dinner available twice weekly—usually Tue and Thu—and costs 190 kn extra, visit or call the museum the day before to reserve). Also on some summer evenings, you can enjoy an outdoor food market with traditional Rovinj foods and live *bitinada* music. The centerpiece is a *batana* boat being refurbished before your eyes (in front of museum, light food, mid-June-early Sept generally Tue and Sat 20:00-23:00).

Sleeping in Rovinj

As throughout Croatia, most Rovinj accommodations (both hotels and *sobe*) prefer multinight stays—especially in peak season (July-Aug). While some places levy surcharges for shorter stays, many are fine with even one-night stays. Don't show up here without a room in August, when Rovinj is packed. Finding these places will challenge even the ablest of route finders. Just ask—locals are happy to help point you in the right direction.

IN THE OLD TOWN

All of these accommodations are on the Old Town peninsula, rather than the mainland section of the Old Town. While it's a delight to sleep deep in the atmospheric center of Rovinj, be warned that this area often comes with some nighttime noise (the town can be quite rowdy in July and August—try requesting a quieter room, and bring earplugs) and requires parking a 10- to 20-minute walk away (for options, see "Arrival in Rovinj—By Car," earlier). Unless otherwise noted, you can assume these places have air-conditioning and do not offer breakfast (for breakfast ideas, see the end of the Eating in Rovinj section).

$$$$ Hotel Adriatic features 18 rooms overlooking the main square, where the peninsula meets the mainland. The only Old Town branch of the big chain of Maistra hotels (described later), this is a posh, four-star splurge with an unbeatable location (includes breakfast, elevator, free parking just outside of town, Trg Maršala Tita, tel. 052/803-510, www.maistra.hr, recepcija@maistra.hr).

$$$$ Porta Antica rents 21 comfortable, nicely decorated but pricey apartments in six different buildings around the Old Town (all but two are on the peninsula; some suffer from nighttime noise)—but conveniently, all are managed from a single reception. Review your options on their website and be specific in your request (RS%, reception and main building on Obala Pina Budičina between Hotel Adriatic and the House of the Batana Boat museum, mobile 099-680-1101, www.portaantica.com, rovinj@portaantica.com, Claudia).

$$$ Casa Garzotto is an appealing option, with four apartments, five rooms, and one large family apartment in three different Old Town buildings. These classic lodgings have modern facilities but old-fashioned charm, with antique furniture and historic family portraits on the walls (includes breakfast, lots of stairs, reception and most apartments are at Garzotto 8, others are a short walk away, tel. 052/811-884, mobile 099-800-7338, www.casa-garzotto.com, casagarzotto@gmail.com).

$$ Villa Markiz, run by sweet Milica and her husband Andrej (who designed the rooms), has four mod, stylish apartments in a beautifully restored old shell in a quiet corner of the Old Town. You'll climb a steep and narrow staircase to reach the apartments, each of which has a small terrace; only the gorgeous top-floor, two-story penthouse apartment has sea views (Pod Lukovima 1, mobile 091-909-8480, https://markizrovinj.com, info@markizrovinj.com). Their **$$ Villa Bianca,** a few steps up the same lane, has two one-bedroom apartments, and they have three other stand-alone apartments in nearby buildings.

$$ Villa Cissa, run by Zagreb transplant Veljko Despot, has three apartments with contemporary decor above an art gallery in the Old Town. Kind Veljko is a fascinating guy who had an illustrious career as a rock-and-roll journalist (he was the only communist-era reporter to interview the Beatles) and record-company executive. Veljko lives off-site, so be sure to clearly communicate your arrival time (cash only, air-con, Zdenac 14, tel. 052/813-080, info@villacissa.com).

$ Hey Rovinj, at the top of town, feels fresh, creative, and youthful. Pleasant Luka manages four apartments and two rooms—all of them nicely equipped and a great value (Trevisol 54, mobile 091-614-3006, www.heyrovinj.com, booking@heyrovinj.com).

$ Casa Casale has three simple but affordable and nicely appointed rooms atmospherically located in a tight lane in the heart of the Old Town. As there's no air-conditioning, thin windows, and lots of outdoor cafés nearby, it can be noisy at night (breakfast included, cash only, steep stairs, Casale 2, tel. 052/814-828, mobile 091-601-6784, info.casale2@gmail.com, Adriano).

ON THE MAINLAND, SOUTHEAST OF THE OLD TOWN

To escape the high prices, nighttime noise, and parking headaches of Rovinj's Old Town, consider the resort neighborhood just south of the harbor. These are a 10- to 20-minute walk from the historic center, but most of that walk is along the very scenic harborfront—hardly an unpleasant commute. While the big Maistra hotels are an option, I prefer cheaper alternatives in the same area. Given the cost and inconvenience of parking if you're sleeping in the Old Town (see "Arrival in Rovinj," earlier, for details), accommodations in this area are handy for drivers. All of these are air-conditioned; unless otherwise noted, breakfast is not provided.

Guesthouses and Small Hotels

These are a bit closer to the Old Town than the Maistra hotels, and offer much lower rates and more personality. The first four are hotelesque and sit up on the hill behind the big resort hotels, while the last two choices are simpler, cheaper, and a bit closer to the Old Town (an easy and scenic 10-minute walk).

$$$$ Arupinum Hotel is an inviting splurge that—in terms of price and comfort—fills a niche between most of my guesthouse listings and the fancy Maistra hotels described later. It has a classy lobby/breakfast room, a small private swimming pool with some poolside tables, and 20 rooms (includes breakfast, elevator, free parking, Luje Adamovića 29, tel. 052/853-755, www.arupinum-rovinj.com, hotelarupinum@providus.hr).

$$ Vila Kristina, conscientiously run by Kristina Kiš and her family, has 10 rooms and five apartments (most with balconies) in a solidly built house along a busy road (air-con, no elevator, Luje Adamovića 16, tel. 052/815-537, www.vila-kristina.com, kis.zoltan@optinet.hr).

$$ Villa Baron Gautsch, named for a shipwreck, is a German-owned pension with 16 tight, cozy rooms. It's nothing fancy, but comes with an inviting shared terrace (includes breakfast, cash only, closed late Oct-Easter, Ronjgova 7, tel. 052/840-538, www.villabarongautsch.com, baron.gautsch@gmx.net, Sanja).

$ Hotel Vila Lili is a family-run hotel on a quiet, very residential-feeling side lane. Its 20 rooms are basic, and the place feels a bit faded, but if you set your expectations right it's a solid budget choice (includes good breakfast, elevator, parking extra, Mohorovičića 16, tel. 052/840-940, www.hotel-vilalili.hr, vila-lili@pu.t-com.hr, Paolo and the Petričević family).

ISTRIA

$ **Rooms Barbieri,** run by outgoing Haidi and her mother Vilma, are a few steps from the waterfront but secluded amidst the trees. There are five simple-but-comfy rooms, most with a nice terrace (breakfast extra, cash only, free parking, Obala Vladimira Nazora 4, mobile 098-976-4482, www.barbieri-rovinj.com, vilmabarbieri@yahoo.it).

$ **Elda Markulin** rents three rooms and four apartments in a modern house a short walk up from the main harborfront road. This is a good option for simple, affordable lodgings (cash only, free parking, Mate Balote 12, tel. 052/811-018, mobile 095-900-8654, markulinelda@gmail.com). To reach it from the Old Town, walk along the waterfront; after you pass the recommended Maestral restaurant on your right, turn left just before the park onto the uphill Mate Balote and follow the road as it curves.

Maistra Hotels

The local hotel conglomerate, Maistra, has several extremely expensive hotels in the lush parklands just south of the old town and on nearby islands. Most of my readers prefer to spend less money for more character at one of my other listings—but the Maistra hotels are top-class and worth considering if you can get a deal. These hotels have extremely slippery pricing, based on the type of room, the season, how far ahead you book, the length of your stay, and little hairs on the back of the manager's neck standing up. (For specific rates, plug your dates into the form at www.maistra.hr.) All hotels have air-conditioning, elevators, and include breakfast in their rates; most have free parking and close during the winter. (The only Maistra hotel in the Old Town—**$$$$ Hotel Adriatic**—is described earlier.) **$$$$ Grand Park Hotel** has more than 200 five-star rooms overlooking a yacht harbor; it's the handiest Maistra hotel for walking into town, via a 10-minute stroll entirely along the stunning harborfront promenade. **$$$$ Hotel Lone** (LOH-neh), with 248 rooms, is the most striking in the collection—the soaring atrium feels like a modern art museum, and room rates can soar here, too. **$$$$ Hotel Monte Mulini** is a "design hotel" with five stars, 99 rooms and 14 suites (all with seaview balconies), a beautiful atrium with a huge glass wall overlooking the cove, and an infinity pool. **$$$ Hotel Eden** offers four stars and 325 upscale, imaginatively updated rooms with oodles of contemporary style; it's a smidge less expensive than most of the chain's hotels. **$$ Island Hotel Katarina** is the castaway's choice, with 110 rooms occupying the hotel's own little island just offshore from the Old Town—complete with a park, beaches, and swimming pool. It's connected by an hourly boat (free for guests) to the Old Town pier; some find this inconvenient, but most who opt to sleep here consider it romantic. Note that it may be closed for renovation in the near future, but for now, it's Maistra's most affordably priced branch. The chain has other branches, but I wouldn't consider them.

Eating in Rovinj

It's expensive to dine in Rovinj, but the food is generally good, with truffle dishes on most menus (see "Istrian Food and Wine" sidebar, earlier). Interchangeable restaurants cluster where Rovinj's Old Town peninsula meets the mainland, and all around the harbor. Be warned that most eateries—like much of Rovinj—close for the winter (roughly mid-Oct to Easter). If you're day-tripping into the Istrian interior, consider dining at one of the excellent restaurants in or near Motovun (see page 150), then returning to Rovinj after dark.

ALONG ROVINJ'S RESTAURANT ROW

The easiest dining option is to stroll the Old Town embankment overlooking the harbor. Window-shop the pricey but scenic eateries along here, each of which has its own personality: Some have sea views, others are set back on charming squares, and still others have atmospheric interiors. I've listed these in the order you'll reach them (all open long hours daily).

$$ Hotel Adriatic, the swanky hotel smack in the middle of town and at the start of this strip, operates a café with cushy outdoor seating and affordable sandwiches, salads, and snacks. If you'd like to nibble a light meal while people-watching, this is the place. They also have a pricier restaurant menu, but I'd skip it (breakfast 7:00-12:00, full menu daily 12:00-23:00, Trg Maršala Tita).

$$$ Scuba is closest to the harbor—so, they claim, they get first pick of the daily catch from arriving fishing boats. They serve both seafood and tasty Italian dishes at reasonable prices in a plain contemporary interior or at outdoor tables with partial harbor views (daily 11:00-24:00, Obala Pina Budičina 6, mobile 098-219-446).

$$$ Veli Jože—named for a mythical Istrian friendly giant—has a smattering of outdoor tables (no real views) and a rollicking, folksy interior decorated to the hilt. They offer a wide variety of pastas and tasty, traditional Istrian cuisine (daily 11:00-24:00, Sv. Križa 1, tel. 052/816-337).

$$$$ Santa Croce, with tables scenically scattered along a terraced incline that looks like a stage set, is well-respected for its seafood and pastas. Classy and sedate, and with attentive service, it attracts a slightly older clientele (no sea views, daily 12:00-15:00 & 18:00-23:00, Sv. Križa 11, tel. 052/842-240).

$$ Lampo is simpler, with a basic menu of salads, pizzas, and pastas. The only reason to come here is for the fine waterfront seating at a reasonable price (daily 11:00-24:00, Sv. Križa 22, tel. 052/811-186).

$$$$ La Puntulina, at the end of the row, is the most scenic option. This upscale restaurant/wine bar features Istrian, Italian, and Mediterranean cuisine served in the contemporary dining room or outside—either on one of the many terraces, or at tables scattered along the rocks overlooking a swimming hole. You're here for the scenery, not the food—quality can suffer at busy times. As the outdoor seating is deservedly popular, reserve ahead (daily 12:00-23:00, closed Jan-March, on the Old Town embankment past the harbor at Sv. Križa 38, tel. 052/813-186, Miriam and Giovanni). You can also order just a drink to sip while sitting down on the rocks.

SPLURGES IN THE OLD TOWN

Offering upscale, international (rather than strictly Croatian) food and presentation, these options are expensive but creative.

$$$$ Monte Restaurant, perched at the top of town (just below the cathedral's bell tower) landed Croatia's first Michelin star. With tables strewn around a covered terrace, this atmospheric place features inventive cuisine that melds Istrian products with international techniques. Come here only if you value a fine dining experience, polished service, and the chance to learn about local food and wines without regard for price. Reservations are a must (daily 18:30-23:00, Montalbano 75, tel. 052/830-203, www.monte. hr, Đekić family).

$$$$ Ulika, a classy hole-in-the-wall run by Inja Tucman, is a split decision. Some people appreciate its mellow, cozy, art-strewn interior, and Inja's opinionated service and flair for surprising diners with unexpected flavor combinations. Others are annoyed by the pretense and the high prices—as portions are small, Inja nudges diners to order multiple courses. If you're willing to go along for the ride, not worry about a hefty bill, and settle in for a long dinner, give it a whirl (daily 13:00-15:00 & 18:30-23:00—except closed for lunch in July, closed late Oct-late April, Porečka 6, mobile 098-929-7541).

AFFORDABLE ALTERNATIVES
ON THE MAINLAND

These options are a bit less expensive than most of those described above. I've listed them in the order you'll reach them as you walk around Rovinj's harbor.

$$$ Bookeria, tucked along a broad but quiet street just off the harbor, feels inventive and fresh. They embrace their book theme, and have mismatched-antique furniture and a fun-to-explore menu of Croatian and international dishes—all well-executed and imaginatively presented. This is also a creative place for breakfast and a great deal at lunch, when they offer an affordable "street food" menu (daily 9:00-23:00, Trg Pignaton, mobile 091-219-0007).

$$ Maestral combines affordable, straightforward seafood, pastas, and pizzas with Rovinj's best view. If you want an outdoor table overlooking bobbing boats and the Old Town's skyline—without breaking the bank—this is the place. It fills a big building on the embankment, surrounded by workaday shipyards, about a 10-minute walk from the Old Town, around the harbor toward Grand Park Hotel (daily 9:00-24:00, closed Oct-March, Obala Vladimira Nazora b.b., tel. 052/830-565).

$$ Sidro, around the harbor with views back on the Old Town, has a typical menu of pasta and fish. But it's particularly well-respected for its Balkan meat dishes such as *ćevapčići*, and a spicy pork-and-onion stew called *mućkalica*. With unusually polite service and a long tradition (run by three generations of the Paoletti family since 1966), it's a popular local hangout (daily 11:00-23:00, closed Nov-Feb, harborfront at Rismondo 14, tel. 052/813-471).

BREAKFAST

Most rental apartments come with a kitchenette handy for breakfasts (stock up at a neighborhood grocery). Cafés and bars along the waterfront serve little more than an expensive croissant with coffee. The best budget breakfast (and a fun experience) is a picnic. Within a block of the market, you have all the necessary stops: mini grocery stores (juice, milk, drinkable yogurt, and so on); market stalls (cherries, strawberries, walnuts, and more, as well as an elegant fountain for washing); a bread kiosk, Pekarna Laste, between the market and the water...plus benches with birds chirping, children playing, and fine Old Town views along the water.

To let someone else do the cooking, several cafés (including the recommended **Hotel Adriatic** and **Bookeria**) offer good breakfasts in a memorable setting.

ISTRIA

Rovinj Connections

BY BUS

Bus service from Rovinj is operated by two different companies, which don't entirely cooperate—to know your options, you'll want to check with both of the side-by-side windows at the station. Autotrans handles most connections (tel. 060-888-611, www.autobusni-kolodvor.com), while Brioni Pula runs a few (tel. 052/365-536, www.brioni.hr; this office also handles Flixbus, which operates buses to Slovenia). For both companies, it's important to confirm specifics when planning your trip. Be aware that bus schedules are dramatically reduced on Saturdays and especially on Sundays, as well as (in some cases) off-season.

From Rovinj by Bus to: Pula (about hourly, 45 minutes), Poreč (5-7/day, 1 hour), Rijeka (5-7/day, 2-3.5 hours), Zagreb (nearly hourly, 3-6 hours).

To Slovenia: In summer, daily Flixbus buses connect Rovinj to Slovenia (2/day, change in Portorož to reach Piran, 4-5 hours direct to Ljubljana); as this connection is changeable, confirm schedules at FlixBus.com and www.ap-ljubljana.si. You can also reach Piran (and other Slovenian destinations) with transfers in Umag and Portorož.

To the Dalmatian Coast: An Autotrans bus departs Rovinj every evening at 19:00 for the Dalmatian Coast, arriving in Split at 6:00 and Dubrovnik at 11:00. There's also an early-morning option departing at 4:40. Additional options may be possible if you change in Pula or Rijeka.

To Venice: Brioni Pula runs two buses daily to Venice—one leaves early and goes all the way to Piazzale Roma, on the island of Venice, while the other leaves in the afternoon and goes to the train station in Mestre (either one about 5 hours).

ROUTE TIPS FOR DRIVERS

Just north of Rovinj, on the coastal road to Poreč, you'll drive briefly along a seven-mile-long inlet dubbed the Limski Canal (Limski Kanal—sometimes called Limski Fjord, but only to infuriate Norwegians). Named for the border (Lim-it) between Rovinj and Poreč, this jagged slash in the landscape was created when an underground karstic river collapsed. Keen-eyed arborists will notice that the canal's southern bank has deciduous trees, and the northern bank, evergreens. Many Venetian quarries once pulled stone from the walls of this canal to build houses and embankments. Supposedly the famed pirate Captain Morgan was so enchanted by this canal that he retired here, founding the nearby namesake town of Mrgani. Local tour companies sell boat excursions into the fjord, which is used to raise much of the shellfish that's slurped down at local restaurants. While the canal isn't worth going out of your way to see, you may skirt it anyway. Along the road above the canal, you'll pass kiosks selling grappa (firewater, a.k.a. *rakija*), honey, and other homemade concoctions. The recommended Matošević winery is a two-minute drive away (see page 156).

Pula

Pula (POO-lah, Pola in Italian)—Istria's biggest city—is an industrial port town with traffic and sprawl...but it has the soul of a Roman poet. Between the shipyards and the concrete apartment blocks, you'll discover some of the top Roman ruins in Croatia, including a stately amphitheater: a fully intact mini-Colosseum that marks the entry to a charmingly scruffy Old Town with ancient temples, arches, and columns.

Strategically situated at the southern tip of the Istrian Peninsula, Pula has long been a center of industry, trade, and military might. In 177 BC, the city became an important outpost of the Roman Empire. It was destroyed during the wars following Julius Caesar's death, then rebuilt by Emperor Augustus. Many of Pula's most important Roman features—including its

amphitheater—date from this time, in the early first century AD. But as Rome fell, so did Pula's fortunes. The town changed hands repeatedly, caught in the crossfire between greater powers—Byzantines, Venetians, and Habsburgs. After being devastated by Venice's enemy, Genoa, in the 14th century, Pula gathered dust as a ghost town...still of strategic military importance, but otherwise abandoned.

In the mid-19th century, Italian unification forced the Austrian Habsburgs—whose navy had been based in Venice—to look for a new home for their fleet. In 1856, they chose Pula, and over the next 60 years, the town's population grew thirtyfold. (Despite the many Roman and Venetian artifacts littering the old town, most of modern Pula is essentially Austrian.) By the dawn of the 20th century, Pula's harbor bristled with Austro-Hungarian warships, and it had become the crucial link in a formidable line of imperial defenses that stretched from here to Montenegro.

As one of the most important port cities of the Austro-Hungarian Empire, Pula attracted royalty, naval officers (including Captain Georg von Trapp, whose wife's death here helped convince him to take his musical clan back to Salzburg)...and a young Irishman named James Joyce who was on the verge of revolutionizing the literary world.

Today's Pula, while no longer quite so important, remains a vibrant port town and the de facto capital of Istria. It offers an enjoyably urban antidote to the rest of this stuck-in-the-past peninsula.

PLANNING YOUR TIME

Pula's sights, while top-notch, are quickly exhausted. Two or three hours should do it: Visit the amphitheater, stroll the circular Old Town, and maybe see a museum or two. As it's less than an hour from Rovinj, there's no reason to spend the night.

Orientation to Pula

Although the city itself is big, the tourist's Pula is compact: the amphitheater and, beside it, the ring-shaped Old Town circling the base of an old hilltop fortress. The Old Town's main square, the Forum, dates back to Roman times.

TOURIST INFORMATION

Pula's TI sits on the main square. It offers information on the town and all of Istria (May-Oct daily 8:00-18:00, later in June-Sept; Nov-April Mon-Sat 9:00-16:00, Sun from 10:00, Forum 3, tel. 052/219-197, www.pulainfo.hr).

ARRIVAL IN PULA

By Car: Pula is about a 45-minute drive south of Rovinj. Approaching town, follow *Centar* signs, then watch for the amphitheater. The easiest parking is in the big lot between the amphitheater and the waterfront (8 kn/hour). There's also street parking nearby (marked with blue lines, generally 5 kn/hour but check signs carefully). For either kind of parking, use the pay-and-display meters.

By Bus: As you exit the bus station, walk toward the yellow mansion, then turn left onto the major street (ulica 43 Istarske Divizije); at the roundabout, bear left again, and you'll be headed for the amphitheater (about a 10-minute walk total).

By Train: The train station is a 15-minute walk from the amphitheater, near the waterfront. Leave the station and walk with the coast on your right until you approach the amphitheater and Old Town.

By Plane: Pula's small airport, which is served by various low-cost airlines, is about 3.5 miles northeast of the center. A handy and affordable **shuttle bus** is coordinated to depart 20 minutes after

Pula

TRAIN STATION

To Rovinj

ULICA SV. PETRA

TRŠĆANSKA ULICA

VODOVODNA ULICA

ULICA 43 IST. DIV.

To Airport & Rijeka

BUS STATION

KUKULJEVIĆEVA

SPLITSKA UL

RIVA

FLAVIJEVSKA

Adriatic Sea

Harbor

P

P

AMPHITHEATER

RAKOVČEVA ULICA

100 Meters
100 Yards

SHIPYARDS

TOWN MODEL

ROMAN RUINS EXCAVATION

AMFITEATARSKA

ISTARSKA ULICA

To Island

THE SHIPYARD PUB

CATHEDRAL

RIVA

KANDLEROVA ULICA

BELL TOWER

THE HOUSE OF ISTRIAN OLIVE OIL

CARRARINA ULICA

ROMAN MAUSOLEUM

DUBROVAČKE / MARTIN

"C8" EXHIBITION SPACE

TEMPLE OF AUGUSTUS

TOWN HALL

Forum Square

OLD TOWN

FORT KAŠTEL

ROMAN THEATER

ARCHAEOLOGICAL MUSEUM OF ISTRIA (closed)

GATE OF HERCULES

FRANCISCAN CHURCH

HOLY CROSS (Archaeology Exhibits)

WC

ZAGREBAČKA ULICA

ROMAN FLOOR MOSAIC

ULICA SERGIJEVACA

ARCH OF SERGIUS

FLANATIČKA ULICA

BASILICA OF ST. MARY FORMOSA

HOOK & COOK

P

Dante Square

CAFÉ ULIKS

FLACIUSOVA UL

ALIGHIERI

National Square

MARKET HALL

KANTINA REST.

ISTRIA

many budget flights arrive—check for details with your airline (30 kn to downtown Pula, some buses go all the way to Rovinj for 150 kn, run by two different companies—check schedule and book at www.brioni.hr or www.fils.hr). **Public bus #23** goes between the airport and Pula's bus station, but it's infrequent (10/day Mon-Fri, 4/day Sat, none Sun, www.pulapromet.hr) and stops along the road in front of the airport rather than at the airport itself (coming from town to the airport, watch for buses to Valtura). Taxis charge exorbitant rates (often 150-180 kn) for the short ride into town—Uber or the shuttle bus are much more affordable (airport code: PUY, tel. 052/550-926, www.airport-pula.hr).

HELPFUL HINTS

Car Rental: All of the big rental companies have their offices at the airport (see airport info above); the TI has a list of a few local outfits with offices downtown.

Local Guide: If you'd like a guide to help you uncover the story of

Pula, **Mariam Abdelghani** leads great tours of the major sites; she also leads tours all around Istria (€80 for a 2-hour city tour, €160 for an all-day tour of Istria in your car, mobile 098-419-560, mariam.abdelghani@gmail.com).

Hop-On, Hop-Off Bus: This route offers a look at some of Pula's sights beyond the center, including the neighborhood of Austrian naval officers' villas, the forested beach areas, and the coastal forts on the outskirts of town (100 kn, daily mid-June-mid-Sept 10:00-18:00, bus begins at the top of each hour next to the amphitheater, shorter hours April-May and Oct, none Nov-March, www.pulacitytour.com).

Pula Walk

This self-guided walk is divided between Pula's two most interesting attractions: the Roman amphitheater and the circular Old Town. Two hours total is plenty. More time can be spent sipping coffee al fresco or dipping into museums.

• *Begin at Pula's main landmark, its...*

▲▲Amphitheater (Amfiteatar)

Of the dozens of amphitheaters left around Europe and North Africa by Roman engineers, Pula's is the sixth-largest (435 feet long and 345 feet wide) and one of the best-preserved anywhere. This is the top place in Croatia to resurrect the age of the gladiators.

Cost and Hours: 70 kn, daily May-Sept 8:00-21:00—often later in July-Aug and for special events, April until 20:00, shorter hours off-season; last entry one hour before closing.

Visitor Information: The 40-kn audioguide, available at the kiosk inside, narrates 20 stops with 30 minutes of flat, basic data on the structure.

Gladiator Shows: About once or twice weekly in the summer, costumed gladiators reenact the glory days of the amphitheater in a show called *Spectacvla Antiqva* (70 kn, 1/week late June-mid-Sept, details at www.pulainfo.hr).

Visiting the Amphitheater: Go inside and explore the interior, climbing up the seats as you like. An "amphi-theater" is literally a "double theater"—imagine two theaters, without the back wall behind the stage, stuck together to maximize seating. Pula's amphitheater was built over several decades in the first century AD under the reign of three of Rome's top-tier emperors: Augustus, Claudius, and Vespasian. It was completed around AD 80, about the same time as the Colosseum in Rome. It remained in active use until the beginning of the fifth century, when gladiator battles were outlawed. The location is atypical but sensible: It was built just outside town (too big for tiny Pula, with just 5,000 people) and near the sea (so its giant limestone blocks could be transported here more easily from the quarry six miles away).

Notice that the amphitheater is built into the gentle incline of a hill. This economical plan, unusual for Roman amphitheaters,

saved on the amount of stone needed and provided a natural foundation for some of the seats (notice how the upper seats incorporate the slope). It may seem like the architects were cutting corners, but they actually had to raise the ground level at the lower end of the amphitheater to give it a level foundation. The four rectangular towers anchoring the amphitheater's facade are also unique (two of them are mostly gone). These once held wooden staircases for loading and unloading the amphitheater more quickly—like the massive corkscrew ramps in many modern stadiums. At the top of each tower was a water reservoir, used for powering fountains that sprayed refreshing scents over the crowd to mask the stench of blood.

And there was plenty of blood. Imagine this scene in the days of the gladiators: More than 25,000 cheering fans from all social classes filled the seats. The Romans made these spectacles cheap or even free—distracting commoners with a steady diet of mindless entertainment prevented discontent and rebellion. (Hmm...*Dancing with the Stars*, anyone?) Canvas awnings rigged around the top of the amphitheater shaded many seats. The fans surrounded the "slaying field," which was covered with sand to absorb blood spilled by man and beast, making it easier to clean up after the fight. This sand *(harena)* gave the amphitheater its nickname...arena.

The amphitheater's "entertainers" were gladiators (named for the *gladius,* a short sword that was tucked into a fighter's boot). Some gladiators were criminals, but most were prisoners of war from lands conquered by Rome, who dressed and used weapons according to their country of origin. A colorful parade kicked off the spectacle, followed by simulated fights with fake weapons. Then the real battles began. Often the fights represented stories from mythology or Greek or Roman history. Most ended in death for

ISTRIA

the loser. Sometimes gladiators fought exotic animals—gathered at great expense from far corners of the empire—which would enter the arena from the two far ends (through the biggest arches). There were female gladiators, as well, but they always fought other women.

While the life of a gladiator seems difficult, consider that it wasn't such a bad gig—compared to, say, being a soldier. Gladiators were often better paid than soldiers, enjoyed terrific celebrity (both in life and in death), and only had to fight a few times each year.

Ignore the modern seating, and imagine when the arena (sandy oval area in the center) was ringed with two levels of stone seating and a top level of wooden bleachers. Notice that the outline of the arena is marked by a small moat (now covered with wooden slats)—just wide enough to keep the animals off the laps of those with the best seats, but close enough so that blood still sprayed their togas.

After the fall of Rome, builders looking for ready-cut stone picked apart structures like this one—scraping it as clean as a neat slice of cantaloupe. Sometimes the scavengers were seeking the iron hooks that were used to connect the stone; in the centuries after the fall of Rome, the material and know-how for smelting iron from ore was hard to come by. Most of this amphitheater's interior structures—such as steps and seats—are now in the

foundations and walls of Pula's buildings...not to mention palaces in Venice, across the Adriatic. In fact, in the late 16th century, the Venetians planned to take this entire amphitheater apart, stone by stone, and reassemble it on the island of Lido on the Venetian lagoon. A heroic Venetian senator—still revered in Pula—convinced them to leave it where it is.

Despite these and other threats, the amphitheater's exterior has been left gloriously intact. The 1999 film *Titus* (with Anthony Hopkins and Jessica Lange) was filmed here, and today the amphitheater is still used to stage spectacles—from Andrea Bocelli to the Foo Fighters—with seating for about 5,000 fans. The loudest concerts have been banned, because the vibrations were damaging the old structure.

Before leaving, don't miss the museum exhibit (in the subterranean hall—follow *exhibition* signs down the chute marked #17). This takes you to the lower level of the amphitheater, where gladiators and animals were kept between fights. When the fight began, gladiators would charge up a chute and burst into the arena, like football players being introduced at the Super Bowl. As you go

Amphorae

In museums, hotels, and restaurants all along the Croatian coast, you'll see amphorae. An amphora is a jug that was used to transport goods when the ancient Greeks ruled the seas, through about the second century BC. Later, the Romans also used their own amphorae. These tall and skinny ceramic jugs—many of them lost in ancient shipwrecks—litter the Adriatic coastline.

Amphorae were used to carry oil, wine, and fish on long sea journeys. They're tapered at the bottom because they were stuck into sand (or placed on a stand) to keep them upright in transit. They also have a narrow neck at the top, often with two large handles. In fact, the name comes from the Greek *amphi pherein*, "to carry from both sides." The taller, skinnier amphorae were generally used for wine, while the fat, short ones were for olive oil. Because amphorae differ according to their purpose and nationality, archaeologists find them to be a particularly useful clue for dating shipwrecks and determining the country of origin of lost ships. This is made easier by later Roman amphorae, which are actually stamped with the place they came from and what they held.

ISTRIA

down the passage, you'll walk on a grate over an even lower tunnel. Pula is honeycombed with tunnels like these, originally used for sewers and as a last-ditch place of refuge in case of attack. In the exhibit, check out the extensive collection of amphorae (see sidebar), find your location—*Pola*—on the replica of a fourth-century AD Roman map (oriented with east on top), and ogle the gigantic grape press and two olive-oil mills.

• *From the amphitheater, it's a few minutes' walk to Pula's Old Town, where more Roman sights await. Exit the amphitheater, cross the street, turn left, and walk one long block along the small wall down the street called Amfiteatarska ulica. When you reach the park on your right, look for the car-sized...*

Town Model

Use this handy model of Pula to get oriented. Next to the amphitheater, the little water cannon spouting into the air marks the pale-blue house nearby, the site of a freshwater spring (which makes this location even more strategic). The big star-shaped fortress on the hill is Fort Kaštel, designed by a French architect during the Venetian era (1630). Read the street plan of the Roman town into this model: At the center (on the hill) was the *castrum,* or military base. At the base of the hill (the far side from the amphitheater) was the forum, or town square. During Pula's Roman glory days, the hillsides around the *castrum* were blanketed with the villas of rich merchants. The Old Town, which clusters around the base of the fortress-topped hill, still features many fragments of the Roman period, as well as Pula's later occupiers. We'll take a counterclockwise stroll around the fortified old hill through this ancient zone.

The huge anchor across the street from the model celebrates Pula's number-one employer—its shipyards.

• *Continue the way you were going and cross the street. At the fork, bear right (on Kandlerova ulica—level, not uphill). Notice the Roman ruins in the field on your right. Just about any time someone wants to put up a new building in Pula, they find ruins like these. Work screeches to a halt while the valuable remains are excavated. At this site, they've discovered three Roman houses, two churches, and 2,117 amphorae—the largest stash found anywhere in the world. (The harbor is just behind, which suggests this might have been a storehouse for offloaded amphorae.) In this case, plans for the new parking garage were scuttled completely. You'll also see some benches inscribed with quotations from the likes of Mark Twain and Isak Dinesen: These are nods to Pula's main library, the yellow building nearby.*

One block farther along, look down the street to your right to see...

The House of Istrian Olive Oil (Kuća Istarskog Maslinovog Ulja)

This shop/museum/tasting room celebrates Istria's burgeoning artisanal olive oil scene. You'll enter a well-stocked shop, showcasing more than 30 local producers of high-end olive oil. Beyond that is a thoughtful, fairly dense museum, with just a few artifacts and lots of reading (much of it also narrated by the included 30-minute audioguide). Exhibits explain the rich history of olive oil production in this region—going back to the Romans—and explains the procedure in ancient, medieval, and modern times. They also offer enjoyable and insightful 20-minute olive oil tastings, which succinctly and effectively train your palate to distinguish top-quality extra virgin olive oil from cut-rate "virgin" and "lampante"-grade olive oil. You'll learn why EU-certified "extra virgin olive oil" isn't always what it's advertised to be...and how to tell the difference.

Cost and Hours: Museum—50 kn, museum plus basic tasting—90 kn, museum plus "gold" tasting with more top-end oils—130 kn; open daily 10:00-18:00, until 22:00 or 23:00 in summer (but tastings only until 20:00); Sv. Teodora 1A, tel. 052/661-235, www.oleumhistriae.com.

• *Continue along the main street as it curves a couple more blocks through gritty, slice-of-life Pula. Soon, on your right, you'll see the...*

Cathedral (Katedrala)

This church combines elements of the two big Italian influences on Pula: Roman and Venetian. Dating from the fifth century AD, the Romanesque core of the church (notice the skinny, slitlike windows) marks the site of an early-Christian seafront settlement in Pula. The Venetian Baroque facade and bell tower are much more recent (early 18th century). Typical of the Venetian style, notice how far away the austere bell tower is from the body of the church. The bell tower's foundation is made of stones that were scavenged from the amphitheater. The church's sparsely decorated interior features

a classic Roman-style basilica floor plan, with a single grand hall—the side naves were added in the 15th century, after a fire.

Cost and Hours: Free, generally open daily 10:00-14:00.

• *Keep walking through the main pedestrian zone, passing tacky souvenir shops and Albanian-run fast-food and ice-cream joints. After a few more blocks, you emerge into the...*

ISTRIA

Forum

Every Roman town had a forum, or main square. Twenty centuries later, Pula's Forum not only serves the same function but has also kept the old Roman name.

Two important buildings front the north end of the square, where you enter. The smaller building

(on the left, with the columns) is the first-century AD **Temple of Augustus** (Augustov Hram). Built during the reign of, and dedicated to, Augustus Caesar, this temple took a direct hit from an Allied bomb in World War II. After the war, the Allied occupiers rebuilt it as a sort of mea culpa—notice the patchwork repair job. It's the only one remaining of three such temples that once lined this side of the square. There's not much to see inside, other than a few fragments of ancient sculptures (10 kn, May-Sept Mon-

Sat 9:00-21:00, Sun until 15:00, shorter hours Oct-April, English labels). The surviving torso from a statue of Augustus, which likely stood on or near this spot, dates from the time of Christ. Other evocative chips and bits of Roman Pula include the feet of a power-ful commander with a pathetic little vanquished barbarian obedi-ently at his knee (perhaps one of the Histri—the indigenous Istri-ans that the Romans conquered in 177 BC).

Head back out to the square. As Rome fell, its long-subjugated subjects in Pula had little respect for the former empire's symbols, and many temples didn't survive. Others were put to new use: Part of an adjacent temple (likely dedicated to Diana) was incorporated into the bigger building on the right, Pula's medieval **Town Hall** (Gradska Palača). If you circle around behind this building, you can still see Roman fragments embedded in the back. The Town Hall encapsulates many centuries of Pula architecture: Roman-esque core, Gothic reliefs, Renaissance porch, Baroque windows... and a few Roman bits and pieces. Notice the interesting combina-tion of flags above the door: Pula, Croatia, Istria (with its mascot goat), Italy (for the large ethnic minority here), and the European Union (which Croatia joined in 2013).

• *Consider dropping by the TI on this square before continuing our stroll down the main drag, Sergijevaca. You'll pass by a small park on your right. For an optional detour to Byzantine times, angle through the park and find a parking lot. Near the end of the lot, on the left-hand side, is a fenced-off grassy field. At the far end of the field is the small...*

Basilica of St. Mary Formosa
(Kapela Marije Formoze)

We've seen plenty of Roman and Venetian bric-a-brac, but this chapel survives from the time of another Istrian occupier: Byzan-tium. For about 170 years after Rome fell (the sixth and seventh centuries AD), this region came under the control of the Byzan-tine Empire and was ruled from Ravenna (now in Italy, across the Adriatic, south of Venice). Much of this field was once occupied by a vast, richly decorated basilica. This lonely chapel—which was the right-most of three tall, long naves—is all that's left. It's rarely open to visit, but you can see the footprint of the entire church in the grass, and part of the left-most wall on the far side of the field.

From here you can look out to sea for a good view of the tower-ing cranes that rise up from the **shipyards** that until recently em-ployed some 2,000 Pulans. One of the last surviving major ship-yards in Croatia, Pula's finally succumbed to the same forces that shut down others: an inability to compete with the lower costs of shipbuilding in Asia. The shipyards were a major part of the iden-tity and economy of the city; any time a new ship was christened, the entire town turned out for a celebration. If you're intrigued by all things maritime, you could walk along the embankment for a better look (after our walk). After dark, those cranes are enlivened by a lightshow (at the top of every hour from 21:00-24:00) created by a local architectural lighting designer who has gained international fame.

• *Turn your back to the shipyards and walk (with the basilica ruins on your right) toward the yard with trees and bushes. Follow Rimski Mozaik signs through a dusty parking lot and into a small yard. Walk to the metal grille, and look down to see the...*

Roman Floor Mosaic (Rimski Mozaik)

This hidden mosaic is a great example of the Roman treasures that lie beneath the old center of Pula. Uncovered by locals who were cleaning up from WWII bombs, this third-century floor was carefully excavated for display right where it was laid nearly two millennia ago. (Notice that the Roman floor level was about six feet below today's.) The centerpiece of the mosaic depicts the punishment of Dirce. According to the ancient Greek legend, King Lykos of Thebes was bewitched by Dirce and abandoned his pregnant queen. The queen gave birth to twin boys (depicted in this mosaic), who grew up to kill their deadbeat dad and tie Dirce to the horns of a bull, to be bashed against a mountain. This same story is famously depicted in the twisty *Toro Farnese* sculpture partly carved by Michelangelo (on display in Naples' Archaeological Museum).

• *Find your way through the adjacent passage (ignore the cut-rate clothing vendors; their stalls look like a private shop, but it's a public passage) to return to the main drag, Sergijevaca. Turn right and continue through Pula's most colorful (and most touristy) neighborhood.*

Sergijevaca and Dante Square (Danteov Trg)

After a block, the stepped lane on the left leads up to the deconsecrated Church of the Holy Cross (Sv. Srca), which is now a museum space housing temporary exhibits from the Archaeological Museum of Istria. Beautifully restored and repurposed as a modern exhibition space, and with good English descriptions, the church is arguably a more satisfying home for the collection. Historians will want to check out the latest exhibits (www.ami-pula.hr).

On the right a block and a half farther, Clerisseauova street leads to the pleasant Dante Square (Danteov Trg). Its centerpiece is a 1930s, Italian-built fountain that resembles a *fasche*, or bundle of sticks—the symbol and namesake for Mussolini's Fascist movement. The irregular dots scattered around the inside of the fountain once supported the names of important Italian fascists, and the big, white, blocky post office across the square is a classic Italian fascist-style building. Remember that from 1918 until 1943—in other words, Mussolini's heyday—Istria was part of Italy.

• *Continuing along Sergijevaca, in a few short blocks you'll arrive at the...*

Arch of Sergius (Slavoluk Sergijevaca)

This triumphal arch, from the first century BC, was Michelangelo's favorite Roman artifact in Pula. Marking the edge of the original Roman town, it was built to honor Lucius Sergius Lepidus. He fought on the side of Augustus in the civil wars that swept the empire after Julius Caesar's assassination. The proto-feminist inscription proudly explains, "Silvia of the Sergius family paid for this with her own money." Statues of Silvia's husband, Lucius, plus her son and her brother-in-law, once stood on the three blocks at the top of the arch. (Squint to see the *Sergivs* name on each block.) On the underside of the arch is a relief of an eagle (the symbol of Rome) clutching an evil snake in its talons.

• *Before going under the arch, look to your left to see a famous Irishman appreciating the view from the terrace of...*

Café Uliks

In October 1904, a young writer named James Joyce moved from Dublin to Pula with his girlfriend, Nora Barnacle. By day, he taught English to Austro-Hungarian naval officers at the Berlitz language school (in the yellow building next door). By night, he imagined strolling through his hometown as he penned short stories that would eventually become the collection *Dubliners*. But James and Nora quickly grew bored with little Pula and moved to Trieste in March 1905. Even so, Pula remains proud of its literary connections. This café—where Joyce likely enjoyed sitting from time to time—carries the Croatian name of his masterpiece, *Ulysses*.

• *Now pass through the arch, into a square next to some remains of the town wall. Cross the street and continue straight ahead for two bustling blocks, along the traffic-free Flanatička street, to...*

National Square (Narodni Trg) and Market Hall

Pula's market hall was an iron-and-glass marvel when inaugurated in the 19th century. This structure is yet another reminder of the

way the Austro-Hungarian Empire modernized Pula with grace and gentility. You'll find meats, cheeses, and smelly fish on the ground floor (Mon-Sat 7:00-13:30, Sun until 12:00), and an inviting food circus upstairs (Mon-Fri 7:00-15:00, Sat until 14:00, sleepy on Sun). All around is a busy and colorful farmers market that bustles until about 13:00, when things quiet down.

• *If you're ready for lunch, consider one of the cheap options inside or near the market hall, or walk one block to Kantina (see "Eating in Pula," later).*

When you're done here, backtrack to the town wall. As you face the Arch of Sergius, take a right and walk uphill under the leafy canopy next to the wall. On our way back to our starting point, we'll pass...

More Roman Monuments

Circling the outside of the old wall to where we began, keep an eye out for more Roman remains. First you'll pass (on your right) a stern, blocky, fascist-style building from 1941—with classic white-stone-and-iron style and a little balcony that seems custom-made for delivering rabble-rousing speeches. Take the left fork around this building, and soon, on your left, you'll reach the **Gate of Hercules** (Herkulova Vrata), with its single, intact stone arch—the oldest surviving monument in town (from the first century BC). If you look carefully, you can pick out the very faded carving of Hercules' head and his club along the top of the arch. Up the steps just beyond the gate, the purple-ish building is the local Italian Cultural Center, a resource for the local cultural minority whose ancestors—from the Romans to Mussolini—so shaped this town.

From here you'll pass more stretches of city wall—though most of what you see here is not the original Roman wall, but fortifications that were beefed up in the 15th and 16th centuries. Soon you reach the **Twin Gates** (Porta Gemina), marking the entrance to a garden that's home to the **Archaeological Museum of Istria** (Arheološki Muzej Istre). The museum should be wrapping up an ambitious, years-long renovation (perhaps sometime in 2020)—check to see if it's open when you visit, since it promises a state-of-the-art look at the city's stunning wealth of ancient monuments.

Up the hill around the right side of the museum—and likely

ISTRIA

not fully accessible during the renovation (but if you're curious, check)—are the remains of a **Roman Theater** (Rimsko Kazalište). If it's not closed off, it's free to visit the ruins. Part of the stage is still intact, along with the semicircle of stone seats (some of which are still engraved with the names of the wealthy theatergoers who once sat in them).

The other attraction you'll see near the museum—marked *Zerostrasse*—is an entrance to the Austro-Hungarian-era **tunnels** that burrow under the hill; this space often hosts special exhibits (open summer only).

Across the street from the Twin Gates, look for the **"C8" exhibition space** (which displays changing exhibits from the museum), as well as a large, round structure that's set deeply into the ground. This is a first-century AD Roman **mausoleum,** which once stood 25 feet higher (see the illustration on the nearby plaque). During Roman times, people would be buried just outside the city walls.

Our walk is nearing its end. If you still have time and energy, there's one more attraction overhead: the hilltop fortress, **Fort Kaštel,** offering a bird's-eye view over the town. This deserted-feeling place, hosting the Historical Museum of Istria, is worth visiting only for the chance to wander the ramparts and enjoy the views over the town and amphitheater (various trails lead up from the streets below).

• *Continuing just another block past the Twin Gates, you'll pop out at the park with the city model. The amphitheater is just to the right.*

Eating in Pula

The best lunch options are in and near the town's **market hall** (toward the end of my self-guided walk route). The top floor of the market is a food circus with a number of cheap and tempting eateries with both indoor and terrace seating. Back outside, around the right side of the market hall, you'll find a pair of fiercely competitive bakeries serving fresh batches of cheap and delicious *burek,* the savory phyllo-dough pastry: One no-name bakery is built into the market hall itself, and Pekarna Corona faces it from across the market square. Remember, in Croatia it's fine to bring your own food to an outdoor café to enjoy at their tables, as long as you buy a drink (and assuming they don't serve food of their own). Browse for some food in the market area, then take your pick of al fresco cafés anywhere in town.

If you prefer a real restaurant, here are some good options.

$$$ Kantina Restaurant, a block away from the market, serves good lunches (including veggie options) and hearty, creative salads, in an elegant vaulted cellar and on a lazy shady terrace. The service can be slow—if you're in a rush, eat at the market hall instead (Mon-Sat 7:00-24:00, Sun 12:00-23:00—except closed Sun off-season, at the end of the pedestrian zone at Flanatička 16, tel. 052/214-054).

$$ Hook & Cook is a fresh and modern-feeling place that offers simple and tasty "street seafood" dishes along the main drag, just steps from the Forum (daily 11:00-21:00, Sergijevaca 18, mobile 099-216-6373).

$$ Alighieri, located on its namesake Dante Square, is a convenient, pleasant spot that does a decent job cranking out Italian classics (daily 7:30-23:00, Danteov Trg 3, tel. 052/381-984).

$$ The Shipyard Pub—huge, boisterous, and trendy—is tucked down a lane at the amphitheater end of the Old Town (just behind the House of Istrian Olive Oil). They have sidewalk tables, a vast and pubby interior, and a huge interior garden—all serving a long list of drinks and gourmet burgers (daily 10:00-23:00, Svetog Teodora 1, mobile 091-200-9116).

Pula Connections

By Bus from Pula to: Rovinj (almost hourly, 45 minutes), **Poreč** (almost hourly, 1.5 hours), **Opatija** (almost hourly, 2 hours), **Rijeka** (nearly hourly, 2-2.5 hours), **Zagreb** (almost hourly, 4 hours), **Split** (5/day, 10 hours), **Venice** (2/day usually in the early morning, 4 hours). To reach **Slovenia,** bus schedules seem always in flux but there are usually options from Pula to **Ljubljana** on Fils Pula (www.fils.hr) and/or Flixbus (www.flixbus.com); to reach **Piran,** you'll likely take the Flixbus to Portorož and change there. The GoOpti shuttle is also a convenient option for destinations in Slovenia or Italy (www.goopti.com; for details, see page 600). In the summer, be aware that bus connections are more frequent on weekdays (fewer departures Sat-Sun). Bus info: tel. 060-304-090.

By Train: Trains from Pula are almost always slower than the bus; check the Croatian Railways website (www.hzpp.hr) for schedules.

ISTRIA

The Brijuni Islands

The Brijuni Islands (bree-YOO-nee, Brioni in Italian)—an archipelago of 14 islands just offshore from the southern tip of the Istrian Peninsula—were a favorite haunt of Marshal Tito, the leader of communist Yugoslavia. The main island, called Great Brijuni (Veli Brijun), was where Tito liked to show off the natural wonders of his beloved Yugoslavia to visiting dignitaries and world leaders. Today the island is a national park that combines serene natural beauty with quirky Yugoslav sights, offering a strange but enjoyable time capsule of the Tito years. It's also a particularly bike-friendly destination, with gentle inclines, well-groomed bike paths, and few cars. Though it can get busy in summer season, at its heart this remains a tranquil, low-key getaway: not a must-see if you have limited time in Istria, but still rewarding, especially if you can't make it to any other of Croatia's bevy of beautiful islands.

Tito wasn't the first to fall in love with Brijuni; visitors see the remains of many previous occupants (Romans, Byzantines, Venetians, Austrians—even dinosaurs). Between the World Wars, a health resort here hosted many notables, from Douglas Fairbanks and John D. Rockefeller to Richard Strauss and Emperor Hirohito. But when Tito took power, he made Brijuni his summer residence from 1949 until 1979—hosting a steady stream of VIP visitors from the East, the West, and the non-aligned world (see sidebar). Brijuni opened to the public as a national park in 1983, just three years after Tito's death.

Getting There: You can get to Great Brijuni Island only on one of the national park's boats. These depart from the town of Fažana, five miles north of Pula and 20 miles south of Rovinj. From Rovinj, drive southeast to Bale, where you'll get on the *ipsilon* highway and continue south. In Vodnjan, watch for the easy-to-miss turnoff (on the right) marked for Fažana and Brijuni. Once in Fažana, follow brown *Brijuni* signs and park along the water (confirm with park ticket office that your parking spot is OK).

Cost and Information: The price, which includes the boat trip and a tour of the island, varies depending on the time of year: June-Sept—230 kn, March-May and Oct—190 kn, Nov-Feb—160 kn. During peak summer season, it's wise to buy tickets in advance online: NP-Brijuni.hr. Tel. 052/525-882.

Hours: From June through September, there are 12 boat departures each day (first boat departure from Fažana at 6:45, last trip at 22:15, last return from Brijuni at 23:00); April-May and Oct, 11/day; Nov-March, 4/day.

English Tour: You're supposed to go to the island with a four-hour guided tour, part of which is spent on a little tourist train. While there's no regularly scheduled English tour, they do happen frequently with demand. It's essential to call or check online a few days ahead to find out if any English tours are planned, and to reserve a space (tel. 052/525-883, izleti@np-brijuni.hr).

If you can't make it on the English tour, you're welcome to join any tour you like (Croatian, German, Italian, etc.). Joining a tour is a good idea especially if you have limited time, as there's lots of ground to cover. It may seem like park officials don't want you to slip away and explore the island on your own, but it's perfectly fine—and in fact Brijuni is great for a slow, scenic wander. You're

Brijuni: Center of the Non-Aligned World

Many visitors to the former Yugoslavia mistakenly assume this country was part of the Soviet Bloc. It most decidedly wasn't. While the rest of "Eastern Europe" was liberated by the Soviets at the end of World War II, Yugoslavia's own, homegrown Partisan Army forced the Nazis out themselves. This allowed the country—and its new leader, the war hero Marshal Tito—a degree of self-determination following the war. Though the new Yugoslavia was socialist, it was not Soviet-style socialism. After formally breaking ties with Moscow in 1948, Tito steered his country toward a "third way" between the strict and stifling communism of the East and the capitalist free-for-all of the West. (For more on Tito's system, see the Understanding Yugoslavia chapter.)

Many other countries also didn't quite fit into the strict East-versus-West dichotomy embraced by the US, USSR, and most of Europe. On July 19, 1956, the Brijuni Declaration—signed by Tito, Jawaharlal Nehru of India, and Abdel Nasser of Egypt—created the Non-Aligned Movement (NAM). Members recognized each other's sovereignty and respected each leader's right to handle domestic issues however he or she saw fit.

As Tito's international prominence grew, so did the list of visitors to his Brijuni Islands hideaway. In addition to Nehru and Nasser, Tito hosted Haile Selassie (Ethiopia), Yasser Arafat (Palestine), Fidel Castro (Cuba), Indira Gandhi (India), Muammar al-Gaddafi (Libya), Queen Elizabeth II (Great Britain), Willy Brandt (West Germany), Leonid Brezhnev (USSR)...not to mention Elizabeth Taylor (US) and Sophia Loren (Italy).

In principle, the NAM was envisioned as a competitor of NATO and the Warsaw Pact. But as the world's politics have changed, many NAM members are now closely allied with other, more powerful nations. And when Yugoslavia broke up, most of the countries that emerged preferred to join NATO and the EU.

So whatever happened to the rest of the NAM? It's still going strong, with 120 member states encompassing virtually all of Africa, the Middle East, Southeast Asia, and Latin America. While the EU and the US wrestle for bragging rights as the world's superpower, the NAM represents more than half of the world's population.

ISTRIA

technically required to take the same boat back with the rest of your tour, but this isn't closely monitored.

It's possible to rent **bikes** on the square where the boat puts in. This is a tempting option for cyclists, as the traffic-free island is a delight to explore on two wheels.

Visiting the Island: After a 15-minute crossing from the mainland town of Fažana, visitors arrive at the island's main harbor, which is a hub of activity and the site of its two hotels.

The **Boathouse** hosts a high-tech permanent exhibit about the history of Brijuni, which offers a good overview of the island; the tours typically spend time here before boarding the return boat. You'll learn about the archipelago's geology, fauna, and flora, and step into a simulated submarine. The exhibit emphasizes the fragility of Brijuni and the need for sustainable tourism.

Outside the harbor area, the island is largely undeveloped. There are virtually no cars—most people get around by bike, golf cart, or the little tourist train you'll board to begin your tour. As you spin around the island, you'll enjoy views over its endlessly twisty coast, with cove after tranquil cove. Your guide will impart both dry facts and eye-rolling legends while you putter past several intriguing sights, periodically giving you a chance to get off the train and explore a few of them up close.

For 20th-century history buffs, the island's highlight is the **"Tito on Brijuni"** exhibit. Dating from 1984—four years after his death, but before the end of Yugoslavia—this exhibit celebrates the cult of personality surrounding the head of this now-deceased nation. The museum (with English descriptions) features countless photos of Tito in every Brijuni context imaginable—strolling, sunbathing, skeet shooting, schmoozing with world leaders and movie stars, inspecting military officers, playing with camels given to him by Muammar al-Gaddafi, and so on. (For more on Tito, and why the dictator remains so beloved in his former lands, see the sidebar on page 740.)

Another high point of the island tour is the **safari,** featuring a diverse menagerie of animals (or their descendants) brought here for Tito as gifts by visiting heads of state. Because many of the non-aligned nations are in Africa, Asia, or other non-European regions, many of these beasts are exotic. Aside from the Istrian ox and Istria's trademark goat, you might see llamas, Somali sheep, Shetland ponies, chamois, and more. There once were elephants, camels, cheetahs, ostriches, monkeys, bears, and bobcats as well, but most of these have gone to the great non-aligned safari in the sky, and their bodies are now preserved at the "Tito on Brijuni" exhibit.

Other attractions you may see on Brijuni: an ancient, gnarled olive tree supposedly dating from the fourth century AD; the remains of a mostly first-century-AD Roman *villa rustica* (country estate); the ruined street plan of a Byzantine fort; a 15th-century Gothic church with an exhibit on frescoes and Glagolitic (early Croatian) script; an Austro-Hungarian naval fort (Brijuni was strategically important back when Pula was Austria's main naval base); and footprints left by a dinosaur who vacationed here 120 million years before Tito.

Birders can look for some of the 250 avian species that live on the island in the summer. Gardeners may spot some exotic, nonnative plant species (more gifts, to go along with all those animals), such as Australian eucalyptus. And Republicans can drool over the golf course, a reminder that Brijuni is attempting to cultivate a ritzy image.

Poreč

Poreč (poh-RETCH, Parenzo in Italian), the tourist capital of the Istrian coast, is the kind of resort that brags about how many hotel beds it has, rather than how many museums or churches pack the cobbled streets of its Old Town. (Think of it as the Croatian Cancun.) The town is too big to be charming, but too small to be exciting. The only reason to come is to see its landmark basilica, slathered with exquisite mosaics. But if you're in a hurry or churched out, I'd skip it.

Getting There: Surrounding Poreč's peninsular Old Town are miles of hotels-and-concrete sprawl. Drivers follow *Centar* and blue *P* signs to the big pay parking lot, then head up to the big boulevard called Zagrebačka (with the grass median). This leads past the **TI** (Zagrebačka 9, tel. 052/451-293, www.myporec.com) to the spacious square named Trg Slobode. From here, Decumanus street marches straight through the middle of the Old Town. To find the basilica, look for the archway with gold mosaics down Sv. Eleuterija street.

▲Euphrasian Basilica (Eufrazijeva Bazilika)

This sixth-century church is a gold mine for fans of Byzantine mosaics.

Cost and Hours: 50 kn, basilica open June-Sept daily 9:00-21:00, until 18:00 off-season, can close for services, no shorts; museum and tower open April-Sept daily 10:00-17:00, likely closed Oct-March; www.zupaporec.com.

Visiting the Basilica: The interior is dominated by gorgeous, glittering mosaics in the apse surrounding the main altar. The top row depicts Jesus surrounded by the 12 apostles, the medallions around the arch celebrate 12 female martyrs, and front and center are Mary and Jesus surrounded by angels and martyrs—including

ISTRIA

Bishop Euphrasius, holding his namesake basilica in his arms (second from left). These date from the 170-year period after the fall of Rome (roughly AD 530-700), when Istria was part of the Byzantine Empire and was ruled from Ravenna (near Venice, across the Adriatic). The more recent (13th-century) canopy over the altar was inspired

by the one in St. Mark's Basilica in Venice. Don't miss another set of mosaics in the floor just inside the door.

For more mosaics, drop into the attached **museum,** with several mosaic fragments scattered around two floors. Or climb the **bell tower** to get a bird's-eye view of Poreč. Both are included in the basilica ticket.

Hill Towns of the Istrian Interior

Most tourists in Croatia focus on the coast. For a dash of variety, head inland. Some of the best bits of the Croatian interior lie within an hour's drive from Rovinj. Dotted with sleepy, picturesque hill towns, speckled with wineries and olive-oil farms, embedded with precious truffles, and grooved by meandering rural roads, the Istrian interior is worth a detour. Tucked below, between, and on top of the many hills are characteristic stone-walled villages, designed to stay cool in summer and warm in winter. Visitors find themselves seduced by the *malvazija* wine, truffles, picturesque tableaus, and laid-back ambience of the Istrian hill towns.

Hill Towns of the Istrian Interior

For a quick visit, focus on the best hill town: Motovun, a popular little burg with sweeping views. With more time, consider venturing deeper into the smaller villages that sit above the Mirna River Valley: the scenic, deserted, lost-in-a-time-warp village of Završje; the rugged, relatively untrampled artists' colony of Grožnjan; or the bigger towns of Buje and Oprtalj. Farther east—on the way to Rijeka—is the extremely remote and minuscule, yet touristy, hamlet of Hum.

One of the interior's main draws is its cuisine—especially the truffles that are found right here, as fresh as you can get. While Rovinj has some fine restaurants, it's worth planning your day around having lunch or dinner in the interior. Review my restaurant options, especially if you want a memorable truffle feast.

During the glory days of the Austro-Hungarian Empire, a twisty railway called La Parenzana (Porečanka in Croatian) connected Trieste to Poreč by way of many of northwest Istria's hill towns. While the train itself is long gone, part of its route has been converted to a rails-to-trails path (you'll see signs for this around the area, and a small museum in Livade). The many bridges and tunnels engineered to make the train line possible have become nostalgic icons of an earlier time. While Croatia hasn't yet developed a serious bicycle-tourism culture, La Parenzana is an impressive first

ISTRIA

effort. Ask locally for the free, EU-funded map of La Parenzana's route, which spans three countries (Italy, Slovenia, and Croatia).

Istrian hill towns can be rough and rugged. Many are abandoned, only recently having been rediscovered by artists. Remember that after Istria shifted from Italy to Yugoslavia following World War II, the "Italian exodus" saw many local peasants leave their homes behind and move into Italy proper—one reason many of these towns are still in such disrepair. Stumbling over cobbles between desolate buildings in a village that was once humming with life, thoughtful travelers are mindful of the pointlessness of forced population shifts.

As you explore, you'll see frequent signs for wineries, olive-oil producers, truffle shops, and *agroturizam*s. Like Italian *agriturismi* or Slovenian tourist farms, these are working farms that try to involve tourists in a meaningful way—sometimes just for a meal or overnight stay, but occasionally actually participating in the daily workings of the farm. For more information, visit Istra.hr.

GETTING AROUND THE ISTRIAN INTERIOR

By Public Transportation: While it's possible to see some parts of inland Istria by public transportation, the rewards are not worth the headaches. The large hill town of Pazin is the region's transit hub, with buses to Rovinj, Pula, Poreč, and Motovun—but not the smaller villages.

By Car: The region is ideal by car. For a quick visit to only the best hill town (Motovun), just zip on the *ipsilon* highway (A-9) to the *Nova Vas* exit, and take the mercifully flat road 44 along the Mirna River Valley straight to Motovun. But for a full day of hill-town hopping in the Istrian interior, follow my suggested route in the "More Hill Towns" section, later.

Motovun

Dramatically situated a thousand feet above vineyards and a truffle-filled forest, Motovun (moh-toh-VOON, Montana in Italian, pop. 531) is the best-known and most-touristed of the Istrian hill towns. And for good reason: Its hilltop Old Town is particularly evocative, with a colorful old church and a rampart walk with the best spine-tingling vistas in the Istrian interior. It's hard to believe that race-car driver Mario Andretti was born in such a tranquil little traffic-free hamlet. Today Motovun's quiet lanes are shared by locals, tourists, and artists—who began settling here a generation ago, when it was nearly deserted.

Orientation to Motovun

Motovun is steep. Most everything of interest to tourists is huddled around its tippy-top. From its little main square, you're just about two blocks in every direc-

tion from a sheer drop-off. This hilltop zone is circled by an old rampart offering a scenic stroll. Motovun has a very modest TI, which serves mainly as a ticket desk for the ramparts (see hours later; www.tz-motovun.hr). If they're not open, the reception desk at Hotel Kaštel kindly dispenses tourist information and town maps.

ARRIVAL IN MOTOVUN

Motovun's striking hilltop setting comes with a catch: Visitors usually have to hike up part of the way. A steep, twisty road connects the base of the hill with the Old Town up top. Where you're directed to park depends on how busy the town is that day (regardless, parking costs 20 kn). On very busy days, you'll park in the lot at the bottom of town and ride a shuttle bus up. If it's less crowded, they'll let you twist most of the way up the hill and park at the upper traffic barrier (or along the road nearby)—a steep 10-minute hike below the main part of town. If you're staying at Hotel Kaštel, you can usually drive almost all the way to the top (follow the procedure explained under "Sleeping in Motovun," later). If you're staying elsewhere in town, ask your *soba* host for advice.

Motovun Walk

The following self-guided commentary will bring some meaning to your hilltop stroll. The walk begins at the traffic barrier partway up the hill (the highest you can drive unless you're sleeping at Hotel Kaštel).

The main drag leading up into town is lined with wine-and-truffle shops. One of the first you'll see is the Lanča family's **Etno-butiga ČA** (just above the parking lot on the right, at Gradiziol 33). This restored 17th-century house has a beautiful view terrace and a wide selection of local wines, brandies, and truffle products (most of them from the Zigante company, just across the valley); they also have a good restaurant with grand views (Pod Napun). Like many people around here, Livio Lanča makes his own mistletoe brandy laced with honey (Easter-Oct daily 10:00-22:00, off-season closed

Motovun

Accommodations
1. Hotel Kaštel & Palladio Restaurant
2. Villa Borgo
3. Villa Maria
4. Houses of Motovun
5. Roxanich Hotel
6. Sobe Nena

Eateries & Other
7. Mondo Konoba
8. Konoba pod Voltom
9. Montona Gallery
10. Etnobutiga ČA Shop
11. Cultural & Educational Center Kaštel

Mon, closed Jan-March, tel. 052/681-767, www.antique-motovun. com.hr).

Hike several steep minutes farther up the hill, passing more local-products shops, truffles, and jewelry boutiques. Soon you'll reach yet another traffic barrier at the base of the town's wall (and the recommended Mondo Konoba restaurant). Continuing up past the barrier, you'll earn grand views on the right—the little town across the valley floor is Livade, the heart of all that truffle commerce—then go through the first of two **defensive gateways.** Inside this passage (under the fortified gate), notice the various insignias from Motovun's history lining the walls: Look for the Venetian lion, the Latin family tombstone, and the seal of Motovun (with a pyramid of five towers being watched over by an angel).

The attic above the gate was a storehouse for weapons in the 15th century, when Motovun first flourished.

Emerging from the gateway, you're greeted by more sweeping views of the valley below on your right-hand side. (A coffee or meal with this view is unforgettable; the upper town's lone ATM is to your left.) Just up and to the left, you'll find another defensive gateway, which is the main entrance into the heart of the **Old Town.** (Inside this gateway, notice the recommended Konoba pod Voltom restaurant.)

To your left as you come through the main gate is the yellow town church, **St. Stephen's.** The crenellated tower is a reminder of a time when this hilltop town need-

ed to be defended. While unassuming from the outside, this austere house of worship has an impressive pedigree: It's based on designs by the famous Venetian architect Andrea Palladio (1508-1580), who greatly influenced the Neoclassical architecture of Washington, DC. The interior is a little gloomy but refreshingly lived-in—used more by locals than by tourists (free, generally open daily 10:00-18:00 and during frequent services).

As you stand on the square in front of the church, imagine Motovun during its annual **film festival,** when it's filled with 20,000 movie lovers from throughout the region and around the world—often including a minor celebrity or two. This square fills to capacity, and films are projected on a giant screen at the far end (generally late July or early Aug, www.motovunfilmfestival.com).

Facing the church is the **Italian Cultural Center,** which plays an important role in this very Italian corner of Croatia. While the building is not open to the public, if your timing is right you'll enjoy beautiful music spilling out from its windows and filling the square. The local *klapa* troupe—with men's voices harmonizing a cappella—practices here with the windows open, filling the square with music. If you happen to hear them, grab a bench and enjoy the show. At the other end of the square is a leafy little piazza dominated by the big, pink **Hotel Kaštel**—the main industry in town.

Head up the little lane between the church and Hotel Kaštel. After a few steps, look on the right for the **Cultural and Educational Center Kaštel,** a thoughtful, modern, well-presented museum all about Motovun that's worth ▲ (25 kn, daily 10:00-18:00, shorter hours or possibly closed off-season, Trg Andrea Antico 7). Sometimes you may have the chance to watch a pasta- and bread-making demonstration (by one of the chefs from the adjacent hotel restaurant). Then circle the courtyard clockwise, checking out a series of strangely fascinating exhibits. You'll learn about the busy watermills that used to churn in the Mirna Valley down below; Josef Ressel, the Czech inventor who lived in Motovun and revolutionized the design of the propeller; and the Parenzana rail line that once connected the isolated villages of Istria to the rest of the world. A small cinema shows off clips from the Motovun Film Festival (founded in 1999 and still going strong), while the room dedicated to Motovun native Mario Andretti has a race-car simulator, one of his actual racing uniforms, and a touching interview where he talks about his early years in this village. You'll also learn about Veli Jože, a legendary Paul Bunyan-type gentle giant tied to Motovun (who's immortalized by a fun wooden sculpture in the courtyard) and see a small diorama of rural life created by local schoolchildren. Taken together, it's an endearing, and surprisingly engaging, celebration of local pride.

Continuing up the lane past the museum, you'll quickly run into the town's **ramparts** (25 kn, daily 9:00-21:00, off-season until 17:00, outside these hours it's free, pay at the TI office on the main square). The lovely walk takes about five minutes. As you breathe in the stunning panorama from above Istria's rolling hills, notice that well-defended Motovun has been fortified three times—two layers of wall up top, and a third down below.

While most of Croatia is overrun by stray cats, Motovun seems populated by dog lovers. If you see or hear dogs in people's backyards, it's a safe bet that they are trained to hunt for truffles in the surrounding forest.

Sleeping in Motovun

Except for the big hotel, all of the places here keep the same rates all year long. Some Motovun accommodations lack air-conditioning; thick old walls and a nice breeze generally keep things cool.

$$$ Hotel Kaštel, dominating Motovun's hilltop (and its tourist industry), is can-do, ideally located, and the only real hotel in this little burg. Most of the 33 colorful, slightly dated rooms have views. True to its name, the building used to be a castle, so the floor plan can be confusing (RS% for room and spa, includes breakfast, air-con, elevator, laundry service, bike rental, Trg Andrea Antico 7, tel. 052/681-607, www.hotel-kastel-motovun.hr, info@hotel-kastel-motovun.hr). Guests have free access to a beautiful indoor pool (and my readers enjoy a discount at the spa, offering a wide range of massages). On arrival at the traffic barrier, tell the attendant there that you have a reservation at Hotel Kaštel; if there's room on top, he'll let you drive up. Otherwise he'll tell you where to park and call the hotel, which will send down a free car to shuttle you up; either way, it's smart to call ahead to the hotel to figure out your options.

$$ Villa Borgo, conveniently located next to the loggia just below Motovun's uppermost gate, has 16 simple but stylish rooms in two buildings; some have views, and all of them have access to a spectacular view terrace (RS%, air-con, staffed until 20:00—call ahead if arriving later, closed Dec-March, Borgo 4, tel. 052/681-708, mobile 098-434-797, www.villaborgo.com, info@villaborgo.com).

$ Villa Maria, in the Sviličić family home, is a good value. They rent two fine rooms with view terraces, a third nonview room, and a studio apartment with access to a little garden. It's on a quiet back lane a steep five-minute walk below the main part of town (breakfast extra, cash only, air-con, facing the defensive gate turn right and go down and around to Borgo 32, tel. 052/681-559, lorenasvilicic@gmail.com, Lorena speaks a little English). Ask them about going on a truffle hunt.

$ Houses of Motovun, just above the parking barrier partway up the hill, has five idiosyncratic rooms that work in a pinch (no breakfast, air-con, check in across the street at Etnobutiga ČA at Gradiziol 33, tel. 052/681-767, mobile 098-955-7978, www.antique-motovun.com.hr, info@antique-motovun.com.hr).

At the Base of Town: These places lack the charm of being right in the center of the Old Town—you have to take the shuttle bus up from the parking lot for 20 kn—but they have other advantages. **$$$$ Roxanich Hotel** is the fanciest place to stay for miles around. Billing itself as a "wine hotel," it's located inside a luxuriously renovated wine cellar from the 19th century. The aesthetic is industrial-chic, and the rooms have colorful, eccentric interiors, many with lovely views over vineyards (includes breakfast, air-con, elevator, pool, parking, Kanal 30, tel. 052/205-700, www.roxanich.hr, reservations@roxanich.hr). **¢ Sobe Nena,** on the other end of the price spectrum, is run by Nevija. It's a good budget option in a tidy house at the very bottom of Motovun's hill. The two rooms are old-fashioned and basic, sharing a bathroom, but there's a fine garden to relax in. Nevija speaks very basic English, but she can call her daughter Doris to translate (no breakfast, cash only, across from the gas station at Kanal 32, tel. 052/681-719, mobile 099-609-0883, sobe.nena@gmail.com).

Eating in Motovun

This small hill town has just a few real restaurants, and most of them are quite good; the first two listings are particularly notable. Every menu is topped by pricey (but tasty) truffle dishes—but keep in mind that these are a better investment when truffles are in season and the flavors are pungent (see sidebar). Remember, there are also several excellent restaurants in the countryside near Motovun, especially just across the valley in Livade—if you're serious about food, be sure to peruse your options in the "More Hill Towns" section, later.

$$$ Mondo Konoba, run by a Croatian-Italian hybrid family and located just below the lower town gate (on the left, at the base of the wall), serves up Sicilian-Istrian fusion cuisine that ranks with any restaurant in the region. Most diners skip the unpretentious, pastel-blue dining room in favor of the inviting little outdoor terrace tucked on the upper level (around the right side), with additional tables across the street at the base of the town wall. The Mondo family's pack of truffle-hunting dogs occasionally pays a visit (daily 12:00-15:30 & 18:00-22:00, closed Jan, Barbakan 1, tel. 052/681-791).

$$$ Konoba pod Voltom is inside the town's upper, main gate (on the right, with the *Taberna* sign above the door). Motovun's most traditional eatery serves excellent, well-presented Istrian food in a cozy dining room. In good weather (June-Sept only), it's hard to beat their view loggia, just below and outside the gate (daily 12:00-22:00, closed Jan, tel. 052/681-923, Martina).

Cheap Food with a View: For budget food with million-dollar views, look for **$ Montona Gallery,** a café with tables along the rampart between the two gates. They serve drinks, ice cream, snacks, pizzas, pastas, burgers, and some Istrian cuisine (daily 9:00-22:00, tel. 052/681-754).

On the Main Square: Hotel Kaštel's **$$ Palladio Restaurant** has ambitiously executed (if hit-or-miss) food and delightful seating right on the leafy main square—but I'd skip the dull interior (RS%, daily 7:00-22:00; also listed under "Sleeping in Motovun," earlier).

More Hill Towns

While Motovun is the top hill town, a charm bracelet of appealing villages sits close by. Dropping by several as you drive can make for a lovely countryside day. Some are better for exploring (Grožnjan, Završje), others better for a meal (Brtonigla, Livade), and others worth a quick stop if you're passing through (Buje, Oprtalj, Hum). I've listed these roughly in the order you'll reach them, coming

Truffle Mania

A mysterious fungus with a pungent, unmistakable flavor is all the rage in Istria. Called *tartufi* in both Croatian and Italian, these precious tubers have been gathered here since Roman times and were favored by the region's Venetian and Austrian rulers. Later on, local peasants ate them as a substitute for meat (often mixed with polenta) during the lean days after World War II.

In 1999, local entrepreneur Giancarlo Zigante discovered a nearly three-pound white truffle. In addition to making Zigante a very wealthy man, this giant truffle legitimized Istria on the world truffle scene. Today, Istria rivals France's Provence

and Italy's Piedmont in truffle production. Most of Istria's truffles are concentrated in the Motovun Forest, the damp, oak-tree-filled terrain surrounding Motovun, Livade, and Buzet.

A truffle is a tuber that grows entirely underground, usually at a depth of eight inches, near the roots of oak trees. Since no part of the plant grows aboveground, they're difficult to find...and, therefore, extremely expensive. Traditionally, Istrian truffle-gatherers use specially trained dogs to find truffles. This is best done at night, when the dog has to rely more on its sense of smell.

There are two general types of truffles: white (more valuable and with a deeper and more pungent flavor—*Tuber magnatum,* known as the "Queen of the Truffles") and black. Each type of truffle has a season when its scent is released, making it easier to find (May-Nov for black, mid-Sept-Jan for white). Once dug up, they look like a tough, dirty pinecone.

Thanks to their powerful and distinctive kick, truffles are often used sparingly for flavor—grated like parmesan cheese, or infused in truffle oil that's sprinkled over a dish. But you'll also find them in cheese, salami, olive oil, tapenade, pâté, and even ice cream. Truffle is commonly served with pasta—sometimes in a rich cream sauce, and other times more simply, just with olive oil. Truffle soufflé and truffle frittata (scrambled eggs) are also popular. Some people find that the pungent, musty aftertaste follows them around all day...and all night, when its supposed aphrodisiac qualities kick in.

If you're a truffle nut, you'll be in heaven here; if not, you may still appreciate the chance to sample a taste. While you do that, ponder how one giant tuber changed the economy of an entire region.

ISTRIA

from the highway and working your way east toward Motovun. While you'll traverse some slow and windy roads, this entire trip is quick—you could do the full circle (not counting Hum) without stops in less than two hours. This route is just a rough framework. Venture off it. Run down leads from locals. Follow intriguing signs to wine tastings, restaurants, and *agroturizam*s. Sniff out some truffles in the Motovun Forest. You will see some other tourists, but this area isn't overrun...yet.

• *From Rovinj, take the fast ipsilon highway (A-9) north. You have two exit options for this area. If you want to enjoy a meal in Brtonigla, take the Nova Vas exit, drive through the middle of Nova Vas, then follow signs for five minutes into Brtonigla. But if you want to head straight to the other towns, take the exit for Buje and skip down to that section.*

BRTONIGLA

Brtonigla (bur-toh-NEEG-lah, Verteneglio in Italian, literally "black soil") is a tiny wine village surrounded by vineyards. It's a bit closer to the sea than the other hill towns in this chapter, and sits above gentle slopes rather than on a dramatic hilltop. This empty-feeling place is home to a luxurious hotel/restaurant and a well-regarded local eatery, but if you're not eating or sleeping here, give it a pass. Once in town, you'll find just a handful of haphazard streets.

Sleeping and Eating in Brtonigla: The family-run **$$$$ San Rocco Hotel and Restaurant** is suitable for a serious splurge. Not long ago, this was the abandoned shell of a traditional Istrian house. Now it's a cushy and elegant hotel with traditional beams-and-stone decor and all the modern amenities. With 14 rooms, an outdoor pool, a big indoor hot tub and sauna, and distant views of the Adriatic, it's a welcoming retreat (air-con, elevator, loaner bikes, Srednja ulica 2, tel. 052/725-000, www.san-rocco.hr, info@san-rocco.hr, Rita and the Fernetich family). Its well-regarded, upmarket **$$$$ restaurant**—open to guests and non-guests alike—features Istrian cuisine served with a modern twist, in a dressy dining room or outside, with poolside elegance (daily 13:00-22:00).

$$$ Konoba Astarea, along the main road toward Buje, is a local favorite for traditional, take-your-time Istrian cuisine with a focus on fish and lamb. While this isn't gourmet cooking (truffles are an afterthought), it's rustic food done very, very well. Anton and Alma Kernjus cultivate a convivial atmosphere that feels like a well-worn neighborhood hangout. Anton ignores the long menu; he'd rather pull up a chair to explain your options. Choose between the warmly cluttered, borderline-kitschy dining room huddled around the blazing open fire, where Alma does a lot of the cooking; the cool and welcoming terrace with faraway sea views; or the relaxing back garden. It's smart to reserve ahead (Thu-Tue 11:00-23:00, closed Wed and Nov, tel. 052/774-384, www. konoba-astarea.com).

• *From Brtonigla, simply follow signs into...*

BUJE

Close to the Slovenian border, Buje (BOO-yeh, Buie in Italian) is big and striking from afar, but functional up close. Still, it's worth a visit if you're passing through and curi-

ous to take a stroll through a hill town that feels more alive and workaday than the norm. Just above the parking lot are the small TI and the town museum (facing each other across the street), and higher up is another parking-lot plaza in front of Buje's pastel-yellow Church of Our Mother of Mercy (marked in Latin, *Mater Misericordiae*). From the nearby terrace, you have (distant) views of the sea. From this square, you can hike on cobbles through everyday neighborhoods. Up and to the left you'll find the squat remains of a mid-15th-century octagonal defensive tower, the small Sv. Martin church with its evocative graveyard, and a viewpoint overlooking the countryside. Up and to the right from the main square is the main Sv. Servol Church, whose big bell tower—visible from miles around—dominates the hilltop. With a rough, unfinished facade, the church shares a fine little piazza with the local elementary school.

Sleeping and Eating near Buje: In Volpia, a nondescript village five minutes outside of Buje (toward Slovenia), you'll find a charming stone country house offering reasonably priced rooms and good food. **$$ La Parenzana,** named for the long-extinct Istrian rail line, rents 16 woody, simple-but-comfortable, Germanic-feeling rooms (no air-con, rental bikes, Volpia 3, mobile 098-434-748, www.laparenzana.com, info@parenzana.com.hr, Alen and Gordan) and also runs a **$$$** restaurant serving up truffle specialties and other dishes cooked over an open fire (daily 12:00-15:00 & 18:00-23:00). The former route of the Parenzana rail line—now a handy hiking and biking trail—runs just behind the property, and the hotel has a sweet little minimuseum about that nostalgic train trip. To get here from Buje, leave town following signs for *Trieste* and *Koper*, then turn off toward *Plovanija*, *Portorož*, and the Slovenian border; after a couple of minutes, watch for *Casa Parenzana* signs to the right.

• *If you're interested in a wine-tasting detour to two of Istria's swankiest wineries (Kabola and Kozlović, both described later), now's your chance: Continue past Buje on the main road, heading at first toward Koper, then watch for signs on the right to Momjan/Momiano. Take this road through the village of Kremenje; soon after, you'll pass Kabola on the right. Kozlović is across the valley around the far side of Momjan.*

To skip the wines and continue on our route, leaving Buje, look for signs that take you along a twisty, narrow road (via Triban) right to Grožnjan.

▲GROŽNJAN

Grožnjan (grohzh-NYAHN, Grisignana in Italian) is your trapped-in-a-time-warp Istrian hill town. Artfully balanced on the tip of a vine-and-olive-tree-covered promontory, Grožnjan is fun to wander and explore. Its stony, leafy, rough-cobbled lanes are lined with art galleries and truffle-and-olive-oil shops. While there are no "sights" to speak of, it's the kind of place that invites you to get lost and leave your itinerary on your dashboard. Not long ago, Grožnjan was virtually forgotten. But now several artists have taken up residence here, keeping it Old World but with a spiffed-up, bohemian ambience.

All roads lead to the convenient and free parking lot, a few steps from the traffic-free village. Distant sea views from the main terrace at the entrance to town remind you that you're not far from the Adriatic. The town church's bell tower is its only landmark. Inside the church, the big painting over the altar shows angels intervening in the Pula amphitheater to save Christians who were thrown to the lions and tigers.

To get the lay of the land, take a 10-minute town wander: Facing the church's front door, go left and loop clockwise through town. Walking along the main street, ulica Umberta Gorjana, you'll pass the first of several truffle shops, then the **TI** (which doesn't have a lot to do; Gorjan 3, tel. 052/776-131, www.tz-groznjan.hr). Just past the TI, on the left (through the gate below the loggia), you'll find the first of two scenic little cafés selling overpriced drinks and cakes with a smashing view.

Back in town, follow the street to the shaded square with two of the town's restaurants, then the Italian Cultural Center. From

ISTRIA

here, explore and follow your nose until you wind up back at the church and view terrace (with another view café). Don't worry about addresses or finding a particular place; you'll find yourself walking in circles, following tempting lanes that end at a sheer drop-off, and quickly see what there is to see. Let your pulse slow and enjoy being a castaway on this isolated, tranquil hilltop.

Eating in Grožnjan: The village has no "destination" restaurant, but if you happen to be here at mealtime, two quite different places share a leafy terrace right in the middle of town (both open daily 8:00-23:00). **$ Café Pintur** is the budget choice, with basic food and low prices (Mate Gorjana 9, tel. 052/776-397, mobile 098-586-188). **$$ Bastia** is a bit more modern and comfortable, with a menu focusing on truffles and its own little lovely courtyard (1 Svibnja 1, tel. 052/776-370).

• *From Grožnjan, backtrack the way you came, keeping an eye out for big, brown signs to Završje. Turn right and follow these signs about 10 minutes to the next stop.*

ZAVRŠJE

If you'd like to visit a nearly deserted hill town, Završje (ZAH-vur-shyeh) is your place. Called "Piemonte d'Istria" in *Italiano*, this mini-Motovun seems to have more truffle-hunting dogs than people. One of the smallest, most com-pact, and most pictur-esquely set hill towns in the area, Završje was once just a double-walled for-tress clinging to the top of its bulbous hill. Over time

ISTRIA

it sprawled just a bit outside its original walls, but it was deserted after World War II and remains almost uninhabited today; only a few locals live here, and virtually all of the buildings are aban-doned skeletons. There's very little to see or do—no museums, no restaurants, and a sporadically open church with a leaning tower and a colorfully painted Baroque altar. But the EU has taken notice of this precious little burg, and has invested in restoring its pretty pink schoolhouse (at the base of the hill, near the parking lot) and posting informative English descriptions scattered around town. Walk up through the village on the main cobbled lane, peering into ruined stone houses and pondering their potential. If I were an entrepreneurial Istrian restaurateur, I'd set up a fancy truffle restaurant here posthaste. A stroll through here today will have a big payoff a decade from now, after little Završje has been redis-covered and repopulated with artists, hotels, and restaurants—as

Istrian Wine Tastings

Istrian wines are beginning to get some attention on the world stage. A few high-class restaurants in New York and London are adding vintages ending in -*ić* to their wine lists, and German, Austrian, and Italian tourists are discovering Istria's wine roads (even if the French remain aloof to them).

A few local wineries have classy tasting rooms that invite passing motorists in for a sample. As this is an emerging scene, serious wine lovers should do their homework before arriving. But if you simply want to splice a few sips into your itinerary, the options below are worth considering. At most places, you can drop by for a few free tastes, though they'd like you to buy a bottle or two for your picnic (most have bottles in the $8-12 range). They understand that it's tough for Americans to carry wine home, so producers that are exporters hope you'll look for their wines back in the US. It's good form to call ahead and let them know you're coming (hotels can help)—particularly if you want to pay for a more serious visit, with a guided tour of the cellar, and local cheeses and other bites paired with each wine. I've organized the wine-tasting options below by area within Istria.

Near Momjan, just north of the Hill Town Loop: An easy 10-minute detour from my recommended hill-town driving loop is the village of Momjan, which is surrounded by some of the most striking vineyards I've seen here. While humble Momjan itself doesn't have much to see, it's flanked by two well-regarded wineries with state-of-the-art tasting facilities. Traditional **Kabola,** near the village of Kremenje (just toward Buje from Momjan), owns the best setting, with a cypress-lined driveway leading to a cluster of picture-perfect stone buildings overlooking gorgeous vineyard tableaus that

it surely will. You'll be able to say, "I was there back when it was a ghost town."

• *If you want to head directly to Motovun, you can simply proceed on the road past Završje and twist down into the valley, on an unpaved road with chunky gravel. You'll pop out on the valley highway just west of Motovun.*

Better yet, for an easier and more scenic approach, backtrack the way you came for a couple of minutes, turning right to follow signs to Oprtalj.

feel like Provence. Kabola produces a wide variety of whites, including several made from *malvazija, pisak* (pinot grigio), and muscat. They also have a full palette of reds—100 percent *teran* and *teran* blends with cabernet sauvignon and merlot. (They also make a 100 percent cabernet sauvignon that's very nice.) Try the rosé that blends *teran* and muscat (free tastings, drop-ins welcome, Mon-Sat 10:00-19:00, closed Sun, Kanedolo 90, tel. 052/779-208, www.kabola.hr). **Kozlović** has a sophisticated, super-modern tasting facility, dramatically perched on a hill overlooking the valley behind Momjan. Arguably Istria's most well-regarded winery, most of their wines are whites (about 85 percent, including lots of *malvazija* and some muscat). They also make exquisite reds (*teran* and blends that knocked my socks off). The staff is more formal, and you must call ahead to make an appointment—tastings are all prearranged to match with light foods (Mon-Sat 10:00-19:00, closed Sun, Vale 78, tel. 052/779-177, mobile 099-277-9177, www.kozlovic.hr).

Between Rovinj and Poreč: Just a minute's drive off the Limski Canal (described under "Rovinj Connections," earlier in this chapter), in the village of Krunčići, **Ivica Matošević** turns out well-respected wines and offers tastings in a humble space without pretense (it's a working facility rather than a snazzy showroom). Its proximity to Rovinj makes it an easy choice if you want a winery visit without scouring the back lanes. Matošević corks up mostly whites, with several varieties of *malvazija* (which they call Alba—Italian for "dawn"), as well as a red blend of *teran* and merlot called Grimalda (after the place where the grapes are grown). Their basic tastings are free if you buy a bottle, or you can call ahead to arrange a cellar tour and a more elaborate tasting paired with local snacks (May-mid-Oct Mon-Fri 9:00-19:00, Sat-Sun 10:00-18:00; off-season Mon-Sat 9:00-16:00, Sun from 10:00; Krunčići 2, tel. 052/448-558, www.matosevic.com). From Rovinj, head up to the Limski Canal (following signs for *Poreč,* but without getting on the highway). After driving along the rim of the canal, then heading inland, watch for the turnoff on the right for *Krunčići* and *Matošević.*

ISTRIA

OPRTALJ

Oprtalj (oh-per-TAL; Portole in Italian) has a particularly scenic approach, along a twisting driveway lined with pointy cypress trees. As a place to visit, the town is midway between cutesy Grožnjan and still-abandoned Završje, with few sights but plenty of atmosphere. Oprtalj lines up along a plateau with a busy road ripping through its middle. Like Motovun, it has a pink loggia across from its main gate, containing an old stone-carved winged lion of St. Mark and other stony fragments from the town's history. If you poke up through the gate and wander the town, you'll find the faintest brush of tourist trappings in what is otherwise an authentic, quiet little burg. Near the gate is the town's *konoba*, with seating under a tree out on the view terrace across the street. The fancy yellow building at the Motovun end of town is the elementary school, named for local hero Milan Šorgo, a

Partisan who was killed during the fighting to retake his native Istria from the Nazis.

• *The road through Oprtalj leads directly down into Livade, then across the valley highway to Motovun.*

LIVADE, ISTRIA'S "TRUFFLE TOWN"

The flat little crossroads village of Livade, sitting in the valley facing the back of Motovun's hill, is home to the first and last name in Istrian truffles. In 1999, Giancarlo Zigante unearthed the biggest white truffle the world had ever seen—2.9 pounds, as verified by *The Guinness Book of World Records*. (The current record-holder, found in central Italy in 2014, weighed nearly 4 pounds.) Zigante's hunk of fungus—revered as if it were a religious relic—kicked off a truffle craze that continues in Istria today (see "Truffle Mania" sidebar, earlier). Today Zigante has a virtual monopoly on Istria's truffle industry, producing a wide range of truffle goodies. If you're a connoisseur, or just curious, make a pilgrimage to this truffle mecca. Livade's White Truffle Days take place on weekends from mid-September through early November; white tents are filled with local producers showing off their truffles, wines, olive oils, and more. While here, you can also drop into Livade's little museum about La Parenzana, the railway that once linked these hill towns.

Eating in Livade: Zigante's large facility here is divided into two parts: The **Zigante Tartufi shop** offers shelves upon shelves of both fresh and packaged truffle products (plus local wines, olive oils, brandies, and more). There's also a little tasting table where you can sample the precious goods (daily 9:00-21:00, off-season 10:00-17:00, Livade 7, tel. 052/664-030, www.zigantetartufi.com). The attached **$$$$ Restaurant Zigante** is the place to splurge on truffles if money really is no object. The decor—inside, or out on the terrace—is white-tablecloth classy, the service is deliberate but friendly, and the truffles, as if on a cooking game show, are prepared in a dizzying variety of ways (daily 12:00-23:00, Livade 7, tel. 052/664-302, www.restaurantzigante.com).

More affordable and less pretentious, **$$$ Konoba Dorjana** is across the roundabout and just down the street from Zigante. This family-run eatery has a cozy old-fashioned dining room around a giant fireplace, an inviting terrace covered by a canopy of ivy, and plenty of truffle options (Thu-Tue 11:00-22:00, closed Wed, Livade 4A, tel. 052/664-093).

Eating near Livade, in Gradinje: A five-minute drive east of Livade, in the hamlet of Gradinje, is a rustic, unpretentious eatery serving up the most affordable truffle dishes around. **$$ Konoba Dolina** (Valley Inn) has a nondescript interior and a pleasant terrace out front. Because it's just beyond the tourist trail, the prices are reasonable and the ambience feels authentic...and the food is utterly delicious. If you want to sample good, hearty, local truffle cuisine with zero pretense, this place is worth the drive (Wed-Mon 12:00-21:00, closed Tue, mobile 091-893-2847). First make your way to Gradinje (go into Livade and turn right at the main round-about, then drive through the countryside for a few minutes). Once in Gradinje, go all the way through town, then look for signs on the left.

• *Motovun (described earlier in this chapter) hovers on the hill just across the valley from Livade. Once you've seen this area, if you have more time and interest, you can carry on another 40 minutes to reach Hum (follow the main valley road east to Buzet, then to Roč, then look for the turnoff on the right to Hum, along the Glagolitic Lane). Most people won't find the Hum detour worth the miles, but it works great if you're headed east anyway (such as to Opatija or Rijeka).*

HUM

According to its marketing plan, Hum (pronounced "hoom," Colmo in Italian) is the "smallest town in the world." Despite its tiny population of 16 people, Hum has a Town Hall, church, school, post office, and all the other trappings of a "town." Smart gimmick. Unfortunately, Hum is also, per capita, the most touristy town in the world—crammed with visitors who come to stroll through its streets, drop

some kunas in its souvenir shops, or dine at its lone restaurant, **$$ Humska Konoba,** with fine outdoor terrace seating (tel. 052/660-005). But despite its quirks and its one-trick commercialism, Hum is engaging. At the far corner of Istria—just up the road from Mount Učka, which forms the natural boundary with the neigh-

ISTRIA

boring Kvarner Gulf—Hum feels incredibly remote, rugged, and (if you don't run into any tour buses) forgotten by modern times.

Getting There: From Motovun, follow the Mirna Valley road east. After you go through Buzet, you'll pass under the village of Roč; watch for the turnoff to Hum on the right. From here, you'll follow the Glagolitic Lane (described next) through the wilderness to Hum.

Nearby: The road between Hum and the Mirna Valley—called the **Glagolitic Lane** (Aleja Glagoljaša)—commemorates a ninth-century alphabet once used for written Croatian. Driving here, watch for giant Glagolitic characters and a sort of "Rosetta Stone" on top of a hill comparing the Glagolitic, Cyrillic, and Roman alphabets. While Glagolitic was abandoned centuries ago in most of Croatia, the area around Hum used it well into modern times. And since the rise of Croatian nationalism during the Yugoslav Wars, the Glagolitic alphabet has been in vogue—schoolchildren even have Glagolitic poetry contests and spelling bees.

• *From Hum, you're very close to the northeast branch of the ipsilon highway (A-8). You can take this either west to Rovinj (via Pazin), or east to the Učka Tunnel, Opatija, and Rijeka.*

Near Istria

The towering Mount Učka separates Istria from the rest of Croatia. And just on the other side of that mountain is a pair of former Habsburg towns that offers a dose of variety (and a convenient pit stop on the way to other Croatian towns). Shot through with the faded elegance of an upper-crust history, Opatija is a welcome change of pace from the salty, stony towns along the rest of the Croatian coast. Its elegant Viennese-style cafés delight coffee-sippers, its parks tickle gardeners, and its beaches lure sunbathers. Nearby, the big industrial port city of Rijeka is an important transit hub; if you wind up changing buses or boats here, consider a quick stroll through its gentrifying urban core.

Opatija

Opatija (oh-PAH-tee-yah) is not your typical Croatian beach town. In the late-19th-century Golden Age of the Austro-Hungarian Empire, this unassuming village was transformed into the Eastern Riviera—one of the swankiest resorts on the Mediterranean. While the French, British, and German aristocracy sunbathed on France's Côte d'Azur, the wealthy elite from the eastern half of Europe—the Habsburg Empire, Scandinavia, and Russia—par-

Opatija

To Rijeka & Učka Tunnel (Istria)

MARKET HALL

Marina

ŠETALIŠTE CARMEN SYLVE

NOVA CESTA

U. EUGENA KUMICIĆA

RADNIČKA ULICA

U. MARŠALA TITA

U. VIKTORA CARA EMINA

VRUKTI

ULICA JURJA DOBRILE

U. VLADIMIRA NAZORA

Angiolina Park

SWISS HOUSE

VILLA ANGIOLINA

OUTDOOR THEATER

Park Margarita

PUT VRUTKI

VELOG JOŽE

NOVA CESTA

Buses to Rijeka

AUTOTRANS

Intercity

MARŠALA TITA

Slatina Beach

HOTEL KVARNER

HOTEL MILENIJ

ABBEY OF ST. JAMES

JURAJ ŠPORER ART PAVILION

STATUE

LUNGOMARE

Adriatic Sea

STAIRS

CHURCH OF THE ANNUNCIATION

Slatina

ULICA

ULICA JOAKIMA RAKOVCA

AMERICAN GARDENS

To Istria (scenic route)

100 Meters
100 Yards

Accommodations	Eateries
❶ Hotel Agava	❺ Ružmarin
❷ Hotel Bristol	❻ Roko
❸ Hotel Savoy	❼ Istranka
❹ Hotel Galeb	❽ Dalla Nonna

ISTRIA

tied in Opatija. Neo-Baroque, Neoclassical, and Art Nouveau villas popped up along its coastline as it became *the* sunny aristocratic playground.

Though the Habsburgs are long gone, Opatija retains the trappings of its genteel past. Most of Croatia evokes the time-passed Mediterranean, but Opatija whispers "belle époque." It may be the classiest resort town in Croatia, with more taste and less fixation on postcards and seashells. Most people don't come to Croatia for this sedate scene. But if rustic seaside villages are wearing on you, cosmopolitan Opatija—which hosts equal numbers of tourists and convention-going businesspeople—is a pleasant return to high-class civilization. You'll notice the clientele here skews a bit older than in other beach towns.

The town is also strikingly situated: tucked beneath thickly forested mountains, with a view across the bay of Rijeka's sprawl. Thanks to its sheltered location nestled under towering peaks, Opatija is protected from the Bora wind, enjoying instead a light, refreshing breeze. This gives Opatija a particularly mild and enjoyable climate—the perfect match for its refined ambience.

Orientation to Opatija

Opatija is basically a one-street town: Ulica Maršala Tita, lined on both sides by stately hotels, follows the seafront. The town's focal point is its beach area, called Slatina. You can walk from one end of the tourist zone to the other in about 20 minutes. (For a handy loop, walk along the bustling main street in one direction, then back along the waterfront promenade—or vice versa.)

TOURIST INFORMATION

Opatija's TI, across from the big Amadria Park Hotel Milenij, is a short walk up ulica Maršala Tita from Slatina (July-Aug daily 8:00-21:00, shorter hours and may be closed Sun off-season; from Slatina, just head a block toward Rijeka and look on the left side of the road, Maršala Tita 128; tel. 051/271-310, www.visitopatija.com).

ARRIVAL IN OPATIJA

Driving in from either Istria or Rijeka, just follow *Opatija* and bull's-eye signs and switchback down, down, down to the water. The handiest place to park is the big, modern Slatina garage, perched just up the hill at the west end of town (well-marked from the main road); there's also a lot behind Hotel Imperial, and ample street parking; all of it costs the same (10 kn/hour). Tow trucks are at the ready for drivers looking for a free ride at the meters. The TI can change bills to coins for meters.

Sights in Opatija

Begin at Opatija's centerpiece, the waterfront beach-and-park area called **Slatina,** with sweeping sea views, a marbled Croatian "Walk of Fame" (with one or two names you might recognize), and a seawater swimming pool. From here, Opatija lines up along its main drag, **ulica Maršala Tita,** still fronted by ornate villas that would seem more at home in Vienna than they do in Croatia. Tourists stroll here hand-in-hand, taking in the views, dipping into pricey boutiques, and snapping photos of the fancy facades as they go. Joining them, you, too, may soon find yourself thinking of this place as the "Monte Carlo of Croatia." (Sure, it's a stretch. But you're on vacation.)

A few steps toward the sea, stretching in either direction along the waterfront, is a scenic promenade called the **Lungomare.** This is another wonderful spot for rocky seafront strolling, and it offers striking views across the bay to Rijeka (which looks much better from afar). Partway along the Lungomare is one of Opatija's trademarks: a **statue** of a woman surrounded by seagulls, called *Greetings to the Sea.* Much as I'd like to relay some romantic legend behind this evocative monument, the truth is that there's no story behind it—like Opatija itself, it's just pretty to look at. Farther along, you'll pass the **Juraj Šporer Art Pavilion,** which hosts temporary art exhibitions (same ticket and hours as the Museum of Tourism, below).

Nearby, drop into the *opatija* (abbey) that gave the town its name, the **Abbey of St. James** (Opatija Sv. Jakov, right along the Lungomare below the TI).

On the dome above the altar is a strangely eerie relief showing St. James standing in a boat, cradling this church in his arm, accompanied by his trademark gourd-on-a-stick, and flanked by palm trees.

Beyond the abbey, you'll pass the Hotel Kvarner, the resort that first put Opatija on the map for the fin-de-siècle rich and famous. Then the Lungomare winds toward the brand-new, upper-crust Angiolina bathing facility (where you can pay royally to rent a chair or umbrella, or enjoy an overpriced drink or meal; www.angiolinaopatija.com). Just above sprawls **Angiolina Park**—the most inviting of Opatija's many manicured parks. Inside the park are two small museums. The first, closer to the water, is located in the **Villa Angiolina,** a mansion with a gorgeous lobby (free to view). The villa houses the mildly interesting **Croatian Museum of Tourism** (20 kn, includes the Šporer Art Pavilion, Tue-Sun July-Sept 10:00-13:00 & 18:00-21:00, shorter hours off-season, closed Mon year-round, www.hrmt.hr). Just uphill through the same garden is **Swiss House,** a separate venue with changing exhibits (open weekends; hours unpredictable, but generally 14:00-19:00). Down-

ISTRIA

The Bora
Or, How to Predict Croatian Coastal Weather

When asked what tomorrow's weather will bring, a salty Croatian fisherman looks to the mountains and feels the stiff wind on his face. "Sun," he says. "The Bora brings good weather."

Like any people whose fate is tied to the sea, coastal Croatians can extrapolate a breeze or a front of clouds into a full-blown weather report. While this is a precise art cultivated over a lifetime, even the casual tourist can learn a few tricks from the natives.

Croatian coastal weather is shaped by a mighty wind called the Bora (named for the Greek Boreas, the North Wind; sometimes called "Bura" in Croatian, or "Burja" in Slovene). Much like France's infamous mistral wind, the Bora has an indelible impact on this region's weather, vegetation, architecture, and tourism.

The Dinaric Mountains, which rise sharply up from the sea along the Croatian Coast, act as a barrier for cold, cloudy weather. As the air on the coastal side of the mountains heats up, the air behind the snow-capped peaks stays cool. To equalize the temperature and pressure differential, the cool air begins to move toward the warm air, creating a white fringe of clouds along the ridge of the mountains—a sure sign that the Bora is about to blow. When all that pent-up air finally escapes, the Bora comes screaming down the slopes to the sea.

The Bora's power is at its peak along the Kvarner Gulf—especially where a gap in the mountains provides a natural funnel toward the sea (such as at Senj and at Karlobag). Farther south, such as in Dalmatia, the inland remains warmer and the Bora is milder (but still strong—Bora winds blowing through the "funnel" near Dubrovnik's airport occasionally force incoming flights to divert to Split).

The Bora is not constant—it's strongest at midday and made

hill (toward the water) from both of these, you'll find an outdoor theater that shows movies or hosts concerts nightly in peak season. Opatija's harbor is just beyond the park.

To add a bit of uphill cardio to your stroll, head back toward Slatina, with the water on your left. Following the road, look for the address 154 Maršala Tita (on the right); you'll see stairs with signs for *Crkva Marijina Nevještenja* (the church) and *Amerikanski vrtovi* (the gardens). At the top of the stairs, go left along the street and you'll shortly see another sign for the **Church of the Annunciation,** a Neo-Romanesque structure from the very end of Opatija's glory days. Pop inside to see the cavernous interior, or have a seat on the benches out front to admire the view of Kvarner Bay.

up of intermittent, fierce gusts that can reach 150 miles per hour. Young children have been known to "fly" through the air for short distances because of the Bora. The Kvarner coastal road is closed several times each year to trucks, buses, and other high-profile vehicles, which can be tipped over by the gusts. The Bora can also wreak havoc on car ferries. After a day or two of a stiff winter Bora, everything is coated with a thin layer of salt, like ash after a volcano.

The good news: As the Bora rushes toward the coast, it sweeps bad-weather clouds away with it—leaving in its wake clear, cooler air and sunshine.

In summer, the much milder version of this wind—which usually bathes the coast in a refreshing breeze each evening, when the interior cools faster than the sea—is called a Maestral. Sporadic mini-Bora gusts at night are known as Burin.

The Bora's unpopular cousin is the wind called Jugo (YOO-goh, meaning "south"). The Jugo originates as a moist air mass gathering over the Adriatic, which creates a low-pressure vortex. Finally it blows northward toward Croatia, bringing with it hot, humid, and stormy weather. Because humid conditions foster disease, an ancient superstition considers the Jugo wind evil, and the refreshing Bora wind good. The Bora and the Jugo are the yin and yang of Croatian winds, blowing in opposite directions and with opposite effects.

Of course, the weather here is anything but predictable. Croatia's coast is made up of a series of microclimates. Each island has its own very specific weather conditions, which is why one island may excel at growing olives, the next one lavender, the next red wine grapes, and the next white wine grapes. If you really want to know what sort of weather is on the way, ask a local.

ISTRIA

A few minutes farther up the road, over the curving pedestrian bridge, you'll come to the **American Gardens** (free entry, Tue-Sun 9:00-13:00 & 15:00-18:00, closed Mon). Created in the 1920s by a rich Hungarian paprika merchant and his wife—who was an illegitimate child of a Habsburg archduke (long story)—the gardens got their name because the pair had once lived in the US. While pleasant to wander around, the real reason you come here is for the views.

The surrounding area has plenty of hiking trails and inviting beaches; if you're looking to kill even more time here, seek advice at the TI.

Sleeping in Opatija

Opatija is chock-a-block full of swanky resort-slash-business hotels. With so many beds—and because Opatija lacks the allure of
places like Dubrovnik and Rovinj—prices are relatively low for the
quality.

Big Chain Hotels: These have the most striking Habsburg
facades in town, and both have luxurious rooms with all the amenities (air-con, elevator, big buffet breakfast included, pay parking garage). **$$$$ Hotel Agava,** part of the Amadria Park chain,
has an impressively restored old shell with a handsome lobby and
café, and 75 businesslike rooms (Maršala Tita 89, tel. 051/278-
200, www.amadriapark.com, hotel.agava@amadriapark.com).
$$$$ Hotel Bristol, part of the OHM group, has 78 rooms. It
maintains its late-19th-century decor inside and out—mixing modern comfort with period moldings, chandeliers, and a cheery yellow
facade (gorgeously restored coffee shop in lobby, Maršala Tita 108,
tel. 051/706-300, www.hotel-bristol.hr, info@hotel-bristol.hr).

Smaller and Family-Run: These two small hotels, run by the
Brko family, are well-located a few steps from the lively Slatina
scene (to the right as you face the water; both have air-con, elevators, and a pay parking garage). While they're a lesser value, they
feel more personal than the hotels listed above. **$$$$ Hotel Savoy,**
overlooking the water, comes with four stars, 32 nicely appointed
rooms, an enticing swimming pool with a great view, a private
beach, and higher prices. Request the type of room you want when
you reserve: Most rooms have balconies and sea views for no extra
charge, but many of these face a noisy nightclub; for more quiet,
you can request a back (nonview) room facing the street (Maršala
Tita 129, tel. 051/710-500, www.hotel-savoy.hr, info@hotel-savoy.
hr). Across the street is **$$$ Hotel Galeb,** with 25 spacious rooms,
three stars, and plenty of character. Guests at the Galeb have access
to the pool and beach at the Savoy (Maršala Tita 160, tel. 051/271-
177, www.hotel-galeb.hr, info@hotel-galeb.hr).

Eating in Opatija

For a good sit-down meal, consider one of the following options.
Several hotels also have refined Vienna-style coffee houses with
late-19th-century appeal; Café Wagner at the Amadria Park Hotel
Milenij is a favorite for its nice outdoor terrace.

$$ Ružmarin, tucked in a residential zone just behind and
above a row of big hotels, is a sane and stylish oasis with an inviting
covered terrace, a modern dining room, and good pizzas, pastas,
and other dishes (daily 10:00-24:00, up the road behind Grand
Hotel Palace at Veprinački put 2, tel. 051/712-673).

ISTRIA

$$ Roko has two popular places side-by-side along the busy main drag. The restaurant is a bit more upscale, but I prefer the cheaper pizzeria at #114, with a cozy stone-and-brick interior, a small terrace, and a busy wood-fired oven turning out tasty Italian meals. If you find this place calming, it may be because it was the home of Opatija native Leo Henryk Sternbach, who invented Valium (daily 11:00-24:00, Maršala Tita 112/114, tel. 051/711-500).

$$$ Istranka does solid regional cuisine including pastas, truffles, soups, meat, and seafood. Their seasonal specialties are particularly enticing, such as porcini mushrooms in autumn (daily 9:00-24:00, hides uphill behind Maršala Tita 83, tel. 051/271-835).

Picnic: To browse for your own picnic, drop by the old-fashioned indoor market hall (*tržnica*, on the left a 10-minute walk up Maršala Tita from Slatina). There's also a convenient Tommy supermarket in the Slatina parking garage, as well as Konzum grocery stores on the main drag. **$ Dalla Nonna** is a nice bakery with takeaway pizza slices, focaccia, and pastries (open long hours daily, Maršala Tita 85).

Opatija Connections

Intercity buses leave Opatija from near the big Slatina square, just above the beach (next to Grand Hotel Palace). Before boarding, buy tickets at the Autotrans office just up the steep road out of town. Most buses leave from the big bus parking lot tucked behind the trees—except buses to Rijeka, which leave from the easy-to-miss bus stop in front of the Autotrans office.

From Opatija by Bus to: Rijeka (2/hour, 30 minutes), **Pula** (almost hourly, 2 hours), **Rovinj** (2/day, 3 hours via Pula), **Zagreb** (3/day direct, 3 hours, more with change in Rijeka). To reach **Split** or **Dubrovnik,** you'll likely need to change in Rijeka. Info: Mobile 060-888-619, Autobusni-Kolodvor.com.

Rijeka

The industrial city of Rijeka (ree-YAY-kah; it translates as "River") became Croatia's biggest port under Austro-Hungarian rule. It's dainty little Opatija's bigger, burlier brother, with a population of 129,000. Remember, this was the primary industrial port of the entire Habsburg Empire (and the proud birthplace of the torpedo in 1866). Like Opatija, much of Rijeka's architecture is reminiscent of the glory days of the Habsburgs. But unlike Opatija, most of Rijeka's buildings outside the gentrifying urban core haven't been renovated—giving much of its sprawl a seedy, gritty, past-its-prime feel.

Rijeka also holds the dubious distinction of being the first-ever fascist state in Europe—in the early 1920s, back when Istria belonged to Italy, this area became the "Free State of Fiume" (its Italian name) as a diplomatic buffer between Italy and Yugoslavia. The charismatic poet and early fascist leader Gabriele D'Annunzio managed to take power in the city, proclaiming its independence... for just 15 months, until he was forced out.

Since Rijeka is a major transportation hub, there's a good chance you'll pass through. While not quite ready for prime time as a tourist destination, it offers an intriguing contrast to the big-name towns that Croatia connoisseurs may enjoy.

Orientation to Rijeka

The bus station, train station, and ferry terminal are within a few blocks of each other in a bustling waterfront business zone. The

sector is crossed by two one-way streets (going in opposite directions): Ivana Zajca (or the Riva, along the waterfront, runs west to east) and Adamićeva (which changes its name a few times as it cuts east to west through town). A block above these two streets is the Korzo, an almost-charming pedestrianized zone

packed with shops, restaurants, and the TI (Korzo 14, tel. 051/335-882, www.visitrijeka.hr).

Sights in Rijeka

If you have time to kill in Rijeka, you can spend it wandering the **Korzo promenade.** The domed yellow tower marks the entrance to the "Old Town," which survives in name only—this area has been heavily rebuilt in modern style and lacks charm. At the top of the Old Town stands Rijeka's **Cathedral of St. Vitus.** A bit higher on the hill and just to the west is the city's museum cluster, with a trio of forgettable collections (maritime, city history, and natural history); a contemporary and modern art museum is in the streets below.

The area of Rijeka perhaps most worth exploring is its lively **waterfront market** area, about a 10-minute walk down from the Korzo (head to the waterfront, turn left, and make your way between the burly buildings). Tucked between bustling open-air produce stands are genteel old Habsburg-era market halls selling fresh fish and meat.

A very steep hike (or drive) above town, you'll find Rijeka's old

fortress (with some nearby historic churches), called Trsat. And yet one more attraction lies underfoot in the city center: Rijeka has renovated a network of underground **tunnels,** constructed by Italians in the 1930s. While there's not much to see, the tunnels can be fun to explore and provide a handy shortcut in case of rain or excessive heat.

Rijeka Connections

BY TRAIN OR BUS

The **train station** is a few blocks west of the Korzo (on arrival, exit the station to the right and walk 10 minutes to the water). The **bus station** is a big parking lot in the middle of the chaos, near the west end of the Korzo. And the **ferry terminal** is at the east end of the waterfront. The Jadrolinija ticket office is at Riva 16. Major car-rental companies also have offices here.

From Rijeka by Train to: Zagreb (3/day direct, 4-5 hours), Ljubljana (2/day direct, 3 hours).

From Rijeka by Bus to: Opatija (local bus #32, 2/hour, 30 minutes; leaves not from main bus station, but from a stop at the east end of the Korzo—at Jelačić Square), Senj (hourly, 1.5 hours), Pula (nearly hourly, 2-2.5 hours), Rovinj (5-7/day, 2-3.5 hours), Zagreb (hourly, 2-3.5 hours), Split (5-6/day, 8 hours), Dubrovnik (4/day, 12-13 hours, includes night buses), Ljubljana (2/day, fewer off-season, 2.5 hours). For schedules, see Arriva.com.hr or call 051/213-821.

ROUTE TIPS FOR DRIVERS
Between Northern Croatia and Dalmatia

The long stretch of Croatian coast from Istria to Dalmatia—between the cities of Rijeka and Zadar—offers twisty seaside roads, functional port towns and fishing villages, some of the country's most rugged scenery, and no real knockout sights. South of Opatija and Rijeka, the Kvarner coastline is stark and desolate—most traces of settlement have been long since blown away by the battering Bora wind (see sidebar). Offshore, sheltered from the elements, are several islands—Krk, Cres, Lošinj, Rab, and Pag—each with its own character and appeal. Still, coastal Croatia offers more bang for your buck to the north (Istria) and the south (Dalmatia).

If you're driving between northern Croatia (Zagreb, Plitvice, Istria, or Opatija) and the Dalmatian Coast (Zadar, from where the expressway zips to Split), you have two options: Use the fast inland A-1 expressway, or follow the slow Kvarner Gulf coastal road all the way down.

The **A-1 expressway** option is boring but faster and far more efficient, especially from Zagreb or Plitvice. If you're coming from

Zagreb, just take A-1 directly to Split; from Plitvice, drive south through Korenica to access A-1 at Gornja Ploča. From Istria or Opatija, you have two options for accessing A-1 that take about the same amount of time: Head east (inland) from Rijeka on A-6 to join A-1; or, more interesting (and better for southern destinations), drive the Kvarner coastal road as far south as Senj, then cut inland and up over the mountains to Otočac, where you can get on A-1.

The two-lane **Kvarner coastal road** (national road #8, a.k.a. E-65) is twisty and slow, but more scenic. Compared to the expressway, you'll lose at least an hour if you're coming from Istria or Opatija, and much more if you're starting in Zagreb or Plitvice. Along this road, you'll enjoy good but not spectacular views—similar to what you'll see in Dalmatia, but less developed. To find this road from Rijeka, just follow signs for *Split* and *Zadar* (being careful not to get on the expressway).

It's striking how desolate it feels as you drive along the Kvarner coastal road. The most appealing spot for a break is **Senj** (pronounced "sehn"—the j is mostly silent, but has a slight *y* sound). Senj has a little harbor and a modest square with a jumble of outdoor cafés. The town is watched over by the boxy fortress of a band of pirates called the Uskoks. These were Serb and Croat refugees forced out of their homes in the interior when the Ottomans invaded in the 16th century. After resettling here in Senj, they became pirates and began terrorizing the Adriatic coastline. While they claimed to target only Ottoman ships, they also harassed anyone who traded with the Ottomans—including the Venetians. Finally the Austrians—bowed by political pressure from Venice—put down the Uskoks. Today Senj is the best jolt of civilization along this road, with busloads of tour groups constantly dropping off here for a coffee-and-WC break. This means that the natives of Senj—perhaps recalling their pirate ancestors—are adept at overcharging and shortchanging visitors. Check your bill carefully against the posted menu prices.

Senj is also the easiest point where the Kvarner coastal road connects to the speedy A-1 expressway that runs parallel to the coast inland. From Senj, a well-traveled road cuts away from the coast and soon begins twisting up the coastal mountain range. After about an hour, you'll arrive at the A-1 expressway, followed by the war-scarred town of **Otočac**.

SPLIT

Dubrovnik is the darling of the Dalmatian Coast, but Split (pronounced as it's spelled) is Croatia's second city, bustling with 178,000 people. If you've been hopping along the coast, landing in urban Split feels like a return to civilization. While most Dalmatian coastal towns seem made for tourists, Split is real and vibrant—a shipbuilding city with ugly sprawl surrounding an atmospheric Old Town, which teems with Croatians living life to the fullest. And life here is good: few cities match Split's combination of urban flair, wonderful climate, mountains, and beaches...as its waves of visitors are finding out.

Though today's Split throbs to a modern, youthful beat, its history goes way back—all the way to the Roman Empire. Along with all the trappings of a 21st-century city, Split has some of the best Roman ruins this side of Italy. In the fourth century AD, the Roman Emperor Diocletian (245-313) wanted to retire in his native Dalmatia, so he built a huge palace here. The palace continued to host the Roman elite until the fall of the empire. Then, in the seventh century, locals fleeing Slavic invaders moved in and made themselves at home, and a medieval town sprouted from the rubble of the old palace. In the 15th century, the Venetians took over the Dalmatian Coast. They developed and fortified Split, slathering the city with a new layer of Gothic-Renaissance architecture.

But even as Split

grew, the nucleus remained the ruins of Diocletian's Palace. To this day, 2,000 people live or work inside the former palace walls. A maze of narrow alleys is home to boutiques and galleries, wonderfully atmospheric cafés, and Roman artifacts around every corner.

For years, Split had a split personality: Was it a no-nonsense, metropolitan transit point; an impressive destination in its own right, with sights to rival Dubrovnik's; or both? While largely lacking Dubrovnik's over-the-top romance, Split settles for being nobody's "second-best." It is its own city, the antidote to all that's quaint and cutesy in Dalmatia. Today Split is stepping up to its role as both an urban hub *and* another tourist gem on Croatia's sun-splashed coast—so on a busy day, when a cruise ship or two is in town, it can be jammed.

PLANNING YOUR TIME

Split deserves at least a full day. Begin by touring Diocletian's Palace, then take a coffee break along the Riva promenade or have lunch in the Old Town. In the afternoon, visit a couple of museums (the Meštrović Gallery, which is a long walk or short bus or taxi ride from the Old Town, is tops), hike on the Marjan peninsula, or hit the beach. As the sun sinks low, promenade along the Riva with the natives and nurse a drink at an atmospheric open-air café.

With a second day (or on your way into or out of town), you could spend some time in nearby Trogir—an enjoyable Dalmatian seaside village just to the north. And if you're connecting to points north on the expressway, you can stop off for a waterfall dip at Krka National Park. (Both are described at the end of this chapter.)

Orientation to Split

Split sprawls, but almost everything of interest to travelers is close to the City Harbor (Gradska Luka). At the top of this harbor is the

Old Town (Stari Grad). Stretching out between the Old Town and the sea is the Riva, a waterfront pedestrian promenade lined with cafés and shaded by palm trees. The main ferry terminal (Trajektni Terminal) juts into the harbor from the east side. Along the harborfront embankment between the ferry terminal and the Old Town are the long-distance bus station (Autobusni Kolodvor) and the forlorn little train station (Željeznička Stanica). West of the Old Town, poking into the Adriatic, is the lush and hilly Marjan peninsula. Spreading up the hillside between Marjan and the Old Town are the characterful little lanes of the Varoš neighborhood.

Split's domino-shaped Old Town is made up of two square sections. The east half was once Diocletian's Palace, and the west half is the medieval town that sprang up next door. The shell of Diocletian's ruined palace provides a checkerboard street plan, with a gate at each end. But the streets built since are anything but straight, making the Old Town a delightfully convoluted maze (double-decker in some places). At the center of the former palace is a square called the Peristyle (Peristil), where you'll find the TI, cathedral, and highest concentration of Roman ruins.

TOURIST INFORMATION

Split has two TI locations: One is in the little chapel on Peristyle square, in the very center of Diocletian's Palace; the other—less crowded and therefore more helpful—is on the Riva at #9, facing the harbor (same hours for both: June-Sept daily 8:00-21:00; April-May and Oct Mon-Sat until 20:00, Sun until 17:00; Nov-March Mon-Fri 9:00-16:00, Sat until 14:00, closed Sun; Peristyle tel. 021/345-606, Riva tel. 021/360-066, www.visitsplit.com).

Helpful handouts include the *Discover Split* newspaper (with a detailed map), plus *Split in Your Pocket* guidebooks and maps.

ARRIVAL IN SPLIT

By Boat, Bus, or Train: Split's ferry terminal (Trajektni Terminal), main bus station (Autobusni Kolodvor), and train station (Željeznička Stanica) all share a busy and practical strip of land called Obala Kneza Domagoja, on the east side of the City Harbor. From any of them, you can see the Old Town and Riva; just **walk** 10 minutes toward the big bell tower. You'll pass travel agencies, baggage-storage offices, people trying to rent out rooms, a post office, shops, and cafés.

Boats arrive at various piers. The **Jadrolinija passenger catamaran** to and from Hvar and Korčula usually docks at the Obala Lazareta embankment, right in front of the Old Town. The **Krilo passenger catamaran** to those destinations usually uses berth #9 at the pier called Gat Sv. Petra, partway along the harbor, and sometimes the Jadrolinija catamaran does as well. Bigger **car ferries** use various docks along the harbor.

By Cruise Ship: Ships either dock along the main harbor in front of the Old Town, or anchor in the harbor and send tenders into the harbor. Either way, it's an easy 5- to 15-minute walk to town.

By Plane: Split's airport (Zračna Luka Split-Kaštela) is across the big bay, 15 miles northwest of the center, near the town of Trogir (airport code: SPU, tel. 021/203-555, www.split-airport.hr). Exiting the airport, turn left to find the airport bus, which departs every 30 minutes or so (30 kn, drops you at the main bus station, described earlier). Near the bus stop is a taxi stand, but the fare is a hefty 250-300 kn between the airport and downtown Split.

By Car: For details on arriving in Split by car, driving between northern Croatia and Split, and driving south to the rest of the Dalmatian Coast, see "Route Tips for Drivers," near the end of this chapter. Dropping rental cars at the airport rather than downtown is wise, as navigating Split's one-way street grid is challenging.

HELPFUL HINTS

Festivals: The summer is busy with special events. The huge **Ultra Europe music festival,** with big-name DJs and electronic music acts, overtakes the city for a weekend in early July (everything's booked up and more expensive—if you're not here for the music, stay away; www.ultraeurope.com). From mid-July through mid-August, the mellow **Split Summer Festival** hosts a variety of plays and concerts at indoor and outdoor venues around town (www.splitsko-ljeto.hr/en). For much of the summer, Split celebrates **Diocletian Days,** when actors walk the streets in ancient garb, a carriage transports "Diocletian" along the Riva, and the Diocletian Games are staged.

Luggage Storage: The strip between the bus station and downtown is lined with a half-dozen luggage storage kiosks, and you'll also find services at the bus and train stations. Just west of the Old Town, Modrulj Launderette (described next) also has a left-luggage service.

Laundry: Conveniently located in the Varoš neighborhood at the west end of the Old Town, **Modrulj Launderette** is a rare self-service launderette near several recommended restaurants and has Wi-Fi—handy if multitasking is your style (full- and self-service, air-con; April-Oct daily 8:00-21:00; Nov-March Mon-Sat 9:00-17:00, closed Sun; Šperun 1—see the "Split" map, tel. 021/315-888).

Bike Rental: There are plenty of choices for bike rentals in Split. One good—if moderately strenuous—option for a ride is a loop around the nearby Marjan peninsula, with a stop at a beach. The city also has a bike-share program (www.nextbike.hr), which is straightforward to use.

Who's Hajduk?: You'll see the word *Hajduk* (HIGH-dook), and a distinctive red-and-white checkerboard circle design (or red-and-blue stripes), all over town and throughout northern Dalmatia. Hajduk Split is the fervently supported soccer team, named for a band of highwaymen bandits who rebelled against Ottoman rule from the 17th to 19th century. Most locals adore Hajduk as much as they loathe their bitter rivals, Dinamo Zagreb.

GETTING AROUND SPLIT

Most of what you'll want to see is within walking distance, but some sights (such as the Meštrović Gallery) are more easily reached by bus or taxi.

By Bus: Local buses, run by Promet, cost 11 kn per ride (or 9 kn if you buy a ticket at a newsstand or Promet kiosk, ask for a *putna karta*; zone I is fine for any ride within Split). For a round-trip within the city—such as going to the Meštrović Gallery and back—buy an 18-kn transfer ticket, which works like two individual tickets (must buy at kiosk). Validate your ticket in the machine or with the driver as you board the bus. Suburban buses to towns near Split (such as Trogir) generally use the suburban bus station (Prigradski Autobusni Kolodvor), a dreary 10-minute walk due north

of the Old Town on Domovinskog rata. Bus information: www.
promet-split.hr.

By Taxi: Taxis start at 20 kn, then cost around 8 kn per kilometer. Figure 60 kn for most rides within the city (for example,
from the ferry terminal to most hotels)—but it can be faster to walk
rather than ride from one end of the Old Town to the other. To call
for a taxi, try Radio Taxi (tel. 021/473-737). Uber is also active in
Split, and is often cheaper than a traditional taxi.

Tours in Split

Walking Tours

Split's Old Town, with fragments of Diocletian's Palace, is made to order for a walking tour, and it seems that Split has dozens upon dozens of tour guides leading cruise-ship excursions around town. My self-guided walk (described next) covers basically the same information you'll get from a guide. But if you'd like to hear it live, join a tour. This is a constantly changing scene, but various fiercely competitive companies offer dueling 1.25-hour walks, leaving regularly throughout the day and into the evening (generally around 90 kn).

Local Guides

You can hire an insider to show you around. **Maja Benzon** is a smart and savvy local guide who leads good walking tours through the Old Town (600 kn/up to 2 hours, 700 kn/3 hours, mobile 098-852-869, maja.benzon@gmail.com). Charming **Nives Fabečić Bojić** is also good and takes your learning seriously (similar rates, mobile 098-904-3366, nfabecic@yahoo.com). You can also hire a guide through the **guides association** (www.guides.hr, info@guides.hr).

Diocletian's Palace Walk

Split's only must-see sight is touring the scattered remains of Roman Emperor Diocletian's enormous retirement palace (Dioklecijanova Palača), which sits along the harbor in the heart of the city. This monstrous complex was two impressive structures in one: luxurious villa and fortified Roman town. My self-guided walk (worth ▲▲▲) takes you through Diocletian's back door and hits all of the main landmarks before leaving through what was the palace's front entrance. The ruins themselves are now integrated with the city's street plan, so exploring them is free—except for the cellars and the cathedral sights/temple, which you'll pay to enter. In peak season, the cellars are open until 21:00, and the cathedral sights generally close at 19:00. Cruise-ship groups typically all arrive right around 9:00, which can make for a terrible crush in the cellars—it can be better to wait until afternoon to visit. Also note that various smaller museums (including the Ethnographic Museum, Emanuel Vidović Gallery, and Split City Museum) are inside the palace walls; these are described later, under "Other Sights in Split."

Background

Diocletian grew up just inland from Split, in the town of Salona (Solin in Croatian), which was then the capital of the Roman province of Dalmatia. He worked his way up the Roman hierarchy and ruled as emperor for the unusually long tenure of 20 years (AD 284-305). Despite all of his achievements, Diocletian is best remembered for two questionable legacies: dividing the huge empire among four emperors (which

DIOCLETIANVS

helped administer it more efficiently, but began a splintering effect that arguably contributed to the empire's decline); and torturing and executing Christians, including thousands right here on the Dalmatian Coast. Diocletian's successor, Constantine, not only legalized Christianity, but also made it the official religion of the empire—effectively making Diocletian's purges some of the last in Roman history.

Diocletian decided to return to his homeland for retirement. Since he was in poor health, the medicinal sulfur spring here was a big plus. His massive palace took only 11 years to build—and this fast pace required a big push (more than 2,000 slaves died during construction). Huge sections of his palace still exist, modified by medieval and modern developers alike.

• *Start in front of the palace, at the east end of the Riva. Near the corner of the harbor, you'll find a car-size model of today's Old Town, which is helpful for orientation. Across the street and a few steps closer to the harbor, find the smaller bronze model of the fully intact Diocletian's Palace. Compare that to the version you see today, looking across the street to the...*

Palace Facade

The "front" of today's Split—facing the harbor—was actually the back door of Diocletian's Palace. There was no embankment in front of the palace back then, so the water came right up to this door—sort of an emergency exit by boat. Looking out to the water, appreciate the palace's strategic location: It's easy to fortify, and to spot enemies approaching either by land or by sea.

Visually trace the outline of the gigantic palace, which was more than 600 feet long on each side. On the corner to the right stands a stumpy, rectangular guard tower (one of the original 16). To the left, the tower is gone and the corner is harder to pick out (look for the beginning of the newer buildings). Mentally erase the higgledy-piggledy two-story houses added 200 years ago, which obscure the grandeur of the palace wall.

Halfway up the facade, notice the row of 42 arched window frames (mostly filled in today). Diocletian and his family lived in the seaside half of the palace. Imagine him strolling back and forth along this fine arcade, enjoying the views of his Adriatic homeland. The inland, nonview half of the palace was home to 700 servants, bodyguards, and soldiers.

• *Now cross over and go through the door in the middle of the palace (known as the Brass Gate; it's easy to miss between the cafés—just follow the tourists, who swarm like ants to the entrance). You'll step down into a cool, dark underground passage.*

SPLIT

Diocletian's Palace

Self-Guided Walk

1. Palace Facade View
2. Cellar Entrance (Below)
3. Passage to Peristyle (Below) & Ethnographic Museum (Above)
4. Peristyle Square
5. Entry Vestibule
6. Cathedral of St. Domnius
7. Jupiter's Temple/ St. John's Baptistery
8. View Up Cardo Street
9. Golden Gate

SPLIT

Diocletian's Cellars (Podrumi)

Since the palace was constructed on land that sloped down to the sea, these chambers were built to level out a foundation for the massive structure above (like a modern daylight basement). The cellars were filled with water from three different sources: a freshwater spring, a sulfur spring, and the sea. Later, medieval residents used them as a dump. Rediscovered only in the last century, the cellars enabled archaeologists to derive the floor plan of some of the palace's long-gone upper sections. These underground chambers now house a strip of souvenir stands. One particularly well-preserved stretch—immediately to the left as you enter the long corridor—are uncluttered and worth paying to enter, as they offer the best look in town at Roman engineering.

Cost and Hours: 45 kn; daily 8:30-21:00, until 22:00 in June-Aug; Nov-March Mon-Sat 9:00-17:00, Sun until 14:00.

Visiting the Cellars: Near the ticket seller, notice the big **topographical map** of the Split area, clearly showing the city's easily defensible location: a natural harbor sheltered by tall mountains. You'll see the former Roman city of Salona, Diocletian's birthplace, just inland.

Step into the complex's vast, vaulted **main hall**—the biggest space in the cellars, with stout pillars to support everything upstairs. When those first villagers took refuge in the abandoned palace from the rampaging Slavs in 641, the elite lived upstairs, grabbing what was once the emperor's wing. They carved the rough holes you see in the ceiling to dump their garbage and sewage. Over the generations, the basement (where you're standing) filled up with layers of pungent waste that solidified, ultimately becoming a precious bonanza for 19th- and 20th-century archaeologists. These days this hall is used for everything from flower and book shows to fashion catwalks—and it was a filming location for *Game of Thrones* (it's where Daenerys Targaryen locked up her dragons).

From here, explore the cellars. Enjoy a scavenger hunt looking for the following items:

In many rooms, look overhead to see the **holes** that once held beams to support floorboards, creating an efficient two-story space.

In one large room are two **petrified beams,** like the ones that once filled those double-decker holes. In the same room, you'll see an **unexcavated wing**—a compost pile of ancient lifestyles, awaiting the tiny shovels and toothbrushes of future archaeologists.

In an adjoining domed room, the headless, pawless black granite **sphinx** is one of 13 that Diocletian brought home from Egypt (only four survive, including a mostly intact one we'll see soon on the Peristyle).

One small room displays a stone **olive-oil press**—a reminder of a local industry that has remained much the same since Roman times.

Back in the other direction, the **bust of Diocletian** (or is it

SPLIT

Sean Connery?) helps you visualize the emperor who left his mark on Split—and on the entire empire.

Near the WCs, look for **original Roman sewer pipes**—square outside and round inside—designed to fit into each other to create long pipes.

When you're finished, your ticket gets you into a whole other labyrinth of chambers—mostly with their ceilings missing, so they're open to the air. To enter this area, walk directly across the main passage and into the **eastern cellars.**

• *When you're finished, head back to the main gallery. Ignore the tacky made-in-Malaysia trinket shops as you head down the passage and up the chunky stairs into the...*

Peristyle (Peristil)

This square was the centerpiece of Diocletian's Palace. As you walk up the stairs, the entry vestibule into the residence is above your

head, Diocletian's mausoleum (today's Cathedral of St. Domnius) is to your right, and the street to Jupiter's Temple (supported by wooden beams) is on your left. The TI is in the small chapel, at the end of the square on the right. Straight ahead, beyond the TI/chapel, is the narrow street that leads to the palace's former main entrance, the Golden Gate.

Go to the middle of the square and take it all in. The red granite pillars—which you'll see all over Diocletian's Palace—are from Egypt, where Diocletian spent many of his preretirement years. Imagine the pillars defining fine arcades—now obscured by medieval houses. The black sphinx is the only one of Diocletian's collection of 13 that's still (mostly) intact.

"Roman soldiers" pose for tips, and every day at noon in summer (mid-June-mid-Sept), an actor playing Diocletian appears at the top of the stairs to address the crowd in Latin for a few minutes.

Without realizing it, you're also standing in the middle of one of Split's most inviting bars, Luxor. The red cushions on the steps ringing the square belong to the bar; if you want to sit on one, you have to buy a drink. To really lounge in Roman style, this is well worth paying for—especially in the cool of the evening, when the Peristyle is less crowded and there's often live music. Come back tonight for a pre- or post-dinner drink.

• *Climb the stairs (above where you came in) into the domed, open-ceilinged...*

Entry Vestibule

Impressed? That's the idea. This was the grand entry to Diocletian's living quarters, designed to wow visitors. Emperors were believed to be gods. Diocletian called himself "Jovius"—the son of Jupiter, the most powerful of all gods. Four times a year (at the changing of the seasons), Diocletian would stand here and overlook the Peristyle. His subjects would lie on the ground in worship, praising his name and kissing his scarlet robe. Notice the four big niches at floor level, which once held statues of the four tetrarchs who ruled the unwieldy empire after Diocletian retired. The empty hole in the ceiling was once capped by a dome (long since collapsed), and the ceiling itself was covered with frescoes and mosaics.

In this grand space, you'll likely run into an all-male band of *klapa* singers, performing traditional a cappella harmonies. Just stand and enjoy a few glorious tunes—you'll rarely find a better group or acoustics. A *klapa* CD is the perfect souvenir.
• *Now go back into the Peristyle and turn right, facing the...*

Cathedral of St. Domnius (Katedrala Sv. Duje)

The original octagonal structure was Diocletian's elaborate mausoleum, built in the fourth century. But after the fall of Rome, it was converted into the town's cathedral (the Venetian-style bell tower was added in the 13th to 16th century). Before you go inside, notice the sarcophagi ringing the cathedral. In the late Middle Ages, this was prime postmortem real estate: Being buried closer to a cathedral improved your chances of getting to heaven.

Cost and Hours: Most visitors will do fine with the 25-kn ticket that includes the three most worthwhile sights: the cathedral interior, the crypt, and—a block away—Jupiter's Temple (described later). If you want to climb the bell tower, get the 40-kn ticket (which also adds the skippable treasury/museum; you can also pay 20 kn just for the tower climb, at the tower door). All of the sights are open similar hours (Mon-Sat 8:00-19:00, Sun

12:30-18:00, cathedral often closed Sat afternoons for weddings; winter daily 8:00-17:00, maybe later on request)—but the cathedral can close unexpectedly anytime for services.

Visiting the Cathedral: To get inside, you usually have to enter from behind: Facing the main door at the bottom of the stairs, circle around the right side—passing the crypt (we'll return here later)—to find the door in the building behind. Buy your ticket here and climb up the stairs.

Once inside, the first flight of stairs leads to the cathedral interior (described below). But first, if you bought the 40-kn ticket and want to see the **treasury/museum,** head up one more flight. The single-room museum contains dusty display cases of vestments, giant psalter books, icon-like paintings, reliquaries, chalices, monstrances, and other church art, with very sparse English descriptions. After visiting, head back down to the cathedral.

Step into the tiny but evocative church **interior.** You'll enter into the apse; head around the side of the altar to reach the main

part of the church. This is the oldest—and likely smallest—building used as a cathedral anywhere in Christendom. Imagine the place in pre-Christian times, with Diocletian's tomb in the center. The only surviving pieces of decor from those days are the granite columns and the relief circling the base of the dome (about 50 feet up)—a ring of carvings heralding the greatness of the emperor. The small red-marble pillars around the top of the pulpit (near the main door) were the only thing scavenged from Diocletian's sarcophagus—his actual remains have never been found.

Diocletian brutally persecuted his Christian subjects. Just before he moved to the Dalmatian Coast, he had Bishop Domnius of Salona killed, along with several thousand Christians. When Diocletian died, there were riotous celebrations. In the seventh

century, his mausoleum became a cathedral dedicated to the martyred bishop. Posthumous poetic justice: Now Christian saints are entombed in Diocletian's mausoleum...and Diocletian is nowhere to be found.

The **sarcophagus of St. Domnius** (to the right of the altar, with early-Christian carvings) was once the cathedral's high altar. To the left of today's main altar is the impressively detailed, Renaissance-era **altar of St. Anastasius,** who is lying on a millstone that is tied to his neck. On Diocletian's orders, this Christian martyr was drowned in AD 302. To the left of St. Anastasius' altar is the **"new" altar of St. Domnius;** his relics lie in the 18th-century Baroque silver reliquary, above a stone relief showing him about to be beheaded.

As you exit, take a moment to study the 13th-century **main doors,** one of the treasures of Romanesque sculpture in Croatia. Carved in walnut wood, the 14 panels on each of the two wings depict 28 scenes from the life of Christ.

Just outside the church, you'll see the entrance to the **bell tower** on your right. The tower is scheduled to be closed for restoration for several years, but it may be open in high season. Climbing its 183 steep steps rewards you with sweeping views of Split, but it's not for claustrophobes or those scared of heights.

To visit the **crypt** *(kripta),* also included with your ticket, exit the main door of the cathedral, go down the stairs, and loop left to find its low-profile entrance. This musty, domed cellar (with eerie acoustics) was originally used to level the foundation of Diocletian's mausoleum. Later, Christians turned it into another chapel, dedicated to the Italian Saint Lucia, who was martyred by Diocletian and is honored with a colorful statue at a small altar. (The legend you'll likely hear about Diocletian torturing and murdering Christians in this very crypt is probably false.) Ponder the contrast of this dark and gloomy space with Santa Lucia, whose name means "light." Notice the freshwater well in the middle of the room. Because this water was believed to have healing properties, the faithful would wash their eyes with it (Santa Lucia is also the patron saint of eyesight).

• *Return to the middle of the Peristyle square. Remember that Diocletian believed himself to be Jovius (Jupiter, Jr.). As worshippers exited the mausoleum of Jovius, they would look straight ahead to the temple of Jupiter. (Back then, there were none of these medieval buildings cluttering up the view.) Make your way through the narrow alley (directly across from the cathedral entry) to explore the small...*

Jupiter's Temple/St. John's Baptistery

About the time the mausoleum became a cathedral, this temple was converted into a baptistery (same ticket and hours as cathedral, or 10 kn on its own). Inside, the big 12th-century baptismal font—large enough to immerse someone (as was the tradition in those days)—is decorated with the intricate, traditional woven-rope *pleter* design that evokes Croatia's nautical heritage. Observant travelers will see examples of this motif all over the country. On the font, notice the engraving: a bishop (on the left) and the king on his throne (on the right). Literally under the feet of the bishop is a submissive commoner—neatly summing up the social structure of the Middle Ages. Standing above the font is a statue of St. John the Baptist counting to four, done by the great Croatian sculptor Ivan Meštrović (see page 196). The half-barrel-vaulted ceiling, completed later, is considered the best-preserved of its kind anywhere. Every face and each patterned box is different.

• *Back at the Peristyle, stand in front of the TI/chapel with your back to the square. The small street just beyond the chapel (going left to right) connects the east and west gates. If you've had enough Roman history, head right (east) to go through the Silver Gate and find Split's busy, open-air Green Market. Or, head to the left (west), which takes you to the Iron Gate and People's Square (see "Other Sights in Split," later) and, beyond that, the fresh-and-smelly fish market. But if you want to see one last bit of Roman history, continue straight ahead up the...*

Cardo

A traditional Roman street plan has two roads: Cardo (the north-south axis) and Decumanus (the east-west axis). Split's Cardo street was the most important in Diocletian's Palace, connecting the main entry with the heart of the complex. As you walk, you'll pass several noteworthy sights: in the first building on the right, a bank with modern computer gear all around its exposed Roman ruins (look through window); at the first gateway on the left, the courtyard of a Venetian merchant's palace (a reminder that Split was dominated by Venice from the 15th century until Napoleon); farther along on the right, an alley to the **City Museum** (described later, under "Other Sights in Split"); and, beyond that on the right, **Nadalina,** an artisan chocolatier selling mostly dark chocolate creations with some innovative Dalmatian flavors—such as dried fig and prosecco.

At the end of the street, just before the Golden Gate, detour a few steps to the left along covered **Majstora Jurja** street, lively both day and night. Near the start of this street, just after its initial jog, stairs climb to the minuscule **St. Martin's Chapel,** burrowed into the city wall. Dating from the fifth century, this is one of the earliest Christian chapels anywhere. St. Martin is the patron saint of soldiers, and the chapel was built for the troops who guarded this gate, though it's now run by Dominican nuns (5 kn, daily 9:00-12:00 & 15:00-18:00).

• *Backtrack to the main drag and go inside the huge...*

Golden Gate (Zlatna Vrata)

This great gate was the main entry of Diocletian's Palace. Its name wasn't literal—rather, the "gold" suggests the importance of this gateway to Salona, the Roman provincial capital at the time. Standing inside the gate itself, you can appreciate the double-door design that kept the palace safe. Also notice how this ancient building has been repurposed: Above, on the outer wall, you can see the bricked-in windows that contain part of a Dominican convent. And at the top of the inner wall is somebody's garden terrace.

Go outside the gate and look back at the fortification. This mostly uncluttered facade helps you visualize how the palace looked before so many other buildings were grafted on. Four miles straight ahead as you exit this gate was Salona, which was a major city of 60,000 (and Diocletian's hometown) before there was a Split. The big statue by Ivan Meštrović is *Bishop Gregory of Nin*, a 10th-century Croatian priest who tried to convince the Vatican to allow sermons during Mass to be said in Croatian, rather than Latin. People rub his toe for good luck (though only nonmaterial wishes are given serious consideration). Beyond the statue you'll find Split's **Gallery of Fine Arts** (described later).

• *Your tour is finished. Now enjoy the rest of Split.*

Other Sights in Split

OLD TOWN PUBLIC SPACES

My self-guided walk took you through Diocletian's Palace, which doubles as the heart of Split. But just a few steps away are some more delightful public zones that are worth exploring.

▲▲▲The Riva

The official name for this seaside pedestrian drag is the "Croatian National

Revival Embankment" (Obala Hrvatskog Narodnog Preporoda)—but locals just call it the Riva (REE-vah, Italian for "harbor"). This is the town's promenade, an integral part of Mediterranean culture. After dinner, Split residents collect their families and friends for a stroll on the Riva. It offers some of the best people-watching in Croatia; make it a point to be here for an hour or two in the evening. The stinky smell that sometimes accompanies the stroll (especially at the west end) is a reminder that the town's medicinal sulfur spas have attracted people here since the days of Diocletian.

At the west end of the Riva, the people-parade of Croatian culture turns right and heads away from the water, up **Marmontova.** Although it lacks the seafront cachet, this drag is equally enjoyable and feels more local. As you walk up Marmontova, on the left is the plain-Jane outer facade of the arcade that defines Trg Republike, a grand and genteel Napoleonic-era square. Duck through the passage across from the fish market to bask in its "poor man's St. Mark's Square" ambience, and maybe to linger over a drink at the recommended Bajamonti café. A bit farther up Marmontova, on the right, look for the whimsical fountain nicknamed "The Teacup," with a hand sporadically squirting water across the sidewalk into a funnel.

At the top of Marmontova are some department stores, a lively café square, and the Croatian National Theater (Hrvatsko Narodno Kazalište, HNK). If you head up the little passage between the theater and the modern church, you'll discover an entirely different—and fully local—convivial scene, in the "Behind the Theater" neighborhood, with lots of tempting eateries (see page 211).

▲People's Square (Narodni Trg)

Locals call this lively square at the center of the Old Town "Pjaca," pronounced the same as the Italian *piazza*. Stand in the center and enjoy the bustle. When Diocletian lived in his palace, a Roman village popped up here, just outside the wall. By the 14th century, a medieval town had developed, making this the main square of Split.

The square has some quirky decorative flourishes. On the wall just to the right of the lane leading to the Peristyle, look for the life-size relief of St. Anthony. Notice the creepy "mini-me" clutching the saint's left leg—depicting the sculptor's donor, who didn't want his gift to be forgotten. Above this strange statue, notice the smaller, faded relief of a man and a woman arguing.

Turn around and face the square. On your left is the city's grand old café, **Gradska Kavana,** which has been a venerable meeting point for generations. Today it's both a café and a restaurant, with disappointing food but some of the best outdoor ambience in town.

Across the square, the white building with the three pointed arches was once the **City Hall,** and now houses temporary exhibitions. The loggia is all that remains of the original Gothic building.

At the far end of the square is the out-of-place **Nakić House,** built in the early-20th-century Viennese Secession style—a reminder that Dalmatia was part of the Habsburg Empire, and ruled by Vienna, from Napoleon's downfall through World War I.

The lane on the right side of the Nakić House leads to Split's **fish market** (Ribarnica), where you can see piles of the still-wriggling catch of the day. Why no flies? It's thanks to the sulfur spring in the nearby spa building (with the gray statues, on the corner). Just beyond the fish market is the pedestrian boulevard, Marmontova (described earlier).

Radić Brothers Square (Trg Braće Radića)

This little piazza hides just off the Riva, between the two halves of Split's historic core. Overhead is a **Venetian citadel.** After Split became part of the Venetian Republic, there was a serious danger of attack by the Ottomans, so octagonal towers like this were built all along the coast. But this imposing tower had a second purpose: to discourage citizens of Split from thinking about rebellion. At its base is a juice bar, invoking the more popular nickname of the square—Voćni Trg (Fruit Square), for the produce that was once sold here.

In the middle of the square is a studious sculpture by Ivan Meštrović of the 16th-century poet **Marko Marulić,** who is considered the father of Croatian literature. Marulić was the first to publish poetry in the Croatian vernacular, which before then had generally been considered a backward peasants' tongue.

On the downhill (harbor) side of the square is **Croata,** a necktie boutique that loves to explain how Croatian soldiers who fought with the French in the Thirty Years' War (1618-1648) had a distinctive way of tying their scarves. The French found it stylish, adopted it, and called it *à la Croate*—or eventually, *cravate*—thus creating the modern necktie. Croata's selection includes ties with traditional Croatian motifs, such as the checkerboard pattern from the flag or characters from the ninth-century Glagolitic alphabet. Though pricey, these ties make nice souvenirs (Mon-Fri 8:00-21:00, Sat until 14:00, closed Sun, Mihovilova Širina 7, tel. 021/346-336).

SPLIT

▲Green Market

This lively open-air market bustles at the east end of Diocletian's Palace. Its placement is logical: Historically, this was where the main road entered Split from the countryside (whereas the fish market, at the opposite end of town, faces the Matejuška fishermen's port). Most vendors set up in the early morning, then stick around until 12:00 or 13:00; a few stay open later, but raise their prices.

The market is big, sprawling, and surprisingly easy for a tourist to miss. It's ringed by souvenir and clothing stands, as if to camouflage the intensely local produce market. Be sure to delve in to find the long tables piled high with produce: grapes, figs, greens (especially *blitva*, Croatia's version of Swiss chard), veggies, and so on. Exploring the area, you'll find flower stands, dried fruits and nuts (handy to pick up a snack), air-cured ham and local cheeses (good for a picnic), jars of pickled vegetables, honey, butchers, and more. A few simple eateries serve up hot roasted meat. Look for the gigantic wheels of dense, chewy bread cooked under a *peka* (copper baking dish), which stay fresh for a few days (buy a wedge for your picnic).

Matejuška Fishermen's Port

While Split's harborfront Riva is where the beautiful people stroll, the city's fishermen roots still thrive just to the west. The neighborhood called Matejuška— at the little harbor where the Varoš district hits the water (a five-minute walk beyond the end of the Riva, with the water on your left)—has long been Split's working fishermen's harbor. The enclosed harbor area is filled with working fishing boats and colorful dinghies that bob

in unison. Along the breakwater, notice the fishermen's lockers, where people who earn their living from the Adriatic still keep their supplies. You'll see the most fishing action here in the mornings.

The far side of the breakwater—all glitzy white marble—is another world, with a pebbly beach, an attractive plaza, and some of the best views looking back on the Riva. This jetty is a popular after-hours hangout for young people. Like Split itself, this is a place where two worlds coexist: the grizzled fishermen mending their nets, and the teenagers laughing and flirting.

Beyond Matejuška, the harborfront embankment (which runs toward the Marjan peninsula) has also been rejuvenated and is now spiffed up with cafés facing moored sailboats, creating a relaxing, scenic, largely tourist-free zone. (Ignore the eyesore of an abandoned skyscraper, formerly the Hotel Marjan; corruption and intrigue swirl around this prime real estate, which is the biggest political hot potato in town.)

MUSEUMS AND OTHER SIGHTS
Ethnographic Museum (Etnografski Muzej)

This museum shows off the culture, costumes, furniture, tools, jewelry, weapons, and paintings of Dalmatia, all with good English explanations. The modest but vibrant collection, with a confusing treehouse floor plan, is displayed in an early medieval palace (parts of which once formed the private residential halls of Diocletian). You'll find it in the upper level of the Old Town, behind Diocletian's entry vestibule.

Cost and Hours: 20 kn; Mon-Sat 9:30-19:00, Sun 10:00-14:00; Oct-May Mon-Fri 10:00-15:00, Sat until 14:00, closed Sun; Severova 7, tel. 021/344-164, www.etnografski-muzej-split.hr.

Visiting the Museum: At the entrance to the courtyard, check out the artsy "golden fleece" gate. The ground floor sports the remains of a seventh-century church, and the exhibits usually include an array of traditional folk dress. Have a look at the old photographs, evocatively preserving now-vanished customs. Your ticket also includes access to the roof of the vestibule (find the stairs outside at the far end of the museum); while it's not high enough to be thrilling, it provides a nice view over the rooftops of Split, and you can peer into the top of the vestibule.

Split City Museum (Muzej Grada Splita)

This museum traces how the city grew over the centuries. While the collection is a bit dull, the good English descriptions can help you better appreciate the layers of history you're seeing in the streets.

Cost and Hours: 25 kn; daily 8:30-21:00, June-Sept until 22:00; Nov-March generally Tue-Sat 9:00-17:00, Sun until 14:00, closed Mon; free audioguide to use on your smartphone; Papalićeva 1, tel. 021/360-171, www.mgst.net.

Visiting the Museum: The ground floor displays Roman fragments (including coins from the days of Diocletian that resemble the kunas in your pocket), temporary exhibits, a model of the Peristyle during Diocletian's time, and the museum's highlight: a semicircular marble table (called a "mensa") used by the Romans. As depicted in Hollywood movies, the Romans ate lying down (multiple people would lounge and feast, while servants dished things up from the straight side). This table has been painstakingly reconstructed from shards and splinters discovered in the cellars.

The next floor focuses on the Middle Ages, with a beauti-

SPLIT

fully restored Gothic ballroom, medieval weapons, and a terrace displaying carved stone monuments. The top floor covers the 16th century to the present.

The 15th-century Papalić Palace, which houses the City Museum, is a sight all its own. At the end of the palace, near Cardo street, look up to see several typical Venetian-style Gothic-Renaissance windows. The stone posts sticking out of the wall next to them were used to hang curtains.

Emanuel Vidović Gallery

This small, somber museum celebrates the work of Split native Emanuel Vidović (1870-1953), who gained fame as a Post-Impressionist painter. Located just a few steps off the Peristyle, it's an easy opportunity to get to know an unfamiliar but locally respected artist.

Cost and Hours: 25 kn; daily 8:30-21:00; Nov-March Tue-Sat 9:00-17:00, Sun until 14:00, closed Mon; Poljana Kraljice Jelene b.b., tel. 021/360-155, www.galerija-vidovic.com.

Visiting the Museum: Buy your ticket and head upstairs to the first floor, where you'll see the reconstruction of Vidović's cluttered studio, filled with objects he created or that inspired him. Elsewhere on the first floor—and upstairs—hang many of his works: hazy, Turner-esque landscapes; church interiors; shimmering street and village scenes from Split and around Dalmatia; and paintings of bizarre dolls. Pause on the top floor to watch an informative video about the artist's life.

Split Synagogue

The tiny, modest synagogue of Split is hidden down a small side street, not coincidentally located just outside the walls of Diocletian's Palace. Ring the bell and climb the stairs to step into the unassuming, lived-in religious home of Split's Jewish community, which numbered around 300 before the Holocaust (and about a hundred today). On the table in front of the ark, look for a replica of a little clay oil lamp that was used to light the menorah. This was discovered in the ruins of ancient Salona, indicating that the Jewish presence here goes back to Roman times. Dating from 1510, this is said to be the third-oldest practicing synagogue in Europe (after ones in Prague and Dubrovnik); a rabbi comes from Zagreb a few times each year.

Cost and Hours: Free but donations requested, loaner yarmulkes; Mon-Fri 10:00-14:00, closed Sat-Sun; Židovski Prolaz 1, tel. 021/345-672, www.zost.hr.

Split Gallery of Fine Arts (Galerija Umjetnina Split)

This collection, beautifully displayed in a finely restored old hospital just behind Diocletian's Palace, features mostly Croatian artwork from the 14th to the 21st century. It's a hodgepodge with few famous works, but provides a nice overview of Croatian artists—best reserved for art lovers. Cross through the courtyard, climb up the stairs, and follow the one-way route through the chronologically displayed collection, which is heavy on the 20th century.

Cost and Hours: 40 kn, more for special exhibits; Tue-Sun 10:00-21:00, shorter hours off season, closed Mon; mod café; go straight out the Golden Gate and a bit to the left—behind the statue of Gregory of Nin—to Kralja Tomislava 15, tel. 021/350-110, www.galum.hr.

Archaeological Museum (Arheološki Muzej)

If you're intrigued by all the big stuff from Split's past (buildings and ruins), consider paying a visit to this collection of its little stuff. A good exhibit of artifacts (mostly everyday domestic items) traces this region's history chronologically, from its Illyrian beginnings through its notable Roman period (items from Split and Salona) to the Middle Ages. About a 10-minute walk north of the Old Town, it's worth the trip for archaeology fans. Don't confuse this with the less-interesting Museum of Croatian Archaeological Monuments, on the way to the Ivan Meštrović Gallery.

Cost and Hours: 40 kn; June-Sept Mon-Sat 9:00-14:00 & 16:00-20:00, closed Sun; Oct-May shorter hours on Sat, closed Sun; Zrinsko Frankopanska 25, tel. 021/329-340, www.mdc.hr/split-arheoloski/eng/index.html.

Game of Thrones Museum

This kitschy little museum cashes in on the popular HBO series and its connection to Split. It showcases replicas of costumes and weapons, some models and photos of sets, plus a few actual props. A knowledgeable guide strolls around, ready to answer questions at any level of geeky detail. It's a bit better than you might expect, but only *GoT* superfans will want to fork over the steep entry fee.

Cost and Hours: 100 kn; daily 9:00-23:00, may be closed Oct-May; Bosanska 9, mobile 099-694-0312, https://game-of-thrones-exhibition-museum-split.business.site.

IVAN MEŠTROVIĆ SIGHTS, WEST OF THE OLD TOWN

The Meštrović Gallery and nearby Kaštelet Chapel are just outside the Old Town. Both sights are covered by the same ticket and have the same hours.

Cost and Hours: 40 kn, can be more during special exhibits; Tue-Sun 9:00-19:00; Oct-April Tue-Sat until 16:00, Sun 10:00-15:00; closed Mon.

Information: Gallery tel. 021/340-800, chapel tel. 021/358-185, www.mestrovic.hr.

SPLIT

Getting There: Both sights are located along Šetalište Ivana Meštrovića. You can take **bus #12** from the little cul-de-sac at the west end of the Riva (departs 1-2/hour, schedule posted in the blue shelter; get off at the stop in front of the gallery, just after your bus passes a museum prominently marked *Muzej Hrvatskih Arheoloških Spomenika*). You can also **walk** (about 30 minutes): Follow the harbor west of town toward the big marina, swing right with the road, and follow the park until you see the gallery on your right (at #46). A **taxi** from the west end of the Old Town to the gallery costs about 60 kn (much more from the east end of the Old Town).

To reach the **chapel**, it's a five-minute walk past the gallery down Šetalište Ivana Meštrovića to #39 (on the left, in an olive grove).

Visitor Information: At the information desk, confirm the departure time for the return bus and ask for the brochure explaining the Kaštelet Chapel (which may not be available once you get there).

Cuisine Art: Café Galerija is just above the ticket office.

▲▲Meštrović Gallery (Galerija Meštrović)

Split's best art museum is dedicated to the sculptor Ivan Meštrović, the most important of all Croatian artists. Many of Meštrović's finest works are housed in this palace, designed by the sculptor himself to serve as his residence, studio, and exhibition space. If you have time, it's worth the trek.

Visiting the Gallery: Each work is labeled, but there's very little description otherwise (and the guidebook is overkill for most visitors).

The following tour will help you navigate the highlights. Before you begin, read the sidebar for background on Meštrović's life; while the collection is presented thematically rather than chronologically, knowing the artist's journey will help make sense of what you'll see.

From the ticket office, climb the stairs toward Meštrović's house, pausing in the **garden** to admire a smattering of sculptures. On the right, see Persephone reaching skyward for freedom—an idea that came to Meštrović while he was imprisoned by the Ustaše in World War II. Beyond her, you'll see Cyclops struggling to hurl a giant shot put, in keeping with Meštrović's theme of the struggles of great men. Tucked behind the trees nearby is an eagle, which was a study for a mountaintop monument honoring one great man in particular, the Montenegrin King Petar II Petrović-Njegoš. To the

SPLIT

left as you face the building is a statue of a woman playing a lute, and reliefs of women playing a lute and harp flank the door of the villa. Much as he enjoyed depicting the travails of men, Meštrović also often sculpted women serenely engaging in music.

Go up another set of stairs to reach the **Entrance Hall.** The sculptures here evoke some of Michelangelo's nudes and were fittingly carved from that great sculptor's favorite medium: Carrara marble. The head of a woman glancing pensively out a window is Meštrović's second wife, Olga, who was one of his favorite models. Notice the smaller black sculptures by the two staircases: on the left, representing birth, and on the right, representing death—Meštrović strove to capture the full range of human experience in his work.

Go to the left to find a pyramid of maternal love called *Madonna and Children.* While the woman is clearly garbed in the head scarf of the Virgin Mary, she cradles not one, but two children; these are Olga and Meštrović's first two kids.

Now enter the **Dining Room** at the end of the main floor. This is the most intimate space in the villa—the only room that still feels even a little bit lived-in. It's decorated with more sculptures of Meštrović and his family. Entering, go straight ahead to the windows, then do a clockwise loop around the room. First look for the self-portrait bust of Meštrović and the bust of a woman in a traditional Dalmatian head scarf—this is Meštrović's mother, another one of his favorite models. Notice that the two giant caryatids carved from Dalmatian stone (embedded with fragments of seashells) are also clad in this traditional garb. On the wall to the right of the fireplace, you'll see two painted portraits of Meštrović—one as a young man (by his contemporary, Vlaho Bukovac), and another shortly before his death. Other busts in the room depict Meštrović's children. A painting of the Last Supper hangs in virtually every Dalmatian dining room, and Meštrović's is no exception—he painted this version himself, on wood. He also designed the furniture in this room.

Now climb the stairs. On the **landing,** look for a large bronze relief panel called *Artist of My People.* The old man and the young boy are linked by the *gusle,* a traditional Balkan stringed instrument. Here, Meštrović uses the *gusle* to represent the oral transmission of history (and specifically, the story of the pivotal Battle of Kosovo in 1389—a date etched into the minds of all Yugoslavs, particularly Serbs). Much as Meštrović dresses his women in traditional peasant clothes, he deeply believes in the regeneration of culture and customs over time. Meštrović's detailed drawings in this room—including some inspired by Dante's *Divine Comedy*—are worth a look.

Next, turn right into the **Secession Room.** Two of the finest

Ivan Meštrović
(1883-1962)

Ivan Meštrović (EE-vahn MESH-troh-veech), who achieved international fame for his talents as a sculptor, was Croatia's answer to Rodin. You'll see Meštrović's works every-

where, in the streets, squares, and museums of Croatia.

Meštrović grew up in a family of poor, nomadic farm workers just inland from Split. At an early age, his drawings and wooden carvings showed promise, and a wealthy family took him in and made sure he was properly trained. He eventually went off to school in Vienna, where he fell in with the Secession movement and found fame and fortune. He lived in Prague, Paris, and Switzerland, fully engaged in the flourishing European artistic culture at the turn of the 20th century (he counted Rodin among his friends). After World War I, Meštrović moved back to Croatia and established an atelier, or workshop, in Zagreb (now a museum).

Later in life—like Diocletian before him—Meštrović returned to Split and built a huge seaside mansion (today's Meštrović Gallery). The years between the World Wars were Meštrović's happiest and most productive. It was during this time that he sculpted his most internationally famous works, a pair of giant Native American warriors on horseback in Chicago's Grant Park. But when World War II broke out, Meštrović—an outspoken supporter of the ideals of a united Yugoslavia—was briefly imprisoned by the anti-Yugoslav Ustaše (Croatia's Nazi puppet government).

After his release, Meštrović fled to Italy, then to the US, where he lectured at prominent universities including Notre Dame and Syracuse. (President Eisenhower personally handed Meštrović his new US passport in 1954.) After the war, the Yugoslav dictator Tito invited Meštrović to return, but the very religious artist refused to cooperate with an atheistic regime. (Meštrović was friends with the Archbishop Alojzije Stepinac, who was imprisoned by Tito.) Meštrović died in South Bend, Indiana.

Viewing Meštrović's works, his abundant talent is evident. He worked in wood, plaster, marble, and bronze, and dabbled in painting. Meštrović's figures typically have long, angular fingers, arms, and legs. Whether whimsical or emotional, Meštrović's expressive, elongated faces—often with prominent noses—powerfully connect with the viewer.

SPLIT

Here are a few themes you'll see recurring in Meštrović's works as you tour his museum:

Religion: Meštrović was a devout Catholic.

Dalmatian Traditions: Meštrović felt a poignant nostalgia for the simple lifestyles and customs of his home region of Drniš, and he used his art to elevate them to be on par with religious and mythological themes. This is most evident in the angular scarves many of his female subjects wear around their heads.

Yugoslav Symbolism: Meštrović was a strong supporter of the first (interwar) incarnation of Yugoslavia. He created sculptures not only in Croatia, but also throughout Yugoslavia, many of them honoring heroes of Yugoslav tradition.

The Secession: Living and studying in Vienna in the early 20th century, Meštrović was exposed to the slinky cultural milieu of the likes of Gustav Klimt.

Struggling Men, Serene Women: While Meštrović frequently sculpted both male and female nudes, they often carry starkly different tones: Meštrović's ripped men tend to be toiling against an insurmountable challenge; his smooth and supple women are celebrating life, often through the medium of music (dancing, singing, playing instruments, and so on).

Tumult: Meštrović's life coincided with a time of great turmoil in Europe. He lived through World War I, the creation of the first Yugoslavia, World War II, the postwar/communist Yugoslavia, and the dawn of the Atomic Age in the United States. This 20th-century angst—particularly surrounding his arrest and exile during World War II—comes through in his work.

Meštrović's works can be found throughout Split, Croatia, and the former Yugoslavia. In Split, in addition to the Meštrović Gallery and Kaštelet Chapel, you'll find his statues of Marko Marulić, Gregory of Nin, and John the Baptist. Zagreb has another fine atelier/museum of Meštrović's works, and the seaside village of Cavtat, just outside Dubrovnik, has one of the sculptor's most cohesive and poignant works, the Račić Mausoleum. And sitting high above Montenegro is the mountaintop Njegoš monument at Lovćen.

SPLIT

works in this room—*Little Girl Singing* and *The Katunarić Family*—show the influence of Meštrović's contemporary, Rodin: smoothed rather than angular features, which make the final product less strictly lifelike, but also more expressive and visually pleasing. Other pieces in this room include several small studies for larger statues, some of which were never completed.

Go back across the landing into the **Long Hall,** lined with life-size figures and a view terrace. The *Vestal Virgin,* sitting with her knees apart and feet together, is demonstrating a favorite pose of Meštrović's. And, once again, we see women finding solace and joy in music: dancing (while playfully tossing her hair), playing a lute, and so on. For contrast, look at the facing wall to see sketches of male nudes. Step out onto the terrace to enjoy the Dalmatian views that inspired the artist.

At the end of the hall—past another small landing with drawings—is the **Study Room,** filled with miniature sculptures Meštrović created to prepare for larger-scale works: *Moses, Prometheus* (the figure tied to a rock, to be eaten by birds for eternity), and *Cyclops* (a large version of which we saw outside). Notice the small study of *Job,* then go into the small side room to see the much larger final version.

Meštrović carved one of his most powerful works, *Job*—howling with an agony verging on insanity—while in exile, as his country was turned upside down by World War II. Like Picasso's *Guernica,* it's a silent scream against the inanity of war. The curator has intentionally placed it in a separate room to emphasize the feeling of alienation. Meštrović sketched his inspiration for this piece (displayed on the wall) while he was imprisoned by the Ustaše.

Head down the stairs and make a U-turn left into the **Sacral Room.** Meštrović was very religious, and here you can see some of his many works depicting biblical figures. The giant, wood-carved *Adam* and *Eve* dominate the room. Also notice the wood-carved relief panels of *Merry Angels* and *Grieving Angels.* (These are similar to the panels you'll see at the Kaštelet Chapel down the road.) Smaller statues around the room include four evangelists (Matthew, John, and two Lukes—but no Mark), Moses, a pietà, and bronze and wooden heads of Christ.

The smaller side room displays another of the gallery's highlights: the quietly poignant **Roman Pietà.** Meštrović follows the classical pyramid form, with Joseph of Arimathea (top), Mary (left), and Mary Magdalene (right) surrounding the limp body of Christ. But the harmony is broken by the painful angles of the mourning faces. Also notice how Jesus' oversized, ruined body drags down those trying to support his dead weight; if he stood up, he'd be towering over all of them. For Meštrović, Christ's suffering was personal: The women wear those traditional Dalmatian head scarves, the features of Joseph are a self-portrait, and Mary Magdalene is modeled after Meštrović's daughter Marija. This sculpture is plaster; there's a bronze version at the Vatican and a marble one on the campus of the University of Notre Dame in the US.

To Kaštelet Chapel: To reach the last part of the Meštrović experience, head down the stairs to the road, cross the street, turn right, and walk about five minutes. You'll see the low-profile entrance to the chapel on the left, through a doorway marked *39*, in an olive grove.

▲▲Kaštelet Chapel

If you're enjoying Meštrović's works, don't miss the nearby Kaštelet Chapel ("Chapel of the Holy Cross"), which brings a new dimension to his oeuvre. Meštrović bought this 16th-century fortified palace to display his 28 wood reliefs of Jesus' life.

You can see how Meštrović's style changed over time, as he carved these over a nearly 30-year span, completing the last 12 when he was in the US. (However, he didn't carve the reliefs in chronological order; the gallery's ticket office has a booklet dating each one.) While the earlier pieces are well-composed and powerful, the later ones seem more hastily done, as Meštrović rushed to complete his opus. He started with the crucifix in 1916. His last two panels, completed in 1953, are on the right as you face the crucifix (the second one, showing the Deposition; and the fourth, showing the Last Supper).

Work clockwise around the room, tracing the life of Christ. Notice that some of the Passion scenes are out of order (a side effect of Meštrović's nonlinear schedule). The beautiful pietà back near the entrance still shows some of the original surface of the wood, demonstrating the skill required to create depth and emotion in just a few inches of medium. Dominating the chapel is an extremely powerful wooden crucifix, with Christ's emaciated arms, legs, fingers, and toes bent at unnatural angles—a typically expressionistic flair Meštrović used to exaggerate suffering.

Activities in Split

▲Hiking the Marjan Peninsula

This huge, hilly, and relatively undeveloped spit of parkland feels like a chunk of Dalmatian island wilderness, a stone's throw from the big city. With out-of-the-way beaches and miles of hiking trails, the Marjan (MAR-yahn) peninsula is where residents go to relax; most people here seem to have their favorite hidden paths and beach coves, so ask around for tips.

From the Varoš neighborhood at the west end of the Old Town, you can hike to various lookout points. If you're in shape, figure about an hour to hike to the top viewpoint, then another 45 minutes back down; some of the best views are from partway up.

Start by climbing the stairs past the recommended Šperun Restaurant, and continue straight up Senjska ulica. Follow the

stairs all the way up for 15 steep minutes to reach a spectacular view terrace (with sweeping vistas over Split), next to a little café/eatery.

These are the best views of the Old Town, though if you like, you can keep ascending for different views: Curl around past the café and follow the

steep pathway up to the small chapel of St. Nicholas. From the chapel, more stairs continue higher to a broad path that cuts through the woods; for the highest viewpoint, follow the steps to the terrace. This top-of-the-world perch offers a 360-degree panorama of Split's urban sprawl, receding layers of jagged and majestic mountains, offshore islands, and the bay behind the Marjan peninsula.

From the top, either head back down the way you came, or—to extend your hike—continue down the stairs at the far end of the view terrace. A path takes you along the length of the peninsula, mostly through trees (read: no views). A series of switchbacks leads back down to the main road running along the perimeter of Marjan; from here, you can turn left to get back to town, or right for an even longer walk around the far end of Marjan.

The peninsula also has some good beaches for a post-hike dip (described next).

Hitting the Beach

Since it's more of a big city than a resort, Split's beaches are less scenic (and less peaceful) than small towns elsewhere along the coast. I'd use my Split time for city sights and culture. However, if the weather's great and you want to go for a dip, here are a few ideas.

East of the Old Town: The most popular, most crowded

beach is **Bačvice,** in a pebbly cove just a short walk east of the main ferry terminal. As it's very shallow, it's often unpleasantly jammed with kids. After dark, it becomes a hopping meat-market nightlife zone for older "kids." Less crowded beaches lie just to the east of Bačvice. Each cove has its own little swimming zone; the fourth cove over, called **Trstenik,** is perhaps the most inviting. A pebbly beach—with free access—flanks the big deck in front of the Radisson Blu Resort, where you can rent a chair, buy a drink at the bar, and use the showers.

West of the Old Town (on Marjan Peninsula): Marjan, the peninsular city park, is ringed with several sunbathing beaches. Along the southern edge of Marjan, and reachable on bus #12, are a couple of good options. First, just below the Meštrović Gallery is a rocky but more local-feeling and less crowded beach called **Ježinac** (Croatian for "sea urchin"...be sure to wear water shoes; this is also nicknamed Obojena Svjetla). Beyond that is **Kašjuni**—also known as Joe's Beach for the touristy beach bar that dominates it. This long, skinny, peninsular beach—which is angled to receive maximum sunrays late in the day—may be connected to Matejuška pier in downtown Split by a handy little shuttle boat in summer (ask locally or check http://joesbeach.com).

Another popular choice, **Bene Beach,** is even farther out, along the northern edge of Marjan—so it offers more shade. You can get to Bene Beach by bus #12, bike, or foot (about a 45-minute walk from the Old Town).

Boat Trips and Bus Excursions

A staggering variety of pop-up travel agencies sell tickets for a wide variety of bus or boat excursions. New companies come and go every year; read online reviews and comparison-shop for a tour that suits your interests.

Boat Trips: Various tour boats line up along the Riva each morning and evening, hawking trips to nearby islands. One of the biggest draws is the **Blue Cave,** on the little island of Biševo. This natural sea grotto with shimmering colors, like the famous Blue Grotto on Capri, can be entered only on a small motorboat. You'll be taken ashore (at a beach bar) to buy your ticket and wait your turn to head into the grotto. Nearby, just south of Vis Island, is the **Green Cave,** a larger, less impressive, but easy-to-visit craggy sea grotto. The **Blue Lagoon** is a shallow, gorgeously colorful bathing area between the island of Drvenik Veli and the tiny offshore islet Krknjaši. And the sandy spit of **Bol,** on the island of Brač, is famous for its long, pristine beach (also known as Zlatni Rat). While all four of these are impressive (and offer enjoyable excuses for a brief Dalmatian cruise), their popularity is quite recent and mostly a product of Instagram- and TripAdvisor-driven hype.

SPLIT

Aside from these standard side-trips, there are a few more interesting or adventurous alternatives—from jet-ski tours (www.jetskisafarisplit.com) to the **Summer Blues catamaran** "sail 'n' swim" cruises with swimming stops, dancing, food, and lots of drinks (www.summer-blues.com). Various companies also offer **kayaking tours** from Split.

Bus Excursions: Popular land-based excursions include the town of **Trogir;** the Roman ruins of **Solin** (ancient Salona); whitewater rafting on the **Cetina River;** the pilgrimage site at **Međugorje; Dubrovnik;** and the waterfalls at **Krka National Park** or **Plitvice Lakes National Park.** As these can sell out (and many leave quite early in the day), it's best to book at least a day or two before.

Nightlife in Split

The Riva

Every night, a flood of humanity flows past the walls of Diocletian's Palace along the town's pedestrian promenade. The Riva is something that makes Split special: It is one of Europe's great public spaces, threaded between Roman ruins and the sea. Find somewhere to sit and watch life go by, ideally over a drink at one of the many outdoor cafés (which are basically interchangeable—just pick one that looks good). Live music enlivens the Riva nightly through the summer.

Old Town Bars

The labyrinthine lanes of the Old Town are packed with al fresco bars and cafés featuring pleasant tables crammed between ancient stone buildings under a starry Croatian sky. Even if you're not interested in drinking, make a point to wander some of these areas after dark just to people-watch and take in the hubbub in these otherwise hidden pockets. Prices and menus are similar at most places (beer, wine, cocktails, coffee drinks); ordering something simply gives you an excuse to sit in a gorgeous outdoor space, nurse a drink, and focus on your travel partner. The action at these places really gets rolling around 22:00 and peaks around 23:00 or 24:00. Bars are supposed to close their outdoor seating areas at 2:00.

On the Peristyle: The obvious choice, particularly for the not-so-young set, is right on the main square of the Old Town, Diocletian's former entry hall. All day long, the Peristyle steps serve as makeshift café tables for the bar called **Luxor,** with red cushions and small tables scattered along the steps. If you sit on a cushion, you're expected to order a drink (but you can sit or stand elsewhere for free). In the evening—as twilight encroaches and floodlights transform the square into one of the most atmospheric public spaces in Europe—live music breaks out (generally starting between 20:00 and 21:00 and continuing until around midnight). The smooth marble tiles of the Peristyle—worn to a slippery sheen by two millennia of visitors—becomes a dance floor, as people salsa, foxtrot, or pop-and-lock their way around the majestic space. Where else can you cut a rug in the grand entry hall of a Roman palace?

"Slavija Square": This is my own nickname for the tight, stepped area that's squeezed in front of Hotel Slavija, near Radić Brothers Square (Trg Braće Radića; from the square's statue of Marulić, enter the Old Town and bear right, following the beat). This area is more youthful and rowdy, with throbbing techno music and cocktails that flow freely. As you approach this area, you'll see classy **La Bodega,** with an outdoor patio neatly framed by a Gothic arch. Facing this, head just to the left and hike up the stairs, which are lined with tables for several lively bars, including the hip **Fluid.** At the top of the stairs, continue a few steps to one of Split's funkiest nightspots (in the enclosed courtyard on the right): **Ghetto,** sporting a sailors' bordello-theme interior, with heart-shaped chairs, red velvet, and vivid graffiti.

Behind the Loggia: For the youngest, trendiest action, head for the zone locals call *Iza Lođa* (Behind the Loggia). From the grand People's Square, follow the beat behind the former City Hall loggia to discover a well-dressed meat-market scene. The main magnet here is the standing-room-only **Gaga,** with a pounding dance beat, indoor and outdoor bar areas, and a laser-light show on the ancient stones above. At the far end of the little square, like a mellow grandparent observing the rowdy younger generation, is **La Linea** (which locals call simply "Taverna")—an old sailors' pub decorated with nautical flags.

Other Areas: Along the north edge of Diocletian's Palace, **Majstora Jurja** street (just inside the wall) is lined with a mellow gaggle of youthful hangouts. Some mood music plays, but the soundtrack here is mostly chatting, laughing, and flirting. The large square at the top of Marmontova, just before the **Zara** store, is crammed with tables belonging to a half-dozen identical-feeling cafés. Nearby (just to the east), the ground floor of the Prima shopping center is home to **Central the Club,** a former movie theater that's been turned into one of Split's top nightclub venues (Trg Gaje Bulata, www.centralclub.hr). Another popular drinking and dancing venue is closer to the waterfront (just below the entrance to

Trg Republike): **Fabrique,** a sprawling, industrial-mod, brick-and-concrete, air-conditioned venue under vaults. They serve affordable drinks (including some local craft beers) and a wide-ranging menu including pub grub; after hours, it becomes a thriving dance club (DJs start spinning around 23:00, Trg Franje Tuđmana 3, www.fgroup.hr).

Clubbing at Bačvice Beach

This family-friendly beach by day becomes a throbbing party area for young locals late at night. Since all Old Town bars have to close by 2:00 in the morning, night owls hike on over to the Bačvice crescent of clubs. The three-floor club complex is a cacophony of music, with the beat of one club melting into the next—all with breezy terraces overlooking the harbor.

Sleeping in Split

Over the last few years, Split has seen an explosion of rooms for rent in and near the Old Town. Most of these are aimed at a wealthy clientele, and prices are high, but I've listed a few old-school *sobe* for those on a tight budget. Checking Airbnb or other property-rental sites is a good idea, too.

Split suffers from perhaps the worst nighttime noise of any destination in this book—bring earplugs, and always ask for a quiet room (if possible).

Many less-expensive Split accommodations, especially outside the Old Town, don't offer breakfast. But just about every café and restaurant in town (including most of my recommendations) sells breakfast; figure around 25 kn for a basic continental breakfast (croissant, juice, coffee), or 45 kn for a heartier one (with eggs).

INSIDE THE OLD TOWN

While the Old Town is convenient and atmospheric, it's also a happening nightlife zone, so you're likely to encounter some noise (especially on weekends). Consider my higher-priced listings in this expensive district only if money is truly no object; those on a budget should give the *sobe* and apartments a careful look.

$$$$ Marmont Hotel is a sophisticated oasis offering four-star comfort, with 21 top-end rooms in a quiet corner of the Old Town. The slight aroma you may notice is from the fish market, just around the corner (includes breakfast, air-con, elevator, sun terrace, Zadarska 13, tel. 021/308-060, www.marmonthotel.com, booking@marmonthotel.com).

$$$$ Palača Judita enjoys an ideal location—right on the appealing People's Square, in the heart of town—but it has good windows (to block out most of the noise) and attentive service. Its

19 lovely rooms are housed in a 16th-century Renaissance palace (includes breakfast, air-con, lots of stairs to the entrance but an elevator goes to the rooms, free parking and porter service, Narodni Trg 4, tel. 021/420-220, www.juditapalace.com, booking@juditapalace.com).

$$$$ Cornaro Hotel is a well-polished, four-star, business-class hotel. Its 156 rooms sprawl through a huge building just north of the Old Town walls, with generous public areas and a wonderful sixth-floor view terrace that's open even to nonguests. This is a good pick for drivers who want big-hotel comforts, but very close to the action (includes breakfast, air-con, elevator, pay parking, entrances at Sinjska 6 and Kralja Tomislava 9, tel. 021/644-200, www.cornarohotel.com, booking@cornarohotel.com).

$$$$ Palace Suites, a boutique hotel right on the lovely People's Square, is a good value at the lower end of this price range. Its 14 rooms come with stone walls, mahogany floors, and contemporary furnishings. There's a rare elevator, and the prices are reasonable for this location and level of comfort (includes breakfast, air-con, Narodni Trg 13, tel. 021/339-040, mobile 091-444-4065, http://palacesuites-split.com, info@palacesuites-split.com).

$$$ Hotel Peristil, with 12 classy rooms over a restaurant, is wonderfully located just steps from the couldn't-be-more-central square of the same name, and some of the rooms have a view of the cathedral. Run by the Caktaš family, it's homey and convenient (includes breakfast, air-con, stairs with no elevator, some noise from nearby bars, just behind TI and inside the Silver Gate at Poljana Kraljice Jelene 5, tel. 021/329-070, www.hotelperistil.com, booking@hotelperistil.com).

$$ Kaleta Apartments, run by the Raić family, consists of several tastefully decorated apartments in a few buildings. Two of the comfortable apartments, with stone walls and beamed ceilings, are squeezed between cafés along a lively area at the back of the Old Town (the good windows do a heroic job of keeping noise to a minimum). Some of their other apartments are slightly farther away—survey your options on their website, and be clear on the location when you book (air-con, Majstora Jurja 4, mobile 099-509-4299, www.kaletaapartments.com, info@kaletaapartments.com).

Memento Travel Agency manages a variety of apartments at different price points (all rooms: RS%, no breakfast, air-con). **$ Split City Breaks** has three rooms near People's Square, and **$$$ Villa Marta** has two rooms and a snazzy apartment (Majstora Jurja 4). They also manage **$$$ Priuli Luxury Rooms,** which feels like a minihotel, with five elegant, nicely equipped rooms just north of the Old Town (at Sinjska 1); three more Priuli rooms (at Vukovarska 5) are a bit farther out and less convenient (mobile 091-390-9416, www.memento.hr, info@memento.hr).

Split Hotels & Restaurants

Accommodations

1. Marmont Hotel
2. Palača Judita & Bepa Café
3. Cornaro Hotel
4. Palace Suites
5. Hotel Peristil
6. Kaleta Apartments & Memento Travel Agency
7. Priuli Luxury Rooms
8. Sobe "Base"
9. Hotel Luxe
10. Villa Ana
11. To Sunrise & Sunset Rooms
12. To Lanterna City Rooms
13. Villa Varoš
14. Hostel Dvor

$ Sobe "Base" faces a hallway from Diocletian's Palace, with budget accommodations at the top of this price range. Tina, dad Ivo, and Anita run a small travel agency where you'll check in. All three rooms overlook the front steps of the cute little Jupiter's Temple. Although this place is in the midst of some bustling bar action, the double-paned windows provide reasonable peace (no breakfast, clearly communicate your arrival time if arriving early or late, air-con, Kraj Svetog Ivana 3, tel. 021/317-375, mobile 098-361-387, www.base-rooms.com, mail@base-rooms.com).

Restaurants & Nightlife
15 Villa Spiza
16 Uje Oilbar
17 Bokeria
18 Bajamonti
19 Ristorante Pizzeria Galija
20 Fast Food None
21 Kantun Paulina
22 D16 Specialty Coffee
23 4Coffee Soul Food
24 Luka & "Behind the Theater" Eateries
25 O'š Kolač
26 Don Dino
27 Cucina Mare & Ćiri Biri Bela
28 Konoba Fetivi
29 Šperun Restaurant
30 Paradox Wine & Cheese Bar
31 Luxor Bar
32 "Slavija Square" Nightlife
33 "Behind the Loggia" Nightlife
34 Majstora Jurja Nightlife
35 Marmontova Nightlife
36 Central the Club
37 Fabrique

SPLIT

OUTSIDE THE OLD TOWN

These good values are within a five-minute walk of the Old Town. They're nearly as convenient as the options there, but less expensive. Of these places, Hotel Luxe has a full-time reception desk; for the others you may need to call ahead to arrange your arrival time.

East of the Old Town

The Lučac neighborhood—which lines up along the busy street

called Kralja Zvonimira—feels urban and a bit gritty, but it's handy to the Old Town. This area also works relatively well for drivers.

$$$$ Hotel Luxe, a modern hotel with a shiny lobby and 30 upscale-mod rooms, is a comfy splurge that combines a convenient location (near the Old Town) with sea views—rare in this city. While it fronts a dreary, busy street, all of its rooms face the quieter back side, and most have views over the harbor. You'll pay extra for a view and/or a balcony (includes good breakfast, air-con, elevator, small gym, whirlpool bath, parking, Kralja Zvonimira 6, tel. 021/314-444, www.hotelluxesplit.com, reservations@hotelluxesplit.com).

$$ Villa Ana has five spacious, comfortable rooms with hotelesque amenities in a smart little freestanding stone house (air-con, a few tight and free parking spots out front, Vrh Lučac 16, tel. 021/482-715, www.villaana-split.hr, info@villaana-split.hr, Danijel Bilobrk). As it's not visible from the main road, it's a little tricky to find (and its address often doesn't work on GPS): It's two long blocks east of the Old Town along busy Kralja Zvonimira. Look for the skinny, driveway-like lane opposite the lonely skyscraper.

¢ Sunrise & Sunset (a.k.a. Aspalathos Arka) are two nicely appointed, modern, simple rooms rented by Nada (who speaks just enough English) and her fluent daughter, Linda. They're tucked in a sleepy residential area just uphill from the main road, and a short walk from the Old Town (no breakfast but kitchenette, air-con, free parking, Omiška 3, mobile 098-957-8069, aspalathosarka@gmail.com).

West of the Old Town

This area includes the atmospheric, inviting, and steep Varoš neighborhood, with twisty lanes climbing up toward the forested peak of the Marjan peninsula. I've listed some well-established options here, but if you're booking your own accommodations (on Airbnb or Booking.com), this is a good area to focus on. It works especially well for nondrivers and those who don't mind a steep hike. Varoš also has a few recommended eateries and the self-service Modrulj Launderette.

$$ Lanterna City Rooms hides in a little alley behind the National (HNK) Theater. With a small patio and five cozy, stone-walled rooms, it's a convenient choice to be close to the action but away from the palace area (breakfast extra, air-con, Ujevićeva poljana 13, mobile 098-954-8013, www.lanternarooms.com, booking@lanternarooms.com).

$ Villa Varoš, run with class by Croatian-American Gregory, has seven rooms and two apartments (with private terraces) on a residential lane just beyond the restaurant-lined Šperun street.

Thin walls and echoey halls can make for a noisy night (no breakfast, air-con, stairs with no elevator, loaner bikes, Miljenka Smoje 1, tel. 021/483-469, mobile 099-215-9538, www.villavaros.hr).

¢ **Hostel Dvor** is classier than your average hostel, with a stylish, white-mod aesthetic and a tranquil atmosphere. It has three private rooms, and even the dorms come with their own en-suite bathrooms (no breakfast, air-con, Radmilovićeva 71, tel. 021/785-908, www.hosteldvor.com, hosteldvor@gmail.com).

Eating in Split

Split's restaurant scene has transformed in recent years, as more and more visitors have driven up quality and variety. Besides a few trendy options, I've included some reliable old standbys. I've concentrated my listings inside Split's Old Town and within the adjacent Varoš district, just a couple of blocks west. Reservations are wise, especially for dinner.

IN AND NEAR THE OLD TOWN
$$ Villa Spiza is a popular, well-run little restaurant serving local cooking from a handwritten menu. It feels fresh, youthful, and energetic, with a very tight interior under beams and only counter seating, plus a couple of sidewalk tables. As they don't accept reservations and are justifiably popular, come at a slow time or plan to wait (daily 12:00-24:00, Petra Kružića 3, mobile 091-152-1249).

$$$ Uje Oilbar is the flagship restaurant of Croatia's popular chain of upscale olive-oil boutiques. Tucked away in a hidden corner of the Old Town, it serves simple plates and boards of Dalmatian *pršut* (prosciutto), cheeses, olives, and, of course, olive oils—50 different types. You can either assemble a filling meal out of a variety of these nibbles, or order a main course—either way, the bill adds up. But the rustic-mod interior, pleasant outdoor seating, and refreshingly good-quality local flavors can make for a memorable meal (also olive-oil tastings, daily 12:00-24:00, Dominisova 3, mobile 095-200-8008, www.oilbar.hr).

$$$$ Bokeria is Split's trendiest foodie hotspot. The bright, spacious, modern bistro atmosphere—with a wall of Aperol bottles and ham hocks hanging over the bar—feels closer to Barcelona than to Split. But the beautifully presented cuisine is a smart melding of Croatian classics with international technique, and the wine list is long. It's a bit too popular for its own good, and the service can be uneven, but it satisfies those looking for a change of pace from traditional *konoba*s. Reserve ahead (daily 9:00-24:00, Domaldova 8, tel. 021/355-577).

$$$$ Bajamonti is the best of the eateries on the beautiful, arcaded square Trg Republike, just off the west end of the Riva. This place has a certain grand-café class, with a checkerboard-tiled, split-level interior—but the best seating is on the square out front, facing the sea. The price sometimes exceeds the quality, but the outside setting is worth the extra kunas (daily 7:30-24:00, Trg Republike 1, tel. 021/341-033, www.restoran-bajamonti.hr).

$$$ Bepa is simple but stylish, and probably the best-value dining option with outdoor tables on the glorious People's Square. Their menu is brief but eclectic—burgers, pastas, big salads, main courses—and it's family-friendly (daily 8:00-24:00, Narodni Trg 1, tel. 021/355-546, www.bepa.hr).

Pizzerias: At the west end of the Old Town, **$$ Ristorante Pizzeria Galija** has a boisterous local following and good wood-fired pizzas, pastas, and salads. They have a woody interior and a terrace (daily 10:00-24:00, air-con, just a block off Marmontova at Tončićeva 12, tel. 021/347-932). For takeaway, you'll see uninspired "pizza cut" (by the slice) windows all over town. For reliably good quality and some interesting options, look for **$ Fast Food None** ("Grandma's"). In addition to pizzas and bruschetta with various toppings, ask if they have a pair of local, pizza-like specialties (with crust on bottom and top, like a filled pizza): *viška pogača*, with tomatoes, onion, and anchovy; and *soparnik*, with a thin layer of spinach, onion, and olive oil. They can also make you a grilled sandwich—just point to what you want (daily 7:00-23:00, just outside Diocletian's Palace on the skinny street that runs along the wall at Bosanska 4, tel. 021/343-067).

Takeaway Grilled Meats: Find perhaps the best budget meal in Split at **$ Kantun Paulina** (Paulina's Corner), a local favorite for takeaway *ćevapčići*—Balkan grilled meats. Everything's fresh, from the *lepinja* flatbread to the meat itself. This is a great place to try this favorite Balkan street food (Mon-Sat 8:30-24:00, Sun from 10:30, Matošića 1). For descriptions of your options, see the "Balkan Flavors" sidebar on page 425.

High-End Coffee: Coffee snobs seeking something a notch above the standard *bijela kava* enjoy a pair of gourmet coffee shops: **D16 Specialty Coffee** (daily 7:00-22:00, Dominisova 16) and **4Coffee Soul Food** (Mon-Fri 7:00-15:00, Sat until 18:00, Sun until 12:00, Hrvojeva 9).

Gelato and Other Sweets: The Old Town teems with interchangeable, uninspired places serving bland ice cream. For something better, venture a couple of minutes north to **Luka,** which

SPLIT

attracts locals with homemade quality and more interesting flavors, such as lavender or rosemary (daily 8:30-24:00, Svačićeva 2; to find it, see "More Options Behind the Theater," below). Nearby, tucked up a lane left of the modern Prima shopping center, is the genteel little shop called **O'š Kolač**—with a delectable variety of top-end cakes (Mon-Sat 8:00-22:00, closed Sun, Ćiril-Metodova 4, tel. 021/480-444). Locals also give the thumbs-up to the ice cream at **Don Dino,** on the pedestrian drag of Marmontova (daily 8:00-24:00, corner of Marmontova and Tončićeva).

More Options Behind the Theater: To leave most of the tourists (and charm) behind, head up to the top of Marmontova pedestrian boulevard and keep going. In the big square, poke up the little covered lane between the yellow National (HNK) Theater and the blocky modern church. You'll pop out in a refreshingly modern, urban zone. The excellent **Luka** gelato and pastry shop (described above) is on your right, and more locals-oriented cafés, bars, "pizza cut" windows, and other eateries are just beyond. Across the square from Luka and left up the street, look for **Stari Plac** (with dessert crêpes); a bit farther up that same street is **$$ Sexy Cow,** where you can order from a tempting menu of decadent top-end hamburgers and wraps (daily 11:00-24:00, Zrinsko Frankopanska 6, tel. 021/780-782).

Also behind the theater is **$$$ Cucina Mare,** a friendly foodie restaurant whose calm patio feels a world away from the bustle of the Old Town. The small menu offers a well-prepared selection of seasonal fish, meat, and vegetarian dishes. You can also order from the menu of their bistro next door, **$$ Ćiri Biri Bela,** with a delectable array of charcuterie plates, fresh juices, and *tartes flambées* (like thin-crust pizzas). They organize Dalmatian cooking classes as well (restaurant daily 18:00-24:00, bistro daily 7:30-14:30, Plinarska ulica 6, tel. 021/209-158, www.cucina-mare.com).

IN VAROŠ, WEST OF THE OLD TOWN

$$ Konoba Fetivi is the locals' choice for unpretentious, quality local food at fair prices just around the corner from several touristy eateries. You can sit in the cozy, air-conditioned interior, or in the larger inner courtyard (daily 12:00-23:00, Tomića Stine 4, tel. 021/355-152).

$$$ Šperun Restaurant has a cozy, Old World ambience and a passion for good Dalmatian food. Owner Damir Banović (with the help of his animated dad, Zdravko) serves a mix of Croatian and eclectic Mediterranean fare, specializing in seafood. A modest table of *antipasti* (starters) in the lower dining room shows you what you're getting, so you can select your ideal meal (not self-service—order from the waiter). This place is known for its warm

SPLIT

welcome and reasonable prices (daily 9:00-23:00—but likely closed Sun Nov-March, air-con, a few sidewalk tables, reservations wise in summer, Šperun 3, tel. 021/346-999).

Wine Bar: Sleek and sophisticated but not pretentious, **$$$ Paradox Wine & Cheese Bar** offers an inviting opportunity to sample some local wines, perhaps on the inviting rooftop terrace. Their well-structured menu lists more than a hundred wines, half of which are available by the glass. They also have a menu of local cheeses, meats, and other accompaniments, which can add up to a light meal (daily 16:00-24:00, Bana Jelačića 3, tel. 021/787-778).

Split Connections

BY BOAT

Split is the transport hub for the Dalmatian Coast, with boats fanning out to nearly anywhere you want to go. You'll find a color map of the Dalmatian coast near the front of this book. Routes and schedules can change, so confirm anything listed here before you make your plans.

Boat Companies: Two major companies run routes from Split. **Jadrolinija,** the national ferry company, runs all car ferries and some high-speed passenger catamarans (tel. 021/338-333, www.jadrolinija.hr). Their most convenient ticket office is at the corner of the harbor, near the entrance to Diocletian's Palace (daily 6:00-20:30). They also have a ticket kiosk at the pier called Gat Sv. Petra, halfway along the harbor, and their main office is in the large terminal building at the far end of the port (open 24/7). **Krilo,** a privately run competitor, also operates catamarans. Krilo's lone ticket office is at the pier called Gat Sv. Petra (window marked *Kapetan Luka;* daily 6:00-20:00, tel. 021/645-476, www.krilo.hr).

Finding Your Boat: The **Krilo catamarans** usually dock at berth #9 (on the pier called Gat Sv. Petra), which is across from the train station, halfway between the main ferry terminal and the Old Town. The **Jadrolinija catamarans** usually use berth #6 at the handy Obala Lazareta embankment just in front of the Old Town (although it may sometimes use berth #9 on Gat Sv. Petra instead—ask on the day of the departure about the vessel name and embarkation point). On the catamarans, boarding typically begins 30 minutes before departure; arrive early in peak season to snare a window seat and to find a place to stow your bag. Big **car ferries**

can arrive or depart from all along the harbor (electronic boards display which dock each boat leaves from).

Fares: Walk-on passage for both catamarans and ferries is affordable. The passenger fare on a trip from Split to Hvar or Korčula costs around 55-110 kn, depending on the type of boat and season. (For a car, figure 380-570 kn for a similar trip.)

Buying Tickets: If you want to take a **fast passenger catamaran** (either Krilo or Jadrolinija), buy your tickets in advance. Tickets sell out quickly in peak season; to avoid disappointment, book at least a day or two in advance (or even further ahead on summer weekends). The first departures of the day—ideal for day-trippers—tend to sell out the fastest, and weekends are the busiest days. Both companies have user-friendly booking websites; you'll be emailed an eticket—just show your phone to the ticket-taker as you board. Note: Jadrolinija tickets cannot be purchased online for same-day departures. These go on sale at 6:00 on the morning of departure, in person only at their various sales offices (see "Boat Companies," earlier).

If catamaran tickets do sell out, slower Jadrolinija **car ferries** ply each route with unlimited room for walk-on passengers. However, this is a less-than-ideal alternative, since car ferries drop you off at ports that are not convenient to the main town on each island (Stari Grad on Hvar, Vela Luka on Korčula), which means an additional bus trip to your final destination. The ticket seller can advise you on alternatives.

Weather Disruptions: Catamarans are the quickest way to the islands, but they're also the most susceptible to inclement weather. In very rough or windy weather, cancellations are possible (decisions are made a couple of hours before departure—ask at the ticket booth what time you should come back to check). In questionable weather, the Krilo is more stable (and provides a more comfortable ride) than Jadrolinija's catamarans; if you have a choice, go with Krilo. If the catamarans aren't running, the slower car ferries go in virtually any weather.

Car Ferry Notes: If you're driving onto a car ferry, it's smart to line up early—ask locally for advice on your particular boat. Unfortunately, there are currently no inter-island connections for cars (for example, from Hvar to Korčula); you'll either have to go back through Split, or take a ferry to the mainland and connect from there, taking another ferry to get to your next island. Jadrolinija has discussed plans to resume the coastal car ferry route 101, which would conveniently connect cities and islands along the coast (Rijeka-Split-Hvar-Korčula-Mljet-Dubrovnik). There are also plans to introduce a reservation system, which would reduce the need to queue; see the company's website (www.jadrolinija.hr) for updates on both of these possibilities.

Sailing Between Croatia and Italy

While adding a dash of Italy to your Croatian vacation is a romantic notion, it can be more complicated than it sounds. Most sea crossings are overnight, and the Italian towns best connected to Croatia—Ancona, Pescara, and Bari—are each a lengthy train ride away from Italy's top sights.

Split is the primary hub for boats to Italy, but there are sometimes also connections from Dubrovnik or Zadar. (Note that in Italian, Split is called "Spalato"—which is also the sound you hear if seasickness gets the best of you.) Almost all boats go to Ancona, Italy, which is on the calf of Italy's "boot." Others go to Pescara, about 100 miles south of Ancona (the "cankle"), and to Bari, near the southeastern tip of Italy (the "heel"). Most trips are overnight and last 8-10 hours; faster daytime catamarans run sporadically. Note that these connections are highly subject to change; do an Internet search to be confident you know all your options.

Slow Night Boats: The lineup of companies that operate night boats to Italy changes from year to year. The most reliable companies are the Italian-based **SNAV** (www.snav.it) and the Croatian national ferry company, **Jadrolinija** (www. jadrolinija.hr). Figure about €40-60 per person for one-way deck passage (about 10-20 percent more in July-Aug, sometimes even more on weekends). Onboard accommodation costs extra (about €40 per person for a couchette in a 4-berth compartment, €60-75 per person in 2-bed compartment with private shower and WC, up to €100 per person in a seaview double).

Trains Within Italy: From **Ancona,** trains zip to Florence (3 hours, change in Bologna), Venice (4 hours, change in Bologna), and Rome (4 hours). From **Pescara,** it's about 4.5 hours to either Rome (direct) or Florence (via Bologna). And from **Bari,** you can hop a train to Naples (4 hours, most transfer in Caserta), Rome (4 hours direct), or Florence (7 hours, most transfer in Bologna). For timetables, check www.trenitalia. com or www.bahn.com.

Northern Italy/Croatia: If you're heading to Istria (in northern Croatia), you may find it's easier to side-trip from there to Venice than it is to head across the Adriatic from Dalmatia. Venice is connected by boat to several seaside towns in northern Croatia and Slovenia. For details, see page 97.

Getting from Split to Dalmatian Destinations

I've roughly explained your options next, but the details change from year to year. The only way to know for sure what works for your trip is to search for your preferred journey on *both* websites: Krilo.hr and Jadrolinija.hr.

To Hvar Island: Note that Hvar Island has two commonly used ports; you want simply "Hvar" (that is, Hvar town), rather than "Stari Grad." Catamarans zip from Split to Hvar town in about an hour, operated by **Jadrolinija** (6-8/day June-Sept, 2/day off-season) and **Krilo** (6/day June-Sept, 3-4/day spring and fall, 1/day off-season). Alternatively, you can reach Hvar Island on a **local car ferry** from Split (7/day in summer, 4/day in winter, operated by Jadrolinija). These car ferries are frequent but take twice as long (2 hours) and are less convenient, since they take you to the town of Stari Grad. From Stari Grad, it's a 20-minute bus ride across the island to Hvar town (public buses generally meet most arriving ferries).

To Korčula Island: As with Hvar, it's important to pay attention to which port on Korčula Island your boat uses: "Korčula" (that is, Korčula town) is far more convenient than "Vela Luka," at the opposite end of the island (a 1-hour bus ride away). To reach Korčula town from Split (about 2.5 hours), the most convenient options are the direct **catamarans** (Krilo usually departs in the morning, 3-4/day May-Oct, 1/day off-season in the afternoon; Jadrolinija usually departs in the afternoon, 1/day June-Sept only). If you're desperate, additional boats head to Vela Luka, including a different Jadrolinija catamaran (generally 1/day, 2 hours) or Jadrolinija's slower **local car ferries** (2/day, 2-3 hours).

To Dubrovnik and Mljet National Park: Krilo runs catamarans each morning, which stop at Hvar and/or Korčula en route (1-2/day early April-late Oct, 4.5 hours to Dubrovnik); one of these also stops at Pomena, handy for Mljet National Park (3 hours). Jadrolinija also offers a catamaran to Dubrovnik (via Hvar and Korčula), but it does not stop at Mljet (runs each afternoon June-Sept, 5 hours).

Uber Boats

Uber has been pilot-testing a program where users can summon a local boat for a private transfer between Dalmatian destinations. It's very pricey—far more expensive than a public boat. But if you have deep pockets, open your Uber app and see what's available.

BY BUS

Each of the following routes is served by multiple companies. Always ask about the fastest option. As with boats, popular buses can sell out in the busy summer months (particularly on weekends);

it's smart to book a day or two ahead. Either stop by the bus station in Split, or book online—many journeys can be purchased at GetByBus.com (they add a 5 percent service fee). The generally English-speaking staff at Split's bus station gives out handy little schedules for popular journeys. Bus info: tel. 021/329-180, ak-split. hr.

By Bus to: Zagreb (at least hourly, 5-8 hours depending on route), **Dubrovnik** (at least hourly, less off-season, 4.5 hours), **Korčula** (1 night bus leaves at 1:00 in the morning and arrives around 7:00), **Trogir** (1-2/hour, virtually any bus bound for Šibenik can stop at Trogir, 30 minutes), **Zadar** (at least hourly, 3 hours), **Mostar** (8/day, 4 hours), **Međugorje** (4/day, 3 hours), **Sarajevo** (5/day, 7.5-8 hours), **Rijeka** (8/day, 7 hours). Zagreb-bound buses sometimes also stop at **Plitvice** (confirm with driver and ask to stop at the national park entrance; about 7/day in summer, 4-6 hours; the best are the direct 4-hour connections with Prijevoz Knežević, described on page 90—check schedules and book ahead at https:// knezevic.getbybus.com; otherwise 4/day in winter, 4-6 hours).

BY TRAIN
From Split, trains go to **Zagreb** (2-4/day, 6 hours; 1 direct night train, 8 hours); in Zagreb, you can transfer to **Ljubljana** (4/day, 9 hours total). Train info: tel. 021/338-525, www.hzpp.hr.

ROUTE TIPS FOR DRIVERS
Driving in the city center can be challenging. Split is split by its Old Town, which is welded to the harbor by the pedestrian-only Riva promenade. This means drivers needing to get 300 yards from one side of the historic core to the other must drive 15 minutes around the center, which can be clogged with traffic. A semicircular ring road and a tunnel under the Marjan peninsula help relieve the situation a bit. If you are driving to the ferry, be warned that traffic in the port can hit a standstill; allow plenty of time to reach your designated ferry queue.

Arriving in Split: Drivers are treated to the ugly side of Split as they approach town (don't worry—it gets better). From the expressway, you'll pass through an industrial zone, then curl through a few tunnels as you twist your way down into Split's striking, bowl-like setting. As you approach downtown on ulica Domovinskog Rata—just before you reach the outermost part of the city wall—you'll come to a fork where you'll have to make a decision about which side of town you want to drive to (east or west); ask your hotel in advance for directions, and be ready for your turn. (While many hotels are individually signposted at the fork, it's a long list and hard to read quickly as you zip past.)

At the main fork, turning to the right (marked with *Centar* signs) takes you along Sinjska street to the **west end** of the Old Town, including the Varoš neighborhood. Or, if you continue straight (marked *Trajekt*—ferry) on Zagrebačka street, you'll eventually reach other *Centar* signs and the **east end** of the Old Town, with the ferry terminal, the bus and train stations, and the Lučac neighborhood. You'll pop out right at the southeast corner of Diocletian's Palace (by the Green Market). For handy but expensive parking, when the road swings left to the ferry terminal, bear right into a pricey little parking lot just outside the palace walls. I'd park here only to unload and find my hotel, then ask about cheaper long-term parking elsewhere.

Connecting Split with Destinations to the North: Thanks to Croatia's A-1 super-expressway, the road trip from Zagreb to Split takes less than five hours. Simply drive up out of the city's bowl-like setting and follow signs to the A-1 expressway north (toward Zagreb; if you're going to Plitvice, get off at Otočac and drive east from there).

Connecting Split with Destinations to the South: If you're heading to Dubrovnik, other Dalmatian Coast destinations, or Mostar, you have two options: the scenic coastal road or the speedy A-1 expressway.

The main **coastal road** twists slowly but scenically along some fantastic scenery, in an area dubbed the "Makarska Riviera." (Along this road is the town of Drvenik, where you can take a ferry to Sućuraj on Hvar Island; from Sućuraj, a long and twisty road traverses the length of the island to Hvar town. If you're going to Hvar Island, taking a car ferry directly from Split to Stari Grad is much faster.) Continuing south, you'll wind up in the town of Ploče.

To save some time, most travelers prefer to take the **expressway** part of the way. To do this, as you leave Split, follow blue expressway signs to *Dubrovnik*. You'll take A-1 south as it cuts inland from the sea, running behind the tall coastal mountain range, near the Bosnian border, all the way to the city of Ploče. (If you're headed to Mostar, stay on the expressway and cross the border at Nova Sela, then follow signs to *Mostar* from there.)

Ploče has an infrequent ferry that runs to the town of Trpanj, on the landward side of the Pelješac peninsula—not far from Orebić, where another boat plods across to Korčula town. If you're headed to Korčula and plan your timing to catch this ferry, it could save you some driving.

Ploče is also where the A-1 expressway ends. Here you'll transfer to slower surface roads the rest of the way to Dubrovnik. Just south of Ploče is the dramatic Neretva River Delta, a scenic and lush zone of farmland. Halfway along the delta, you'll see the

turnoff to Metković, the gateway town on the main, heavily tour
isted road between Croatia and Mostar.

South of the Neretva River Delta—after twisting up to a high
perch overlooking the delta—is a border crossing. Here begins an
odd little stretch of coastline that's technically in Bosnia, around
the town of Neum (for details on Neum—and the bridge under
construction to bypass it—see sidebar on page 360). Have your
passport ready; the border can be a quick wave-through, but at busy
times you may have to wait. After a few miles in Neum, you'll cross
back into Croatia, and shortly come to a crossroads where, if you
like, you can turn right and detour a few minutes to the impressively walled little villages of Ston and Mali Ston, at the base of the
Pelješac peninsula. If you're headed to Korčula, continue beyond
Ston to the far end of the Pelješac peninsula, where the ferry put-
ters from Orebić to Dominče, near Korčula town.

After Ston, you're less than an hour from Dubrovnik. Along
the way, you'll have fine views of Mljet and the Elaphite Islands.
As you near Dubrovnik, you'll pass through the town of Trsteno,
which has a good arboretum. When you cross the giant, modern
bridge, you'll know Dubrovnik is just around the bend; for arrival
tips, see page 281.

Near Split

Two destinations are easy, worthwhile side trips from Split: the
small town of Trogir, and farther north, the swimmable waterfalls
at Krka National Park.

Trogir

Just 12 miles northwest of Split, across
a giant bay, is Trogir, a tiny, medieval-
architecture-packed town surrounded by
water. This made-for-tourists village is
appealing, though it lacks the real-world
heart and soul of Split. Trogir is popular with yachters; the proud masts of tall
ships line the harbor three deep. Although
Trogir is nothing to jump ship for, it's an
easy day trip for those looking to get away
from urban Split.

GETTING THERE

The easiest option in summer is to take the **Bura Line boat,** which avoids traffic and includes a fun Adriatic minicruise. The boat departs Split from the end of the little pier directly in front of the Riva (34 kn one-way, 4/day mid-May–mid-Oct only, 1 hour, stops at Čiovo Island en route, www.buraline.com).

Alternatively, you can take the **bus** (around 25 kn one-way, 30 minutes). Your best bet is to head to Split's main bus station (along the harbor) and hop on a northbound bus (for example, to Šibenik, Zadar, or Rijeka—just go to the ticket window and ask for the next bus that stops at Trogir). Be warned that this doesn't always work perfectly: Occasionally these buses show up already full, and during the busiest summer months, long-distance bus drivers may prefer to sell your seat to someone paying for a longer trip. If you're desperate, it's possible to take local bus #37, but I wouldn't—you have to catch it at the inconveniently located suburban bus station, a boring 10-minute walk north of the Old Town, and its frequent stops between there and Trogir mean it's a very long journey (at least an hour).

Drivers find Trogir an easy stopover. There's a handy pay parking lot on the left just before Trogir; you can walk into town in five minutes (pass the bus station and cross the bridge).

Orientation to Trogir

Trogir is a small island wedged between the mainland and the much bigger Čiovo Island. Busy bridges connect it to the rest of the world at its east end, and a big soccer field squeezed between imposing watchtowers anchors the west end. In the middle is a tight medieval maze of twisty marble-stone lanes.

Tourist Information: At the main square, named for Pope John Paul II (Trg Ivana Pavla II), you'll find the TI (open long hours daily except closed Sun off-season, tel. 021/885-628).

Arrival in Trogir: Buses drop you off at the mainland market, just across the canal from the island. Cross the bridge into town and wander straight ahead for two blocks (bearing left); you'll run into the main square.

Sights in Trogir

On the main square is the town's centerpiece, the **Cathedral of St. Lawrence** (Katedrala Sv. Lovre). Built from the 13th through the 17th century, the cathedral drips with history. The bell tower alone took 200 years to build, leaving it a textbook lesson in Dalmatian architectural styles: straightforward Gothic at the bottom, Venetian Gothic in the middle, and Renaissance at the top. The ca-

thedral's front entryway—the ornately decorated, recently restored
Radovan's Portal—is worth a gander. Inside, it's dark, very old-
feeling, and packed with altars. The treasury features some beautiful 15th-century carved-wood cabinets filled with ecclesiastical art
and gear.

The town's other sights are the **Town Museum** (Muzej
Grada), a few blocks north (toward the mainland) from the main
square; and the **Monastery of St. Nikola** (Samostan Sv. Nikole), a
few blocks south (toward Čiovo Island).

But Trogir isn't for museum going; it's for aimless strolling.
And the best place for that is the wide, beautifully manicured **harborfront promenade** along the southern edge of town (Obala bana
Berislavića). Lined with expensive restaurants, and clogged with
giddy, ice-cream-licking tourists, this promenade is the highlight
of a visit to Trogir. Often the enormous yachts of the rich and famous stern-tie into the good life here, giving wanderers something
to gaze at and yak about. At the far end of the promenade, the
Kamerlengo Fortress has a lookout tower with fine views over the
town and region.

Sleeping in Trogir

Some travelers prefer sleepy Trogir to bustling Split. It's also
very close to the Split airport. Here are some good options:
$$$ Hotel Pašike is a family-run boutique hotel with 13 rooms,
lots of character, and over-the-top traditional formality (Splitska
4, tel. 021/885-185, mobile 091-484-8434, www.hotelpasike.com,
Buble family). **$$ Hotel Concordia,** with 11 outmoded-but-tidy,
slightly overpriced rooms at the end of the embankment, is run
with warmth by the Bulum family (Obala bana Berislavića 22, tel.
021/885-400, www.concordia-hotel.net). **$ Palaća Stafileo** has
six apartments in a 15th-century Venetian palace buried in a quiet
part of town (Subićeva 7a, tel. 021/885-680, mobile 098-131-3171,
www.trogironline.com/stafileo).

Krka National Park

While Plitvice has Croatia's best
waterfalls, they're not the only option. An hour north of Split, an
easy detour off the expressway, is
the glittering canyon of Krka National Park. This sprawling park—
where the Krka (pronounced
KUR-kah) River spreads out and
splits into many fingers cut deep

into the parched limestone, with shimmering blue waters and forested bluffs—could occupy a nature lover for days. But its claim to fame is easy to reach and enjoy in just a few hours: the multitiered Skradinski Buk waterfall. While not as magical or as expansive as Plitvice's cascades, Skradinski Buk is bigger (a single grand run, rather than sprinkled throughout a canyon)—and, crucially, at Skradinski Buk, swimmers are allowed to dive into its lowest pool (June-Sept only). If you could barely resist the urge to jump into the ponds at Plitvice, this is your chance. (Note: Because the footing is uneven and the services for swimmers are basically nonexistent, I'd recommend this only for hardy paddlers who enjoy a good, rugged swimmin' hole.)

Cost and Hours: The ticket price changes by season—200 kn in June-Sept (or 150 kn after 16:00), 100 kn in April-May and Oct, 30 kn in Nov-March—and includes the boat from Skradin to Skradinski Buk and the shuttle bus from Lozovac to Skradinski Buk, but not boats or shuttle buses to other parts of the park. The park is open daily 8:00-20:00, May and Sept until 19:00, April and early Oct until 18:00, shorter hours off-season. The last boat from Skradinski Buk back to Skradin departs 30 minutes before closing time.

Information: Tel. 022/771-688, www.npkrka.hr.

Crowd-Beating Tips: In high season (especially July-Aug), crowds can be a problem. If you anticipate crowds, it's best to visit the park either first thing in the morning or in the late afternoon, after most of the day-trippers have left. It's also possible to book tickets online before your visit, to avoid ticket-buying lines.

Getting There: By **car,** it's easy—about an hour north of Split, just off the expressway (see exit information for both major park entrances below). By **public transportation,** the easiest option is to take the direct bus from Split to Skradin, where you can buy your park ticket and hop on the boat to Lozovac and the waterfalls (5-6/day in summer, first departure around 8:00, 1.5 hours; you can ride the boat back to return on this same bus, or you can take the bus from Lozovac to Šibenik and return to Split from there). The other option is to first take the bus from Split to the city of Šibenik; from there, buses go to both the Skradin entrance (for the boat trip) and the Lozovac entrance (closer to the waterfalls). Check the specifics for any of these connections locally (at the Split TI or bus station). Alternatively, consider paying for an **excursion** from Split (or other cities in Dalmatia), which includes door-to-door transportation and the park entrance fee; this often doesn't cost much more than doing it on your own, but you'll have to stick to a set itinerary.

Visiting the National Park: The national park sprawls over 42 square miles, with five entrances; assuming your interest is the Skradinski Buk waterfall, you can ignore all but two of them. The most efficient entrance is the **Lozovac entrance** (Šibenik exit from A-1 expressway, then a seven-mile, 15-minute drive). Here you'll find a large and free parking lot, and you can take a shuttle bus straight down to the waterfall area (leaves every 15 minutes or so, 10-minute ride on a very twisty and steep road). If you have more time and would prefer to approach the falls by boat, you can use the **Skradin entrance** (Skradin exit from A-1, then a three-mile drive). From the glassy Skradin visitors center, you can hop on an hourly boat for the 20-minute trip to Skradinski Buk (included in your park ticket; boats depart every 2 hours off-season, Oct-April).

Due to increased crowds in recent years, visitors must follow a one-way route through the Skradinski Buk area. If coming by boat, you're not allowed to head straight for the waterfalls—you're required to first hike steeply up to the top of the complex, at the Ethno Village, then loop back down around to the waterfalls. If coming from the Lozovac parking lot, the shuttle bus drops you off near the Ethno Village.

At the **Ethno Village** area (with a few houses displaying traditional lifestyles) is a large terrace with free WCs and grand views down over the falls. From here, a roughly circular, 1.5-mile **waterfall boardwalk** path takes you up, down, and around the various cascades, through forests, over gurgling streams, and to a variety of thrilling viewpoints. Near the bottom of the falls—close to the boat dock from Skradin—is a pay WC popular with swimmers, a large outdoor eating area (mostly table-service restaurants and a few snack stands), and the bridge that cuts across the pool at the bottom of the falls. From this bridge, you'll spot people enjoying the park's most popular activity: swimming near the falls.

Swimmers are allowed only in this one, large pool at the bottom of the final cascade (and only June-Sept—it's strictly forbidden Oct-May). While swimming is permitted, it's not exactly encouraged; there are no lifeguards, no real beach, no showers, and no official changing rooms (you have several options: wear your swimsuit to the park; pay a small fee to change in the cramped WC 100 yards away from the pool; awkwardly change into your suit under a towel...or do as many Europeans do, and just skip the towel). When you're ready to get in, make your way across the uneven, root-embedded ground and find a place to gingerly slip in. The water can be chilly, and you'll smell the fishy aroma from the pounding spray, but it's generally clean. As you wade into the pool, watch your footing—the same travertine dams that create those grand waterfalls can be very treacherous to walk on, with dramatically uneven surfaces, occasional sharp edges, and slippery moss. Once you've tiptoed past the initial rocky gauntlet, you can plunge into the deeper section—noticing that the closer you get to the falls, the stronger the current pushes you back.

SPLIT

Other Excursions in the Park: Aside from hiking and swimming, another popular attraction at Krka is its variety of excursions by boat or minibus to farther-flung parts of the park. These excursions are not covered by the entrance ticket. Options include a two-hour cruise to **Visovac Island,** with its picturesque Franciscan monastery; a 3.5-hour cruise to **Visovac Island and Roški Slap** (another, less striking waterfall where you can swim); and a 2.5-hour trip to the **Krka Monastery** and ruins of two fortresses. Other excursions take you to the ancient Roman ruins (amphitheater and military camp) at **Burnum.**

HVAR

Hvar's hip cachet, ritzy "Croatian Riviera" buzz, and easy proximity to Split have turned this tidy Dalmatian fishing village into one of the most popular destinations in the country. The island has, for better or for worse, been transformed into Croatia's answer to Mykonos, Ibiza, or St-Tropez. While the infrastructure still lags behind, the rows of yachts tied up five-deep in the harbor—and the steady string of jet-set twentysomethings dressing up for a night on the town—don't seem to notice. Budget travelers may be stymied by Hvar's pervasive "quality is worth paying for" mantra. But the setting is undeniably gorgeous, and the island provides a cosmopolitan contrast to its humbler rival, Korčula.

Hvar's straightforward main town, also called Hvar, melts into the harbor rather than dominating it. Its quirky museums are enjoyable. The formidable fortress hovering above town provides restless beach bums with a good excuse for a hike—and rewards hikers with stunning views.

Happening Hvar becomes a rollicking party town after hours. In jam-packed August, the entire town seems to be hopping to the same thumpa-thumpa beat...much to the aggravation of those looking for a sleepy island getaway. Hvar has become popular for celebrity-spotting—from Beyoncé, Tom Cruise, and Bill Gates to Giorgio Armani, Ellen DeGeneres, and Britain's Prince Harry. Islanders brag that their laid-back attitude is perfect for high-profile visitors who just want to be left alone.

Despite Hvar's newfound fame, it has plenty of history. Its tongue-twisting name comes from the ancient Greek settlement here: Pharos. Greeks from the island of Paros migrated here in the fourth century BC, attracted by the fertile farmland. Since then, it's been occupied by Slavs, Venetians, Habsburgs, and—today—tourists, all of whom have left their mark.

But Hvar town is just the beginning. Hvar Island—which insists it's both the sunniest and greenest in Dalmatia—entertains those who stay here long enough to do some exploring. Known for its excellent wines (grapes love the island's perfect combination of wind and sunshine), stony terraces, and fragrant lavender fields, Hvar Island's gentle climate is appreciated by tourists and farmers alike. The small archipelago called the Pakleni Islands, just offshore, rounds out Hvar's appeal.

PLANNING YOUR TIME

Don't overdose on Dalmatian islands. On a quick visit, overnighting on one island is enough—choose either Hvar or Korčula, and give it at least two nights and a full day. (If you're efficient, you can squeeze in a brief visit to Hvar on the way to Korčula.) On a longer, more relaxed vacation, sleep in both towns.

With a full day on Hvar, do your sightseeing—or hike to the fortress (with little shade)—in the morning, before the weather gets too hot and while the sights are open (many close for an afternoon siesta). Use the rest of the day to relax, swim at the beaches, explore the Old Town, or take a trip out to the Pakleni Islands (this excursion works well in the late afternoon—take a dip while it's still hot, then hike over to Vlaka for your dinner reservation at Dionis). The cool of the early evening is another good time to hike up to the fortress, which is an ideal vantage point for watching the sunset.

If time is short, well-connected Hvar is easy to see on the run (for example, a few hours en route between Split and Korčula—just keep in mind that many sights close at 12:00 or 13:00).

Be warned that July and especially August are peak-of-the-peak season. When you ask locals about crowds in August, they just roll their eyes and groan. It can be impossible to find a room, and the "undiscovered" back lanes and "hidden" offshore islands are jam-packed with loud, partying tourists. In summer, consider giving Hvar a miss. The ideal times for a visit—with the right balance of weather and crowds—are late May through the end of June, and mid-September through early October. Like other little coastal towns, it's shut tight in winter.

Orientation to Hvar

"Hvar" is pronounced almost like it's spelled, but the *H* is nearly silent. If you struggle with it, just say "far" (but don't say "huh-var," which just sounds silly to locals).

Hvar town (with about 3,600 residents) clusters around its

harbor. The harbor's eastern embankment (to the left, as you face the water) is where the big boats put in and is home to the boat ticket offices, most travel agencies and tourist services, and the post office. At the top of the harbor is Hvar's generous main square, St. Stephen's Square (Trg Svetog Stjepana). The Old Town scampers up the

hills in either direction from the square. Overlooking the town and harbor is a mighty hilltop fortress. Sprawling in both directions from the Old Town are nondescript residential zones packed with good-value apartment rentals, many with sensational sea views.

TOURIST INFORMATION

Hvar's TI is in the big Arsenal building right on the main square, a few steps from the harbor (mid-April-Oct daily 8:00-20:00; Nov-mid-April Mon-Fri until 15:00, Sat until 13:00, closed Sun; off-season hours can vary with demand; Trg Svetog Stjepana, tel. 021/741-059, www.tzhvar.hr).

ARRIVAL IN HVAR

If you're staying at a private room or apartment outside the Old Town, clearly communicate your arrival time to your host, and ask for directions. Some hosts may offer to come pick you up, but because only a few vehicles have permission to enter the Old Town area, most will meet you at the bus station (a scenic 5- to 10-minute stroll from the harbor, through the middle of the main square—see details next).

By Boat: Passenger boats to **Hvar town** arrive on the harbor's eastern embankment. Simply exit your boat and walk to the left along the water—you'll run right into St. Stephen's Square. Many *soba* hosts suggest meeting you at the town bus station. To find this from the boat dock, simply walk along the embankment to St. Stephen's Square, then walk all the way through the square and up the street to the left of the cathedral. You'll pop out at a little parking lot and your waiting host.

Car ferries to Hvar Island arrive just outside the town of **Stari Grad,** across the island from Hvar town. Buses are timed to meet arriving boats and take passengers over the island's picturesque spine to Hvar town (20 minutes, 27 kn; off-season, not every ferry is met by a bus—confirm).

By Bus: Hvar's bus station is just beyond the far end of St. Stephen's Square from the harbor. As you get off your bus, you can see the main tower of the cathedral—marking the town center, a two-minute walk away. The island's few taxis usually hang out at the bus station.

By Car: Car ferries arrive at the town of Stari Grad. There are two ways to drive from Stari Grad to Hvar town: the speedy, newer road via Dubovica (and a long tunnel) to the south; or the slower, windy road (through prettier, less-traveled terrain) via Brusje to the north. In Hvar, you can park by the bus station. Be warned that the car ferries can be crowded in summer—waiting two hours or more is not unusual.

A second ferry crossing is at the opposite tip of Hvar Island, connecting the island's settlement of Sućuraj to the mainland town of Drvenik. But the road connecting Sućuraj to Hvar town is long, twisty, and challenging to drive—most visitors prefer arriving and departing at Stari Grad instead. If you do need to drive from Hvar town to Sućuraj, give yourself about 1.5 hours, and add about an hour to get to the boat dock before everyone else making the same trip.

HELPFUL HINTS

Boat Tickets: Tickets for the fast catamarans to Split and Korčula Island (operated by Jadrolinija and Krilo) sell out quickly in peak season. Buy them a day or two ahead online, or stop by the ticket office in Hvar to book. For details, see "Hvar Connections," later.

Live Music: The **Hvar Summer Festival** fills the entire peak season (June-Sept) with frequent concerts, most of them hosted in the tranquil cloister of the Franciscan Monastery. Ask the TI for a Summer Festival program with the latest schedule. Other festivals include the **Lavender Fest,** which packs the little village of Velo Grablje with demonstrations and a general celebration of the traditional harvesting of the fragrant herb (last weekend in June).

Addresses: Everyone in Hvar ignores house numbers ("b.b." in an address means "without number") and even street names. Making things more complicated, the town recently renamed and renumbered many streets and addresses...so you now have twice as many ways to get lost. (Locals tend to ignore both the old and the new systems.) Navigate with maps—a good one is available free at the TI—and by asking for directions.

Laundry and Baggage Storage: A no-name, hole-in-the-wall outfit in the town center offers convenient but very expensive laundry, bag storage, and showers—handy if you're day-tripping here and want to swim in the sea. It hides beneath the market at the cathedral end of the main square (unpredictable hours, but generally daily June-Aug 7:00-23:00, May and Sept

Hvar Town

Mala Garška Bay

PODSTINE

PUT PODSTINE

⑫ ⑪

Blue Lagoon
Podstine Bay

ZASTUP

BISKUPA DUBOKOVIĆA

⑩

⑰

⑯

Majerovica Bay

⑤⓪

Adriatic Sea

TO Vira

TOWN WALLS

ŠETALIŠTE

ANTE

HANČEVIĆA

ŠETALIŠTE ANTE HANČEVIĆA

③

㉑

BENEDICTINE CONVENT

IVANIĆA

BOŽE

㉒

④

BUS STATION

P

VINKA PRIB.

②

⑬

①

㉘

PAPARAVA

㉖

GRODA

P. HEKTOR

Trg. Miličaćh

⑲

㉛ ⑳

㉜ ㉗

⑳

㉖

㉙

㉞

⑮

St. Stephen's Square

CATHEDRAL OF ST. STEPHEN

FABRIKA

Harbor

ARSENAL

ROIĆ DUŠKA

㉓

NOVAK JURA

㉕

BRAĆE BOŽITKOVIĆ

BUZOLIĆ ŠIME TOME

POST

BOAT LANDING

㉝

ROSSO

PAVAO

Cemetary

⑭

JADROLINIJA OFFICE

DINKA

ŠETALIŠTE — ŠIME BUZOLIĆ

㉔

KOVA.

⑦

PLICKOG USTANKA

100 Meters

100 Yards

HVAR

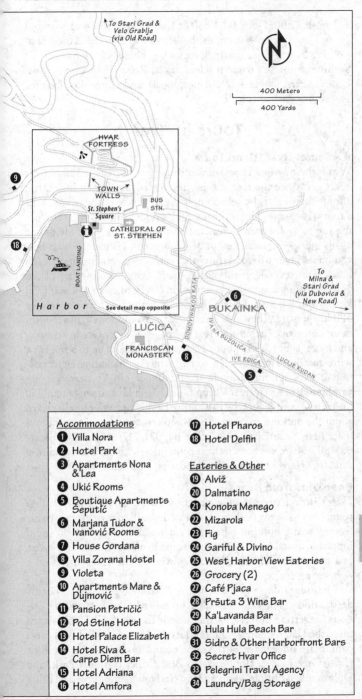

400 Meters
400 Yards

To Stari Grad &
Velo Grablje
(via Old Road)

HVAR FORTRESS

TOWN WALLS

St. Stephen's Square

BUS STN.

CATHEDRAL OF ST. STEPHEN

BOAT LANDING

Harbor   See detail map opposite

To Milna & Stari Grad (via Dubovica & New Road)

BUKAINKA

LUČICA

FRANCISCAN MONASTERY

DOMOVINSKOG RATA

VIA NA BUZOLIĆA

IVE ROICA

LUCIJE RUDAN

Accommodations
1. Villa Nora
2. Hotel Park
3. Apartments Nona & Lea
4. Ukić Rooms
5. Boutique Apartments Šeputić
6. Marjana Tudor & Ivanović Rooms
7. House Gordana
8. Villa Zorana Hostel
9. Violeta
10. Apartments Mare & Dujmović
11. Pansion Petričić
12. Pod Stine Hotel
13. Hotel Palace Elizabeth
14. Hotel Riva & Carpe Diem Bar
15. Hotel Adriana
16. Hotel Amfora
17. Hotel Pharos
18. Hotel Delfin

Eateries & Other
19. Alviž
20. Dalmatino
21. Konoba Menego
22. Mizarola
23. Fig
24. Gariful & Divino
25. West Harbor View Eateries
26. Grocery (2)
27. Café Pjaca
28. Pršuta 3 Wine Bar
29. Ka'Lavanda Bar
30. Hula Hula Beach Bar
31. Sidro & Other Harborfront Bars
32. Secret Hvar Office
33. Pelegrini Travel Agency
34. Laundry/Bag Storage

HVAR

until 21:00, Oct 8:00-13:30 & 16:00-19:00, shorter hours and no laundry off-season, to the left as you face the cathedral at Trg Svetog Stjepana 1—look for big, blue *toilet* sign).

Summer Fun: You name it, Hvar has it. Various agencies in town rent cars, scooters, bikes, motorboats, and more—just look for signs or ask at the TI.

Tours in Hvar

▲▲Secret Hvar Island Tours

While the town of Hvar is beautiful, most tourists without a car never get to see the rest of this stunning island. For an insightful, affordable peek at the refreshingly unglitzy side of the island, take a tour with Secret Hvar. Owner Siniša prides himself on introducing you to undiscovered corners that most tourists miss. He or one of his guides—guaranteed to be a long-term Hvaranin—can take you on a **"Hvar off-road tour"** that includes a *peka* lunch, a beach break, and several off-the-beaten-path sights, making use of old gravel farming roads that you wouldn't want to drive yourself (750 kn/person, 8 hours; 4-hour version skips the lunch and beach for 500 kn/person). They also offer a **"Hvar island tour"** that focuses more on towns, including Hvar town, Jelsa, Stari Grad, Vrboska, and more (about 2,500 kn for 1-3 people, tour lasts up to 5 hours); a **wine-tasting** trip with visits to two wineries, including eight tastings and enough finger food to call it dinner (600 kn/person for up to 4 hours); or a private **walking tour** around Hvar town (about 750 kn/up to 2 hours). Stop by their office below the Park Hotel to learn about the options, or contact Siniša to arrange a meeting time and place (Trg Sv. Stjepana 4A, office tel. 021/717-615, Siniša mobile 095-805-9075, www.secrethvar.com, info@secrethvar.com). Siniša can also arrange hiking, biking, boating, and other trips.

Boat Trips from Hvar

Hvar's little harbor is its connection to the world. The churning waters here swarm with boats big and small: luxury yachts, rustic fishing boats, hulking passenger catamarans, sporty RIBs (rigid inflatable boats) offering a quick escape to offshore islets and coves, and cut-rate tour boats that can slowly trundle 150 tourists on a sightseeing cruise.

Joining a day-trip excursion is a handy way to reach nearby destinations (generally available June-Oct). The best-selling options for getting off Hvar Island include the nearby Pakleni Islands (described later, under "Sights and Activities in Hvar"). Local companies also offer many of the same excursions as in Split: the Blue Cave, Green Cave, Bol beach on Brač, Mljet National Park, and Dubrovnik. Multiple companies around town offer these and other excursions, and salespeople along the embankment hawk various boat trips.

Sights and Activities in Hvar

IN AND NEAR THE OLD TOWN

▲▲St. Stephen's Square (Trg Svetog Stjepana)

Hvar's main square is a relaxed and relaxing people zone surrounded by inviting cafés filled with deliriously sunbaked tourists. For a quick tour, begin by the harbor and face the cathedral. Sit on the stone wall with your back to the water.

To your right is the **Arsenal** building (housing the TI)—a reminder of Hvar's nautical importance through history, thanks to its ideal location on the sailing route between Venice and the Mediterranean. During the town's seafaring heyday, ships were repaired and supplied in this huge building that still dominates the town. The beautiful barrel-vaulted space inside is used for special exhibits and private events. You can climb the stairs to the terrace atop the Arsenal for fine views over the square.

Many of Hvar's buildings date from the 16th and 17th centuries, when it was an important outpost of the Venetian Republic. During the Venetian period, the population was segregated: To the left of the square lived the well-to-do patricians, protected within the city wall (from the fortress, crenellated walls reach down to embrace this neighborhood—not quite visible from here). To the right, outside the wall, dwelled the humble plebeians—who worked hard and paid high taxes but had no say in government. In the 16th century, these two populations came to blows. The Venetians finally decided enough was enough and sent a moderator to restore peace. As a symbol of the reconciliation, part of the Arsenal building was converted into a **communal theater** (see below).

Looking left, the building with the arches and short tower is the **Loggia,** all that remains of a 15th-century palace for the rector (who ruled the island as a representative of Venice). This was the town's court of justice, and important decisions were announced from the stepped pillar in front (with the flagpole). This pillar also served as the town pillory, for publicly humiliating prisoners. During Habsburg control in the early 20th century, most of the palace was torn down to build the town's first resort hotel; today, the Palace Elisabeth Hotel still stands just behind the Loggia.

Now look behind you. Across the tiny, enclosed marina, a park fills a little pier. Standing in the park is a bust of Hvar native **Ivan Vučetić,** who moved to Argentina and pioneered the science of fingerprinting in the 1890s. Embedded in the pavement in the middle of the park is a giant fingerprint (not quite visible from here). This park is a delightfully green and shaded spot to escape the bustle of town.

Now turn back around, facing the square, and walk toward the cathedral, stopping at the first street on the left. You can see the top of a **Venetian palace,** with its distinctive Venetian-style windows. A descendant of the former owner recently bought back this palace and has been restoring it—but renovations have taken longer than expected since workers began to uncover layer after layer of Hvar's history: blocks of stone from the Greek island of Paros, Illyrian coins, and Roman mosaics. If you were to head two blocks up this street, you'd run into the yellow **Benedictine Convent** and its loveable lace museum; if you continued beyond the convent, you'd reach the trailhead for the **fortress** up above (all described later). But before leaving the square, visit the cathedral (see below).

Then poke around Hvar's **back streets.** As you wander, especially on the left (north) side of the square, look up to find more characteristic Venetian windows. You'll also spot stone tabs jutting from house facades. The ones with holes were used to hang color-coded curtains: white for a birth, black for a death. Also notice the gleaming white limestone everywhere. It's quarried locally, and an often-repeated legend that the US White House was built of this same stone is false but temptingly plausible.

Cathedral of St. Stephen (Sv. Stjepan)

Hvar's centerpiece is its Renaissance-era cathedral, with a distinctive three-humped gable (representing the Holy Trinity) and open-work steeple. The interior comes with a few tales from Hvar's storied past; you can see the bronze doors (described next) without buying a ticket.

Cost and Hours: 10 kn, daily 9:00-12:00 & 17:00-18:30 except closed to tourists during services and Sun 10:00-11:00.

Visiting the Cathedral: The **bronze entrance doors,** completed by a popular Croatian sculptor in 1990, combine religious themes with important elements of life on Hvar. On the left door, top to bottom, you'll see the Creation; Madonna and

Baby Jesus surrounded by the circle of stars (representing the European Union—reflecting Croatians' desire to be considered part of Europe); vineyards (both literal and as a symbol of heaven); and a procession of penitence, a fixture of life among religious locals. On the right door, you'll see a dove (representing peace and the Holy Spirit); the crucified Christ; fishermen (an actual part of Hvar life, but also representing the Church's "fishers of men" evangelical philosophy); and a boat, sailing into the future.

Inside, buy your ticket, pick up a free English information sheet, and work your way counterclockwise around the church **interior.** In the chapel to the right of the main altar, the tabernacle embedded in the yellow marble "cloth" (under the big crucifix) holds an important piece of Hvar history: a crucifix that supposedly shed tears of blood on the eve of a major 1510 uprising of the plebeians against the patricians. (This spooked the rebels enough to postpone the uprising a few months.)

Behind the main altar are wooden choir stalls rescued from an earlier Gothic church that was destroyed during an Ottoman attack in 1571. Notice the two pulpits: The right one, with St. Paul and his sword, is for reading or singing the Epistles; the left one, with the eagle (representing St. John), is used for reading the Gospels.

The chapel to the left of the main altar features the tomb of St. Prosperus, Hvar's co-patron saint, who shares the credit with the more famous St. Stephen. People pray to Prosperus for good health. On his feast day, May 10, the lid is opened and you can actually see his preserved body. The figures flanking his tomb represent Faith and Strength.

▲Historic Hvar Theater

Head up the stone stairs right by the TI to visit this beautiful small theater, dating back to 1612. The oldest public theater in Europe, it was built as a symbol of reconciliation between warring factions in Hvar's 17th-century population: Here, plebeians and patricians would (almost) mix and enjoy cultural events together. Today, it continues to host community events and changing art exhibitions.

Cost and Hours: 50 kn, daily 9:00-21:00, usually closed Nov-April, tel. 021/741-009.

Visiting the Theater: The theater reopened in 2019 after a decade of renovations, and decorative touches such as the ceiling painting are more vibrant than they've been in centuries. Notice the stone inscription over the main door, which suggests the aspiration behind the theater's founding: *Anno secundo pacis,* the "second year of peace" after conflict. Inside, you're free to stroll around, poke into the box seats, and maybe even head up on stage to belt an aria. From the double level of box seats, the upper crust could watch each other (which was often as entertaining as the performance), and they didn't have to mix *too* much with the commoners, who sat in rows in front of the little stage. Much of the present appearance of the theater still dates from the early 1800s; look for the faded mural painted in 1819 on the wall at the back of the stage.

▲Benedictine Convent (Benediktinski Samostan) and Lace Museum

Hvar's most endearingly quirky sight is this nun-run attraction, inside a convent where 13 Benedictine sisters spend their lives (they never go outside). When they're not praying, the sisters make lace by using fibers from the *agava* (a cactus-like plant with broad, flat, tapered, spiny leaves—see the sample just outside the door). First, they tease the delicate threads out of the plant, then wash, bleach, and dry them. Finally, they weave the threads into intricate lace designs. The painstaking procedure is made even more challenging by Hvar's unpredictable weather: The humid, southerly Jugo wind causes tangles, while the dry northern Bora wind makes the fibers stiff and difficult to work with.

Cost and Hours: 10 kn, skimpy 15-kn multilingual booklet, extremely expensive samples for sale; Mon-Sat 10:00-12:00 & 17:00-19:00, closed Sun; generally closed Oct-May, but try ringing the bell to the right of the main door during these same hours—use the door in the yellow building; tel. 021/741-052.

Visiting the Convent: The museum is very small, and skippable if you're not interested in lace. But if you come, you'll see astonishingly delicate samples of the nuns' work, both new and old. Some yellowed specimens date from the late 19th century (the oldest ones are in the back room). The sisters are particularly happy to make lace for bishops and cardinals. And when the *other* Benedict—the XVI—became pope in 2005, they created a lace papal emblem for him as a gift.

Rounding out the museum are ecclesiastical gear, some bishops' vestments (with the Baby Jesus below them wearing an *agava*-lace shirt), ancient kitchenware discovered in this house, a stone sink and baptismal font, an actual well, and some amphora jugs. Out in front of the building is a statue of St. Benedict, the patron saint of Europe, reading his daily routine in a book: *ora et labora* (pray and work).

▲Franciscan Monastery (Franjevački Samostan)

Starting in the 15th century, this monastery was a hospice for sailors who contracted illnesses on treacherous sea journeys. These days it's worth the 10-minute stroll from the Old Town to visit its offbeat museum, Hvar's most famous painting, an ancient tree, and a pair of monks.

HVAR

Cost and Hours: 35 kn; Mon-Sat 9:00-15:00 & 17:00-19:00, closed Sun; usually closed Nov-April.

Visiting the Monastery: Out front, notice the statue of a kneeling **St. Francis**—the twin of the prayerful St. Benedict, who stands in front of the Benedictine Convent.

As you enter, notice that the **cloister**'s floor is slanted inward to capture rainwater. Pipes took this pure water out to the waterfront, where ships could use it to replenish their supplies. This space is a popular venue for summer concerts.

Inside, the focal point of the monastery is its impressive painting of *The Last Supper* (c. 1640). The U-shaped table in the painting provides the framework for some bold experimentation with perspective. Facing Jesus, front and center, is Judas, identified by several clues. In his left hand (hard to see) is a bag of coins, and his right hand is dipping bread into wine (after Jesus had predicted that the one who did this would betray him). The yellow of his garment symbolizes betrayal, and the red indicates that the betrayal led to the spilling of blood. Under the table by Judas is a cat, representing lust. On the lower right, we see a beggar (accompanied by a dog, symbolizing fidelity)—likely a self-portrait by the artist, grateful to the monks who nursed him back to health.

Through the door to the right of *The Last Supper,* look for the little **museum** of currency from the fourth century BC (Greek coins with an image of Zeus) through today (see the rapid evolution of Croatia's currency since the country's independence), as well as a collection of amphora jugs.

Retracing your steps back out toward the entrance, find the room filled with paintings by Venetian masters and modern Croatian artists (and see more interpretations of Jesus from medieval to modern times). Next, head into the relaxing garden to find the outside attraction: an enormous **cypress tree** whose gnarled branches are held up by big supports. Scientists believe this ancient tree—estimated at 250 years old—was struck by lightning, which caused the branches to spread out and become flatter than usual.

Wrap up your visit with a peek into the colorful and unusual little **chapel** off the cloister, with a separated choir.

▲▲Hvar Fortress (Fortica Hvar)

Visiting this mighty castle above the Old Town is a good excuse for a sturdy 30-minute hike to break up your lazy Hvar day. The main reason to come here is for the views, which are sensational—particularly at sunset.

Cost and Hours: 50 kn, daily June-mid-Sept 8:00-22:00, Easter-May and mid-Sept-Oct until 20:00, Nov-Easter much shorter hours and sometimes closed.

Getting There: From the Old Town, hike up the steep street called Groda to the road passing above town. Once on that road, look for the nearby gate with the picture of a castle for another steep hike up a switchback trail (stay on the main path—side paths that seem like shortcuts are actually dead ends). The entrance is around behind, but cheapskates enjoy the views for free from the little dirt mound on the seaward side of the fort.

Visiting the Fortress: This large fortification was built over several generations, beginning in the 13th century. In the 14th century, Spanish engineers did their part to bulk up the fortress (earning it the nickname "Španjola"). In 1571, the townspeople fled here for sanctuary during an attack by the Ottomans (prior to the famous Battle of Lepanto). Just a few years later, the fortress was devastated when lightning hit a gunpowder store. In the 19th century, the occupying Austrians put their own touches on the castle. Today it's used as a catering facility and tourist attraction.

Inside the fort, there's little in the way of posted descriptions, but the views over town are magnificent. You can also climb down

into the prison, sip a drink at the café/bar, and visit the one-room marine archaeological collection (hiding inside the blocky central part of the fortress; look for *amphorae* and *muzej* signs). This display features booty found at three different Dalmatian shipwrecks, including a collection of amphora jugs. According to the exhibit, one out of every 50 voyages in antiquity ended in a shipwreck. (And you thought flying was dangerous.)

The complex on the higher hill nearby was built by Napoleon (which is also its nickname among locals). In the 1970s, it was converted into an astronomic and seismographic observatory.

Strolling and Swimming

With typically Dalmatian crystal-clear water, Hvar is a great place to swim. Also typically Dalmatian, virtually all of the swimming areas are rocky or pebbly. As you walk along the coastline in either direction from town, you'll spot concrete pads and ladders trying to seduce you into the cool blue (these are generally open to the public;

you may have the option
of renting a beach chair).
Whether or not you plan
to swim, make a point of
following either of the two
paths along the waterfront
for a while: The views of
distant islands, the scents
of Mediterranean forest,

and the sun sparkling off the sea are reason enough to come to
Hvar.

East of the Old Town: This delightful path leads past swimmers, sunbathers, and boats bobbing just offshore. You'll pass a
tiny, crowded, pebbly beach in the cove just before the Franciscan
Monastery. Farther along—after about a 20-minute walk—you'll
reach the town's main beach, **Pokonji Dol,** which faces a small,
barren island of the same name topped with a lonely little lighthouse. This is an easy choice, but because it's close to town, this
beach can be quite crowded, and it has large underwater rocks. Locals prefer to go a bit farther. However, after Pokonji Dol, the path
becomes more challenging, offers little shade, and is not as well-
marked. Bring water and wear good shoes if planning to venture
this far. If you continue eastward along the coast, you'll find more
beaches—first the pleasant and peaceful beach nicknamed **Robinson,** after the beach restaurant that dominates it, and then the
even better one at the charming resort village of **Milna** (2.5 miles
from Hvar town). Beyond Robinson, the waterfront path to Milna
is challenging and very poorly marked, so if you want to go to the
beach there, consider taking a taxi, water taxi (about 50 kn one-way
between Hvar and Milna), or the bus (any bus taking the new road
to Stari Grad stops at Milna).

West of the Old Town: This path leads past a cactus garden
and children's play area, then along a series of bays—one of them
dominated by the huge Hotel Amfora (with a row of private caban-
as, below the trail). On the next bay over, the popular **Hula Hula**
beach bar serves light meals and cocktails on platforms and rocks
over the beach, with chill-out music all day and a live DJ in the evening (see "Nightlife in Hvar," later). The farther you get from town,
the more remote-feeling the beaches become, ending at the beach
nicknamed the Blue Lagoon, near the mellow cocktail bar under
Pod Stine Hotel. The hotel's private beach is another inviting place
for a swim; you'll pay royally to rent a chair, but it's comfortable and
scenic and offers easy access to the water. The rocky floor here is
perfect for snorkeling, and a nearby dive shop rents gear.

Many sun worshippers—especially the clothing-optional

crowd—prefer to take a water taxi to the beaches of the nearby **Pakleni Islands,** across the bay from Hvar town (described later).

MORE SIGHTS ON HVAR ISLAND

If you have more time, Hvar is an interesting island to explore. The best way to efficiently hit several sights in a single day is to take a trip with Secret Hvar (listed earlier, under "Tours in Hvar"). Otherwise, consider one of these outings—which are best by car.

If you do leave town, you'll quickly reach a dramatically mountainous landscape with rugged soil that has been carefully worked by centuries of Hvaranins. Heaps of stones big and small—like hundreds of giant molehills—pockmark the landscape. These piles of unwanted rocks were created when the land was cleared for farming. You'll also see a few little stone huts (called *trim*), some of them centuries old. These provided farmers with shelter from sun or storms and gave them a cool place to take a nap during a hot day's work.

Stari Grad

Literally "Old Town," this was the island's original settlement, dating back some 2,400 years. Today it's a likably humble, workaday port town almost entirely lacking Hvar's glamor-girl charm...and crowds. Simple fishing boats rather than luxury yachts bob in its harbor, and its flat, labyrinthine street plan disperses the few tourists who venture here.

From the harbor, head up through town to the tallest **bell tower;** it marks the Church of St. Stephen, which watches over its own quiet little square. Beyond that is the much smaller Church of St. John, the core of which likely dates from the fifth or sixth century. It offers great acoustics and displays a replica of a Roman mosaic that was discovered during excavations just behind the building. (Loop around behind the church to see the scant foundations.)

Closer to the harbor is a large square fronted by a long, stout **fortress,** which was the personal palace of local landowner and poet Petar Hektorović, who dominates much of the story of Stari Grad. Of the many covered canals leaving the harbor and twisting through town, one runs right into this palace.

Running parallel to the harbor is the street called **Srinjo Kola,** which means "Middle Street" in the local dialect. This was once the town's main street for commerce—notice the display windows that abut many of the doorways. These days, many homes here are abandoned.

Finally, back near the harbor, seek out the shop called **Fantazam,** where artist Zoran Tadić assembles various discarded organic materials (bones, hair, feathers, and other animal body parts) into wholly unique and grotesque statues of mythical beasts. Zoran hangs out in his courtyard working when the weather is good and invites the curious in to peek at his gallery (Ivana Gundulića 6, mobile 098-953-2967, www.fantazam.com).

While many visitors to Hvar see only the main town and the road to Stari Grad (en route to the island's main car-ferry port), drivers may enjoy heading east of Stari Grad to some nearby settlements. Driving eastbound on the main road from Stari Grad takes you into a plain with fertile **farm fields.** This unassuming patch of land is one of the only agricultural areas in Europe still divided according to its original plots, dating all the way back to the first ancient Greek settlers.

Eating near Stari Grad: For a memorable, rustic, middle-of-nowhere meal, head for the village of Dol (a couple of miles beyond Stari Grad, just off the main road). **$$ Konoba Kokot,** run by the Pavičić family, sources almost everything they serve right here: They raise lambs, have a prolific produce garden, make their own sheep's-milk cheeses, and—best of all—hunt wild boar in the surrounding countryside. You can call ahead to arrange a classic *peka* meal, but the highlight here is the "boar burger"—a perfectly seasoned patty of wild boar meat. If you'd like a meal out in the countryside, it's worth the taxi trip (reservations smart, daily 18:00-24:00, mobile 091-511-4288).

Vrboska

On the opposite side of the farm fields from Stari Grad is the sea-front village of Vrboska, nicknamed Little Venice (this endearing hyperbole is typical of local pride). While the name is a stretch, this appealing town does have a canal with picturesque bridges, the fortress/church of St. Mary's (built during a time of Turkish naval threat), a good wine-tasting opportunity, and an island with a lone palm tree. Even better, there are no tourists here. This is where locals from the town of Hvar go to escape the crowds.

Wine Tasting: To sample some of the island's well-reputed wines in a fun, rustic setting, find **Vina Pinjata,** 30 paces above the Church of St. Mary. Call or email ahead to be sure Marija is available, and enjoy the warm reception (also serves meals, tel. 021/774-262, mobile 091-955-1667, konobapinjata@gmail.com).

Hike from Velo Grablje to Milna

For a vigorous but mostly downhill hike in the interior of Hvar Island, you can bus to a partially abandoned town, walk down through a ravine to a nearly empty village, then pop out along the sea at Milna for a bus ride back to Hvar. Allow a half-day for the

Hvar Wine and Lavender

The hillsides of Hvar Island are striped with the faint outlines of an elaborate network of terraces, once used to cultivate grapes for wine. But in 1910, a phylloxera pest infestation devastated vineyards and decimated the island's winemaking industry. Many vintners moved to the US, Australia, and Argentina, where they became pioneers in wine production. Today winemaking on Hvar is at only about 5 percent of its historic peak, and the focus is on quality, not quantity. In general, the south side of the island gets more intense sun, which leads to smaller and sweeter grapes—and, in turn, higher-alcohol and better-quality wine.

Several well-respected vintners are putting Hvar on the oenophiles' map. Top producers include the large Plinković operation (which also has vineyards on the mainland) and Andro Tomić. The **Tomić** winery is well set up for visitors curious to taste a few wines, including their fruity rosé, their Beleca red blend, and their exquisite *prošek* dessert wine, called Hektorovich. While it's smart to call ahead to tell them you're coming, drop-ins are typically welcome (daily 9:00-20:00, shorter hours off-season, on the road into the town of Jelsa, just above the Hvar Hotel, tel. 021/768-160, www.bastijana.hr).

In the 1930s, in an effort to boost the economy, the island began producing lavender. This was mostly exported for industrial use to Germany and the UK (peaking in the 1960s and 1970s, when Hvar Island was responsible for 10 percent of the world's total lavender production). The lavender industry dramatically improved the quality of life on Hvar, but devastating forest fires in 1984, 1997, 2003, and 2007 burned up much of this cash crop. As the island's tourism industry expands, it has become less critical to the economy to replant after each fire, so many lavender farmers have left their fields fallow. These days most lavender is produced for the sake of tradition...and for tourists.

whole trip, including about two hours for the hike itself. This is best for hardy hikers and those who enjoy getting away from touristy beaches to explore the artifacts of an earlier age of Hvar; most of the route is in a ravine without sea views. As this is a challenging trail with little shade, wear good shoes and load up on water, sunscreen, and anything else you might need before setting out.

To reach the start of the hike, take the one daily bus that uses the scenic old road to Stari Grad (generally departs Hvar town at 12:10 in summer, 12:20 in winter—confirm at TI or bus station), and get off about five miles east of Hvar town at the village of Velo Grablje. From the Velo Grablje stop, hike down the switchback road into the town. For a more scenic arrival, stay on the bus a few hundred yards longer and ask the driver to let you off at Vidikovac (vee-DEE-koh-vats), a viewpoint restaurant with panoramic vistas across the far side of the island; from here, cross the road and walk down the gravel path into town.

Velo Grablje, once famous for its lavender-oil production, is now a near-ghost town on a rugged plateau with far-off views of the sea. Most people migrated to Hvar town in the 1970s and 1980s, though seven natives still reside here.

From Velo Grablje, follow the medieval foot-path through the ravine downhill about two miles to the abandoned village of **Malo Grablje.** After the phylloxera epidemic, most people from this village moved down to Milna, on the sea (where tourism provided them with better prospects). The last holdout left in 1968. But the grandson of the first villager who left returned to Malo Grablje and opened a rustic restaurant called **$$$ Konoba Stori Komin** (open 16:00-23:00 only, run by Berti Tudor—the surname of virtually everyone who originated in this village, possible to call ahead to arrange a *peka* dinner, mobile 091-527-6408). Even if the *konoba* is closed, you can explore the streets of Malo Grablje. (After a *New York Times* article brought international attention to Berti's *konoba* a few years back, they paved the road to the village just for his guests. To eat here without the hike, you can come by taxi for dinner.) Poke into the ruined buildings to find a giant, still-functioning olive press. The humble church hosts a Mass twice per year, when people from Milna return to their ancestral village. Next to the church is a huge reservoir and cistern for catching rainwater.

Leaving Malo Grablje, follow the gravel road down into the beach town of **Milna.** The seafront path from Milna back to Hvar (about 2.5 miles) is extremely rugged and can be nearly impossible to follow; unless you're very adventurous, it's best to walk along the main road (not very scenic) or take a public bus back to Hvar (any bus that goes between Stari Grad and Hvar along the new road stops along the road above Milna—departs Stari Grad in summer at 16:05 and 18:50, schedule may be different in winter, reaches Milna about 10-15 minutes later, but confirm times at Hvar TI before heading out). You can also take a water taxi between Milna and Hvar for about 50 kn one-way.

Note: It's possible to drive from Milna up to Malo Grablje and Velo Grablje, but the road consists of very rough gravel and rock—not advisable with a rental car.

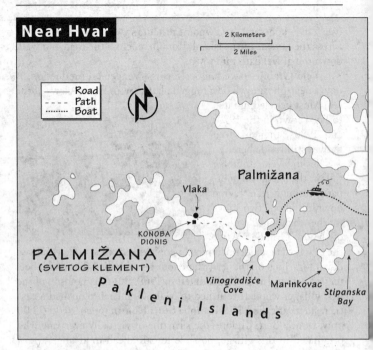

Near Hvar

2 Kilometers

2 Miles

— Road
--- Path
···· Boat

N

Vlaka

Palmižana

KONOBA
DIONIS

PALMIŽANA
(SVETOG KLEMENT)

P a k l e n i   I s l a n d s

*Vinogradišče
Cove*

Marinkovac

*Stipanska
Bay*

NEAR HVAR
Pakleni Islands (Pakleni Otoci)

These islands, just offshore from Hvar town, are a popular and easy back-to-nature day-trip destination. The name means the "Devil's Islands" in Croatian, but in the local dialect, *pakleni* refers to the resin used to seal the hulls of ships (which had to be boiled—hence the hellish connection). These days, the islands harbor some popular nude beaches: The island of Jerolim and the bay of Stipanska (or is it *Strip*anska?) on the island of Marinkovac are particularly good places to spot—or sport—some bare skin. While the beaches used to be predominantly nude, local cap-

tains figured out that they get more business if they don't adver-tise the nudist connection—so the beaches are now more mixed than they once were. For a bit more civilization, set your sights on the biggest island, known as **Palmižana** (pahl-mee-ZHAH-nah; sounds like "parmesan-a") for its main settlement (the island's offi-cial name is Svetog Klement, but nobody calls it that). The beach at Palmižana is a popular swim destination because it's partly "sandy"

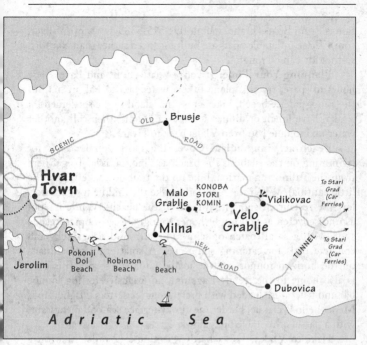

(translation: smaller pebbles). The only real town on this island is also named Palmižana, basically a modest marina and a handful of cafés huddled around a beach. From there, you can hike through the woods and scramble your way to some postcard-perfect hidden coves.

Getting There: Every summer morning, **excursion boats** ferry tourists out to the islands from the harbor in front of the Hvar TI—just look for signs to the specific island, beach, or cove that you want. It costs about 60 kn round-trip per person to Palmižana; most boats take people over between 9:00 and 14:00, then go back to fetch them around 16:00 or 19:00 (schedule fluctuates wildly with demand—they run more or less constantly in peak season; figure about 20 minutes each way to Palmižana). This works well, provided you want to spend the entire day stranded on a tropical island. Note that you need to come home with the same company that brought you—confirm their return options. Visiting Jerolim or Marinkovac costs 50 kn round-trip.

An efficient sightseer might prefer just a few hours of island time—enough for a quick dip, a hike, and maybe a meal. For this purpose, you can pay double for a faster, private **water taxi** to zip you there in just 15 minutes and then pick you up whenever you like. This is also handy for reaching or returning from Konoba Dionis (described later) at Vlaka, which isn't connected by regular boats. Most accommodations have a line on taxi boats; one option is Primi Boats (Frano, mobile 091-515-5385, www.primi-hvar.com). These inflatable boats are built for speed rather than comfort, so the ride can be rough.

Planning Your Time: If you're relatively fit and have a few hours to spare, try this plan: Take a water taxi to Palmižana, hit the Vinogradišće beach, hike across the island to the settlement of Vlaka, have lunch or dinner at Konoba Dionis, then call another water taxi to take you from Vlaka back to Hvar.

Beach at Vinogradišće Cove: The most popular spot for swimming on the island is the beach at Vinogradišće. To get here from the Palmižana marina, hike up the trail (to the left, past the little cantina). When the road forks, take the middle fork and follow the restaurant signs (they're all at the beach). While it's not as undiscovered as you might hope, Vinogradišće is a picturesque spot, with a small patch of semi-sand surrounded by rocks and concrete pads for catching some rays. A smattering of sailboats on the horizon rounds out the idyllic Croatian scene. This cove is also home to the trendy Laganini, an exclusive-feeling lounge bar and fish house loaded with pretentious jet-setters. Higher up is Meneghello, a classic, borderline-funky terrace seafood restaurant, with a passel of rentable bungalows.

Hike to Vlaka: For a hardy 45-minute (2-mile) hike on a rough trail with some pleasant views—and a restaurant reward at the end (Konoba Dionis)—trek across the top of the island to the little settlement of Vlaka (wear good shoes and bring water). From Palmižana, first follow signs to *Meneghello*. After you pass Meneghello Restaurant and some of its bungalows, go right at the fork in the path (following the faint red marking on the wall to *Vlaka*). You'll climb up to the crest of the island, on a very narrow and rocky trail. A few side paths fork down to various bays, but stay on the main trail along the island's spine (generally marked with red-painted rocks). You'll periodically break through the trees for views over secluded coves and nearby islands. Finally, the path leads down along yet another pretty cove before sending you back over the top of the island to Vlaka and Konoba Dionis.

Eating at Vlaka: The culinary highlight of the island is **$$$$ Konoba Dionis,** a charming stone hut with just six tables on a covered terrace overlooking vineyards, an olive grove, and the distant sea. The electricity comes from a generator, and the water comes from the sky—so the cuisine is straightforward, traditional Dalmatian dishes, and the focus is on relaxation. Their "aubergine pie" is a tasty eggplant lasagna (daily 12:00-23:00, closed mid-Oct-mid-May, mobile 098-167-1016, www.dionis-hvar.com). Tourists often make the long journey over to Dionis, only to find it's already full—reservations (especially for lunch) are a must.

Shopping in Hvar

Little souvenir kiosks are everywhere on Hvar. The big item here is lavender, produced on the island for the last century or so (see "Hvar Wine and Lavender" sidebar, earlier). In addition to making things smell good, lavender is acclaimed by some locals for its medicinal properties: Massage some lavender oil on your temples to cure a headache, or rub it on your chest for asthma. You'll see it sold in bottles or sachets—a fragrant souvenir that helps keep your luggage smelling fresh, too. Hvar town also has plenty of jewelry shops selling coral and other pieces made from semiprecious stones.

Nightlife in Hvar

This island town is known for its nightlife, so it teems with the young and the restless (that is, the loud).

Mellow Nightlife

Strolling the harbor, then continuing out of town along the waterfront promenade, is a fine way to pass a warm, starry evening. The best views are from the harbor's east side.

Consider a pre- or post-dinner drink with the best view over the harbor from the fourth-floor bar/terrace at the recommended **Hotel Adriana** (on the waterfront at Obala Fabrika 28, tel. 021/750-200). Slip into your comfortable chair and watch the lights of the village glimmer below.

Pršuta 3 wine bar, along a tight restaurant-lined lane right in the heart of town, has an older clientele and seating outside and in. It's a cozy and chill place to hang out, socialize, and sip some of the island's wines with light food (about 25 wines available by the glass, cash only, nightly 18:00-late, Hektorovića 5, mobile 098-969-6193).

Ka'Lavanda, a sophisticated cocktail bar, climbs the steps just inside the Old Town's eastern wall, directly uphill from the cathedral tower. The atmosphere is magic: floodlit stone walls and cushy chairs under flowering trees (overpriced but creative cocktails, long hours daily, Dr. Mate Miličića 7, mobile 099-447-7799).

Lively Nightlife

Hvar has Dalmatia's most happening "après-beach" scene. Expect very high prices for drinks, and prepare to share the nightspots with a very flush, well-dressed, international jet-set crowd. On balmy summer evenings, partying is best enjoyed in three stages. (Note that virtually all the places below are closed from about early October through early May.)

Stage 1: Watch the sunset from the groovy **Hula Hula** beach bar, with drinks—and tables—"on the rocks" (literally). Don't ex-

HVAR

pect a relaxed vibe here—in summer, it's absolutely jam-packed with young partiers (drinks, meals, and snacks; open long hours daily with a live DJ and dance-club ambience in the evening, hopping until about 23:00; for directions, see "Strolling and Swimming," earlier in this chapter). When I asked if older guests would be comfortable here, they smirked and said, "When they come here, everybody feels young!"

Stage 2: Head for the rowdy bars in the center of town, along the harbor (including **Sidro**—known for its cheap drinks and friendly service—as well as **Seven, Nautica Bar, Aloha,** and so on). Each one has a few tall tables with skinny stools just across the promenade, perched over the harborfront. Just uphill from this strip of bars, on the ground floor of Hotel Park, is the big, spacious, and more upscale-feeling **Central Park Club Bar,** with Tuscan living-room ambience.

Stage 3: If you're still going strong—and don't mind paying dearly for the chance to rub elbows with a celebrity—continue to one of Hvar's famous late-night clubs. The most established (and the one that put Hvar on the global nightlife heatmap) is **Carpe Diem,** an exclusive-feeling cocktail bar along the harbor, just past Hotel Riva (Carpe Diem also has its own beach bar on Stipanska Island, www.carpe-diem-hvar.com).

Sleeping in Hvar

In keeping with its posh reputation, Hvar has some of the most expensive accommodations in Croatia. Book as far ahead as possible in July and especially August (when all accommodations boost their rates). As usual, *sobe* and apartments are a more affordable option than hotels, but there are relatively few in the center of town; you'll have to walk 10 to 20 minutes to reach most of them. The ones I've listed are cozy, well-equipped, well-run, and worth the walk.

Unlike Dubrovnik, Korčula, or Rovinj, Hvar is a place where sleeping in the Old Town can have more minuses than pluses. In July and August, it's chaotic and extremely noisy, and you might actually prefer having to walk up out of town to escape the bustle. (The Old Town hotels I've listed suffer a bit from the clamor, though my three recommended *sobe* manage to avoid the worst of it.) In shoulder season, the center of town becomes more desirable.

For most places I recommend, plan on climbing several steps and/or trudging up steep suburban streets. The farther and steeper you're willing to walk, the better the price and views (some come with glorious seaview balconies, even if you're on a budget). Many of my listings are tucked away in residential areas, so they can be very tricky to find; online maps might not help, so get clear directions from your host, ask locals as you go, or—better yet—arrange for your host to meet you on arrival. While some will meet you on the boat, others prefer to greet you at the bus station (5-10 level minutes of walking).

Unless otherwise noted, all of these listings have air-conditioning (essential in summer) and don't offer breakfast. Except for some of the big Sunčani Hvar branches, assume all come with lots of stairs and no elevator. While pricier hotels accept credit cards, the *sobe* are cash only. Several of the *sobe* are run by old-timers who speak minimal English, but in each case a younger relative is standing by to help translate.

Soba **Tips:** It's standard for *sobe* and apartments to charge 30 percent more for stays shorter than three nights. This is rarely waived in high season, but you can try to negotiate your way out of this at other times. While I've recommended some reliable, well-established options, good alternatives abound on booking sites like Airbnb and Booking.com.

IN THE OLD TOWN

The first two (along with Sunčani Hvar's Hotel Palace Elisabeth, described later) are the only real hotels in the Old Town. I'd consider these only if you're determined to sleep in a real hotel, at high prices, in a central (but potentially noisy) location. The last three are a few short but steep blocks above the main square. Note that Sunčani Hvar's Riva and Adria hotels, described later, are also relatively near the center, facing each other across the harbor.

$$$$ Villa Nora is as central as can be, with nine spacious rooms filling an old townhouse squeezed between the two restaurant streets in the heart of Hvar. It's fairly quiet after the restaurants close down around midnight. Natalija and her crew are helpful hosts and pride themselves on providing a generous breakfast (Frane Primija 2, tel. 021/742-498, mobile 092-217-7466, www.villanora.eu, info@villanora.eu).

$$$$ Hotel Park sits right in the heart of town, just above the harbor. Its 15 nicely furnished rooms (most of them very spacious suites, some with sea views for extra) offer a small-hotel alternative to the big boys, and its restaurant/breakfast terrace, overlooking the harbor, will slow your pulse. Despite its bottom-floor nightclub and locale near the harborfront disco zone, good windows minimize the noise (air-con, Sv. Marak 2, tel. 021/718-337, www.hotelparkhvar.com, info@hotelparkhvar.com).

$$ Apartments Lea, across the lane from Nona—listed below—has three fresh, modern, well-equipped apartments (Nike Karkovića 7, mobile 099-267-9916, dragojevic.lea55@gmail.com).

$$ Ivana and Paško Ukić offer four cozy, renovated apart-

HVAR

ments (with kitchens) and one double room. The house is wonderfully buried deep in the Old Town (a few steep blocks above the main square) and shares a quiet square with a little church (Matija Ivanića 10, daughter Lidija's mobile 097-780-3700, ivanaukic@net.hr). From the cathedral, walk three blocks up toward the fortress, then look for the little church (Sv. Duh) to your left.

$ Apartments Nona (Grandma), filling the former home of Ivanka's grandmother and run by great-granddaughter Marija, rents four beautiful, new-feeling apartments just high enough up to evade the downtown bustle. Some of the apartments have their own private terrace—a rarity in the heart of Hvar (Nike Karkovića 18, mobile 091-517-7038, ivanka.hvar@gmail.com).

EAST OF THE OLD TOWN, IN BUKAINKA

The quiet residential neighborhood called Bukainka sits on a high plateau just east of the harbor, hemmed in by the main road to Stari Grad. Most houses here have peek-a-boo water views—ask. To reach this area, plan on a steep 10- to 15-minute uphill walk from the Old Town and waterfront. While I've located these carefully on the Hvar Town map, earlier, the streets here are confusing—especially for drivers—and online maps tend to be erroneous, though parking is relatively easy. Ideally, ask if your host will meet you on arrival.

$ Boutique Apartments Šeputić, run by enterprising Dino, rents seven modern, colorful apartments, all with kitchens and most with balconies offering exceptional views. This listing is the farthest from the center, best for hardy walkers (car and scooter rentals, Ive Roića 16, mobile 098-526-099, www.seputic.hr, info@seputic.hr).

$ Marjana Tudor, a Slovene who married into Hvar, rents four nicely equipped apartments (some with views) in a new building high above town (Ivana Buzolića 11, mobile 091-559-4977, www.hvar-apartment-rent.com, marjanatudor@yahoo.com).

$ Charming **Ivanka Ivanović,** next door, rents five pleasantly low-key apartments and two rooms in a big, modern house with view balconies (Ivana Buzolića 9, tel. 021/741-332, mobile 091-517-7038, www.ivanovic-hvar.com, ivanka.ivanovic@st.t-com.hr).

$ House Gordana sits above the little bay in front of the Franciscan Monastery. Kind Marija Barbarić's five rooms are modest but well-kept. All rooms come with balconies, and some have views (breakfast available for extra charge, Šima Buzolića Tome 49, tel. 021/742-182, mobile 098-923-4823, www.house-gordana-hvar.com.hr, housegordana@gmail.com).

¢ Villa Zorana Hostel is relatively civilized by Hvar's party-hearty hostel standards, with six affordable private rooms in addition to its bunks. There's an outdoor kitchen and pleasant common space with views from the terrace (Domovinskog rata 20, mobile 091-723-1737, www.villazorana.com, villazorana@gmail.com).

WEST OF THE OLD TOWN
In Zastup

Several similar places line the street called ulica Biskupa Jurja Dubokovića, the main road leading west of town, about a 10- to 15-minute walk from the Old Town (directly above and behind hotels Pharos and Amfora). I've listed my favorites, in the order you'll reach them. Pansion Petričić is a bit farther out and higher up.

$ Violeta, a guesthouse-like building with a reception area, five rooms, and three apartments, is the priciest and closest to town. The lodgings are new-feeling and minimalist-white, and most have views. The namesake owner speaks limited English, but her daughter-in-law Iva helps (Biskupa Jurja Dubokovića 22, mobile 091-896-2898, violeta.marusa@gmail.com).

$ Apartments Mare, warmly run by Marica and Đani (Gianni) Dujmović, has seven apartments with seaview terraces in the main building, plus four more freestanding cottages in a delightful, well-tended back garden. They make their own olive oil, wine, and grappa that you can sample in their atmospheric cellar (Biskupa Jurja Dubokovića 34, tel. 021/741-454, mobile 091-552-2014, www.apartments-mare-hvar.com, maricadujmovic@gmail.com).

$ Ana Dujmović, a lesser value, has eight older but well-appointed apartments with balconies, all overlooking an olive grove and most with sea views (BBQ terrace, Biskupa Jurja Dubokovića 36, mobile 098-838-434, www.visit-hvar.com/apartments-ana-dujmovic, ana.dujmovic@st.t-com.hr).

¢ Pansion Petričić, high up in a residential zone, offers million-dollar views for an amazingly low price. Proudly run by raconteur and former sailor Živko (with wife Marija and big but friendly dog Lex), it has four simple, old-fashioned, small rooms plus two apartments, which all have fantastic sea views (Biskupa Jurja Dubokovića 25, tel. 021/742-481, www.hvar-petricic.com, z.petricic@inet.hr).

In Podstine, Beyond Zastup

$$$$ Pod Stine Hotel ("Under Stones") feels like the sunny hideout of a reclusive writer. At the edge of town overlooking a tiny arboretum and a beautiful cove, this small resort features smart contemporary decor, 54 upscale-feeling rooms, a cocktail terrace, a small pool, and a gorgeous, momentum-killing private beach. If you don't mind the 20-minute walk along the waterfront promenade into town—which, if you're truly on vacation, is more of a delight than a chore—it's a far more intimate and enjoyable splurge than the big hotels. Particularly in July and August, when hotels closer to town can feel rowdy, its location is a refreshing escape (closed late Oct-late April, elevator, parking, free use of spa facilities—including gym and swimming pool, good restaurant, Put Podstina 11, tel. 021/740-400, www.podstine.com, hotel. podstine@gmail.com).

SUNČANI HVAR HOTELS

Most of the big hotels in town are operated by the same company, Sunčani Hvar. Most of them have been elaborately renovated with trendy decor (with increased prices to match); however, a couple of remaining, unrenovated branches offer a taste of the drab old communist days. Prices vary dramatically depending on the season, view, size, how recently the rooms were renovated, and the direction the wind is blowing. I've based the price rankings below on a two-night stay for a standard double room in mid-September; check specific rates on their website (www.suncanihvar.com). As these hotels tend to be both overpriced and impersonal, I'd save some serious kunas and enjoy more local color by sleeping in one of the *sobe* or apartments listed earlier. But if you prefer a well-located home base with big-hotel amenities, here are your options: **$$$$ Hotel Palace Elisabeth** owns a prime location a few steps off the main square, overlooking the harbor; its 45 five-star rooms are the top of Hvar's luxury ladder. **$$$$ Hotel Riva,** along the embankment where the big boats dock, is only slightly less posh, with 54 rooms, artsy decor, and nude sketches in the halls; this branch comes with serious disco noise from the adjacent Carpe Diem nightclub. **$$$$ Hotel Adriana,** across the harbor from Hotel Riva, has 59 super-plush rooms, a full-service spa, and killer views from the rooftop bar. **$$$$ Hotel Amfora** has perhaps the best family-resort feel—not too fancy (like the Riva or Adriana), and with 324 rooms and a sprawling swimming pool complex that reaches down to the beach. **$$ Hotel Pharos** has a hip motel vibe, with 200 rooms circling an inviting swimming lagoon. **$ Hotel Delfin** is the only "budget" choice, since its 55 rooms still await renovation...but until then, it's one of the worst-reviewed hotels in Dalmatia (skip it). You can book any of the Sunčani Hvar hotels through the same office: tel. 021/750-555, www.suncanihvar.com, reservations@suncanihvar.com.

Eating in Hvar

Like everything else in Hvar, restaurants are expensive—sometimes shockingly so. While the town has a few "local" eateries, most places cater at least somewhat to deep-pocketed tourists. My listings favor restaurants that are respected by natives and at least pretend that they're trying to cultivate return business. There are plenty of rip-off places in Hvar, which find creative ways to pad the bill (a cover charge is otherwise rare in Croatia, but commonplace here). But I've also described a few areas where you might feel OK getting ripped off a bit in exchange for a memorable setting. No matter where you dine, reservations are smart July through September.

$$ Alviž is a lowbrow restaurant that owns Hvar's most unromantic location—just outside the Old Town near the bus station—but the food and welcoming atmosphere make it every Hvaranin's top recommendation for a satisfying, untouristy meal. Say hello to owner Katarina, then dine on affordable pizzas, pastas, and other dishes in a woody interior or on a welcoming terrace out back with a busy open grill. The food is simple but delicious, including one of the best *pašticada*s I've had (daily 18:00-24:00, closed mid-Oct-April, across parking lot from bus station, Hanibala Lucića 1, tel. 021/742-797).

$$$ Dalmatino delivers on its promise of high-end Dalmatian cooking done very well. It has unusually attentive service, class without pretense, and a fine sense of hospitality (with free local shots to start and end the meal). With most of its tables tucked along a lane just a block off the harbor, it lacks sea views, but the good food at reasonable-for-Hvar prices more than compensates. It's justifiably popular and important to reserve ahead, using the form on the website (Mon-Sat 12:00-24:00, closed Sun and off-season, Sveti Marak 1, www.dalmatino-hvar.com).

$$$ Konoba Menego, owned by the Kovačević family and run with the help of efficient Marijo, offers the chance to try typical cuisine from Dalmatia and throughout Croatia. (Owner Dinko stubbornly refuses to serve anything that's not authentically Dalmatian—including Coca-Cola, spaghetti, or beer.) The user-friendly menu lists the town or region of origin for each specialty. Portions are small, so think of it as Croatian tapas: Two people can order three or four dishes to share, or they can split a larger combination plate—the fisherman's plate is excellent. Dine on the cozy, cave-like terrace or in the atmospheric dining room, with air-dried ham *(pršut)* hanging from the rafters. They don't take reservations, so arrive early or be prepared to wait on the steps out front (Mon-Sat 11:30-14:00 & 18:00-23:00, closed Sun and mid-Oct-March, on the steep lane called Groda leading up to the fortress, tel. 021/717-411, www.menego.hr).

$$ Mizarola is a classic, casual Hvar eatery hiding out at the top corner of town, behind some rollicking party bars. In a pleasant interior patio and up on a terrace, it serves affordable pizzas, pastas, and simple main dishes (daily 11:00-24:00, ulica Vinka Pribojevića 2, mobile 098-799-978).

$$ Fig was started by two friends who wanted to bring "culinary diversity" to Hvar, and it's a good choice if you need a break from the Dalmatian standards. Nestled on a lane above the main square, its menu ranges from Mexican pulled pork to coconut curry soup, with several options for vegetarians (daily 10:00-23:00, Ivana Frane Biundovića 3, tel. 021/717-203, www.figrestaurants.com).

Along the Harbor, East of Town: Several bars and eateries face the busy yacht-lined embankment (past Hotel Riva). Two restaurants, while overpriced, are worth considering for a splurge meal with a view. These both feel posh and dressy, with high-end seafood menus. I'd pay these prices only if you can snare an outdoor, seaview table (reserve ahead). **$$$$ Gariful** ("Carnation") is well-established, with a lovely terrace right next to the catamaran berth. While you should eat outside, take a peek in the small dining room, where the catch of the day is swimming around beneath the floor (daily 10:00-23:00, tel. 021/742-999). Just past Gariful, **$$$$ Divino** has perhaps even better outdoor seating: perched above the harborfront promenade with lots of sea-view tables (daily 12:00-14:00 & 19:00-24:00, Put križa 1, mobile 091-437-7777).

With a View, West of Town: The best views are from the harbor's far (west) side. Troll the handful of **$$$$** restaurants past Hotel Adriana and choose what looks best. Everything here is equally overpriced—but you're here for the view, not high cuisine.

Hvar's Restaurant Row: The streets just above the main square (to the left as you face the cathedral) are full of restaurants slinging similar Dalmatian and Mediterranean fare in an upscale atmosphere. Outdoor tables make it easy to window-shop. Most places here value style over substance, though quality is usually fine.

Picnics: This may be the only truly budget option in town (other than some disappointing pizza-by-the-slice windows). A big, handy **Konzum** supermarket is near the bus station (daily 7:00-20:00, Sun 8:00-13:00), and a smaller grocery store is on the town square. There's no shortage of scenic places to enjoy an al fresco munch: on a stone bench by the Arsenal, overlooking the main square, or on the embankment that runs along the harbor. But please be considerate and discreet; Hvaranins grow understandably irritated by tourists who sprawl out on the main square right in front of a grocery store, munching their picnic like it's their own living room.

Breakfast: If you're sleeping in a *soba*, you're on your own for breakfast. Small **$ bakeries** are scattered around town. Many restaurants advertise breakfast deals—ask your *soba* host if they have a deal with anyone. For perhaps the most appealing setting—watching Hvar wake up while you eat—grab an outdoor table at **$$ Café Pjaca,** on the main square across from the TI (daily 7:00-23:00, cool modern decor).

Hvar Connections

BY BOAT

For nondrivers, the handiest boat connections from Hvar are on speedy catamarans, which leave from the harbor in the heart of Hvar town. The big, slow car ferries depart from the port of Stari Grad, a 20-minute drive or bus ride from Hvar town. Note that these boat schedules are subject to great variation; confirm departure and ticketing information on each company's website.

Buying Tickets: Remember, buy tickets for the catamarans at least a day or two ahead (or even earlier on summer weekends). The route to Dubrovnik is particularly popular and can sell out as much as three days ahead in peak season. You can book online for both Krilo (www.krilo.hr) and Jadrolinija (www.jadrolinija.hr, but Jadrolinija does not allow same-day bookings; visit the ticket office instead). Each also has a ticket office in town. Krilo tickets are sold at the Pelegrini travel agency facing the harbor at the opposite end of Hotel Riva (Riva 20, tel. 021/742-743, www.pelegrini-hvar.hr). The Jadrolinija ticket office is on the embankment where the catamarans dock (tel. 021/741-132). Note that both of these typically close for a couple of hours around lunchtime (usually 13:00-15:00).

Fast Catamarans from Hvar Town: Frequent catamarans connect Hvar town to **Split** in about an hour (on Krilo: 6-8/day June-Sept, 2/day off-season; on Jadrolinija: 6/day June-Sept, 3-4/day spring and fall, 1/day in winter). Heading southbound, there are fewer options: to **Korčula** (1 hour; on Krilo: June-Sept 3/day, 2/day spring and fall, 1/day in winter; on Jadrolinija: 1/day June-Sept only); to **Mljet National Park** (on Krilo: Pomena dock, 2 hours, 1/day early April-late Oct); and to **Dubrovnik** (3 hours; on Krilo: 1-2/day early April-late Oct; on Jadrolinija: 1/day June-Sept only). Jadrolinija runs a different catamaran to **Vela Luka,** at the far end of Korčula island (2.5 hours, plus a 1-hour bus ride to Korčula town, daily year-round).

Slower Car Ferries from Stari Grad: If you're in a pinch, you can head to Stari Grad to catch a big Jadrolinija car ferry to Split (7/day in summer, 4/day in winter, 2 hours).

OVERLAND CONNECTIONS

Hvar's **buses** only connect you to other parts of the island. For farther-flung destinations (such as Dubrovnik, Mostar, Sarajevo, or Zagreb), you'll take a boat to Split, then connect by bus from there. In summer, frequent buses cross the island between Hvar town and Stari Grad, and there's always a bus coordinated to meet the big ferries at Stari Grad (in which case you want Stari Grad's "Trajekt" stop rather than its Old Town stop); off-season, not every boat is coordinated with a bus. Most of the Stari Grad buses use the new road and stop at Milna, while one per day uses the old road.

Drivers heading north can drive 20 minutes to Stari Grad and catch the car ferry right to Split. If you're heading south (or to Mostar), you can also drive the very twisty roads (about 1.5 hours) down the length of Hvar Island to the town of Sućuraj, where you can catch the car ferry to Drvenik; from Drvenik, you can drive along the mainland or catch a different ferry to Korčula town (before making the trip, confirm all ferry schedules at the Hvar TI and get advice about how long in advance you need to line up).

KORČULA

The island town of Korčula (KOHR-choo-lah) boasts an atmospheric Old Town, a smattering of fine little museums, and a dramatic, fjord-like mountain backdrop. Humbler than its glitzy big sister Hvar, Korčula—while certainly on the tourist trail—has an appealing (and occasionally frustrating) backwater charm. At its heart, Korčula is a traditional, blue-collar, salt-of-the-earth shipbuilding and fishing town with a dim patina of tourism. All things considered, Korčula is the most enjoyable Back Door stopover between Rovinj and Dubrovnik.

Like some other small Croatian coastal towns, Korčula was founded by the ancient Greeks. It became part of the Roman Empire and was eventually a key southern outpost of the Venetian Republic. The town's "mini-Dubrovnik" vibe isn't an accident: Venice would have liked to claim the *real* Dubrovnik, but when that failed, they fortified Korčula instead...as if to create a Dubrovnik of their very own. Four centuries of Venetian rule left Korčula with a quirky Gothic-Renaissance mix and a strong siesta tradition. Korčulans take great pride in the (dubious) claim that Marco Polo was born here in 1254—the explorer remains the town's poster boy. Korčula is also known for its traditional *Moreška* sword dance.

You'll discover that there are two Korčulas: the tacky seaside resort and the historic Old Town. Savvy visitors ignore the tourist sprawl and focus on Korčula's medieval quarter, which pokes into the sea on a picture-perfect peninsula. Tiny lanes branch off the humble main drag like ribs on a fishbone, a street plan that's designed to catch both the breeze and the shade. All in all, this laid-back island village is an ideal place to take a vacation from your busy vacation.

PLANNING YOUR TIME

For general Dalmatian Island tips, see "Planning Your Time" for Hvar (page 225).

Korčula deserves the better part of a day. Spend the morning wandering the medieval Old Town and exploring the handful of tiny museums. In the afternoon, kick back at a café or restaurant and bask on the beach. If you're here on a Thursday, be sure to catch the performance of the *Moreška* dance (also Mon in height of summer). With a second day, unwind longer, or consider an excursion—either a trip around the island or a side-trip to Mljet Island and its national park (sold by various travel agencies around town).

If you're trying to choose between Hvar and Korčula, why not do both? For example, if heading south, you can take an early boat from Split to Hvar, have much of the day there, then take the evening boat on to Korčula to set up for a day or two of vacation. If you're in a rush, you could arrive late, spend one night on Korčula, spend the day seeing the town, then zip out on the evening catamaran to Dubrovnik (possible June through Sept).

While Korčula is reasonably well-connected to the rest of Dalmatia in the summertime, things get more challenging off-season. If planning a trip in shoulder season, carefully check your transportation options.

Orientation to Korčula

The long, skinny island of Korčula runs alongside the even longer, skinnier Pelješac Peninsula. The main town and best destination on the island—just across a narrow strait from Pelješac—is also called Korčula.

Korčula town is centered on a compact peninsula called Stari Grad (for "Old Town"), which is connected to the mainland at a big staircase leading to the Great Land Gate. In the area in front of this staircase, you'll find ATMs, travel agencies, the Jadrolinija ferry office, the Konzum supermarket, an occasional outdoor produce market, and other handy tourist services.

Stretching to the south and east of the Old Town is **Shell Bay,** surrounded by a strip of tourist shops and resort hotels. There's not much of interest in this zone except for two pebble beaches and a little path with some pleasant swimming and sunning places along the rocks.

To the west of the Old Town is the serene waterfront street **Put Svetog Nikole,** where you'll find a few *sobe* (including some

Korčula

100 Meters
100 Yards

WESTERN FERRY DOCK

OLD TOWN WALLS

ŠET. PETRA KANAVELIĆA

OBALA DR. FRANJO TUĐMANA

KRILO TICKET BOOTH

Foot ferry to Orebić

A. ROŽANOVIĆA

ŠPANIĆEVA

SVETOG ROKA

KORČ. BRAT

LENTIČA

V. FORETIĆA

TOWN MUSEUM

RAFA ARNERIJA

D. MIROŠEVIĆA

DEPOLO

MARCO POLO HOUSE

DON PAVLA

ISMAELLI

St. Mark's Square

KORČ. STAT. 1214

 St. MARK'S CATHEDRAL

CHURCH MUSEUM

BISKUPIJE

GIUNIO

MARKA ANDRIJIĆA

OD TEATRA

J. BANIČEVIĆA

ŽITNICA

TOWN HALL

L. BABLIĆA

ST. MICHAEL'S

KAPOROVA

ICON MUSEUM

ALL SAINTS' CHURCH

KNEZEV PROLAZ

GREAT LAND GATE

DOBRO.

To 6

PUT SV. NIK.

FOSA

POST

RAMPADA

Pomirenja Square

STAIRCASE

EASTERN FERRY DOCK

PLOKATA 19 TAVNJA 1921

HRVATSKE BRATSKE ZAJEDNICE

JADROLINIJA OFFICE

KORČ. BROD.

MARCO POLO MUSEUM

To Bus Station, Dominče Ferry Dock, Vela Luka & 8

Accommodations

1. Carpe Diem Rooms
2. M&J Central Suites
3. Sobe Nina
4. Tedeschi Rooms & Pizzeria
5. Royal Apartments
6. To Depolo Rooms & Kiwi Rooms
7. Hotel Fabris
8. To Hotel Korsal & HTP Korčula Properties
9. Hotel Korčula de la Ville

Eateries & Other

10. Adio Mare
11. Aterina
12. Pizzeria Amfora
13. Filippi
14. Silk
15. Grocery
16. Cukarin Sweet Shop
17. Buffet "Massimo" Bar
18. Bokar Wine Bar
19. Korkyra Info
20. Moreška Outdoor Theater
21. Marco Polo Gift Shop

KORČULA

recommended under "Sleeping in Korčula," later), inviting swimming areas, great views of the historic center, benches placed just so, and more locals than tourists.

TOURIST INFORMATION

Korčula's TI is on the main street in front of the entrance to the Old Town (daily June-Sept 8:00-21:00, May and Oct until 17:00, Nov-April until 15:00, may be closed weekends off-season; Ulica Plokata 19. Travnja 1921, tel. 020/715-701, www.visitkorcula.eu; Hana and slyly smiling Smilija).

ARRIVAL IN KORČULA

By Boat: The fast catamarans to **Korčula town** dock at the embankments on either side of the Old Town peninsula (depending on conditions). From either cat-amaran landing, it's just a two-minute walk to where the peninsula meets the mainland and the services described under "Orientation to Korčula," earlier.

Car ferries use the **Dominče** dock two peninsulas east of Korčula, about a five-minute drive (or 30-minute walk) from town. Taxis (75 kn) and infrequent buses connect this dock with Korčula town.

Additional boats from Split and Hvar town arrive at **Vela Luka,** at the far end of Korčula Island. Each boat arriving at Vela Luka is met by a bus waiting to bring travelers to Korčula town (about 1 hour).

By Bus: The bus station is a short stroll from the Old Town. If you leave the station with the bay on your right, you'll reach the town center. If you leave with the bay on your left, you'll get to hotels Korsal, Liburna, Park, and Marko Polo.

By Car: See "Route Tips for Drivers" at the end of this chapter. Once in Korčula town, you can park affordably on top of the big Tommy supermarket. From here, you can ride the elevator down and walk straight out the front door into town (about a 5- to 10-minute downhill walk). There's also parking along the marina, but it's pricey and jammed.

HELPFUL HINTS

Boat Tickets: Don't dawdle buying your boat tickets to leave Korčula—they can sell out. Fortunately, all three of the major boat companies serving Korčula (Jadrolinija, Krilo, and Nona Ana) let you buy tickets online. For details, see "Korčula Connections," later.

Travel Agencies: Korčula has several travel agencies where you can book an excursion, browse shelves of books and souvenirs, and get information about car rental and other activities. The dominant company is **Korkyra Info,** which offers a wide variety of activities and services (such as car, bike, and kayak rental). Popular options include excursions to Mljet National Park and wine-tasting trips around Korčula Island. They're also the local sales point for the Nona Ana catamaran to Mljet and Dubrovnik (though you can also book those tickets online). Look for their main office on the little circular square facing the Old Town (Trg Petra Šegedina 3A, tel. 020/711-750, www.korkyra.info).

Transfers: An "Electric Car Transfer" service (that is, a golf cart) can take footsore tourists to distant hotels or parking lots (50 kn/group), or on a little panoramic loop for some high-up views down over Korčula (75 kn/person). To summon them, call 099-321-9160.

Laundry and Baggage Storage: Conveniently located at the bus station, you can drop off your laundry at **Na 90°** for full-service wash/dry; they also offer luggage storage (generally daily 7:00-21:00, mobile 099-325-4448).

Sights in Korčula

Korčula's few sights cluster close to one another in its historic core. I've listed them roughly in order from the Great Land Gate (the Old Town's main entry) to the tip of the peninsula. Museums are officially closed November through April, but most will usually open by request (ask the TI to call for you...or just try knocking on the door).

▲▲*Moreška* Dance

Lazy Korčula snaps to life when locals perform a folk dance called the *Moreška* (moh-REHSH-kah). The dance dates back at least to the mid-17th century, and the current troupe has been performing it since the 1960s. With local dancers all dressed up in traditional costume and the action interspersed with live music, it's a fun evening out...a bit of small-town community theater that keeps an age-old custom alive.

As the seating (metal chairs on concrete steps) has poor visibility, it's worth showing up a bit early to snare a good seat, close to the action. The program can vary, but usually kicks off with a jaunty musical piece performed by a local band, often followed by a brief performance of some hauntingly beautiful *klapa* songs by a choir. Then the *Moreška* begins: The evil king enters, clutching a fair maiden against her will. The good king challenges him, some amateur acting ensues, both kings' armies file in, and before long, the armies begin circling each other. After much clashing of swords, one side prevails...and a good time is had by all.

Cost and Hours: 100 kn, June-mid-Oct every Thu at 21:00, July-Aug also Mon, in outdoor theater next to the Great Land Gate—to the left as you face the gate, or in a nearby congress center in bad weather; buy tickets from travel agency, at your hotel, or at the door.

▲Great Land Gate (Veliki Revelin)

A noble staircase leads up to the main entrance to the Old Town. Like all of the town's towers, it's adorned with the Venetian winged lion and the coats of arms of the doge of Venice (left) and the rector of Korčula (right). You may be able to climb the tower (find the stairs around the left side) to visit a small exhibit with costumes and photos from the *Moreška* dance, then head up to the top level to enjoy panoramic town views (20 kn, July-Aug daily 9:00-21:00, June and Sept until 15:00, unpredictable hours off-season).

Pass through the gate into a little square ringed with Korčula history. On the left is the 16th-century **Town Hall and Rector's Palace.** The seal of Korčula (over the center arch) symbolizes the town's importance as the southernmost bastion of the Venetian Republic: St. Mark standing below three defensive towers. The little church on the other side of the square is dedicated to **St. Michael** (Crkva Sv. Mihovila). Throughout Croatia, many towns have churches dedicated to St. Michael just inside the town gates, as he is believed to offer saintly protection from enemies. Notice that a passageway connects the church to the building across the street—home to the Brotherhood of St. Michael, one of Korčula's many religious fraternal organizations. (Another such organization, located farther down this street, hosts the Icon Museum, described later.)

• *Now begin walking up the...*

Street of the Korčulan Statute of 1214 (Ulica Korčulanskog Statuta 1214)

This street is Korčula's backbone, in more ways than one: While most medieval towns slowly evolved with twisty, mazelike lanes, Korčula was carefully planned to resemble a fish skeleton. The streets to the west (left) of this one are straight, to allow the refreshing northwesterly Maestral winds into town. To the east (right), they're curved (notice you can't see the sea) to keep out the bad-vibe southeasterly Jugo winds. As in Croatia's other seafaring towns, the various winds—and weather in general—are highly important to locals.

The street's complicated name honors a 1214 statute—the oldest municipal legal document of any Croatian town—with regulations about everyday life and instructions on maintaining the city walls, protecting nature, keeping animals, building a house, and so on. As you head up the street, look up to notice some interesting decorations on the houses' upper floors—artifacts from an earlier time, when residents were proud and wealthy citizens of the Republic of Venice.

• *Speaking of Venice, if you continue up the street, you'll reach St. Mark's Square (Trg Sv. Marka). From here, you're a few steps from the next four sights.*

▲St. Mark's Cathedral (Katedrala Sv. Marka)

Korčula became a bishopric in the 14th century. In the 19th century—36 bishops later—the Habsburgs decided to centralize ec-

clesiastical power in their empire, and they removed Korčula's bishop. The town still has this beautiful "cathedral"...but no bishop. On the tympanum above the main door (outside), you'll see another Venetian statue of St. Mark (flanked by Adam and Eve, who support jutting stone tabs that hold fierce lions). Inside, notice the pointed Gothic arches on the ground floor and the rounded Romanesque arches above. Churches like this were commonly built entirely in the Romanesque style but later retrofitted with some pointed arches for better support. Above the main altar, you'll find an original Tintoretto painting. At the altar to the far left, find the statue of St. Rok (better known by his Italian name, San Rocco) pointing to a wound in his leg. This French saint is very popular in Croatia; it's believed he helps cure disease. As you leave, notice the weapons on the wall near the door; these were used in pivotal battles near strategically situated Korčula.

Cost and Hours: 15 kn, 25 kn combo-ticket with Church Museum; open daily 9:00-19:00, closed during church services, generally closed Nov-April but may be open Mon-Fri 9:00-12:00 after Easter.

Tower Climb: To huff up 70 stairs for great views over town, you can pay 25 kn to climb the bell tower (entrance left of main door).

▲Church Museum (Opatska Riznica)

This small museum has an eclectic and fascinating collection. Go on a scavenger hunt for the following items: a ceremonial necklace from Mother Teresa (who came from North Macedonia, not far from here—she gave this necklace to a friend from Korčula), some 12th-century hymnals, a coin collection (including a 2,400-year-old Greek coin minted here in Korčula), some Croatian modern paintings, a bishop's throne, three amphora jugs, and two framed reliquaries with dozens of minuscule relics. Lovers of clay pots and old kitchen stuff should ask at the gift shop to see the kitchen.

Cost and Hours: 25 kn combo-ticket with cathedral, 25-kn guidebook covers both museum and cathedral; Mon-Sat 9:00-19:00, sometimes open Sun morning, same off-season hours as cathedral.

▲Town Museum (Gradski Muzej)

Housed in an old mansion, this museum does a fine job of bringing together Korčula's various claims to fame. The house is arranged like a traditional Dalmatian home: shop on the ground floor, living quarters in the middle floors, kitchen on top.

Cost and Hours: 20 kn; July-Sept Mon-Sat 9:00-21:00, closed Sun; Oct-June Mon-Fri 10:00-14:00, closed Sat-Sun; tel. 020/711-420. If it's locked, try knocking.

Visiting the Museum: Some things may have been moved during renovations, but here's an idea of what you will see. A lapidarium features fragments of Korčula's stone past (see the first-century Roman amphora jugs). Look for a scant display of ancient Greek artifacts and an exhibit on the *Moreška* dance. Other exhibits include a display on Korčula's long-standing shipbuilding industry, with models of modern steel ships built here (the town still builds ship parts today). There's also a furnished living room and, in the attic, a kitchen. This was a smart place for the kitchen—if it caught fire, it was less likely to destroy the whole building. Notice the little WC in the corner. A network of pipes took kitchen and other waste through town and out to sea.

Marco Polo's House (Kuća Marka Pola)

Actually a more recent building on the site of what may or may not have been the property of the adventurer's family, the attraction of "Marco Polo's House" has been a stubby tower you can climb for an uninspiring view...and nothing else. Until a major renovation is completed to expand the exhibit, there's little reason to choose this over the Marco Polo Museum (described later).

Cost and Hours: 20 kn; July-Aug daily 9:00-21:00, irregular hours Easter-June and Sept-Oct but likely until 14:00, closed Nov-Easter; just north of cathedral on—where else?—ulica Depolo.

Nearby: Across the street from the house's entrance, you'll

Marco Polo

Korčula's favorite son is the great 13th-century explorer Marco Polo. Though Polo sailed under the auspices of the Venetian Republic (which included Korčula), locals proudly claim him as their own. Marco Polo was the first Westerner to chronicle his travels to China; he brought back amazing stories and exotic goods (like silk) that Europeans had never seen before. After his trip, Marco Polo fought in an important naval battle against the Genoese near Korčula (1298). He was captured, taken to Genoa, and imprisoned. He told his story to a cellmate, who wrote it down, published it, and made the explorer a world-class and much-in-demand celebrity. However, just as historians have wondered whether Polo made up parts of his tale, his Korčula origins might be a fabrication; there's no solid evidence he was actually born here.

find a **Marco Polo gift shop** selling various items related to the explorer—herbs, brandies, honey, and so on. Each one comes with a little tag telling a legend about M.P.—for example, how the word "million" was based on his middle name, Emilio (because no existing word was superlative enough for his discoveries). This is one of several such shops you'll see all over town.

▲Icon Museum (Zbirka Ikona)

Korčula is known for its many brotherhoods—centuries-old fraternal organizations that have sprung up around churches. The Brotherhood of All Saints has been meeting every Sunday after Mass since the 14th century, and they run a small but interesting museum of icons. These golden religious images were brought back from Greece in the 17th century by Korčulans who fought the Ottomans on a Venetian warship.

Brotherhoods' meeting halls are often connected to their church by a second-story walkway. Use this one to step into the Venetian-style **All Saints' Church** (Crkva Svih Svetih). On the rafters under the loft in the back of the church, notice the models of boats and tools—donated by Korčula's shipbuilders. Above the loft, notice the KKK-like white cloaks of the brotherhood. Look closely at the painting to the right of the altar. See the guys in the white robes kneeling under Jesus? That's the Brotherhood, who commissioned this painting.

Cost and Hours: 25 kn, hours depend on demand—generally May-Oct Mon-Sat 9:00-13:00 & 18:00-19:00, longer hours in peak season, closed Sun, closed Nov-April—but try ringing the bell, on Kaprova ulica at the Old Town's southeast tip—look for *Ikone* sign.

KORČULA

▲Old Town Walls

For several centuries, strategic Korčula was one of the most important southern outposts of the Venetian Republic. The Republic of
Dubrovnik began at the Pelješac Peninsula, just across the channel.
Korčula's original town walls date from at least the 13th century,
but the fortifications were expanded over several centuries to defend against various foes of Venice—mostly Ottomans, pirates, and
Ottoman pirates.

By the late 19th century, Korčula was an unimportant
Habsburg beach town, and the walls had no strategic value. The
town decided to quarry the top half of its old walls to build new
homes (and to improve air circulation inside the city). Though today's walls are half as high as they used to be, the town has restored
many of the towers, giving Korčula its fortified feel. Each one has
a winged lion—a symbol of Venice—and the seal of the rector of
Korčula when the tower was built.

• *Back out near the main gate of town, you'll find Korčula's final sight.*

▲Marco Polo Museum

While not quite a serious "museum," this exhibit offers an engaging interpretation of the life story of the (supposedly) Korčula-born
explorer. Considering that this attraction is basically a kid-friendly
publicity stunt for the local chain of Marco Polo gift shops, it's far
better than it could be, offering a brisk overview of the adventure,
suspense, and romance of one of the Western world's most swash-
buckling characters.

Cost and Hours: 60 kn, daily mid-June-late Sept 10:00-
21:00, shorter hours in shoulder season, closed Nov-April, Plokata
33, mobile 098-970-5334.

Visiting the Museum: You'll borrow a long-winded but
evocative audioguide (or just read the descriptions) and walk past
life-size dioramas of seven scenes from Marco Polo's adventures,
including setting sail from Korčula on his 24-year eastern odyssey,
crossing the deserts of Asia, coming to the court of Kublai Khan,
falling in love with Princess Cocacine, fighting a naval battle—and
being captured—off the coast of Korčula, and telling his tales in
prison. While pretty low-tech (it feels a bit like a walk-through
Pirates of the Caribbean, but with figures that don't move), it com-
pensates for the otherwise near-total lack of information about this
town's would-be favorite son. Though pricey, the museum is worthwhile if you're curious to learn more about Marco Polo, or simply
want an excuse to get out of the blazing sun or pouring rain.

KORČULA

ACTIVITIES IN KORČULA
Swimming

The water around Korčula is clean and suitable for swimming. You'll find pebbly beaches strewn with holiday-goers all along Put Svetog Nikole, the street that runs west from the Old Town. (The big, circular plaza where the embankment meets the Old Town is a pebbly kids' beach.) While this shoreline doesn't have much flat land for sunning yourself, you can generally find a relatively comfy rock to recline on. Other good swimming spots are at the tip of the Old Town peninsula, or southeast of town around Shell Bay.

To really commit some quality time to a beach, get out of town. The following options are good and fairly easy to reach; for details on any of these, ask at the TI, or try Taxi Boat Korčula (mobile 095-895-2204, www.taxi-boat-korcula.com):

Lumbarda, a nearby small town, has some good beaches and can be reached by bus, taxi, or boat (described later, under "More Sights on Korčula Island").

Stupe Island, just east of Korčula town, is home to the trendy Moro restaurant, which presides over a fine beach and runs a shuttle boat from the Old Town (120 kn round-trip, 3/day, 15 minutes each way, runs roughly June-Sept, also possible by taxi boat). When Leonardo DiCaprio came to Korčula on his yacht, he rented out this entire island.

Badija Island, immediately offshore from the boat dock at Dominče, is a fun place either to relax at the beach or go for a one-hour hike (60 kn round-trip, 2/hour, mid-June-early Sept). The island also has a 14th-century Franciscan monastery and a gallery of local artwork (40 kn, daily May-late Oct 10:00-18:00).

Excursions

Various companies offer day-long excursions, including trips around the island (either by car or by boat) and side trips to Dubrovnik or the national park on Mljet Island. Korkyra Info is the dominant outfit (see "Helpful Hints," earlier), but several other companies offer trips. There are also tour companies offering more active excursions, including canoe trips, snorkeling, kayaking, and other adventures—look for fliers around town.

Other Activities

All over town, you'll see travel agencies where you can rent a car, bike, scooter, boat, sea kayak, or anything else you want for some vacation fun. Local captains take tourists on

KORČULA

cruises to nearby bays and islands to get out on the water, swim, and enjoy a local-style "fish picnic." Inquire at any travel agency, or simply talk to a captain at the harbor (near the eastern ferry dock, at Shell Bay; figure about 200 kn per hour regardless of number of people). If you're a wine lover, consider hiring a driver to take you on a tour of Korčula Island, including stops at some wineries (ask at TI or travel agency).

MORE SIGHTS ON KORČULA ISLAND

Korčula Island may be one of Croatia's most beautiful. It mingles rugged mountains, lush forests, picturesque and tasty vineyards, gorgeous hidden beaches, and an almost Hawaiian ambience. If you have a car, the island is worth a half-day spin. Or you can easily take the bus or a taxi boat to Lumbarda.

▲Lumbarda

For a break from Korčula town, venture about three miles southeast to Lumbarda, a tranquil and tidy, end-of-the-road resort village. Lumbarda makes up for its lack of the stirring, fortified oldtown vibe of Korčula town by offering a lazy vacation personality that encourages visitors to linger.

There's not much to see in the town itself; most visitors come to hit the **beach.** While you can swim around Lumbarda's wide harbor, it's worth venturing farther out of town to one of its pleasant and pristine beaches. The best two cling to the little peninsula that juts out east of town: the pebbly **Bilin Žal** (literally "White Stone") to the north, and the sandy **Vela Pržina** (Old Sand) to the south. Both beaches are about a 20- to 30-minute walk (or a short drive) from Lumbarda. If you're coming on the bus from Korčula town, stay on the bus through Lumbarda's town-center stop, and carry on one more stop to the end of the line, which is a bit closer to the beaches. With your back to Lumbarda, walk right for sand, left for pebbles (ask locals—or other beachgoers—for specific directions).

Lumbarda is also known for its **wine**—specifically the *grk* white wine, the grapes for which grow only in this village's unique climate. It's named for the Greeks who introduced it. Several wineries drape the hillsides above Lumbarda; my favorite for a visit and tasting is **Bire** (BEE-reh; drivers will see the turnoff on the right just before entering the town of Lumbarda). The setting is beautiful: a series of stone buildings bunny-hopping down the hill toward town, with an inviting tasting room. You can sample their *grk, plavac,* and rosé wines for a small fee (Mon-Sat 10:00-12:00 & 16:00-18:00, closed Sun, generally closed Oct-May, mobile 098-344-712, www.bire.hr).

Getting There: From Korčula town, you can get to Lumbarda by water taxi (75 kn round-trip) or by bus (hourly Mon-Sat in summer, fewer buses Sun, 15 minutes, 17 kn one-way, 25 kn round-trip). A land taxi costs about 100 kn one-way.

North Coast

On the road that hugs the island's northern coast, from Korčula town to the village of Račišće, you'll find a series of beautiful tableaux over tranquil coves and tiny offshore islands, with the looming Pelješac Peninsula as a dramatic backdrop.

Korčula Island Spin

If you'd like to see more (beyond Lumbarda and the coastal zones), head west and drive the length of this long, skinny island (29 miles by just 5 miles).

Driving up and out of Korčula (pausing for grand views at the pullout just above the Tommy supermarket), you'll pass through Žrnovo and eventually twist your way up to humble **Pupnat.** This oldest village on the island has a Tito-era Partisan monument and a cluster of old 12th- and 13th-century slate-roof houses. From here, you can continue along the main road, or wind down the steep side road to the tranquil and gorgeous bay of **Pupnatska Luka,** with an inviting pebbly beach fronted by beach bars. Ponder how the ancient Greeks—impressed by the thick forests here—called this island "Black Korkyra."

Farther west are two of Korčula island's main wine-growing towns: **Čara,** an otherwise nondescript concrete town, overlooks a broad basin striped with vineyards. Farther along, **Smokvica** is also all about grapes. In both towns, you'll spot several wineries that invite passersby in for a sample. Korčula produces mostly white wines, using local grapes called *pošip* (which tend to produce dry wines), *korčulanka,* and *rukatac* (smaller grapes that produce sweeter, higher-alcohol wines).

From Smokvica, detour down along the south coastal road, via **Brna** (deep yet sheltered, this stunning cove is a favorite spot for super-wealthy yachters to drop anchor) and then **Prižba.** The scenic road passes the parking pads of cantilevered rental villas that are a popular place for Czechs, Poles, and other Central Europeans to set up for a week or two of fun in the Adriatic sun. A string of tiny islets hovers just offshore, and farther behind is the big island of Lastovo. Facing the open sea, this area is popular for fishing.

Then twist your way back up into the interior (passing old terraces), dropping down into the island's biggest town, **Blato**—filling a low-slung valley and huddled around the base of a small hill. Its atmospheric tree-lined streets take you through a landlocked, workaday town that seems blissfully oblivious to the tourism all around it. Literally "Mud," Blato is named for the flood plain that surrounds it—now efficiently drained and used for abundant agriculture.

The road ends at **Vela Luka,** a working-class town surrounding a picturesque harbor. Enjoy a coffee, wine, or beer as you watch the bobbing fishing vessels, then head back across the island to Korčula town.

Nightlife in Korčula

This town is much sleepier than Hvar, but you'll still find a fair number of late-night discos in the summertime, including one near the eastern base of the Old Town peninsula and others along the waterfront between the historic center and the resort hotels (east of town). Just below the Great Land Gate, Caffe Bar Step often has live music outside.

The best setting for drinks is at **Buffet "Massimo,"** a youthful-feeling cocktail bar in a city-wall tower at the very tip of the Old Town peninsula. You can have a drink on one of three levels: the downstairs bar, the main-floor lounge, or the tower-top terrace (terrace is only for cocktail-sippers—no beer or wine; climb the ladder at your own risk). If you're up top, notice the simple dumbwaiter for hauling up drinks (daily 9:00-late, closed Nov-April, tel. 020/715-073).

For a no-stress opportunity to sample local wines right in the Old Town, you'll find **Bokar Wine Bar** near the tip of the peninsula (just steps from Massimo, above). They have a tight interior, fun sidewalk tables on an atmospheric lane, a small selection of wines, and knowledgeable servers who enjoy offering suggestions (daily 10:00-24:00, closed Nov-April, Antuna Rozanovića, mobile 099-404-1052, Peter).

Sleeping in Korčula

SOBE

Korčula has a wide variety of *sobe;* they're fairly basic but affordable and very local. Unless otherwise noted, these places have air-conditioning, accept only cash (no credit cards), and don't provide breakfast. Apartments come equipped with kitchens, and *sobe* often have refrigerators and kettles. For something more substantial, several cafés in town offer a basic breakfast for around 50 kn; ask your *soba* host for suggestions.

In the Old Town

Sleeping in the Old Town nestles you squarely in the historic heart of Korčula, in immediate proximity to all the sights. The likely trade-offs: steep and tight staircases, small rooms in centuries-old houses, and (with a few exceptions) no sea views.

$$$$ Carpe Diem sits deep in the center of Korčula's Old Town. Rather than individual rooms, you rent out the entire beautifully restored historic townhouse, which sleeps up to five on five steep floors. It's a worthwhile splurge for those wanting to have their own traditional Korčula home that's thoughtfully appointed with modern conveniences, including a washing machine and a sauna (air-con, Antuna Rozanovića 8, mobile 091-769-7007, nikola.curac@du.htnet.hr, Nikola and Marija Curać).

$$ M&J Central Suites, run by Marko and Jelena, are cozy and central. Their four tight but nicely appointed and well-equipped apartments (all with laundry facilities—washing machine and drying lines) fill in a nicely renovated house right in the middle of the Old Town; they also have a small double room with a private bathroom across the hall (air-con, near Konoba Marko Polo restaurant at Jakova Baničevića 13, mobile 098-160-9644, mjcentralsuites@yahoo.com).

$ Sobe Nina, run by Nina and her son Mate (who works at the pizzeria downstairs), offers four simple rooms and a few pricier apartments (some with views) in a building along the seawall. It's a lesser value, worth considering if you're in a pinch (air-con, cheap self-serve washing machine, next to Marco Polo shop at Šetalište Petra Kanavelića 3, mobile 098-912-7638, matekurtovic@yahoo.com).

$ Ivo and Katja Tedeschi, who also run a recommended pizzeria, rent three small, simple rooms (two with views) and a big, low-ceilinged, top-floor seaview apartment up lots of steep stairs just inside the seawall (RS%, air-con, Don Iva Matijace 26, tel. 020/711-354, mobile 091-566-6924, acc.tedeschi@gmail.com).

West of the Old Town

The pleasant residential neighborhood west of the Old Town, along the waterfront drag called Put Svetog Nikole, comes with an easy, level walk into town and gorgeous views of the peninsula. The main advantages to sleeping here are a bit more space and (in many cases) sea views. I've listed places in the order you'll reach them as you walk along the water—from one minute (the first listing) to 10 minutes (last listing) away from the Old Town.

$$ Royal Apartments, spacious and hotelesque, are conscientiously run by Zvonko and Marija Jelavić, who enjoy socializing with their guests in the small square out front. It's nicely situated facing a little beach, just steps from the Old Town peninsula (closed mid-Oct-mid-April, car rental possible, well-marked with green awning just west of Old Town at Trg Petra Šegedina 4, mo-

KORČULA

bile 098-184-0444, www.korcularoyalapartments.com, royalapt@ ica.net).

¢ Rezi and Andro Depolo, possibly distant relatives of Marco, rent four comfy, good-value rooms on the bay west of the Old Town. Three of the rooms offer beautiful views, and the five-minute stroll into town is pleasant and scenic. Friendly, English-speaking Rezi works to make her guests feel welcome (walk along waterfront from Old Town with bay on your right to the yellow house at Put Svetog Nikole 28—it's set back from the street but well-signed; tel. 020/711-621, mobile 098-964-3687, www.family-depolo.com, rezi.depolo@gmail.com).

¢ Kiwi Rooms, run by gregarious, English-speaking Nado Andrijić and his artist wife Marica, has two bright, tight, and nicely decorated rooms with gorgeous seaview balconies facing the monastery steeple. While there's no air-conditioning, they often get a good breeze and there's only a bit of road noise (Put Svetog Nikole 42, tel. 020/711-608, mobile 091-543-8265, kiwirooms@ yahoo.com).

HOTELS

These two hotels—the only ones not run by the big, local hotel chain (see "HTP Korčula," below)—are the town's lone compromise between *sobe* and big hotels.

$$$$ Hotel Fabris, beautifully located overlooking a little beach where the Old Town peninsula meets the picturesque waterfront promenade, has 10 tight but well-equipped rooms with stone walls, varnished wood, and lots of stairs (more for seaview balcony, Hrvatske Bratske Zajednice 6, tel. 020/716-755, https://thefabris. com, info@thefabris.com, Zlatko).

$$$ Hotel Korsal has 19 rooms filling three buildings just above the touristy promenade connecting the Old Town to the resort area, a 10-minute walk from downtown. The decor is bright, colorful, and nautical; you can choose between seaview rooms and "comfort garden" rooms, which are big and have private decks but lack views (includes breakfast, closed Nov-April, Šetalište Frana Kršinića 80, tel. 020/715-722, www.hotel-korsal.com, info@hotel-korsal.com).

HTP Korčula

This company owns Korčula's five big hotels. While overpriced and (mostly) distant from the historic heart of Korčula, they have high capacity and could work in a pinch. You can reserve rooms at any of them through the website or main office (includes breakfast, tel. 020/726-336, www.korcula-hotels.com, marketing@htp-korcula. hr). **$$$ Hotel Korčula de la Ville** has by far the best location, right on the waterfront alongside the Old Town. It has a fine seaside terrace restaurant and friendly staff. The 20 rooms are on two floors: The more expensive "first-floor" rooms (actually on the third floor) have big windows and views, while the cheaper "second-floor" rooms (actually on the fourth) have tiny windows and no views (reception tel. 020/726-900). Three more HTP Korčula hotels cluster a 15-minute walk away, around the far side of Shell Bay. While relatively inconvenient to the Old Town, they share a nice beach: **Hotel Marko Polo** has 94 rooms, air-conditioning, an elevator, and a big pool; **Hotel Liburna,** with a clever split-level design that reflects the skyline of the Old Town, has 109 rooms, most of them accessible by elevator; and **Hotel Park**—the oldest of the bunch, and still awaiting renovation—has 134 cheaper rooms. About 15 minutes' walk farther (30 minutes total) is the recently spiffed-up **Port 9 Resort;** while distant, it's a fun place to be on vacation, and it is connected to town by boats and a shuttle service (www.port9resort.com).

Eating in Korčula

Korčula lacks the burgeoning culinary scene of Hvar; while a few top-end places try to lure the yachting crowd, most options are interchangeable *konoba*s—simple restaurants serving pastas and seafood dishes. Note that almost all these places close from mid-October to Easter (if you're here off-season, call ahead or ask around to find out what's open). Skip the eateries around Shell Bay, east of the Old Town.

$$$ **Adio Mare,** with fine seafood and friendly service, is the best of Korčula's many traditional restaurants. You'll step into a stone tavern-like dining room sporting long, shared tables and a thick vine scaling one wall. But if the weather's nice, ask to sit in the enchanting rooftop garden terrace, where you'll dine romantically above the fray below (Mon-Sat 12:00-23:00, Sun from 18:00, on the main drag just past Marco Polo's House, tel. 020/711-253).

$$$ **Aterina,** with a youthful spirit, fills a hidden little square just inside the Old Town walls. It's deservedly proud of its original recipes, fresh products, and warm welcome (assured by Nataša). Here you can assemble small plates of local Dalmatian bites (mostly seafood-based, though usually with some good vegetarian options) or order full courses. The "little bit of everything" sampler plate makes a fine meal. Ask about the day's specials (daily 12:00-24:00, Trg Korčulanskih Klesara i Kipara 2, mobile 098-986-1856).

$$ **Pizzeria Amfora,** on a side lane off the people-parade up Korčula's main drag, features delicious and well-priced pastas and pizzas, and less successful wok dishes—nothing fancy, just good ol' comfort food. Squeeze into the small dining room or enjoy the

sidewalk tables (daily 10:00-24:00, ulica od Teatra 4, tel. 020/711-739).

Along the Seawall: A wide variety of restaurants line up scenically along the Old Town's eastern seawall, providing al fresco dining with salty views. Their tables, spilling out along the wall and overlooking the water, are ideal for romantic harborside meals. Dine here if it's hot, as there's often a pleasant breeze. Of the high-end options in this area, **$$$$ Filippi** is the most worth considering. Serving a limited but enticing menu of quality Dalmatian and international cuisine, but with warm service that skips the snobby pretense of some of its rivals, it's a fine place to splurge (assemble your own wine flight from the wine list, daily 12:00-24:00, closed Nov-March, tel. 020/711-690, www.restaurantfilippi.com). For something less expensive, consider **$$ Silk**—named for the Silk Road explorations of local boy Marco Polo—with surprisingly good Asian street food (order at the window and choose a bench; all outdoor seating, but no waterfront tables; daily 11:30-23:00, Baničevića 17, tel. 020/721-111). There's also easygoing **$$ Pizzeria Tedeschi,** which serves up good pizzas closer to the base of the peninsula (daily 9:00-24:00, tel. 020/711-586).

Picnics: Just outside the main gate, you'll find a lively produce market and a big, modern, air-conditioned **Konzum** supermarket (Mon-Sat 7:00-21:00, Sun 8:00-20:00). A short stroll from there down Put Svetog Nikole takes you to rocky seafront perches with the best Korčula views. There are also many inviting picnic spots along the Old Town embankment.

Sweet Shop: For good local sweets, stop by **Cukarin,** which sells tasty traditional cookies such as the delicious flourless (and gluten-free) *amareta* almond cake; the Marko Polo cake (flourless chocolate cake with buttercream); and the walnut-cream-filled *klašun.* They also sell homemade wine, liqueur, honey, and jam (Mon-Sat 8:30-14:00 & 17:00-22:00, closed Sun and Nov-March, a block behind the Jadrolinija office on Hrvatske Bratske Zajednice, tel. 020/711-055).

Korčula Connections

Korčula is tethered to the rest of the Dalmatian Coast by a few tenuous boat connections. Service becomes quite sparse off-season, and everything has been in flux in recent years, so it's important to research your options carefully online. If you're here during a lull in the sailing schedule, buses (which make the short crossing on the Dominče-Orebić ferry) are your ticket out of town.

BY BOAT
Fast Passenger Catamarans

For most travelers, the key connections are the fast passenger catamarans. These are run by three different companies, and the only way to fully understand all of your options is to check the websites for all three: Krilo (www.krilo.hr), Jadrolinija (www.jadrolinija.hr), and—to Mljet and Dubrovnik—Nona Ana (www.gv-line.hr). You can—and should—buy tickets on these websites. Ideally, buy your tickets a day or two ahead—or more than that, in peak season. Boats sell out at busy times.

Ticket Offices: While booking online is easy, each company also has a sales point in Korčula: Jadrolinija's well-marked ticket office is right where the Old Town peninsula meets the mainland (for this company only, you must buy tickets in person for same-day departures); Krilo has a ticket kiosk on the western embankment (open limited hours: 9:00-10:30 & 17:00-19:00); and Nona Ana sells tickets through the Korkyra Info travel agency (see "Helpful Hints," earlier).

Departure Point: On most days, before 17:00, the speedy catamarans depart from the eastern embankment. After 17:00, and somewhat randomly at other times, they may use the western embankment instead. Ask in the morning which dock your catamaran uses.

Catamarans from Korčula Town North to Hvar and Split: Jadrolinija and Krilo run fast catamarans north, some stopping first at **Hvar** town (1 hour), all terminating at **Split** (2.5 hours). Krilo has more connections (in summer 3/day to Hvar, 4/day to Split, fewer departures in spring and fall, 1/day year-round) than Jadrolinija (1/day June-Sept only).

Catamarans from Korčula Town South to Mljet and Dubrovnik: All three companies make the run to **Dubrovnik** (2 hours). If you want to get to the national park on **Mljet,** check the schedule carefully: You want a boat that stops at Pomena or Polače (30 minutes), *not* at Sobra. Krilo has two different southbound boats departing around the same time in the morning (2/day late May-early Oct, one with a stop at Pomena, Mljet; 1/day early April-late May and late Oct, also stops at Pomena; none offseason). Jadrolinija's Dubrovnik-bound boat departs in the evening (no stop on Mljet, June-Sept only). And Nona Ana departs in the afternoon, but only four times per week from July through September; this boat also stops at Polače on Mljet.

Boarding Tips: In some cases, companies might run two different catamarans that depart around the same time. Passengers tend to stand in one big line until the first boat arrives, at which point an attendant shouts the two different departures to divvy the

KORČULA

line into two. Be ready for this: Know your boat's departure time and its name, which are both printed on your ticket; if the boat that pulls up isn't the one on your ticket, don't get on it.

Other Boats

In addition to the catamarans, Korčula Island has an assortment of other boat connections. The first one leaves from Korčula town, while the rest depart from other points on the island.

Passenger Ferry from Korčula Town to Orebić: Državna Brodska boats leave from the Old Town's western embankment, connecting Korčula with Orebić on the Pelješac Peninsula in 15 minutes (15 kn, hourly July-Aug, 10/day in June and Sept, 7/day in Oct and March-May). This is handy mostly for those meeting a driver at Orebić for a wine-tasting Pelješac drive on the way to Dubrovnik.

Car Ferry from Dominče (near Korčula Town) to the Mainland: The island of Korčula is connected to the mainland by a small car ferry that runs between Dominče—about a mile east of Korčula town—and Orebić, across the channel on the Pelješac Peninsula (15-minute crossing, departs Dominče at the top of most but not all hours—check carefully in Korčula, departs Orebić at :30 past most hours).

Boats from Vela Luka North to Hvar Town and Split: Additional boats connect to points north, but they depart from the port at Vela Luka, an hour away from Korčula town, at the opposite end of the island. A Jadrolinija **fast catamaran** goes daily from Vela Luka to both Hvar town and Split; unfortunately, on most days it departs extremely early, with no bus connection from Korčula to get you there in time—if you're desperate, you could pay about 450 kn for an early-morning taxi or sleep overnight in Vela Luka (Mon-Sat departs at 5:30, Sun at 8:05; 45 minutes to Hvar, 2 hours to Split). A **car ferry** also travels daily from Vela Luka to Split—it's slower but generally departs at a more convenient time; at least one daily connection is coordinated with a bus from Korčula (2/day, 3 hours, no stop at Hvar town). Since getting to Vela Luka from Korčula town is a hassle, carefully confirm these boat schedules at the Korčula TI or Jadrolinija office, and understand all of your options before you get up early to make the trip.

BUS CONNECTIONS

All buses from Korčula town (except those to Vela Luka) first drive to Dominče, where they meet the car ferry to cross over to Orebić, on the Pelješac Peninsula. Once across, it takes just over an hour to drive the length of the Pelješac Peninsula and meet the main coastal road.

From Korčula Town by Bus to: Dubrovnik (2/day, 3.5 hours, likely departs at 6:45 and 15:35; July-Aug extra departure at 8:35 on Wed, Fri, Sun); **Vela Luka** (at far end of island, Mon-Fri 6/day, Sat 5/day, Sun 3/day, 1 hour). An inconveniently timed bus departs Korčula nightly at 19:45, stopping in **Split** (5 hours, arrives after midnight) and then continuing overnight to **Zagreb** (arrives around 7:00 the next morning).

ROUTE TIPS FOR DRIVERS

If you're driving via the mainland, you'll first cross on the car ferry from Dominče to Orebić (described earlier), which is on the vineyard-strewn Pelješac Peninsula. Consider dropping into a winery as you traverse the long, narrow Pelješac Peninsula (about a 1.5-hour drive to the main coastal road). Where the peninsula meets the mainland, you'll see the cute little "Great Wall of Croatia" town of Ston. For more on the Pelješac Peninsula and Ston—including a self-guided driving tour of the vineyards between here and Dubrovnik—see page 357.

If you're heading south to **Dubrovnik,** the coastal road zips you right there (about an hour from Ston). If you're heading north to **Split,** soon after joining the coastal road you'll actually pass through Bosnia-Herzegovina for a few miles (around the town of Neum; for details, see page 458). A bridge now under construction near Neum will eventually bypass the Bosnian stretch of road.

Because of the ferry crossing and the long drive along the Pelješac Peninsula, driving **between Split and Korčula** is time-consuming and tiring. Instead, I prefer to take the longer car ferry the whole way between Split and Vela Luka, at the far end of Korčula Island (described earlier; allow 1 hour for the drive from Korčula town to Vela Luka). The scenic and relaxing three-hour boat ride from Vela Luka to Split saves you more than that much driving time.

If you're headed north, note that there's also a car ferry from Dominče north to **Drvenik** on the mainland (about halfway to Split).

DUBROVNIK

Dubrovnik is a living fairy tale that shouldn't be missed. It feels like a small town today, but 500 years ago, the city was a major maritime power, with the third-biggest navy in the Mediterranean. Still jutting confidently into the sea and ringed by thick medieval walls, Dubrovnik deserves its nickname: Pearl of the Adriatic. Within the ramparts, the traffic-free Old Town is a fun jumble of steep alleys, low-impact museums, al fresco cafés, and kid-friendly squares. After all these centuries, the buildings still hint at old-time wealth, and the central promenade (Stradun) remains the place to see and be seen.

The city's charm is the result of its no-nonsense past. Busy merchants, the salt trade, and shipbuilding made Dubrovnik rich. But Dubrovnik's most valued commodity was always its freedom— even today, you'll see the proud motto *Libertas* displayed all over town (see *"Libertas"* sidebar).

Dubrovnik flourished in the 15th and 16th centuries, but an earthquake (and ensuing fire) destroyed nearly everything in 1667. Most of today's buildings in the Old Town are post-quake Baroque, although a few palaces, monasteries, and convents displaying a rich Gothic-Renaissance mix survive from Dubrovnik's earlier Golden Age. Dubrovnik remained a big tourist draw through the Tito years, bringing in much-needed hard currency from Western visitors. Consequently, the city never acquired the hard socialist patina of many other Yugoslav cities.

As Croatia violently separated from Yugoslavia in 1991, Dubrovnik became the only coastal city to be pulled into the fighting (see "The Siege of Dubrovnik" sidebar, later). Imagine having your youthful good memories of romping in the surrounding hills re-

Libertas

Libertas—liberty—has always been close to the heart of every Dubrovnik citizen. Dubrovnik was a proudly independent republic for centuries, even as most of Croatia fell under Venetian or Hungarian rule.

In the Middle Ages, the city-state of Dubrovnik (then called Ragusa) bought its independence from whichever power was strongest—Byzantium, Venice, Hungary, the Ottomans, the Vatican—sometimes paying off more than one at a time. Dubrovnik's ships flew whichever flags were necessary to stay free, earning the derisive nickname "Town of Seven Flags." It was sort of a Hong Kong or Singapore of the Middle Ages—a spunky, trading-oriented statelet that maintained its sovereignty while being completely surrounded by an often-hostile mega-state (in Dubrovnik's case, the Ottoman Empire). Dubrovnik persevered partly because the sultans were always susceptible to bribery (or "tribute"): They were more than happy to let Dubrovnik thrive...provided they got their cut.

As time went on, Dubrovnik's status grew. Europe's big-league nations were glad to have a second major seafaring power in the Adriatic to balance Venice; Dubrovnik emerged as an attractive alternative at times when Venetian ports were blockaded by the Ottomans. A free Dubrovnik was more valuable than a pillaged, plundered Dubrovnik.

In 1808, Napoleon conquered the Adriatic and abolished the Republic of Dubrovnik. After Napoleon was defeated, the fate of the continent was decided at the Congress of Vienna. But Dubrovnik's delegate was denied a seat at the table. The more powerful nations, no longer concerned about Venice and fed up after years of being sweet-talked by Dubrovnik, were afraid that the delegate would play old alliances off each other to reestablish an independent Republic of Dubrovnik. Instead, the city became a part of the Habsburg Empire and entered a long period of decline.

Libertas still hasn't died in Dubrovnik. In the surreal days of the early 1990s, when Yugoslavia was reshuffling itself, a movement for the creation of a new Republic of Dubrovnik gained some momentum (led by a judge who, in earlier times, had convicted others for the same ideas). Another movement pushed for Dalmatia to secede as its own nation. But now that the dust has settled, today's locals are content and proud to be part of an independent Republic of Croatia.

DUBROVNIK

placed by visions of tanks and warships shelling your hometown. The city was devastated, but Dubrovnik was repaired with amazing speed. The only physical reminders of the war are lots of new, bright-orange roof tiles. Locals are often willing to talk openly about the experience with visitors—offering a rare opportunity to grasp the realities of war from an eyewitness perspective.

Though the war killed tourism in the 1990s, today the crowds are most decidedly back—far exceeding prewar levels. In fact, Dubrovnik's biggest downside is its popularity. When several cruise ships are in town, it can be mobbed. And, with more and more locals priced out of the Old Town and moving to the suburbs, the center can feel, at times, like a very pretty but soulless theme park. But those who dig deeper find that the city still has a strong sense of identity and a lovable personality. And, like Venice, Dubrovnik rewards those who get off the beaten path and savor the town early and late, when cruisers and day-trippers have cleared out. If you

Greater Dubrovnik

To Bosnia-Herzegovina

1 Kilometer

1 Mile

Mount Srđ

CABLE CAR

Bosanka

"CABLE CAR" BUS STOP

JADRANSKA CESTA

PLOČE

STRADUN

FRANA SUPILA

PETRA KREŠIMIRA FRANA SUPILA

BANJE BEACH

Pile Gate Bus Stop

OLD TOWN
See detail map

To Elaphite Islands

Lokrum

ST. JAKOB BEACH
To Cavtat

VLAHA BUKOVCA

To Airport & Montenegro

---

haven't discovered your own secluded, laundry-draped back lane... then you haven't looked hard enough.

For many, Dubrovnik makes an ideal home base. Build some slack into your Dubrovnik stay for a wide array of worthwhile side trips (outlined in the Near Dubrovnik, Montenegro, and Mostar chapters).

PLANNING YOUR TIME

Dubrovnik's museums aren't major draws; the real attraction here is the Old Town and its relaxing, breezy ambience. While Dubrovnik could easily be "seen" in a day, a second or third day to unwind (or even more time, for side trips) makes the long trip here more worthwhile. I enjoy staying at least three or four nights, for maximum side-tripping flexibility.

To hit all the key sights in a single day, start at the Pile Gate, at the entrance to the Old Town. Walk around the city's walls to get your bearings (before it gets too hot and crowded), then work your way down the main drag (following my "Stradun Stroll"). As you explore, drop in at any museums or churches that appeal to you. Ride the cable car to the top of Mount Srđ for the sunset, then descend to the Old Town for dinner. With a second day, spread out these activities, hit the beach, or take a boat excursion from the Old Port (Lokrum Island, just offshore, requires the least brainpower). With even more time, fit in side trips to a pair of particularly striking international destinations: Bosnia-Herzegovina's Mostar and Montenegro's Bay of Kotor.

Orientation to Dubrovnik

Nearly all of the sights worth seeing are in Dubrovnik's traffic-free, walled **Old Town** (Stari Grad, STAH-ree grahd) peninsula. The main pedestrian promenade through the middle of town is called the **Stradun** (STRAH-doon); from this artery, the Old Town climbs steeply uphill in both directions to the walls. The Old Town connects to the mainland through three gates: the **Pile Gate,** to the west; the **Ploče Gate,** to the east; and the smaller **Buža Gate,** at the top of the stepped lane called Boškovićeva. The **Old Port** (Gradska Luka), with leisure boats to nearby destinations, is at the east end of town. While greater Dubrovnik has about 50,000 people, the population within the Old Town is around 1,500; most property owners here have converted their homes into tourist apartment rentals.

The **Pile** (PEE-leh) neighborhood, a pincushion of tourist services, is just outside the western end of the Old Town (through the Pile Gate). In front of the gate, you'll find the main TI, ATMs, a post office, taxis, buses (fanning out to all the outlying neighborhoods), a bus-ticket kiosk, a cheap Konzum grocery store, and a DM pharmacy. This is also the starting point for my "Stradun Stroll."

A mile or two away from the Old Town are beaches peppered with expensive resort hotels. The closest area is **Boninovo Bay** (a 20-minute walk or 5-minute bus trip from the Old Town), but most cluster on the lush **Lapad Peninsula** to the west (a 15-minute bus trip from the Old Town). Across the bay from the Lapad Peninsula is **Port Gruž,** with the main bus station, ferry terminal, and main cruise port. (Additional cruise ships tender to the Old Port.) While accommodations prices in these areas can be lower, you'll be competing with lots of other day-trippers (and cruise passengers) on your daily "commute" into your Old Town sightseeing. I prefer to stay within walking distance of the walls.

TOURIST INFORMATION

Dubrovnik's main TI is just outside the Old Town's **Pile Gate,** at the far end of the big terrace with the modern video-screens sculpture (June-Sept daily 8:00-21:00, April-May and Oct until 20:00, off-season until 19:00 and shorter hours on Sun; Brsalje 5, tel. 020/312-011, www.tzdubrovnik.hr). There are also locations at **Port Gruž,** across the street from the Jadrolinija ferry dock (same hours except closes earlier in off-season, Obala Ivana Pavla II, tel. 020/417-983); in the **Lapad** resort area, at the head of the main drag (Masarykov put 2, in Dvori Lapad building, tel. 020/437-460); on two of the Elaphite Islands, **Lopud** (Obala Iva Kuljevana 12, tel. 020/322-322) and **Šipan** (Luka b.b., tel. 020/758-084); and at the arrivals area of the **airport.** While not an official TI, the handy **Cultural Information Desk** (at the base of the Bell Tower, on Luža Square) is more central and can answer many questions (open long hours daily).

All TIs sell the Dubrovnik Card and hand out two similar booklets: the annual *Dubrovnik Riviera Info* (lots of glossy photos and telephone directory) and the monthly *The Best in Dubrovnik* (with a current schedule of events and performances, and bus and ferry schedules).

Sightseeing Passes: If you'll be doing any sightseeing at all, choose between Dubrovnik's two passes. (Since you can't buy individual tickets for the Rector's Palace, Rupe Museum, or Maritime Museum, you'll have to get one of these passes to see any of them.) Assuming you're climbing the City Walls—Dubrovnik's top attraction—you might as well buy the **Dubrovnik Card,** which covers several major museums, the walls, and public transit. To squeeze all of your sightseeing into one day, get the 24-hour pass (250 kn, includes unlimited transit); with more time, consider one of the longer tickets, which cover the same sights and add a few more bonuses and discounts—including for side-tripping to Cavtat (300 kn/3 days includes 6 transit rides, 350 kn/7 days includes 10 transit rides; cards sold at TIs and many sights and hotels; slightly cheaper if you purchase online). The 130-kn **"nine museum ticket"** is good for a week and covers several major museums.

ARRIVAL IN DUBROVNIK

Most of Dubrovnik's arrival points—ferry dock, cruise terminal, bus station—are at **Port Gruž,** about 2.5 miles northwest of the Old Town. To get into town, hop on a bus (#1a, #1b, #1c, #3, or #8) or take a taxi (around 70-80 kn) to the Pile Gate, at the entrance to the Old Town.

By Boat

Passenger **catamarans** and car **ferries** all arrive at Port Gruž, two miles northwest of the Old Town. On the road in front of the ferry terminal, you'll find a bus stop (wait on the embankment side of the street) and a taxi stand. Across the street is the Jadrolinija office (with an ATM out front) and a TI.

Some **cruise ships** anchor just offshore from the Old Port, then send their passengers into the Old Town on tenders. Others put in just beyond the bus station at Port Gruž, where you can catch a bus or taxi to the Old Town.

By Bus

Dubrovnik's main bus station (Autobusni Kolodvor) is just beyond the ferry terminal along the Port Gruž embankment. On arrival, walk straight ahead through the bus stalls then bear right at the main road to the city bus stop, or hop in a taxi.

Alternate Bus Stop for Outbound Buses: For buses that are leaving Dubrovnik toward regional destinations to the south (such as the airport or Cavtat), there's another bus stop that's much closer to the Old Town, saving you the long journey out to the main bus station. The **"cable car" bus stop** (a.k.a. "fire station" bus stop) is just uphill from the Buža Gate, overlooking the old wall, right next to the bottom station of the cable car up to Mount Srđ.

By Plane

Dubrovnik's small airport (Zračna Luka) is near a village called Čilipi, 13 miles south of the city. A bus meets arriving flights for most major airlines and takes you to the main bus station (55 kn, 40 minutes), with public-bus connections to the Old Town. Legitimate cabbies charge around 250-270 kn for the ride between the airport and the center, though some cabbies charge more than 300 kn; consider arranging your transfer in advance with one of the drivers listed under "Tours in Dubrovnik—Private Drivers" or through your *soba* host (airport code: DBV, tel. 020/773-333, www. airport-dubrovnik.hr).

To get *to* the airport, you can take the same bus, which typically leaves from Dubrovnik's main bus station 1.5 hours before each Croatia Airlines or Austrian Airlines flight, or two hours before other airlines' international flights (the schedule is posted the day before—ask at the TI). The airport-bound bus departs from the main bus station and stops at the "cable car" bus stop just above the Old Town's Buža Gate (see "By Bus," earlier).

By Car

Coming from the north, you'll drive over the modern Tuđman Bridge (which most locals, mindful of their former president's tarnished legacy, call simply "the New Bridge").

To Port Gruž: To get to the main bus station, ferry terminal (with some car-rental drop-off offices nearby), and Lapad Penin-sula, take the left turn just after the bridge, wind down to the wa-terfront, then turn left and follow this road along the Port Gruž embankment.

To the Old Town: Continue straight after the bridge. You'll pass above the Port Gruž area, then take the right turnoff marked *Dubrovnik* (with the little bull's-eye). You'll go through a tunnel, then turn left for *Grad/Old City*. This road passes the big Old Town parking garage (described next), then twists around over the top of the Old Town, until you can see the lower station for the cable car. Here you have two choices, which will determine which one-way loop you'll get stuck in: If you want to reach the Pile Gate (at the eastern end of the Old Town), make a sharp right turn just before the cable car (watch for *Grad/Old City* signs), then turn right again (passing the entrance to the small "tennis court" parking lot) to curl around the back of the city wall and pop out at the Pile Gate (with another small parking lot), then back up out of town toward Boninovo Bay and Lapad. Or, if you want to head east of the Old Town, continue straight past the cable-car station for a long, scenic drive above the Viktorija area, then (after a sharp right turn) past luxury hotels and to the Ploče Gate.

Parking: Near the Old Town, parking costs are exorbitant— maybe even more than you're paying for accommodations (rates are constantly in flux and may exceed what's listed here). Ideally, make Dubrovnik either the first or last stop of your car rental, so you won't have to pay to park here. But if you must, ask your *soba* host for their best advice (many have a line on relatively reasonable op-tions, though they may be distant).

There are a few small parking lots **near the City Walls**—so expensive and crowded that they're useful only for dropping off luggage before retreating to a more affordable alternative. The most expensive is just behind the DM pharmacy near the Pile Gate (75 kn/hour, no daily rate); somewhat cheaper—but still pricey and often full—is the "tennis court" lot, huddled behind the wall at the Buža Gate, at the very top of the Old Town (50 kn/hour or 600 kn/24 hours—you have to buy the daily ticket at a Tisak kiosk or the machine, www.sanitat.hr).

For longer-term parking, choose between close and expensive or far and cheap: The **Old Town parking garage** costs 40 kn/hour or 480 kn/day in July-Aug, 35 kn/hour or 420 kn/day in June and September, and less off-season (Zagrebačka ulica, see map on page 279 and "To the Old Town," earlier, for directions). Important: If you'll be staying overnight, request a daily ticket *(dnevna karta)* at the ticket office within 15 minutes of when you park—this is es-sential to avoid exorbitant hourly rates. From this garage, it's about a 10-minute downhill walk to the Old Town—and a much steeper,

DUBROVNIK

20-minute hike back up. Or you can park at the big lot at **Port Gruž,** just north of the Jadrolinija ferry terminal (15 kn/hour, 200 kn/day); from here, you can take a bus or taxi to the Old Town's Pile Gate.

HELPFUL HINTS

Festivals: Dubrovnik is most crowded during its **Summer Festival,** a month and a half of theater and musical performances held annually (July 10-Aug 25, www.dubrovnik-festival.hr). This is quickly followed by the **Late Summer Festival,** designed to continue the festivities into September.

Crowd-Beating Tips: Dubrovnik has been discovered—especially by cruise ships (bringing more than one million passengers yearly—on very busy days, there may be four ships in at once, sending 9,000-plus passengers ashore). Cruise-ship crowds descend on the Old Town roughly between 8:30 and 14:00 (the streets are most crowded 9:00-13:00). Bad-weather days are a perfect storm, when people who'd otherwise hit the beach instead sightsee in the Old Town, along with all the cruise passengers. On busy days, try to avoid the big sights—especially walking around the City Walls—during these peak times, and hit the beach or take a siesta midday, when the town is hottest and most crowded. It can also make sense to schedule out-of-town side trips for busy cruise days; check the day-by-day cruise schedule at www.portdubrovnik.hr. There's a lot of talk about how Dubrovnik could strategically limit the number of cruise passengers allowed in town—but until that happens, your best strategy is to be aware and to avoid the busiest places.

No Euros: Dubrovnik's merchants (even some of the city's top sights, such as the City Walls and cable car) can be stubborn about accepting only kunas—no euros.

Wine Shop: For the best wine-tasting selection in a cool bar atmosphere, don't miss **D'Vino Wine Bar** (described later, under "Eating in Dubrovnik"). If you want to shop rather than taste, **Vinoteka Miličić** offers a nice variety of local wines in a shoebox space. Jolly Dolores can explain your options, most of which are their own Miličić wines, and she can bubble-wrap bottles for transport (daily June-Aug 9:00-22:00, shorter hours off-season, near the Pile Gate end of the Stradun, tel. 020/321-777).

Laundry: Dubrovnik's laundry services have a tendency to rack up bad reviews and go out of business. One place that has stuck around is the pricey self-service **Laundry Spin,** a steep hike up above the Old Town in the tunnel just outside the Buža Gate (daily 8:00-20:00, Wi-Fi, Iza Grada b.b., tel. 020/456-855).

Car Rental: The big international chains have offices at the airport; a few also have branches near the Port Gruž embankment, or in Lapad hotels. In addition, the many travel agencies
closer to the Old Town also have a line on rental cars. Be sure
the agency knows if you're crossing a border (such as Bosnia-
Herzegovina or Montenegro) to ensure you have the proper
paperwork.

Best Views: Walking the **City Walls** late in the day, when the city
is bathed in rich light, is a treat. The cable car up to **Mount
Srđ** provides bird's-eye panoramas over the entire region,
from the highest vantage point without wings. The **Fort of
St. Lawrence,** perched above the Pile neighborhood cove, has
great views over the Old Town. The **panoramic cruises** that
loop around the Old Town are another fine choice. A stroll
up the road east of the walls offers nice views back on the Old
Town (best light early in the day). Better yet, if you have a car,
head south of the city in the morning for gorgeously lit Old
Town views over your right shoulder; various turnoffs along
this road are ideal photo stops. The best one, known locally
simply as **"panorama point,"** is where the road leading up and
out of Dubrovnik meets the main road that passes above the
town (look for the pullout on the right, usually crowded with
tour buses). Even if you're heading north, in good weather it's
worth a quick detour south for this view.

GETTING AROUND DUBROVNIK

If you're staying in or near the Old Town, everything is easily walkable. But those sleeping in outlying areas will want to get comfortable using the buses. Once you understand the system, commuting
to the Old Town is straightforward (though the buses can be quite
crowded).

By Bus: Libertas runs Dubrovnik's public buses. Tickets,
which are good for an hour, are cheaper if you buy them in advance
from a newsstand or your hotel (12 kn, ask for *autobusna karta*,
ow-toh-BOOS-nah KAR-tah) than if you buy them from the bus
driver (15 kn). A 24-hour ticket costs 30 kn (only sold at special
bus-ticket kiosks, such as the one near the Pile Gate bus stop).

When boarding, validate your ticket (insert it in the machine
next to the driver with the orange arrow facing out and pointing
down). Because most tourists can't figure out how to validate their
tickets, it can take a long time to load the bus (which means drivers
are understandably grumpy, and locals aren't shy about cutting in
line).

All buses stop near the Old Town, just in front of the Pile
Gate (buy tickets at the newsstand). From here, they fan out to various
parts of town; the routes you're most likely to use are buses #1a,

Game of Thrones in Dubrovnik

Fans of the HBO television series *Game of Thrones* may feel the tingle of déjà vu during their visit to Dubrovnik. For years, much of the series was filmed here. Many locals have been extras, and they grew accustomed to seeing Peter Dinklage strolling down the Stradun in full costume.

On the show, Dubrovnik and the surrounding coastline and islands provided a setting for two main storylines: the royal family intrigue at King's Landing; and Daenerys Targaryen's conquest of the continent of Essos, from idyllic Qarth to Slaver's Bay. Of course, in most cases, the real-life Croatian settings were dressed up with special effects—the sea, rocks, and bottoms of the buildings were real, while the fanciful towers and spires (and the dragons) were pure fantasy. For die-hard *GoT* geeks, here are some specifics (spoilers ahead!):

The real-life, mostly ruined Fort of St. Lawrence, perched on a rocky bluff, was the base of the (mostly digital) Red Keep. It looks over a pleasant cove that stood in for Blackwater Bay, the site of a calamitous naval battle in season two, and some poignant Stark family goodbyes in the series finale. The City Walls saw frequent airtime as the mighty fortifications of King's Landing—the site of many strategic (and scenic) conversations between the royals and their advisors. And in the epic Battle of King's Landing, Drogon strafed these walls and bastions with dragon fire.

Several of the streets in Dubrovnik's Old Town—especially St. Dominic's street (ulica Svetog Dominika), connecting the main drag to the Ploče Gate—become the crowded market streets of King's Landing. The real-life Rupe Ethnographic Museum, in the upper reaches of the Old Town, served as the exterior of Littlefinger's brothel. And Cersei was humiliated by being forced to walk naked through town, beginning at the top of the grand staircase below the Jesuit St. Ignatius Church (which I now think of as the "Steps of Shame! Shame! Shame!").

More locations are farther afield: Trsteno Arboretum (described in the next chapter) was where Sansa Stark had many

#1b, #1c, #3, and #8 to Port Gruž (cruise port, ferry terminal), or buses #4 or #6 to the resort cove at Lapad. For information, visit www.libertasdubrovnik.hr.

By Taxi: Taxis start at 25 kn, then charge 8 kn per kilometer. The handiest taxi stand for the Old Town is just outside the Pile Gate. The biggest operation is Radio Taxi (tel. 020/411-411). Uber, which is often cheaper, also works well in Dubrovnik.

heart-to-hearts with Olenna and Margaery Tyrell. The eventful "Purple Wedding" of Joffrey and Margaery was filmed in Gradac Park. The epic duel between Oberyn Martell and The Mountain took place at the amphitheater below Hotel Belvedere. The island of Lokrum played host to the Qarth garden party, and the tower where Daenerys' dragons were held captive was Minčeta Tower (in the City Walls).

Filming also took place in Split, where Diocletian's cellars became the dungeon where Daenerys safely locked up her dragons. And the fortified town of Klis, just north of Split, was the location for the slaving town of Mereen.

Game of Thrones stopped filming in Dubrovnik two seasons before the series ended. For the rest of its run, they used archival footage and digital reconstructions. For the apocalyptic penultimate episode, "The Bells," a full-scale, multiblock reconstruction of Dubrovnik was built in Northern Ireland...and then blown to bits by Daenerys and her dragon. (Knowing that the real Dubrovnik withstood a real-life military siege not that long ago made watching this episode even more poignant.)

To please *GoT* pilgrims—sometimes called "set jetters"—various companies offer walking tours of filming locations (see "Tours in Dubrovnik," later). A shop on Boškovićeva street (just above Prijeko street) has a replica of the Iron Throne (a great photo op, but only if you buy an overpriced souvenir). The monastery on Lokrum Island hosts a small museum of *Game of Thrones* memorabilia, and Split recently opened a *Game of Thrones* Museum (see page 193).

Game of Thrones kicked off a new trend of Hollywood filming in Dubrovnik. The town stood in for the casino city of Canto Bight in *Star Wars: The Last Jedi;* 2018's *Robin Hood* was shot here; and *Mamma Mia: Here We Go Again* was filmed on the nearby "Greek island" of Vis. For the latest on what's been filmed here, ask around town.

Tours in Dubrovnik

Walking Tours

Two companies—**Dubrovnik Walks** (www.dubrovnikwalks.com) and **Dubrovnik Walking Tours** (www.dubrovnik-walking-tours.com)—offer similar one-hour walking tours of the Old Town several times daily (90-100 kn). I'd skip these tours—they're pricey and brief, touching lightly on the same information explained in this chapter. Both companies (and others) also offer themed tours covering *Game of Thrones* locations, wartime Dubrovnik, and the historic Jewish quarter. For the latest offerings, pick up their fliers

Dubrovnik at a Glance

▲▲▲**Stradun Stroll** Charming walk through Dubrovnik's vibrant Old Town, ideal for coffee, ice cream, and people-watching. See page 290.

▲▲▲**City Walls** Scenic mile-long walk along top of 15th-century fortifications encircling the city. **Hours:** June-July daily 8:00-19:30, progressively shorter hours off-season. See page 301.

▲▲▲**Mount Srđ** Napoleonic fortress above Dubrovnik with spectacular views and a modest museum about the recent war. **Hours:** Mountaintop—always open; cable car—daily June-Aug 9:00-24:00, progressively shorter hours off-season; museum—same hours as cable car. See page 318.

▲▲**Red History Museum** A smart look at the social and political history of socialist Yugoslavia, located in the Port Gruž area. **Hours:** Daily 9:00-22:00, Nov-April 10:00-18:00. See page 321.

▲**Franciscan Monastery Museum** Tranquil cloister, medieval pharmacy-turned-museum, and a century-old pharmacy still serving residents today. **Hours:** Daily 9:00-18:00, Nov-March until 14:00. See page 307.

▲**Rector's Palace** Sparse antique collection in the former home of rectors who ruled Dubrovnik in the Middle Ages. **Hours:** Daily 9:00-18:00, Nov-April until 16:00. See page 309.

▲**Cathedral** Eighteenth-century Roman Baroque cathedral and

(sales kiosks by Pile Gate bus stop, in front of TI) or check their websites.

Dubrovnik Food Tours, run by friendly Hamo (who used to live in Southern California) and his team, offer combination history/food walking tours as well as day trips into the countryside (www.dubrovnikfoodtours.com).

Local Guides

For an in-depth look at the city, consider hiring your own local guide. **Roberto de Lorenzo** and his mother **Marija Tiberi** are both warm people enthusiastic about telling evocative stories from medieval Dubrovnik, including some off-the-beaten-path stops tailored to your interests (500 kn/2 hours, mobile 091-541-6637, dubrovnikgardens@gmail.com); ask about guided transfers to Bosnia-Herzegovina, Split, or beyond. **Tea Batinić** wrote a book about Dubrovnik, runs an art gallery, and brings a free-spirited joy to treasury filled with unusual relics, such as a swatch of Jesus' swaddling clothes. **Hours:** Church—daily 8:00-17:00; treasury—generally open same hours as church, both have shorter hours off-season. See page 311.

▲**Dominican Monastery Museum** Another relaxing cloister with precious paintings, altarpieces, and manuscripts. **Hours:** Daily 9:00-18:00, Nov-March until 16:30. See page 313.

▲**Synagogue Museum** Europe's second-oldest synagogue and Croatia's only Jewish museum, with 13th-century Torahs and Holocaust-era artifacts. **Hours:** Daily 9:00-20:00; mid-Nov-April Mon-Fri 10:00-15:00. See page 315.

▲**War Photo Limited** Thought-provoking photographic look at contemporary warfare. **Hours:** May-Sept daily 10:00-22:00, April and Oct Wed-Mon until 16:00, closed Tue; closed Nov-March. See page 315.

▲**Serbian Orthodox Church and Icon Museum** Active church serving Dubrovnik's Serbian Orthodox community and museum with traditional religious icons. **Hours:** Church—daily 8:00-21:00, Oct-April until 18:00; museum—may be closed for renovation, ask at icon shop near cathedral for status. See page 316.

▲**Rupe Granary and Ethnographic Museum** Good folk museum with tools, jewelry, clothing, and painted eggs above immense underground grain stores. **Hours:** Wed-Mon 9:00-16:00, July-Aug until 20:00, closed Tue. See page 317.

her tours (600 kn/2 hours, mobile 098-285-398, teabatinic@gmail. com). **Štefica Curić Lenert** is a sharp professional guide who offers a great by-the-book tour and an insider's look at the city (550 kn/1.5 hours, other tour options explained on her website, reserve at least one day ahead, www.dubrovnikprivateguide.com, stefica. curic.lenert@gmail.com). If these guides are busy, they can refer you to another good guide for a similar price.

From Dubrovnik

For information on tour boats and guided big-bus excursions from Dubrovnik to nearby destinations, see the next chapter.

Private Drivers

If you're more comfortable having someone else do the driving to sights near Dubrovnik, hire your own driver. While the drivers listed here are not licensed tour guides, they speak great English and offer commentary as you roll, and can help you craft a good day-long itinerary to Mostar, Montenegro, or anywhere else near Dubrovnik (typically departing around 8:00 and returning in the early evening).

Friendly **Pepo Klaić** is enjoyable to get to know and has a knack for making the experience both informative and meaningful. Ask about what it was like growing up inside the walls of Dubrovnik's Old Town (around €230 for Bay of Kotor or Mostar, airport transfer for about €30—cheaper than a taxi, these prices for up to four people—more expensive for bigger group, mobile 098-427-301, www.dubrovnikshoretrip.com, pklaic@gmail.com). **Petar Vlašić** does similar tours for similar prices, and specializes in wine tours to the Pelješac Peninsula, with stops at wineries along the way (€35 airport transfers, €190-200 for 2-person trip to Pelješac wineries, €230 to Mostar or €250 to Montenegro including local guide, these prices for 1-3 people—more for larger groups, mobile 091-580-8721, www.dubrovnikrivieratours.com, info@dubrovnikrivieratours.com).

If your destination is Mostar, likable Bosnian driver **Ermin Elezović** will happily pick you up for less than the Dubrovnik-based drivers (€140 for one-way transfer from Dubrovnik to Mostar with a few brief sightseeing stops en route, more for round-trip to Mostar with same-day return to Dubrovnik; for contact information and details, see page 433).

Stradun Stroll

Running through the heart of Dubrovnik's Old Town is the 300-yard-long Stradun promenade—packed with people and lined with sights. This self-guided walk (rated ▲▲▲) offers an ideal introduction to Dubrovnik's charms. It takes about 30 minutes, not counting sightseeing stops.

• *Begin at the busy square in front of the west entrance to the Old Town, the Pile Gate.*

Pile Neighborhood

This bustling area is the nerve center of Dubrovnik's tourist industry—it's where the real world meets the fantasy of Dubrovnik (for details on services offered here, see "Orientation to Dubrovnik," earlier). Behind the odd, modern, mirrors-and-LED-screens monument (which honors the "Dubrovnik Defenders" who protected the city during the

1991-1992 siege) is a long and leafy café terrace. Wander over to the balustrade at the terrace's end and take in the imposing walls of the Pearl of the Adriatic. (*Game of Thrones* fans might feel a twinge of déjà vu for Blackwater Bay.) The huge, fortified peninsula just outside the City Walls is the **Fort of St. Lawrence** (Tvrđava Lovrijenac), Dubrovnik's oldest fortress. Imagine how this fort and the stout walls worked together to fortify the little harbor—and the gate just behind you. You can climb 208 steps up to this fortress for great views over the Old Town (50 kn, covered by same ticket as City Walls on the same day)...or just hike up to the little terrace in front of the door, which has views nearly as good. The view from up top offers a perfect illustration of how Dubrovnik's walled Old Town is shaped like a V—with two formerly separate hill towns joined by a covered-over canal.

• *Back along the busy main drag, cross over the moat (now a shady park) to the round entrance tower in the City Walls. This is the...*

Pile Gate (Gradska Vrata Pile)

Just before you enter the gate, notice the image above the entrance of **St. Blaise** (Sveti Vlaho in Croatian) cradling Dubrovnik in his arm. You'll see a lot more of Blaise, the protector of Dubrovnik, during your time here—he is to Dubrovnik what the winged lion of St. Mark is to Venice.

Inside the first part of the gate, dead ahead you'll see another image of Blaise. Turn left and go down the ramp, to the little hole in the wall. Step through it to enter a tranquil **playground park,** where locals play with their toddlers in serenity (surrounded by tourists). Back inside the gate, look for the **white map** (next to the tourist map) that shows where each bomb dropped on the Old Town during the siege. Once inside town, you'll see virtually no signs of the war—a testament to the townspeople's impressive resilience in rebuilding so well and so quickly.

• *Continue down the ramp and pass the rest of the way through the gate. On the other side, you'll find a lively little square surrounded by landmarks.*

St. Savior Square

The giant, round structure in the middle of the square is **Onofrio's Big Fountain** (Velika Onofrijea Fontana). In the Middle Ages, Dubrovnik had a complicated aqueduct system that brought

DUBROVNIK

Dubrovnik's Old Town

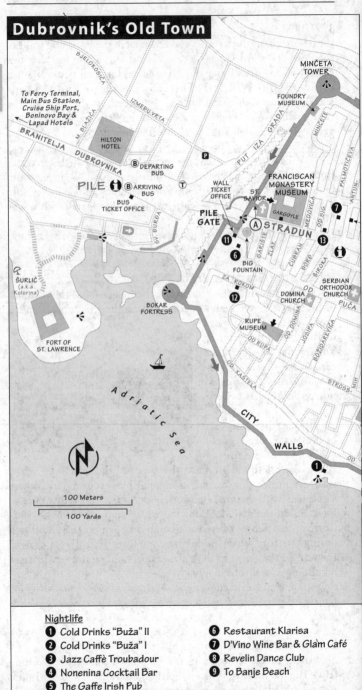

BJELOKOSIĆA

IZMEĐU VETA

To Ferry Terminal,
Main Bus Station,
Cruise Ship Port,
Boninovo Bay &
Lapad Hotels

BRANITELJA DUBROVNIKA

M. BLAŽIĆA

HILTON
HOTEL

P

B DEPARTING
BUS

PILE

B ARRIVING
BUS

BUS
TICKET OFFICE

SV. ĐURĐA

T

MINČETA
TOWER

FOUNDRY
MUSEUM

PUT IZA GRADA

MINČETE

WALL
TICKET
OFFICE

ST.
SAVIOR

FRANCISCAN
MONASTERY
MUSEUM

PALMOTIĆEVA

ANTUN-

7

OD SIG

GARGOYLE

A STRADUN

13

ČUBRAN

ŽUPAN

BOŠK

SIROKA

ŠIROKA

MEDOVIĆA

GARIŠTE

ZLAT

PILE GATE

11

6

BIG
FOUNTAIN

ŠURLIĆ
(a.k.a.
Kolorina)

BOKAR
FORTRESS

FORT OF
ST. LAWRENCE

ZA ROKOM

12

OD DOMINA

DOMINA
CHURCH

RUPE
MUSEUM

OD RUPA

SERBIAN
ORTHODOX
CHURCH

PUČA

OD JOSIPA

BOŽIDAREVIĆA

OD KAŠTELA

A d r i a t i c   S e a

CITY

WALLS

STROSS. MIH.

OD

1

N

100 Meters

100 Yards

Nightlife

1. Cold Drinks "Buža" II
2. Cold Drinks "Buža" I
3. Jazz Caffè Troubadour
4. Nonenina Cocktail Bar
5. The Gaffe Irish Pub
6. Restaurant Klarisa
7. D'Vino Wine Bar & Glàm Café
8. Revelin Dance Club
9. To Banje Beach

Other

10 Sloboda Theater

11 Visia Cinema

12 Jadran Cinema

13 Vinoteka Miličić Wine Shop

14 Laundry

15 DEŠA Shop

16 Life According to KAWA Shop

water from the mountains seven miles away. The water ended up here, at the town's biggest fountain, before continuing through the city. Three things helped make little, independent Dubrovnik very siege-resistant: this plentiful supply of water, large reserves of salt (a key source of Dubrovnik's wealth, from the town of Ston— see page 357), and a massive granary (now the Rupe Granary and Ethnographic Museum, described later).

Stand with your back to the fountain and face the small **Church of St. Savior** (Crkva Svetog Spasa). Townspeople built this votive church to thank God after Dubrovnik made it through a 1520 earthquake. When the massive 1667 quake destroyed the city, this church was one of the only buildings left intact—its Renaissance interior stands at odds against the predominantly Baroque styles in other town churches. And during the Yugoslav Wars, the church survived another close call when a shell exploded on the ground right in front of it (you can still see faint pockmarks from the shrapnel).

To the left of the church, a steep stairway leads up to the imposing **Minčeta Tower.** It's possible to enter here to begin Dubrovnik's best activity, walking around the top of the City Walls (tickets are sold across the square)—but this walk ends near a better, less crowded entry point.

The big building to the right of the Church of St. Savior is the **Franciscan Monastery Museum.** This tourable building has a delightful cloister and one of Europe's oldest continually operating pharmacies (described later; enter through the gap between the small church and the door of the big church). Historically, the monastery's **Franciscan Church** was the house of worship for Dubrovnik's poor people, while the Dominican Church (down at the far end of the Stradun, where our walk ends) was for the wealthy. Services were staggered by 15 minutes to allow servants to drop off their masters there, then rush up the Stradun for their own service here. If you peek inside the church, you'll find a Baroque interior—typical of virtually all of the town's churches, which were rebuilt after the 1667 quake.

Back outside, still with your back to the round fountain, look up and notice the **bell tower** of the Franciscan Church—with its rounded top—which is integrated into the structure of the building. If your travels have taken you beyond Dubrovnik, you'll notice the difference from other Croatian towns, where church steeples follow Venetian convention: Set apart from the church, and with a pointy top. This is just the first of many contrasts we'll see between Dubrovnik and Venice—two powerful, rival maritime republics.

Finally, notice the stubby little shin-high, mustachioed **gargoyle** embedded in the wall, just left of the Franciscan Church's door. You may see a commotion of tourists trying to balance on the small, slippery surface of the gargoyle's head. Tour guides enjoy spinning a variety of tall tales about this creature—for instance, if you can balance on one leg for three seconds, your fondest wish comes true—but these are a recent invention.

• *When you're finished taking in the sights on this square, continue along...*

The Stradun

Dubrovnik's main promenade—officially called the Placa, but better known as the Stradun—is alive with locals and tourists alike.

This is the heartbeat of the city: an Old World shopping mall by day and sprawling cocktail party after dark, when everybody seems to be doing the traditional evening stroll—flirting, ice-cream-licking, flaunting, and gawking. A coffee and some of Europe's best people-watching in a prime Stradun café is one of travel's great $5 bargains.

When Dubrovnik was just getting its start in the seventh century, this street was a canal. Romans fleeing from the invading Slavs lived on the island of Ragusa (on your right), and the Slavs settled on the shore. In the 11th century, the canal separating Ragusa from the mainland was filled in, the towns merged, and a unique Slavic-Roman culture and language blossomed. While originally much more higgledy-piggledy, this street was rebuilt in the current, more straightforward style after the 1667 earthquake. The ensuing fire raged for three weeks and consumed much of the city.

The distinctively shaped doors—with P-shaped shop windows built right in, to provide maximum views of goods, but minimum access—indicate that this was the terrain of the merchants...and it still is.

The austerity of Dubrovnik's main drag disappoints some visitors. Rather than lavishing funds on ostentatious palaces, as in Venice, Dubrovnik seems to downplay its wealth. For much of its history, Dubrovnik paid a hefty tribute to the sultan of the Ottoman Empire to maintain its independent status. Flaunting wealth would have raised Ottoman eyebrows...and, likely, Ottoman taxes.

Think about the stark contrast between restrained Dubrovnik and its rival Venice, which was desperate to impress. Venice was surrounded by Italians, Austrians, Germans—some allies, some rivals, but all Christian. Dubrovnik sat five miles from the frontier of the Ottoman Empire; leaving the city felt like leaving the known world and the safety of what we'd today call "Western Civilization."

Let me guess—the Stradun is crowded, right? When multiple cruise ships drop anchor, their passenger excursions into town feel more like incursions. But try some attitude adjustment: The maritime republic of Dubrovnik has always been a crossroads of merchants, sailors, and other travelers from around the world. While today they may be following their tour guides' numbered paddles rather than trading exotic spices, the legions of visitors are still part of the city's tapestry of history.

If you're here on a summer evening (June-Sept), you might hear the rat-a-tat-tat of a drum echoing through the streets from the Stradun. This means it's time to head for this main drag to get a glimpse of the colorfully costumed **"town guards"** parading through (and the cavalcade of tourists running alongside them, trying to snap a clear picture). You may also see some of these characters standing guard outside the town gates. Begun only recently, this "tradition" is part of the local tourist board's efforts to make their town even more atmospheric.

• *Branching off from this promenade are several museums and other attractions. At the end of the Stradun is the lively Luža Square. Its centerpiece is the 20-foot-tall...*

Orlando's Column (Orlandov Stup)

Dubrovnik erected this column—a northern European symbol—in 1417, soon after it had shifted allegiances from the oppressive Venetians to the Hungarians. Whenever a decision was made by the Republic, the town crier came to Orlando's Column and announced the news. The step he stood on indicated the importance of his message—the higher up, the more important the news. It was also used as the pillory, where people were publicly punished. The thin line on the top step in front of Orlando is exactly as long as the statue's forearm. This mark was Dubrovnik's standard measurement—not for a foot, but for an "elbow."

• *Now stand in front of Orlando's Column and orient yourself with a...*

Luža Square Spin-Tour

Orlando is looking toward the **Sponza Palace** (Sponza-Povijesni Arhiv). This building, from 1522, is the finest surviving example of Dubrovnik's Golden Age in the 15th and 16th centuries. It's a combination of Renaissance (ground-floor arcade) and Venetian Gothic (upstairs windows). Houses up and down the main promenade used to look like this, before the 1667 earthquake and fire. This used to be the customs office *(dogana)*, but now it's an exhaustive archive of the city's history, with temporary art exhibits and a war memorial. The poignant **Memorial Room of Dubrovnik Defenders** (inside and on the left) has photos of dozens of people from Dubrovnik who were killed fighting Yugoslav forces in 1991. A TV screen and images near the ceiling show the devastation of the city. Though the English descriptions are pointedly—if unavoidably—slanted to the Croat perspective, it's compelling to look in the eyes of the brave young men who didn't start this war...but were willing to finish it (free, long hours daily in peak season). Beyond the memorial room, the impressive **courtyard,** which hosts temporary exhibits, is worth a peek (25 kn, generally free after-hours).

To the right of Sponza Palace is the town's **Bell Tower** (Gradski Zvonik). The original dated from 1444, but it was rebuilt when it started to lean in the 1920s. The big clock may be an octopus, but only one of its hands tells time. Below that, the golden circle shows the phase of the moon. At the bottom, the old-fashioned digital readout tells the hour (in Roman numerals) and the minutes (in five-minute increments). At the top of each hour (and again three minutes later), the time is clanged out on the bell up top by two bronze bell-ringers, Maro and Baro. (If this all seems like a copy of the very similar clock on St. Mark's Square in Venice, locals are quick to point out that this clock predates that one by several decades.)

The clock still has to be wound every two days. Notice the little window between the moon phase and the "digital" readout: The clock-winder opens this window to get some light. The Krasovac family was in charge of winding the clock for generations. During the 1991-1992 siege, their house was destroyed—with the winding keys inside. For days, the clock bell didn't run. But then, miraculously, the keys were discovered lying in the street. The excited Dubrovnik citizens came together in this square and cheered as the clock was wound and the bell chimed, signaling to the soldiers surrounding the city that they hadn't won yet.

To the right of the Bell Tower, you'll see the entrance to the **Sloboda theater** (marked *Luža*), which hosts cultural events (such as folk-dancing shows) in the summer, and movies year-round. There's also the helpful Cultural Information Desk inside. Next to that, **Onofrio's Little Fountain** (Mala Onofrijea Fontana) is

DUBROVNIK

The Siege of Dubrovnik

In June 1991, Croatia declared independence from Yugoslavia. Within weeks, the nations were at war (for more on the war, see the Understanding Yugoslavia chapter). Though warfare raged in the Croatian interior, nobody expected that it would reach Dubrovnik.

As refugees from Vukovar (in northeastern Croatia) arrived in Dubrovnik that fall, telling horrific stories of the warfare there, local residents began fearing the worst. Warplanes from the Serb-dominated Yugoslav People's Army buzzed threateningly low over the town, as if to signal an impending attack.

Then, at 6:00 in the morning on October 1, 1991, Dubrovnik residents awoke to explosions on nearby hillsides. The first attacks were focused on Mount Srđ, high above the Old Town. First the giant cross was destroyed, then a communications tower (both have been rebuilt and are visible today). This first wave of attacks cleared the way for Yugoslav land troops—mostly Serbs and Montenegrins—who surround-

ed the city. The ragtag, newly formed Croatian army quickly dug in at the old Napoleonic-era fortress at the top of Mount Srđ, where just 25 or 30 soldiers fended off a Yugoslav takeover of this highly strategic position.

At first, shelling targeted military positions on the outskirts of town. But soon, Yugoslav forces began bombing residential neighborhoods, then the Pearl of the Adriatic itself: Dubrovnik's Old Town. Defenseless townspeople took shelter in their cellars, and sometimes even huddled together in the city wall's 15th-century forts. It was the first time in Dubrovnik's long history that the walls were actually used to defend against an attack.

The people of Dubrovnik refused to flee their town. Though severely outgunned and outnumbered, Dubrovnik's defenders managed to hold the fort atop Mount Srđ, while Yugoslav forces controlled the nearby mountaintops. All supplies had to be carried up to the fort by foot or by donkey. Dubrovnik wasn't prepared for war, so its citizens had to improvise their defense. Many brave young locals lost their lives when they slung old hunting rifles over their shoulders and, under cover of darkness, climbed the hills above Dubrovnik to meet Yugoslav soldiers face-to-face.

After eight months of bombing, Dubrovnik was liberated by the Croatian army, which attacked Yugoslav positions from the north. By the end of the siege, 100 civilians were dead, as well as more than 200 Dubrovnik citizens who lost their lives actively fighting for their hometown (much revered today as "Dubrovnik Defenders"); in the greater Dubrovnik area, 420 "Defenders" were killed, and another 900 wounded. More than two-thirds of Dubrovnik's buildings had been damaged, and more than 30,000 people had to flee their homes—but the failed siege was finally over.

Why was Dubrovnik—so far from the rest of the fighting—dragged into the conflict? Yugoslavia wanted to catch the city off-guard, gaining a toehold on the southern Dalmatian Coast so they could push north to Split. They also hoped to ignite pro-Serb passions in the nearby Serb-dominated areas of Bosnia-Herzegovina and Montenegro. But perhaps most of all, Yugoslavia wanted to hit Croatia where it hurt—its proudest, most historic, and most beautiful city, the tourist capital of a nation dependent on tourism. It seems their plan backfired. Locals now say, "When Yugoslavia attacked Dubrovnik, they lost the war"—because images of the historic city under siege swayed international public opinion *against* Yugoslavia.

The war initially devastated the tourist industry. Now, to the casual observer, Dubrovnik seems virtually back to normal. Aside from a few pockmarks and bright, new roof tiles, there are scant reminders of what happened here more than two decades ago. But even though the city itself has been repaired, the people of Dubrovnik are forever changed. Imagine living in an idyllic paradise, a place that attracted and awed visitors from around the world...and then watching it gradually blown to bits. It's understandable if Dubrovnik's citizens are a little less in love with life than they once were.

It's clear that in the case of this siege, the Croats of Dubrovnik were the largely innocent victims of a brutal surprise attack. But keep in mind the larger context of the war: The cousins of these Croats, who were defending the glorious monument that is Dubrovnik, bombarded another glorious monument—the Old Bridge of Mostar. It's just another reminder that the "good guys" and "bad guys" in these wars are far from clear-cut.

Dubrovnik has several low-key attractions related to its recent war, including the museum in the ruined fortress atop Mount Srđ and the Memorial Room of Dubrovnik Defenders in the Sponza Palace on Luža Square. Another sight, War Photo Limited, expands the scope to war photography from around the world.

DUBROVNIK

the little brother of the one at the other end of the Stradun. The big building beyond the fountain is the **City Hall** (Vijećnica). The terrace at the near end of City Hall is occupied by the **Gradska Kavana,** or "Town Café." This hangout—historically Dubrovnik's favorite spot for gossiping and people-watching—has seating all the way through the wall to the Old Port.

Behind Orlando is **St. Blaise's Church** (Crkva Sv. Vlaha), dedicated to the patron saint of Dubrovnik. You'll see statues and

paintings of St. Blaise all over town, always holding a model of the city in his left hand. According to legend, a millennium ago St. Blaise came to a local priest in a dream and warned him that the up-and-coming Venetians would soon attack the city. The priest alerted the authorities, who prepared for war. Of course, the prediction came true. St. Blaise has been a Dubrovnik symbol—and locals have resented Venice—ever since.

The church, like most churches in this city, was built following the 1667 earthquake and fire. And, while we've heard plenty on this walk about Dubrovnik's rivalry with Venice, there's no denying that the Venetians were some of Europe's top cultural trendsetters at that time. So Dubrovnik invited a Venetian architect to design the church dedicated to their favorite saint. That's why St. Blaise's looks like it would be right at home reflected in a Venetian canal...right down to its bulbous dome, which seems to have been transplanted here from the top of St. Mark's.

Just down the street from the "Town Café" is the Rector's Palace, and then the cathedral (both described later, under "Sights in Dubrovnik"). Just before the palace, on the left, notice the statue of Dubrovnik poet **Marin Držić** (1508-1567). This beloved bard's most famous work concerns "Uncle Maro," an aristocrat who's as stingy as he is wealthy. His son cleans out his savings account and goes on a bender in Rome...until his father gets wind of it and comes calling. The shiny lap and bright nose of this statue, erected in 2008, might lead you to believe it's good luck to rub his schnoz—and, sure enough, you'll see a steady stream of tourists doing just that. But the truth is that when the statue went up, local kids were drawn to his prominent proboscis, and couldn't resist climbing up on his lap and grabbing it. Tourists saw the shine and assumed they were supposed to do it, too. A legend was born.

• *Your walk is finished. From here, you've got plenty of sightseeing options (all described next). As you face the Bell Tower, you can go up the street to the right to reach the Rector's Palace and cathedral; you can walk straight ahead through the gate to reach the Old Port; or you can head through the gate and jog left to find the Dominican Monastery Museum. Even more sights—including an old synagogue, an Orthodox church, a modern exhibit of war photography, the medieval granary, and the ruins of an old foundry—are in the steep streets between the Stradun and the walls.*

Sights in Dubrovnik

Keep in mind that many of Dubrovnik's museums require you to have either a "nine museum ticket" or a Dubrovnik Card (which also covers the City Walls and public transit); for details on both options, see "Tourist Information," earlier.

▲▲▲CITY WALLS (GRADSKE ZIDINE)

Dubrovnik's single best activity is strolling the scenic mile-and-a-quarter around the City Walls. As you meander along this lofty perch—with a sea of orange roofs on one side and the azure sea on the other—you'll get your bearings, peer into secluded gardens, and snap pictures like mad. Bring your map, which you can use to pick out landmarks and get the lay of the land. Speed demons can walk the walls in about an hour; strollers and shutterbugs should plan on longer.

Cost: 200 kn to enter walls, also includes the Fort of St. Lawrence outside the Pile Gate (kunas or credit cards only—no euros).

Hours: From April through October, the walls open daily at 8:00; the closing time depends on the season (April-May and early Sept until 18:30, June-July until 19:30, Aug until 19:00, late Sept until 18:00, Oct until 17:30). Off-season (Nov-March), the walls are open daily 9:00-15:00. The "closing time" indicates when the walls shut down, *not* the last entry. Attendants begin circling the walls 30 minutes after the posted closing time to lock the gates, so if you want to make it all the way around, ascend at least 30 minutes before the posted closing if you're speedy, and an hour or more before if you want to linger.

Entrances and Strategies: There are three entry points for the wall (see "Dubrovnik's Old Town" map), and wall walkers are required to follow the one-way route counterclockwise. One good strategy is to begin at the far side of the Old Town, using the entrance **near the Ploče Gate** and Dominican Monastery (this is where my self-guided tour of the walls begins). This entrance is the least crowded, and you'll tackle the steepest part (and enjoy some of the best views) first. The most popular—and most crowded—entrance is **just inside the Pile Gate,** next to the Church of St. Savior (for this location, you must buy your tickets at the desk across the square from the stairway entry). If you manage to arrive before the hordes descend, it can make sense to enter here and get this (most congested) section out of the way first. Finally, there's a small entrance **near St. John's Fort** overlooking the Old Port (next to the Maritime Museum).

Avoiding Crowds: Because this is Dubrovnik's top attraction, it's extremely crowded. Your best strategy is to avoid the walls when cruise ships are in town. During busy times, your best bet is to hit the walls around 8:00, or just before 17:00 (to avoid both the worst heat and the worst crowds). Crowds are worst from about 9:30 until 11:00, then decrease ever so slightly. They pick up again in the late afternoon (around 17:00), peaking about an hour before closing time (18:30 in high season).

Tips: Because your ticket is scanned as you enter, you can't leave and re-enter the wall later; you have to do it all in one go. If you have a Dubrovnik Card—even a multiple-day one—you can only use it once to ascend the walls.

Heat Warning: The walls can get deliriously hot—all that white stone and seawater reflect blazing sunshine something fierce, and there's virtually no shade (except at a few wall-top cafés). It's essential to bring sunscreen, a hat, and water (the Onofrio public fountains are near both the Pile and Ploče entrances). A few shops and cafés along the top of the wall (mostly on the sea side) sell drinks, but it's cheaper to bring what you'll need with you. Pace yourself: There are several steep stretches, and you'll be climbing up and down the whole way around. Particularly on the hottest days (commonly in July-Aug), the walls are best avoided between about 9:00 and 16:00—those first-aid workers you'll see stationed near the entry points aren't just hanging out for fun. If you have trouble with the heat, save the walls for a cloudy day.

Background: There have been walls here almost as long as there's been a Dubrovnik. As with virtually all fortifications on the Croatian Coast, these walls were beefed up in the 15th century, when the Ottoman navy became a threat. Around the perimeter are several substantial forts, with walls rounded so that cannonballs would glance off harmlessly. These stout forts intimidated would-be invaders during the Republic of Dubrovnik's Golden Age, and protected residents during the 1991-1992 siege.

○ Self-Guided Tour: It's perfectly fine to just wander the walls and take in the views over Dubrovnik rooftops. But this brief tour should help give you bearings to what you're seeing, as you read Dubrovnik's unique and illustrious history into its street plan.

Part 1—Ploče Gate to Pile Gate: Begin by ascending near the **Ploče Gate** (go through the gate under the Bell Tower, walk along the stoutly walled passageway between the port and the Dominican Monastery, and look for the wall entrance on your right). Buy your ticket, head up, turn left, and start walking counterclockwise. After climbing some stairs, you'll walk with Mount Srd and the cable car on your right. After passing the roofline of the Dominican Monastery's cloister on the left, you're walking above what was the poorest part of medieval Dubrovnik, the domain of the craftsmen—with narrow, stepped lanes that had shops on the ground floor and humble dwellings up above. Peering down all of the tight lanes, look for the many little stone ledges sticking out next to windows. These were used to hang banners during the city's Golden Age.

As you walk, keep an eye on the different-colored **rooftops** for an illustration of the damage Dubrovnik sustained during the 1991-1992 siege. It's easy to see that nearly two-thirds of Dubrovnik's roofs were replaced after the bombings (notice the new, bright-orange tiles—and how some buildings salvaged the old tiles, but have 20th-century ones underneath). The

pristine-seeming Old Town was rebuilt using exactly the same materials and methods with which it was originally constructed.

The path you're on alternates between straight stretches and stairs; as you walk you're rewarded with higher and higher views. Nearing the summit, you pass a juice bar (you can use the WCs if you buy a drink). At the very top, enjoy the best possible view of the Old Town—you can see the rooftops, churches, and the sea. Stuck behind a traffic jam of selfie sticks, ponder the increasing

DUBROVNIK

narcissism of our age...then snap a selfie to post to Instagram. For an even better view, it's worth hiking up 63 crowded stone stairs to the top of **Minčeta Tower.** From either viewpoint, observe the valley-like shape of Dubrovnik. It's easy to imagine how it began as two towns—one where you are now, and the other on the hilly island with the church spires across the way—originally separated by a seawater canal. Notice the relatively regular, grid-like pattern of houses on this side, and the more higgledy-piggledy arrangement on the far side (a visual clue that the far side is older).

The **sports court** at your feet is a reminder that Dubrovnik is a living city. (Anyone can play here—B.Y.O. ball.) Underneath the sports court are the remains of a medieval foundry—the centerpiece of Dubrovnik's least-known museum. (You can visit the **Foundry Museum,** described later, after you've descended the walls).

While around 1,500 people currently reside within these walls, that number used to be much higher. Nowadays, renting out your house to tourists is far more lucrative than living there yourself. And life is much easier in the suburbs—imagine the challenges that come with living in such a steep medieval townscape well into the 21st century. Delivery trucks rumble up and down the Stradun early each morning, and you'll see hardworking young men delivering goods on handcarts throughout the day.

Looking up at the fortress atop **Mount Srđ**—seemingly custom-made for keeping an eye on a large swathe of coastline—the strategic position of Dubrovnik is clear. Independent Dubrovnik was not just this walled city, but an entire region.

Now continue downhill (you've earned it), noticing views on your right of the bustling Pile Gate area and the Fort of St. Lawrence (we'll reach better views of both of these soon). You'll pass an overpriced shop (with a pay-to-view movie about the war). And then, as the wall walk levels off, you'll pass an exit (on the left); if you're bushed and ready to head back to town, you can leave here—but once you leave, you can't re-enter on the same ticket, and some of the best views lie ahead. It's much better to carry on straight for part 2.

Part 2—Pile Gate to Old Port: This is the most crowded section, where many people enter—be patient. While you're waiting, pause to enjoy the full-frontal view of the **Stradun,** barreling right at you. In the Middle Ages, merchants lined this drag, and before that, this was a canal. At your feet is Onofrio's Big Fountain, which supplied water to a thirsty town. From here, you can see a wide range of church steeples representing the cosmopolitan makeup of a thriving medieval trade town (from left to right): Dominican, Franciscan (near you), the town Bell Tower, St. Blaise's (the round dome—hard to see from here), Serbian Orthodox (twin domed steeples), cathedral, and (high on the hill) Jesuit St. Ignatius. Sit and watch the river of humanity, flowing constantly up and down one of Europe's finest main streets. Now do a 180 for a good view of the Pile Gate chaos, with a steady stream of buses lumbering up and down the hill, tethering the Old Town to Port Gruž and the Lapad resort zone.

Carry on through the guard tower and along the wall, climbing uphill again. Looking to the wall ahead of you, notice that—after you pass along a straighter, lower stretch—this wall scampers up a mighty foundation of solid rock. You've left the canal that once separated the two parts of Dubrovnik, and now you're ascending what used to be a separate, very steep, rocky island. This stretch tickles *Game of Thrones* fantasies—many King's Landing scenes were filmed along here.

Climbing higher and looking to your left, into town, you'll see that this area is still damaged—not from the 1991-1992 siege, but from the 1667 earthquake. Notice that, unlike the extremely dense construction on the poorer far side of town, this area has more breathing space and larger gardens. Originally this was also densely populated, but after the quake, rather than rebuild, the wealthy folks who lived here decided to maximize green space. Grates cover the openings to old wells and grain stores that once supplied homes here—essential for surviving a siege.

As the walkway summits and levels out, you reach a drink stand. On the right are stunning views of the **Fort of St. Lawrence,** which worked in concert with these stout walls to make Dubrovnik virtually impenetrable. (That fort is also climbable, and covered by the same ticket as the walls.)

Past the drink stand, you'll stroll past locals' backyards, peering into their inviting gardens and checking the status of their drying laundry. Farther along, at the picturesque little turret, is a popular juice bar and an ice-cream stand. Looking outside the wall, you'll spot tables and umbrellas clinging to the rocks at the base of the wall. This is the recommended Cold Drinks "Buža" II, the best spot in town for a scenic drink. (You can't enter from atop the wall—you'll have to wait until later.) On the horizon is the isle of Lokrum and—often—cruise ships at anchor, sending passengers to and fro on tenders. After passing Buža, look down on the left to see another sports court, wedged between the walls—the best they can do in this vertical town.

Soon you'll see the *other* Buža (nicknamed "Little Buža"); just above it, notice the little statue of St. Blaise, Dubrovnik's patron, enjoying some shade under the turret.

Rounding the bend over Little Buža, look left to see the facade of the Jesuit St. Ignatius Church. Notice that the homes in this area are much larger. These are aristocratic palaces—VIPs wanted to live as close as possible to the cathedral and Rector's Palace, which are just below—and this also happens to be the oldest part of town, where "Ragusa" was born on a steep offshore island.

Continue around the wall, passing two more snack bars (the second is more elaborate, with a better menu, more shade, and pay WCs). Behind the second snack bar are more quake-ruined houses. Eventually you pop out at a high plateau, where *The City Walls— Continuation* signs lead down to the next part. From here you could drop down to the exit (though the final stretch of our wall walk is a snap—at the fork, go right, through the hole in the wall). In the little plant-filled square at the bottom of the next staircase is a sweet cat hospice, with a donation box for feeding some homeless feline residents.

Part 3—Old Port to Ploče Gate: At the start of the next stretch, you'll come to the entrance of the **Maritime Museum.** If you have a museum ticket or Dubrovnik Pass, here's a chance to escape the sun, use a clean WC, and learn about Dubrovnik's 2,500-year seafaring past (see description, later).

Next, walk along the top of the wall overlooking the **Old Port.** Imagine how this heavily fortified little harbor (facing away from Dubrovnik's historic foes, the Venetians) was busy with trade in the Middle Ages. Today it's still the economic lifeline for town—watch the steady stream of cruise-ship tenders injecting dose after dose of tourist cash. The Old Port is so charming partly because they prohibit huge, glitzy yachts from mooring here. All of the boats here must be under a certain size, and belong to locals—humble fishing and pleasure craft.

After circling your way to the middle of the port, immediately above the main pier, the path turns sharply left and heads straight for the Bell Tower—with a good glimpse of the bell ringers, Maro and Baro. Continuing, you'll look down into the inner passage that insulated the wall from the town center. On the sea side, look for the outdoor tables of the unsigned **360°**, a cocktail bar/restaurant catering to high rollers. Gussied-up jet-set diners enjoy coming here for extremely expensive, Michelin-starred fare.

Just past 360°, you'll come face to face with the vertical walls of the Dominican Church before finding the stairs back down to where you started this wall walk. Nice work. Now head on down and reward yourself with an ice-cream cone...and some shade.

The "Other" Wall Climb: Your ticket for the City Walls also includes the Fort of St. Lawrence just outside the Old Town (valid same day only; fort described on page 291). If you've already bought a 50-kn ticket there, show it when buying your main wall ticket and you'll pay only the difference.

Foundry Museum (a.k.a. Gornji Ugao Tower)

This easy-to-miss sight, tucked high up below the City Walls' tallest tower, offers a glimpse at a medieval foundry that was established in 1545. Used for the production of cannonballs and gunpowder (essential elements of an independent ministate), the foundry was intentionally located at the very top of town—still barely within the walls, but a safe distance from most residents. Damaged in the great 1667 quake, it was buried under a garbage dump and then under a playground, until it was finally excavated in 2008. Explanations are sparse, and it can be difficult to make sense of what you're seeing, so a visit here is best for archaeology buffs.

Cost and Hours: 30 kn, same hours as City Walls, closed Nov-March, last entrance one hour before closing.

Getting There: You'll enter the complex through the base of the Minčeta Tower, at the top (northernmost) point of the Old Town (follow any of the stepped lanes all the way up to the landward side of town, turn left, and walk along the inside of the wall until you can't walk anymore).

Visiting the Foundry: Visitors walk through the inside of Minčeta Tower, including two levels of casements, then along a private little inner stretch of the City Wall. Below the tower, look for the foundry's foundations, including its four furnaces, molds for church bells and gigantic cannonballs, and a pile of original casting sand (a volcanic material imported from Italy, essential for the working of any foundry). Exhibits include a few of the original items that were cast here, such as buckles, keys, needles, horseshoes, and musket shot.

NEAR THE PILE GATE
▲Franciscan Monastery Museum
(Franjevački Samostan-Muzej)

In the Middle Ages, Dubrovnik's monasteries flourished. As a part of their charity work, the monks at this monastery took on the responsibility of serving as pharmacists for the community. Visiting here today, you'll stroll through a delightful cloister and walk through a one-room museum with an old pharmacy.

Cost and Hours: 40 kn, daily 9:00-18:00, Nov-March until 14:00, Placa 2, tel. 020/321-410.

Visiting the Museum: Enter through the gap between the small church and the big monastery. Just inside the door (before the ticket-seller), a century-old **pharmacy** still serves residents; it's one of the world's oldest continually operating pharmacies. Notice the antique jars, advertisements (including one of the first known aspirin ads), and other vintage pharmacist gear.

Turn left and walk clockwise to explore the peaceful, sun-dappled **cloister.** Examine the capitals at the tops of the 60 Roman-

esque-Gothic double pillars. Each one is different. Notice that some parts of the portals inside the courtyard are made with a lighter-colored stone—these had to be repaired after being hit during the 1991-1992 siege. The damaged 19th-century frescoes along the tops of the walls depict the life of St. Francis, who supposedly visited Dubrovnik in the early 13th century. If you look closely, in a few panels you may see two layers of (different) scenes; beneath the 19th-century frescoes, restorers have found even more precious fragments of some early-18th-century paintings; where possible, these are also being resurrected.

In the far corner stands the monastery's original medieval **pharmacy,** opened in 1317. The Franciscans have been operating a pharmacy here ever since. On display are jars, pots, and other medieval pharmacists' tools. Notice the display of old pharmacists' books from the 16th, 17th, and 18th centuries—expertise imported from as far away as Venice, Frankfurt, Amsterdam, and Bologna. The sick would come to get their medicine at the little window (on the left side), which limited contact with the pharmacist and reduced the risk of passing on disease. On the right wall, look for the glass case marked *venena*—where poisons were locked away and carefully doled out, with a record of who had what.

Around the room, you'll also find some relics, old manuscripts, and a detailed painting of early-17th-century Dubrovnik. In the painting, notice that at the top of Mount Srđ—the highly strategic locale where Napoleon built a fortress that was key during the 1991 siege (see "The Siege of Dubrovnik" sidebar, earlier)—is a chapel. Though Dubrovnik was always heavily fortified, they avoided putting a fortress on the mountaintop—fearing it might seem overly provocative to the Ottoman Empire that surrounded them, and upon whose favor they depended for their autonomy.

Leaving the museum room, turn left and walk to the end of this corridor. Look up to see a tomb with a privileged position, affixed high on the wall. The **Gučetić-Gozze** family donated vast sums to help rebuild the monastery after the devastating 1667 earthquake. As thanks, the Franciscans helped them get just that much closer to God when they passed on, offering them this final resting place that was elevated...in every sense.

NEAR LUŽA SQUARE

These sights are at the far end of the Stradun (nearest the Old Port). As you stand on Luža Square facing the Bell Tower, the Rector's Palace and cathedral are up the wide street called Pred Dvorom to the right, and the Dominican Monastery Museum is through the gate by the Bell Tower and to the left.

▲Rector's Palace (Knežev Dvor)

In the Middle Ages, the Republic of Dubrovnik was ruled by a rec-

tor (similar to a Venetian doge), who was elected by the nobility. To prevent any one person from becoming too powerful, the rector's term was limited to one month. Most rectors were in their 50s—near the end of the average life span and when they were less likely to shake things up. During his term, a rector lived upstairs in this palace. Because it's been plundered twice (most recently by Napoleon's forces, who stole all the furniture), this empty-feeling museum isn't as interesting as most other European palaces. What little you'll see was donated by local aristocrats to flesh out the pathetically empty complex. The palace collection (with paid admission and good English explanations) is skippable, but it does offer a glimpse of Dubrovnik in its glory days. The palace's exterior and courtyard are viewable at no charge.

Cost and Hours: 100 kn, covered by 130-kn "nine museum

ticket" and by Dubrovnik Card; daily 9:00-18:00, Nov-April until 16:00; Pred Dvorom 3, tel. 020/322-096.

Visiting the Palace: The **exterior** is decorated in the Gothic-Renaissance mix (with particularly finely carved capitals) that was so common in Dubrovnik before the 1667 earthquake. Above the entrance is the message *Obliti privatorum publica curate*—loosely translated, "Forget your personal affairs and concern yourself with the affairs of state." This was a bold statement in a feudal era before democracy, when aristocrats were preoccupied exclusively with their self-interests. (It also feels tragically relevant today.)

Standing at the main door, get a free look at the palace's impressive **courtyard**—a venue for the Summer Festival, hosting music groups ranging from the local symphony to the Vienna Boys' Choir. During Dubrovnik's Golden Age, this courtyard was open to the public. People would wander in and out—gossiping, washing their laundry in the fountain (on the left), and bringing food to family members imprisoned in the cells. In the courtyard stands the only secular statue created during the centuries-long Republic. Dubrovnik republicans, mindful of the dangers of hero-worship, didn't believe that any one citizen should be singled out. They made only one exception—for Miho Pracat (a.k.a. Michaeli Prazatto), a rich citizen who donated vast sums to charity and willed a fleet of ships to the city. But notice that Pracat's statue is displayed in here, behind closed doors, not out in public.

If you pay to go **inside,** you'll ramble through a few rooms of dull paintings on the ground floor, then go into the green-stucco courtroom (with explanations of the Republic's unique judiciary system, and portraits and bios of some of its key politicians). Next, you'll see one of the palace's highlights: the original bronze bell-ringers from the town Bell Tower (Maro and Baro). Like antique robots (from the Renaissance, 1477-1478), these eerily lifelike sculptures could pivot at the waist to ring the bell. Nearby you'll see stone-

work that used to decorate city buildings. Farther along, massive iron chests (including a few with elaborate locking mechanisms) are displayed inside some old prison cells, which supposedly were placed within earshot of the rector's quarters, so he would hear the moans of the prisoners...and stay honest. Leaving the prison, you'll enter the courtyard described earlier, where you can get a better look at the Pracat statue.

On the mezzanine level (stairs near the main entrance, above the prison—notice the "hand" rails), you'll find a decent display of furniture, beautiful 18th-century sedans used to tote around V.I.R.s (Very Important Ragusans), a wimpy gun exhibit, votive offerings (mostly silver), an 18th-century coin collection (with magnifying glasses to make out the detail), and an interesting painting of "Ragusa" in the early 17th century—back when its stout walls were surrounded by a moat.

Head back down to the courtyard and ascend the grand stairway to the upper floor (with more "hand" rails). Upstairs, you'll explore old apartments that serve as a painting gallery. The only vaguely authentic room is the red room in the corner, decorated more or less as it was in 1500, when it was the rector's office. Mihajlo Hamzić's exquisite *Baptism of Christ* painting, inspired by Italian painter Andrea Mantegna, is an early Renaissance work from the "Dubrovnik School" (see "Dominican Monastery Museum" listing, later). This area also often displays temporary exhibits.

Back in the courtyard, you can go up the smaller stairs to the Domus Christi collection of old pharmacist tools and pots.

Handy WCs are just off the courtyard next to the shop, through which you'll exit.

▲Cathedral (Katedrala)

According to legend, Dubrovnik's original 12th-century cathedral was funded largely by the English King Richard the Lionheart.

On his way back from the Third Crusade, Richard was shipwrecked nearby. He promised God that if he survived, he'd build a church on the spot where he landed—which happened to be on Lokrum Island, just offshore. At Dubrovnik's request, Richard agreed to build his token of thanks inside the city instead. It was the finest Romanesque church on the Adriatic...before it was destroyed by the 1667 earthquake. This version is 18th-century Roman Baroque.

Cost and Hours: Church—free, daily 8:00-17:00; treasury—20 kn or 75-kn combo-ticket with Bishop's Palace (see next), generally open same hours as church; both have shorter hours off-season.

Visiting the Cathedral: Inside, you'll find a painting from the school of Titian *(Assumption of the Virgin)* over the stark contemporary altar.

DUBROVNIK

Behind the altar is a quirky **treasury** *(riznica)* packed with 187 relics (pay and enter to the right of the altar). Examining the treasury collection, notice that there are three locks on the treasury door—the stuff in here was so valuable, three different VIPs (the rector, the bishop, and a local aristocrat) had to agree before it could be opened. On the table near the door are several of St. Blaise's body parts (pieces of his arm, skull, and leg—all encased in gold and silver). In the middle of the wall directly opposite the door, look for the crucifix with a piece of the True Cross. On a dig in Jerusalem, St. Helen (Emperor Constantine's mother) discovered what she believed to be the cross that Jesus was crucified on. It was brought to Constantinople, and the Byzantine emperors doled out pieces of it to Balkan kings. Note the folding three-paneled altar painting (underneath the cross). Dubrovnik ambassadors packed this on road trips (such as their annual trip to pay off the Ottomans) so they could worship wherever they traveled.

On the right side of the room, the silver casket supposedly holds the actual swaddling clothes of the Baby Jesus. Dubrovnik bishops secretly passed these clothes down from generation to generation...until a nun got wind of it and told the whole town. Pieces of the cloth were cut off to miraculously heal the sick, especially new mothers recovering from a difficult birth. No matter how often it was cut, the cloth always went back to its original form. Then someone tried to use it on the wife of a Bosnian king. Since she was Muslim, it couldn't help her, and it never worked again. True or not, this legend hints at the prickly relationships between faiths (not to mention the male chauvinism) here in the Balkans.

Bishop's Palace (Biskupska Palača)

Just across the plaza from the cathedral's main entrance, this building once belonged to an illustrious family, but in the 19th century was taken over by Dubrovnik's bishops. After many decades of restoration, it's now one of the only places in town where you can get an idea of how Dubrovnik's aristocracy once lived.

Cost and Hours: 75-kn combo-ticket includes entrance to cathedral treasury, daily 10:00-22:00, Nov-March until 17:00.

Visiting the Palace: The bishop still occupies the upper floors of the house; the lower floors display the bishopric's art collection. The medieval, Renaissance, and Baroque paintings mostly appeal to art lovers, but the historic interiors are the real draw here. Notice the frescoes in the entrance hall, then climb the stairs to the tourable rooms. Branching off to the right from the main staircase, you can see an arched Gothic ceiling—one of the few that survived the 1667 earthquake. Notice the charming details, such as the faces carved in the stonework at the bottom of door arches on the first floor. The standout is the room with the spectacular, Renaissance-era wooden ceiling; it also survived the earthquake, and is one of the only such ceilings on the eastern Adriatic.

▲Dominican Monastery Museum (Dominikanski Samostan-Muzej)

You'll find many of Dubrovnik's art treasures—paintings, altarpieces, and manuscripts—gathered around the peaceful Dominican Monastery cloister inside the Ploče Gate.

Cost and Hours: 30 kn, daily 9:00-18:00, Nov-March until 16:30, art buffs enjoy the 50-kn English book.

Visiting the Museum: As you climb the **stairs** up to the monastery, notice that the spindles supporting the railing are solid up until about two feet above the ground. This was to provide a modicum of modesty to ladies on their way to church—and to prevent creeps down below from looking up their skirts.

Buy your ticket, then turn left and work your way clockwise around the cloister. The room in the far corner contains paintings from the **"Dubrovnik School,"** the Republic's circa-1500 answer to the art boom in Florence and Venice. Though the 1667 earthquake destroyed most of these paintings, about a dozen survive, and five of those are in this room. Just inside the door, don't miss the triptych by Nikola Božidarović with St. Blaise holding a detailed model of 16th-century Dubrovnik (left panel)—the most famous depiction of Dubrovnik's favorite saint. You'll also see reliquaries shaped like the hands and feet that they hold.

Continuing around the courtyard, duck into the next room. At the far end of the room is a painting by **Titian** depicting St. Blaise, Mary Magdalene, and the donor who financed this work.

At the next corner of the courtyard is the entrance to the striking **church** at the heart of this still-active monastery. (The church may be closed, or its art removed for renovation.) If it's open, step inside and face the altar. The interior is decorated with modern stained glass, a fine 13th-century stone pulpit that survived the earthquake (reminding visitors of the intellectual approach to scripture that characterized the Dominicans), and a precious 14th-century Paolo Veneziano crucifix hanging in the arch above the altar. Perhaps the finest piece of art in the church is the *Miracle of St. Dominic,* showing the founder of the order bringing a child back to life (to the left as you face the main altar). Behind the altar, find the Vukovar Cross, embedded with panels painted by different artists from the Croatian school of Naive Art—offering an enticing taste of this unique and fascinating style (for more on Naive Art, see page 55). It was painted in the Realist style (late 19th century) by Vlaho Bukovac.

NEAR THE OLD PORT (STARA LUKA)

The picturesque Old Port, carefully nestled behind St. John's Fort, faces away from what was Dubrovnik's biggest threat, the

Venetians. At the port, you can haggle with captains selling excursions to nearby towns and islands (described in the next chapter) and watch cruise-ship passengers coming and going on their tenders. The long seaside building across the bay east of the Ploče Gate is the Lazareti, once the medieval quarantine house. In those days, all visitors were locked in here for 40 days before entering town. A bench-lined harborside walk leads around the fort to a breakwater, providing a peaceful perch. From the breakwater, rocky beaches curl around the outside of the wall.

Maritime Museum (Pomorski Muzej)

In the 15th century, when Venice's nautical dominance was peaking, Dubrovnik emerged as another maritime power and the Mediterranean's leading shipbuilding center. The Dubrovnik-built "argosy" boat (from "Ragusa," an early name for the city) was the Cadillac of ships, even mentioned by Shakespeare. This worthwhile museum, built into Dubrovnik's walls, fits in tidily with a wall walk. It traces the long history of Dubrovnik's most important industry with contracts, maps, paintings, navigational devices, and models—all well-described in English. The main floor takes you through the 18th century, and the easy-to-miss upstairs covers the 19th and 20th centuries.

Cost and Hours: Covered by 130-kn "nine museum ticket" and by Dubrovnik Card; hours flex on demand—usually Tue-Sun 9:00-18:00, Nov-Feb until 16:00, closed Mon year-round; 5-kn English booklet or elaborate 60-kn book, good WCs at entry, upstairs in St. John's Fort, at far/south end of Old Port, tel. 020/323-904.

DUBROVNIK

Aquarium (Akvarij)

Dubrovnik's aquarium, housed in the cavernous St. John's Fort, is an old-school place, with 31 tanks on one floor. A visit here allows you a close look at the local marine life and provides a cool refuge from the midday heat.

Cost and Hours: 60 kn, kids-20 kn, daily July-Aug 9:00-21:00, progressively shorter hours off-season until 9:00-16:00 Nov-March, English descriptions, ground floor of St. John's Fort, enter from Old Port, tel. 020/323-978.

BETWEEN THE STRADUN AND THE MAINLAND

The first two museums are a few steps off the main promenade toward the mainland.

▲Synagogue Museum (Sinagoga-Muzej)

When the Jews were forced out of Spain in 1492, a steady stream of them passed through here en route to today's Turkey. Finding Dubrovnik to be a flourishing and relatively tolerant city, many stayed. Žudioska ulica ("Jewish Street"), just inside the Ploče Gate, became the ghetto in 1546. It was walled at one end and had a gate (which would be locked at night) at the other end. Today, the same street is home to the second-oldest continuously functioning synagogue in Europe (after Prague's), which contains Croatia's only Jewish museum. The top floor houses the synagogue itself. Notice the lattice windows that separated the women from the men (in accordance with Orthodox Jewish tradition). Below that, a small museum with good English descriptions gives meaning to the various Torahs (including a 14th-century one from Spain) and other items—such as the written orders *(naredba)* from Nazi-era Yugoslavia, stating that Jews were to identify their shops as Jewish-owned and wear armbands. (The Ustaše—the Nazi puppet government in Croatia—interned and executed not only Jews and Roma, but also Serbs and other people they considered undesirable; see page 23.) Of Croatia's 24,000 Jews, only 4,000 survived the Holocaust. Today Croatia has about 2,000 Jews, including a dozen Jewish families who call Dubrovnik home.

Cost and Hours: 50 kn, daily 9:00-20:00, mid-Nov-April until 15:00, Žudioska ulica 5, tel. 020/321-204.

▲War Photo Limited

The brainchild of photojournalist Wade Goddard, this thought-provoking museum attempts to show the ugly reality of war through raw, often disturbing photographs taken in the field around the world (not just Dubrovnik). Use the loaner guide to understand the well-displayed images on two floors; a small permanent exhibit (on the top floor) captures the Yugoslav Wars through photography

DUBROVNIK

and video footage. Each summer, the gallery also houses various temporary exhibits.

Cost and Hours: 50 kn; May-Sept daily 10:00-22:00; April and Oct Wed-Mon until 16:00, closed Tue; closed Nov-March; Antuninska 6, tel. 020/322-166, www.warphotoltd.com.

BETWEEN THE STRADUN AND THE SEA
▲Serbian Orthodox Church and Icon Museum (Srpska Pravoslavna Crkva i Muzej Ikona)

Round out your look at Dubrovnik's major faiths (Catholic, Jewish, and Orthodox) with a visit to this house of worship—one of

the most convenient places in Croatia to learn about Orthodox Christianity. Remember that people from the former Yugoslavia who follow the Orthodox faith are, by definition, ethnic Serbs. With occasional lingering hard feelings about the Yugoslav Wars, this church serves as an important reminder that not all Serbs are aggressors.

Dubrovnik never had a very large Serb population (an Orthodox church wasn't even allowed inside the town walls until the mid-19th century). During the Yugoslav Wars, most Serbs fled, created new lives for themselves elsewhere, and saw little reason to return. But some old-timers remain, and Dubrovnik's dwindling, aging Orthodox population is still served by this **church.** The candles stuck in the sand (to prevent fire outbreaks) represent prayers: The ones at knee level are for the deceased, while the ones higher up are for the living. The gentleman selling candles encourages you to buy and light one, regardless of your faith, so long as you do so with the proper intentions and reverence. To better appreciate this church, read "The Serbian Orthodox Church" sidebar.

Cost and Hours: Free but donations accepted; daily 8:00-21:00, Oct-April until 18:00, liturgy Sun 10:00-11:00; Od Puča.

Nearby: A few doors down (at Od Puča 8) is the **Icon Museum,** which may be closed for renovation—ask at the icon shop next door to the cathedral entrance. When open, this small collection features 78 different icons (stylized paintings of saints, generally on a golden background—a common feature of Orthodox churches) from the 15th through the 19th centuries, all identified in English. In the library—crammed with old shelves holding some 12,000 books—look for the astonishingly detailed calendar, with portraits of hundreds of saints.

The Serbian Orthodox Church

This book emphasizes the Catholic areas of the former Yugoslavia, but don't overlook the rich diversity of faiths in this region. Dubrovnik's Serbian Orthodox church—as well as Orthodox churches in Kotor (in Montenegro), Sarajevo, and Ljubljana—offer invaluable opportunities to learn about a faith that's often unfamiliar to American visitors.

Orthodox churches carry on the earliest traditions of the Christian faith. Orthodox and Catholic Christianity came from the same roots, so the oldest surviving early Christian churches (such as the stave churches of Norway) have many of the same features as today's Orthodox churches.

Notice that there are no pews. Worshippers stand through the service, as a sign of respect (though some older parishioners sit along the walls). Women stand on the left side, men on the right (equal distance from the altar—to represent that all are equal before God). The Orthodox Church uses essentially the same Bible as Catholics, but it's written in the Cyrillic alphabet. Following Old Testament Judeo-Christian tradition, the Bible is kept on the altar behind the iconostasis, the big screen in the middle of the room covered with curtains and icons (golden paintings of saints), which separates the material world from the spiritual one. At certain times during the service, the curtains or doors are opened so the congregation can see the Holy Book.

Orthodox icons are not intended to be lifelike. Packed with intricate symbolism, and cast against a shimmering golden background, they're meant to remind viewers of the metaphysical nature of Jesus and the saints rather than of their physical form. You'll almost never see a statue, which is thought to overemphasize the physical world (and smacks of worshipping graven images). Orthodox services generally involve chanting (between the priest and the congregation), and the church is filled with the evocative aroma of incense.

The incense, chanting, icons, and standing are all intended to heighten the experience of worship. While many Catholic and Protestant services tend to be more of a theoretical consideration of religious issues, Orthodox services strive to help the worshipper transcend the physical world and join in communion with the spiritual one.

▲Rupe Granary and Ethnographic Museum (Etnografski Muzej Rupe)

This huge, 16th-century building was Dubrovnik's biggest granary, and today houses the best folk museum I've seen in Croatia. *Rupe* means "holes"—and it's worth the price of entry just to peer down into these 15 cavernous underground grain stores, designed to maintain the perfect temperature to preserve the seeds (63 degrees

DUBROVNIK

Fahrenheit). Look down through the hefty grates on the main floor. When the grain had to be dried, it was moved upstairs—where today you'll find a surprisingly well-presented Ethnographic Museum covering Dubrovnik's many traditions and festivals, and displaying tools, jewelry, clothing, instruments, painted eggs, and other folk artifacts from its colorful history. English explanations are scant; it's worth downloading the museum's app for the audioguide. The museum hides several blocks uphill from the main promenade, toward the sea (climb up Široka—the widest side street from the Stradun—which becomes Od Domina on the way to the museum).

Cost and Hours: Covered by 130-kn "nine museum ticket" and by Dubrovnik Card, Wed-Mon 9:00-16:00, July-Aug until 20:00, closed Tue, Od Rupa 3, tel. 020/323-013.

OUTSIDE THE OLD TOWN
See the "Greater Dubrovnik" map for the locations of these sights.

▲▲▲Mount Srđ
After adding Dubrovnik to his holdings, Napoleon built a fortress atop the hill behind the Old Town to keep an eye on his new subjects (in 1810). During the city's 20th-century tourism heyday, a cable car was built to effortlessly whisk visitors to the top so they could enjoy the fine views from the fortress and the giant cross nearby. Then, when war broke out in the 1990s, Mount Srđ (pronounced like "surge") became a crucial link in the de-fense of Dubrovnik—the only high land that locals were able to hold. The fortress was shelled and damaged, and the cross and cable car were destroyed. Minefields and unexploded ordnance left the hilltop a dangerous no-man's-land. But more recently, the mountain's fortunes have reversed. The landmines have been removed, and in 2010, the cable car was rebuilt to once again connect Dubrovnik's Old Town to its mountaintop. Visitors head to the top both for the spectacular sweeping views and to ponder the exhibits in a ragtag museum about the war.

Warning: While this area has officially been cleared of landmines, nervous locals remind visitors that this was once a war zone. Be sure to stay on clearly defined paths and roads.

Expect Changes: International developers have plans to build a luxury golf resort on the mountain plateau behind Mount Srđ.

You may see construction and, while it likely won't affect the cable car, it may eventually take over the fort and museum.

Getting to the Top: The **cable car** is easily the best option for reaching the summit of Mount Srđ (170 kn round-trip, 90 kn one-way, kunas or credit cards only—no euros; at least 2/hour—generally departing at :00 and :30 past each hour, more frequent with demand, 3-minute ride; daily from 9:00, June-Aug until 24:00, Sept until 22:00, May until 21:00, April and Oct until 20:00, Feb-March and Nov until 17:00, Dec-Jan until 16:00; doesn't run in Bora wind or heavy rain, last ascent 30 minutes before closing, tel. 020/325-393, www.dubrovnikcablecar.com). The lower station is just above the Buža Gate at the top of the Old Town (from the main drag, huff all the way to the top of Boškovićeva, exit through gate, and climb uphill one block, then look right). You may see travel agencies selling tickets elsewhere in town, but there's no advantage to buying them anywhere but here. The line you may see at the cable-car station is not to buy tickets, but to actually ride up. For tips on avoiding a long wait, see below.

If you have a **car,** it's possible to drive up—though the road can be crowded. From the high road above the Old Town, watch for the turnoff to *Bosanka,* which leads you to that village, then up to the fortress and cross—follow signs for *Srđ* (it's twisty but not far—figure a 20-minute drive from the Old Town area). If you're coming south from the Old Town, once you reach the main road above, you'll have to turn left and backtrack a bit to reach the *Bosanka* turnoff. For **hikers,** a switchback trail (used to supply the fortress during the siege) connects the Old Town to the mountaintop—but it's very steep and provides minimal shade. (If your knees are solid and it's not too hot, you could ride the cable car up, then hike down.)

Crowd-Beating Tips: The cable car has a limited capacity, and lines can get long when several cruise ships are in town. On busy days, it's best avoided entirely in the morning, especially 9:30-11:00. Things may quiet down in the mid- to late afternoon. But then there's another rush before sunset—which is, understandably, the most popular time to ascend. Be warned that the line to go back down the cable car stacks up as soon as the sunset ends (see "Sunset Tips," later).

Mountaintop: From the top cable-car station, head up the stairs to the panoramic terrace. The bird's-eye **view** is truly spectacular, looking straight down to the street plan of Dubrovnik's Old

DUBROVNIK

Town. From this lofty perch, you can see north to the Dalmatian islands (the Elaphite archipelago, Mljet, Korčula, and beyond); south to Montenegro; and east into Bosnia-Herzegovina. Gazing upon those looming mountains that define the border with Bosnia-Herzegovina—which, centuries ago, was also the frontier of the huge and powerful Ottoman Empire—you can appreciate how impressive it was that stubborn little Dubrovnik managed to remain independent for so much of its history.

The **cross** was always an important symbol in this very Catholic town. After it was destroyed in the siege, a temporary wooden one was erected to encourage the towns-people who were waiting out the siege below. During a visit in 2003, Pope John Paul II blessed the rubble from the old cross; those fragments are now being used in the foundations of the city's newest churches. Nearby stands a huge red, white, and blue flagpole—the colors of the Croatian flag.

To reach the museum in the old fortress, walk behind the cable-car station along the rocky red soil toward the gigantic antenna.

Fort and Museum: The Napoleonic-era Fort Imperial (Trđava Imperijal) houses the **Dubrovnik During the Homeland War (1991-1995) Museum** (30 kn, daily 8:00-18:00, Nov-late March until 16:00). While interesting (and occupying an important location, where the Dubrovnik Defenders burrowed in to fight for their city), the museum's descriptions are rabble-rousing and one-sided ("Serbian and Montenegrin aggression"). Still, it offers an insightful look at the conflict.

The hallway on the right as you enter leads to a changing photo exhibition showing slices of life during the siege. The hallway on the left has the permanent exhibits, where photos, documents, and artifacts tell the story (with English descriptions) of the overarching war with Yugoslavia and how the people defended this fortress. The descriptions are too dense and tactical for casual visitors, but you'll see lots of photos and some actual items used in the fighting: primitive, rusty rifles (some dating from World War II) that the Croatians used for their improvised defense, and piles of spent mortar shells and other projectiles that Yugoslav forces hurled at the fortress and the city. Look for the wire-guided Russian rockets. After being launched at their target, the rockets would burrow into a wall, waiting to be detonated once their operators saw the opportunity for maximum destruction. The tattered Croatian flag seems soaked in local patriotism. A video screen shows breathless international news reports from the front line during the bombing.

After seeing the exhibit, climb up a few flights of stairs to the **rooftop** for the view. The giant communications tower overhead flew the Croatian flag during the war, to inspire the besieged residents below. You might see some charred trees around here—these were claimed not by the war, but more recently, by forest fires. (Fear of landmines and other explosives prevented locals from fighting the wildfires as aggressively as they might otherwise, making these fires more dangerous than ever.)

Sunset Tips: Mount Srd is a popular vantage point for enjoying the sunset over the Dalmatian islands. There are two viewpoints at the cable-car station: one at the cabin level and another upstairs. Another good vantage point is from near the cross (where some people scramble down onto the dangerously steep, rocky slope below). But, if you're going to tour the museum at the fort anyway, consider timing your visit to be on its rooftop for sunset. It tends to be less crowded and has fine views over the islands. The only disadvantage is that you're farther away from the cable car—and as soon as the sun sets, the line back down begins to form. While the line moves quickly, you may be in for a bit of a wait. Be warned that, up on the arid and breezy mountaintop, the temperature can drop quickly once the sun sets (bring a sweater).

Eating: Boasting undoubtedly the best view in Dubrovnik, **$$$$ Restaurant Panorama** has drop-dead astonishing views over the rooftops of the Old Town and to the most beautiful parts of three different countries. While there's glassed-in seating inside, in good weather I'd exit the building to find the outdoor terrace— the Old Town floats just under your nose. Prices are high, but you can dine affordably if you stick to basic pasta dishes. If riding the cable car late in the day, this is a great place for a breezy dinner; it's often cooler up here than down in the Old Town, and the views can't be beat. There's a rush on tables just after sunset; if you're planning to be here around that time, it's smart to reserve a table ahead of time (open same hours as cable car, tel. 020/312-664).

▲▲Red History Museum

This well-done museum is somewhat inconveniently located in the Port Gruž area, but it's worth the trip for a crash course on 20th-century Croatian (and Yugoslav) history. Focusing on socialism in theory and practice through accessible explanations and everyday objects, the exhibits also address the repressive aspects of living in the Yugoslav socialist regime. Overall, while there's a lot of reading and most of the exhibits aren't very interactive, the museum offers an excellent intellectual counterpoint to a sea-and-sun itinerary.

Cost and Hours: 50 kn, daily 9:00-22:00, Nov-April

10:00-18:00, Svetog Kriza 3, mobile 091-540-1704, www.
redhistorymuseum.com. It's straightforward to get here with public
transportation: from Pile Gate, take bus #1a, #1b, #1c, or #3, get
off at the main bus station, then walk 10 minutes back in the direction you came, looking for Hotel Petka. The museum is just up the
street behind the hotel.

Visiting the Museum: Concise but smart English explanations chart the rise of socialist/communist ideas in the territory
of former Yugoslavia, then their eventual dominance thanks to
Tito and the Partisans' victory in World War II. The museum does
a particularly good job integrating political and social history to
show how society developed—for example, through the urban
planning that created whole new sections of cities and guaranteed
modern housing for everyone. You'll walk through rooms of what
would have been a typical family home. Spend some time in the
kitchen, featuring cupboards stacked with former Yugo products
that have a lot of nostalgic value today.

You might have some assumptions challenged as you learn
how good life could be in socialist Yugoslavia. The country had
the world's second-fastest-growing economy (after Japan's) starting in the 1950s, and many citizens saw their standard of living
increase dramatically. One exhibit details the "required vacations"
that every family got, usually at a government-run Adriatic seaside
resort. This was quite an adjustment for many poor or rural people,
who had never had a vacation in their lives. The museum also explores the cultural side of socialist Yugo, such as education, film,
pop music, and sports (the tall Yugoslavs were—and remain—a
basketball powerhouse).

The museum doesn't shy away from the dark side to the regime. The secret police were a powerful force, and political freedoms were tightly curtailed. One room tells about Goli Otok, the
Alcatraz of Tito's Yugoslavia, via filmed recollections of two men
who spent time at the prison. The exhibits finish up with a long
wall of old photos and individuals' memories—both positive and
negative—of living under socialism.

Activities in Dubrovnik

Swimming and Sunbathing

If the weather's good and you've had enough of museums, spend a
sunny afternoon at the beach. There are no sandy beaches on the
mainland near Dubrovnik, but there are lots of suitable pebbly options, plus several concrete perches.

The easiest and most atmospheric place to take a dip is right
off the **Old Town.** From the Old Port and its breakwater, uneven
steps clinging to the outside of the wall lead to a series of great

sunbathing and swimming coves (and even a showerhead sticking out of the town wall). Another delightful rocky beach hangs onto the outside of the Old Town's wall (at the bar called Cold Drinks "Buža" I; for more on this bar, and how to find it, see "Entertainment in Dubrovnik," later).

A more convenient—and crowded—public beach is **Banje,** just outside the Ploče Gate, east of the Old Town. This public beach (watched over by an upscale bar/restaurant/lounge) is ideal for sunbathing and wading, with a spectacular backdrop of Dubrovnik's Old Town. To reach the beach, leave the Old Town through the Ploče Gate, walk about five minutes gradually uphill on the main road, then watch for the staircase marked *Banje Beach* (while the stairs pass through the bar, it is public access). The bar itself is slick and swanky, serving pricey food and drink. You can also rent a very expensive sun bed, but it's much more affordable to bring your own towel and find a comfy patch of sand. Pay showers are nearby.

My favorite hidden beach—**St. Jakob**—takes a lot longer to reach, but if you're up for the hike, it's worth it to escape the crowds. Figure about a 25-minute walk (each way) from the Old Town. Go through the Ploče Gate at the east end of the Old Town, and walk along the street called Frana Supila as it climbs uphill above the waterfront. At Hotel Argentina, take the right

(downhill) fork and keep going on Vlaha Bukovca. Eventually you'll reach the small church of St. Jakob. You'll see the beach—in a cozy protected cove—far below. Curl around behind the church and keep an eye out for stairs going down on the right. Unfortunately, these stairs are effectively unmarked, so it might take some trial and error to find the right ones. (If you reach the rusted-white gateway of the old communist-era open-air theater, you've gone too far.) Hike down the very steep stairs to the gentle cove, which has rentable chairs and a small restaurant for drinks (and a WC). Enjoy the pebbly beach and faraway views of Dubrovnik's Old Town. In peak season, water taxis may be ferrying beachgoers between this beach and the Old Port, offering an easier trip (around 30 kn one-way).

Other, even more distant beaches are worth considering. If you're staying at—or visiting—the resort zone of **Lapad Bay,** you'll find a fine beach there (near Hotel Kompas).

Locals prefer to swim on **Lokrum Island,** because there are (relatively) fewer tourists. While there are no sandy or even pebbly beaches, there are several rocky ones, with ladders to lower yourself gingerly into the water. As the rocks here can be particularly jagged, you'll want to wear good water shoes, and beware of uneven footing (both underwater, and on your way to the ladders). For details on taking a boat to Lokrum, see the next chapter.

Finally, for the best sandy beach in this part of Croatia, you'll have to take a boat to the island of Lopud, then hike (or ride a golf cart) across the spine of the island to the gorgeous **Šunj Beach.** Making an all-day trek out here (by public ferry) is worth doing only if you're desperate for a long, lingering day at the beach. If you're cruising the Elaphite Islands, you'll likely stop on Lopud for two or three hours—enough time for a quick dip at Šunj. For more on Lopud and Šunj Beach, see the next chapter.

Sea Kayaking

Paddling a sleek kayak around the outside of Dubrovnik's imposing walls is a memorable experience. Several outfits in town offer half-day tours (most options 250-350 kn); popular itineraries include loops along the City Walls, to secluded beaches, and around Lokrum Island; many include a break for snorkeling (they provide goggles), and some are timed to catch the sunset while bobbing in the Adriatic. Well-established companies include **Adriatic Kayak Tours** (www.adriatickayaktours.com), **Outdoor Croatia** (https://outdoorcroatia.com), **Adria Adventure** (www.kayakingcroatia.com), and **Adventure Dubrovnik** (www.adventuredubrovnik.com)—but new companies pop up all the time...check online or look for fliers locally.

Shopping in Dubrovnik

Most souvenirs sold in Dubrovnik—from lavender sachets to plaster models of the Old Town—are pretty tacky. Whatever you buy, prices are much higher along the Stradun than on the side streets.

Jewelry: A classy alternative to the knickknacks is a type of local jewelry called *Konavoske puce* ("Konavle buttons"). Sold as earrings, pendants, and rings, these distinctive and fashionable filigree-style pieces consist of a sphere studded with small posts. Though they're sold around town, it's least expensive to buy them on Od Puča street, which runs parallel to the Stradun two blocks toward the sea (near the Serbian Orthodox Church). The high concentration of jewelers along this lane keeps prices reasonable. You'll find the "buttons" in various sizes, in both silver (affordable) and gold (pricey).

You'll also see lots of jewelry made from red coral, which can only be legally gathered in small amounts from two small islands

in northern Dalmatia. If you see a particularly large chunk of coral, it's likely imported. To know what you're getting, shop at an actual jeweler instead of a souvenir shop; **Clara Stones** at Nalješkovićeva 3 is reputable.

Local Arts and Crafts: DEŠA, a humanitarian organization that supports people in rural areas around Dubrovnik, is

a nice place to buy traditional crafts like embroidery, treats such as candied almonds and oranges, and cosmetics. Their shop is in the Lazareti, the old quarantine house just outside the Ploče Gate (Mon-Fri 9:00-17:00, closed Sat-Sun, shorter hours off-season).

A shop called **Life According to KAWA,** also outside the Ploče Gate, is a great place to browse for characteristic, hipster-aesthetic local souvenirs and handicrafts. They've got everything from artisanal sea salt and jewelry, to ceramics and Dubrovnik-themed ironic T-shirts. They also stock a fridge full of local microbrews and some carefully selected local wines and foods (daily 9:00-21:00 in peak season, until 22:00 in shoulder season, Maestra Đela Jusića 2, tel. 020/696-958).

Along **Zlatarska** street in the Old Town, you can find a couple of shops with clothes and accessories made by local designers.

Gift-Shop Chains: Several gift shops in Dubrovnik (with additional branches throughout Dalmatia) hawk fun, if sometimes made-in-China, items. Look for these chains, which are a bit classier than the many no-name shops around town: **Aqua** sells pleasant nautical-themed gifts, blue-and-white-striped sailor shirts, and other gear. **Bonbonnière Kraš** is Croatia's leading chocolatier, selling a wide array of tasty candies. **Uje** has artisan olive oils and other boutiquey edibles.

Entertainment in Dubrovnik

MUSICAL EVENTS

Dubrovnik annually hosts a full schedule of events for its Summer Festival (July 10-Aug 25, www.dubrovnik-festival.hr), which is quickly followed by its Late Summer Festival. But the town also works hard to offer traditional music outside of festival time. The Cultural Information Desk, inside the Sloboda theater lobby at the

DUBROVNIK

bottom of the Bell Tower on Luža Square, is a good source of information on events (open long hours daily). For the latest, check the listings in *The Best in Dubrovnik* guide, or ask the TI.

Here are a few good choices:

Spirited **Linđo folk-music** concerts are performed for tourists twice weekly in the Lazareti (former medieval quarantine building), just outside the Ploče Gate (120 kn, usually Tue and Fri at 21:30, www.lindjo.hr).

The **Dubrovnik Symphony Orchestra** performs crowd-pleasing classics twice weekly in summer (and once weekly through winter)—usually at the Rector's Palace in good weather, or the Dominican Monastery in bad weather (100-400 kn, typically at 21:00, www.dso.hr).

Various historic **churches** around town host touristy but enjoyable concerts (generally 100 kn, each venue hosts about 3/week at 21:00, mobile 098-244-264). Venues include St. Savior, just inside the Pile Gate; the simpler Domina Church, just up Od Domina street from the Stradun; and the little Rosario Church near the Dominican Monastery at the Ploče Gate.

Also consider the folk dancing and market each Sunday morning at Čilipi, a small town near the airport (see the next chapter). Dubrovnik-based companies offer excursions that include transportation there and back.

NIGHTLIFE

Dubrovnik's Old Town is one big, romantic parade of relaxed and happy people out strolling. The main drag is a fun scene, brightly lit and packed with shops, cafés, and bars, all open late. And if you walk away from the crowds or out on the port, you'll be alone with the magic of the Pearl of the Adriatic. Everything feels— and is—very safe after dark.

If you're looking for a memorable bar after dark, consider these:

▲▲▲Drinks with a View

Cold Drinks "Buža" offers, without a doubt, the most scenic spot for a drink. Perched on a cliff above the sea, clinging like a barnacle to the outside of the City Walls, this is a peaceful, shaded getaway from the bustle of the Old Town...the perfect place to watch cruise ships disappear into the horizon. *Buža* means "hole in the wall"—and that's exactly what you'll have to go through to reach these places. There are two different Bužas, both open every

day in summer from 9:00 until the
wee hours (closed in bad weather
and off-season; both have drinks for
around 40-50 kn). **Buža II** (nicknamed "Big Buža") is the older and
more appealing of the pair. Filled
with mellow tourists and bartenders
pouring wine and beer into plastic
cups, Buža II comes with castaway
views and Frank Sinatra ambience.
When the seats fill up—as often
happens around sunset—you can
order a drink at the bar and walk
down the stairs to enjoy it "on the
rocks"...literally. **Buža I**—also called Mala (Small) Buža—is mellower, plays hip or edgy rather than romantic music, and has concrete stairs leading down to a beach on the rocks below. While
lacking Buža II's shade, Buža I is less claustrophobic and often a bit
less crowded, making it a viable alternative.

Getting There: Both Bužas are well away from the bustle of
the main drag, along the seaward wall. To reach them from the
cathedral area, hike up the grand staircase to St. Ignatius' Church,
then go left to find the lane that runs along the inside of the wall.
To find the classic Buža II, head right along the lane and look for
the *Cold Drinks* sign pointing to a literal hole in the wall. For the
hipper Buža I, go left along the same lane, and locate the hole in
the wall with the *No Toples No Nudist* graffiti.

Cocktails and People-Watching

Bunićeva Poljana, the little square tucked behind the cathedral, is
jammed with tables from a half-dozen cafés, which fill with tourists and locals each evening. Live jazz is provided nightly by **Jazz
Caffè Troubadour,** but as their drink prices are outlandish, most
people prefer to sit at a nearby place...you can hear the music just
as well from there (or from anywhere in this part of the Old Town,
for that matter).

Nonenina, a few steps in front of the cathedral on Pred Dvorom, is an outdoor lounge with a fine vantage point for people-
watching (daily 9:00-late, across from Rector's Palace).

The Gaffe Irish Pub, with a chummy, pubby interior and a
small courtyard, is a rollicking spot to drain a pint and watch some
rugby (Miha Pracata 4, tel. 020/640-152).

Restaurant Klarisa, tucked in a tight back corner of the Old
Town (behind St. Claire's Convent, just up Gariște ulica from Onofrio's Big Fountain), has live jazz each night outside. You can pay

for an overpriced meal or drink, or just loiter and enjoy (Poljana Paska Miličevića 4, tel. 020/413-100).

D'Vino Wine Bar is an ideal place to nurse a drink while learning about Croatian wine, nibbling local tapas, and socializing (plus listening to occasional live music—see www.dvino.net for details); also see full listing under "Eating in Dubrovnik," later. **Glam Café,** just across the street, has a similar vibe and stocks a nice assortment of local microbrews.

Nightclubs

Two night spots are just beyond the Ploče Gate at the east end of town. Head under the Bell Tower, up the street past the Dominican Monastery. After crossing the bridge, look (on the left) for the entrance to **Revelin**—a dance club that fills one of the city wall's fortress towers (www.clubrevelin.com). Then continue up the street until you reach **Banje Beach,** a bar/lounge/dance club overlooking one of the city's most scenic beaches (www.banjebeach.com). Note that some exclusive bars and clubs may charge admission on weekends.

MOVIES

The Old Town has a variety of movie theaters showing American blockbusters (usually in English with Croatian subtitles, unless the film's animated or for kids; for the schedule, see www.kinematografi.org). Two modern cinemas in town have comfortable seating and show current movies: the **Sloboda,** right under the Bell Tower on Luža Square (open outside of the summer outdoor movie season—see next); and **Visia,** just inside the Pile Gate (year-round).

In good summer weather, head for the fun outdoor **Jadran** cinema, where you can lick ice cream (B.Y.O.) while you watch a movie with a Dubrovnik-mountaintop backdrop. This is a cheap, casual, and very Croatian scene, where people smoke and chat, and the neighbors sit in their windowsills to watch the movie (most nights late June-mid-Sept, shows begin shortly after sundown; in the Old Town near the Pile Gate). Another outdoor movie venue, **Slavica,** is farther out of town, on the road leading away from the Pile Gate.

Sleeping in Dubrovnik

You basically have two options in Dubrovnik: a centrally located room in a private home *(soba);* or a resort hotel on a distant beach, a bus ride away from the Old Town. Dubrovnik hotels are generally a rotten value, and you'll have to commute into your sightseeing on crowded buses. For this reason, I heavily favor a central *soba.*

No matter where you stay, prices are much higher mid-June through mid-September, and highest in July and August. Reserve well ahead for these peak times.

SOBE (PRIVATE ROOMS): A DUBROVNIK SPECIALTY

In Dubrovnik, you'll almost always do better with a *soba* or apartment than with a hotel. Before you choose, carefully read the information on page 773. All of my favorite *sobe* are run by friendly English-speaking Croatians and are inside or within easy walking distance of the Old Town.

All of my listings are air-conditioned and come with private facilities, and most have kitchenettes. A few are in family homes, but you can be as anonymous as you like. These *sobe* accept cash only (no credit cards), and you're on your own for breakfast—I've listed some suggestions later, under "Eating in Dubrovnik."

My four long-time personal favorites here are Dubrovnik Gardens, Jadranka Benussi, Van Bloemen Apartments, and Villa Ragusa. These all enjoy conscientious management, a fine location, and good value for the price. Book these early—they're often full. I've also listed several almost-as-good options.

To search from home, you can use the regular booking sites (such as Airbnb or Booking.com)—but if you want to book one of the places I've listed here, **please book direct** (by sending them an email), which saves both you and your host money. These hosts respond to email quickly, and many will offer you a discounted rate if you book direct. Another good place to search is www.dubrovnikapartmentsource.com, run by an American couple and offering a range of carefully selected, well-described accommodations.

In the Old Town, Above the Stradun Promenade

These options are located at the top of town, high above the Stradun, just far enough away from nighttime noise. The first four are within a few steps of each other, along a little block dubbed by some "Rickova ulica." If you don't mind the very steep hike up, you'll find this area to be a handy home base. When one of these places is full, they work together to find space for you. The last two listings are a few blocks over, just as nice, and equally steep. Because all of these hosts live off-site, be sure to let them know when you'll arrive so they can let you in.

$$ Villa Ragusa offers a good value in the Old Town. Pero Carević renovated a 600-year-old house at the top of town. The five comfortable, modern rooms come with wooden beams and antique furniture. There are three doubles with bathrooms (including a top-floor room with rooftop views over the Old Town for no extra

DUBROVNIK

Old Town Hotels & Restaurants

BJELOKOSICA

To ⑫

IZMEÐU VRTA

To Ferry Terminal,
Main Bus Station,
Cruise Ship Port,
Boninovo Bay &
Lapad Hotels

M. BLAŽICA

BRANITELJA DUBROVNIKA

HILTON
HOTEL

㉘

P

Ⓑ DEPARTING
BUS

PILE ⓘ

Ⓑ ARRIVING
BUS

BUS
TICKET OFFICE

SV. ÐURÐA

Ⓣ

MINČETA
TOWER

FOUNDRY
MUSEUM

PUT IZA GRADA

MINČETE

PALMOTIĆEVA

FRANCISCAN
MONASTERY
MUSEUM

MEDOVIĆA

ANTUN

ⓘ

WALL
TICKET
OFFICE

ST.
SAVIOR

Ⓐ

GARGOYLE

ODSIG.

STRADUN

GARIŠTE

ZLAT.

⑰

㉒

⑮

⑬ ㉖

ŠURLIĆ
(a.k.a.
Kolorina)

FORT OF
ST. LAWRENCE

BOKAR
FORTRESS

BIG
FOUNTAIN

ČUBRAN.

PORB.

ŠIROKA

ⓘ

ZA ROKOM

DOMINA
CHURCH

OD DOMINA

SERBIAN
ORTHODOX
CHURCH

PUĆA

RUPE
MUSEUM

OD RUPA

JOSIPA

㉕

BOŽIDAREVIĆA

OD KAŠTELA

STROSS.

STROSS. MIH.

Adriatic Sea

CITY

⑪

N

WALLS

OD

100 Meters

100 Yards

Accommodations

❶ Villa Ragusa &
   Apartments Paviša

❷ Raič Apartments

❸ Apartment Nina Old Town

❹ Apartments Martecchini

❺ Plaza Apartments

❻ Minerva Apartments

❼ Fresh Sheets Kathedral B&B

❽ Van Bloemen Apartments & Gianni

❾ Dubrovnik Gardens

❿ Renata Zijadić Rooms &
   Cogito Coffee

⓫ City Walls Hostel

⓬ To Benussi Rooms

⓭ Hotel Stari Grad

⓮ To Viktorija Apartments, Hotel
   Excelsior & Grand Villa Argentina

DUBROVNIK

Eateries

15 Nishta
16 Dalmatino
17 Fat Cats
18 Restaurant Dubrovnik
19 Kopun
20 Azur
21 Lady Pi-Pi
22 D'Vino Wine Bar
23 Oliva Pizzeria

24 Tabasco Pizzeria
25 Spaghetteria Toni
26 Buffet Škola
27 Produce Market
28 Grocery (2)
29 Congo
30 Gradska Kavana
31 The Gaffe Irish Pub

charge—request when you reserve) and two singles that share a bathroom (extra for breakfast at an atmospheric café just down the stairs, Žudioska ulica 15, mobile 098-765-634, www.villaragusadubrovnik.com, villa.ragusa@du.t-com.hr).

$$ Apartments Paviša, next door to Villa Ragusa and run by Pero Paviša, has three good, older-feeling rooms at a higher price (Žudioska ulica 19, mobile 098-427-399, www.apartmentspavisa.com, pero.pavisa@gmail.com). Pero also rents two more rooms in the Viktorija neighborhood, about a 15-minute mostly uphill walk east of the Old Town. While it's a long-but-scenic walk into town, the views from these apartments are spectacular (same prices and contact as in-town rooms, Kralja Petra Krešimira IV 60, bus stop nearby).

$$ Ivana and Anita Raič are sisters renting four simple, well-priced apartments with kitchenettes and modern, stylish, pastel flourishes (Žudioska ulica 16, Ivana's mobile 098-996-0858, www.apartments-raic.com, ivanaraic@gmail.com).

$$ Apartment Nina Old Town is bright and modern, with simple furnishings, a small kitchen, and lots of stairs...which reward you with a top-floor terrace and fantastic views (Žudioska ulica 14, mobile 092-118-5053, ninamatic8@gmail.com).

$$ Apartments Martecchini has three units closer to the main drag (Kovačka 2, mobile 095-587-6036, www.apartmentsmartecchini.com, cizek1981@gmail.com, Petra).

$ Plaza Apartments, run by Lidija and Maro Matić, rents three well-appointed, heavily perfumed apartments on a plant-filled lane—the steepest and most appealing stretch of stairs leading up from the Stradun. Lidija's sweet personality is reflected in the cheerful rooms, which are a great value if you don't mind the hike (RS%, all apartments have kitchenettes and laundry machines, climb the stairs past Dolce Vita gelato shop to Nalješkovićeva 22, tel. 020/321-493, mobile 091-517-7048, lidydu@yahoo.com).

$ Minerva Apartments has three cozy, budget-priced units a block over, near the top of a similar lane, in the home of Dubravka Vidosavljević-Vučić (laundry machine, Antuninska 14, mobile 091-252-9677, duvivu@gmail.com).

In the Old Town, near the Cathedral and St. John's Fort

The following places are south of the Stradun, mostly clustering around the cathedral and St. John's Fort, at the end of the Old

Port. To find the Van Bloemen and Zijadić apartments from the cathedral, walk toward the big fort tower along the inside of the wall (follow signs for *akvarji*); for Dubrovnik Gardens, climb up the grand staircase to the Jesuit St. Ignatius Church.

$$$$ Fresh Sheets Kathedral, well-run by Canadian-Croatian couple Jon and Sanja, rents six bright, stylish, modern rooms in an ideally located building—next door to the cathedral and squeezed between two of Dubrovnik's most happening squares (better for those who enjoy being out late). All have views over interesting squares and landmarks in the heart of the Old Town. While pricey, the hospitality, well-appointed rooms, and great location can make it worthwhile (Bunićeva Poljana 6, mobile 091-896-7509, www.freshsheetskathedral.com, stay@freshsheetskathedral.com).

$$$ Van Bloemen Apartments are well-run by a Brit named Marc and his Croatian wife Silva, who offer four welcoming apartments just inside the big fort. While a bit pricey, the apartments are roomy, well-equipped, and homey-feeling, each with a bathroom and kitchen. The decor is eclectic but tasteful, drawing from Marc and Silva's extensive art collection; the stairwell has a virtual mini museum of historic Dubrovnik maps and documents (RS%, near the aquarium at Bandureva 1, tel. 020/323-433, mobile 098-619-282, www.karmendu.com, mvanbloe@gmail.com).

$$ Dubrovnik Gardens, conscientiously run by Roberto and his mother Marija (also recommended tour guides—see "Tours in Dubrovnik," earlier), is unique and a top value. From the big square in front of the Jesuit St. Ignatius Church, you'll enter through a hidden door to reach a rare private garden—a peaceful oasis smack-dab in the heart of the bustling city. Two units have their own exclusive slice of the garden: a cozy freestanding cottage (can work for a family of up to four); and an elegant, bright, spacious, artistically appointed studio apartment. Each unit has full access to its own garden, where you can even order food from the neighboring restaurant (the recommended Kopun)...very cool, particularly in a city with virtually no green space. They also have a bigger, antique-furnished, two-room apartment (garden views but no access, up several flights of stairs, sleeps up to four; all units have kitchenette, mobile 091-541-6637, www.dubrovnikgardens.com, dubrovnikgardens@gmail.com).

$ Renata Zijadić offers three older but well-located rooms with slanting floors. She rents an affordable, older, simple double with an ornate cabinet and no views, and two over-priced apartments that are worth considering if you're in a pinch or would like a great view over the Old Port (follow signs for wall access and walk up the steps marked *ulica Stajeva*, with the empty lot on your right, going over the street to find

Stajeva 1; mobile 095-532-3505, www.dubrovnik-online.net/house_renata, renatadubrovnik@yahoo.com).

¢ **City Walls Hostel** is a good budget option in the Old Town. The 18 bunks (two 6-bed dorms, one 4-bed dorm, and a double room) sit above a tight common area. Located at the very top of Dubrovnik just inside the City Walls, this bright and cheery place is a steep hike up from the main drag (closed Nov-March, includes breakfast, lockers, kitchenette, Svetog Šimuna 15, mobile 091-799-2086, www.citywallshostel.com, citywallshostel@gmail.com).

Outside Pile Gate, Just West of the Old Town

While the area in front of the Pile Gate is a congested tourist hub, one of my favorite Dubrovnik lodgings sits high on the hill above the chaos, offering a warm welcome to travelers hardy enough to make the hike.

$$$ Jadranka Benussi rents two apartments in a quiet, traffic-free neighborhood. Her delightful stony-chic home, complete with a leafy terrace, is a steep 10-minute hike above the Old Town—close enough to be convenient, but far enough to take you away from the bustle and into a calm residential zone. Jadranka speaks good English, enjoys visiting with her guests, and gives her place a modern Croatian class unusual for a *soba*. This is one of your most comfortable home bases in Dubrovnik, if you don't mind the walk (kitchenettes, Miha Klaića 10, tel. 020/429-339, mobile 098-928-1300, www.dubrovnik-benussi.com, jadranka@dubrovnik-benussi.com). To find Jadranka's house, first go to the big Hilton Hotel just outside the Pile Gate. Walk up the little stepped lane called Marijana Blažića at the upper-left corner of the Hilton cul-de-sac. When that lane dead-ends, go left up ulica Don Iva Bjelokosića (more steps) until you see a little church on the left. Jadranka's house is just before this church.

HOTELS

If you must stay in a hotel, you have only a few good options. There are just two hotels inside the City Walls—and one of them charges $500 a night (Pucić Palace, www.thepucicpalace.com). Any big, resort-style hotel within walking distance of the Old Town will run you at least €200. These inflated prices drive most visitors to Boninovo Bay or the Lapad Peninsula, a bus ride west of the Old Town. The following are good choices for those who don't mind spending a lot on big-hotel amenities.

$$$$ Hotel Stari Grad is petite and boutique; it appeals to those with deep pockets. It has eight extremely stylish rooms a half-block off the Old Town's main drag. The rooftop breakfast terrace enjoys an amazing view over orange tiles (air-con, lots of stairs, Od Sigurate 4, tel. 020/322-244, www.hotelstarigrad.com, info@hotelstarigrad.com).

$$$$ Adriatic Luxury Hotels is a chain with several plush hotels near Dubrovnik. Location-wise, the most enticing are **Hotel Excelsior** (Frana Supila 12) and **Grand Villa Argentina** (Frana Supila 14)—which are a scenic 10-minute walk outside the Ploče Gate, east of the Old Town—as well as the **Hotel Bellevue** (on Boninovo Bay, a short bus ride or long walk west of the Old Town; see "Greater Dubrovnik" map, earlier). For top-of-the-top luxury lodgings without regard for the price tag, browse their options at www.adriaticluxuryhotels.com.

Eating in Dubrovnik

Dubrovnik's restaurant scene is hit-or-miss. Many places are in business only to extract money from people who are passing through

on a cruise ship. However, I've carefully selected the following gems, ranked from **$** budget to **$$$$** splurge, which are better run and more likely to treat you like a return customer. All of my recommendations are in or near the atmospheric Old Town. Anywhere you dine, breezy outdoor seating is a no-brainer, and scrawny, adorable kittens beg for table scraps. In general, seafood restaurants are good only at seafood; if you want pasta, go to a pasta place.

$$ Nishta ("Nothing"), featuring a short menu of delicious vegan-fusion cuisine with Asian, Indian, and Mexican flair, offers a welcome change of pace from the Dalmatian seafood-pasta-pizza rut. Busy Swiss owner/chef Gildas cooks, while his wife Ruža and their staff cheerfully serve a steady stream of return diners. This tiny place—which has been a reliably delicious and improbably affordable crowd-pleaser for years—has just a few cramped indoor and outdoor tables. Even if you're a carnivore, it's worth a visit; reserve a day ahead in peak season (Mon-Sat 11:30-22:00, closed Sun and possibly Jan-Feb, on the restaurant-clogged Prijeko street—near the Pile Gate end of the street, tel. 020/322-088, www.nishtarestaurant.com).

$$$ Dalmatino offers some of the best traditional Dalmatian cooking in the city, presented with modern class. This is quality food at prices that, while not cheap, won't blow your budget. While there are only a few outdoor tables tucked along the alley, the dining room is spacious and sophisticated, but not stuffy. This is a rare Dubrovnik eatery that's open year-round—a good sign (daily 11:00-23:00, on the Prijeko "restaurant row" at #15, tel. 020/323-070, Robert).

$$ Fat Cats, the sister restaurant to D'Vino Wine Bar (see below), offers good-value tapas-style dishes often inspired by international street foods. Their "big bites" are good for sharing, and soups, salads, and lighter "small bites" round out the inventive menu (daily 8:00-23:00, on the Prijeko restaurant row at #30, tel. 020/684-676).

$$$$ Restaurant Dubrovnik, well-regarded for its Dalmatian and international cuisine, is the place for a fine-dining experience without blowing your entire budget. And in good weather, the setting is gorgeous: Their expansive terrace is tucked deep in the Old Town, under floodlit old houses and drying laundry (though when they close the roof in bad weather, it loses much of its appeal). If you're going to splurge, this is worth serious consideration. Reserve ahead (daily 12:00-23:00, open for dinner only July-Aug, Marojice Kaboge 5, mobile 099-258-5871, www.restorandubrovnik.com).

$$$$ Kopun just feels special, with an off-the-beaten-path setting on a gravelly square facing the Jesuit St. Ignatius Church. They serve up regional specialties (mostly seafood) with a touch of class. Several dishes make use of the restaurant's namesake, *kopun*—a rooster that's castrated young and plumps up (daily 11:00-23:00, Poljana Ruđera Boškovića 7, tel. 020/323-969, www.restaurantkopun.com).

$$$ Azur, tucked near the Buža bars just inside the City Walls, offers a break from the standard regional fare. The menu presents Mediterranean cuisine with an Asian twist (for example, swordfish in a black curry sauce). Owner Vedran has created a hit with discerning locals and travelers alike with careful preparation and service. Book ahead for an outside table (Tue-Sun 11:00-23:00, closed Mon, Pobijana 10, tel. 020/324-806, www.azurvision.com).

$$$ Lady Pi-Pi, named for a comical, anatomically correct, and slightly off-putting statue out front, sits high above town, barely inside the wall. The clientele skews a bit younger, and many of the tasty dishes are prepared over an open grill. Several tables overlook the rooftops of Dubrovnik, but these fill up fast, and no reservations are possible—come early or be prepared to line up. The nonview tables, on a stony, vine-strewn terrace, are nice but nothing special (daily 9:00-22:30, closed Oct-April and in bad weather, Peline b.b., tel. 020/321-154).

Wine Bar with Food: Just a few steps off the main drag, **$$$ D'Vino Wine Bar** has a relaxed atmosphere and a smart, easygoing approach to Croatian wines. Run by gregarious Aussie-Croat Sasha and his capable staff (including cheerful Anita), this cozy bar encourages you to slow down and really be on vacation.

Their user-friendly menu describes more than 60 wines by the glass and highlights small producers. The various three-taste flights make a good introduction to Croatian wines, and they can do full-blown tastings (customized to your schedule and interests—ask). Their tasty appetizers—cheese-and-meat and *antipasti* plates—pair perfectly with the wines and can easily add up to a tasty lunch or dinner; the smoked duck or swordfish plates go well with the reds. Sit in the get-to-know-your-neighbor interior or linger at the sidewalk tables. And if you just want a takeaway coffee, they've got you covered there, too. Reservations are smart after about 18:00 (daily 10:30-late, Palmotićeva 4a, tel. 020/321-130, www.dvino. net). D'Vino also offers all-day wine tours to the Pelješac Peninsula (see the next chapter for more on this region) and fun activities—check their website for the latest.

Pizza: Dubrovnik seems to have a pizzeria on every corner. Little separates the various options—just look for a menu and outdoor seating option that appeals to you. **$$ Oliva Pizzeria,** just behind St. Blaise's Church, puts out consistently good food (Lučarica 5, daily 10:00-23:00, tel. 020/324-594); around the side is a handy takeout window for slices. Close to the Old Town, but just far enough away to be frequented mostly by locals, **$$ Tabasco Pizzeria** is tucked at the corner of the parking lot beneath the cable-car station. Unpretentious and affordable, this is the place to come if the pizza is more important than the setting—though the outdoor terrace does have views of the City Walls...over a sea of parked cars (daily 9:30-23:00, Hvarska 48A, tel. 020/429-595). A few other lowbrow places (good for diners on a budget) line Hvarska downhill from here.

Pasta: $$ Spaghetteria Toni is nothing fancy; it's just a reliable old standby that offers good pastas (including a few creative choices) at reasonable prices. Choose between the cozy 10-table interior or the long alley filled with outdoor tables (daily in summer 11:00-23:00, closed Sun in winter, closed Jan, Nikole Božidarevića 14, tel. 020/323-134).

Sandwiches: Just a few steps off the Stradun, **$ Buffet Škola** is a rare bit of preglitz Dubrovnik, serving takeaway or sit-down sandwiches on homemade bread. Squeeze into the hole-in-the-wall interior, or sit at one of the outdoor tables (skip the overpriced ham-and-cheese boards, daily 8:00-24:00, shorter hours off-season, Antuninska 1, tel. 020/321-096).

Ice Cream: Dubrovnik has lots of great *sladoled,* but my favorite is the top-quality, artisan stuff at **Gianni.** They also make delicious cakes and pastries, and have vegan options too (daily 10:00-23:00, shorter hours off-season, Kneza Damjana Jude b.b., mobile 095-392-6323, www.gianni-dubrovnik.com).

The Old Town's "Restaurant Row," Prijeko Street: The

street called Prijeko, a block toward the mainland from the Stradun promenade, is lined with eateries, many with a huckster out front trying to lure in diners. Don't be sucked into this vortex of mediocre food at inflated prices. The only places worth seeking out here are Nishta, Dalmatino, and Fat Cats (described earlier), which distinguish themselves with quality cooking. Still, it can be fun to take a stroll along here—the atmosphere is lively, and the sales pitches are entertainingly desperate.

Dinner Experiences: My most memorable dinner in Dubrovnik came not at a restaurant but at Marija and Zlatko's house. This charming, talented couple runs **$$$$ Dubrovnik Eat with Locals,** where they serve you a delicious, traditional, home-cooked dinner on their rustic patio. Come hungry: You'll join your hosts and a few other guests for an all-inclusive, whole-evening feast that you won't soon forget. Their place is in the Montovjerna neighborhood, an easy 15-minute walk from Pile Gate, or a short taxi ride (by reservation only, can accommodate dietary restrictions, mobile 095-385-5344, www.dubrovnikeatwithlocals.com, marija.papak@gmail.com).

Picnic Tips: Dubrovnik's lack of great restaurant options makes it a perfect place to picnic. You can shop for fresh fruits and veggies at the open-air produce market (each morning near the cathedral, on the square called Gundulićeva Poljana). Supplement your picnic with basic supplies from **Konzum grocery store** (one location on the market square near the produce vendors, another near the bus stop just outside Pile Gate, both open Mon-Sat 8:00-22:00, Sun until 21:00). Good picnic spots include the shaded benches overlooking the Old Port; the Porporela breakwater (beyond the Old Port and fort—comes with a swimming area, sunny no-shade benches, and views of Lokrum Island); and the green, welcoming park in what was the moat just under the Pile Gate entry to the Old Town.

Premade Gourmet Picnics: Canadian expat Alex runs **$$$$ Piknik Dubrovnik,** which can hand you a high-end, ready-made picnic in an insulated backpack, with plenty of tips on where to enjoy it. While it's not cheap, it's a hit with adventurous foodies (around 700 kn/2 people, arrange at least 24 hours in advance, mobile 098-175-1103, www.piknikdubrovnik.com, piknikdubrovnik@gmail.com). Alex also offers guided trips and picnics in the countryside around Dubrovnik.

Gourmet Coffee: If you're craving something a notch above the standard *bijela kava*, head for **Cogito Coffee**—an artisanal coffee shop (part of a Zagreb-based chain), tucked under a little tunnel near the bottom of the Maritime Museum stairs, near the Old Port (daily 9:00-19:00, Pustijerne 1).

BREAKFAST

If you're sleeping in a *soba*, you'll likely be on your own for breakfast. Fortunately, you have plenty of cafés and pastry shops to choose from, and your host probably has a favorite he or she can recommend. For something substantial, several restaurants in inviting locations serve up eggy breakfasts for around 65 kn. Choose a fine perch along the Stradun and pay a bit too much for the privilege of watching the town wake up and the cruise passengers file in (**Congo,** at Placa 6, opens before anyone else at 7:00—handy if you're departing early). Locals who meet along here each morning—catching up with their friends as they stroll by—call this their low-tech version of "Facebook." Another scenic perch is just around the corner: **Gradska Kavana,** tucked between the Bell Tower and Rector's Palace (served daily 8:00-11:30, Pred Dvorom 1). **D'Vino Wine Bar** (described earlier) has a short but appealing menu of more interesting breakfast options, and a shady alley to hang out in (served daily 8:00-11:00). And if you'd like an even wider menu of affordably priced breakfast options—in a less atmospheric setting—try **The Gaffe Irish Pub** (served daily 9:00-11:00, Miha Pracata 4, tel. 020/640-152).

Dubrovnik Connections

While ferries and catamarans have traditionally used Dubrovnik's Port Gruž (a bus ride away from the Old Town), a planned redevelopment could relocate some or all boats to the far end of the port, under the big bridge. Ask locally for the latest.

By Catamaran: Speedy catamarans connect Dubrovnik to points north. As these are operated by three companies and the schedules tend to change from year to year, it's important to check all three websites to fully understand your options: Krilo (www.krilo.hr), Jadrolinija (www.jadrolinija.hr), and Nona Ana (www.gv-line.hr). Boats sell out: Purchase tickets online at least a day or two ahead (or longer) at very busy times. (Note that Jadrolinija requires you to buy tickets in person, at Port Gruž, for same-day departures.)

Catamarans take about 1.5 hours to **Mljet National Park** (use the Polače or Pomena docks—not Sobra), 2 hours to **Korčula,** 3 hours to **Hvar,** and 4-5 hours to **Split.**

The **Krilo** catamaran runs twice each afternoon through the summer to Korčula and Split; both depart at the same time, but only one of them stops en route at both Pomena on Mljet and Hvar town—be sure you get on the right one (2/day late May-early Oct; 1/day early April-late May and rest of Oct; none off-season). The **Jadrolinija** catamaran departs in the early morning and stops at Korčula, Hvar, and Split (1/day June-Sept only). The **Nona Ana** also has a short season (June-Sept) and doesn't reach as far north, departing each morning for Polače on Mljet Island; in July and August only, it continues to Korčula (4/week, 2.5 hours). Off-season (Oct-May), the boat goes only to Šipan (one of the Elaphite Islands near Dubrovnik) and Sobra (on Mljet, but far from the national park).

By Bus to: Split (1-2/hour, less off-season, 4.5 hours), **Korčula** (summer: 2/day generally around 9:00 and 15:00, may also be a later bus 2/week in summer, 3.5 hours; off-season: 1/day at 15:00), **Rijeka** (5/day, 13 hours), **Zagreb** (15/day, overnight options, 10 hours), **Kotor** in Montenegro (8/day in summer, less off-season, 2-2.5 hours—or can take much longer due to border delays), **Mostar** (5/day in summer, less off-season, 3-4 hours), **Sarajevo** (1-2/day, 7 hours; includes a night bus in summer only at 22:30), **Pula** and **Rovinj** (1/day overnight departing at 15:30, 15 hours to Pula, 16 hours to Rovinj). Schedules are subject to change—confirm locally before making the trip to the bus station. You can check schedules and buy tickets at www.getbybus.com. For additional bus information, check www.libertasdubrovnik.com or call 060-305-070 (a pricey toll line, but worth it).

By Plane: To quickly connect remote Dubrovnik with the rest of your trip, consider a cheap flight. For information on Dubrovnik's airport, see "Arrival in Dubrovnik: By Plane," earlier.

By Car: For tips on driving along the Dalmatian Coast between Dubrovnik and Split, see page 216.

Can I Get to Greece from Dubrovnik? Your best bet is to fly. There are direct flights to Athens on Aegean and Croatia Airlines. Even though Croatia and Greece are nearly neighbors, no direct boats connect them, and the overland connection is extremely long and rugged.

What About Italy? Flying is the easiest option, though there are only a few direct flights (to Rome, Venice, or Naples; airlines include Croatia Airlines, Volotea, EasyJet, and Vueling). You can take a direct night boat from Dubrovnik to Bari, or head to Split for more boat connections (for more on all of these boats, see page 214). The overland connection is too long (figure 5 hours to Split, then 5 hours to Zagreb, then 7 hours to Venice).

NEAR DUBROVNIK

Excursions from Dubrovnik's Old Port • Cavtat • Trsteno Arboretum • Pelješac Peninsula • Mljet National Park

The longer you linger, the clearer it becomes: Dubrovnik isn't just a town, it's an entire region. Stretching up and down the glimmering Dalmatian Coast from Dubrovnik are a variety of worthwhile getaways.

Just offshore from the city's Old Town—and accessible via scenic boat trip from its historic port—are enticing islands and villages, where time stands still for lazy vacationers: the playground islet of Lokrum and the archipelago of the Elaphite Islands. The serene resort town of Cavtat, just south of Dubrovnik, has some of the best art treasures of this part of Dalmatia (including a stunning mausoleum designed by Ivan Meštrović). Nearby, the medieval canals and waterwheels of the Konavoski Dvori area offer a welcome and refreshing escape from sunbaked coastal towns.

To the north is a lush arboretum called Trsteno, with a playful fountain, a 600-year-old aqueduct, a villa, a chapel...and, of course, plants galore. Poking into the Adriatic is the vineyard-covered Pelješac Peninsula, where friendly vintners are eager to impress you with their wines, and where the mighty little town of Ston lures you to climb its sprawling fortifications. And out at sea is the sparsely populated island called Mljet, a third of which is carefully protected as one of Croatia's most appealing national parks, where you can hike, bike, kayak, and swim to your heart's content. Best of all, there's no better place to "come home to" than Dubrovnik—after a busy day exploring the coastline, strolling the Stradun to unwind is particularly sweet.

Dubrovnik Day Trips at a Glance

The international excursions to Bosnia-Herzegovina and Montenegro—which are worth considering for overnight stops—are covered in their own chapters.

In Bosnia-Herzegovina

▲▲▲Mostar The side trip with the highest degree of cultural hairiness—but, for many, also the greatest reward—lies to the east, in Bosnia-Herzegovina. With its iconic Old Bridge, intriguing glimpse of European Muslim lifestyles, and still-vivid examples of war damage, Mostar is unforgettable. Allow a full day or more (best reached by bus or car).

Međugorje Devout Catholics may want to consider a trip to this pilgrimage site in Bosnia-Herzegovina, with a holy hill that some believe is visited regularly by an apparition of the Virgin Mary. Allow a full day or more (car or bus).

In Montenegro

▲▲The Bay of Kotor For rugged coastal scenery that rivals anything in Croatia, head south of the border to Montenegro. The Bay of Kotor is a dramatic, fjord-like inlet crowned by the historic town of Kotor, with twisty Old World lanes, one of Europe's best town walls, and oodles of atmosphere. Allow a full day or more (car or bus).

The Montenegrin Interior A visit to Montenegro's scruffy but historic former capital, Cetinje, comes with a twisty drive up a mountain road and across a desolate, forgotten-feeling plateau. Allow a few hours' side-trip from Kotor (car).

Budva Riviera Montenegro's best stretch of sandy beaches isn't worth a special trip, but it's a fun excuse for a drive if you've got extra time to kill. A highlight is the famous resort peninsula of Sveti Stefan. Allow a few hours' side-trip from Kotor (car).

On the Mainland near Dubrovnik

▲Cavtat A charming resort/beach town, unassuming Cavtat

holds a pair of wonderful and very local art experiences: an elabo-rate mausoleum de-signed by the sculptor Ivan Meštrović, and the house and museum of Cavtat-born modern painter Vlaho Bukovac. Allow a few hours (boat or bus).

▲**Pelješac Peninsula** This long, narrow, scenic spit of land—between the main coastal road and Korčula Island—is a favorite of wine lovers, who can joyride through its vineyards and sample its prod-uct (or just enjoy the beautiful scenery). Allow a half-day to a full day (car).

▲**Trsteno Arboretum** Plant lovers will enjoy this surprisingly en-gaging botanical garden just outside Dubrovnik, punctuated by a classical-style fountain and aqueduct. Allow a half-day (bus or car).

Konavoski Dvori This rugged, forested landscape of ancient ca-nals and still-spinning waterwheels is a refreshing spot for a coun-tryside meal. Allow a few hours (car).

Ston A small town with giant fortifications, Ston (on the Pelješac Peninsula) is worth a short stop to scramble up its extensive walls. Allow an hour (car or bus).

Off the Coast of Dubrovnik
▲**Mljet National Park** While this largely undeveloped island is time-consuming to reach from Dubrovnik, Mljet offers an oppor-tunity to romp on a pristine island without tacky tourist towns. This is for serious nature lovers eager to get away from civilization to hike, swim, and kayak. Allow a full day (boat).

Lokrum Island The most convenient excursion from Dubrovnik, this little island—just a short hop offshore from the Old Port—is a good chance to get away from (some of) the tourists. Allow a few hours (boat).

Elaphite Islands This inviting archipelago offers a variety of is-land experiences without straying too far from Dubrovnik. With more time, Korčula (for a small town) or Mljet (for a back-to-na-ture experience) are better, but the "Elafiti" are more convenient. Allow a half-day to a full day (boat).

PLANNING YOUR TIME

Give yourself at least two nights (one full day) to experience Dubrovnik itself. But if you can spare the time, set up in Dubrovnik for several nights and use your extra days for some of the excursions described in this chapter. (This also gives you the luxury of keeping an eye on the weather reports and saving the most weather-dependent activities for the sunniest days.) For suggestions on how much time to allow per destination, see the "Dubrovnik Day Trips at a Glance" sidebar. Use a map to strategically line up these attractions—for example, you can easily do Trsteno, Ston, and the Pelješac Peninsula on a drive between Dubrovnik and Korčula, while Cavtat pairs nicely with a trip to the airport or Montenegro.

I've listed day trips in this chapter in order of ease from Dubrovnik—the further down the list, the more difficult to reach

Near Dubrovnik

(Montenegro and Mostar, the most time-consuming, are covered in their own chapters).

GETTING THERE

Cavtat and the Elaphite Islands are easy to reach by private **excursion boat** from Dubrovnik's Old Port; Cavtat also works by bus. A **city-run boat** links the Old Port to nearby Lokrum. **Public ferries** connect Dubrovnik's Port Gruž to the Elaphite Islands (the most appealing is Lopud). The other destinations are farther afield, best reached by **boat** (Mljet) or by **car** or **bus** (Montenegro, Mostar, Trsteno, Pelješac Peninsula).

NEAR DUBROVNIK

I've listed public transportation options for each, but consider **renting a car** for the day. Or you can splurge for your own **private driver** (see page 288); to make it more affordable, rally other travelers to accompany you and split the cost.

Alternatively, a variety of travel agencies in Dubrovnik offer **guided excursions** (by bus and/or boat) to nearby destinations. Popular itineraries include everything mentioned in this chapter, plus Korčula (in its own chapter) and others. While these excursions can be a convenient way to see otherwise difficult-to-reach destinations, the quality can be hit-or-miss. The biggest companies are efficient mass-tourism machines—you'll be jammed into buses and boats until every seat is filled, and the guides typically do their spiel (mostly a memorized script) in several languages. Smaller outfits offer a more casual experience with more personal attention, but lack the polish of the big players. Since this scene is constantly evolving, check online reviews, look around for fliers, and ask locals for tips. (Be aware that many small travel agencies simply sell seats on the big companies' trips.)

Excursions from Dubrovnik's Old Port

At Dubrovnik's salty Old Port, captains set up tiny booths to hawk touristy boat trips. It's fun to chat with them, page through their sun-faded photo albums, and see if they can sell you on a short cruise. In addition to the islands noted below, you can also take a boat from the Old Port to **Cavtat** (described later).

PANORAMA CRUISE

The basic option is a 50-minute "panorama cruise" out on the water and back again (75 kn, departures about every hour). You'll loop around the City Walls—which offer a unique view on Dubrovnik's stout defenses—and do a circuit around Lokrum Island as well. Understandably, these cruises are most popular at or shortly before sunset.

You could just hop on whichever boat is departing next, but I enjoy the **Sv. Ivan,** a cargo boat dating from 1878. Prowling its decks and leaning back against rope railings just feels right in this seafaring town (60 kn for 50-minute panorama cruise; RS%—20 percent with this book; look for their desk among the many sales kiosks at the Old Port, mobile 098-427-177, www.dubrovnik-panoramacruise.com).

LOKRUM ISLAND

This island, a protected natural area just offshore from the Old Town, provides a handy escape from the city. When the Old Town just gets too jam-packed with tourists, locals hop a boat out here for some peace and quiet. They call it the "Island of Love," because it offers many se-cluded spots popular with courting couples. The main attractions here are hiking (on shaded paths that curl up, over, and around the thickly wooded island) and sunbathing (on jagged, rocky beaches—many of which are designated nude beaches).

Getting There: Lokrum is reachable only by an official city-run boat, which departs twice hourly from the end of the pier in Dubrovnik's Old Port. The hefty boat-ticket price also includes your admission to the island (150 kn round-trip, 15-minute cross-ing, runs daily mid-June-Aug 9:00-20:00, shorter hours in shoul-der season, stops running Nov-March).

Visiting the Island: From the Lokrum boat dock, walk up to the pink building—the visitors center—to buy a map of the is-land. Continuing up, you'll reach a fork: To head across the nar-row middle of the island, continue straight ahead, where you'll find a monastery-turned-Habsburg-palace. This building is gradually being converted into a free **museum.** Already in place are exhibits on Richard the Lionheart and his reputed historical connections to this island (according to legend, he was shipwrecked on his way back from the Third Crusade and landed safely on Lokrum), and on *Game of Thrones.* You'll see "behind the scenes" footage from filming in the Dubrovnik area, and you can pose for photographs with an Iron Throne. Additional exhibits may be completed by the time you visit. (For more *GOT*-related sights, see the sidebar on page 286.)

Nearby is a small **botanical garden.** Just beyond this area, un-even rocks lead to ladders where you can ease yourself into the sea. There's also a small lake (fed by an underwater canal from the sea) called the "Dead Sea" (Mrtvo More) that's suitable for swimming.

Another option from the boat dock is to hook left and curl around the cove to the island's most popular beach, on the **Bay of Portoč,** that's famous for its nude sunbathing. If you'd like to (care-fully) subject skin that's never seen the sun to those burning rays, follow the *FKK* signs from the boat dock for about five minutes to the slabs of waterfront rock, where naturists feel right at home.

NEAR DUBROVNIK

Continuing past this beach, you can work your way up and over to the other side of the island (on very rocky trails).

For an even more serious hike, head right from the boat dock for the two-hour hike that goes all the way around the island, and consider a detour to its highest point (at 315 feet above sea level), capped by Fort Royal, an old Austro-Hungarian military fortification.

You can bring your own picnic, but you'll also find a few cafés and restaurants scattered around the island, mostly along the main path from the boat dock to the monastery/museum complex. The island also has WCs and showers for swimmers.

ELAPHITE ISLANDS (ELAFITI)

This 13-island archipelago, just north of Dubrovnik, is popular among day-trippers because it allows you to hit three different islands in a single day: Koločep, Lopud, and Šipan. These "Deer Islands" (supposedly named for their shape—though I don't see it) are a bit overhyped and can't hold a candle to some of the more distant Dalmatian islands, such as Mljet, Korčula, and Hvar. But they're a decent choice if you need a break from Dubrovnik's crowds and want a lazy day cruising Dalmatia. Along the way, you'll discover fishing ports, shady forests, inviting beaches, and forgotten escape mansions of old Dubrovnik aristocracy. The two smaller islands (Koločep and Lopud) are traffic-free, making them a restful backwater getaway. While there's little to actually see on these islands, each church, beach, and walking path is well-signed, making it easy to just wander. Bring decent footwear for hiking uneven trails, and pack along swimwear. Each island has some sort of beach relatively near the boat dock; on a hot day, you could just wear your swimsuit on the boat and make a point to take a dip at each stop.

Getting There: The easiest way to cruise the Elafiti is to buy an excursion at Dubrovnik's Old Port, which usually includes a

"fish picnic" cooked up by the captain as you cruise (about 300 kn with lunch, several boats depart daily around 10:30-11:00, return around 15:45-19:30; companies prefer you to reserve and pay a 50-kn deposit the day before). For a bigger and more memorable ship—and a more corporate experience—you can pay a bit more to go on the *Karaka* or the *Sirena*, modern replicas of the traditional cargo ships once built here in Dubrovnik (advertised along with the others at the Old Port).

Regardless of which company you go with, you generally spend about two to three hours on Lopud and about an hour each on Koločep and Šipan, with about 2.5 hours on the boat. To get to the Elaphite Islands without a tour (on a cheap ferry), you'll sail from Dubrovnik's less convenient Port Gruž.

Koločep

The nearest island to Dubrovnik, and the sleepiest, Koločep's harbor arcs away from its boat dock. Walking around it, you'll quickly reach a small main square with al fresco cafés spilling out onto the seawall; beyond that is a sandy beach in front of a hotel, with rentable chairs. Near the boat dock, well-signed steps lead up into the hills, passing several small churches and Koločep's little museum of ecclesiastical art (the only museum I saw on the Elafiti).

On a short visit, you'll barely have time to stroll the harbor; if your excursion leaves you here a bit longer, consider a low-impact **hike** over the spine of the island to the village of Gornje Čelo, on the opposite side (about 1.5 miles away). You'll climb up stairs past an old guard tower, pass a pink stucco church near a cemetery, then follow the narrow path between high stone walls and past olive groves. You'll wind down to a little port town with an inviting beach; looping around to Placet takes you to a wall of dramatic cliffs. *Donje Čelo* signs lead you back to your boat.

▲Lopud

The main attraction of the Elaphite Islands, Lopud feels like a humbler Cavtat without all the great art. But Lopud's trump card is its fine beaches, especially Šunj—one of the nicest beaches in southern Dalmatia (a long hike or short golf-cart ride from the main boat dock). Lopud feels bigger, more vital, and more inviting than the other two islands. Most excursions give it far more time than Koločep or Šipan; it's also accessible by public ferry, and may be worth considering for an all-day beach getaway.

Your boat docks near the stout Franciscan monastery, which pokes out into the sea, dominating the townscape. From there, a picturesque promenade winds past several beaches (sand, then pebbles, then sand) and the entrance to a lush garden, before stretching all the way to a luxury hotel. Near the boat dock, you'll find a **TI** (Obala Iva Kuljevana 12, tel. 020/322-322).

For beach bums, the main attraction on Lopud is at the other end of the island: **Šunj Beach.** This gorgeous, shallow, sandy beach—hemmed in on both sides by forested cliffs—splays serenely between beach bars and ritzy yachts that drop anchor to take a dip. The almost entirely sandy floor and gentle

NEAR DUBROVNIK

incline makes this beach ideal for waders and families. The catch is that it takes a bit of effort to reach: It's a moderately strenuous 1.5-mile walk over the scraggly spine of the island. Otherwise, golf carts zip arriving tourists over to the beach for a small fee. To find the golf carts, follow the promenade as far as the abandoned Grand Hotel, then head inland (on a drab, poorly maintained concrete trail), following signs for *Šunj Beach*. From here, you can either flag down a golf cart or continue to hike the rest of the way. Given its distance from the main boat dock, it's not worth attempting to visit Šunj if you're on Lopud for less than two hours.

Šipan

By far the biggest island (at just over six square miles), and the northernmost, Šipan has two different port towns. Your ship will

most likely use the one facing Lopud, called Suđurađ (named for the local patron saint, George). Suđurađ's harbor is watched over by the fortified, castle-like 16th-century villa of a local aristocrat. A beach beckons just across the bay from the boat dock. Next to the harbor,

the small Church of St. George—with a large covered porch—has a vivid fresco over the altar of George slaying the dragon while being watched over by two other locally revered saints, Blaise (Dubrovnik's protector) and Nicholas (the patron saint of sailors).

If you need an excuse for a short hike, head from the harbor straight up the street away from the water, following signs for the Church of Sv. Duh (Holy Spirit). After passing through a humble residential zone, you'll arrive at a stout, fortress-like church, with raw-stone walls. If it's open, poke inside to see the rough-and-tumble interior. The stairs to the right of the altar lead up to the rooftop, where you can see the large, fertile valley that sits in the middle of this island. If you're tempted to ring the bell, resist—locals ring it only when a member of their community dies.

South of Dubrovnik

A variety of worthwhile stopovers line up along the main road south of Dubrovnik, toward the border with Montenegro, in the region called Konavle.

Cavtat

This sleepy resort town—filling a wooded peninsula just 12 miles to the south, and rated ▲—offers a milder alternative to bustling Dubrovnik. With its strategic location sheltered inside a nearly 360-degree bay, this settlement was thriving long before there was a Dubrovnik. The Greeks called it Epidaurus, while the Romans called it Epidaurum—but these days, it's Cavtat (TSAV-taht). The town is best known as a handy spot to find a room when Dubrovnik's booked up. But even those suffering from beach-resort fatigue will enjoy a side trip to Cavtat, which is home to two gems of Croatian art: a breathtaking hilltop mausoleum by the great Croatian sculptor Ivan Meštrović, and the former home-turned-museum of the Cavtat-born, early-20th-century painter Vlaho Bukovac.

GETTING TO CAVTAT

Boats to Cavtat leave about hourly from Dubrovnik's Old Port (60 kn one-way, 100 kn round-trip, about 45 minutes each way, hourly return boats from Cavtat). The boat deposits you right along Cavtat's main seafront promenade.

You can also reach Cavtat by public **bus #10**, which leaves from Dubrovnik's main bus station and also stops at the "cable car" bus stop above the Old Town (1-2/hour, 30-40 minutes, 28 kn). The bus brings you to Cavtat's parking lot (described next). Returning by bus from Cavtat, hop off at the Dubrovnik bus stop that's along the main road high above the Old Town—about a 5- to 10-minute walk down into town. (Note that the bus to or from Cavtat does *not* stop at Dubrovnik's Pile Gate.)

For variety, consider going to Cavtat by boat (buy a one-way ticket), then returning by bus.

Drivers find Cavtat an easy detour when heading to points south, including Montenegro or the airport; the town is well-signed off the main road. The big parking lot is at the back of Cavtat's peninsula, just around the corner from the main part of town and seafront promenade.

Orientation to Cavtat

Cavtat is set within an idyllic, horseshoe-shaped harbor hemmed in by a pair of peninsulas. Tucked around the back side of the peninsula is the parking lot and **TI** (Zidine 6, tel. 020/479-025, www. visit.cavtat-konavle.com). Cavtat is basically a one-street town, but that street is a fine pedestrian promenade running along the harbor, with a few narrow lanes winding steeply up into the hill. Capping the hill above town is a cemetery with the Meštrović mausoleum.

Sights in Cavtat

Waterfront Wander

Strolling along Cavtat's waterfront, you'll be immersed in a wrap-around bay and surrounded by Europeans vacationing well. At

the near end of the promenade, notice the big water-polo court roped off in the bay; the core of the Croatian national water polo team comes from Cavtat and Dubrovnik. Across the street is **St. Nicholas Church,** with a humble, dull interior (though hanging high in the altar area are Vlaho Bukovac's paintings of the four evangelists). About halfway along the drag, at the little square called Trg Tuđmana, one of the narrow lanes leading up the hill (appropriately named Bukovčeva) takes you to the fine **Vlaho Bukovac House** (described below). At the end of the main waterfront area is the **Church of Our Lady of the Snows,** commemorating a freak—and seemingly miraculous—midsummer snowstorm in ancient Roman times, believed to have been a sign sent by the Virgin Mary. Inside, above the altar, is a Vlaho Bukovac painting (from 1909) of Mary and the Baby Jesus watching over Cavtat.

Climbing the steep steps up to the right of the church leads you up to Ivan Meštrović's **Račić Mausoleum** (described later). With more time, consider continuing around the peninsula to its pointy tip for distant views of Dubrovnik's Old Town. This is one of the favorite spots in this area for watching the sunset. (If you continue all the way around the point, in about 20 minutes you'll wind up back at the parking lot at the start of town.)

▲Vlaho Bukovac House (Kuća Bukovac)

One of the joys of travel is learning about locally beloved artists who are little known outside their homelands. Cavtat proudly introduces you to native son Vlaho Bukovac (1855-1922), who grew up in this very house and went on to become the most important Croatian painter of the modern period. Bukovac moved to New York City with his uncle at age 11, beginning a life of great adventure. After a brief career as a sailor (traveling to Peru and San Francisco), he trained as an artist in Paris, then in Zagreb. For his last 20 years, Bukovac spent his summers in Prague and his winters here in Cavtat.

Cost and Hours: 30 kn, April-Oct Mon-Sat 9:00-18:00, Sun until 14:00, off-season shorter hours and closed Mon, Bukovčeva 5, tel. 020/478-646, www.migk.hr.

Visiting the Museum: Touring the collection (with good English explanations), you'll get to know Bukovac's life and his works. Bukovac's paintings are mostly realistic (in accordance with his formal Salon training in Paris), but shimmer with a hint of Post-Impressionism; his later works echo the slinky Art Nouveau Slavic pride of the Czech painter Alfons Mucha, who was Bukovac's contemporary.

From the ground floor (with temporary exhibits), head up to find old furniture, early sketches, and portraits of Bukovac and

his family. The top floor houses one big atelier room filled with canvases from various periods, allowing you to survey his impressive artistic development with a sweep of the head. Look for the painting of his children's disembodied heads hanging on the wall—macabre but strangely tender. Throughout the house are murals painted by Bukovac in his early days, offering a glimpse of a burgeoning artist who would go on to make Cavtat very proud.

▲▲Račić Family Mausoleum (Mauzolej Obitelji Račić)

This harmonious masterwork of Croatia's greatest artist is the gem of Cavtat, and worth ▲▲▲ to fans of Ivan Meštrović's powerful sculptures. To learn more about Meštrović before you visit, read the sidebar on page 196.

Cost and Hours: 20 kn, Mon-Sat 10:00-17:00, closed Sun and Nov-March, www.migk.hr.

NEAR DUBROVNIK

Getting There: Capping the hill above town, it's a steep 10-minute walk from the Cavtat waterfront. From the Church of Our Lady of Snows at the far end of the waterfront, climb up the stairs (following *mauzolej* signs). You can also wrap all the way around the fine waterfront promenade, to the back of the peninsula, and climb the stairs up near the restaurant and rocky beach.

Visiting the Mausoleum: Over the course of one tragic year, all four members of the wealthy Račić family—father, mother, son, daughter—died in the 1918-19 flu pandemic. From 1920 to 1922, in accordance with their will, Ivan Meštrović was commissioned to craft their final resting place. He used the opportunity to create a cohesive meditation on Christian faith and death, made entirely of brilliant white stone from the island of Brač.

As you enter, take a moment to appreciate how the interior ponders birth, life, and death. The four inner walls of the octagonal hall hold the tombs of the departed; above each tomb, an angel lovingly carries their souls up to heaven—spiriting them into a cupola studded with angel heads. The floor has symbols for the four evangelists: Matthew (angel), Mark (lion), Luke (bull), and John (eagle). The chapel to the left holds a crucifix; to the right, an altar to St. Rok (the patron saint of illness, to whom the chapel is dedicated—the dog licking the wound in his leg is his symbol). Straight ahead is an altar with Mary holding the Baby Jesus above a relief of the Lamb of God, and below that, Jesus' body being taken down from the cross. Flanking this altar, notice the bases of the twisting candelabras: alternating angels, with agonized and mournful expressions, look down to honor the dead.

The chapel rewards those who linger over the details, such as the bronze doors, with four saints, Glagolitic inscriptions, and the 12 Apostles. The saints chosen for this door preach both ecumenism and Yugoslav unity: Cyril and Method (the Byzantine missionaries who first brought Christianity to this region), along with a Catholic bishop (Bishop Gregory of Nin) and an Orthodox saint (St. Sava). Taken together, the mausoleum is an astonishing display of talent, especially considering it was Meštrović's first architectural work.

Nearby: The mausoleum sits in the middle of a tranquil cemetery that's still used for the funerals of Cavtat residents. As you exit the mausoleum, bear left into the cemetery and look for five communal graves for the poor—with smaller markers and flower-pots lined up along large plinths. Also in this cemetery is the grave of the artist Vlaho Bukovac.

IN THE COUNTRYSIDE NEAR CAVTAT
Čilipi

This nearby village—five miles from Cavtat and the namesake for Dubrovnik's airport—hosts a Sunday-morning folk festival through the summer (Easter-Oct, starting at 9:00). There's a special Mass at the church, an open-air market, and—starting at 11:15—a costumed folk-dancing show (tel. 020/771-007, www. cilipifolklor.hr).

Konavoski Dvori

The rugged terrain stretching south of Dubrovnik, toward the Montenegrin border, huddles under steep limestone peaks—a sure recipe for lots of rushing water. This area's name—Konavle—comes from the ancient Roman word for "channels." And since antiquity, these foothills have been a popular place for settlement and for primitive industry, with canals, aqueducts, and spinning millwheels designed to harness the constant flow of high-mountain runoff. Today, a short detour from the main highway takes you to Konavoski Dvori (Palaces of Konavle), where you can stroll through a well-preserved network of medieval canals and even step into a reconstructed 400-year-old mill (open sporadically).

As the road passes through Gruda (about 18 miles, or 30 minutes, south of Dubrovnik), turn off and head up into the village of Ljuta (whose name means "Angry," for the fierce flow of the river by the same name). The steep, wooded terrain is laced with nature trails that follow gurgling canals—handy for a pre- or post-meal wander. The main reason most people come here is for a meal at one of two destination restaurants: the traditional, unpretentious **$$$ Konoba Vinica Monković** (mobile 099-215-2459, www. konobavinica.com) and the fancier, more elaborate complex of **$$$$ Restaurant Konavoski Dvori** (huge terraces, trout ponds, tel. 020/791-039, www.esculaprestaurants.com). At either place (both open long hours daily in good weather, closed off-season), it's smart to reserve in advance for an outdoor table, along the gurgling canals. Most locals come here for a *peka* meal—meat slow-simmered under a copper baking lid covered in glowing coals—which should also be requested when you book your table. While not worth a trip on its own, this experience works well with a visit to Cavtat or Montenegro, and offers an opportunity to escape the crowds and heat of Dubrovnik's Old Town and spend some time in the cool, refreshing countryside.

North of Dubrovnik

These attractions are on or near the northbound highway from Dubrovnik, on the way to Split or Mostar. (For more ideas along the back roads toward Mostar, see page 458.)

Trsteno Arboretum

Take a stroll through the shaded, relaxing botanical garden in Trsteno (worth ▲), just up the coast from Dubrovnik. Nongardeners may find it a bit dull, but Trsteno is a horticulturalist's heaven.

Cost and Hours: 50 kn, daily 7:00-19:00, Nov-April 8:00-16:00, tel. 020/751-019.

Getting There: Trsteno is best reached by car, particularly if you're taking your time driving to Dubrovnik from the north (the main coastal road goes through the town of Trsteno, right past the well-marked arboretum). You also have two bus options from Dubrovnik (20-30 minutes). Any long-distance northbound bus can drop you in Trsteno—ask about the next bus at the main station. Alternatively, the slower local buses #12, #15, and #22 also reach Trsteno. Coming back from Trsteno to Dubrovnik is trickier: Wait at the bus stop with the glass canopy by the park entrance and wave down any Dubrovnik-bound bus that passes (roughly hourly).

Visiting the Arboretum: Spread over 63 acres on a bluff overlooking the sea, this arboretum features hundreds of different Mediterranean, Asian, and American plants (each one labeled in six languages, including English). The whole complex is laced with easy footpaths and sprinkled with fun attractions—a column-studded Renaissance Garden, a desolate villa, a little chapel, an old mill and olive-oil press, and a seaview pavilion. *Game of Thrones* fans will recognize it as the backdrop of many park-set scenes at King's Landing.

As you wander, the world melts away and you're alone with the sounds of nature: wind, water, birds, and frogs. The garden's centerpiece is the whimsical 18th-century Neptune Fountain, featuring the god of the sea flanked by water-spouting nymphs and fishes as he holds court over a goldfish-stocked, lily-padded pond. Circling around behind the fountain, you'll discover that it's fed by an impressive 230-foot-long aqueduct that was built in the 15th century.

Pelješac Peninsula

North of Trsteno, the skinny, 55-mile-long Pelješac (PEHL-yeh-shahts) Peninsula—practically an honorary island, and rated ▲—splits off from the Croatian coastline as if about to drift away to Italy. (The far tip of Pelješac comes within a stone's throw of Korčula Island.) This sparsely populated peninsula, famous for its rugged terrain—and the grapes that thrive here—is worth a detour for wine lovers. But its heavily fortified town of Ston, just a short side-trip from the main coastal road, merits a stretch-your-legs visit for anyone. Notice that if you're connecting from Korčula to anywhere else in Croatia by car, you'll probably be taking the ferry to the Pelješac Peninsula anyway; consider slowing down to sample a few wines, to scramble up the walls at Ston, or to have a meal at Mali Ston.

Getting There: Buses between Dubrovnik and Korčula traverse the Pelješac Peninsula, but drivers have the option of stopping where they like (such as at Ston or a winery). Some public buses also stop at Ston.

STON

The town of Ston, at the base of the peninsula, is the gateway to Pelješac. This "Great Wall of Croatia" town is famous for the impressive wall that climbs up the mountain behind it (about a half-mile encloses the town itself, while another three miles clamber up the hillsides). The unassuming town was heavily fortified (starting in 1333) for two reasons: to defend its strategic lo-

cation, where mountains and bays create a bottleneck along the road from Dubrovnik to Pelješac, near the Republic of Dubrovnik's northern boundary; and to protect its impressive salt pans. Filling a low-lying plain that sprawls in front of Ston's doorstep, these pans provided Dubrovnik with much of its wealth, back in the days when salt was worth more than its weight in gold. The pans would be flooded with saltwater, then sealed and left to evaporate—leaving the salt easy to harvest.

Today, the sleepy town—with more than its share of outdoor cafés and restaurants—is notable mainly for the chance to scram-

NEAR DUBROVNIK

Peljesac Peninsula

To Ploče

Trpanj

Peljesac

415

POSTUP

DRIVING TOUR BEGINS

Orebić

Postup

414

To Split

Korčula

118

Dominče

Lumbarda

To Vela Luka

Korčula

PLAVAC MALI

Potomje

414

TUNNEL

DINGAČ

Trstenik

Adriatic Sea

- - - Peljesac Wine Country Drive
🍇 Wine Region
🍷 Recommended Winery

① Kapetanova Kuća Restaurant
② Peninsula Wine Bar
③ Vina Matković, Madirazza, Violić & Matuško Wineries
④ Grgić Winery

See Mljet National Park detail map

Pomena

Polače

Mljet National Park

ble up its massive **fortifications** (park your car in the big lot, then cross the street into town and look right; the entrance to the walls is in the big tower). For a short wall experience, you can just do a circle around the stout lower walls (about 30 minutes); for a more serious hike, you can climb all the way up and over to Mali Ston (figure an hour or more). Be warned that the walls can be blazing hot—with all that glistening limestone reflecting heat—and there's virtually no shade (70 kn to enter walls regardless of how far you walk, daily June-July 8:00-19:00, shorter hours off-season).

Other than the walls, there's not much to do in Ston. The town's deserted feel is a result of a devastating 1996 earthquake, from which Ston is still rebuilding. But there are several inviting cafés for a lazy drink and various places to grab a sandwich or pizza slice. If you want a serious sit-down meal, skip Ston's mediocre offerings and head over to Mali Ston instead.

Eating in Mali Ston: From Ston, the walls scamper over a ridge to its little sister, the bayside village of Mali Ston (Small Ston). Surrounded by a similar, but smaller, fortified wall, Mali

Ston is known for its many mussel and oyster farms, and for its good restaurants. **$$$$ Kapetanova Kuća** is a memorable place with a fine location on Mali Ston's waterfront. Celebrity chef Lidija Kralj prides herself on her unpretentious but delicious food, made with fresh produce from the restaurant's own garden. For dessert, her bizarre *makaruli*—macaroni cake—is tastier than it sounds (daily 11:00-23:00, tel. 020/754-264).

Near the entrance to Kapetanova Kuća's parking lot, look for the simple **oyster shack/souvenir kiosk,** where local women sell fresh oysters and mussels from the adjacent bay and Pelješac wine decanted into plastic water bottles—all for cheap.

PELJEŠAC WINE COUNTRY DRIVE

The sparsely developed Pelješac Peninsula is blanketed with vineyards. Wine is the draw here, and a variety of vintners open their doors for passing visitors to sample their products. While it's a bit distant from Dubrovnik (about a two-hour drive to the heart of the wine-producing area), it's a worthwhile pilgrimage for wine lovers—or even just wine likers—and an easy stop-off for those driving from Korčula. Pelješac is an overlooked gem, and feels like a throwback to an age when wine tastings were relaxed, chatty, and fun, rather than corporate and rushed.

Guided Tours of Pelješac: I've outlined a self-guided driving tour of the region next, but if you don't have a car—or if you

A Bridge Too Far?

As you drive along the coast between Split and Dubrovnik, you may be surprised to reach a border checkpoint for Bosnia-Herzegovina at the resort town of Neum—at least until the opening of a bypass bridge now under construction. How is it that Bosnia wound up with its very own five-and-a-half-mile stretch of the Dalmatian Coast?

During the heyday of the Republic of Dubrovnik, the city's leaders granted this land to the Ottoman Empire to provide a buffer between Dubrovnik's holdings and the Republic of Venice, to the north. (They knew the Venetians would never dare to enter the territory of the Ottomans, their feared enemy.) Later, as the borders of Europe were being redrawn in modern times, Bosnia retained possession of this strip of land.

For years, coastal Bosnians and their Croatian neighbors have coexisted, albeit with a bit of friction. Prices for hotel rooms, groceries, and other staples are slightly cheaper in Neum, whose rest stops lure tourist buses with low prices and generous bus-driver kickbacks. Visitors are inconvenienced by having to go through a passport checkpoint as they enter Bosnia and again, just a few minutes later, as they exit Bosnia. On busy days, lines can back up at this border—have your passport and rental car's "green card" (proof of insurance) ready.

As Croatia extends its expressway southward, the most logical approach would be a route through Bosnia to Dubrovnik. But instead, they're building a 1.5-mile-long bridge from just north of Neum to the Pelješac Peninsula, where it will rejoin the coastal road back in Croatia, just south of Neum—completely bypassing Bosnian territory.

After many years of false starts, construction began on the Pelješac Bridge in 2018, to the tune of an estimated $500 million—most of which will be funded by the European Union. But the bridge remains controversial: It's a very expensive way to avoid a tiny strip of land. Environmentalists worry about the impact the bridge will have on the delicate ecosystem around Mali Ston. And Bosnian government officials have objected to the plan, saying that the bridge will illegally cut off Bosnian access to the sea. Even so, the bridge has its champions...and barring delays, it should be completed by 2022.

want an insider's view—consider hiring a guide to take you for a spin around Pelješac. **Sasha Lušić,** who runs the D'Vino Wine Bar in Dubrovnik, is a gregarious Aussie-Croat. He prides himself on taking you to a wide variety of vintners who represent the best of what's happening here. Sasha's tours, which flex from day to day based on his customers' interests and stamina, can go late into the evening (other options include cheaper half-day tours to areas closer to Dubrovnik—prices depend on what's included—and traditional *peka* lunch or sunset seaside dinner; you might get one of his well-trained associates, www.dvino.net, sasha@dvino.net). Other Dubrovnik-based drivers also do good wine tours (which also include worthwhile scenic stops), including **Petar Vlašić** (see page 290).

Planning Your Drive: I've arranged this tour to start near the western tip of Pelješac (Orebić, just across the channel from Korčula). If you're doing it from Dubrovnik, begin by driving to the village of Potomje (you can skip the section between there and Orebić) and backtrack to the wineries on this route from there. I've included some of Croatia's finest (and largely undiscovered) vineyards. For a primer before you start, see the "Croatian Wine" sidebar on page 30 and the "Sampling Pelješac Wines" sidebar in this section.

If you're crossing from Korčula Island, you'll begin the tour in **Orebić.** It's basically one main road from here back to Ston (where you'll meet up with the main coastal road to Dubrovnik or Split), so you can't really get lost—though we will make an off-the-beaten-path vineyard detour.

From Orebić to Potomje: Follow the main road (toward Dubrovnik and Split) up, up, up for about 15 minutes to a dramatic **viewpoint** (there's a pullout on the right with benches—watch for the giant wine bottle). Looking back toward Korčula, the jagged cliffs to your left are the Pelješac Peninsula (where we're about to drive), and the island poking out to the left is Mljet National Park. Straight ahead, behind Korčula, is the island of Lastovo. On a clear day, you can almost see to Italy. Below you and to the right, you can see some vineyards in the **Postup** area; to the left (not quite visible from here) are the vineyards of **Dingač.** These are the two best wine-growing regions of Pelješac: Both areas are steeply angled, so they catch a maximum amount of sun, which creates very sweet grapes that produce high-alcohol, very dark (actually called "black" in Croatian) wine with strong legs (or, as Croatians call them, "tears"). The rugged, rocky limestone provides natural irrigation (since water can flow freely through it), and the high winds here keep off bugs and other pests. It all adds up to extremely healthy vines; because disease is rare, pesticides are not needed.

Continuing along the road, you'll crest the hill and pass the turnoff for Trpanj (where ferries connect to the mainland); soon after, watch on the left for the **Peninsula Wine Bar.** Owned by local vintners Boris and Baldo, and run by Toni, this place feels like a glorified truck stop. But it's ideal for one-stop shoppers who want to learn about and try wine from a variety of producers. They usually have about 60 wines available. You can sample wine by the taste (look for tasting flights listed on the chalkboard), by the glass

Sampling Pelješac Wines

Most Pelješac wines are made with *plavac mali* (little blue) grapes, a distant relative of California zinfandel (they're called "son of zinfandel") and Italian *primitivo*. These wines are usually quite "big," with lots of tannins and high alcohol content (thank the warm climate for that).

Reds from the *plavac mali* grape are the real draw here, even though they account for just a third of the production (most are whites, with a few rosés). Winery staff enjoy explaining that this small area has three entirely different terroirs. The flat, easy-to-harvest Potomje valley produces cheaper, lower-quality wines; bottles are generally labeled simply with the type of grape (for example, *plavac mali*). Just over the mountains are the steep, sea-facing, sun-drenched Dingač and Postup areas (Dingač wines, a notch up in quality, tend to have more finesse than the coarser Postup wines). Bottles from these areas are usually labeled with the region rather than the grape.

Some vintners are starting to blend the *plavac mali* grape with other red grapes, like cabernet franc, merlot, and marselan, which creates a softer, less robust wine.

(most about 25 kn), or by the bottle (most around 50 kn). Tastings are free if you buy a few bottles. They also offer tastings of local olive oil and grappa, and serve burgers (daily 9:00-23:00, closed Nov-March, tel. 020/742-503, www.peninsula.hr).

After the wine bar, you'll drop down into a **plateau** surrounded by cliffs. The vines you'll see in this so-called "continental" area are the same *plavac mali* grapes as in Postup and Dingač, but they receive less sun and are less sweet. Notice that many of the vines appear to be almost wild; these are older vineyards, which aren't irrigated, so they must let the vines grow this way to help them survive the hot summer months. This method maximizes yield but reduces quality. Newer vineyards are irrigated and use guide wires, and generally look more manicured.

Wine Tasting in Potomje: Soon you'll arrive in the village of **Potomje,** a good stop for wine tasting. Four wineries here welcome visitors and offer a helpful introduction to Pelješac wines; taken together, they deliver a good range in experience, from mom-and-pop to state-of-the-art: Madirazza, Matuško, Vina Matković, and Violić. Violić is an appealingly Back Door experience, and worth saving for last.

All are staffed by friendly English speakers who are eager to introduce you to their wines; while the tastings are free, it's good form to buy a bottle or two. (If you want a more elaborate tasting with food pairings or for a small group, call ahead.) Unless otherwise noted, these places are open around 8:00-20:00, but close earlier in shoulder season and are generally closed in winter (Nov-March—but call ahead and they may be able to open for you, cash only). Most wineries also have various brandies to try (including *travarica*, an herb-infused brandy).

Drive through Potomje to the far end of town, where you'll see the big, pink building of the **Madirazza** winery, your first stop. Notice the roses that line the vineyards—like a canary in a coal mine, these are more quickly affected by disease than the vines, offering an early-warning system in the event of an unwanted infestation. Madirazza wines are oaky and fairly acidic (mobile 098-212-163, www.dingac.hr, Mina).

Across the main road from Madirazza's parking lot is a smaller road (marked with *Matuško* and *Tunel Dingač* signs) leading to the **Matuško** winery. This handsome winery sports a library-like tasting room and makes finer, less coarse wines than Madirazza's. The range of wines available to taste is exceptional (including a chardonnay and tasty rosé—although red is what they do best and most). If you ask nicely, you can visit the sprawling network of atmospheric cellars where tour groups sip wines between aging barrels (good place for a WC stop, tel. 020/742-393, mobile 098-428-676 www.matusko-vina.hr).

Leaving Matuško, it's a two-minute drive to the next stop; make two lefts and a right on the country road; your destination, **Vina Matković,** will be on the left. The gentle owner, Željka, can pour you a sample of their well-balanced and reasonably priced wines (reds only, don't miss her blend with marselan grapes, June-Oct daily 9:00-21:00, call ahead at other times, mobile 091-211-1230, http://iskrenavinamatkovic.com).

Backtrack past Matuško to the road that leads to the tunnel. As you face the entrance to the tunnel, turn left, following *Boris Violić* signs to the unassuming **Violić** family home and winery. Offering a good contrast to the polished and more mainstream-feeling wineries described above, chatty Boris Violić-Matuško and his charming wife Marine invite passing visitors to slow down and enjoy some home-style hospitality. In addition to sampling their wines (four reds and two whites made the "old-fashioned" way), consider buying some brandy, olive oil, or their delicious grandma-made treats (Potomje 6, mobile 091-575-4422).

When you're ready to move on, look for the **tunnel** through the mountain marked *Tunel Dingač*, with the picture of a donkey. Before this tunnel was dug, beasts of burden trod surefootedly up and over this mountain to carry the grapes from Dingač, on the far side, to this village. The donkey remains a symbol of this wine-growing region. In the 1970s, this tunnel was built to make everyone's lives easier. Take advantage of it by driving through the mountain and into another world.

Dingač Vineyards: Popping out at the sea, you're in the heart of the **Dingač** vineyards. Turn left (toward *Borak*) and drive on the one-lane road above all those vines, with a green and jagged waterline that looks almost Celtic. (Drive carefully: While it's a paved road, it's narrow, with a very steep shoulder.) Croatia's best reds are lovingly raised right here, soaking up ample sunshine as they struggle against a very rocky soil (ideal for wine grapes).

Locals explain that these grapes are bathed in sunlight from every angle—not just the sun above, but also the reflection of those rays from both the sea and the white soil. Dingač never freezes (unlike the valley), and rainfall runs off immediately through its porous limestone soil, making these plants very disease-resistant. By the time they are harvested, Dingač grapes are withered by the sun—halfway to raisins, packed with sugar, and ideal for producing top-quality and highly alcoholic wines. At the fork, continue down to the right, toward *Dingač/Borak;* at the next fork, when the Borak road turns sharply down and to the right, keep going straight onto the smaller road.

As you drive, keep enjoying dramatic views of Mljet Island. When you enter an area of trees, look across the harbor to see a building perched on a cliff over the water—that's our next stop. Soon you'll come to the village of Trstenik; at the T-intersection, make a sharp right turn, then turn left to pass along its little waterfront. At the far end of town, on the way up the hill, turn into the parking lot for the **Grgić** winery. Perhaps the best-known and best-regarded Croatian vintner, Mike Grgić's facility is less appealing than the

others we've visited, and you have to pay a small fee for the tasting...but the fame of the wine may be worth it for some. (See page 30 for the story of how Grgić revolutionized both American and

Croatian winemaking.) This place is surprisingly humble. Keeping things simple, Grgić does a white wine (*pošip,* with grapes grown on Korčula but produced here) and a red wine; breaking with convention, he names his red simply *plavac mali* partly to help promote this largely unknown and underappreciated grape. He also sells wines from his California winery, Grgich Hills, at or below their California prices (daily 9:00-19:00, tel. 020/748-090, www.grgic-vina.com).

From Grgić Winery to Ston: Exiting the Grgić winery, turn right (uphill) and twist up to the main road, where you'll turn right, toward Ston. Cresting the hill, you'll see the other side of the peninsula and the channel separating it from the mainland—as if to emphasize the narrowness of this spit of land. From here, you'll continue straight along all the way to Ston. You may be tempted by the *vino* signs in **Janjina,** but these are aimed mainly at Croatians buying table wine in bulk—100 liters at a time.

Leaving Janjina, keep following signs for *Ston* and *Dubrovnik.* You'll twist down and follow the **Bay of Ston,** which is famous for its shellfish production. Here where the Neretva River (which runs under Mostar's Old Bridge) empties into the sea, conditions are perfect for cultivating mussels, oysters, and clams. (You'll spot many such farms out in the bay—look for the areas roped off with buoys.) The road climbs up once more, passing the aptly named Bella Vista viewpoint café (which overlooks the dock for the ferry to the national park on Mljet Island), before continuing into the walled town of **Ston** (described earlier).

Leaving Ston, turn right (toward Dubrovnik) once you hit the main road; from here, it's about an hour back into town. En route, watch out for the speed traps at the towns of Doli and Orešac.

Mljet National Park

Carefully protected against modern development, the island hideaway of Mljet National Park (rated ▲) offers a unique back-

to-nature escape. With ample opportunities for hiking, swimming, biking, and kayaking—and without a nightclub, tacky T-shirt, or concrete "beach" in sight—Mljet (muhl-YAYT) is appreciated by active, outdoorsy travelers looking to escape some of the crowds and find their own pristine corner of Dalmatia.

Though Mljet Island is one of Dalmatia's largest, it has fewer than 1,500 residents. Nearly three-quarters of the island is covered in forest, leaving it remarkably untamed. Aside from its beautiful national park, Mljet has inspired some of the most memorable tales of the Croatian coast—the poet Homer, his protagonist Ulysses, and the Apostle Paul all spent time here...or so the locals love to boast.

PLANNING YOUR TIME

While back-to-nature travelers invest an overnight here, it's perfectly doable to visit Mljet as a day trip—most logically from either Dubrovnik or Korčula. In summer, this can be done by public catamaran: on the Nona Ana from Dubrovnik to Polače, or on the Krilo from Korčula to Pomena. At other times—or from other home bases—you may find it easier to sign up for a package excursion through a local tour company.

No matter how you arrive, one day is plenty to get a nice taste of Mljet. There are three top experiences: the **boat trip to the Island of St. Mary;** the **bike ride around the Great Lake** (allow about 1 hour, plus photo and swimming stops); and **swimming at the Small Bridge,** or at your choice of secluded cove around either of the park's two lakes.

Hikers can also do the easy walk around the Small Lake or the more strenuous summit to the park's highest point, Montokuc. If you enjoy **kayaking,** the Great Lake is a good place to do it. And if you have your own snorkeling gear (no rentals on the island), the coral reef near Soline (where the Great Lake meets the Adriatic) is a popular spot.

These activities can be done in any order. However, it can be smart to visit the Island of St. Mary first; that way, once back on the main island, you'll know exactly how much time you have left to bike, swim, hike, or kayak before heading back to your boat.

Mljet en Route from Korčula to Dubrovnik: In summer, when the catamarans are running at full schedule, it's possible to squeeze the national park into this journey: Ride the morning Krilo from Korčula to Pomena, and find somewhere to stow your bag (see "Arrival in Mljet," later); spend the day enjoying the park; head back to Pomena to get your bag and ride the shuttle to Polače; take the Nona Ana to Dubrovnik in time for a late dinner. As the catamaran schedule is always in flux, carefully confirm this will work; the Korčula TI is helpful in sorting out the logistics. This can also be done in reverse: Take the morning Nona Ana catamaran from Dubrovnik to Polače, ride a taxi over to Pomena to drop your bag at the hotel, and take the Krilo to Korčula in the afternoon.

Off-Season Visits: Be warned that everything here is very seasonal and weather-dependent, so visiting outside of peak season

(June-Sept) will come with some frustration (and the park is officially closed Nov-Feb). However, locals say that off-season visitors particularly enjoy the island's many orchids, which bloom only outside of summer.

Orientation to Mljet

The island of Mljet is long (23 miles) and skinny (less than two miles wide). The national park occupies the western third of the island. You're likely to reach Mljet via one of three port towns: **Polače** (POH-lah-cheh) and **Pomena** (POH-meh-nah) are the main entry points into the national park, while **Sobra** (SOH-brah) is much less convenient (a 35-minute drive across the island from the park). The Nona Ana catamaran from Dubrovnik puts in at both Polače and Sobra; the Krilo catamaran and most excursions use Pomena; and car ferries to the mainland use Sobra. Day-trippers should simply ignore the rest of the island and focus on the national park.

Polače and Pomena flank the heart of the national park—a pair of adjoining "lakes" (actually large saltwater lagoons fed by canals from the Adriatic) called **Great Lake** (Veliko Jezero) and

Small Lake (Malo Jezero). These two bodies of water meet at the aptly named **Small Bridge** (Mali Most), where you can rent kayaks and bikes. A 15-minute walk or five-minute pedal along the Great Lake from the Small Bridge brings you to **Pristanište** (meaning, roughly, "transit hub"), which is connected by shuttle bus to Polače. In the middle of the Great Lake sits the **Island of St. Mary,** which is served by national park shuttle boats (included in your ticket) from both the Small Bridge and Pristanište. Everything's well-signed, and it's hard to get lost if you use the free orientation map that comes with your ticket. But if you want to do some serious hiking, you can invest in a detailed park map (available at the entry kiosks).

Beyond Pomena and Polače, the national park has a few small settlements. **Babine Kuće** is on the lakeside path, between the Small Bridge and Pristanište; **Soline,** a lonely fishing village, sits along the channel where the Great Lake connects to the sea; and the cliff-climbing town of **Goveđari** is home to many of the people who work at the park, but is not interesting to tourists.

Cost and Hours: To enter the park, you'll pay an entrance fee of 125 kn (June-Sept) or 70 kn in shoulder season. This includes access to the park's trails and beaches, plus the boat to the Island of St. Mary and the shuttle bus from Polače to Pristanište. The park is open daily June-mid-Sept 7:00-21:00, until 19:00 in shoulder season, and closed Nov-Feb.

TOURIST INFORMATION

The **national park ticket kiosks,** where you buy your ticket, can help you plan your day (tel. 020/744-041, www.np-mljet.hr). The only **official TI** is in Polače, across from where the Nona Ana cata-maran docks (tel. 020/744-186). The island's lone hotel, the **Hotel Odisej** in Pomena, also acts as a tourist information point (tel. 020/362-111). The island's general-information website is www.mljet.hr.

ARRIVAL IN MLJET

At Polače (on the catamaran from Dubrovnik): Exit to the right, pass the TI, and walk a few minutes up (through some scant ruins of what, at one time, was the third largest Roman palace in Croatia) to the blue national park kiosk. Here you can buy your entry ticket and catch a minibus to the Pristanište transit hub at the Great Lake (coordinated with boat arrival). If the line for the shuttle bus is too long—not uncommon on busy mornings—ask them to point you to the old Roman trail that leads about 30 minutes through the woods to Pristanište, where you can hop on the hourly boat to the Island of St. Mary.

At Pomena (on the catamaran from Korčula, or an excursion):

Exit the boat to the left (passing Hotel Odisej), hike uphill, and look for the national park kiosk on your left. Buy your ticket here, then continue up past some restaurants and grocery stores (last chance to stock up on water and snacks). Just after you leave town, a stepped path on your right leads through the woods to the Small Lake, about a 10-minute walk. When you reach the lake, turn left and follow the shore another five minutes to the Small Bridge. Use the Small Bridge as a home base for the rest of your day.

Note that there's no official bus between Polače and Pomena, but Hotel Odisej operates a handy and comfortable shuttle to coincide with the Dubrovnik catamaran (45 kn one-way; not covered by park ticket). The island also has some minibus-taxis (mobile 098-505-654). A low-capacity "tourist train" (just a big golf cart) occasionally loops around the Great Lake, but it's too small to be practical.

At Sobra: If you come on a car ferry into Sobra, it's about a 35-minute drive on twisty roads to reach the Polače/Pomena tourist hub. If you're not bringing a car to Mljet, don't get off the boat in Sobra—there are no convenient bus connections to the national park, and a taxi will run you around 350 kn. In a pinch, there's typically an afternoon speedboat connecting Polače and Sobra.

Returning to Your Boat: At the end of the day, Dubrovnik-bound boats depart from Polače. If you're in the Small Bridge area, you have two choices: The easiest is to walk to Pomena and pay for the shuttle to Polače (just a few minutes in an air-conditioned van, book at Hotel Odisej); or you can walk or ride the boat to Pristanište, then hop on the shuttle bus to Polače from there. If you're hiking up to Montokuc, you can hike from the summit all the way down to Polače.

HELPFUL HINTS

Bike Rental: At both Polače and Pomena, you'll see companies advertising bike rentals, but these places are separated from the Great Lake's beautiful bike path by hilly terrain. Unless you like hills, wait to rent your bike until you reach the Small Bridge.

Kayak Rental: You can rent basic kayaks next to the Small Bridge. Enjoy the calm waters: Motorized boats (beyond the official park boats, and the occasional locally owned dinghy) are not allowed on the lakes.

Bag Storage: Pomena has no official baggage storage, but the Hotel Odisej or the national park ticket kiosk are generally willing to watch your bag for the day...if you ask sweetly.

Eating in the Park: You'll find several small eateries in both **Pomena** and **Polače.** Once at the lakes, you may spot a very basic ice-cream truck at the **Small Bridge** (but nothing else there).

The Tales of Mljet

For a mostly undeveloped island, Mljet has had a surprisingly busy history. Home to Illyrians, Greeks, Romans, Slavs, Venetians, Habsburgs, Yugoslavs, and now Croatians, the island has hosted some interesting visitors (or supposed visitors) that it loves to brag about.

Around the eighth century BC, the Greek epic poet Homer possibly spent time here. He was so inspired by Mljet that he used it as the setting for one of the adventures of his hero Ulysses (a.k.a. Odysseus). This is the island where Ulysses fell in love with a beautiful nymph named Calypso and shacked up with her in a cave for seven years. Today there's a much-vaunted Ulysses' Cave (Odisejeva Spilja), a 40-minute hike below the island's main town, Babino Polje (at the far end of the island—skip it unless you're a Ulysses groupie).

Flash forward nearly a millennium, when a real-life traveler found his way to Mljet. According to the Bible (Acts 28), the Apostle Paul was shipwrecked on an island called "Melita"—likely this one—for three months. While on the island, Paul was bitten by a deadly snake, which he threw into a fire. The natives were amazed that the poison didn't affect him, and he proceeded to cure their ailments. This event was long believed to have happened on the similarly named isle of Malta, in the Mediterranean Sea. But more recently, many historians began to believe that Paul was on Mljet. The most convincing argument: Malta never had poisonous snakes. Incidentally, Mljet no longer does, either—the Habsburgs imported an army of Indian mongooses to rid the island of problematic serpents. Because of this historical footnote, people from Mljet are nicknamed "mongooses" by other Croatians.

The heroics continue with today's "mongooses." There have been more than 100 fires on the island in recent decades (most caused by lightning, some by careless visitors), but only three have spread and caused significant damage. That's because the people of Mljet—well aware of the fragility of the island that provides their income—are also a crack volunteer firefighting force, ready to spring into action and save their home at the first wisp of smoke.

The lakefront towns of **Babine Kuće** and **Soline** both have some nice eateries with great views. And the **Island of St. Mary** has the **$$** Restaurant Melita (with a menu of typical Dalmatian dishes) and an adjacent, simpler **$** pizzeria (with basic pizzas and sandwiches).

Services: Because the island has limited access to fresh water, there are no showers for swimmers here...be prepared for a salty ride back to Dubrovnik. The Small Bridge has some pit toilets with no running water, and no formal changing areas for swimmers (wear your swimsuit under your clothes, brave the tight and smelly WCs, or discreetly change under a towel). The restaurant on the Island of St. Mary has a pay WC (with actual running water). In Pomena, you can discreetly use the bathroom in the lobby of Hotel Odisej.

What to Bring: With so many tempting **swimming** spots in the park, you'll certainly want to bring a swimsuit and towel. If you have **snorkel gear,** this is a good place to use it (you can't rent it on the island). There are a few lunch options on the island (see earlier), but packing a **picnic** gives you more flexibility. With limited refreshment available once inside the park, bring plenty of **water.**

Overnighting on Mljet: This chapter is designed for day-trippers, but if you'd like to spend the night, consider the island's lone hotel. **$$$ Hotel Odisej,** with 157 rooms, sits right on Pomena's waterfront. It's a predictably comfortable home base, with helpful staff (closed late Oct-late April, tel. 020/362-111, www.adriaticluxuryhotels.com). The park also has a variety of rustic **$** *sobe* **and apartments** in its various villages; some are listed at www.mljet.hr.

Sights at Mljet National Park

▲▲The Lakes

The "Great Lake" and "Small Lake," with shimmering turquoise waters, are saltwater bays—fed by the sea and affected by ocean currents. Scientists love these lakes, which contain various shellfish species unique to Mljet. One of them—the biggest shellfish in the Mediterranean, which grows up to three feet long—is the noble pan shell, which naturally filters the water here, keeping it crystal-clear.

Swimmers love the lakes, too. There are two channels where it's fun to see (and swim in) the tidal currents: at the Small Bridge,

and at the footbridge (near Soline) where the Great Lake connects to the Adriatic. The most popular and most satisfying place to take a dip is at the little beach near the Small Bridge, with warm water, a mostly level and only slightly rocky bottom, and—best of all—a narrow channel where you can ride the current between the two lakes. Crossing between them, you'll notice that the Small Lake is always a few degrees warmer than the Great Lake or the sea. Circling either lake, you'll see plenty of other opportunities to take a dip.

▲The Island of St. Mary (Sv. Marija)

From the Small Bridge or Pristanište, you can hop on a boat for the 15-minute crossing to the Great Lake's Island of St. Mary (included in park ticket, boats depart about hourly—schedule posted at park entrances and at boat docks). While this island-within-an-island isn't too exciting, it's a fun excuse for a boat ride and an easy hike.

Benedictine monks lived on Mljet starting in the 12th century and founded a monastery on this island. Though the monastery complex has been modified over the ages, fragments of the original Romanesque structure still survive.

From the boat, turn left and find the stairs up to the tall, austere, limestone church interior, with its gracefully rounded arches, and peek into the adjoining cloister. From there, an easy stepped trail leads up to the top of the island, passing remains of old fortifications, some Roman ruins, and a rugged stone stable with the island's only permanent residents: a handful of donkeys. From the summit, you can hike steeply down the other side—passing more tiny chapels and a miniature cemetery—to reach the inviting promenade at the back of the island, popular with swimmers. The promenade leads back around to the boat dock.

You'll have about an hour to explore between boats, but it only takes half that to see everything. So relax with an overpriced drink (or meal) at the restaurant by the boat dock or the nearby pizzeria.

▲Biking Around the Great Lake

The Great Lake is surrounded by a mostly paved, mostly level, five-mile path that's enjoyable for a bike ride. You can do the entire loop in about an hour, not counting photo, swimming, or eating stops. The entire lakeshore is nicely manicured, with strategically placed information boards, benches, and places to get in the water. It's all well signed and the ride is easy—just stay on the main path, which is almost always within sight of the lake.

Rent a bike at the Small Bridge, then head clockwise around the Great Lake (with the water on your right). You'll curl along the lakeshore, through the charming waterfront village of Babine Kuće (with some appealing restaurants), then climb a little hill and continue around. At about the halfway point, you come to a little footbridge that crosses the channel where the Great Lake meets the sea; you'll need to carry your bike across the bridge to continue the loop. Before crossing the footbridge, you can detour (about a half-mile) to the humble fishing village of Soline (with more restaurants); if you continue even farther, you'll come to the popular snorkeling area of the largest coral reef in the Mediterranean Sea. (It's a brown, not-too-striking "pillow coral"—less exciting than it sounds.)

Across the footbridge, the rough path curls around a gorgeous bay, overlooking the Island of St. Mary. Continuing on, the path gets better as it takes you back around to the Small Bridge.

Note: The unpaved path around the Small Lake is rough and rocky, making biking there more difficult, but it's a pleasant walk (1.25 miles, about 30 minutes).

Hiking to Montokuc

The most rewarding hike takes you up to the national park's highest point, Montokuc. At 830 feet above sea level, this is a serious hike—skip it unless you're in good shape, and be sure to bring water. There are several trails up, including two along the lakeshore of the Great Lake, one in the village of Soline, and one in Polače. If you're doing this or any other hike, the park map is essential (sold at park entry kiosks and other merchants).

Mljet Connections

By Catamaran: Two convenient passenger catamarans connect Mljet to other major destinations. Schedules can vary from year to year, and both of these boats can sell out in peak season; check the schedules and book tickets at one of the websites below.

The **Krilo catamaran** uses the dock at Pomena; through the high season (early April-late Oct), it heads south every morning to Dubrovnik (1.5 hours) and north each afternoon only to Korčula (1 hour), Hvar (2 hours), and Split (3 hours; www.krilo.hr).

The **Nona Ana catamaran** heads from Polače to Dubrovnik each afternoon in summer (June-Sept, 1.5 hours, www.gv-line.hr). On some days in the peak months of July and August, the Nona Ana also heads north in the morning to Korčula (4/week, 1 hour). In winter (Oct-May), the boat runs only from Sobra to Dubrovnik, making it pointless for day-trippers to the national park.

By Car Ferry: For drivers, a car ferry connects the town of Prapratno (near the base of the Pelješac Peninsula, not far from

Ston) to Sobra on Mljet (for schedules, see www.jadrolinija.hr). Once at Sobra, it's a 35-minute drive to the park.

By Excursion: Many destinations are more conveniently connected to Mljet by excursion than by public transit. While you don't need a guide to enjoy the island, the simple convenience of round-trip transportation makes this worth considering—particularly if the catamarans are booked up.

MONTENEGRO

Crna Gora

MONTENEGRO

*The Bay of Kotor • Kotor • The Montenegrin Interior •
The Budva Riviera*

If Dubrovnik is the grand finale of a Croatian vacation, then Montenegro is the encore. One of Europe's youngest nations awaits just south of the border, with dramatic scenery, friendly locals proud of their unique land, and a rough-around-the-edges appeal.

Crossing the border (with passport ready), you know you've left sleek and tidy Croatia for a place that's gritty, raw, and a bit exotic. While Croatia's showpiece Dalmatian Coast avoided the drab, boxy dullness of the Yugoslav era, less affluent Montenegro wasn't so lucky. Between the dramatic cliffs and time-passed villages, you'll drive past grimy, broken-down apartment blocks and some truly unfortunate concrete architecture. Montenegro is also a noticeably poorer country than its northern neighbor.

Historically, Montenegro has been even more of a crossroads of cultures than Croatia. In some ways, there are two Montenegros: the remote, rugged, rustic mountaintop kingdom that feels culturally close to Serbia; and this chapter's focus, the sun-drenched coastline of strategic importance that has attracted a steady stream of rulers over the millennia. At one point or another, just about every group you can imagine has planted its flag here—from the usual suspects (Venetians, Austrians, Russian czars) to oddball one-offs (Bulgarian kingdoms, Napoleon's Ljubljana-based Illyrian Provinces). In spite of their schizophrenic lineage, or maybe because of it, Montenegrins have forged a unique cultural identity that defies many of the preconceived notions of the Balkans. Are they like Serbs or Croats? Do they use the Cyrillic or the Roman alphabet? Do they follow the Roman Catholic rite or the Eastern Orthodox one? Yes, all of the above.

Since Montenegro gained independence in 2006, its coast has become a powerful magnet for a very specific breed of traveler: multimillionaires from Russia and the Middle East, who have chosen to turn this impressionable, fledgling country—with its gorgeous coastline—into their very own Riviera. The Tivat airport is jammed with charter flights from Moscow, signs along the coast advertise Russian-language radio stations, and an extravagant luxury-yacht marina caters to the rich near Tivat (Porto Montenegro, www.portomontenegro.com). And so Montenegro finds itself in an awkward position: trying to cultivate an image as a high-roller luxury paradise, while struggling to upgrade what is—in places—inadequate infrastructure. Glittering new €500-a-night boutique hotels are built, but they might suffer power and water outages. Lower your expectations, and don't assume that a fancy facade and high prices come with predictable quality.

Still, nothing can mar the natural beauty of Montenegro's mountains, bays, and forests. For a look at the untamed Adriatic, a spin on the winding road around Montenegro's steep and secluded Bay of Kotor is a must. The area's main town, also called Kotor, has been protected from centuries of would-be invaders by its position at the deepest point of the fjord—and by its imposing town wall, which scram-

bles in a zigzag line up the mountain behind it. Wander the winding streets of Kotor, drop into some Orthodox churches, and sip a coffee at an al fresco café.

With more time, romantics can corkscrew up into the mountains to sample the Balkans' best smoked ham at Njeguši and visit the remote, original capital of the country at Cetinje, beach bums can head for the Budva Riviera, and celebrity-seekers can daydream about past glories at the striking hotel-peninsula of Sveti Stefan. Find more information at the Montenegro.travel website.

GETTING TO MONTENEGRO

This chapter is designed for day-tripping to Montenegro from Dubrovnik; all of the sights are within about a three-hour drive of Dubrovnik, and within about an hour of each other. If you're arriving in Montenegro by cruise (as many visitors do these days), see the "Cruising into Kotor" sidebar, later.

By Car: Driving is the best option, giving you maximum flexibility for sightseeing—but be aware of possible border delays (see "Helpful Hints," later). I've narrated a self-guided driving tour of the Bay of Kotor, and another for the most accessible slice of the Montenegrin interior. Even if you don't have a rental car during your Dubrovnik visit, consider renting one just for the day to visit Montenegro. Perhaps most satisfying—but more pricey—is to hire your own Dubrovnik-based driver to bring you here (my favorites are recommended on page 289). While this is expensive (around

Montenegro Almanac

Official Name: After being part of "Yugoslavia," then "Serbia and Montenegro," it's now the Republic of Montenegro (Republika Crna Gora)—which means "Black Mountain." It might have gotten its name from sailors who saw darkly forested cliffs as they approached, or it may have been named for a mythical mountain in the country's interior.

Size: 5,415 square miles (slightly smaller than Connecticut). Montenegro is home to about 650,000 people. Of these, the vast majority are Eastern Orthodox Christians (45 percent Montenegrins, 29 percent Serbs), with minority groups of Muslims (including Bosniaks and Albanians, about 11 percent total) and Catholics (1 percent).

Geography: Montenegro is characterized by a rugged, rocky terrain that rises straight up from the Adriatic and almost immediately becomes a steep mountain range. The country has 182 miles of coastline, about a third of which constitutes the Bay of Kotor. The only real city is the dreary capital in the interior, Podgorica (190,000 people). Each of Yugoslavia's six republics had a town named after Tito, and Titograd (now Podgorica) was Montenegro's.

Snapshot History: Long overshadowed by its Croatian and Serbian neighbors, Montenegro finally achieved independence on June 3, 2006, in a landmark vote to secede from Serbia—its influential and sometimes overbearing "big brother."

Red Tape: Americans and Canadians need only a passport (no visa required) to enter Montenegro.

€250 for the day), you can try to team up with other travelers to share the cost.

By Bus: Bus service between Dubrovnik and Montenegro is good in the summer (8/day, 2.5 hours or longer with border delays), but decreases off-season. It's possible to day-trip from Dubrovnik to the town of Kotor, but it's a long day on the bus: The first morning bus departs Dubrovnik at 7:00, usually arriving in Kotor between 10:00 and 11:00 (depending on the wait at the border). In summer, there may be additional morning buses, departing at 8:15, 10:00, and/or 11:00—but these can be even more susceptible to border delays. From Kotor, return buses typically depart at 14:40 (reaching Dubrovnik around 17:15) and at 18:00 (arriving in Dubrovnik around 21:00). Keep in mind that if you ride the bus, you can't stop to explore the sights along the way. As the schedule is always in flux, it's important to confirm times carefully at the Dubrovnik TI or bus station. Sit on the right side of the bus on your way to Montenegro, and the left side on the way home. The website

Economy: Upon declaring independence in 2006, Montenegro's economy was weak. But the privatization of its economy (including its dominant industry, aluminum) and the aggressive development of its tourist trade (such as soliciting foreign investment—mostly Russian—to build new luxury hotels) have turned things around. In fact, in recent years, Montenegro has had one of the highest foreign investment rates in Europe. Still, it remains a poor place: Montenegro's unemployment rate hovers around 15 percent, and its per-capita GDP is $17,800.

Currency: Though it's not a member of the European Union, Montenegro uses the euro as its currency (€1 = about $1.20).

Language and Alphabet: The official language is Montenegrin, which is nearly identical to Serbian but predominantly uses "our" Roman alphabet (rather than Cyrillic). Still, you'll see plenty of Cyrillic here—catering to both the country's large Serb minority as well as Russian tourists and investors.

Telephones: Montenegro's country code is 382. When calling from another country, first dial the international access code (00 from Europe, 011 from the US), then 382, then the area code (minus the initial zero), then the number.

Flag: It's a red field surrounded by a gold fringe. In the middle is the national seal: a golden, two-headed Byzantine eagle topped with a single crown, holding a scepter in one hand and a ball in the other (symbolizing the balance between church and state). The eagle's body is covered by a shield depicting a lion with one paw raised (representing the resurrected Christ).

MONTENEGRO

BusTicket4.me is useful for sorting out Montenegro bus connections.

It's also possible to take a bus from Montenegro to **Mostar** in Bosnia-Herzegovina; it's a long journey via Trebinje in the mountainous interior (9 hours), or somewhat shorter via Dubrovnik (5.5 hours). For details, see "Kotor Connections," later.

By Excursion: As a last resort, consider taking a package excursion that follows basically the same route covered in this chapter (sold by various travel agencies in Dubrovnik; see page 346).

PLANNING YOUR TIME

Assuming you have your own car, for a straightforward one-day plan, drive to Kotor and back (figure about nine hours, including driving time and sightseeing stops). To extend your time, you can add as much Montenegro as you like. Get an early start (to avoid lines at the border, I'd leave Dubrovnik as early as 7:30). It takes about two hours to drive from Dubrovnik to Kotor (add about 1.5 hours if you stop in Perast for the boat trip out to the island). Kotor is worth two or three hours. From Kotor, you can return directly to Dubrovnik (about 1.5 hours if you use the ferry shortcut—see the "Lepetane-Kamenari Ferry" description later in this chapter); or drive another hour up to Njeguši and Cetinje in the Montenegrin interior, or a half-hour to the Budva Riviera (from either place, figure about 2.5-3 hours back to Dubrovnik). To cram everything into one extremely long day, you can do Dubrovnik-Perast-Kotor-Cetinje-Budva Riviera-Dubrovnik.

HELPFUL HINTS

Border Delays: The main Croatian-Montenegrin border is at Debeli Brijeg. When it's not busy, this border is relatively straightforward—just stop, have your passport scanned, and show your car's "green card" (proof of insurance). There can be long delays here on very busy days, especially on Saturdays in August, and to a lesser degree in July and early September. On the busiest days, the line can be hours long; however, locals in Dubrovnik tend to exaggerate how often the border is seriously backed up. Long waits are rare if you avoid the morning crush of tour buses.

To avoid the worst waits, you have three options. The best is to get an early start (reach the border by 8:00—which means leaving Dubrovnik around 7:30); get a later start (leaving Dubrovnik around 9:00); or use the secondary crossing, called Konfin, which is generally less busy. Big buses are not allowed at Konfin, but savvy locals know about it, so on the busiest days, it can be backed up too. While the Konfin border might save you time, it's a bit less straightforward (with a few turn-offs rather than a straight shot on the main road) and takes a few more miles. I've narrated a scenic route ("Konfin Border Detour") in my self-guided driving tour, later. Once you've crossed into Montenegro, if you're finding that the roads are unpleasantly crowded, another strategy for avoiding delays and crowds is to reverse the loop of my driving tour (explained later).

Afternoon Delays: The Debeli Brijeg border crossing can also be severely delayed coming back to Dubrovnik in the afternoon. (Lines are worst in summer around 16:00 or 17:00—when a long chain of excursion buses all head back at the same time.) If this happens, use the secondary (and typically less crowded) Konfin border crossing. To avoid delays, some people like to make their way back to Dubrovnik in the early afternoon, perhaps stopping for dinner in Konavle; others prefer to linger for dinner in Kotor, and come back later, after the lines have thinned out.

Local Guide: While many Dubrovnik-based drivers/guides can bring you to Montenegro, if you really want the Montenegrin perspective, consider hiring a local guide here. I spent a great day learning about this area from **Stefan Đukanović,** a young, energetic, knowledgeable guide who speaks good English and has an infectious enthusiasm for his homeland. Hiring Stefan is a great value. The catch is that he can't come and get you in Dubrovnik, so it works best if you drive yourself to Montenegro and pick him up when you get there. Stefan is also an excellent choice if you're arriving in Kotor by cruise ship (guiding only: €80/half-day, €100/day, extra for driver if going outside of Kotor; several shore excursions possible—contact for details and rates, mobile 069-297-221 or 069-369-994, www.miroandsons.com, djukan@t-com.me).

MONTENEGRO

The Bay of Kotor

With dramatic cliffs rising out of the glimmering Adriatic, ancient towns packed with history and thrilling vistas, an undeveloped ruggedness unlike anything in Croatia, and a twisty road to tie it all together, the Bay of Kotor represents the best of Montenegro. To top it off, it's easy to reach by car from Dubrovnik. (Don't forget your passport.)

Bay of Kotor Driving Tour

The Bay of Kotor (Boka Kotorska—literally the "Mouth of Kotor"; sometimes called Boka Bay) is Montenegro's most enjoyable and convenient attraction for those based in Dubrovnik. This self-guided day trip—worth ▲▲—narrates the drive from the Croatian border to the town of Kotor, in the Bay of Kotor's deepest corner. If you're doing the drive in peak summer season, consider following my itinerary *in reverse* to avoid crowds; I'll tell you below precisely where you need to deviate to do the route in reverse.

The Montenegrin border is about 40 minutes south of Dubrovnik. Simply follow the main coastal road south (signs to *Ćilipi*), past Cavtat and the airport.

From Dubrovnik to the Border
As you leave Dubrovnik, the jagged cliffs on your left eventually give way to a pastoral countryside called **Konavle** (meaning "canal," recalling how the Romans built aqueducts through this area to supply their settlement at today's Cavtat). This farming region—effectively Dubrovnik's hinterland—was badly damaged during the Yugoslav Wars, when the Yugoslav People's Army invaded from

MONTENEGRO

Cruising into Kotor

With cruise-ship crowds reaching capacity in nearby Dubrovnik, the Montenegrin town of Kotor has emerged as a hugely popular port of call on Mediterranean cruises. If your ship is stopping in Kotor, here are some pointers.

Arrival in Kotor by Cruise Ship: It's easy. Ships either dock at or tender to the long pier that juts out directly in front of the Old Town. All passengers are funneled out of the same port gate, with the Old Town straight ahead. As you leave the port gate, look left to find an **ATM** in a freestanding orange kiosk (the main square of the Old Town, less than a five-minute walk away, also has ATMs; Montenegro uses the euro). As soon as you pass the port gates, expect to be accosted by a mob of taxi drivers. (For the best rate, ignore the cabbies on the dock. Cross the street, turn left and walk about 200 yards to the Kamelija Shopping Center, where there is a taxi stand with less aggressive cabbies.) To enter the town, walk down the dock with the water on your right about 100 feet until you see traffic lights and a crosswalk on your left. Cross the street and stop by the TI kiosk for a free map and local information. Then go through the main gate, where you could start my self-guided walk.

Amenities: Free **Wi-Fi** is available near the TI kiosk. The two **pharmacies** in the Old Town are open long hours daily (for locations, see the "Kotor" map, later).

Sightseeing Options: The **Old Town of Kotor** itself is the obvious place to spend your day, though seeing everything—including my self-guided orientation walk and all of the museums—won't take you more than a couple of hours. Add a couple more hours if you're up for the stiff hike to the fortress above town (and maybe another hour or so to recover). With more time, you may want to venture farther afield. The easiest choice is **Perast,** where you can explore a seaside village and ride a small boat out to one of the islands in the middle of the fjord (see details later in this chapter); allow about four hours total for the round-trip to Perast and the island. Public buses connect Kotor town to Perast, or you can spring for a taxi (legitimate cabbies charge €20-25 one-way or €40-50 round-trip, including waiting time; negotiate a fixed price up front). For either of these trips—or to reach other, more distant Montenegrin destinations explained in this chapter—consider hiring a **local guide;** I recommend Stefan Đukanović (see "Helpful Hints," earlier in this chapter).

Sail-in and Sail-away: Cruisers visiting Kotor are treated to a spectacular sail-in and sail-away, through the fjordlike bay and the narrow Verige Strait. If the weather's good and you enjoy dramatic scenery, this is not a day to sleep in or to nap during the sail-away.

the south, forcing villagers to flee to safety in Dubrovnik. But it's bouncing back, and is home to many appealing *konoba*s (taverns) serving traditional local food. To stop off here (perhaps for dinner at the end of your Montenegro day), see "Konavoski Dvori" on page 355.

Soon after the turnoff for the Bosnian border, on the right, you'll pass **Kupari,** with one of the few buildings in the area that still has war damage. Originally Tito's villa, the building later became a vacation home for Yugoslav military officers. Now it's a ruin, awaiting investors.

From Kupari, you'll curl around the picturesque **Bay of Cavtat,** where some of the world's richest people tie up their yachts. Partway along the bay, after the village of Plat, you'll pass (on the left) an electrical plant, which harnesses the power of an underground river to generate more than enough clean energy for the entire city.

After the pleasant resort town of **Cavtat** (described on page 351), then the airport, you have the option of turning off (on the right, toward *Molunat*) to take advantage of the less crowded border crossing at Konfin (described next). Otherwise, just cruise along the main road until you reach the primary Debeli Brijeg border crossing. (If there's a line when you arrive, it's easy to backtrack to the alternate crossing: Just after the town of Gruda, follow signs for *Pločice*, then *Vitaljina*, then *Herceg Novi*, joining up with the route described next.)

Optional Konfin Border Detour

This is your first option to avoid big crowds and long waits at the border. If you're doing this drive in the peak of summer, or you arrive at the primary border crossing and find a lengthy line, then consider this slightly longer and more scenic route that takes you to the usually uncongested secondary border, at Konfin.

Soon after passing the airport, take the turnoff on the right for *Molunat.* You'll pass through a tranquil, nearly Tuscan landscape of pointy cypresses, vineyards, olive groves, and fig trees. Just before the village of Radovčići, on the right, watch for **Kojan Koral,** a horse farm that hosted movie-star equines for *Game of Thrones.* They offer horseback rides and ATV safaris (https://kojankoral.com).

Farther along, you'll enjoy fine views (on the right) down on the dramatic, elongated peninsula of **Molunat.** Notice that the H-shaped peninsula forms two protected bays. The larger one, facing north (toward Dubrovnik), is used to harbor ships in winter, while the smaller, south-facing one is better in summer.

When the road reaches a T-intersection, turn left for *Dubrovnik* and *Park Prevlaka*, then follow signs right for *Đurinići*, then right again for *Vitaljina*. As you continue on this road—through the vil-

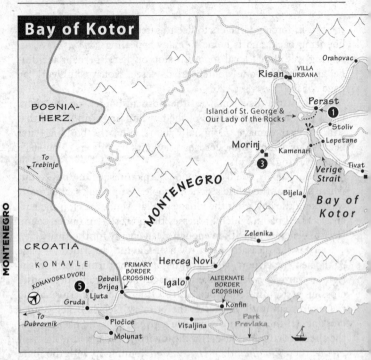

Bay of Kotor

lages of Đurinići, Višnjići, and Vitaljina—high on the mountains to your left is the point locals call **Tromeđe** (Three Borders), where Croatia, Bosnia-Herzegovina, and Montenegro converge.

Continue straight along this road all the way to the border, following signs for *Herceg Novi* and *GP Konfin*. You'll pass a turn-off on the right for **Park Prevlaka,** an old Austro-Hungarian and Yugoslav army fortress that has been converted into a park; you can see it at the tip of the peninsula poking out on your right—the southernmost point in Croatia.

Before long, you'll arrive at the Croatian border post, and then the Montenegrin one. After entering Montenegro, you'll curve along the small bay into Igalo, where you can resume the self-guided driving tour; see Igalo, next.

• *From either border, you can make it to Kotor in about an hour without stopping, but with all the diversions en route you should plan for much more time. Navigating on this tour is really simple: It's basically the same road, with no turnoffs, from Dubrovnik to Kotor. First, you'll approach the coast at the town called...*

Igalo

Driving through Igalo, keep an eye out (on the right) for a big concrete hotel called **Institut Dr. Simo Milošević** (no relation to war-criminal Slobodan). This internationally regarded spa is one of the world's premier treatment facilities for arthritis and nerve disorders. Especially popular among Scandinavians, it can host more than 1,000 patients at once. Yugoslav President-for-Life Tito had a villa nearby and took treatments here.

• *A couple of miles beyond Igalo, you enter the biggest city you'll see today...*

Herceg Novi

The drab economic and industrial capital of the Bay of Kotor, Herceg Novi (with 25,000 people) is hardly the prettiest introduction to this otherwise striking landscape. Herceg Novi flourished during the Habsburg boom of the late 19th century, when a railroad line connected it to Dubrovnik, Sarajevo, and Vienna. Back then, Austrians vacationed here—but more recent development has been decidedly less elegant than the Habsburgs'. While there is a walled Old Town core to Herceg Novi, it's not worth stopping to see; skip the turnoff for the town center, carrying on along the main road toward Budva.

Passing above Herceg Novi's Old Town, keep an eye out on the right for the town's stout 15th-century **fortress,** which was built by the Ottomans—who controlled this area, but never made it deeper into the bay.

Also in Herceg Novi, watch for tropical trees. Locals pride

MONTENEGRO

The History of Kotor

With evidence of prehistoric settlements dating back to 2500 BC, the Bay of Kotor has been a prized location for millennia. Its unique bottleneck shape makes the Bay of Kotor the single best natural harbor between Greece and Venice.

One of the earliest known civilizations in Kotor (third century BC) was that of the Illyrians, whose Queen Teuta held court here until her lands were conquered by the Romans. After the Roman Empire split in the fourth century AD, Montenegro straddled the cultural fault line between West (Roman Catholic) and East (Orthodox Christian). As Rome crumbled in the sixth and seventh centuries, the Slavs moved in—some Orthodox, some Catholic.

By the 10th century, Montenegro's Slavs had organized into a sovereign state, affiliated with the Byzantine (Eastern Roman) Empire. Thanks to its protected location, medieval Kotor became a major city of the salt trade. The area further flourished in the 14th century, under the Serbian emperor Dušan the Mighty. Notorious for his aggressive law enforcement—chopping off the hand of a thief, slicing off the nose of a liar—Dušan made the Bay of Kotor a particularly safe place to do business. If a visiting merchant was robbed, the nobleman who controlled that land would be ruthlessly punished. Soon 2,000-horse caravans could pass without a worry along this fjord.

But the Serbian Empire went into steep decline after Dušan. As the Ottomans threatened to invade in the 15th century, Kotor's traders turned to Venice for help. The Venetian Republic would control this bay for nearly 400 years, and it was never taken by the Ottomans.

In the early 19th century, when Venice fell to Napoleon, the Bay of Kotor came briefly under the control of France, then Russia, then Austria. With the decline of feudal traditions and trading wealth, the Bay of Kotor entered a period of architectural stagnation—preserving many time-warp towns that travelers appreciate today.

When Montenegro became part of Yugoslavia following World War I, the Serbs (who felt a cultural affinity with the Montenegrins that wasn't always reciprocated) laid claim to the Montenegrin coast as their own little patch of seafront. This Serb connection helped Montenegro avoid the initial violence of the breakup of Yugoslavia. But a few years later, the Montenegrins decided it was time to part ways. For the rest of the story, see the "Montenegro: Birth of a Nation" sidebar, later.

themselves on their particularly mild climate, sheltered by the fjord. They claim that it never drops below 50 degrees Fahrenheit. Town symbols include banana trees and the mimosa flower, which blooms all winter long. Each February, as much of Europe (and most of Montenegro) is under a blanket of snow, Herceg Novi proudly hosts a Mimosa Festival.

Despite its tropical cachet, Herceg Novi is basically a mess. (Don't worry—the drive gets much prettier later on.) Why so much ugliness compared to Croatia? For one thing, Tito viewed Croatia's Dalmatian Coast as a gold mine of hard Western currency—so he was inclined to keep it Old World-charming. But in Montenegro, a heritage of corruption and bribery spurred some unfortunate construction. ("Would five thousand dinars convince you to ignore my new hotel's code violations?") From an architectural point of view, it's a sad irony that gorgeous Dubrovnik was devastated by bombs while the gritty cities of Montenegro survived the war essentially unscathed. Today, Montenegro is encouraging the construction of top-end resort hotels to lure high rollers from around the world (such as James Bond, who came to "Montenegro" to join a poker tournament at the Casino Royale—actually filmed in the Czech Republic). But this new development is poorly regulated, threatening to turn Montenegro into a charmless, concrete Costa del Sol-style vacation zone. Enjoy the Bay of Kotor's pristine areas (which we'll enter soon) while you still can.

MONTENEGRO

• As you go through Herceg Novi, at the roundabout, follow signs for Budva, Kotor, and Trajekt/Ferry.

After the tunnel, you'll pass through **Zelenika**, once the end of the line for the Habsburg rail line from Vienna, which first brought tourism to this area.

You'll carry on through a few more dreary towns. Entertain yourself by gazing across the strait on your right to look for caves burrowed into the cliff face at sea level. These once provided shelter for Yugoslav warships. Also along this cliff, you'll see naval barracks. In **Bijela**, you'll pass a big industrial shipyard on your right; in addition to the rusty, hard-working ships you'll likely see here, this slip also services luxury yachts—another example of Montenegro's odd juxtaposition of gritty industry and nouveau wealth.

Eventually, you'll emerge into a more rustic setting. This fjordside road is lined with fishing villages, some now developed as resorts (including a few with severe communist-era touches). Each waterfront house seems to have its own little boat dock sticking out into the glassy water.

Soon you come to the town of **Kamenari**, where a ferry crosses the narrow strait to Lepetane. At this point, if the traffic is moving right along and congestion is minimal, keep going along the main road. (You'll come back across on this ferry later on.)

However, if you find yourself stuck behind a column of slow-

*moving tour buses (most likely in summer) and want to break out of the rut, consider **reversing the direction** of the remaining loop. To do this, take the ferry now from Kamenari to Lepetane and drive to Kotor to sightsee there. (Choose between the scenic but slow road to Kotor through Prčanj, or the faster road through Tivat.) Then return from Kotor to Dubrovnik by way of Perast, Risan, and so on (reversing the order of the remaining stops), back to Kamenari.*

If you stick to the route outlined below, watch for a convenient pullout on the right two minutes after leaving Kamenari (just after the Kostanjica sign; likely packed with tour buses, by the Verige 65 restaurant) and stop to check out the narrowest point of the fjord, the...

Verige Strait

Any would-be invaders had to pass through this strategic bottleneck to reach the port towns inside the bay. It's narrow enough to carefully monitor (not even a quarter-mile wide), but deep enough to accommodate even today's megaships (more than 130 feet deep). Because this extremely narrow strait is easy to defend, whoever controlled the inside of the fjord was allowed to thrive virtually unchecked.

Centuries before Christ, the Bay of Kotor was home to the Illyrians—the mysterious ancestors of today's Albanians. In the third century BC, Illyrian Queen Teuta spanned this strait with an ingenious shipwrecking mechanism to more effectively collect taxes. To this day, many sunken ships litter the bottom of the bay. (Teuta was a little too clever for her own good: Her shrewdness and success, not to mention her encouragement of piracy, attracted the attention of the on-the-rise Romans, who seized most of her holdings.)

In later times, chains were stretched across the bay here to control the entrance (the name Verige comes from a Slavic word for "chain"). Later still, the Venetians placed cannons on either side of the strait, with a clear shot at any entering ships. Looking across the wide part of the bay, notice the town of Perast (by the two islands). Perast—where we'll be stopping soon—was also equipped with cannons that could easily reach across the bay. This extensive defense network succeeded in keeping the Ottomans—and any other would-be invaders—out of the bay.

• *Continue driving around the fjord. You'll pass through the village of...*

Morinj

This town is known for two starkly different reasons: First, it's the home of a recommended restaurant with fine food in a gorgeous setting (Konoba Ćatovića Mlini); another, more casual eatery sits nearby (both described later, under "Eating in Kotor"). And second, it was the site of a concentration camp for Croat prisoners captured during the 1991-1992 siege of Dubrovnik. Some 300 civil-ians from in and near Dubrovnik were forcibly brought here, where they lived in horrifying conditions. After the war, six of the guards from this camp were convicted of war crimes.

• *After going through Morinj and some other small villages, you'll pass through the larger resort town of...*

Risan

Back in Greek times, when the Bay of Kotor was known as *Sinus Rhizonicus,* Risan was the leading town of the bay. Later, during the Illyrian Queen Teuta's brief three-year reign, Risan was her capital. Today the town is still home to the scant remains of Teuta's castle (on the hilltop just before town), but it's mostly notable for its giant, abandoned communist eyesore—Hotel Teuta.

In the town center, historians may want to turn off to the left (at the brown *Roman Mosaics* sign) for a quick look at a few partly intact mosaic floors of the second-century AD Roman **Villa Urbana** (€5, daily 8:00-17:00, off-season until 15:00). You'll enter through a small modern building to access the large, covered foot-print of the villa. Between the knee-high stone walls are mosaics of checkerboards, stylized marine life (including calamari), and—most significant—a small mosaic of reclining Hypnos, the god of dreams.

• *Continue on to Perast. As you approach the town, take the right fork (marked with a brown sign) directly down into Perast; or you can first take the left fork to pass above town for sweeping views over the bay, then backtrack down into the town center.*

Perast

Called the "Pearl of Venetian Baroque," little Perast is a handy and scenic spot to stretch your legs and consider a boat trip. In high

season (June-Oct), you're required to pay to park near the entrance of town, and then walk 10 level minutes or ride the free shuttle bus into the town center; at other times, you may be allowed to drive along the waterfront road and park for free in front of the church.

Remember that Perast, with its cannons aimed at the Verige Strait across the bay, was an essential link in the Bay of Kotor's fortifications. In exchange for this important duty, Venice re-warded Perast with privileged tax-free status, and the town became

MONTENEGRO

extremely wealthy. Ornate mansions proliferated here during its 17th- and 18th-century heyday. But after Venice fell to Napoleon, and the Bay of Kotor's economy changed, Perast's singular defensive role disappeared. With no industry, no hinterland, and no natural resources, Perast stagnated—leaving it a virtual open-air museum of Venetian architecture.

Go to the tallest steeple in town, overlooking a long and narrow harborfront square. Perast is centered on its too-big (and incomplete) **Church of St. Nicholas**—dedicated to the patron saint of fishermen. It was originally designed to extend out into the sea (the old church, still standing, was to be torn down). But Napoleon's troops came marching in before the builders got that far, so the plans were scuttled—and this massive partial-church was instead simply grafted on to the existing, modest church.

Go inside (free, treasury-€1, sporadic hours, generally daily June-Sept 9:00-18:00, until 14:00 off-season and closed Dec-March except by request—ask locals around the church if someone can let you in; closed during Mass). Beyond the small sanctuary, you'll find a treasury with relics and icons. Look for the priceless crucifix from the school of the 18th-century Venetian artist Giovanni Battista Tiepolo (#1, in the center display case), with Jesus on one side, and Mary and the saints on the other. Beyond the treasury is what was to be the main apse (altar area) of the unfinished massive church (notice it's at a right angle

to the altar of the existing smaller church). The rough, unadorned brick walls make it clear that they didn't get very far. Check out the model of the ambitious but never-built church. The Baroque main altar is by Bernini's student Francesco Cabianca, who lived in this area and was always trying to earn money to pay off his gambling debts. The small room at the end displays old vestments.

You can pay €1 to climb the **church tower** for the view. I'd skip the Town Museum, farther down the waterfront (fills a grand old hall with paintings, furniture, model ships, and other historical bric-a-brac).

Eating in Perast: For a seafront meal, window-shop the restaurants with seating out on the water. **$$$ Conte,** filling a pier in the middle of town, is a classic choice (tel. 032/373-687).

• *Before leaving Perast, take a close look at the two islands just offshore (and consider paying a visit).*

St. George (Sv. Đorđe) and Our Lady of the Rocks (Gospa od Škrpjela)

These twin islands—one natural, the other man-made—come with a fascinating story.

The **Island of St. George** (the smaller, rocky island with trees and a monastery—closed to tourists) was once part of the fortifica-

tion of the Bay of Kotor. Nearby was an underwater reef with a small section poking above the surface. According to legend, two fishermen noticed a strange light emanating from the reef in the early-morning fog. Rowing out to the island, they discovered an icon of Our Lady. They attempted to bring it ashore, but it kept washing back out again to the same spot. Taking this celestial hint, local seamen returning home from a journey began dropping rocks into the bay in this same place. The tradition caught on, more and more villagers dropped in rocks of their own, and eventually more than a hundred old ships and other vessels were loaded with stones and intentionally sunk in this spot. And so, over two centuries, an entire island was formed in the middle of the bay.

Flash forward to today's **Our Lady of the Rocks** (the flat island with the dome-topped Catholic church). In the 17th century, locals built this Baroque church on this holy site and filled it with symbols of thanks for answered prayers. Step inside (free entry) to explore the collection: silver votive plaques—many of them with images of ships in storms or battles—given by appreciative sailors who survived; 1,700 silver and gold votive plaques from other grateful worshippers; 68 canvases by local Baroque painter Tripo Kokolja; and a huge collection of dried wedding bouquets given by those who had nothing else to offer (the church is a popular place for weddings). Take a close look at the main altar. That legendary icon, which refused to budge from this spot, still caps the altar today. The faithful squeeze into the very tight space behind the altar, where a hole in the back of the structure lets them reach through and touch the original reef where the icon was found. Give it a try—if you dare.

The adjacent **museum** is an entertaining mishmash of items. The entry price includes a fun little tour by Davorka, Nataša, or Sandra (€2, May-Oct daily 9:00-17:00, off-season opens sporadically with boat arrival—or call ahead to Davorka's mobile 069-621-322). Just inside, study the models of both islands. The artificial one—the one you're on—is shaped vaguely like a boat. The collection comprises a wide range of ancient artifacts, including a glass case displaying fragments dating—staggeringly—from 3500

MONTENEGRO

BC (found in the hills just above Perast). There's also a small modern-art gallery with various depictions of the two islands created by artists who came here and were inspired by this place; paintings of ships commissioned by local sailors (notice that most have a saintly image of Mary and the Baby Jesus hovering nearby); and other gifts given through the ages. Upstairs, near

the gift-shop counter, look for the amazing embroidery made by a local woman who toiled over it for more than 25 years. She used her own hair for the hair of the angels—which you can see fade from brown to gray as she aged (beginning at around 3 o'clock and going clockwise, you'll see the subtle change in color).

Getting There: Boats to Our Lady of the Rocks leave from in front of St. Nicholas' Church in Perast—look for the guys milling around the harborfront with boats ready to go. The going rate is €5/person round-trip, but Zoran (who has the boat with the red awning marked *Taxi Boat Perast*) offers an RS% discount—€4/person if you show this book. If it's quiet, they'll drop you on the island for about 30 minutes before returning to get you.

• *When you're ready to move on, continue driving around the fjord. After the large town of Orahovac, you'll see part of the bay roped off for a mussel farm; these farms do best when located where mountain rivers spill into the bay. And a hundred or so yards later, you cross a bridge spanning the don't-blink-or-you'll-miss-it...*

Ljuta River

According to locals, this is the shortest river in the world—the source is under the cliff just to the left of the bridge, and it meets the sea just to the right. Short as it is, it's hardly a trickle—in fact, its name means "Angry River" for its fierce flow during heavy rains. The river actually courses underground for several miles before emerging here. Like the Karst area south of Ljubljana, this is a karstic landscape—limestone that's honeycombed with underground rivers, caves, and canyons.

• *Immediately after the bridge, look for the turnoff (on the right) to the recommended Restoran Stari Mlini (Old Mill)—a tranquil spot for a meal or drink. Fittingly, the restaurant sits right where the river comes tumbling out—the perfect spot to harness that hydropower.*

Continuing along the fjord, as you pass through the town of Dobrota, look across the bay to the village of...

Montenegro: Birth of a Nation

Montenegro, like Croatia and Slovenia, was one of the six republics that constituted the former Yugoslavia. When these republics began splitting away in the early 1990s, Montenegro—always allied closely with Serbia, and small enough to slip under the radar—decided to remain in the union. When the dust had settled, four of the six republics had seceded, leaving only two united as "Yugoslavia": Serbia and Montenegro.

At first, Montenegrin Prime Minister Milo Đukanović was on friendly terms with Serbia's Slobodan Milošević. But in the late 1990s, as Milošević's political stock plummeted, Montenegro began to inch away from Serbia. Eager to keep its access to the coast (and the many Serbs who lived there), Serbia made concessions that allowed Montenegro to gradually assert its independence. In 1996, Montenegro boldly adopted the German mark as its official currency to bail out of the inflating Yugoslav dinar.

By 2003, the country of Yugoslavia was no more, and the loose union was renamed "Serbia and Montenegro." Thus began a three-year transition period that allowed Montenegro to test the waters of real independence. During this time, Serbia and Montenegro were united only in defense—legislation, taxation, currency, and most governmental functions were separate. And after three years, Montenegro would be allowed to hold a referendum for full independence.

That fateful vote took place on May 21, 2006. In general, ethnic Montenegrins tended to favor independence, while ethnic Serbs wanted to stay united with Serbia. To secede, Montenegro needed 55 percent of the vote. By the slimmest of margins—half a percent, or just 2,300 votes—the pro-independence faction won. On June 3, 2006, Montenegro officially declared independence. (To save face, two days later, Serbia also "declared independence" from Montenegro.)

Today, Montenegrins are excited to have their own little country and enthusiastic about eventually joining the European Union. But many view independence as an epilogue rather than a climax. Shortly after the referendum, I asked a Montenegrin when the countries would officially separate. He chuckled and said, "Three years ago."

Prčanj

This town is famous as the former home of many centuries' worth of wealthy sea captains. When the Bay of Kotor was part of the Austrian Empire, Emperor Franz Josef came to Prčanj. Upon being greeted by some 50 uniformed ship captains, he marveled that such a collection of seafarers had been imported for his visit...not realizing that every one of them lived nearby.

• *Keep on driving. When you see the giant moat with the town wall, and* *the smaller wall twisting up the hill above, you'll know you've arrived in **Kotor** (described later).*

Before leaving Kotor, make a decision about where you want to go next. You have three basic options: Budva Riviera; the mountainous Montenegrin interior; or back to Croatia (see the next section).

*Continuing past Kotor's Old Town, you'll follow the edge of the fjord. At the far end of town (and the fjord), you'll come to a roundabout. Bearing left at the roundabout takes you toward the handy tunnel to the **Budva Riviera**—or, along this same road, if you turn right after the cemetery and just before the tunnel, you'll take the extremely twisty road up, up, up into the **Montenegrin interior** (Njeguši and Cetinje).*

Once you're finished in Montenegro, it'll be time to head to the...

Lepetane-Kamenari Ferry

To return to Dubrovnik, you can go back the way you came. Or, for a quicker route, consider the ferry that cuts across the narrow part of the fjord (between the towns of Lepetane and Kamenari). The boat departs from the town of Lepetane.

From Kotor, you have two options to reach the ferry: The easiest option is to leave Kotor, bear left at the roundabout at the far end of town, and take the tunnel toward Budva. Once through the tunnel, follow signs into Tivat, and continue straight through Tivat on the main road to reach Lepetane, which is a few miles beyond the end of town. Or, for a more challenging but more scenic route, simply turn right at the roundabout and continue driving on the waterfront road clockwise around the bay (through Prčanj and Stoliv) until you land in Lepetane. This road is extremely narrow (one lane, with an Adriatic shoulder) and can be exhausting. However, it also offers grand views back across the fjord at Kotor, Perast, and other picturesque towns you came through earlier.

No matter how you approach, remember that "ferry" is *trajekt* (it's also signed for *Herceg Novi*—the city across the bay). The boat goes continuously (in slow times, you may have to wait briefly for enough cars to show up), and the crossing takes just four minutes (it takes longer to load and unload all the cars than it does to cross). A small car and its passengers pay €4.50 each way.

On your way back to Dubrovnik after the ferry, if there are long lines at the primary border crossing—or you want a quieter, more scenic return—use the Konfin alternate crossing described earlier: After exiting Igalo, just before the border, take the first left after the Hipermarket and Petrol gas station (following small yellow sign to *Višnjići*)—watch for the turnoff on the left that's marked *granični prijelaz Konfin*. From the Konfin border, follow signs to *Dubrovnik* (on back roads at first, later merging with the main road).

Kotor

Butted up against a steep cliff, cradled by a calm sea, naturally
sheltered by its deep-in-the-fjord position, and watched over by
imposing fortifications, the town of Kotor is as impressive as it is
well-protected. Though it's enjoyed a long and illustrious history,
today's Kotor is a time-capsule retreat for travelers seeking an unspoiled Adriatic town.

The ancient town of Catarum—named for the Roman word
for "contracted" or "strangled," as the sea is at this gnarled fjord—
was first mentioned in the first century AD. Like the rest of the
region, Kotor's next two millennia were layered with history as it
came under the control of foreign powers: Illyrians, Romans, Serbs,
Venetians, Russians, Napoleonic soldiers, Austrians, Tito's Yugoslavia...and now, finally, Montenegrins. Each group left its mark,
and Kotor has its share of both Catholic and Orthodox churches.

Through all those centuries, Kotor avoided destruction by
warfare. But it was damaged by earthquakes—including the same
1667 quake that leveled Dubrovnik (known here as the "Great
Shaking"), as well as a devastating 1979 earthquake from which
the city is still cleaning up.

With an extremely inviting Old Town that seems custom-built
for aimless strolling, Kotor is an idyllic place to while away a few
hours. Though it's sometimes called a "little Dubrovnik," Kotor is
more low-key, less ambitious, less historic, flatter, and much smaller than its more famous neighbor. And yet, with its own special
spice that's exciting to sample, Kotor is a hard place to tear yourself
away from.

Orientation to Kotor

Kotor (or Cattaro in Italian) has a compact Old Town shaped like a
triangle. The two sides facing the bay are heavily fortified by a thick
wall, and the third side huddles under the cliff face. A meandering
defensive wall climbs the mountainside directly behind and above
town. While only 3,000 people live within the Old Town walls,
greater Kotor has a population of about 12,000.

The Old Town's mazelike street plan is confusing, but it's so
small and atmospheric that getting lost is more fun than frustrating. The natives virtually ignore addresses, including the names of
streets and squares. Most Old Town addresses are represented simply as "Stari Grad" (Old Town) and a number, useless if you're trying to navigate by streets. To make matters worse, a single square
can have several names—so one map labels it Trg od Katedrale
(Cathedral Square), while another calls it Pjaca Sv. Tripuna (Pi-

MONTENEGRO

Kotor

"PARKING BENOVO"

NORTHERN GATE

Škurda River

TOWN WALLS

ST. NICHOLAS' CHURCH

ST. MARY'S

WALK ENDS

WC

4 · BAZAAR

ST. LUKE'S

9 · 3

Access to Upper Town Walls

To Parking Benovo", "Parking Urc" & Perast

Square of Arms

WC

7 · St. Luke's Square

Trg od Kina

KARAMPANA WELL

MARITIME MUSEUM OF MONTENEGRO

WALK BEGINS

MAIN TOWN GATE

1

2

6

CHURCH OF OUR LADY OF HEALTH

"PARKING RIVA"

POST

Trg od Brašna

Pjaca Sv. Tripuna

CATHEDRAL OF ST. TRYPHON

CRUISE SHIP PORT

JADRANSKI PUT

8

10

Pjaca od Salate

Access to Upper Town Walls

Bay of Kotor

100 Meters

100 Yards

5

To Bus Station, Budva & Cetinje

SOUTHERN GATE

N

Accommodations
1 Hotel Vardar
2 Hotel Villa Duomo
3 D&Sons Apartments
4 Hotel Marija
5 Old Town Hostel

Eateries & Other
6 City Restaurant
7 Cesarica
8 Produce Market
9 The Old Winery
10 Pharmacy (2)

azza of St. Tryphon). My advice: Don't fret about street or square names. Simply navigate with a map from the TI and by asking locals for directions. Thanks to the very manageable size of the Old Town, this is easier than it sounds.

TOURIST INFORMATION

The TI is in a kiosk just outside the Old Town's main entrance gate (daily May-Oct 8:00-20:00, Nov-April until 17:00, tel. 032/325-950, www.tokotor.me).

ARRIVAL IN KOTOR

By Car: Approaching town, you'll first see Kotor's substantial wall, which overlooks a canal. You can park in one of three pay lots, which are all priced around €1/hour: "Parking Riva," along the bay immediately across from the main gate, is the closest to the Old Town and a bit more expensive (to the right just after crossing the bridge by the wall); "Parking Benovo," in the lot across the canal (on the left just before the bridge by the wall—you'll be sent back here if the first lot is full); or "Parking Urc" (a bit farther out and along the water). All three are easily walkable from the Old Town entrance. Be sure you've parked legally, in one of these designated lots; while locals brazenly leave their cars anywhere they like, tourists get towed without remorse.

By Bus: The bus station is about a half-mile (10-minute walk) south of the Old Town. Arriving here, simply exit to the right and walk straight up the road—you'll run into the embankment and town wall.

Sights in Kotor

Because of its tangled alleys and irregular street plan, Kotor feels bigger than it is. But after a few minutes of strolling, you'll discover you're going in circles and realize it's quite compact. (In fact, aimless wandering is Kotor's single best activity.) As you ramble, keep an eye out for these key attractions. I've listed them roughly in the order of a counterclockwise route through town, beginning outside the main entrance gate.

▲Main Town Gate (Glavna Gradska Vrata)

The wide-open **square** fronting the bay and waterfront marina now welcomes visitors. But for centuries, its purpose was exactly the opposite: As the primary point of entry into this heavily fortified town, it was the last line of defense. Before the embankment was built, the water came directly to this door, and there was only room for one ship to tie up at a time. If a ship got this far (through the gauntlet we saw back at the Verige Strait), it was carefully examined here again to levy taxes before its passengers could disembark. This double-checkpoint was designed to foil pirates who might fly the flag of a friend to get through the strait, only to launch a surprise attack once here. (The pirates' primary booty wasn't silver or gold, but men—kidnapped for ransom, or, if ransom wasn't paid, as slaves to row on ships.)

Check out the pinkish **gate** itself. The oldest parts of this gate date from 1555. It once featured a Venetian lion, then the double-headed eagle of the Habsburg Empire. But today, most of the symbolism touts Tito's communism (notice the stars and the old

MONTENEGRO

Yugoslav national seal at the top). The big date (November 21, 1944) commemorates this area's liberation from the Nazis by Tito's homegrown Partisan Army. The provocative Tito quote *(tuđe nećemo svoje nedamo)* means, roughly, "Don't take what's ours, and we won't take what's yours."

• *Notice the* **TI** *in the kiosk just to the left of the gate. Then go through the gate into town. You'll emerge into the...*

Square of Arms (Trg od Oržja)

Do a quick spin-tour of the square, which is ringed with artifacts of the city's complex history. Looking to the left, you'll see a long building lined with cafés. This was once the palace of the rector, who ruled Kotor on behalf of Venice. Princes could watch the action from their long balcony overlooking the square, which served as the town's living room. Later, the palace became the Kotor Town Hall. Beyond the

long building, two other buildings poke out into the square (on either side of the lane leading out of the square). The one on the right is the Venetian arsenal, the square's namesake. The yellowish one on the left is the "French Theater," named for its purpose during the time this area was under Napoleon's control. Directly across from the gate you just came through, you'll see the town's Bell Tower, one of Kotor's symbols. The odd triangular structure at its base was once the town pillory, where wrongdoers would be chained and subjected to public ridicule of the rudest kind imaginable. In the little recessed square just right of that, you'll spot the recommended, copper-roofed Hotel Vardar. ATMs around this square dispense euros, which may be handy since Montenegro is surrounded by nations that use other currencies.

• *Walk down the long part of the square directly ahead of where you entered (toward Hotel Vardar). Take the broad lane angling off to the right (paved with red-and-white-striped tiles), which leads past mansions of Kotor's medieval big shots. Cross a square (Trg od Brašna) and turn left down the little lane at its end. After one short block, you'll hit Pjaca Sv. Tripuna (a.k.a. Trg od Katedrale), home to the...*

▲Cathedral of St. Tryphon (Katedrala Sv. Tripuna)

Even though most of today's Kotorians are Orthodox, Kotor's most significant church is Catholic. According to legend, in 809, Venetian merchants were sailing up the coast from Nicea (in today's Turkey) with the relics of St. Tryphon—a third-century martyr and today's patron saint of gardeners. A storm hit as they approached the Bay of Kotor, so they took shelter here. Every time they tried to leave, the weather worsened...so they finally got the message that St. Tryphon's remains should remain in Kotor.

Cost and Hours: €3, daily 9:00-18:00, possibly later in summer; Dec-Feb 10:00-16:00; Mass on Sun at 10:00.

Visiting the Cathedral: Take in the cathedral's **exterior.** The church has been rebuilt after four different earthquakes—most extensively after the 1667 quake, when it achieved its current Renaissance-Baroque blend. That earthquake, which also contributed to Dubrovnik's current appearance, destroyed three-quarters of Kotor's buildings. A fire swept the city, and all of the dead bodies attracted rats (and with them, the plague)—a particularly dark chapter in Kotor's history.

Why are the two **towers** different? There are plenty of legends, but the most likely answer is that restorers working after 1667 simply ran out of money before they finished the second one. Notice the Church of Our Lady of Health way up on the hill above this church—built in thanks to God by survivors of the plague (it also serves as part of the town fortifications—described later).

Within the cathedral, the **nave** of the church is marginally interesting, with stout columns; surviving Byzantine-style frescoes under the arches—all that's left of paintings that once covered the church; and a fine 15th-century silver-and-gold altar covered by a delicate canopy.

But the best part is the **reliquary** upstairs. Find the stairs near the cathedral's main entrance and walk up to the chapel. Behind the Baroque altar (by Bernini's student Francesco Cabianca, whose work we saw in Perast) and the screen are 48 different relics. In the center is St. Tryphon—his bones are in a silver casket, and his head is in the golden chalice next to it. In the small room up the stairs, examine the fascinating icon of the Madonna and Child from the 15th century (it's in a freestanding wooden frame with a crucified Jesus on the other side; to find it, you may have to look around back or rotate the frame). The painting exemplifies this town's position as a bridge between Western and Eastern Christianity: The faces, more lifelike, are Western-style (Catholic) Gothic; the stiff, elongated bodies are more Eastern (Orthodox) and Byzantine-style. From here, take a slow walk around the upper gallery of the church to see its displays of relics (such as arms and feet covered in silver), paintings, vestments, and other ecclesiastical items.

• *Exit the church, veer right, and exit the square on the street near the recommended City Restaurant, marked by trees. In a block, you'll wind up on a little square that's home to the...*

Maritime Museum of Montenegro (Pomorski Muzej Crne Gore)

Like so many Adriatic towns, Kotor's livelihood is tied to the sea. This humble museum covers three floors and explores that important heritage. As you climb the stairway, notice the evocative maps and etchings of old Kotor. Portraits of salty swashbucklers, traditional costumes, and 98 coats of arms representing aristocratic families who have lived here (ringing the main room upstairs) are all reminders of the richness of Kotor's history. You'll see a display of rifles and swords (some with fun ornamental decorations illustrating the art of killing) and lots of model ships. The museum is housed in the Gregorina Palace, one of dozens of aristocratic mansions that dot the Old Town—yet another reminder of the historically high concentration of wealth and power in this little settlement.

Cost and Hours: €4, includes English audioguide; July-Aug Mon-Sat 9:00-20:00, closes earlier off-season, Sun until 13:00 year-round; on Trg Grgurina, tel. 032/304-720, www. museummaritimum.com.

• *Turn right out of the museum, and make a right again on the first lane. After 10 yards, you'll pass a well on your left called the...*

Karampana

This well served as Kotor's only public faucet until the early 20th century. As such, it was also the top place in town for gossip, like the office water cooler. It's said that if your name was mentioned here, you knew you had arrived. Today, though the chatter is no longer raging on this square, the town's gossip magazine is called *Karampana*. While the pump still works (swing the pendulum once and keep it there), it's sometimes disconnected to prevent tourists from swinging it back and forth too aggressively.

• *Continue straight past the well into the next square...*

▲St. Luke's Square (Trg Svetog Luke)

There are two Serbian Orthodox churches on this pretty square, each with the typical Orthodox church features: a squat design, narrow windows, and portly domes. Little **St. Luke's Church**

(Crkva Sv. Luka), in the middle of the square, dates from the 12th century. Locals debate long and hard as to whether St. Luke's was originally built as a Catholic church or an Orthodox one. (Although it looks Orthodox, it was constructed at a time when even Catholic churches were built in the Orthodox style.) Regardless of its origin, during the Venetian era the church did double duty as a house of worship for both. These days, it's decidedly Orthodox. Step into the humble interior (free, daily May-Oct 10:00-20:00, Nov-April 8:00-13:00 & 17:00-19:00).

The bigger and much-newer **St. Nicholas' Church** (Crkva Sv. Nikola), was built in 1909—because of its Neo-Byzantine design, it has similarly spherical domes and slitlike windows (free, same hours as St. Luke's).

Before entering, notice how the Orthodox crosses on the steeples of St. Nicholas' Church differ from the cross seen in Roman Catholic churches (known as a Latin cross). In addition to the standard crossbar, Orthodox crosses often also have a second, smaller crossbar near the top (representing the *I.N.R.I.* plaque that was displayed above Jesus' head). Sometimes Orthodox crosses also feature a third, angled crossbar at the bottom. Many believe that rather than being nailed directly to the cross, Jesus' feet were nailed to a crossbar like this one to prolong his suffering. The slanted angle represents Jesus' forgiveness of the thief crucified to his right (the side that's pointing up)...and suggests where the unrepentant thief on his left ended up.

Stepping into these (or any other Orthodox) churches, you'll immediately notice some key differences from Catholic churches: no pews (worshippers stand through the service as a sign of respect), tall and skinny candles (representing prayers), and a screen of icons, called an iconostasis, in the middle of the sanctuary to separate the material world from the holy world (where the Bible is kept). For more about Orthodox worship, see the sidebar on page 317.

Before continuing, enjoy this square's lazy ambience. The big building fronting the square is a music school, and the students practicing here fill this already pleasant public space with an appealing soundtrack.

• *Go down the street to your left as you face St. Nicholas and keep an eye out for the banners announcing the Kotor bazaar, on your right. In the ruins of a Dominican monastery destroyed in the 1667 quake, you'll find a little marketplace selling souvenirs. If you continue on down the street you'll wind up back at the Square of Arms. But first try getting lost, then found again, in Kotor's delightful maze of streets.*

The town's final attraction is above your head. To go there directly, face St. Nicholas' Church, turn right, and walk straight for two blocks until you reach St. Mary's Church (named for one of four Catholic saints who came from the Bay of Kotor—which some faithful locals call the Bay of Saints). If you skirt the church along its right side—down the narrow lane with two arches—you'll find the entrance to the town walls.

▲▲Town Walls (Gradske Zidine)

Kotor's fortifications begin as stout ramparts along the waterfront, then climb up the sheer cliff face behind town in a dizzying zigzag line. If there's a more elaborate city wall in Europe, I haven't seen it. A proud Kotorian bragged to me, "These fortifications cost more to build than any palace in Europe."

Imagine what it took to create this "Great Wall of Kotor." The wall is nearly three miles long and sits on some extremely inac-

cessible terrain. It was built in fits and starts over a millennium (9th-19th centuries, though most of it was completed during the Venetian occupation in the 17th and 18th centuries). Its thickness varies from 6 to 50 feet, and the tallest parts are 65 feet high. Sections higher on the hill—with thinner walls, built before the age of gunpowder—are the oldest, while the thick walls along the water are most recent. It was all worth it: The fortified town survived many attacks, including a two-month Ottoman siege in 1657.

If you're in great shape, consider scrambling along the walls and turrets above the Old Town.

Cost and Hours: Entry to the walls is €8, generally daily 8:00-20:00.

Hiking the Walls: If you go all the way up to the top fortress and back again, it'll take around an hour and a half round-trip (depending on how fast you go). This involves climbing 1,355 steps (an elevation gain of more than 700 feet)—don't overestimate your endurance or underestimate the heat. ("Am-I-*that*-out-of-shape?" tourists routinely find themselves winded and stranded high above town.) Bring plenty of water, along with a hat and sunscreen, and wear sturdy shoes. Most of the way, there's both a ramp and uneven stairs, but the

route is in poor repair, with a lot of rough, rocky patches.

It's best to tackle the walls clockwise. (Even if you're not doing the hike, you can visually trace this route.) Find the entrance at the back-left corner of town (near St. Mary's Church, through the alley with the two arches over it). Pay the entry fee and begin hiking up. On the way up, you might see the sign explaining that the fortress reconstruction was funded by the United States in 2004—if you're a US taxpayer, consider this hike your tax dollars at work.

First climb as high as the **Church of Our Lady of Health** (Crkva Gospe od Zdravlj). This is the halfway mark—about 20 minutes from the base at a good pace. While some believe this church has miraculous healing powers, everyone agrees it offers some of the best views down over Kotor.

From this church, you can either cut back down toward the Old Town, or—if you're not exhausted yet—keep hiking up to the tippy-top **Fortress of St. John** (figure another 30 minutes from the church, if you're in decent shape). Built on the remains of fortifications from the Illyrians (you can scan the third-century BC remains just beyond the fort), this was the headquarters for the entire wall network below it. There's not much to see here, but it is fun to play "king of the castle" exploring the ruined shell—and the views, with 360 degrees of Montenegrin cliffs, are spectacular.

Once you've finished touring the wall, enjoy your reward: a downhill walk with head-on views of the Bay of Kotor. On the

way down, watch your step on the slippery-even-when-dry marble stairs, highly polished by the feet of centuries of visitors. At the round terrace below the church, you can head to the right (back the way you came); or, for a different path, head left following *powder magazine* signs, then down (right) at the fork. The ticket-seller warned me that he's often seen people wipe out on the very last step on their way down—so exhausted after the demanding hike that they let their guard down.

MONTENEGRO

Sleeping in Kotor

Kotor is an enjoyable place to spend the night. (Given its popularity as a cruise port, and among side-trippers from Dubrovnik, only a tiny fraction of visitors bother to sleep here.) However, the town has two big disadvantages: inexplicably high prices (you'll sleep more affordably in Dubrovnik) and lots of nighttime noise from boisterous bars. Assume it'll be loud anywhere, and pack earplugs.

$$$ Hotel Vardar has 24 rooms with mod bathrooms smack-dab in the middle of the Old Town. This classic old copper-roofed hotel has been renovated from top to bottom, leaving it tastefully chic and at the top of this price range. While convenient, the dead-central location can come with some noise, especially on weekends—request a quieter room (elevator, Stari Grad 476, tel. 032/325-084, www.hotelvardar.com, info@hotelvardar.com).

$$$ Hotel Villa Duomo is a stylish refuge just down the street from the cathedral. The 13 stony-chic rooms share an interior terrace where breakfast is served in good weather (Stari Grad 358, tel. 032/323-111, www.villaduomo.com, villaduomo@yahoo.com).

$$ D&Sons Apartments has six good, upscale apartments along an atmospheric, café-lined lane at the back edge of the Old Town (no breakfast but kitchenettes, Stari Grad 490, mobile 069-050-094, www.dandsons.com, dandsons@t-com.me, Dražan).

$ Hotel Marija, an Old World throwback on an Old Town square, offers 17 rooms and wood-paneled halls. Request a quieter room in the back (on Trg od Kina, Stari Grad 449, tel. 032/325-062, http://hotelmarija.me, hotel.marija.kotor@t-com.me).

¢ Old Town Hostel is a budget option in the Old Town, filling a stony, labyrinthine 13th-century building with options ranging from 10-bed dorms to overpriced private rooms. There's youthful conviviality in the lounge and an inviting pool (no breakfast but kitchen in each room, Stari Grad 284, tel. 032/325-317, mobile 067-205-647, www.hostel-kotor.me, info@hostel-kotor.me).

Eating in Kotor

In coastal, Italian-influenced Kotor, the cuisine is very similar to Croatia's: seafood, pasta, and pizza. There are a few local specialties to look for, and at the top of the list is *Njeguški pršut*, the delicious smoked ham from the village of Njeguši high in the mountains above town (described later, under "The Montenegrin Interior"). While *pršut* (prosciutto) is beloved throughout the Balkans, *Njeguški pršut*'s rich, salty, smoky flavor is perhaps the best. It goes well with the local cow's cheese—smoked, of course.

Montenegro produces some surprisingly good (and expensive) wines. The biggest producer in the country—and one of the biggest in the Balkans—is Plantaže Podgorica, which corks up some 20 million bottles each year. While that kind of volume often doesn't come with quality, Plantaže's vintages are quite good and worth trying (if not impossible to avoid). The most popular red-wine grape is the dry, medium-bodied *vranac* (VRAH-nahts), which is distantly related to Italian *primitivo*, Californian zinfandel, and Croatian *plavac mali*. For white, you'll see the dry, fruity *krstač* (kur-STACH), similar to riesling.

As far as choosing restaurants in Kotor, there's not much to recommend. Truly great cuisine is rare here—I'd just settle for something scenic and functional. For a better-quality, memorable meal in a romantic setting, drivers can consider heading to Konoba Ćatovića Mlini or Restoran Stari Mlini (described later).

Simple Meals near the Cathedral: Find a shady perch at **$$ City Restaurant,** with breezy outdoor tables next to the Cathedral of St. Tryphon. Its well-varnished picnic tables are set within the little forest in the Old Town, and more tables fill a small square out front (daily 8:00 until late; mobile 069-378-179).

Local Fish: Buried deep in the Old Town, **$$$ Cesarica** offers unpretentious seafood in a casual, stony interior. They enjoy bragging that the owner, Petar, was a fisherman, so he has a line on the freshest ingredients (daily 9:00-23:00, Stari Grad 375, mobile 069-049-733).

Market: Just outside the Old Town wall, facing the harbor, is a lively open market that hops each morning (typically 9:00-14:00, busiest on Sat). This is a great place to gather ingredients for a picnic, including the delicious local smoked ham, *Njeguški pršut*.

Wine Bar: Montenegrin vintages are in the spotlight at **$$$$ The Old Winery** (Stara Vinarija), which fills an inviting space on a tight Old Town lane with convivial indoor and outdoor seating. It's a chance to enjoy a limited but appealing range of dishes that work well with wines from throughout the former Yugoslavia (about 50 wines available by the glass; frequent live music in season—piano in the morning, blues after 21:00; Stari Grad 483, mobile 067-500-738).

NEAR KOTOR

These very scenic options are situated on or near the bayside road, handy for dinner on your way back to Croatia. The first two restaurants sit in oasis-like settings near running water, which helps keep them cool during the hot summer months. Another dinner option on the way home to Dubrovnik—just over the Croatian border—are similar restaurants in Konavoski Dvori (see page 355).

In Ljuta

$$$$ Restoran Stari Mlini has a cozy interior and wonderful outdoor seating scattered around a spring-fed stream near an old, namesake water mill. Surrounded by trickling water, you'll dine on local cuisine, with an emphasis on seafood. If you prefer freshwater fish, you can choose your own trout from the pond (daily 12:00-24:00, tel. 032/333-555).

Near the Verige Strait, in Morinj

$$$$ Konoba Ćatovića Mlini is a memorable place worth the trek. Hiding in a sparse forest off the main fjordside road, this

oasis is situated amidst a series of ponds, streams, waterfalls, and bubbling springs, with both indoor and outdoor seating. The traditionally clad waiters are stiffly formal, mindful of the restaurant's good reputation. Family-run for 200 years, it's a local institution, yet it feels like a well-kept secret. Reservations are essential in summer (extensive wine list, daily 12:00-21:00, tel. 032/373-030, www.catovica-mlini.com). At the town of Morinj, watch for burgundy *Konoba Ćatovića Mlini* signs leading away from the water.

$$ Tramontana is a more affordable, still very scenic option overlooking a beach with grand fjord views, right along the main waterfront road on the way out of Morinj (daily 8:00-23:00, mobile 068-737-737).

Kotor Connections

From Kotor by Bus to: Perast (hourly, usually at :15 past the hour, every 2 hours on Sun, 30 minutes, departs from small bus stop near Old Town rather than bus station—ask TI for location), **Herceg Novi** (2/hour, 1 hour), **Budva** (2-3/hour, 40 minutes), **Cetinje** (2/hour, 1 hour), **Dubrovnik** (7/day in summer, less off-season, 2.5 hours—or can take much longer due to border delays), **Mostar** (2-3/day via Trebinje—likely at 11:00 and 22:00, 9 hours; also 1/day via Dubrovnik—likely at 14:40, 5.5 hours), **Zagreb** (2/day, including overnight option, 13-16 hours). Bus info: Tel. 032/325-809, AutobuskaStanicaKotor.me.

The Montenegrin Interior

Although Montenegro is trying to cultivate a glitzy beach-break cachet, for most of its history it has been thought of as a rugged mountain kingdom. While the coast—the focus of most of this chapter—was traditionally Venetian or Austrian, the true heart of Montenegro beat behind the sheer wall of mountains rising up from that seafront. And romantics, caught up in misty Balkan fantasies, still think of this inland area as the "real" Montenegro.

While the Bay of Kotor is the most accessible and appealing part of the country, those with more time might enjoy a detour up into the mountains. For a quick look at this area, the easiest loop takes you to the historic capital of Cetinje—a dull little town in its own right, but a fine excuse for a mountain joyride. You could do this whole loop in about 2.5 hours without stopping (about an hour from Kotor to Cetinje, then another hour to Budva, then a half-hour back to Kotor)—but if you want to stretch your legs in Njeguši or Cetinje, allow more time.

Montenegro Driving Tour

The Road into the Mountains

The road to Cetinje twists you up the mountain face that stretches high above Kotor—it's an incredibly scenic, white-knuckle drive. (Particularly since it can be clogged with cruise excursion buses, timid drivers may want to skip it.)

From Kotor, leave town toward Budva (bearing left at the roundabout). At the edge of Kotor, after the cemetery but before the big tunnel, take a right (marked for *Cetinje*) and begin your ascent. Cresting the first hill, go left to get to Cetinje (also marked for *Njeguši*). You'll wind up and up (past a small Roma encampment) on 25 numbered switchbacks. The road is a souvenir from the Habsburg era (1884). While Venetian rule brought sea trade, Austrian rule brought fortresses and infrastructure. After switchback #13, you'll pass an old customs house marking the former border between the Austro-Hungarian Empire and the Kingdom of Montenegro—a reminder that the coastline was not historically an integral part of Montenegrin cultural identity. As you near the top, look across the canyon to the left to spot the impossibly rough little donkey path that once was Cetinje's connection with the coast... like a tenuous umbilical cord tethering the mountainous interior to the outside world.

As you crest the hill, the vegetation changes—you're high above the Adriatic, with commanding views of Kotor and its bay (and great photo-op pullouts; the best is just after switchback #25).

Continuing inland, you find yourself in another world: poor, insular, and more Eastern (you'll see more Cyrillic lettering). Country farmhouses sell smoked ham, mountain cheese, and *medovina* (honey brandy). Before long, you reach a broad plain and the hamlet of...

Njeguši

The humble-seeming village of Njeguši (NYEH-goo-shee) is actually well-known among Montenegrins, with two very important claims to fame. This was the hometown of the House of Petrović-Njegoš, the dynasty that ruled Montenegro for much of its history (1696-1918). The family's favorite son was Petar II Petrović-Njegoš (1813-1851). Aside from ruling the country, Petar II is remembered most fondly as a great poet and playwright—sort of the Montenegrin Shakespeare.

Njeguši is also famous for producing its own special type of air-dried ham, called *Njeguški pršut*. Locals explain that, because this meadow overlooks the sea on one side and the mountains on the other, the wind changes direction 10 times each day, alternating between dry mountain breeze and salty sea air—perfect for seasoning and drying ham hocks. For good measure, the *pršut* is also smoked with beech wood. The blocky, white buildings lining the road that look like giant Monopoly houses are actually smokehouses, jammed with five layers of hanging ham hocks—thousands of euros' worth—silently aging. (More industry than you realize hides out in sleepy villages.) A couple of traditional restaurants at the heart of the village are happy to serve passing tourists a lunch of this local specialty. For more on *pršut*, see the sidebar on page 537.

From Njeguši to Cetinje

Continuing through Njeguši toward Cetinje, you'll twist up into more mountains—soon arriving in an even more rugged and inhospitable landscape than you passed on the road that brought you here from the coast. Eyeing this desolate scenery, you can understand why the visiting Lord Byron said of this place, "Am I in paradise or on the moon?" Along the mountain road that drops you down into Cetinje, each rock has the phone number of a vulture-esque road-repair service *(auto slep)* spray-painted onto it. Low-profile plaques mark the site of Tito-era ambush assassinations.

Keep an eye out (on the horizon to the right) for the pointy peak of the mountain called **Lovćen,** which is capped by an elaborate mausoleum, designed by the great Croatian sculptor Ivan Meštrović, and devoted to King Petar II Petrović-Njegoš. With more time, you could actually drive up to the top of this mountain for sweeping views across Montenegro.

Soon you reach the outskirts of...

Cetinje

Cetinje (TSEH-teen-yeh)—the historic "Old Royal Capital" of
Montenegro—is a fine but fallen-on-hard-times little burg that sits
cradled in a desolate valley surrounded by mighty peaks. The home
of the Montenegrin king since the 15th century, the city was destroyed and rebuilt several times. Under Tito, it provided shoes and
refrigerators for the country, but when Yugoslavia disintegrated, so
did the viability of Cetinje's economy. Many of its younger generation have left for employment along the coast in the tourism
industry.

Park in the town center and stroll the main street (Njegoševa).
At the end of this drag is the main square (Balšića Pazar), surrounded by low-key sights with sporadic opening hours: the **Ethnographic Museum** (traditional costumes and folk life), **Historical Museum** (tracing the story of Montenegro), **Njegoš Museum**
(dedicated to the beloved poet-king Petar II Petrović-Njegoš),
and **National Museum,** which honors King Nikola I, who ruled
from 1860 until 1918. While his residence is as poor and humble
a royal palace as you'll see in Europe, Nikola I thought big. He
married off five of his daughters into the various royal families of
Europe.

A short walk from the palace is the birthplace of the town,
Cetinje Monastery. It's dedicated to St. Peter of Cetinje, a legendary local priest who
carried a cross in one hand
and a sword in the other,
established the first set
of laws among Monte-
negrins, and inspired his
people to defend Christian
Montenegro against the
Muslim Ottomans. The
monastery also holds the
supposed right hand of St. John the Baptist. You are free to wander respectfully through the courtyard and church of this spiritual
capital of Serbian Orthodox Montenegro.

From Cetinje Back to the Coast

To avoid backtracking down the same twisty road you came up,
consider heading more directly back toward the coast from Cetinje.
Just follow signs for *Budva*. A few miles outside of Cetinje along
this road, look for the good **$$ Restoran Konak,** which serves
up tasty traditional dishes with indoor and outdoor seating (daily
8:00-23:00, tel. 041/761-011).

Continuing along this road, you'll pop out high above the
Budva Riviera. Looking out to sea, you'll spot the distinctive pen-

insula of Sveti Stefan off to the left, and the town of Budva to the right. If you have more time, linger along the coast to visit these sights (described next). Otherwise, head right to return to Kotor or Dubrovnik.

The Budva Riviera

Montenegrins boast, "Croatia's got islands, but we've got beaches!" Long swaths of coarse-sand and fine-pebble beaches surround the resort town of Budva, just south of Kotor. This 15-mile stretch of coast, called the "Budva Riviera," is unappealingly built up with a mix of cheap and luxury resort hotels—making it pale in comparison to the jagged saltiness of the Bay of Kotor or the romantic tidiness of Dalmatia. This region is a mecca for super-wealthy Russians, staking their claim to this patch of Adriatic seafront. But the area isn't without its charms. Aside from the pleasant Old Town of the region's unofficial capital, Budva, you'll discover a near-mythical haunt of the rich and famous: the highly exclusive resort peninsula of Sveti Stefan, an alluring view from afar, but difficult to visit. For me, more time in Kotor or an earlier return to Dubrovnik would be more satisfying than the trek to the Budva Riviera. But beach lovers who have plenty of time and a spirit of adventure will find this area merits a look.

GETTING TO THE BUDVA RIVIERA

Budva is about a 30-minute drive south of **Kotor.** The easiest approach is to continue past Kotor along the fjord, left at the roundabout, then through the tunnel (following *Budva* signs; exiting the tunnel, notice the sign in Cyrillic letters for Russki Radio 107.3—catering to Russian jet-setters). First, you'll reach the town of **Budva** (turn right at traffic light, following brown *Stari Grad* signs to the Old Town; parking is well-marked in modern complex next to Old Town). Continuing around the bay, you'll pass the busy, modern resort cluster of Bečići before reaching **Sveti Stefan.**

Sights on the Budva Riviera

Between the strings of resort hotels are two towns that deserve a quick visit.

Budva

The Budva Riviera's best Old Town has charming Old World lanes crammed with souvenir shops and holiday-making Serbs and Russians. While less appealing than Kotor, Budva at least offers a taste of romance between the resort sprawl.

Budva began as an "emporium" (market and trading center) for Greek seamen, and extremely valuable jewelry uncovered here indicates that some important people spent time here. Today, Budva's layout is simple and intuitive—a peninsula (flanked by beaches) with a big Venetian-style bell tower.

From the parking lot, head inside the Old Town walls and wander up the main drag, Njegoševa. Out at the tip of town, you'll pop out into a small café-lined square with a **Catholic church** (on the left, with an unusually modern 1970s mosaic behind the altar depicting St. John preaching on the Montenegrin coast) facing the Orthodox **Holy Trinity Church,** with gorgeous and colorful Orthodox decorations inside. Beyond that is a huge **citadel** that's imposing on the outside but dull on the inside; it's not worth paying to tour its museum of model ships, antiquarium (old library), restaurant, and less-than-thrilling sea views.

Sveti Stefan

Like a mirage hovering just offshore, the famously exclusive luxury hotel that makes up the resort peninsula of Sveti Stefan beckons curious travelers to come, see, snap a photo...and then wish they'd spent more time elsewhere. While scenic, there's not much to actually experience at Sveti Stefan (unless you've got more than a thousand bucks to rent a room); while it's a great photo op, it disappoints many who make the trip.

Once an actual, living town (connected to the mainland only by a narrow, natural causeway), Sveti Stefan was virtually abandoned after World War II. The Yugoslav government developed it into a giant resort hotel in the 1950s. As old homes were converted to hotel rooms, the novelty of the place—and its sterling location, surrounded by pebbly beaches and lush scenery—began to attract some seriously wealthy guests.

During this resort's heyday in the 1960s and 1970s, it ranked alongside Cannes and St-Tropez as a place to see and be seen

MONTENEGRO

on Europe's beaches. You could rent a room, a house, a block of houses, or even the entire peninsula. Anonymity was vigilantly protected, as the nicest "rooms" had their own private pools (away from public scrutiny), lockable gates, and security guards. Lured by Sveti Stefan's promise of privacy, celebrities, rock stars, royalty, and dignitaries famously engaged in bidding wars to decide who'd be granted access to the best suites: Whoever put the most money in a sealed envelope and slipped it to the manager, won. (According to local legend, Sly Stallone's money talked.) Guests were pampered—indulged no matter how outrageous their requests. Sophia Loren, Kirk Douglas, Doris Day, and Claudia Schiffer are just a few of the big names who basked on Sveti Stefan's beaches.

By the late 2000s, Sveti Stefan had experienced a dramatic decline. The Yugoslav Wars scared visitors away, its cachet faded, and the resort grew a bit rough around the edges. Then the Indian company Aman Resorts swept in with ambitious plans to restore the island to its former status as one of the world's most exclusive, crème-de-la-crème resorts (www.aman.com). These days, no-neck thugs guard the causeway, letting only guests (no exceptions, don't bother asking) cross over into the fantasy world of Sveti Stefan. If you're desperate to check it out, you can reserve a table at the expensive restaurant. If you want to relax on the beaches flanking the causeway, most areas charge €30-50 per person for the day, but there are a few free areas—ask the guard for pointers.

Across the water from Sveti Stefan, on its own little cove, is one of Tito's former vacation villas (Villa Miločer, also part of the Aman resort). From here, you can enjoy the promenade that runs from the beach in front of the villa and to the next cove; eventually, this path will let you stroll along the water all the way to Budva.

Getting to Sveti Stefan: Sveti Stefan is just three miles beyond Budva. Coming around the bay from Budva (following signs toward *Bar*), you'll pass above the peninsula on the main road, watching for the well-marked pullout on the right that offers classic views. After snapping your photos, if you want to get closer, continue down and turn off to the right, following signs to *Hotel Sveti Stefan;* you can park in the pay lot and walk along the beach as far as the causeway.

From Sveti Stefan to Dubrovnik: Figure 1.5 hours to the Croatian border (if you go via Tivat—rather than Kotor—and use the shortcut ferry between Lepetane and Kamenari, described earlier in this chapter), then another 45 minutes to Dubrovnik.

BOSNIA-HERZEGOVINA

Bosna i Hercegovina

BOSNIA-HERZEGOVINA

The 1990s weren't kind to Bosnia-Herzegovina: War. Destruction. Genocide. But apart from the tragic way it separated from Yugoslavia, the country has long been—and remains—a remarkable place, with ruggedly beautiful terrain, a unique mix of cultures and faiths, kind and welcoming people who pride themselves on their hospitality, and some of the most captivating sightseeing in southeastern Europe.

Little Bosnia-Herzegovina is a country with three faiths, three languages, and two alphabets. While the rest of Yugoslavia has splintered into countries dominated by one ethnicity, Bosnia remains a mix of scattered communities, with large contingents of all three major Yugoslav groups: Muslim Bosniaks, Eastern Orthodox Serbs, and Catholic Croats. These same three factions fought each other in that brutal war 25 years ago, and today they're still working on reconciliation.

A visit here offers a fascinating opportunity to sample the cultures of these three major faiths within a relatively small area. In the same day, you can inhale incense in a mystical-feeling Serbian Orthodox church, hear the subtle clicking of rosary beads in a Roman Catholic church, and listen to the Muslim call to prayer echo across a skyline pricked by minarets. Few places in Europe cram so much diversity into such a small area.

About half of the people in Bosnia are "Bosniaks"—that is, Muslims. And that makes travel in Bosnia an illuminating and unique foray into a culture that's both devoutly Muslim and fully European. Here, just a short drive from the touristy Dalmatian Coast, you can step into a mosque and learn about Islam directly from a Muslim. The country also holds one of the most important pilgrimage sites of the Roman Catholic world: Međugorje, where six residents have reported seeing visions of the Virgin Mary.

Bosnian coffee *(bosanska kafa)* is not just a drink, but a complex ritual that captures this culture's deliberate, stop-and-smell-the-tulips approach to life. Similar to what you might call "Turkish coffee," this unfiltered brew is prepared—and enjoyed—according to a very specific routine: The fine grounds are stirred with water in a small copper-plated kettle with a long, straight handle (called a *džezva*). When it's ready to drink, it's done slo-o-o-owly: Carefully decant the coffee—easy now, don't pour off too many grounds—into a small ceramic cup. If you take sugar, put the sugar cube in the cup first, then pour the coffee over it. Sip your coffee gradually, and swirl the cup periodically to agitate and recaffeinate your brew. (If it's prepared—and drunk—properly, you won't even wind up with mud at the bottom of the cup.) Nibble on the Turkish delight candy *(rahatlokum)* that usually accompanies Bosnian coffee, and take time to chat with your travel partner or a new Bosnian friend. The point is not to slam down caffeine, but to have an excuse to slow your pulse and focus on where you are and who you're with.

Bosnian coffee is just one of the many facets of local culture that were adopted from the Ottomans (from today's Turkey) who ruled here for centuries. Thanks largely to this influence, Bosnian culture is permeated with a soulfulness that's rare in Europe. The Bosnian language features an entire lexicon of words that have no clear translation in other tongues or cultures.

Sarajevans embrace the concept of *raja*, meaning an unpretentious humility that stems from being one with a community or a circle of friends. *Merak* is enjoyment, particularly a relaxed atmosphere that arises when you're among friends—perhaps while listening to *sevdah* music (explained below) and sipping Bosnian coffee. Enjoying the company of friends while going out for snacks is called *mezetluk* (related to the Greek *mezedes*, or tapas-like small plates). And the insult *papak* (literally "hoof") means primitive, naive, tacky, or generally "outsider"—such as wearing white socks with dark shoes (a stereotypical Bosnian faux pas).

My favorite Bosnian word is *ćeif* (pronounced "chayf"), which means a sense of well-being while engaged in a highly idiosyncratic routine. These rituals—from the way someone spins their worry beads, to their own unique procedure for preparing and drinking coffee or smoking a water pipe, to a dervish whirling in a worshipful trance—might be considered "OCD" (or simply "annoying") by many Americans...but Bosnians understand that it's simply *ćeif*. As long as your *ćeif* is not hurting anyone, it's tolerated—because everyone has one.

Sevdah—sometimes called "the Bosnian blues"—is a traditional folk music that mingles powerful emotions: sad and happy, convivial and nostalgic. Bosnians explain how the passionate, mournful strains of *sevdah* (which sounds distinctly eastern) pair perfectly with falling in love, drinking with friends, or contemplating loss. *Sevdah* is also the word for a poignant, melancholic mood—sort of the counterpoint to *merak*. Balancing these moods, Bosniaks explain, is key to emotional satisfaction.

To strike up a conversation, ask your new Bosnian friend to tell you more about what any of these terms means. All of them are examples of how Bosnians celebrate the "little things" that make life worth living...things that mainstream American and European cultures, all too often, see as barriers to progress.

In keeping with their generally relaxed culture, Bosnians are known for their gregarious sense of hospitality and their sharp sense of humor. Even during the darkest days of the war, they found ways to joke about the horrors unfolding around them. And today, they're quick to chuckle at their complicated political system and shambolic economy. Pointing to an ATM, your new Bosnian friend may say, "That's what we call our 'wailing wall.'" And they like to quip about their unfortunate circumstances in life: "Just our luck. Bosnia has so many Muslims—but no oil."

This unique Muslim culture seems fitting in this porous and mountainous land, where streams and rivers trickle endlessly. After all, the very name "Bosnia" comes from a term that means "running water" or "saturated"—and Muslim culture prizes constantly flowing water. While Christians bless still water and call it holy, for Muslims, the power of nature is in its movement; they prefer water to be continually flowing, cleansing, replenishing, circulating. Just as a dervish whirls to connect with the spirituality of the earth and the heavens, so, too, should water be in motion. When the Ottomans arrived here from their Turkish homeland, they must have felt right at home.

Bosnia rearranges your mental furniture more than any other country in this book. It offers an enticing glimpse at a completely different, very eastern worldview. And it comes with some in-your-face lessons about recent history.

While repairs are ongoing, you'll still be confronted by vivid and thought-provoking scars of the Yugoslav Wars, especially outside of the tourist zones. Poignant roadside memorials to fallen soldiers, burned-out husks of buildings, unmistakable starburst patterns in the pavement, and bullet holes in walls are a constant reminder that the country is still recovering—physically and psychologically. Driving through the countryside, you'll pass between Muslim, Croat, and Serb towns—each one decorated with its own provocative sectarian symbols. Bosnia teaches an essential lesson about how real—and destructive—war and interethnic strife truly are.

Of all the former Yugoslav states, Bosnia is where you'll sense the most nostalgia for communist-era leader Marshal Tito (at least, in the Bosniak-dominated parts of Bosnia, like Mostar and Sarajevo). This is likely because Bosniaks suffered the most from the breakup of Yugoslavia. It was only under Tito—who made it clear that ethnic division mattered far less than Yugoslav unity—that Bosniaks felt protected and respected.

And there's another throwback to the past here: In Bosnia, you'll be exposed to more cigarette smoke than in most of Europe. Hotels and restaurants permit smoking to an unusual degree.

In this book, I focus on a few user-friendly Bosnian destinations within easy reach of the Dalmatian Coast: the Turkish-flavored city of Mostar (with its restored Old Bridge—one of Europe's most inspiring sights), some nearby attractions offering a more complete view of Herzegovina (Blagaj, Počitelj, and Stolac), the Catholic shrine at Međugorje, and—just over the Croatian bor-

BOSNIA-HERZEGOVINA

Bosnia-Herzegovina Almanac

Official Name: Bosna i Hercegovina (abbreviated "BiH")—that's Bosnia and Herzegovina, the country's two regions. For simplicity, I generally call the whole country "Bosnia" in this book.

Size: 19,741 square miles (about the size of West Virginia). Bosnia is home to about 3.9 million people. In both size and population, Bosnia is comparable to Croatia. Someone who lives in Bosnia-Herzegovina, regardless of ethnicity, is called a "Bosnian." A southern Slav who practices Islam is called a "Bosniak." Today, about half of all Bosnians are Bosniaks (Muslims), about a third are Orthodox Serbs, and nearly 15 percent are Catholic Croats.

Geography: Bosnia and Herzegovina are two distinct regions that share the same mountainous country. Bosnia constitutes the majority of the country (in the north, with a continental climate), while Herzegovina is the southern tip (about a fifth of the total area, with a hotter Mediterranean climate). The nation's capital, Sarajevo, has an estimated 310,000 people; Mostar is Herzegovina's biggest city (with approximately 130,000 people) and unofficial capital.

Snapshot History: Bosnia-Herzegovina's early history is similar to the rest of the region: Illyrians, Romans, and Slavs (oh, my!). In the late 15th century, the Ottoman Empire began a 400-year domination of the country. Many of the Ottomans' subjects converted to Islam, and their descendants remain Muslims today. Bosnia-Herzegovina became part of the Austro-Hungarian Empire in 1878, then Yugoslavia after World War I, until it declared independence in the spring of 1992. The bloody war that ensued came to an end in 1995. There were about 100,000 identified Bosnian casualties of the Yugoslav Wars, but many estimates of total casualties are double that number. (For de-

der—an excellent Roman museum near Metković. A longer trip from Dalmatia—and well worth the trek—is the Bosnian capital of Sarajevo, with a spectacular mountain-valley setting, a multilayered history, powerful wartime stories, and a resilient populace of proud Sarajevans eager to show you their city.

Bosnia is highly recommended as a detour—both geographical and cultural—from the Croatian and Slovenian mainstream. Inquisitive visitors come away from a visit to Bosnia with a more nuanced understanding of the former Yugoslavia. And Bosnia offers lower prices and a warmer welcome than you'll find on the Croatian coast. Overcome your jitters and dive in.

BOSNIAN HISTORY

With its mountainous landscape, remote from the more mainline areas of the western Balkans, Bosnia's evolution has followed tails, see the Understanding Yugoslavia chapter.)

Red Tape: To enter Bosnia-Herzegovina, Americans and Canadians need only a passport.

Economy: The country's economy has struggled since the war—the per-capita GDP is around $12,800, and the official unemployment rate is around 21 percent.

Currency: The official currency is the convertible mark (*konvertibilna marka,* abbreviated KM locally, BAM internationally). The official exchange rate is $1 = about 1.50 KM. But merchants are usually willing to take euros, and (in Mostar) they'll often accept Croatian kunas, roughly converting prices with a simple formula: 2 KM = €1 = 7 kn (= about $1.20).

Telephones: Bosnia-Herzegovina's country code is 387. If calling from another country, first dial the international access code (00 in Europe, 011 in the US), then 387, then the area code (minus the initial zero), then the number.

Flag: The flag of Bosnia-Herzegovina is a blue field with a yellow triangle along the top edge. The three points of the triangle represent Bosnia-Herzegovina's three peoples (Bosniaks, Croats, Serbs), and the triangle itself resembles the physical shape of the country. A row of white stars underscores the longest side of the triangle. These stars—and the yellow-and-blue color scheme—echo the flag of the European Union (a nod to the EU's efforts to bring peace to the region). While this compromise flag sounds like a nice idea, almost no Bosnian embraces it; each group has its own unofficial but highly prized symbols and flags (such as the fleur-de-lis for the Bosniaks, the red-and-white checkerboard shield for the Croats, and the cross with the four C's for the Serbs)—many of which offend the other groups.

a unique course. Even in the present day, the people of Bosnia struggle with being outsiders—afloat on an oddball cultural island flanked by the Roman Catholic West (Croatia) and the Orthodox East (Serbia), borrowing elements from both but not fully belonging to either.

After periods of rule by the Illyrians and the Romans, Bosnia fostered its own thriving Slavic civilization during the Middle Ages. The local Bogomils were a homegrown branch of Christianity that was neither Catholic nor Orthodox—and was viewed with suspicion by both sects. Literally "dear to God," the Bogomil faith was simple, ascetic, and somewhat mystic, combining elements of Slavic, Illyrian, and Celtic traditions. The Bogomils—who comprised a majority of the population of medieval Bosnia—had a thriving civilization. Vivid artifacts of the Bogomil kingdom still survive, such as their engraved burial grave markers, called *stećaks* (some of the best-preserved are in Stolac, near Mostar—see page 466).

When the Ottomans (from today's Turkey) took over this land in the 15th century, they tolerated different faiths, but offered generous economic and political incentives to those who converted to Islam. In negotiating their religious freedoms with the sultans, Bosnia's Roman Catholics (who identified as Croats) and Eastern Orthodox (who identified as Serbs) both had the support of larger church hierarchies outside of Bosnia. But the Bogomils had no bargaining power, and were more likely to swap one monotheistic faith for another—creating the Muslim South Slav ethnicity that would come to be known as "Bosniak."

Under the Ottomans, Bosnia flourished. The Ottoman sultans invested in infrastructure (primarily bridges—including Mostar's Old Bridge—and fountains) and architecture, including many mosques, hammams (baths), caravanserais (inns), madrassas (theological schools), and so on. Bosnian Muslims rose through the ranks of the empire, becoming military generals, religious leaders, beloved poets, and even grand viziers (advisers to the sultans).

After four centuries of rule, the Ottoman Empire entered a steep decline. The Bosniak military hero Husein Gradaščević—nicknamed "The Dragon of Bosnia" (Zmaj od Bosne)—led an armed uprising in the 1830s. Though he died in battle, his movement eventually brought about the end of the archaic Ottoman system of rule in Bosnia, leading to a greater degree of autonomy.

But Bosnia was bound for even bigger changes. Unable to manage their vast holdings, in 1878 the Ottomans passed control of Bosnia-Herzegovina to their Habsburg rival, the Austro-Hungarian Empire (which already controlled neighboring Croatia and Slovenia). The Habsburgs quickly moved to modernize Bosnia, erecting buildings and investing in infrastructure. Sarajevo, Mostar, and many other Bosnian cities still show the impressive results of these efforts, which pulled Bosnia into the modern world. Habsburg rule piped in mainstream European culture for the first time. Now Bosnian urbanites and aristocrats exchanged their ornate Turkish gowns for snazzy Austrian business suits...which they wore with their old fezzes and turbans.

Of course, not everybody bought what the Habsburgs were selling. Fierce underground resistance movements—such as the Black Hand—were determined to bring about self-rule for the South Slavs. Just 40 years after the Habsburgs took over, their empire began to topple—losing a Great War that began when the Habsburg heir, Archduke Franz Ferdinand, was assassinated in Sarajevo (see sidebar on page 503).

Following World War I, Bosnia was swept up in the movement to create a union of the South Slavs. The original incarnation of Yugoslavia, called "the Kingdom of the Serbs, Croats, and Slovenes," ignored the Bosniaks both in name and in political influence—they were merely along for the ride.

During World War II, Bosnia was part of the so-called "Independent State of Croatia" (run by the Nazis' puppet Ustaše government). Hitler's right-hand man, Heinrich Himmler, came to Bosnia to assess where the Bosniaks might fit into the Führer's ethnic vision. He determined that they were "Croats with Muslim culture"—that is, Aryans who would be conscripted to fight. The Nazis created an SS Hanjar/Handschar unit (named for a Turkish knife), issuing the conscripts a Germanic-style uniform with a ceremonial fez. The unit fought fiercely against Tito's Partisan Army, and participated in the Ustaše's genocidal efforts against Serbs, Jews, and other "undesirables." But as the war wore on, more and more of these troops became disillusioned with the Nazi cause and deserted in large numbers.

Some of the most dramatic WWII battles between the Yugoslav Partisans and the Nazis took place here in Bosnia. One of the most famous was the Battle of the Neretva, in which Tito ingeniously saved more than 4,000 of his wounded troops—effectively turning the tide of the war (for more on this battle, see page 525).

The postwar communist country of Yugoslavia was born in the Bosnian town of Jajce on November 29, 1943, when Partisan generals met to outline the future of a hoped-for post-Nazi state. But in the new incarnation of Yugoslavia, many Bosniaks still felt like second-class citizens. Local Muslims recall that Yugoslav government-issued textbooks reinforced negative stereotypes. For example, they might say, "Sasha [a typically Serb name] is working," but "Mujo [a typically Muslim name] is a bad boy."

Even after the outbreak of violence between breakaway republics Slovenia and Croatia and Serb-dominated Yugoslavia in 1991, things stayed strangely calm in Bosnia. But when the Bosnian conflict finally erupted in 1992, it was war of the most brutal kind. A three-way war exploded between Bosnian Croats (supported by Croatia proper), Bosnian Serbs (supported by Serbia proper), and Bosniaks (who, caught in the crossfire, realized they had no real European allies). The early to mid-1990s saw the worst human, architectural, and cultural devastation in Bosnian history. Sarajevo, Srebrenica, and Mostar became synonymous with sectarian strife, horrific sieges, and shocking genocide. (For more details on the war, see page 747 of the Understanding Yugoslavia chapter.)

The Dayton Peace Accords that ended the conflict here in 1995 gerrymandered the nation into three separate regions: the Federation of Bosnia and Herzegovina (FBiH, shared by Bosniaks and Croats, roughly in the western and central parts of the country), the Republika Srpska (RS, dominated by Serbs, generally to the north

BOSNIA-HERZEGOVINA

and east), and the Brčko District (BD, a tiny corner of the country, with a mix of the ethnicities). For the most part, each of the three native ethnic groups stay in "their" part of this divided country, but tourists can move freely among them.

On your visit, tune into the many ways that the Bosniaks, Croats, and Serbs of Bosnia are working to coexist. To satisfy the country's various factions, the currency uses both the Roman and the Cyrillic alphabets, and bills have different figureheads and symbols (some bills feature Bosniaks, others Serbs). Until recently, the alphabet used on road signs changed with the territory: Roman alphabet in Muslim and Croat areas, Cyrillic alphabet in Serb lands. Now all road signs throughout Bosnia-Herzegovina are required to appear in both alphabets—though

that doesn't prevent vandals from spray-painting over the alphabet they don't like. License plates also used different alphabets, but this led to vandalism. Today's license plates use only letters that are common to both alphabets.

Towns with mixed populations are either effectively divided in half, or have buildings clearly marked with symbols indicating the ethnicity of the occupant. Until very recently small-town schoolhouses operated "two schools under one roof," with separate entrances and staggered shifts for the Bosniak and Croat kids... who, virtually from birth, were constantly reminded they were very different from each other. In some towns still today, a beautifully restored Orthodox church may sit across from the battered footprint of a long-gone mosque, or vice versa.

Bosnia has a central government, but each population group also has its own autonomous government and sub-agencies, resulting in four essentially redundant bureaucracies. The country is also divided into 10 state-like cantons, each of which also has some governmental authority. Imagine the inefficiency. On top of all this, Bosnia is still navigating the complex transition from communism to capitalism, and rebuilding from a devastating war. It's a miracle that things here work at all.

A quarter-century later, the delicate compromises that were necessary to end a horrifying war have become almost too complicated to maintain. For Bosnia-Herzegovina to fully recover, all three groups must learn to truly set aside their differences and work together. Pessimists (who are abundant in this region) don't like

Fundamentalist Islam in Bosnia?

Islam is a hot topic in today's Europe, where some citizens scapegoat Muslim immigrants. And even though Bosnia's Muslims are indigenous, they're not immune to criticism—especially from their Serb and Croat rivals. While Bosniaks have a long history as a peace-loving people, critics allege that elements of the population are experimenting with some alarming fundamentalist Islamic ideologies.

These allegations have some basis in fact. During the war and genocide of the 1990s, many Bosniaks felt abandoned by Europe and the US, who were too timid to step in and "take sides" to end the violence. In his people's darkest hour, desperate Bosnian President Alija Izetbegović recruited assistance from the only group willing to offer help: Muslim fundamentalists from the Middle East and North Africa. Several hundred mujahideen (Islamic jihadists) came to Bosnia to train Bosniak soldiers—and participated in bloody massacres of Serbs and Croats. They brought with them the dangerous ideas of Wahhabism, an ultraconservative movement bent on "purifying" Islam, often through violent means. According to unsubstantiated rumors, Izetbegović was even in contact with Osama bin Laden. In some cases, the mujahideen offered donations to widows of šehids (Bosniak martyrs).

Today, while waning, these groups' influence persists. At the legitimate end of the spectrum, Muslim countries have helped to fund the postwar reconstruction of Bosnia—especially the rebuilding of mosques and madrassas. Just as the end of atheistic, communist Yugoslav rule kick-started a passion for Catholicism in Croatia and the Orthodox faith in Serbia, many Muslims in Bosnia are today actively pursuing their faith. You may even see women wearing traditional Muslim headscarves—a rare sight before the war, when most Bosniaks dressed just like their Serb and Croat neighbors. (But note that many veiled women are likely Muslim tourists from elsewhere.)

As for the mujahideen fighters, most left the country after the war, as dictated by the Dayton Peace Accords. But small pockets of Wahhabists still live in remote areas in the mountains. The vast majority of Muslims in Bosnia denounce the Wahhabists—just as any peaceful, moderate country looks with concern upon its lunatic fringe.

Bosnia's chances, and Bosnian Serbs still talk loudly about secession (Republika Srpska's president, Milorad Dodik, is an outspoken separatist). But others see signs of hope, such as the young people from the three faiths now beginning to cautiously intermingle, as their ancestors did for centuries. Will Bosniak, Serb, and Croat youth manage to transcend the fear and anger that tainted their parents' and grandparents' country in the 20th century? That history is yet to be written.

BOSNIAN FOOD

Bosnia-Herzegovina dines on grilled meat, stewed vegetables, soft cheeses, and other foods you may think of as "Turkish" or "Greek." On menus, look for the word *domaća*—"homemade." Another key term is *pod saća*, which means "under the bell" (similar to *peka* in Croatia); this means that it has been slow cooked under a copper lid covered with hot coals. For a rundown of the most common items you'll eat in Bosnia—and throughout the Balkans—see the "Balkan Flavors" sidebar.

Dolma is a bell pepper stuffed with minced meat, vegetables, and rice. A *sarma* or *sarmica* is similar, but stuffed in cabbage leaves rather than in a pepper, while *japrak* is stuffed grape leaves. *Begova ćorba* ("nobleman's stew") is a meaty vegetable soup. *Grah* is bean soup. And one Bosnian institution—which you'll see at roadside truck stops across the country—is the whole lamb grilled on a spit.

While Balkan cuisine favors meat, a nice veggie complement is *đuveđ* (JOO-vedge)—a spicy mix of stewed vegetables, flavored with tomatoes and peppers. And the best salad option is *šopska salata*—a Greek-style salad of tomatoes, cucumbers, onions, and peppers, smothered in grated feta-like *sirene* cheese. *Srpska salata* ("Serb salad") is often the same thing, but may have extra cheese.

Bosnian desserts—typically sweetened with honey rather than sugar—are another local treat. Drop by a sweets shop and peruse your options. *Baklava*, a phyllo-dough pastry with nuts and honey, is a familiar choice. *Kadaif* is similar, but made with shredded sheets of dough. *Tulumba* is a pastry cylinder drenched in honey, and *tufahija* is an apple stuffed with walnuts, soaked in honey, and topped with whipped cream. *Smokvača* is a dense, very sweet fig pie. You'll also see blocks of nougat-like *halva*, made from sesame paste. And every cup of Bosnian coffee comes with a Turkish delight candy.

Bosnia produces some wine, but it's mostly consumed domestically. Sarajevso Pivo, brewed in the capital, is the favored brand of beer. In Bosnia, "coffee" is *kafa* (not *kava*, as in Croatia and Slovenia). While you can easily get espresso-style coffee, *bosanska kafa* (unfiltered "Bosnian coffee") is more local—and more fun to drink. (For tips on this ritual, see earlier.)

BOSNIAN LANGUAGE

Technically, Bosnia-Herzegovina has three languages—Bosnian, Serbian, and Croatian. But all three are mutually intelligible variants of what was until recently considered a single language: Serbo-Croatian. The Croatian survival phrases on page 35 will work

Balkan Flavors

All of the countries of the Balkan Peninsula—from Slovenia to Greece—have several foods in common: The Ottomans who

controlled much of this territory for centuries imported some goodies that remained standard fare here long after they left town. Whether you're in Bosnia-Herzegovina, Slovenia, Croatia, Montenegro, or Serbia, it's worth seeking out some of these local flavors.

A popular, cheap fast food you'll see everywhere is *burek* (BOO-rehk)—phyllo dough filled with meat, cheese, spinach, or apples. *Burek* rivals pizza-by-the-slice as the most popular takeaway snack food in southeastern Europe. The best *burek* is *pod sača*—cooked under a baking lid.

Grilled meats are a staple of Balkan cuisine. You'll most often see *ćevapčići* (cheh-VAHP-chee-chee), or simply *ćevapi* (cheh-VAH-pee)—minced meat (typically a mix of lamb and beef) formed into a sausage-link shape, then grilled. There are variations: Sarajevo-style *(sarajevski ćevapi)* is typically eaten with grilled onions and stuffed into a pita-like flatbread called *somun;* Banja Luka-style *(banjalučki ćevapi)* is one long, continuous *ćevap* with hot peppers on the side.

Ražnjići (RAZH-nyee-chee) is small pieces of steak on a skewer, like a shish kebab. *Pljeskavica* (plehs-kah-VEET-suh) is similar to *ćevapčići,* except the meat is in the form of a hamburger-like patty. *Pileći* is chicken, and *piščančje* is grilled chicken breast. *Sudžukice* are sausages, and *ćufte* are meatballs.

You can't eat any of this stuff without the ever-present condiment *ajvar* (EYE-var). Made from red bell pepper and eggplant, *ajvar* is like ketchup with a kick. Many Americans pack a jar of this distinctive sauce to remember the flavors of the Balkans when they get back home. (You may even be able to find it at specialty grocery stores in the US—look for "eggplant/red pepper spread.")

Particularly in Bosnia, another side dish you'll see is the soft, spreadable—and tasty—cheese called *kajmak. Lepinje* is a pita-like grilled bread, which is often wrapped around *ćevapčići* or *pljeskavica* to make a sandwich. *Uštipci* is a fry bread that's especially popular throughout Bosnia-Herzegovina.

Ajvar, kajmak, lepinje, and diced raw onions are the perfect complement to a "mixed grill" of various meats on a big platter—the quintessence of Balkan cuisine on one plate.

just fine throughout Bosnia-Herzegovina. Bosniaks and Croats use basically the same Roman alphabet we do, while Serbs use the Cyrillic alphabet. You'll see both alphabets on currency, official documents, and road signs, but the Roman alphabet predominates in virtually every destination covered in this book. Most people also speak English.

MOSTAR & NEARBY

Mostar • Blagaj • Počitelj • Metković • Stolac • Međugorje

Mostar (MOH-star) encapsulates the best and the worst of the former Yugoslavia. During the Tito years, its residents—Catholic Croats, Orthodox Serbs, and Muslim Bosniaks—enjoyed an idyllic mingling of cultures, all living together in harmony. Their differences were spanned by an Old Bridge that epitomized an optimistic vision of a Yugoslavia in which ethnic differences were accepted and celebrated. But then, as the country unraveled in the early 1990s, Mostar was gripped by a gory three-way war among those same peoples...and that famous bridge crumbled into the Neretva River.

Mostar is still rebuilding, and the bullet holes and destroyed buildings are ugly reminders that the last time you saw this place, it was probably on the night-

ly news. Western visitors may also be struck by the immediacy of the Muslim culture that permeates Mostar, where minarets share the horizon with church steeples. During the Ottomans' 400-year control of this region, many Slavic subjects converted to Islam. And, although they retreated in the late 19th century, the Ottomans left behind a rich architectural, cultural, and religious legacy that has forever shaped Mostar. Five times each day, loudspeakers on minarets crackle to life, and the call to prayer warbles through the streets. In parts of the city, you'd swear you were on an old Ottoman street in Turkey.

Scars of war aside, Mostar's setting is stunning: straddling the banks of the gorgeous Neretva River, with tributaries and waterfalls carving their way through the rocky landscape. The sightseeing—mosques, old Turkish-style houses, and that spine-tingling Old Bridge—is more engaging than much of what you'll find in Croatia or Slovenia. And it's cheap: Hotels, food, and museums cost less than half of what you'll pay in Dubrovnik or Ljubljana.

In this chapter, I've also included some worthwhile attractions near Mostar: the river spring and whirling dervish house at Blagaj, the striking fortified hill town of Počitelj, and workaday Stolac, which sits upon some very impressive history. The top Croat sight in Bosnia-Herzegovina is Međugorje, where Catholic pilgrims flock from around the world to hear tales of a Virgin Mary apparition. And just over the Croatian border, near Metković, is a fine Roman museum. All of these places are within a half-hour's drive of Mostar; take your pick of detours on the drive between Mostar and the coast.

A visit to Mostar gets more uplifting all the time: Mostarians are rebuilding at an impressive pace, tentatively reintegrating, and working hard to make Mostar tourist-friendly. Mostar is well on its way to reclaiming its status as one of the premier destinations on the Balkan Peninsula.

PLANNING YOUR TIME

Bosnia-Herzegovina is a major cultural detour on your Dalmatian vacation—but it's easy to reach, just a three-hour drive or four-hour bus ride from Dubrovnik or Split. To fit a Mostar overnight into your itinerary, consider a round-trip plan that takes you south along the coast, then back north via Bosnia-Herzegovina (for example, Split-Hvar-Korčula-Dubrovnik-Mostar-back to Split).

Mostar's Old Town is packed with day-trippers at midday, but empty in the morning and evening. You can get a good feel for Mostar in just a few hours, but a full day—and, ideally, an overnight—gives you time to linger and ponder. My self-guided walk provides a framework for a visit of any duration. With extra time, venture to the western (Croat) part of the city, which most tourists miss.

If you're day-tripping from Dubrovnik (a common plan), you have several choices. The easiest option is to hire a driver, or take a package excursion with a company based in Dubrovnik. If you have your own car, Mostar is a fairly easy side-trip (with the option of going down and back by different routes, outlined in this chapter)—or it works great on the way to Sarajevo, or even for those heading overland to Split. In summer, it's typically possible to do a same-day round-trip using public buses (though it's a long day)—

but, because the specific bus connections change from year to year, carefully check your options.

GETTING AROUND HERZEGOVINA

By Car: Coming with your own car gives you maximum flexibility, and a number of interesting routes connect Mostar to the coast (but be aware that GPS is often wrong in Mostar; for detailed route information, see "Route Tips for Drivers," later). If you do plan to drive here, let your car-rental company know in advance, to ensure you have the appropriate paperwork for crossing the border. If you're not up for driving yourself, consider splurging on a **driver** to bring you here (for drivers based in Dubrovnik, see the Dubrovnik chapter; for a Mostar-based driver, see "Helpful Hints," later). Drivers may suggest several detours en route. Do your homework to know which ones interest you (for example, Međugorje isn't worth the extra time for most visitors), and don't hesitate to say that you want to just max out on time in Mostar itself.

By Bus: Public buses connect Mostar with destinations on the Dalmatian Coast (particularly Split and Dubrovnik), but doing Mostar as a one-day side-trip from Dubrovnik only works in peak season (June-Aug) due to limited buses; otherwise you'll need to pay for an excursion, drive yourself, or spend the night. For bus details, see "Mostar Connections," later.

By Package Tour: Taking a package excursion from a Dalmatian resort town sounds like an efficient way to visit Mostar or Međugorje. But it has its cons: Count on lots of hours on a crowded bus, listening to a lackluster, multilingual tour guide reciting a memorized script, and precious little time in the destinations themselves. I'd pick an itinerary focusing on Mostar itself, and avoid tours that include a pointless boat trip on the Neretva River or time in Međugorje. Those that add a quick visit to the worthwhile town of Počitelj are a better deal. Ask for details at any travel agency in Dalmatia.

Orientation to Mostar

Mostar (pop. 130,000) fills a basin surrounded by arid mountains and split down the middle by the emerald-green Neretva River. Bosniaks live mostly on the east side of the river (plus a strip on the west bank) and Croats in the modern sprawl to the west—though the populations are beginning to mix again. Virtually all of the sights are in the Bosniak zone, but visitors move freely throughout the city, and don't even notice the division. The cobbled, Turkish-feeling Old Town (called "Stari Grad" or "Stara Čaršija") surrounds the town's centerpiece, the Old Bridge.

The skyline is pierced by the minarets of various mosques, but

Mostar

To "Kolodvor" Bus Stop

WALK ENDS

Trg Musala

MUSALA BRIDGE

Zrinjevac Park

Spanski Trg

NIKOLE ŠUBIĆA ZRINSKOG

To the Rondo

ADEMA BUĆA

BUNUR BRIDGE

BULEVAR

P

200 Meters
200 Yards

M-6.1

To the Rondo & Medugorje

KNEZA MIHAJLA VIŠEVIĆA HUMSKOG

BULEVAR

6

RADE

P

CAFÉ

River

MARRIOTT HOTEL

BELL TOWER

FRANCISCAN CHURCH

FUTURE SYNAGOGUE

P

WALK BEGINS

ONEŠĆUKOVA

7

MUJE BJELAVCA

Accommodations
1 Muslibegović House
2 Shangri La Mansion
3 Villa Anri
4 Pansion Čardak & Pansion Nur
5 Hotel Kriva Ćuprija
6 Villa Fortuna
7 Villa Botticelli

Eateries & Other
8 Bridge-View Eateries
9 Restoran Hindin Han
10 Tima-Irma
11 Nacionalni Restoran Aščinica Balkan (2)
12 Saray
13 Urban Grill
14 Ali Baba Nightclub
15 Oscar Nightclub
16 Black Dog Pub
17 Grocery
18 Laundry

MOSTAR & NEARBY

To Main
Bus Station

To
Sarajevo

H. MASALA

BRAĆE

MARŠALA

M-17

MUSLIBEGOVIĆ
HOUSE
❶

Cemetery

ĐIKIĆA

⓬

MUSEUM OF WAR &
GENOCIDE VICTIMS
1992-1995

KARAĐOZBEG
MOSQUE

TITA

BIŠĆEVIĆ
TURKISH
HOUSE

FEJIĆA

⓱

New
Muslim
Cemetery

ORTHODOX
CHURCHES
(CONSTRUCTION SITE)

⓫

SINAN
PASHA
MOSQUE

Neretva

TEPA
MARKET

BAJATOVA

BOSNASEUM

⓫

KOSKI MEHMET-
PASHA MOSQUE

KUJUNDŽILUK

MUSEUM OF
HERZEGOVINA

BITANGE

⓭

⓲

CAFÉ DE
ALMA

COPPERSMITHS'
STREET

HAMMAM
MUSEUM

❽

⓮

ℹ

GALLERY ON THE BRIDGE &
MUSEUM OF THE OLD BRIDGE

ONEŠĆUKOVA

⓯

⓾

❷

❺

❾

OLD
BRIDGE

⓰

❹

CROOKED
BRIDGE

GOJKA VUKOVIĆA

FOOTPATH

River

KAJTAZ
HOUSE

M-17

❸

BULEVAR

M-6.1

To H.M. Brkica Bridge,
M-17, Airport, Blagaj,
Počitelj & Stolac

LUČKI BRIDGE

To
Dubrovnik

MOSTAR & NEARBY

none is as big as the two major Catholic (Croat) symbols in town, both erected after the Yugoslav Wars: the giant white cross on the hilltop (marking the place from where Croat forces shelled the Bosniak side of the river, including the Old Bridge); and the enormous (almost 100-foot-tall) bell tower of the Franciscan Church of Sts. Peter and Paul. A monumental Orthodox cathedral on the hillside across the river, destroyed during the war, is now being rebuilt.

A note about safety: You'll see bombed-out buildings everywhere, even in the core of the city. A few are marked with *Warning! Dangerous Ruin* signs; for safety's sake, never wander into any building that appears damaged or deserted. Also, pickpockets operate in the tourist zone; watch your valuables, especially around the Old Bridge.

TOURIST INFORMATION

The virtually worthless TI shares a building with a tour office, but it does give out a free town map and a few brochures on Mostar and Herzegovina (sporadic hours, a block from the Old Bridge at Rade Bitange 5, tel. 036/580-275, www.turizam.mostar.ba).

ARRIVAL IN MOSTAR

By Bus or Train: The **main bus station** sits next to the giant but mostly deserted **train station**, north of the Old Town on the east side of the river. At the bus station, you'll find ticket windows and a left-luggage counter in the Autoprevoz lobby facing the bus stalls. You can check schedules and buy tickets in this office for most buses *except* the many connections operated by Globtour, whose office is nearby (exit Autoprevoz, turn left, and walk to the end of the bus-station area; look for *Mediteran Tours* sign). Because these two companies don't cooperate well, you may have to check with both to get the complete schedule; most departures with either company are also listed at GetByBus.com. To find your way to the town center, walk through the bus stalls and parking lot and turn left at the big road, which leads you to the Old Town area in about 15 minutes. A taxi into town costs about 5-10 KM.

It's possible (though unlikely) that you'll arrive at Mostar's secondary bus station, called **Kolodvor**, on the west/Croat side of town. From here, it's a dreary 20-minute walk into town: Turn right out of the bus station area, turn left down the busy Dubrovačka street, and head straight to the river (which you can follow south into the Old Town). Globtour buses that stop at Kolodvor will likely continue to the main bus station; those run by other companies probably won't (in either case, ask).

For details on both stations, see "Mostar Connections," later.

By Car: There are two good options for **parking** close to the Old Town, as you approach on the main drag called the Bulevar. For both options, be ready to turn just before the giant church tower. The cheaper, slightly farther option is the "Campanile" parking lot: Turn left on Franjevačka just before the church, then turn right immediately after the bell tower. This takes you to a cheap parking lot (2 KM all day), with pay WCs and café. The nearby church is also the starting point for my self-guided walk.

For a speedy, targeted visit, you can pay more for a parking lot closer to the Old Bridge: Approaching on the Bulevar, just before the church, turn right on Onešćukova and go two short blocks to where it dead-ends at the Old Town cobbles; on the left is a fancy pay lot (2 KM/hour, 20 KM/24 hours).

For tips on driving to Mostar from the Dalmatian Coast, see "Route Tips for Drivers," later.

HELPFUL HINTS

Local Cash: Need convertible marks (KM)? There are plenty of ATMs around town, but a convenient one is to the left of Fortuna Tours (see next) on Coppersmiths' Street. But on a short visit, you can generally skip a trip to the ATM, as many vendors here also accept Croatian kunas and euros.

Travel Agency: The handy **Fortuna Tours** travel agency, right in the heart of the Old Town (at the top of Coppersmiths' Street), can book a local guide or arrange a transfer, and answer basic questions (long hours daily, Kujundžiluk 2, tel. 036/551-887, main office tel. 036/552-197, www.fortuna.ba, headoffice@fortuna.ba).

Laundry: A very central laundry service is **Laundry Lahor** (daily 9:00-17:00, Maršala Tita 137, mobile 060-320-3448).

Local Guides: Hiring a guide is an excellent investment to help you understand Mostar. I've enjoyed working with **Alma Elezović,** a warm-hearted Bosniak who loves sharing her city and her wartime stories with visitors (€25/person, up to €80/group for 2-3-hour tour, mobile 063-282-142, http://almasguidedtours.blogspot.com, aelezovic@gmail.com). If Alma is busy, she may send you with her son **Jaz** (pronounced "yahz"), who speaks perfect English and offers a younger generation's perspective. Ask them about the "Mostarian nights" Ottoman-themed evenings they sometimes organize, which include dinner at a Turkish house.

Another good guide is sharp, funny **Adisa Ibrulj Muhić** (same prices as Alma, mobile 061-271-623, adisaibrulj@gmail.com).

Local Driver: Ermin Elezović, husband of local guide Alma (see above), is a gregarious, English-speaking driver who enjoys taking visitors on day trips from Mostar. You can also hire him for a transfer between Mostar and destinations anywhere in Croatia (prices for 2 people: €110 for one-way transfer to Sarajevo, €140 one-way to Dubrovnik, or €160 one-way to Split with a few brief sightseeing stops on the way; he can also drive you to Split airport or the Korčula ferry and is available for longer trips for around €1/kilometer—contact Ermin and Alma for help planning a multiday itinerary; mobile 061-908-597, elezovicermin@gmail.com).

Sights in Mostar

CENTRAL MOSTAR

Mostar's major sights line up along a handy L-shaped axis. I've laced them together as an enjoyable orientation walk: From the Franciscan Church, you'll walk straight until you cross the Old Bridge (see map for starting point). Then you'll turn left and walk basically straight (with a couple small detours) to the big square at the far end of town. This walk is designed to help you see both the main tourist zones and the parts of workaday Mostar that many visitors miss.

• *Begin at the...*

▲Franciscan Church of Sts. Peter and Paul

In a town of competing religious architectural exclamation points, the spire of this church is the tallest. The church, which adjoins a

working Franciscan monastery, was built in 1997, after the fighting subsided (the same year as the big cross on the hill). The tower, which looks like a minaret on steroids, is modeled after typical Croatian/Venetian, campanile-style bell towers.

Step inside the church to see the cavern-ous interior, still not fully decorated. (Sunday Mass here is an inspiration.) Downstairs—but often closed to the public—is another sanctuary, with naked concrete walls that make it feel like a bomb shelter, as well as a small museum documenting the history of Franciscans in Mostar. Seeing photos of older versions of this church—one destroyed by WWII fighting in 1945 (when many friars were killed by communists), and the other destroyed by the Yugoslav Wars in 1992—is a reminder that Mostarians of all stripes have suffered loss over time.

It's possible to ascend the church's 350-foot-tall **bell tower**—called the Mostar Peace Bell Tower. You'll ride the elevator up about 250 feet, then hike up 148 steps around the bells (some of which were salvaged from the original church) to reach fine views over the city. On the way up, you'll see information panels about various interesting sights around Herzegovina (6 KM, Mon-Sat 9:00-19:00, Sun from 13:00; closed Nov-March but you can ask at nearby Campanile coffee bar about a visit).

• *The church fronts the busy boulevard called the...*

▲Bulevar

"The Boulevard" was once the modern main drag of Mostar. In the early 1990s, this city of Bosniaks, Croats, and Serbs began to fracture under the pressure of politicians' propaganda. In October 1991, Bosnia-Herzegovina—following Croatia's and Slovenia's example, but without the blessing of its large Serb minority—began a process of splitting from Yugoslavia. Soon after, the Serb-dominated Yugoslav

People's Army invaded. Mostar's Bosniaks and Croats joined forces to battle the Serbs and succeeded in claiming the city as their own, forcing out the Serb residents.

But even as they fended off the final, distant bombardments of Serb forces, Mostar's Bosniaks (Muslims) and Croats (Catholics) turned their guns against each other. This street became the front line—and virtually all its buildings were destroyed. The area to the east of here (toward the river) was held by Bosniaks, while the western part of town was Croat territory.

While many of the buildings along here have been rebuilt, some damage is still evident. Stroll a bit, imagining the hell of a split community at war. Neighbors, friends, and even families fought among themselves. Mortar craters in the asphalt leave poignant scars. During those dark war years, the Croats on the hill above laid siege to the Bosniaks on the other side, cutting off electricity, blocking roads, and blaring Croatian rabble-rousing pop music and propaganda speeches from loudspeakers. Through '93 and '94, when the Bosniaks dared to go out, they sprinted past exposed places, for fear of being picked off by a sniper. Local Bosniaks explain, "Night was time to live"—cloaking themselves in black clothes, under cover of darkness. When people were killed along this street, their corpses were sometimes left here for months, because it wasn't safe to retrieve the bodies. Tens of thousands fled, many taking refuge elsewhere in Europe, in the US, and in Canada.

The stories are shocking, and it's difficult to see the war impartially. But looking back on this complicated war, I try not to broadly cast one side as the "aggressors" and another as the "victims." Bosniaks were victimized in Mostar, just as Croats were victimized during the siege of Dubrovnik. And, as the remains of a destroyed Orthodox cathedral on the hillside above Mostar attest, Serbs also took their turn as victims. Every conflict has many sides, and it's the civilians who often pay the highest toll—no matter their affiliation.

Head down Oneŝćukova street, across the Bulevar from the church. A few steps down on the left, the vacant lot with the menorah-ornamented metal fence will someday be the **Mostar Synagogue.** While the town's Jewish population has dwindled to a handful of families since World War II, many Jews courageously served as aid workers and intermediaries when Croats and Bosniaks were killing each other. In recognition of their loving help, the community of Mostar gave them this land for a new synagogue.
• *Continue past the synagogue site, walking two short blocks along a row of modern storefronts. Soon, you'll enter the Old Town and follow the canyon of the...*

Radobolja River Valley

Cross the small river called Radobolja, which winds over waterfalls and several mills on its way to join the Neretva, and enter the city's cobbled historic core (keeping the river on your right). As you step upon the smooth, ankle-twisting river stones, you suddenly become immersed in the Turkish heritage of Mostar. Around you are several fine examples of Mostar's traditional heavy limestone-shingled roofs. From the arrival of the Ottomans all the way through the end of World War II, Mostar had fewer than 15,000 residents—this compact central zone was pretty much all there was to the city. It wasn't until the Tito years that it became industrialized and grew like crazy. As you explore, survey the atmospheric eateries clinging to the walls

of the canyon—and choose one for a meal or drink later in the day (I've noted a couple under "Eating in Mostar," later).

Walk straight ahead until you reach a break in the buildings on your right. Belly up to the wall (you may have to squeeze between souvenir stands). The mosque you see across the river is one of 10 in town. Before the Yugoslav Wars there were 36, and before World War II there were even more (many of those damaged or destroyed in World War II were never repaired or replaced, since Tito's communist Yugoslavia discouraged religion). But the recent war inspired Muslims to finally rebuild. Each of the town's reconstructed mosques was financed by a Muslim nation or organization (this one was a gift from an international association for the protection of Islamic heritage). Some critics (read: Croats) allege that these foreign Muslim influences—which generally interpret their faith more strictly than the typically progressive and laid-back Bosniaks—are threatening to flood the country with a rising tide of Islamic fundamentalism. For more on this debate, see page 423.

• *Look upriver. Spanning the river below the mosque (partly obscured by trees) is the...*

▲Crooked Bridge (Kriva Ćuprija)

This miniature Old Bridge was built nearly a decade before its more famous sibling, supposedly to practice for the real deal. Damaged—but not destroyed—during the war, the original bridge was swept away several years later by floods. The bridge you see today is a reconstruction.

• *Continue on the same street deeper into the city center. After a few steps, take a detour to the left, to the area I like to call...*

"Hammam Square"

Heading up this relatively calm eddy off the rushing river of the main tourist strip, you'll emerge into a small square. The glimmering domes mark the hammam, or bathhouse, built in the classical Ottoman style some 400 years ago. Destroyed during World War II, it was rebuilt a few years ago by a Turkish organization (as if restaking their original Ottoman claim here) and now operates as the **Hammam Museum** (4 KM, hours unpredictable but may be daily May-Oct 9:00-19:00, Nov-April until 17:00). Inside, under the beautiful dome, are artifacts once used in baths like this one—soaps, tea sets, artfully crafted copper soap boxes, towels, and so on—with helpful English explanations of Turkish bathing culture.

As you face the hammam, notice the long building to your right. If you go in the door near the left end of this building, then cross straight through the courtyard, you'll pop out at a **terrace** where various restaurants offer mediocre food with stunning views of the Old Bridge—a great spot for a floodlit dinner.

Near the right end of that same long building is one of Mostar's best-kept secrets. At **Café de Alma,** soulful Jaz ("yahz") loves to explain the rich heritage and traditions around Bosnian coffee (which you may think of as "Turkish coffee"). For 3 KM, he'll show you his coffee roaster (the only one in Mostar), then grind and pour you a cup of Bosnian coffee. The coffee is good, but learning about this important facet of Bosnian life is even better. He also has teas and handmade syrups for refreshing drinks, sells bags of his coffee (either beans or ground), and can organize coffee workshops to get you in touch with Bosnian culture (daily 9:00-18:00, closed Mon in winter and sporadically at other times).

• Head back to the main drag and continue toward the bridge, passing several more market stalls. Because the bridge itself can be crowded with tourists (and pickpockets), I'd hike down to the riverbank below to read the following description while enjoying a dramatic view of the stunning structure. To get there, hook right at the Šadrvan restaurant, then watch for the steps down to the river on your left.

▲▲▲Old Bridge (Stari Most)

One of the most evocative sights in the entire region, this iconic bridge confidently spanned the Neretva River for more than four centuries. Mostarians of all faiths love the bridge and speak of "him" as an old friend. Traditionally considered the point where East meets West, the Old Bridge is as symbolic as it is beautiful. Dramatically arched and flanked by two boxy towers, the bridge is stirring—even if you don't know its history.

Before the Old Bridge, the Neretva was spanned only by a rickety suspension bridge, guarded by *mostari* ("watchers of the bridge"), who gave the city its name. Commissioned in 1557 by the Ottoman Sultan Süleyman the Magnificent, and completed just nine years later, the Old Bridge—the longest single-span stone arch on the planet—was a technological marvel for its time. Because of its graceful keystone design—and the fact that there are empty spaces inside the structure—it's much lighter than it appears. And yet, nearly 400 years after it was built, the bridge was still sturdy enough to support the weight of the Nazi tanks that rolled in to occupy Mostar. Over the centuries, it became the symbol of the town and region—a metaphor in stone for the way the diverse faiths and cultures here were able to bridge the gaps that divided them.

All of that drastically changed in the early 1990s. Beginning in May 1993, as the city became engulfed in war, the Old Bridge frequently got caught in the crossfire. Old tires were slung over its sides to absorb some of the impact from nearby artillery and shrapnel. In November 1993, Croats began shelling the bridge from the top of the mountain (where the cross is now). The bridge took several direct hits on November 8; on November 9, another shell caused the venerable Old Bridge to lurch, then tumble in pieces into the river. The mortar inside, which contained pink bauxite, turned the water red as it fell in. Locals said that their old friend was bleeding.

The decision to destroy the bridge was partly strategic—to

cut off a Bosniak-controlled strip on the west bank from Bosniak forces on the east. (News footage from the time shows Bosniak soldiers scurrying back and forth over the bridge.) But there can be no doubt that, like the Yugoslav Army's siege of Dubrovnik, the attack was also partly symbolic: the destruction of a bridge representing the city's Muslim legacy.

After the war, city leaders decided to rebuild the Old Bridge. Chunks of the original bridge were dredged up from the river. But the limestone had been compromised by soaking in the water for so long, so it couldn't be used (you can still see a few chunks of the old Old Bridge on the riverbank below). Having pledged to rebuild the bridge authentically, restorers cut new stone from the original quarry, and each block was hand-carved. Then they assembled the stones with the same technology used by the Ottomans 450 years ago: Workers erected wooden scaffolding and fastened the blocks together with iron hooks cast in lead. The project was overseen by UNESCO and cost over $13 million, funded largely by international donors.

It took longer to rebuild the bridge in the 21st century than it did to build it in the 16th century. But on July 23, 2004, the new Old Bridge was inaugurated with much fanfare and was immediately embraced by both the city and the world as a sign of reconciliation.

Since its restoration, another piece of bridge history has fully returned, as young men once again jump from the bridge 75 feet down into the Neretva (which remains icy cold even in summer). Done both for the sake of tradition and to impress girls, this custom carried on even during the time when the destroyed bridge was temporarily replaced by a wooden one. Now the tower on the west side of the bridge houses the office of the local Divers Club, a loosely run organization that continues this long-standing ritual. On hot summer days, you'll see divers making a ruckus and collecting donations at the top of the bridge. They tease and tease, standing up on the railing and pretending they're about to jump...then get down and ask for more money. (If he's wearing trunks rather than Speedos, he's not a diver—just a teaser.) Once they collect about €30, one of them will take the plunge. Recently, this custom has gotten even more attention: Each autumn the bridge becomes the venue for a Red Bull-sponsored cliff diving contest.

• *Now begin to walk across the Old Bridge. Watch your footing—the big, chunky steps, spaced at awkward intervals, seem designed to trip up distracted tourists.*

Inside the Halebija Tower at the near end of the bridge, up the stairs (above the Divers Club), the **War Photo Exhibition** displays 50 somber, poignant wartime images taken by photojournalist Wade Goddard. While small, the collection of black-and-white images puts a human face on the suffering by focusing not on the conflict itself, but on the everyday people whose lives were ripped apart by the war (6 KM, daily July-Sept 9:00-21:00, March-June and Oct-Nov 11:00-18:00, closed Dec-Feb).

From the top of the bridge, see how many of the town's 10 mosques you can spot (I count seven minarets).

• *Once across the bridge, three exhibits are on your right; unless you have a special interest, I'd skip these and save your time for the more worthwhile sights described later.*

Exhibits near the Old Bridge

The **Gallery on the Bridge,** a bookstore operated by the local Islamic cultural center, fills a former mosque for the soldiers who guarded the bridge. Explore the good, free photo exhibition of war-torn Mostar. The shop sells an impressively wide range of books about the former Yugoslavia and its troubled breakup. You can pay 4 KM to watch a seven-minute montage of videos and photos of the bridge—before, during, and after the war (entry free, daily 8:00-22:00).

Just beyond the bookstore, tucked into the corner on the right, look for the stairs leading up to the **Museum of the Old Bridge** (Muzej Stari Most). Located within one of the Old Bridge's towers, this museum features a 45-minute film and photos about the reconstruction of the bridge, archaeological findings, and a few other paltry exhibits about the history of the town and bridge, all in English. The museum offers more detail than most casual visitors need (10 KM, daily 10:00-18:00, closed Nov-March, lots of stairs, tel. 036/551-6021).

• *After the Old Bridge, the street swings left and leads you along...*

▲▲Coppersmiths' Street (Kujundžiluk)

This lively strip, with the flavor of a Turkish bazaar, offers some of the most colorful shopping this side of Istanbul. You'll see Mostar's characteristic bridge depicted in every possible way, along with blue-and-white evil eyes (believed in the Turkish culture to keep bad spirits at bay), old Yugoslav Army kitsch (including spent bullet and shell casings engraved with images of Mostar), and hammered-copper decorations—continuing the long tradition that gave the street its name. Partway up, the homes with the colorfully painted facades double as galleries for local artists. The artists live and work upstairs, then sell their work right on this street. Pop into the *atelier d'art* Đul Emina on the right (under wooden beams) to meet Sead Vladović and enjoy his impressive iconographic work. This is the most touristy street in all of Bosnia-Herzegovina, so don't expect any bargains. Still, it's fun. As you stroll, check out the fine views of the Old Bridge.

• *Continue uphill; on the right, you'll soon reach...*

BosnaSeum

This earnest museum has a mixture of ethnographic and historical exhibits which, while a bit dry, do a decent job of showcasing Bosnia's cultural diversity and complex history. English explanations are few, but you can ask at the main desk if a guide will take you through the museum. Without a guide, the exhibits may seem pretty inert—best saved for a hot or rainy day.

Cost and Hours: 10 KM, daily 9:00-22:00, until 17:00 off-season, mobile 067-114-968, www.bosnaseum.com.

Visiting the Museum: Stroll past a series of rooms, the most interesting of which are essentially life-size dioramas recreating the dwellings of Muslim, Orthodox, and Catholic families. One room focuses on a typical Muslim house from the 18th century, while another shows a home from a Croat village. You'll also see exhibits on national and regional costumes from around the country; traditional crafts such as copperwork, blacksmithing, and woodworking; and old photos from both the Ottoman and Austro-Hungarian periods.

Toward the end you'll come across a large model of a "typical" Herzegovinian village, which is impressive for its painstaking intricacy. There are rooms dedicated to Tito's Yugoslavia, with a bust of the marshal himself, and one depicting the destruction Mostar suffered in the 1990s. The museum admirably avoids any sort of nationalist perspective; instead it pays respect to the three major religious groups and their shared history.

• *Farther ahead, after the street levels out, about halfway along the street on the left-hand side, look for the entrance to the...*

▲Koski Mehmet-Pasha Mosque (Koski Mehmet-Paša Džamija)

Step into this courtyard for a look at one of Mostar's many mosques. Dating from the early 17th century, this mosque is notable for its cliff-hanging riverside location, and because it's particularly accessible for tourists.

Cost and Hours: 6 KM to enter mosque, 12 KM includes minaret climb, daily in summer 8:00-21:00, progressively shorter hours off-season. If it seems crowded with tour groups, you can enter a very similar mosque later on this walk instead (which has most of the same features).

Visiting the Mosque: The mosque displays the essential elements of all Islamic places of worship. The **fountain** (*šadrvan*) in the courtyard allows worshippers to wash before entering the mosque, as directed by Islamic law. This practice of ablution is both a literal and a spiritual cleansing in preparation for being in the presence of Allah. It's also refreshing in this hot climate, and the sound of running water helps worshippers concentrate.

The **minaret**—the slender needle jutting up next to the dome—is the Islamic equivalent of the Christian bell tower, used to call people to prayer. In the old days, the *muezzin* (prayer leader) would climb the tower five times a day and chant, "There is no god but God, and Muhammad is his prophet." In modern times, loudspeakers are used instead. Climbing the minaret's 89 claustrophobic, spiral stairs is a memorable experience, rewarding you at the top with the best views over Mostar—and the Old Bridge—that you can get without wings.

Because this mosque is accustomed to tourists, you don't need to take off your shoes to enter (but stay on the green carpet), women don't need to cover their heads, and it's fine to take photos inside. Near the front of the mosque, you may see some of the small, overlapping rugs that are below this covering (reserved for shoes-off worshippers).

Once **inside,** notice the traditional elements of the mosque. The niche *(mihrab)* across from the entry is oriented toward Mecca—the direction all Muslims face to pray. The small stairway *(mimber)* that seems to go nowhere is symbolic of the growth of Islam—Muhammad had to stand higher and higher to talk to his growing following. This serves as a pulpit for the cleric. No priest ever stands on the top stair, which is symbolically reserved for Muhammad.

The balcony just inside the door is traditionally where women worship. Historically, Muslim men decided prayer would go better without the distraction of bent-over women between them and Mecca. These days, women can also pray on the main floor with the men, but they must avoid physical contact.

Muslims believe that capturing a living creature in a painting or a sculpture is inappropriate. (In fact, depictions of Allah and the prophet Muhammad are strictly forbidden.) Instead, mosques are filled with ornate patterns and Arabic calligraphy (of the name

The Muslims of Bosnia

Muslims have been an integral part of Bosnia's cultural tapestry for centuries. During the more than 400 years under Ottoman rule, the Muslim Turks did not forcibly convert their subjects (unlike some Catholic despots at the time). But many local Slavs were persuaded to become Muslims, for lower taxes and better business opportunities. Within 150 years of the start of Ottoman rule, half of the population of Bosnia-Herzegovina was Muslim. These people constitute an ethnic group called "Bosniaks," and many of them are still practicing Sunni Muslims today. Most Bosniaks are Slavs—of the same ethnic stock as Croats and Serbs—but some have ancestors who married into Turkish families.

The actions of a small but attention-grabbing faction of Muslim extremists have burdened Islam with a bad reputation

in the Western world. But judging Islam based on ISIS and al-Qaeda is a bit like judging Christianity based on the Oslo gunman and the Ku Klux Klan. Visiting Mostar is a unique opportunity to get a taste of a fully Muslim society, made a bit less intimidating because it wears a more-familiar European face.

Here's an admittedly simplistic outline designed to help travelers from the Christian West understand a very rich but often misunderstood religion that's worthy of respect:

Muslims, like Christians and Jews, are monotheistic. They call God "Allah." The most important person in the Islamic faith is Muhammad, Allah's most important prophet, who lived in the sixth and seventh centuries AD. Jesus is also one of the most revered prophets in Islamic tradition.

The "five pillars" of Islam are the same among Muslims in Bosnia-Herzegovina, Turkey, Iraq, the US, and everywhere else. Followers of Islam should:

1. Say and believe this basic statement of faith: "There is no god but God, and Muhammad is his prophet."

2. Pray five times a day.

3. Give to the poor (annually about 2.5 percent of one's income).

4. Fast during daylight hours through the month of Ramadan. Fasting develops self-control and awareness, and is a step toward achieving selflessness.

5. Make a pilgrimage (hajj) to Mecca. Muslims who can afford it and are physically able are required to travel to Mecca at least once in their lifetimes.

"Muhammad" and important prayers and sayings from the Quran). You'll also see some floral and plant designs, which you'd never see in a more conservative, Middle Eastern mosque.

Before leaving, ponder how progressive the majority of Mostar's Muslims are. Most of them drink alcohol, wear modern European clothing (you'll see very few women wearing head scarves or men with beards—and those you do see are likely tourists from the Middle East), and almost never visit a mosque to pray. In so many ways, these people don't fit our preconceived notions of Islam...and yet, they are Muslims all the same.

The mosque's **courtyard** is shared by several merchants. When you're done haggling, head to the **terrace** behind the mosque for the best view in town of the Old Bridge (entrance included in mosque ticket).

• *Just beyond this mosque, the river-stone cobbles of the Old Town end. Take a right and leave the cutesy tourists' world. Walk up one block to the big...*

▲▲New Muslim Cemetery

In this cemetery, which was a park before the Yugoslav Wars, every tomb is dated 1993, 1994, or 1995. As the war raged, more exposed cemeteries were unusable. But this tree-covered piece of land was relatively safe from Croat snipers. As the casualties mounted, locals buried their loved ones here under cover of darkness. Many of these people were soldiers, but some were civilians. Muslim graves typically don't display images of the deceased, but here you'll see photos of war dead who were young members of the Muslim community. The fleur-de-lis shape of many of the tombstones is a patriotic symbol for the nation of Bosnia.

• *For an optional sightseeing stop, you can head up the wide stairs to the right of the cemetery (near the mosque). At #4 (on the right, just before and across from the bombed-out tower), you'll find the...*

Museum of Herzegovina (Muzej Hercegovine)

This humble little museum is made worthwhile by a deeply moving **film** that traces the history of the town through its Old Bridge: fun circa-1957 footage of the diving contests; harrowing scenes of the bridge being pummeled, and finally toppled, by artillery; and a stirring sequence showing the bridge's reconstruction and grand reopening in 2004—with high-fives, Beethoven's *Ode to Joy*, fireworks, and more divers. (This includes much of the same footage as the similar film at the Gallery on the Bridge, described earlier, but doesn't focus solely on the wartime damage.)

The museum itself displays fragments of this region's rich history, including historical photos and several items from its Ottoman period. There are sparse English descriptions, but without a tour guide the exhibits are a bit difficult to appreciate. Topics include the Turkish period, Herzegovina under the Austro-Hungarian Empire, village life, and (in the basement) local archaeology. One small room commemorates the house's former owner, Džemal Bijedić, who served as prime minister of Yugoslavia for several years until he was killed in a mysterious plane crash in 1977. (If Bijedić had lived, many wonder whether he might have succeeded Tito...and succeeded in keeping Yugoslavia together.)

Cost and Hours: 5-KM museum entry includes 12-minute film, no narration—works in any language, ask "film?" as you enter; Mon-Fri 8:00-16:00, closed Sat-Sun; Bajatova 4—walking up these stairs, it's the second door that's marked for the museum, under the overhanging balcony, tel. 036/555-215, www.muzejhercegovine.com.

• *Backtrack to where you left the Old Town. Notice the Tepa Market, with locals buying clothing and produce, in the area just beyond the pedestrian zone. Now continue into the modern town, with the market on your left (bear right at the fork). You'll head along the lively street called Braće Fejića. (There's no sign, but the street is level and busy with cafés.) You're in the "new town," where locals sit out in front of boisterous cafés sipping coffee while listening to the thumping beat of distinctly Eastern-sounding music. Stroll down this street for a few blocks. On the left, just after the handy Konzum supermarket (a block or so before the big minaret), side-trip a block to the left to reach...*

▲Bišćević Turkish House (Bišćevića Ćošak)

Mostar has three traditional Turkish-style homes that are open for tourists to visit. The Bišćević House is the oldest, most interesting, and most convenient for a quick visit, but two others are described at the end of this listing. Dating from 1635, the Bišćević House is typical of old houses in Mostar that mix Oriental style with Mediterranean features.

Cost and Hours: 4 KM, daily 9:00-19:00, generally closed Dec-Feb—but you can arrange a visit by calling ahead to Fortuna Tours at tel. 036/552-197; house is at Bišćevića 13.

Visiting the House: First you'll step through the outer (or animals') garden, then into the inner (or family's) garden. This inner zone is surrounded by a high wall—protection from the sun's rays, from thieves...and from prying eyes, allowing women to take off the veil they were required to wear in public. Enjoy the geometrical patters of the smooth river stones in the floor (for example, the five-sided star), and keep an eye out for the house's pet turtles. It's no coincidence that the traditional fountain (*šadrvan*) resembles those at the entrance to a mosque—a reminder of the importance of running water in Muslim culture. The little white building is a kitchen—cleverly located apart from the house so that the heat and smells of cooking didn't permeate the upstairs living area.

Buy your ticket and take off your shoes before you climb up the wooden staircase. Imagine how a stairway like this one could be pulled up for extra protection in case of danger (notice that this one has a "trap door" to cover it). The cool, shady, and airy living room is open to the east—from where the wind rarely blows. The overhanging roof also prevented the hot sun from reaching this area. The loom in the corner was the women's workplace—the carpets you're standing on would have been woven there. The big chests against the wall were used to bring the dowry when the homeowner took a new wife. Study the fine wood carving that decorates the space.

Continue back into the main gathering room (*divanhan*). This space—whose name comes from the word "talk"—is designed in a circle so people could face each other, cross-legged, for a good conversation while they enjoyed a dramatic view overlooking the Neretva. The room comes with a box of traditional costumes—great for photo fun. Put on a pair of baggy pants and a fez and really lounge.

Other Turkish Houses: If you're intrigued by this house, consider dropping by Mostar's two other Turkish houses. The newer **Muslibegović House** (Muslibegovića Kuća) dates from 1871, just a few years before the Ottomans left town. This homey house—which also rents out rooms to visitors (see "Sleeping in Mostar," later)—has many of the same features as the Bišćević House. If they're not too busy, Sanela or Gabriela can give you an English tour (4 KM, mid-April-mid-Oct daily 11:00-18:00, closed to visitors off-season, just two blocks uphill from the Karađozbeg Mosque at Osman Đikića 41, tel. 036/551-379, www.muslibegovichouse. com). To find it, go up the street between the Karađozbeg Mosque and the cemetery, cross the busy street, and continue a long block uphill on the alley. The wall with the slate roof on the left marks the house.

The **Kajtaz House** (Kajtazova Kuća), hiding up a residential alley a few blocks from the Old Bridge, feels lived-in because it still is (in the opposite direction from most of the other sights, at Gaše Ilića 21).

• *Go back to the main café street and continue until you see (on the left) a sculpture of a mother and a child in a cage. This is the...*

▲Museum of War and Genocide Victims 1992-1995 (Muzej žrtava rata i genocida 1992-1995)

Bosnia is about more than just the 1990s Yugoslav Wars—there are mountain landscapes, a fascinating mix of cultures, hearty food, and friendly people. But if Mostar is the only place you visit in the country, then this museum is an essential stop to learn about the violent disintegration of the former Yugoslavia.

Cost and Hours: 10 KM, daily 9:00-22:00, shorter off-season, mobile 061-462-898.

Visiting the Museum: The museum focuses on the individual stories of people who suffered and died during the war in Bosnia. Testimonies, all translated into English, are often linked to an item, such as a jacket, letters to family, or a diary, that belonged to a victim. Good descriptions explain the complicated demographics of Yugoslavia and give biographies of convicted war criminals whose bloodthirsty attempt to change those demographics drove the conflict. You'll also see a few movies, including one about the siege of Sarajevo, and objects that were used to torture people. Downstairs is a grisly room exploring the mass graves and forensic research carried out to identify bodies.

While a visit here can be disturbing, the museum does an excellent job of making the war meaningful for people who didn't live through it. Its personal, poignant exhibits help remind us that one of the first steps toward mass atrocities is to dehumanize people— and as with the sculpture of the mother and child in a cage out front, it warns that dehumanization is ongoing today.

• *Across the street from the museum you'll find...*

▲Karađozbeg Mosque (Karađozbegova Džamija)

The city's main mosque was completed in 1557, the same year work began on the Old Bridge. This mosque, which welcomes visitors, feels less touristy than the one back in the Old Town. Before entering the gate into the complex, look for the picture showing the war damage sustained here. You'll see that this mosque has most of the same elements as the Koski Mehmet-Pasha Mosque (described earlier), but some of these decorations are original. Across the street is another cemetery with tombstones from that terrible year, 1993.

Cost and Hours: 5 KM to enter mosque, 5 KM more to climb minaret, daily 9:00-18:00, Oct-April 10:00-16:00. You'll need to remove your shoes, but women don't have to cover their heads, and photos are allowed inside.

• *Now leave the tourists' Mostar and continue into modern, urban Mostar along the street in front of the Karadozbeg Mosque. This grimy, mostly traffic-free street is called...*

▲Braće Fejića

Walking along the modern town's main café strip, enjoy the opportunity to observe this workaday Bosniak town. Notice many cafés that serve drinks but no food. People generally eat at home before going out to nurse an affordable drink. (Café ABC has good cakes and ice cream; the upstairs is a popular pizza hangout for students and families.)

At the small mosque on the left, obituary announcements are tacked to the stone wall on the corner, listing the bios and funeral times for locals who have recently died. A fig tree grows out of the mosque's minaret, just an accident of nature illustrating how that plant can thrive with almost no soil (somehow, the Bosniaks can relate). Walking farther, look back and up to see a few ruins—still ugly more than two decades after the war. There's a messy confusion about who owns what in Mostar. Surviving companies have no money. Yugo Bank, which held the mortgages, is defunct. No one will invest until clear ownership is established. Until then, the people of Mostar sip their coffee in the shadow of these jagged reminders of the warfare that wracked this town a couple of decades ago.

Near the end of the pedestrian zone, through the parking lot on the right, look for the building with communist-era reliefs of 12th-century Bogomil tomb decor—remembering the indigenous culture that existed here even before the arrival of the Ottomans.

When you finally hit the big street (with car traffic), head left one block to the big **Trg Musala** (literally, "Place for Prayer"). Historically, this was where pilgrims gathered before setting off for Mecca on their hajj. This is a great scene on balmy evenings, when it's a rendezvous point for the community. The two busts near the fountain provide perfect goal posts for budding soccer stars.

• *For a finale, you can continue one block more out onto the bridge to survey the town you just explored. From here, you can backtrack to linger in the places you found most inviting. Or you can venture into...*

The Dawn of War in Mostar

Mostar was always one of the most stubbornly independent parts of the former Yugoslavia. It had one of the highest rates of mixed-ethnicity marriages in all of Bosnia-Herzegovina. In the early 1990s, Mostar's demographics were proportioned more or less evenly—about 35 percent of its residents were Bosniaks, 34 percent Croats, and 19 percent Serbs. But this delicate balance was shattered in a few brutal months of warfare.

On April 1, 1992, Bosnia-Herzegovina—led by Muslim president Alija Izetbegović—declared independence from Yugoslavia. Very quickly, the Serb-dominated Yugoslav People's Army moved to stake their claim on territory throughout the country, including the important city of Mostar. On April 3, Serb forces occupied the east end of town (including the Ottoman Old Town), forcing many residents—predominantly Croats and Bosniaks—to hole up in the western part of the city. Meanwhile, Serbian and Croatian leaders were secretly meeting to divvy up Bosnian territory, and by early May, they'd agreed that Croatia would claim Mostar.

Several weeks later, when the joint Croat-Bosniak forces crossed back over the river, the Serb forces mysteriously withdrew from the city (having been directed to capitulate), and retreated to the mountaintops above town. The Croats and Bosniaks, believing they'd achieved peace, began putting their city back together. During this time, some factions also rounded up, tortured, and killed Serbs still living in Mostar. Many Bosniaks moved back to their homes on the east side of town, but, rather oddly, many of the Croats who had previously resided there instead stayed in the west—in many cases, moving into apartments vacated by Serbs who had fled.

On May 9, 1993—the Yugoslav holiday of "Victory over Fascism Day"—Mostarians were rocked awake by the terrifying sounds of artillery shells. Croat military forces swept through the city, forcibly moving remaining Bosniaks from the west part of town into the east. Throughout that summer, Bosniak men were captured and sent to concentration camps, while the Croats virtually sealed off the east side of town—creating a giant ghetto with no way in or out. The long and ugly siege of Mostar had begun.

WESTERN (CROAT) MOSTAR

Most tourists stay on the Bosniak side of town. But for a complete look at this divided city, it's well worth strolling to the west side. While there's not much in the way of sightseeing here, and much of this urban zone isn't particularly pretty, it does provide an interesting contrast to the Muslim side of town. As this is the location of some of Mostar's new shopping malls, this area feels more vital each year, and a few of the tree-lined streets seem downright elegant.

Crossing the river and the Bulevar, the scarred husks of destroyed buildings begin to fade away, and within a block you're immersed in concrete apartment buildings. When the city became divided, the Muslims holed up in the original Ottoman Old Town, while the Croats claimed this modern Tito-era sprawl. The relative lack of war damage here makes it clear which side of town had it worse. Also notice that there are more pizza and pasta restaurants than *ćevapčići* joints—even the food over here is more Croat than Bosniak.

Looking at a map, you'll notice that many streets on this side of town are named for Croatian cities (Dubrovačka, Splitska, Vukovarska) or historical figures (Kneza Branimira, Kralja Tomislava, and Kralja Petra Krešimira—for the dukes who first united the Croats in the ninth and tenth centuries). This side of town also has several remnants of Mostar's brief period of Habsburg rule (1878-1918). During this time, the empire quickly expanded what had been a sleepy Ottoman backwater, laying out grand boulevards and erecting genteel buildings that look like they'd be at home in Vienna.

All streets converge at the big roundabout (about a 15-minute walk from the Old Town) called the **Rondo,** which is a good place to get oriented to this neighborhood. Overlooking this lively intersection is the stately Hrvatski Dom ("Croatia House") cultural center. Notice how even the street signs are politically charged: *Centar* signs pointedly direct traffic *away* from the (Bosniak) Old Town, and many road signs point toward Široki Brijeg—a Croat stronghold in western Herzegovina.

The adjacent **Park Zrinjevac,** a pleasant place to stroll, was the site of an infamously ill-fated attempt at reconciliation. In the early 2000s, idealistic young Mostarians formed the Urban Movement of Mostar, which searched for a way to connect the still-feuding Catholic and Muslim communities. As a symbol of their goals, they chose Bruce Lee, the deceased kung-fu movie star, beloved by both Croats and Bosniaks for his characters' honorable struggle against injustice. A life-size bronze statue of Lee was unveiled with fanfare in this park in November of 2005—but was almost immediately vandalized. The statue was repaired and may or may not have been returned to its pedestal (which you'll still find in the park).

Several interesting sights lie close to this roundabout. A block toward the Old Town from the Rondo (on Kralja Višeslava Humskog), look for the big **Muslim cemetery** with tombstones from the early 1990s. These are the graves of those killed during the first round of fighting, when the Croats and Bosniaks teamed up to fight the Serbs.

If you head from the Rondo down Kneza Branimira (across from the park), you'll enjoy an inviting boulevard shaded by plane trees. When first built, this street was called **Štefanijino Šetalište**—"Stéphanie's Promenade," after the Belgian princess who married Austria's Archduke Rudolf (the heir apparent of the Habsburg Empire until he died in a mysterious murder-suicide pact with his mistress).

If you head up Kralja Petra Krešimira IV from the Rondo, after two long blocks on the left you'll see an abandoned, derelict park leading to a gigan-

tic **Partisan Cemetery and Monument.** This socialist-style monument spreads all the way up the hill. It oozes with symbolism trumpeting the pivotal WWII Battle of the Neretva, when Tito and his Partisan Army turned the tables on Nazi forces (just 30 miles north of here—see page 525). It was designed by Bogdan Bogdanović, who created many such monuments and memorials throughout Yugoslavia, and dedicated by Tito himself in 1965. From the terrace at the top, which is scattered with symbolic gravestones for those who gave their lives to free Yugoslavia from the Nazis, small streams once trickled down to the large enclosure at the bottom, ultimately flowing beneath a stylized broken bridge representing the Bridge at the Neretva. Today the monument is overgrown and ignored—a tragic symbol of post-Tito ethnic discord. Local Croats—who have little nostalgia for the Yugoslav period, which they now view as a time of oppression—seem to intentionally neglect the place. This formerly hallowed ground is a mess of broken concrete and a popular place for drunken benders, garbage dumping, and drug deals (be careful if you decide to explore—and avoid it after dark). A stroll here comes with a poignant reflection on how one generation's honored war dead can become the next generation's unwanted burden.

Nightlife in Mostar

Though Mostar is touristy, it's also a real urban center with a young population looking for fun. The courtyard next to the Hammam Museum (on "Hammam Square") is a fun place to observe them in action. The Old Bridge is another popular meeting place for locals as well as tourists. A stroll from the Old Bridge down the café-lined Braće Fejića boulevard to the modern **Trg Musala** at the far end of town (described earlier) gives a great peek at Mostarians socializing away from the tourists. Wherever you wind up, order a cocktail or try a Turkish-style hubbly-bubbly (*šiša*, SHEE-shah). Ask to have one of these big water pipes fired up for you and choose your flavored tobacco: apple, cappuccino, banana, or lemon.

Ali Baba is an actual cave featuring a fun, atmospheric, and mellow hangout scene (look for the low-profile entrance along Coppersmiths' Street, just down from the Old Bridge— watch for signs tucked down a rocky alley).

Oscar Nightclub is a cara-vanserai for lounge lizards—an exotic world mixing babbling streams, terraces, lounge chairs, and big sofas where young and old enjoy cocktails and *šiša* (open "nonstop" as long as the weather is good—usually June-mid-Sept, closed off-season, up from the Old Bridge on Oneščukova street, near the Crooked Bridge at the end of the pedestrian zone).

Black Dog Pub, the brainchild of Seattleite Stefan (who moved to Mostar as part of a humanitarian NGO during the war), fosters a lively, youthful scene that feels more international than "traditional Bosnian." They serve more than 40 local microbrews (including several from the Oldbridz Brewery)—some on tap— and have live music most nights from around 20:00. While they don't serve food, they can call in an order for you at a neighboring restaurant. Stefan makes a point of hiring locals from every different ethnic background, and his bar has become a hangout for Mostarians from both sides of town as well as tourists. Sit in the convivial interior or head out to the riverside terrace (daily in summer 9:00-24:00, from 15:00 off-season, just across the Crooked Bridge from Oneščukova street).

Sleeping in Mostar

Most of my listings are small, friendly, accessible, affordable guesthouses in or very near the Old Town. Prices are deceptively low here—don't overlook my lowest-priced listings, which are essentially as comfortable as the pricier ones. Many hotels and pensions in town promise "parking," but it's often street parking out front—private lots are rare. Mostar's Old Town can be very noisy on weekends, with nightclubs and outdoor restaurants rollicking into the wee hours. If you're a light sleeper, consider Villa Fortuna, the Muslibegović House, or Shangri La, which are quieter than the norm. If you're looking for something more luxurious, check online to see if the new Marriott near the Old Bridge has opened.

$$$$ The **Muslibegović House,** a Bosnian national monument open to tourists during the day, is in an actual Turkish home dating from 1871. The 10 homey rooms and two suites combine classic Turkish style (elegant and comfortable old beds, creaky wooden floors with colorful carpets, lounging sofas, shoes left at the outer door) with modern comforts (air-con, flat-screen TVs). Situated on a quiet residential lane just above the bustle of Mostar's main pedestrian drag and Old Town zone, this is a memorable experience (includes a tour of the house, closed Nov-March, 2 blocks uphill from the Karađozbeg Mosque at Osman Đikića 41, tel. 036/551-379, www.muslibegovichouse.com, muslibegovichouse@gmail.com; Sanela, Gabriela, and stoic boss Tađudin).

$ **Shangri La Mansion** fills a gorgeously restored Austro-Hungarian building on a hill above the Old Town, accessed by a steep driveway next to a war ruin. The 12 rooms come in different sizes, but they're all modern and nicely appointed. Thoughtfully run with modern flair by Nermin, it also has a beautiful rooftop garden that's ideal for relaxing (breakfast extra, air-con, free parking, Kalhanska 10, mobile 061-169-362, www.shangrila.com.ba, info@shangrila.com.ba).

$ **Villa Anri,** between the Old Town and the Bulevar, feels bigger and a bit more hotelesque than other Mostar pensions. The stony facade hides eight rooms (six with balconies) combining old Herzegovinian style and bright colors. The big draw is the rooftop terrace, shared by two rooms, which enjoys grand views over the Old Bridge area (cash only, air-con, free parking, Braće Đukića 4, tel. 036/578-477, http://villa-anri-mostar-ba.book.direct, villa.anri@gmail.com).

$ **Pansion Čardak,** run by kind and gregarious Suzana and Nedžad Kasumović, has seven pleasant rooms sharing a kitchen in a stone house set just back from the bustling Crooked Bridge area. Their top-floor rooms, while a bit more expensive, are beautifully decorated and feel luxurious (cash only, breakfast extra at nearby restaurant, air-con, free parking, Jusovina 3, tel. 036/578-249, mobile 061-385-988, www.pansion-cardak.com, info@pansion-cardak.com).

$ Pansion Nur, run by Niyaz, has four simpler rooms and a shared kitchen (cash only, no breakfast, air-con, free parking, Jusovina 8b, mobile 062-160-872, www.pansion-nur.com, info@pansion-nur.com).

$ Hotel Kriva Ćuprija ("Crooked Bridge"), by the bridge of the same name, is tucked between waterfalls in the picturesque gorge a few steps from the Old Bridge. It's more hotelesque, impersonal, and expensive than my other listings in this price range. The 26 rooms are stylish (though many suffer from nearby nightlife noise), and their restaurant has atmospheric outdoor seating (RS%, air-con, call to reconfirm if arriving after 19:00, enter at Onešćukova 23 or Kriva Ćuprija 2, tel. 036/360-360, mobile 061-915-915, www.hotel-mostar.ba, krivacuprijamostar@gmail.com, Sami and Jasna). They also have three big apartments in a building across the river.

¢ Villa Fortuna is an exceptional value, located in a nondescript urban neighborhood a few minutes' walk farther away from the Old Bridge. Owners Nela and Mili Bijavica rent eight tasteful, modern rooms plus six apartments above the main office of Fortuna Tours. The courtyard in front offers free, secure parking, and in back there's a pleasant garden with a traditional Herzegovinian garden cottage (RS%, breakfast extra, nonsmoking, air-con, Rade Bitange 34, tel. 036/580-625, mobile 063-299-189, www.villafortuna.ba, villa_fortuna@bih.net.ba).

¢ Villa Botticelli, overlooking a charming waterfall garden just up the valley from the Crooked Bridge, has five colorful rooms at affordable prices (breakfast extra, air-con, Muje Bjelavca 6, enter along the street facing the Crooked Bridge, mobile 063-319-057, www.villabotticelli.com, info@villabotticelli.com, sweet Snježana and Zoran).

Eating in Mostar

Most of Mostar's tourist-friendly restaurants are conveniently concentrated in the Old Town. If you walk anywhere that's cobbled, you'll stumble onto many tempting restaurants charging the same reasonable prices and serving rustic, traditional Bosnian food. The menus at most places are virtually identical—though quality and ambience can vary greatly. As eateries tend to come and go quickly here, and little distinguishes these places anyway, don't be too focused on a particular spot. Grilled meats are especially popular—read the "Balkan Flavors" sidebar, on page 425, before you dine. Most local wines are made with one of two indigenous grapes:

blatina (literally "muddy"; a thick, heavy, earthy red) and *žilavka* (literally "root"; a bright, fairly acidic white).

ON THE EMBANKMENT, WITH OLD BRIDGE VIEWS

For the best atmosphere, find your way into the several levels of restaurants that clamber up the riverbank and offer perfect views of the Old Bridge. This is the most memorable setting for dining in Mostar—but the quality of the food is uniformly low, and prices are relatively high (figure 8-18 KM for a meal). If you want a good perch, it's fun and smart to drop by earlier in the day and personally reserve the table of your choice.

To reach two of the most scenic eateries, go over the Old Bridge to the west side of the river, and bear right on the cobbles until you get to the Hammam Museum. To the right of the old Turkish bathhouse is the entrance to a lively courtyard surrounded by cafés. Crossing straight through the courtyard, you'll find stairs leading down to several riverfront terraces belonging to two different restaurants: **$ Babilon** (my choice for better food) and **$ Teatar.** Poke around to find your favorite bridge panorama before settling in for a drink or a meal. Two other places (including a pizzeria) are a bit closer to the bridge—to reach these, look for the alley on the left just before the bridge tower.

IN AND NEAR THE OLD TOWN

While they lack the Old Bridge views, these places are just as central as those listed above and serve food that's generally a step up.

$ Restoran Hindin Han is pleasantly situated on a woody terrace over a rushing stream. It's respected locally for its good cooking—with a wide variety, from grilled meats to seafood—and fair prices (Sarajevsko beer on tap, daily 11:00-24:00, Jusovina 10, tel. 036/581-054). To find it, walk west from the Old Bridge, bear left at the Šadrvan restaurant, cross the bridge, and you'll see it on the left.

$ Tima-Irma, run by the frenetic one-woman show Irma, grills up the best *ćevapčići* and other meats that I've had in Mostar. Its touristy, very scenic location—along the main shopping drag, a couple of blocks from the Old Bridge—belies the quality of the food (long hours daily, Onešćukova b.b., mobile 066-905-070).

$ Nacionalni Restoran Aščinica Balkan ("Balkan National Restaurant/Cafeteria") is a convenient cafeteria-style eatery with two handy locations. They serve up tasty, home-cooked Bosnian specialties; you can order from the menu, but it's more fun to order a "mix" *(mješanac)* plate from the display case—the small 10-KM plate is plenty for a light meal (Bosnian coffee, tempting dessert display case, daily 7:00-24:00, one location right at the end of the Old Town cobbles before the market, the other a couple of blocks away on the new town's main drag at Braće Fejića 57, tel. 036/551-868).

$ Saray is an untouristy, nondescript little eatery just uphill from the Karađozbeg Mosque in the modern part of town. They have a basic menu of very cheap and tasty grilled meats—specializing in the classic *ćevapčići*—and outdoor seating overlooking a playground that offers good people- and kid-watching while you eat (daily 7:00-23:00, Karađozbegova 3, mobile 062-322-962).

$ Urban Grill's food is nothing special—it has basically the same menu as other places in town—but its terrace enjoys one of Mostar's best unobstructed views of the Old Bridge (Bosnian coffee, daily 8:00-22:00, enter along the main cobbled Old Town drag at Mala Tepa 26, mobile 063-410-990).

In the West (Croat) Side of Town: While less charming and romantic, a stroll to the west side of town offers an interesting contrast to the cutesy Old Town—and a completely different array of restaurants. Here you'll find more pizza and pasta than grilled meats, as well as shiny new shopping centers with modern food courts. For more on this neighborhood, see "Sights in Mostar," earlier.

Mostar Connections

BY BUS

Mostar has two different, autonomous bus terminals, each served by different companies. Mostar's **main bus station** (Autobusna Stanica) is on the east/Bosniak side of the river, about a 15-minute walk north of the Old Town (for details, see "Arrival in Mostar," earlier). Most buses you're likely to take use this station; for information on the other station (on the west/Croat side of town), see the end of this section.

Schedules and Tickets: Tracking down reliable schedule information in Mostar is tricky, but you can research timetables (and purchase tickets) at GetByBus.com, which usually succeeds in listing most of your options. At the main station, two primary companies operate independent offices, providing schedule information and tickets only for their own buses—visit both before buying tickets. As you face the bus station, near the left end is the Bosniak company **Autoprevoz** (tel. 036/551-900, www.autoprevoz.ba); they also sell tickets for a few other companies (including Eurolines and Bogdan Bus). Near the right end is the Croat-owned **Globtour** (look for *Mediteran Tours* sign, tel. 036/550-065, www.globtour. com), which sells tickets only for its own buses. Local and regional connections (not listed below) are operated by Mostar Bus, whose buses depart across the street from the main bus station (www. mostarbus.ba). Note that buses to seasonal destinations (such as along the Dalmatian Coast) run more frequently in peak season, roughly June through mid-September.

From Mostar's Main Bus Station: Both Autoprevoz and Globtour operate buses to **Sarajevo** (9/day on Autoprevoz, 4/day on Globtour, 3 hours), **Zagreb** (4/day on Autoprevoz, 4/day on Globtour, 9 hours, includes a night bus), and **Split** (3/day on Autoprevoz, 2/day on Globtour, 4 hours; additional departures by Eurolines in summer). Globtour exclusively handles buses to **Međugorje** (5/day, 40 minutes), and **Dubrovnik** (2/day, 3-4 hours).

That important **Dubrovnik** connection is tricky: Most days, all Dubrovnik buses depart early in the day, making an afternoon return from Mostar to Dubrovnik impossible. However, in summer (June-Aug), Eurolines typically adds two more departures each day—including a handy 17:30 departure, which makes day-tripping from Dubrovnik workable (tickets sold at Autoprevoz office).

Globtour also runs a handy bus to Montenegro's **Bay of Kotor.** Two buses leave around the same time, at 7:00; one takes the inland route, via Herzegovina and Trebinje, passing only one border (but with much less coastal scenery). This takes longer but is more likely to be on time, arriving in Kotor around 16:00. The other option takes the coastal route via Dubrovnik, with four borders and more scenery, and is scheduled to arrive at 13:00—but often arrives late. Another connection to Kotor (using the inland route) leaves at 16:00, arriving around 1:00 in the morning.

From Mostar's West/Croat Bus Station: A few additional buses, mostly to Croatian destinations and to Croat areas of Bosnia-Herzegovina, depart from the west side of town. These use a makeshift "station" (actually a gravel lot behind a gas station) on Vukovarska street, called "Kolodvor." It's about a 15-minute walk due west of the main bus station. Most buses using the Kolodvor station are operated by the Euroherc company. In addition to one daily bus apiece to **Zagreb, Split,** and **Sarajevo,** this station has several departures to **Metković** (at the Croatian border, with additional connections to Croatian destinations) and to **Međugorje.** Additionally, some Croat buses leave from a bus stop near the Franciscan church. But since the connections are sparse, the location is inconvenient, and the "station" is dreary, I'd stick with the main bus station and ignore this option unless you're desperate.

BY TRAIN
While the bus is preferable for almost every destination, there is a train to **Sarajevo** that makes the connection faster and costs less. While you'll enjoy a higher vantage point for this scenic journey, the train spends more time in tunnels—so you'll wind up seeing less (generally 2/day, about 2 hours, check the schedule at www. zfbh.ba).

ROUTE TIPS FOR DRIVERS FROM DUBROVNIK TO MOSTAR
You have two options for the drive between Dubrovnik and Mostar: easy and straightforward along the coast, or adventurous and off-the-beaten-path through the Herzegovinian mountains. I've narrated each route coming from Dubrovnik to Mostar, but you can do either one in reverse. (For driving directions from Mostar to Sarajevo, see the end of the Sarajevo chapter.)

Option 1: Main Coastal Road
The vast majority of traffic from Dubrovnik to Mostar follows the coastal road north, then cuts east into Bosnia. Because this is one of the most direct routes, it can be crowded (allow about 2.5 hours, not counting photo and sightseeing stops, or border delays). It's also a bit inconvenient, as you have to cross the border three times (into and out of Bosnia at Neum, and into Bosnia again at Metković).

Crowd-Beating Tip: At busy times—particularly in the peak of summer (July-Aug), and especially on weekends—northbound traffic can back up at Neum (worst around 9:00-11:00, when day-trippers from Dubrovnik are clogging the roads). If busy borders have been the norm (you can try asking savvy locals—but it's hard to predict), try leaving Dubrovnik early (before 8:00) or later (around 10:00, or leave earlier but make some stops—such as Trsteno or Ston—en route; your goal is to reach the border after 11:00). Another way to beat the crowds is to take the lesser-known border crossing between the Croatian town of Slano ("Salty") and the Bosnian town of Ravno ("Flat")—you'll meet up with my "Rugged-but-Scenic" route, described later, near the Vjetrenica cave (see "Near Dubrovnik" map on page 345). This misses the scenery of the Neretva Delta and the option of seeing the Roman museum near Metković, but if you expect the Neum borders to be backed up, it will save some time.

The Drive Begins: Head north out of Dubrovnik, passing some of the places mentioned in the Near Dubrovnik chapter: **Trsteno** (with its arboretum), and **Ston** and **Mali Ston** (with a mighty wall and waterfront restaurants, respectively). After passing the Ston turnoff, you'll see the long, mountainous, vineyard-draped **Pelješac Peninsula** across the bay on your left. (Note: Between Trsteno and Ston—about 30 minutes after crossing the bridge out of Dubrovnik—you'll curve around the bay town of Slano, where you can take the alternate border crossing to Ravno, Bosnia.)

Soon you'll come to a surprise border crossing, at **Neum.** Here you'll cross into Bosnia-Herzegovina—then, six miles later, cross back out again (for details on this odd little stretch of Bosnian coast, see page 360).

You won't be back in Croatia for long. Just north of Neum, the main coastal road jogs away from the coast and around the striking **Neretva River Delta**— the extremely fertile "garden patch of Croatia," which produces a significant portion of Croatia's fruits and vegetables. The Neretva is the same river that flows under Mostar's Old Bridge upstream— but in Metković, it spreads out into 12 branches as it enters the Adriatic, flooding a vast plain and creating a bursting cornucopia in the middle of an otherwise rocky and arid region. Enjoying some of the most plentiful sunshine on the Croatian coast, as well as a steady supply of water for irrigation, the Neretva Delta is as productive as it is beautiful.

At the Neretva Delta, turn off for the town of **Metković.** If you're interested in Roman ruins, it's worth a brief detour to see the Narona Archaeological Museum in Vid (see listing later in this chapter). Otherwise, just carry on straight through Metković to reach the border into **Bosnia-Herzegovina,** then continue straight on the main road (M-17) directly into Mostar. As you drive, you'll see destroyed buildings and occasional roadside memorials bearing the likenesses of fresh-faced soldiers who died in the Yugoslav Wars of the mid-1990s.

Along the way are a few interesting detours, all described later in this chapter: In Čapljina, you can turn off to the left to reach Međugorje. If you stay on the main road, keep your eyes peeled soon after the Čapljina turnoff for a mountaintop castle tower (on the right side of the road), which marks the medieval town of Počitelj. With extra time, just before Mostar (in Buna), you can detour a few miles along the Buna River into Blagaj.

Approaching **Mostar** on M-17, you'll pass the airport, then carry on straight toward *Sarajevo*. Be warned that GPS doesn't have a good handle on Mostar, so follow these directions instead:

Skip the first turnoff for *Centar,* when you're still far from town. Rather, stay on the main Sarajevo-bound road, and then, as you begin to enter Mostar's urban sprawl, take the left turn for *Centar* and *Posušje.* When you come to the traffic light, you can turn right to reach the east side of the river (for the Muslibegović House or Shangri La); or continue straight and then bear right onto the Bulevar to reach the west side of the river (for my other accommodations, or parking near the Old Bridge, see "Arrival in Mostar," earlier).

Once in town, signage can be confusing; if you get lost, try asking for directions to "Stari Most" (STAH-ree most)—the Old Bridge.

Option 2: Rugged-but-Scenic Backcountry Journey Through Serb Herzegovina

While the coastal route outlined above is the most common way to connect Dubrovnik to Mostar, I enjoy getting out of the tourist rut by twisting up the mountains behind Dubrovnik and cutting across the scenic middle of Herzegovina. This route feels much more remote, but the roads are good and the occasional gas station and restaurant break up the journey—and, because you're going through just one border crossing (instead of three), it takes about the same amount of time as the main route, described above.

I find this route particularly interesting because it offers an easily digestible taste of the **Republika Srpska** part of Herzegovina—controlled by the country's Serb minority, rather than its Bosniak and Croat majorities. You'll see Orthodox churches and monasteries, the Cyrillic alphabet, and various symbols of the defiantly proud Serb culture (such as the red, white, and blue flag with the four golden C's). You can't get a complete picture of the former Yugoslavia without sampling at least a sliver of Serb culture. (Because this road goes through the Serbian part of Herzegovina, it's not popular among Bosniaks or Croats.) If you want a little taste of Republika Srpska, consider just day-tripping into Trebinje—especially on Saturday, when the produce market is at its liveliest.

The Drive Begins: From Dubrovnik, head south toward Cavtat, the airport, and Montenegro. Shortly after leaving Dubrovnik, watch for—and follow—signs on the left directing you to *Brgat Gornji.* (Signage completely ignores the large Serb town of Trebinje, just past this obscure border village.) As you climb up over the mountains and cross the border into Bosnia-Herzegovina, notice the faint remains of a long-abandoned old rail line cutting sharp switchbacks up the slope. This once connected Dubrovnik to Mostar and Sarajevo.

Carry on across the plateau, where you may begin to notice Cyrillic lettering on signs: You've crossed into the Republika Srp-

ska. About 20 minutes
after the border, you'll
come upon **Trebinje**
(Требиње)—a pleasant
and relatively affluent
town that's a good place
to stretch your legs, get
some convertible marks
(ATMs are scattered
around the town center),
and maybe nurse a coffee

while people-watching on the big, leafy, inviting main square. Out
on the square, a smattering of humble open-air market stalls sell
local produce (Saturday is the biggest market day, but there's always some action). From the bottom of the square, you can stroll
through the fortified gate into the sleepy, almost completely untouristy Old Town (called Kaštel), with more cafés and the town
mosque (vengefully demolished during the war, but later rebuilt).
The Trebišnjica River is spanned by the graceful, Ottoman-built
Arslanagica Bridge.

Overlooking the town from its hilltop perch is the striking
Orthodox Church of **Nova Gračanica,** built to resemble the historically important Gračanica Monastery in Kosovo. If you have
time, drive up to the church's terrace for great views over Trebinje
and the valley, and step inside the church to immerse yourself in a
gorgeously vibrant world of Orthodox icons.

Whether you stop in Trebinje or not, from here you'll follow signs for *Mostar* and *Ljubinje.* You'll trace the course of the
Trebišnjica River into a high-altitude karstic basin, where evocative
old waterwheels power a primitive irrigation system. From here,
the river flows down to the coast—providing hydroelectric power
for Dubrovnik—before detouring south and emptying into the sea
near Herceg Novi, Montenegro...one river, three countries, in just
a few miles. This area is blanketed with vineyards and dotted with
old monasteries. Passing the village of Mesari ("Butchers"), you'll
also see flocks of sheep. In this part of the Balkans, Croats were
traditionally the city-dwellers, while Serbs were the farmers. There
used to be sheep like these in the pastures near Dubrovnik, but
when the Serbs left during the war, so did the sheep.

Pull over at one of the humble, slate-roofed Orthodox chapels
by the road. (There's one in Staro Slano.) In the cemeteries, many of
the gravestones are from 1991—when soldiers from this area joined
the war effort against Dubrovnik.

The large, flat, sunken field you're driving along is called **Pop-
ovo Polje** ("Priests' Field"). Watch for the turnoff to **Vjetrenica**
(near Zavala), a karstic cave. It's less spectacular than the famous

caves in Slovenia, but has interesting water features that may be worth touring for spelunkers with time to kill (www.vjetrenica.ba).

At the fork, carry on toward **Ljubinje** (Љубиње), twisting up through even higher mountains. In this humble burg, roadside stands with *med* signs advertise homegrown honey. Also keep an eye out for drying tobacco. The partially built houses you'll see are a form of "savings" in the Balkans, where people don't trust banks: Rather than deposit money in an account, they spend many years using any extra funds to gradually add on to a new house.

Continuing toward Mostar, you'll pass through more desolate countryside, then your ears will pop (and you'll pass a red, white, and blue sign marking the "border" of Republika Srpska) as you drop down into the town of **Stolac** (Столац); the town's mosque minaret tells you that you've crossed from Serb territory into Bosnia's Muslim-Croat Federation. Stolac is home to some fascinating history, and worth a stroll if you have the time (see later in this chapter). Leaving Stolac toward Mostar, keep an eye out (on the left, just before the *Poprati* sign) for its interesting **necropolis**—a cluster of centuries-old traditional Bosnian tombstones (worth a quick photo-op stop, and described later).

Past Stolac, you'll climb up the hill, going through the village of Poprati. Soon you'll have the option of either turning off to the right to head directly to **Mostar,** or continuing along the main road to reach Čapljina, where you'll turn right to go past **Počitelj** on your way into Mostar. Either way, **Blagaj** (see below) is worth considering as a detour before ending in Mostar. (If you want to go to **Međugorje**—described later—go through Čapljina and follow signs.)

Near Mostar

There's plenty to see within a short drive of Mostar. Ideally try to splice one or two of these stops into your trip between Mostar and the coast (see my "Route Tips for Drivers," above, for tips on linking them up).

BLAGAJ

Blagaj (BLAH-gai, rhymes with "pie") was the historical capital of this region until the arrival of the Ottomans. This is the site of a mountain called Hum, which is topped by the ruins of a hilltop castle that once belonged to Herzog ("Duke") Stjepan, who gave Herzegovina its name.

Deep in Blagaj is an impressive cliff face with a scenic house marking the source of the Buna River. The building, called the **Tekija,** is a former monastery for Turkish dervishes (an order that emphasizes poverty and humility, famous for the way they whirl

Near Mostar

- - - - Backcountry Driving Route
.... Coastal Driving Route

Note: Driving route road width exaggerated for clarity

To Bari, Italy

25 Kilometers
25 Miles

in a worshipful trance). Built in the 15th century and recently restored, the house is surrounded by a modern visitors-center complex with a café, gift shop, and WCs. It costs €2.50 to enter and look around the Tekija, which feels similar to the tourable Turkish houses in Mostar (for a description, see the Bišćević Turkish House listing under "Sights in Mostar"). You'll take your shoes off and tiptoe across a patchwork of small rugs from room to room. Gazing out the windows at the towering cliff stretching to heaven, and hearing the constant, steady flow of water, it's easy to imagine how this could be considered a very spiritual place.

After seeing the house, stroll a bit along the river, which is crossed by several footbridges offering a grand view back on the Tekija and cliff. A handful of sprawling, touristy restaurants—with open-air terraces right along the refreshing river—serve up traditional Bosnian food, including trout pulled from their own river-fed ponds.

Getting There: Blagaj is easiest to see on the way to or from Mostar—just turn off from the main road and follow the Buna River, following *tekija* signs to the big parking lot.

POČITELJ

Počitelj (POTCH-ee-tell) is an artists' colony filled with a compelling mix of Christian and Muslim architecture. Ideally situated right along the main Mostar-to-Croatia road, it's one of the most popular rest stops for passing tour buses, so it's hardly undiscovered. But it's still worth a stop for its dramatically vertical townscape and beautifully restored Ottoman architecture.

Park your car and hike across the river-stone cobbles to the open square at the base of town, with a handy restaurant, lots of gift shops, and aggressive vendors. The multi-domed building is an old hammam (bath-house). Then hike up the steep stairs (dodging costumed vendors, and enjoying fine aerial views on those hammam domes) to reach the **mosque.** You can pay 3 KM to enter (women must cover their heads). The interior is bigger, though not necessarily better decorated, than the mosques in downtown Mostar (for a description of a typical Bosnian mosque interior, see the Koski Mehmet-Pasha Mosque listing under "Sights in Mostar"). A photo on the porch shows the building circa 1993, destroyed to its foundation.

Continue up the stairs behind the mosque, which lead steeply all the way up to the fortress, which was originally built in the

15th century by Hungarian King Mátyás Corvinus (who pushed the Ottomans back, briefly reclaiming some territory—including this region—for the forces of Christian Europe). There's virtually nothing to see inside (the

stairs inside the tower are extremely steep and narrow—tread carefully), but the views are sensational. The best views are from the flat terrace out front. It's clear just how strategic this location is, between steep cliffs and with perfect views up and down the Neretva Valley.

METKOVIĆ

This dusty and depressed Croatian border town—which sits where the lush Neretva River Delta meets a wall of limestone hills—is best-known as the place where most people cross the border into Bosnia. There's nothing to see in Metković itself, but if you're interested in ancient ruins, the nearby Narona Archaeological Museum is worth a short detour.

▲Narona Archaeological Museum
(Arheološki Muzej Narona)

In Roman times, the province of Dalmatia (roughly today's Croatia and Bosnia) was sparsely populated. There were only two real towns of note. The main city was Salona, the birthplace of Diocletian, near today's Split. The second city was Narona, which stood on a plain at the foot of the mountains, powered by tributaries of the Neretva River.

Today Narona is mostly unexcavated, sitting under a tiny village called Vid near Metković. In the 1990s, archaeologists discovered a treasure trove of Roman statues in a dilapidated barn here. They carefully excavated this cache—the largest collection of marble Roman statues from this period—and built a state-of-the-art museum to show them off in situ (with English explanations). The centerpiece is the foundation of a temple of Augustus, dating from around 10 BC, with 15 Roman statues. You'll also see plenty of Roman carvings, pottery fragments, and good descriptions. Out front, under glass, is a mosaic floor. The museum is in a blocky, can't-miss-it building that stands at the entrance to the otherwise ramshackle hill town of Vid. (The square in front of the museum was the site of Narona's forum.)

Cost and Hours: 40 KM; June-Sept Tue-Sun 9:00-19:00; Oct-May Tue-Fri until 16:00, Sat until 17:00, Sun until 13:00; closed Mon year-round; Naronski Trg 5 in Vid, tel. 020/691-596, www.a-m-narona.hr.

Getting There: Driving through Metković toward the Bos-

MOSTAR & NEARBY

nian border, turn left over the last bridge before you reach the checkpoint. At the next roundabout, turn right, following signs for *Vid*. After crossing the river in Vid, the museum is straight ahead. It's less than 10 minutes from the main road.

Eating: Across the street from the museum, the rustic **$$ Đuđa i Mate** specializes in local Neretva River cuisine—frogs and eels (though they also have an extensive menu of typical Croatian dishes). There's a covered terrace near the restaurant, but I prefer the covered seating down by the river (daily 8:00-22:00, tel. 020/687-500).

STOLAC

One of the most historic spots in Herzegovina, Stolac (STOH-lats) was a cradle of early Balkan civilization. Unless you're fascinated by archaeology, Stolac isn't worth a long detour—but since it's on the way between Mostar and Dubrovnik (on the back-roads route), consider stopping off if you have time to spare.

About 15,000 to 16,000 years ago—long before the Greeks or Romans arrived in this region—the Illyrians lived in this area's caves, where they left behind some drawings. On a hill above the modern town are the overgrown remains of the once-fearsome dry-stone Illyrian fortress that watched over this strategic road in the third and fourth centuries BC. The Romans were later supplanted by the local Bogomil civilization, an indigenous Christian society. Stolac's most impressive attraction dates from this era: On the outskirts of town (on the road toward Mostar), you'll find a **necropolis** with a bonanza of giant tombstones called *stećak*s (from the 13th-15th century), engraved with evocative reliefs. Soon after these were erected, the Ottomans arrived, and conversions to Islam followed.

Archaeological treasures aside, today's Stolac is a workaday village with little tourism—it trudges along, largely oblivious to the ancient treasures embedded all around. The town was particularly hard-hit during the Yugoslav Wars, when it was taken over by Croat forces and its majority Muslim residents forced to flee to Mostar. The war-crimes tribunal in The Hague had an entire division devoted to "Stolac Crimes"—at least 80 civilians were killed here. The mosque and surrounding area were completely leveled; it's now rebuilt, and the town's population is divided evenly between Croats and Bosniaks. Tension still hangs heavy in the air. Local Croats have erected crosses in front of several buildings in town, and the main square features a giant monument engraved with the names of Croats killed in the fighting here. The new, super-modern Catholic church spire rockets up over town, evoking the one-upmanship of the similar steeple in Mostar.

Local Guides: If you're interested in learning more, it's well worth hiring local guide **Sanel Marić,** who works for a local organization that strives to help the people of Stolac transcend the scars of the war. He can show you some of the ancient sights around town and fill you in on recent events (€40 for a tour around town, mobile 061-071-830, sanel.marich@gmail.com). If Sanel is busy, his colleague **Edin Buzaljko** also does great tours of Stolac (same price, mobile 061-308-476, edobuzz@gmail.com).

Eating in Stolac: To grab a bite here, consider two traditional eateries. **$ Restoran Han** is right in the heart of town, while **$ Old Mill** occupies a beautiful setting overlooking waterfalls on the road up the Bregava River.

MEĐUGORJE

Međugorje is an unassuming little village "between the hills" (as its name implies) that ranks with Lourdes, Fátima, and Santiago de Compostela as one of the most important pilgrimage sites in all of Christendom. To the cynical non-Catholic, it's just a strip of crassly commercial hotels, restaurants, and rosary shops leading up to a dull church, all tied together by a silly legend about a hilltop apparition. But if you look into the tear-filled eyes of the pilgrims who've journeyed here, it's clear that to them the power of this place is real. Strolling through the grounds, you can hear the hushed sounds of prayer whispering through the bushes.

For true believers, Međugorje represents a once-in-a-lifetime opportunity to tread on sacred soil: a place where, over decades, the Virgin Mary has appeared to six local people. Even though the Vatican has declined to officially recognize the apparitions, it does acknowledge the faithful devotion of the hundreds of thousands of Catholics who come here each year. More than 30 million pilgrims have visited Međugorje since the sightings began—summer and winter, war (which didn't touch Međugorje) and peace, rain and shine. People make the trek here from Ireland, Italy, Germany, Spain, the US, and just about anywhere else that has Catholics.

Planning Your Time: Unless you're a pilgrim (or think you might be a pilgrim), skip Međugorje—it's an experience wasted on

MOSTAR & NEARBY

Međugorje Mary

What compels millions to flock to this little village in the middle of nowhere? The official story goes like this: On the evening of June 24, 1981, two young women were gathering their sheep on the hillside above Mostar. They came across a woman carrying a baby who told them to come near. Terrified, they fled, only to realize later that this might have been a vision of the Virgin Mary. They returned the next night with some friends and saw the apparition again.

In the three-plus decades since, six different locals (including the two original seers) claim to have seen the vision, and some of them even say they see it regularly to this day. They also say that Mary has given them 10 secrets—predictions of future events that will portend Judgment Day. Written on a piece of parchment, these are kept safely at the home of one of the seers. They have said they will reveal each of these secrets, 10 days before the event occurs, to the local parish priest, who will then alert the world.

Doubting Thomases aren't convinced. One cause for suspicion is that the six seers, before witnessing the visions, were sometimes known to be troublemakers. (In fact, they later admitted that they went up the hill that fateful night not to chase wayward sheep, but to sneak a smoke.) One investigator suggested that they invented the story as a prank, only to watch it snowball out of control once they told it to the local priest.

For decades, the Vatican declined to confirm the sightings as miraculous in nature. (Priests were allowed to accompany pilgrimages to Međugorje, but not to *lead* them.) But in 2019, Pope Francis officially authorized Međugorje as a pilgrimage site.

nonbelievers. The only "attractions" are an unexceptional modern church, a couple of hilltop hikes, and pilgrim-spotting.

If you do go, the easiest way is to take a day-trip excursion from the Dalmatian Coast (sold from Split, Dubrovnik, and Korčula). By public bus, you can day-trip into Međugorje from Split, but not from Dubrovnik. Consider spending the night here, or sleep in Mostar two nights and day-trip into Međugorje.

Orientation to Međugorje: Međugorje (MEDGE-oo-gor-yeh, sometimes spelled "Medjugorje" in English) is basically a one-street town—most everything happens in the half-mile between the post office (where the bus stop is) and the main church, St.

James (Crkva Sv. Jakova). On the hills behind the church are two trails leading to pilgrimage sites. Many travel agencies line the main strip; at any of these, you can find a room, rent a car, hire a local guide, buy ferry tickets for Croatia, and use the Internet.

Sights in Međugorje: The center of pilgrim activity is St. James' Church, which was built before the apparitions. The interior, like the outside, is modern and monochromatic—with a soothing yellow color and stained-glass windows lining the nave. Out front are posted maps that are useful for getting oriented, and a white statue of the Virgin Mary that attracts a lot of attention from pilgrims. Notice the long row of multilingual confessional booths.

As you face the church, you'll see two trails leading up into the hills. Behind and to the left of the church is **Apparition Hill** (at Podbrdo), where the sightings occurred (a one-mile hike, topped by a statue of Mary). Directly behind the church is the **Great Hill** (Križevac, or "Cross Mountain"), where a giant hilltop cross, which predates the visions, has become a secondary site of pilgrimage (1.5-mile hike). If you wonder why they don't make these rocky paths easier to climb, remember that an act of pilgrimage is supposed to be challenging. In fact, pilgrims often do one or both of these hikes barefoot, as an act of penitence.

Around back of the church is a makeshift amphitheater with benches, used for outdoor services. Beyond that is a path, lined with

scenes from the life of Jesus. Farther along, on the right, is an elongated, expressionistic statue of the **Resurrected Savior** (Uskrsli Spasitelj), also known as the "Weeping Knee." Miraculously (or not), the statue's right knee is always wet—go ahead and touch the spot that's been highly polished by worshippers and skeptics alike.

Believers and nonbelievers alike appreciate the parade of kitsch that lines the **main street** leading up to the church. While rosaries are clearly the big item, you can get basically anything you want stamped with Catholic imagery (Mary is particularly popular, for obvious reasons).

Sleeping and Eating in Međugorje: In town, the main street is lined with straightforward, crank-'em-out eateries catering to tour groups. For something a little more atmospheric and fun, head for **$$ Gardens Restaurant** (near the post-office end of the main drag), with a drinks-only bar, a classy upstairs dining room,

MOSTAR & NEARBY

and a garden terrace (Antunovića 66, tel. 036/650-499, www. clubgardens.com).

Just outside town, **Herceg Etno Selo** is an appealing "ethno-village" of new-but-old-looking Bosnian dry-stone buildings wedged between industrial areas and office parks. With slate roofs, inviting ponds, playgrounds, a vineyard, a small farm, and a big amphitheater, this sprawling complex includes an industrial-size **$$** restaurant (well-executed Bosnian and Croatian food) and a 71-room **$$** hotel (Tromeđa b.b., tel. 036/653-400, www.etno-herceg. com, info@etno-herceg.com). Leaving town, follow signs for *Split/Ljubuški*, and look for it on the left between warehouses.

SARAJEVO

Spectacularly set in a mountain valley, blanketed with cute Monopoly houses and prickly with minarets, Sarajevo (sah-rah-YEH-voh) is a sight to behold. It's a cruel irony that for a few short years, Sarajevo became synonymous with sectarian strife. For virtually its entire history, this beautiful city was a model of the opposite: Muslims, Catholics, Orthodox Christians, and Jews living together in cooperation and harmony. (One of its many nicknames is "Little Jerusalem.") Squeezed into its narrow valley, Sarajevo never even had the option of splitting itself up into ethnic ghettos, so people lived side-by-side. To this day, there are several places in the city where you can see a mosque, synagogue, Catholic church, and Orthodox church with a turn of the head.

Sarajevo is the delightful product of a rich history. The Ottoman-style Old Town, the Baščaršija, feels transplanted here from Istanbul. Then you'll turn a corner and suddenly feel lost in an almost Viennese cityscape. Strolling its streets is the next best thing to a time machine.

Though torn by war in the early 1990s, today's Sarajevo is a comfortable and safe place to visit. Listen to the Muslim call to prayer and watch Catholic and Orthodox church bells playfully jostle above the skyline. Step into historic houses of worship from each of this region's four major faiths, noticing the similarities. Visit the street corner where World War I began, climb up into the hills to the Olympic stadium that commanded the world's attention in 1984, or take the cable car even higher for sweeping views over one of Europe's most stunningly set capitals. Make friends with a gregarious Sarajevan—it's easy to do—and ask him the best way to prepare and drink Bosnian coffee. Ponder the scars of war, hunch over to squeeze through the tunnel that was the besieged Sarajevans' one lifeline to the world, and listen to a local relate personal stories from the harrowing time of the siege. Play a game of giant chess with the jeering old-timers in an urban park. Shop your way through the copper-laden canyons of the Turkish-style bazaar, bartering down the price of a hand-hammered Bosnian coffee set. Relax in a hidden caravanserai, take a slow drag on a *šiša* (water pipe spewing sweet plumes of fruity smoke), and sample some honey-dripping pastry treats. For dinner—or just a snack—nibble on some of the best *burek* (savory, flaky pies) and *ćevapi* (grilled sausages) this side of the Bosphorus. Go ahead—it's OK to enjoy Sarajevo...and there's a lot to enjoy.

PLANNING YOUR TIME

Sarajevo demands a minimum of a day. Side-tripping here from Mostar lets you scratch the surface, but you won't regret having one, two, or even three nights here. With whatever time you have, begin in the characteristic Ottoman quarter, the Baščaršija.

I've described two self-guided walks. If you only have time for one, take the first one, which provides a good orientation to Sarajevo and takes you all the way through town, with opportunities to stop at virtually all of the important sights (except the Sarajevo War Tunnel Museum, which requires a long but worthwhile detour). The second walk focuses on the urban, downtown zone called "Sniper Alley," with some harrowing tales of the Siege of Sarajevo and a pair of museums.

Note that Sarajevo is a 2-hour trip by car or train beyond Mostar, making it a logistical dead-end that's not really on the way to other destinations in this book. To maximize efficient use of your time, consider flying in or out of here (for example, Croatia Airlines has reasonably priced flights to Zagreb). But be aware that in winter, heavy morning fog sometimes grounds flights.

Orientation to Sarajevo

With approximately 310,000 people (660,000 in the greater Sarajevo area)—filling a city that held up to 525,000 at its prewar peak—Sarajevo is barely contained by its valley. It's surrounded by steep mountains on all sides, with typical communist-concrete sprawl and cute houses scampering up the valley walls (more recently joined by wartime cemeteries occupying what once were forested parks). It's a long, skinny city, lining up along its humble Miljacka River and main thoroughfare. You can trace the city's historical and architectural development from east to west, starting with the historic Old Town core, called the Baščaršija. West of that is the Austrian-feeling part of town (along Ferhadija street), and beyond that, the modern, concrete skyscraper zone called Marijin Dvor. From here, the city's busy main drag rumbles west (it's called Zmaja od Bosne close to downtown, and Bulevar Meše Selimovića farther out; in wartime it was known as "Sniper Alley").

Terminology: The terminology for the various parties involved in the Yugoslav Wars is particularly sensitive—and can vary depending on whom you're talking to. During the siege, the citizens of Sarajevo were majority Muslim/Bosniak, but also included Croats, Serbs, Jews, and others; many think of themselves not as a specific ethnicity, but as "Sarajevans" or "Bosnians." Meanwhile, the army surrounding the city was made up almost entirely of Serbs, but not all Serbs supported them—so to call them simply "Serbs" is incomplete. Sarajevans (conscientious not to disrespect the many Serbs who were among those besieged) prefer to call the aggressors "the Bosnian Serb Army," "Army of Republika Srpska" (abbreviated VRS), "Karadžić's forces," or "Četniks." But the term "Četnik" is a loaded one: It was first used to describe the fierce Serb fighting force that ethnically cleansed parts of Yugoslavia during World War II. The troops who surrounded the city evoked this earlier image and called themselves "Četniks," and many Sarajevans have followed suit. However, in other contexts, calling a Serb (who was not involved in the siege) a "Četnik" is a serious insult.

TOURIST INFORMATION

Sarajevo's helpful TI is on the main pedestrian drag through the old Ottoman quarter (May-Aug Mon-Fri 9:00-21:00, Sat-Sun until 18:00; Sept-April Mon-Fri 10:00-17:00, Sat-Sun until 16:00; Sarači 58, tel. 033/580-999, www.sarajevo-tourism.com). Pick up the *Sarajevo Navigator* monthly planner.

ARRIVAL IN SARAJEVO

By Bus or Train: Sarajevo's bus and train stations sit next to each other on one very long, urban block up from the Marijin Dvor area (former "Sniper Alley," US Embassy, Holiday Inn, and museums). They're about 2.5 miles west of the Baščaršija (Old Town, with my recommended hotels).

The **train station** looks out over a desolate-feeling plaza; simply walk out front, buy a tram ticket from the kiosk or the driver, and ride tram #1 to the Baščaršija. Alternatively, you can pay 6-10 KM for a taxi.

The **bus station** (Autobusna Stanica Sarajevo) has a small tick-

Sarajevo

ZETRA ARENA

ZETRA OLYMPICS CENTER

KOŠEVO STADIUM

KOŠEVO

GABELINA

ŠUMBULA

AVLIJA REST.

ČEKALUŠA

ALIPAŠINA

KOŠEVO

TRAIN STATION

ARAZ TWIST TOWER

HABSBURG

MEMORIAL TO THE CHILDREN OF SARAJEVO

Srebrenica Genocide Memorial Square

Park

WALK ENDS

BBI MALL

POST

Željeznička Stanica

To Bus Station

US EMBASSY

KRANJČEVIĆA

HOSPITAL

MARIJIN DVOR

BOSNIAN PRESIDENCY

ALIPAŠINA MOSQUE

FRANCA LEHARA

RUNNING STR.

MARIJIN DVOR BLDG.

MARŠALA TITA

SIRIUS TRAVEL

To Airport, Sarajevo War Tunnel Museum & Mostar

WALK BEGINS

FORMER HOLIDAY INN

ST. JOSEPH

HISETA

Skenderija

ZMAJA OD BOSNE

Univerziter

"SNIPER ALLEY"

Muzeji

SARAJEVO CITY CENTER

River

SKENDERIJA BRIDGE

HISTORICAL MUSEUM

BOSNIAN PARLIAMENT

Marijin Dvor

SKENDERIJA

TITO CAFÉ

WALK ENDS

NATIONAL MUSEUM

WOODROW WILSON PROMENADE

ARS AEVI BRIDGE

ICAR MONUMENT

Miljacka

PUT MLADIH

GRBAVICA

ROMEO & JULIET BRIDGE

To Jewish Cemetery

SARAJEVO

et lobby, a left-luggage desk *(garderoba)*, and a smattering of kiosks and cafés. Exit the building straight ahead, keeping the busy street on your right. Walk about 100 yards, then hook left around the big post office (near a row of cafés). You'll wind up at the big plaza in front of the train station, with the stop for tram #1 (explained above).

By Car: If you're driving into Sarajevo from Mostar, see "Route Tips for Drivers" at the end of this chapter.

By Plane: Sarajevo's small, sleepy airport sits on the south-

SARAJEVO

western edge of town (airport code: SJJ, tel. 033/289-100, www.
sarajevo-airport.ba). A bus coordinated with flight arrivals and departures connects the airport with the city center; check the airport
website for details (5 KM). If the airport bus times are inconvenient, you could take city transit: Walk straight out the front door
of the airport and continue on foot about 10 minutes directly ahead
to the Dobrinja neighborhood, where you can catch bus #103 to the
Latin Bridge in the Old Town, or bus #31E to near the old City
Hall, also in the Old Town (both run about 3-4/hour, buy ticket

from kiosk or driver). For a taxi, the fair metered rate to downtown is around 15-20 KM, but most taxi drivers demand 30 KM; ask for an estimate up front, and avoid cabbies who suggest a highball figure. If you'll be at the airport, it's convenient to visit the nearby War Tunnel Museum (pay no more than 10 KM for the taxi ride there from the airport).

GETTING AROUND SARAJEVO

Almost everything that's worth seeing in town (with the notable exception of the War Tunnel Museum) is within long walking distance of each other. But you may need to make use of the city's **public transportation** network, which includes trams, buses, and trolley buses. A single ticket costs 1.80 KM (buy at kiosk or on board, good for one ride only—if you transfer, you must buy a new ticket; when boarding, validate your ticket by stamping it in the green box). A day ticket for 5.30 KM is good for one calendar day (sold only at the kiosk behind the Catholic cathedral). The handy tram #3 does a big loop from one end of town to the other, starting in the Old Town (several stops, including at the Latin Bridge/Latinska Ćuprija, at the City Hall/Vijećnica, at the Baščaršija stop near the main square on Kovači street, and behind the cathedral), then along the main drag (the former "Sniper Alley") to the west end of town (Ilidža stop, a short taxi ride to the Sarajevo War Tunnel Museum), and back again (7.5 miles and 40 minutes one-way). Tram #1 is also useful, connecting the train and bus stations with "Sniper Alley" and the Old Town.

Sarajevo is an excellent **taxi** town, with cheap fares and generally honest cabbies. Figure 1.90 KM for the drop, then 1.20 KM per kilometer. Short rides within town are typically a steal at 5-10 KM. To ensure you're getting an official, regulated taxi, confirm that the license plate starts with the letters "TA," and be sure the driver turns on the meter.

HELPFUL HINTS

Laundry: The centrally located **LaundroLounge,** tucked into a courtyard at Baseskije 63, is run by friendly Juliet (Mon-Sat 9:00-18:00, closed Sun, shorter hours in winter, mobile 061-632-344).

Local Guidebook: Look for the informative, pocket-sized book called *The Siege of Sarajevo 1992-1996* (by Amir Telibećirović; see "Local Guides," next). Designed to help visitors better understand this city's complex and tragic wartime story, it's concisely written, filled with powerful black-and-white photographs, and sold at bookstores around town.

Useful App: The city and local historians have teamed up to create a surprisingly good app you can download to your phone—

War and Peace in Sarajevo

When the Ottomans arrived in this valley in the 15th century, what had been a humble settlement of Bogomil kings and Franciscans from Dubrovnik was swiftly converted into a major trading center—thanks to its strategic location between the Croatian coast and the Ottoman-held lands farther east. Sarajevo's location was near silver and coal mines, and came with an ample supply of fresh spring water and runoff from the mountains all around—providing constantly running water, which is so prized in Muslim culture. The Ottomans harnessed that water to build baths and fountains for Sarajevo's mosques. The town became a thriving population center and, eventually, the capital of the area.

As the Ottoman Empire declined in the late 19th century, the Habsburgs took over—dispatching urban planners and architects to spiff up the burg to Viennese standards. During its brief 40 years under the Austro-Hungarian Empire, Sarajevo was modernized and grew quickly. But the Habsburgs, too, fell from power—thanks to a war that started with the assassination of their heir in this very city (see "The Shot Heard 'Round the World" sidebar, later in this chapter).

During the Yugoslav era, Sarajevo enjoyed a privileged status as a town that exemplified Tito's idealistic vision of the various Yugoslav ethnicities living and working together. It was chosen to represent Yugoslavia as the host of the 1984 Winter Olympics.

But then, less than a decade after its moment in the limelight, its fate took an appalling turn, as Sarajevo again seized the world's attention—for the worst possible reasons. As Yugoslavia broke apart, multiethnic Bosnia became ground zero for hashing out old ethnic grudges. Sarajevans woke up one morning in the spring of 1992 completely surrounded by the heavy artillery of Radovan Karadžić's Bosnian Serb army and paramilitary groups. Overnight, their besieged city became a shooting gallery, with Sarajevan civilians as the targets. During the longest siege in modern European history (three years and eight months), people here were bombarded to the edge of madness and picked off in the streets by distant snipers. The Sarajevans—Bosniaks, Croats, and Serbs alike—were forced to improvise to create shelter, heat, food, and entertainment. They dug a half-mile-long tunnel to get basic supplies and did whatever they could to keep going. For more on this dark time, see "The Siege of Sarajevo" sidebar, later.

Since 1996, peace has returned to Sarajevo. While you'll see some completely restored historical buildings and glass skyscrapers, there are also skeletons of bombed-out buildings, and lots of bullet holes and shrapnel scars. Sarajevo is a city in transition—and much remains to be done.

Guide2Sarajevo. It has tours for dozens of sights, offline maps, and GPS functionality to help you navigate the city. Get it at Guide2Sarajevo.com.

Tours in Sarajevo

▲▲▲Local Guides

With such a powerful and challenging-to-grasp recent history, and with the ready availability of extremely good and affordable local guides, it's virtually obligatory to hire a guide for your Sarajevo time. For the price of joining an organized walking tour in many European cities, you can hire your very own Sarajevan for the day, who will likely be willing to speak frankly about their experiences during the siege. **Amir Telibećirović** is a journalist, siege veteran, and historian who explains Sarajevo's sights and history—from ancient to recent—with brilliant clarity. Amir can add immeasurably to your Sarajevo experience (30 KM or €15/person for a tour of any length, or 50 KM/€25 for just one person, mobile 061-304-966, teleamir@gmail.com). If Amir is busy, **Orhan Hadžagić** likes to focus on the traditional way of life in Sarajevo, walking through undiscovered residential areas with stories about history and everyday customs (€60/3 hours for groups up to 4, mobile 062-333-623, hadzagic@gmail.com). **Jadranka Šuster** is also worth considering for her professional, by-the-book approach (€40/2 hours, €15/extra hour, €120/all day, more for 4 or more people; also offers special activities such as cooking classes, food and drink tours, coppersmithing, and wood-burning crafts; mobile 061-828-400, sarajevotour@gmail.com).

Insider Tours

This company runs various itineraries around the city, departing from their office near the Latin Bridge (at Zelenih Beretki 30, open Mon-Fri 8:00-18:00—or 9:00-17:00 in winter, Sat-Sun 9:00-14:00). Options include their **introductory free tour** (tips expected, 1.5 hours, daily at 9:30 and 16:30); a longer version, typically with smaller groups, called the **Sarajevo Grand Tour** (€12, 3 hours, daily at 10:30); **Eat, Pray, Love,** an experiential tour that includes some food tasting and visits to Sarajevo's main houses of worship (€30, 4 hours, most days at 10:00); **Times of Misfortune,** detailing the siege (€27, includes entrance to War Tunnel Museum, 3 hours, daily at 11:00); a more specific tour of the **War Tunnel Museum** (€15, includes museum admission, 2 hours, daily at 14:00); **Sarajevo Assassination,** focusing on Franz Ferdinand and Princip sites (€19, 3 hours); **Islam You Did Not Know,** designed to demystify Bosnian Muslim culture (€15, 2 hours); a side-trip to **Tito's bunker** in the town of Konjic (€40, half-day); and other tours available on request (such as their Jewish tour, €25, 4 hours). They also offer excursions to other parts of Bosnia, including the Srebrenica massacre site, a river-rafting trip, Olympics sights, Mostar and nearby towns, and a combo-tour of the scenic and historic towns of Jajce and Travnik. Call ahead to confirm the schedule and to reserve—book at least an hour ahead for the in-town walks, or a day ahead for the out-of-town trips (tel. 033/534-353, mobile 061-190-591, www.sarajevoinsider.com).

TravelPlus is another reputable company offering a variety of tour itineraries, including to Sarajevo's Olympics sites in the mountains (tel. 033/238-811, www.travelplus.ba).

Adventure Excursions

Sarajevo's setting lends itself to adventure travel—hiking, mountain biking, river rafting, skiing, and so on. **Green Visions** can take you on an eco-friendly excursion into the spectacular Bosnian countryside (mobile 061-213-278, www.greenvisions.ba).

Walks in Sarajevo

Below I've outlined two different self-guided walks that, when taken together, provide a useful spine for visiting virtually all of the sights mentioned under "Sights in Sarajevo," later (except the War Tunnel Museum, which is farther out). The first walk covers the historic core of town, including most of the museums. The second (which begins an easy five-minute walk from where the first leaves off) focuses on the Siege of Sarajevo.

▲▲▲WELCOME TO SARAJEVO

This walk begins where most tourist visits do, in the Ottoman-influenced Old Town—the Baščaršija—then strolls through history as it traverses the Habsburg quarter.

I've split the walk into three parts. If you're in a hurry and want to focus on the Old Town, just do Parts 1 (Ottoman zone) and 2 (Habsburg quarter); Part 3 takes you deeper into the workaday urban core, including some sights relating to the siege, and is designed to help you connect to the "Sniper Alley" area. Doing the entire walk without entering any of the sights could take as little as two hours—but with sightseeing stops, it can fill an entire day.
• *Begin at the main square of the Old Town (Baščaršija), with the wooden fountain at the top.*

Part 1: Ottoman Old Town (Baščaršija)

Pigeon Square: Though it's nicknamed for its many winged residents, this square is officially called Baščaršija. Literally translated as "Main Marketplace," this unmistakably Ottoman-flavored

Sarajevo Self-Guided Walk
Old Town Section

WAR CHILDHOOD MUSEUM

LOGAVINA

MEHMED-PAŠE SOKOLOVIĆA

PEHLIVANUŠA

JOSIPA ŠTADLERA

SARAJEVO ROSES

OLD SYNAGOGUE & BOSNIAN JEWISH MUSEUM

MULA

MARKALE COVERED MARKET

BOSNIAK INSTITUTE

GAZI HUSREV-BEY BIBLIOTEKA

Katedrala

CATHOLIC CATHEDRAL

WALK PART 2 BEGINS

WALK PART 2 ENDS & PART 3 BEGINS

MULA MUSTAFE BAŠESKIJE

SREBRENICA EXHIBITION

ETERNAL FLAME

MARKET HALL

FERHADIJA

BUS INFO OFFICE

HOTEL EUROPE

To Bosnian Central Bank, Maršala Tita Street & Rest of Walk

Liberation & Izetbegović Square

SERBIAN ORTHODOX CATHEDRAL

GAZI HUSREV-BEY BEZISTAN BAZAAR

ŽELENIH BERELKI

HOTEL CENTRAL

INSIDER TOURS OFFICE

GIMNAZIJSKA

ISTROSMAJEROVA

River

MUSIC PAVILION

To Čobarnija Bridge

OBALA KULINA BANA

Drvenija

DRVENIJA BRIDGE

Miljacka

ĆUMURIJA BRIDGE

MJEDENICA

square has given its name to the entire Old Town. Sit for a while and watch kids (and kids-at-heart) play with the namesake pigeons.

The centerpiece fountain (notice the small faucet at the base), called **Sebilj,** is an icon of Sarajevo. According to local legend, visitors who drink water from this fountain will return to Sarajevo someday. The original was built in 1753, but this restored version dates from the 19th century. Although it's the centerpiece of the "Turkish" Old Town, the fountain is more Persian in style. The Ottoman Empire (of which Sarajevo was a part) enjoyed influences from throughout both the Islamic and the European cultures: art, literature, and poetry from Persia (today's Iran); religious influence (that is, Sunni Islam) from the Arabic world; diplomacy from the Germanic world; and herbal pharmacology and music from the Jewish world.

Turn with your back to the fountain and walk down the long, narrow square. Look for the tight little lane on the left, just be-

fore the mosque. This is the wonderfully authentic **Coppersmiths' Street** (Kazandžiluk), where craftsmen still carry out their work, hammering beautiful works of art out of copper—you can hear their little hammers tapping from their workshops. It's just the place to buy a copper Bosnian coffee set that you'll never use. This might be the most touristy street in Sarajevo, so the prices aren't a bargain, but it's a fun stroll.

Walk all the way down Coppersmiths' Street—jogging right with the street—until you pop out around the corner, on **Locksmiths' Street** (Bravadžiluk). Locals call this lane "Ćevapi Street" for its many *ćevabdžinica* (shops selling the tasty minced-meat, grilled sausages called *ćevapčići*). You'll also see several *buregdžinica* (shops selling the savory phyllo-dough pastry called *burek;* my favorite, the recommended Buregdžinica Sač, is just down a side lane off of this street).

Look left, to the yellow-and-brown-striped building at the end of the block. This is one of the city's main landmarks, the **City Hall** (Vijećnica)—the best example of Austrian Historicist-style architecture from the 40 years of Habsburg rule. While it looks Islamic, it was designed by a Czech architect who went to Morocco to find inspiration—so it has no connection at all to local culture. Later it became the City Library and was also the local Nazi headquarters during World War II. But this landmark building—and its books—was destroyed by shells in 1992; in 2014, it reopened after a years-long restoration. Visitors are welcome to take in its gorgeous interior (described later). This building is also the place where, on June 28, 1914, the Habsburg heir, Archduke Franz Ferdinand, began a fateful drive through town. (We'll see where that trip ended later on this walk.)

Now turn right and walk a half-block down Locksmiths' Street, popping out at the bottom of the square where we started this walk. On your right is the **Baščaršija Mosque,** the first of many we'll see throughout town (though this one is closed to the public). Kitty-corner from the mosque, notice the copper domes on the roof of the covered market hall (Brusa Bezistan). Dating from 1551, this market hall now holds the **City History Museum,** with a great model of late-19th-century Sarajevo and other good exhibits (worth visiting for an introduction to the city, and described later under "Sights in Sarajevo").

• *Across from the mosque's gate, walk down the main street through town.*

Sarači Street: Lined with shops, more *ćevapi* joints, tempting desserts, and the TI, this busy pedestrian street is a handy artery for sightseeing. Like so many streets in the Baščaršija, this is named for a type of craftsman who worked here—in this case, leathermakers. After a short block, on the left, is the **TI.** Across the street is the lane called **Prote Bakovića,** crammed with characteristic (if touristy) eateries. Bakovića also leads to the **Old Serbian Orthodox Church,** well worth a visit (described later). None of the four Serbian Orthodox Churches in Sarajevo was vandalized during the siege, though they were all damaged by shrapnel launched at nearby targets by the Bosnian Serb Army.

It's easy to miss the many **courtyards** *(han)* that burrow between blocks in the Old Town. Directly across Sarači street from Prote Bakovića, go down the little alley next to the TI. You'll pop into an atmospheric courtyard called **Trgovke,** which is especially popular with *šiša* bars (also known as *nargila,* hookah, hubbly bubbly, or water pipe). They're not an indigenous tradition—having been imported from the Middle East—but they've become popular and make an inviting scene after dark. As twilight twinkles, local twenty-somethings lounge here on divans, chilling like sultans (or, at least, pashas) as they deeply inhale pungent, fruity smoke. In the corners and tucked down little alleys, miniature potbellied stoves churn day and night, providing glowing coals to power the pipes. Even without taking a direct drag, it's like cotton candy for your lungs. While there's no marijuana in these particular hookahs, the mellow hubbub, air rich with sickly sweet smoke, dueling music played at top volume, and floodlit minarets rocketing overhead are plenty mind-bending. Also on this courtyard, look for the Egoist design shop, with some fun and hip Sarajevo stuff for sale.

From where you entered the courtyard, turn right to find a narrow alley (next to Damask Nargila Bar) leading back out to Sarači street. Turn left and continue along Sarači. After a few steps, on the right (at #77), dip into the courtyard of the **Morića Han,** an old Ottoman caravanserai—like an inn, where passing merchants could find food and accommodations. It serves a similar purpose today, with several atmospheric café tables offering the chance to taste the high-octane, unfiltered "Bosnian coffee"; stop here now if you need to get caffeinated for all the sightseeing coming up.

Head back out to Sarači. A few steps farther along, look left for Kolobara Han, a pizzeria filling a garden courtyard.

Keep going, and soon you'll come to (on the left) the walled courtyard of Sarajevo's top mosque, the **Gazi Husrev-Bey Mosque**—definitely worth a visit, and described later. This is just the first of many mentions you'll see of Gazi Husrev-Bey (1480-1541), a Muslim aristocrat who poured money into the local community. (*Bey* is an Ottoman aristocratic title, like "Lord" or "Sir.") Many of the landmarks of the Old Town were built as part of Husrev-Bey's *vakuf,* or religious endowment; you'll notice plaques to this effect all over town. Thanks to his patronage, Sarajevo became the biggest city in the European part of the Ottoman Empire. If you'd like to pay your respects to this John-D-and-Catherine-T-

SARAJEVO

style benefactor, his tomb is just to the left of the mosque (also described later).

Across the street from the mosque's middle gate (at #33, labeled *Muzej Gazi Husrev-Bey*) is the **Kuršumilja Madrasa,** originally built as an Islamic theological school by Husrev-Bey in the 1530s. Step into the outer courtyard for a better look at the building, which has multiple chimneys poking up above the roofline. Students lived in simple dorms, each one individually heated by its own stove. You can peek into the inner courtyard from the door, or pay 3 KM to go in and peruse its interesting but dry exhibit about Husrev-Bey (including a good film about his life and legacy) and the history of the building. The main classroom, straight ahead from the entrance, has a Star of David chandelier, suggesting the deep interfaith respect through much of Sarajevo's history (everything described in English, daily 9:00-13:00 & 13:30-20:00). The modern school next door (the yellow building, to the right) still teaches the Islamic faith.

Still in the courtyard, as you face the madrasa, look left to see the sparkling-new library, **Gazi Husrev-Bey Biblioteka.** While local Muslim bigwigs (the modern-day versions of Husrev-Bey) don't have the money to invest as they'd like in their home country, other Middle Eastern countries (in this case, Qatar) are keeping this tradition of endowment alive. Throughout Bosnia, many destroyed-then-rebuilt mosques and Muslim cultural institutions come with a plaque noting which Islamic country paid to resurrect it. In addition to being a fully operational archive and library, this gorgeous new complex includes a large auditorium and a museum that displays its treasures—including precious books that were hidden away in a bank vault to survive the siege (3 KM, Mon-Fri 9:00-18:00, Sat 8:00-16:00, closed Sun, www.ghb.ba).

Head back out to Sarači street and continue a couple of short blocks. The stone building on the left is another covered bazaar, this one still functioning as a market, the **Gazi Husrev-Bey Bezistan.** Cut through the market hall—maybe browsing for a scarf, purse, necklace, watch, or sunglasses—and pop out the far end, turning right to find a field (squeezed between the market and Hotel Europe) littered with ruins from a 16th-century Ottoman caravanserai, called **Tašlihan.** Funded by (surprise, surprise) Gazi Husrev-Bey, this caravanserai hosted passing travelers, traders, and merchants—logically, since it was located next to the bazaar—until it was badly damaged by an 1879 fire.

• *Now walk back past the end of the covered market, take the first right, and walk a short block down to the...*

Miljacka River: The last building on your left before the riverfront houses the **Sarajevo 1878-1918 Museum** (described later). The museum outlines the brief but prolific four decades of Austrian Habsburg rule here—and, more importantly, the story of how Gavrilo Princip's assassination of the Habsburg heir, Archduke Franz Ferdinand, took place right on this corner. The shooting set off a chain reaction of allegiances and grudges that swiftly pulled all of Europe—and, eventually, much of the world—into a Great War that would end the age of empires and inaugurate a new era of modern nations. (For the full story, see "The Shot Heard 'Round the World" sidebar, later.)

Go across the street to the **Latin Bridge** (Latinska Ćuprija)—so named because during Ottoman times, this was an area popu-

lated by many Catholics (who said Mass in Latin). After World War I, the bridge was renamed "Principov Most" for the assassin who had asserted Bosnian Serb nationalism against the Habsburgs. But after the 1992-1996 siege, Sarajevans decided that Princip was too controversial a figure, and went back to the old name.

Looking down, you'll see that the Miljacka is hardly a rushing river (like the Neretva in Mostar)—up here in the Bosnian highlands, this is still just a trickle. While not navigable for trade, the river's current was harnessed to spur the development of the old Ottoman town. From here, you're near three sights that may be worth a detour later. Looking across the bridge to the left, you'll see the minaret of the copper-domed **Emperor's Mosque** (Careva Džamija)—the city's most elegant and oldest, built in 1457 to honor the Ottoman Sultan Mehmet the Conqueror (though it's been rebuilt and expanded many times since then). Just behind the mosque, a short walk from here, is the huge **Sarajevska Brewery.** Because it's fed by a natural spring, this was one of the few factories that was able to keep working through the siege. It also has a fine little museum about the history of Sarajevsko Pivo, one of Bosnia's top beers, and an atmospheric old beer hall serving pub grub (see "Eating in Sarajevo," later). Those intrigued by Sarajevo's spiritual history might consider a five-minute detour from here to the **Tomb of the Seven Brothers** (described later; go straight across the river and up the hill, past the park with the charming little music pavilion/tea house, to the top of the parking lot).

• *Part 1 of our walk is finished. To continue with Part 2—and see a very different side of Sarajevo—backtrack all the way through the covered market (or the walkway through the caravanserai ruins) to the main drag where we started, and turn left.*

SARAJEVO

This street has now changed its name from Sarači to Ferhadija. Without the slightest transition, you step from the extremely Ottoman-feeling "little Istanbul" of the Baščaršija into the Viennese-feeling Habsburg Quarter. Notice the Sarajevo: Meeting of Cultures *sign underfoot. You're encouraged to stand here and snap a selfie in one direction, with an Ottoman backdrop—then turn 180 degrees and snap a selfie in the other, with an Austrian backdrop.*

Part 2: Habsburg Sarajevo (Ferhadija Street)

With the precipitous decline of the Ottoman Empire in the late 1800s, the Habsburgs—who ruled the vast Austro-Hungarian Empire from Vienna—saw an opportunity to fill the vacuum left in this part of Europe. With the swirl of a pen in 1878, Bosnia went from Ottoman to Austrian rule. As they had throughout their realm, the Habsburgs stepped in and immediately began to modernize Sarajevo, rolling out new infrastructure and buildings like crazy. While they ruled Sarajevo for only 40 years, the Habsburgs left it a far more modern city than they'd found it.

Just a couple of steps along Ferhadija, an alley on the right leads up to the **Old Synagogue and Bosnian Jewish Museum** (described later)—offering a fascinating look at another of this city's many faiths. Just beyond that is the wrenching **War Childhood Museum** (also described later).

Just a bit farther, set back from the street on the left, is the small but pretty **Ferhadija Mosque.** If you go around behind the mosque and duck into the **Hotel Europe,** you'll find a genteel, chandeliered, Viennese-style coffeehouse interior. The architect who gave Sarajevo its Austrian look—including this hotel—was actually a Czech, Karel Pařík. He lived here for nearly 60 years and designed some 70 buildings in town, including the City Hall, the big Evangelical Church across the river, and the National Museum where this walk ends.

Continuing two more blocks along Ferhadija street, on the right, you can't miss the **Catholic Cathedral** (described later). Notice that this is the fourth different house of worship we've seen (Muslim, Orthodox Christian, Jewish, Catholic) in just the short distance since we began our walk. The silver statue out front celebrates Sveti Ivan Pavao II. "Papa"—that's St. John Paul II—came here on April 12, 1997, Bosnia's first-ever papal visit.

Around the right side of the cathedral is the very sobering **Srebrenica Exhibition,** documenting the heinous genocidal activities at that eastern Bosnian town. This sight is a must for visitors who want to better understand the atrocities that went on in this country in the 1990s.

Directly in front of the cathedral's main steps, look for the big **Sarajevo rose** in the pavement—a distinctive starburst indentation that's colored in red, and carefully preserved as a memorial, even after the surrounding pavement was replaced. Immediately following the war, about 1,000 of the impact craters in the streets of Sarajevo were filled with a red resin, instantly creating a poignant memorial. As the city has rebuilt, most of these Sarajevo roses have been replaced with new asphalt. Only a few remain, and those are tended to by a local preservation group. Another one is around the left side of the cathedral, just before the side door. I'll point out two more Sarajevo roses through the rest of this walk.

Behind the cathedral is an old Ottoman bathhouse *(hammam)*, with telltale copper domes. Today it's part of a private cultural center called the **Bosniak Institute.** It sometimes houses special exhibits; if one is going on, you can look around inside.

A block farther along Ferhadija, on the left, is a parklike square once called Liberation Square—since renamed **Liberation and Izetbegović Square** to honor the wartime Bosnian president. The square is ringed with busts of important Bosnian writers, and the *Multicultural Man Builds the World* statue in the middle—of a naked man doing jumping jacks, with a highly polished member—was donated by an Italian artist to beautify the war-torn city. You'll see many such examples of donated public art throughout Sarajevo—quite a few of them are "white elephants" not en-

tirely embraced by the cynical, siege-hardened Sarajevans. At the far end of the square, old-timers gather to play giant-size chess—carefully strategizing while a rogues' gallery of onlookers cheers and jeers for each move. It's an enjoyable scene that testifies to the resilience of the Bosnian spirit—and the ability of unemployed locals to find ways to entertain themselves.

At the end of the square is yet another house of worship: The bold facade and towers of the **Serbian Orthodox Cathedral.** This was built from 1863 to 1869, during

Ottoman rule. In this ecumenical city, the funds came from all quarters: donations from the Romanovs, Russia's ruling family; from the Ottoman sultan; and from a Serbian prince. Like many houses of worship in this town, the church's architecture demonstrates the mingling of faiths: It looks like an Orthodox church with a Catholic bell tower. (Bell towers are atypical enough for Orthodox churches, but this one even uses Catholic-style Roman numerals.) The interior is cavernous and lavishly decorated, with beautifully painted domes and a stirring iconostasis—it's well worth a look for a taste of a modern Orthodox church (2 KM, daily 8:00-17:30).

Continuing along Ferhadija, just after the park on your right is an elegant yellow **market hall.** Go through (or alongside) this hall and emerge on the other side, then walk to the right one block

along the busy street. On the left side of this street, look for Sarajevo's **Markale covered market.** Browse your way through humble tables, heavy with produce, to the back corner, where a stone plaque and names engraved on a glass wall recall a pivotal moment in the Siege of Sarajevo. This busy, completely untouristy market gained infamy as the site of two cruel bombings that targeted civilians and claimed more than a hundred innocent lives—Sarajevans who were simply shopping for paltry foodstuffs to keep their families fed and alive through impossibly tough conditions. Sixty-seven Sarajevans died during an attack on February 5, 1994 (plus another 144 wounded), and 43 more died (and 90 wounded) on August 28, 1995. (The blast pattern from one of the bombings, in the floor, is protected by a glass case.) These ruthless bombardments were a turning point in the siege—when the international community began to sit up, pay attention, and realize that this was not simply a standard-issue war between equal parties, but a barbaric siege that was destroying the lives of countless peace-loving civilians who wanted no part of the violence. It was the 1995 attack, in part, that prompted NATO air strikes against Karadžić's forces two days later. "Operation Deliberate Force" ultimately led to the Dayton Peace Accords, which finally ended the violence—although Sarajevans wish NATO hadn't been quite so "deliberate" as to wait three and a half years before taking action.

Head back to the main walking street, Ferhadija, and continue on your way. As you walk, look for **another Sarajevo rose** in the pavement in front of the Parfois shop (at #12, on the left; this one was reconstructed after the street was repaved). The plaque next to the door of the shop explains that on May 27, 1992, 26 *Građana Sarajeva* (citizens of Sarajevo) were killed by an artillery shell while waiting in line to buy bread at a bakery here.

The street angles and takes you up to an intersection with the busy Maršala Tita street, named for the WWII Partisan military hero and president-for-life of communist Yugoslavia—Marshal Tito. On the right at the corner is an **eternal**

flame honoring Partisan fighters. If you're here in cold weather, you may notice that the practical Sarajevans—who learned during the lean years of the siege never to waste resources—use it to warm up as they pass by. • *Part 2 of our walk is finished. If you're pooped, or just want more time to check out the sights in this part of town, now's the time to bail out. But if you want to continue, Part 3 will send you in the direction of "Sniper Alley" (covered in my other self-guided walk).*

Part 3: Maršala Tita Street

Crowded with cars, trucks, trams, and buses, this artery feels more urban and less atmospheric than the Ottoman and Austrian zones we just left. During the siege, this was one of the safest major boulevards in town, since it's relatively narrow and well-protected from snipers by tall buildings. The exposed side streets were blocked off to create what was called a "Road of Life," where people could walk without fear of being picked off by distant gunmen. We'll follow this street several blocks to ground zero of the former war zone.

After a block, on the right, his-and-hers Atlases flank the doors of the **Bosnian Central Bank** building—where the nation's convertible mark currency is administered.

Farther along, on the left, is **McDonald's**,

which caused an uproar when it finally opened here in July of 2011. The opening was delayed for four years, as local *ćevapi* vendors—scandalized by the notion of a multinational conglomerate challenging the loyalty of Bosnian palates—did whatever they could to block it. For weeks after it opened, there were long lines down the street of Sarajevans curious to try the American burgers. But within a few weeks, the furor died down, the crowds dispersed, and the *ćevapi* sellers were satisfied that Bosnians wouldn't abandon the grilled meats they've enjoyed for centuries.

One block later, the street opens up. On the left is the slick BBI Centar shopping mall. On the right is a fine park with perhaps the most emotionally devastating memorial in this tragedy-laden city: the **Memorial to the Children of Sarajevo.** Look closely at the symbolism-packed fountain. The glass sculpture in the middle represents a sandcastle, but one that is not—and never will be—finished...the innocent play of a child cut short by an untimely death.

The footprints embedded in the concrete basin belong to the young siblings of children who were killed in the war. The silver pillars to the left can be spun to see names of young victims of the fighting. Nearly 1,600 children were among those killed during the siege.

Scattered in the hillsides of the **park** beyond the fountain, notice a few Ottoman-style gravestones, shaped like turbans—the earliest dating from the early 17th century. In the pavement at the far end of this park—about 30 yards before the crosswalk—look for a Sarajevo rose.

Leaving the park, continue down the busy street. The brown-and-orange building on the left is the **Bosnian Presidency** (the local "White House"). During the early days of the war, this building was the focus of street-by-street fighting; if the Bosnian Serb forces had claimed it, they could have declared victory. At one point, they were within 50 yards of this building, but the defense held. As part of the compromise to end the war, today Bosnia's "Presidency" is made up of a committee of three members: one Bosniak, one Croat, and one Serb, with a rotating chairmanship. Difficult as it is to get things done with one president, imagine how impossible the situation is when you need agreement among three people who are predisposed to mistrust each other. While critical for ending the war, this compromise has made it even more difficult to move forward with postwar recovery.

In the park beyond the Presidency is the 16th-century Alipašina Mosque. A long walk directly up the hill from here (with your back to the mosque, about a mile up Alipašina street) would take you to the **Zetra Olympics Center** (not worth a detour now, but worth considering if you're curious and have time later). This complex includes Koševo Stadium, which held the opening ceremony for the 1984 Olympics (and, in 1997, hosted visits by both Pope John Paul II and the band U2—both of whom had spoken out in support of the besieged Sarajevans); and Zetra Arena, which was used for Olympic skating events (this is where ice dancers Jayne Torvill and Christopher Dean thrilled the world with their "Bolero" routine) and for the closing ceremony. Today the complex houses a museum about those games. Poignantly, the stadium that once commanded the world's attention is now surrounded by a vast field of headstones—mostly of Sarajevans killed during the war. The ice arena's basement was used as a makeshift morgue, and its wooden seats were used to build coffins for the deceased.

• *Our walk is finished. From here, you can circle back to any of the sights you haven't yet seen. If you have stamina and interest left, you can continue directly on to the next walk, which covers the main sights of the Siege of Sarajevo. The starting point is just a five-minute walk away: Simply continue following Maršala Tita street, jogging left with the road and passing another park (with a conspicuously modern sculpture that was another artist's "white elephant" gift to Sarajevo). Soon after, you'll reach the major intersection with the huge, glassy Sarajevo City Center shopping mall on your left. Here Maršala Tita becomes the city's main thoroughfare (Zmaja od Bosne)—where the next walk begins.*

▲▲"SNIPER ALLEY": THE SIEGE OF SARAJEVO

This walk, which leads you through the broad boulevards and skyscraper jungle of modern Sarajevo, is designed to help you appreciate some of the key sites of the Siege of Sarajevo, and to provide an interesting way to get to the Historical Museum (which further illustrates the way people lived during the siege) and the National Museum. The walk begins in the shadow of the Bosnian Parliament building, which you can reach by walking five minutes from the end of the previous self-guided walk or by riding a tram to the Marijin Dvor tram stop. This neighborhood is officially called Marijin Dvor (roughly "Maria's Castle," after a nearby palace that was built for an aristocrat's wife)—a strangely romantic name for a modern downtown turned war zone. These days it's better known

The Siege of Sarajevo

Most travelers know that Bosnia-Herzegovina was torn apart by a war when Yugoslavia broke up in the early to mid-1990s (see the Understanding Yugoslavia chapter). But few realize that in that country's capital, Sarajevo, the "war" was not conventional fighting between armies, but a medieval-style siege designed to cut off the city from food, water, electricity, telephone, medicine, and other critical supplies. The Siege of Sarajevo lasted for more than 1,300 days, making it the longest siege in modern European history (longer than the infamous WWII-era Siege of Leningrad, a.k.a. St. Petersburg). How could a modern city of some 300,000 people be cut off in this way?

In early 1992, the people of Bosnia-Herzegovina voted in favor of independence from Yugoslavia; although many Serbs boycotted the ballot box, 64 percent of Bosnians turned out, and 98 percent of them voted yes. Over the next month, Bosnian Serb leader Radovan Karadžić and Bosnian President Alija Izetbegović traded heated rhetoric about what the new nation of Bosnia-Herzegovina would look like. Meanwhile, each one built a make-shift army: Izetbegović's Bosnian Army asserted control over Sarajevo's city center, while Karadžić's well-supplied Bosnian Serb troops from the Yugoslav People's Army fortified their positions on the hills ringing the capital.

On April 1, a Serb militia group invaded the town of Bijeljina in eastern Bosnia, massacring many innocent civilians. On April 5, some 100,000 Sarajevans—of all ethnic stripes—came to the busy intersection in front of the Bosnian Parliament to stage a peace rally. Karadžić watched nervously from his office in the Holiday Inn across the street. When the protesters turned their attention to his building, he commanded his snipers to open fire on the unarmed crowd, killing six. Karadžić fled to the hills above town, while Izetbegović's police moved in and arrested the snipers. After Izetbegović refused Karadžić's ultimatum to release the snipers, Karadžić began shelling the city.

For the next month, the situation degraded in other parts of the country, as Bosnian Serb paramilitary groups carried out ethnic cleansing. On May 2, 1992, the Bosnian Serb Army began their advance on the capital in earnest, bombarding Sarajevo's city center, blowing up its central post office to disable telephone communication, and erecting barricades, completely cutting off the Sarajevans from the outside world. The city was defended by a motley collection of policemen, professional soldiers who had defected from the Yugoslav army, and even criminal street gangs. About 12 percent of the army was made up of Serbs. It wasn't necessarily a "pro-Bosnia" army—just Sarajevans desperate to preserve their way of life. This wasn't patriotism: It was survival.

Both sides dug in for a long struggle. Yugoslavia's leader, Slobodan Milošević, sent a ruthless general, Ratko Mladić, to take command of the Bosnian Serb forces. His orders: "Target the Muslim neighborhoods...Shell them until they're at the edge of madness." Snipers monitored exposed streets, immediately firing upon any Sarajevan who dared to walk past.

Horrifying as the tales of besieged Sarajevo are, it's equally uplifting to hear about the irrepressible human spirit shown during these times. The people of Sarajevo survived thanks to the tireless efforts of those who dug and used a tunnel to break the siege (described later, under "Sights in Sarajevo"); and to international relief organizations, including the Red Cross as well as Islamic, Orthodox, Catholic, Jewish, and secular humanitarian groups.

Food was a major concern. The UN took responsibility for humanitarian aid through the siege, and about 90 percent of food was provided by UN airlifts. Sarajevans remember European Community-donated mystery meat in *ICAR* cans, which they ate happily while trying not to think of where it came from (now immortalized by a monument behind the Historical Museum).

Amazingly, people did not simply give up. Even if they lacked basic resources, they continued dressing well and keeping up appearances—if only to preserve their own sanity. Barbers, for example, had a very valuable skill that they could barter for other goods and services.

Throughout even the darkest days of the siege, Sarajevans had art galleries, cafés for socializing, and even a film festival (the famous Sarajevo Film Festival, still going strong, began in 1993). One well-known figure—Vedran Smailović, the "Cellist of Sarajevo"—played his instrument in the bombed-out ruins around town. In 1993, a Miss Sarajevo beauty pageant was held in a basement; at the end, all of the contestants held up a banner pleading, "Don't let them kill us." (The pageant was immortalized in U2's "Miss Sarajevo" music video.)

Sarajevans managed to keep their sense of humor even through the difficult times. When tensions were running high before the war broke out, one night a pro-Serb vandal spray-painted on a Sarajevo post office, "This is Serbia!" The next day, it was rebutted with a new message: "No, this is a post office, you idiot!" On another occasion, someone graffitied on a building: "Tito, come back!" The next day's response: "No thanks, I'm not crazy!" And on the day that Sarajevo beat Leningrad's record for the longest siege of modern times, a local radio station proudly played Queen's "We Are the Champions."

In mid-1995, thanks to NATO bombing raids and joint action by the Croatian and Bosnian armies, the siege started to weaken. On Feb. 29, 1996—the four-year anniversary of the independence referendum that had sparked the war—the government officially declared that the siege was over. It's impossible to know exact figures, but most estimates suggest that about 300,000 to 350,000 lived through the siege, including around 50,000 to 70,000 Serbs who decided to stay in their home city. During the siege, about 10,000 Sarajevans died—including nearly 1,600 children—and 56,000 to 70,000 were wounded.

as "Sniper Alley," the nickname given by foreign journalists who covered the besieged city.

• *Begin your visit to this part of Sarajevo with a...*

"Sniper Alley" Spin-Tour: Stand near the engraved medieval tomb at the corner of the big intersection in front of the Bosnian Parliament (the tall, glassy building). Look up to the hillside across the river. Midway up that hill, the patch of land with the grave markers is the city's main **Jewish cemetery;** during the siege, Karadžić's snipers found this an ideal position from which to rain bullets down on the innocent civilians below. People would cross this street only at night, by cover of darkness, or occasionally by running behind a moving UN armored vehicle that provided cover. A quarter-century ago, if you stood here long enough to read this paragraph, you'd be dead.

Spin to the right to see the blocky glass skyscraper—the **Bosnian Parliament,** rebuilt after being utterly destroyed during the war.

Looking farther to the right, up the big boulevard, you'll see the prominent, bright-yellow facade of the **Holiday Inn** (now labeled *Hotel Holiday*). When it was built for the 1984 Olympics, this was the premier hotel in Sarajevo, fit for visiting dignitaries. But less than a decade later, the first shots of the Bosnian War were fired right here. As tensions were rising throughout Bosnia-Herzegovina, tens of thousands of peace protesters filled this street on April 5,

1992. Karadžić instructed snipers positioned in the hotel to open fire on the unarmed crowd, killing six and wounding many others. Later, the hotel housed foreign journalists and dignitaries, and was therefore virtually the only safe space in the entire city center—though even this enclave suffered its share of incidental damage. (It's been renovated since the war.)

Turning to the right, you see the Catholic **Church of St. Joseph** (another building designed by the Czech architect Karel Pařík). The street to the left of the church, with a clear view from the sniper's nest in the Jewish cemetery, is called Tršćanska (Trieste Street)—but locals began calling it Trćanska, or "Running Street," when it was deadly to walk at a normal pace. Behind the church stands a **hospital.** While the side of the hospital facing away from the hillside sniper's nest was a safe place for injured and ill Sarajevans to recover, the side facing the hill was exposed to sniper fire...a lesson learned in the worst possible way when snipers shot through the windows to kill patients lying in their beds.

Finally, looking to the right you'll see the gigantic **Sarajevo City Center** shopping mall—super-modern and exclusive-feeling, this seems to trumpet to the world that Sarajevo's recovery is well underway. It was built (like so much in modern-day Sarajevo) by investors from the Middle East, who view Sarajevo as a comfortably Muslim enclave in the heart of Europe.

• *From here, if you want to go straight to the Historical Museum, continue up the main street past the Bosnian Parliament, then carry on two long blocks to reach the museum (on your left). But for a more interesting approach—dotted with significant siege locations—take the scenic back way along the river. With your back to the church, walk three minutes down the street to the river and the...*

"Romeo and Juliet Bridge": This span was originally named Vrbanja Bridge, but now it's officially called Suada Dilberović and Olga Sučić Bridge for the two young women who were the first documented victims of the Siege of Sarajevo. Dilberović was a Dubrovnik-born Bosniak pursing her medical degree at the University of Sarajevo, and Sučić was a Croat resident of Sarajevo;

both were killed by sniper bullets while standing on this bridge during the Holiday Inn peace-rally massacre. But this bridge is better known internationally as "Romeo and Juliet Bridge," for two other victims of the war. Two young Sarajevans—Admira Ismić (a Bosniak) and Boško Brkić (a Serb)—were lovers who wanted to escape to a better life together. Brkić used his connections with Serb officials to obtain promise of safe passage out of the city. On May 19, 1993, the couple made it as far as this bridge before snipers opened fire; both were hit and fell to the ground. Boško died instantly; Admira crawled to her beloved, and died clutching his body in her arms. The bodies could not be retrieved and buried for fear of further sniper attacks, so they lay on the bridge for another week, locked in a heart-wrenching embrace. After four days, American war correspondent Kurt Schork issued a dispatch describing the corpses, grabbing the attention of people around the world with this example of the horrifying conditions in the Bosnian capital. The ill-fated "Romeo and Juliet of Sarajevo" have been immortalized in film, song, and news accounts. Sarajevans embrace the couple for the way they embodied a united Sarajevo—with people of various ethnicities living together under siege. As

Ismić's father said in Schork's dispatch, "Love took them to their deaths. That's proof this is not a war between Serbs and Muslims. It's a war between crazy people, between monsters."

Directly across this bridge is the **Grbavica** neighborhood, the closest Bosnian Serb forces got to the city center during the siege—which is why the area we just passed through was so deadly. The snipers were just a couple of blocks away. Notice the bullet holes that still pockmark the buildings facing Grbavica.

• *Now stroll along the river for a couple of blocks, with the river on your left, along the...*

Woodrow Wilson Promenade (Vilsonovo Šetalište): Though this was a deadly no-man's-land a few decades ago, today it's a pleasant, tree-lined riverside park. But here in Sarajevo, even a pretty park has a sinister edge: The trees here survived only because they were too close to enemy lines to safely cut down for fuel.

• *Enough siege talk. Stow your guidebook and just enjoy this romantic walk for a while. I'll meet you at the next bridge.*

The **Ars Aevi Bridge** was designed by Paris' Pompidou Centre architect Renzo Piano, who has also drawn up plans for the nearby future home of Sarajevo's contemporary art museum.

At this bridge, turn right and head away from the river. You'll pass through a field that's the future site for the Ars Aevi museum

noted above. (Meanwhile, its collection is at the Skenderija cultural complex.) Just beyond the field, tucked into the back wall of the Historical Museum, are the outdoor tables of the **Tito Café.** This kitschy hangout celebrates the dictator of communist Yugoslavia with preachy red flags, lots of old photos, camouflage stools, and a bust of the beloved leader, as well as an old jeep and other Yugoslav military vehicles scattered out front. (The tank you'll see out front is a WWII-era relic, which was actually put into use again during the siege.) The clientele seems split between those who really do miss Tito, and those who are here ironically...but either way, they're having fun. (While nursing a drink here, read the "Tito" sidebar on page 740.)

In the park between the café and the river, look for the now-deteriorating **monument** shaped like a giant tin can with an *ICAR* label. This is a (somewhat ironic) thank-you for international relief supplies sent to Sarajevo during the siege, including the canned meat that sometimes appeared in care packages from the European

Community. Understandably, Sarajevans have a love-hate nostalgia for this
"siege Spam."

From the big can, take the sidewalk
through the park back toward the main
drag. On the left, look for another ironic monument, a big **stone slab,** on the
left (next to the stairs to the Historical
Museum). This reads, "Under this stone
there is a monument to the victims of
the war and cold war."

The stairs next to this slab lead
up to the gloomy concrete home of the
Historical Museum, with a quirky but
interesting collection of everyday items used by Sarajevans to survive the siege (described later).

Exiting the Historical Museum, you're facing the side of the
genteel mansion housing the **National Museum.** Across the street
from the Historical Museum, you can see the sleek, low-slung **US
Embassy** building, which fills a huge walled complex in the heart
of downtown—keeping a cautious eye on a city that has seen more
than its share of turmoil over the past generation or two. Hovering
just beyond the embassy is the 580-foot-tall **Avaz Twist Tower,**
which has a fine view from its 36th floor (see "City Views," later in
this chapter).

• *Our walk is finished. From here, you can visit the Historical Museum;
walk or ride a tram (#2, #3, or #5) back to your starting point in the
Old Town; or, for perhaps the most poignant siege sight in town, take a
taxi or tram #3 (plus a short taxi ride) out to the War Tunnel Museum
(described later).*

Sights in Sarajevo

I've organized Sarajevo's main sights as you'll reach them while you
follow my self-guided walks.

IN THE OTTOMAN OLD TOWN (BAŠČARŠIJA)
City Hall (Vijećnica)

This Karel Parík-designed masterpiece of Neo-Moorish style was
one of the main landmarks of Habsburg-era Sarajevo. Destroyed
during the siege, it was meticulously rebuilt thanks partly to donations from Spain, Austria, and Hungary (the three big Habsburg
countries). It once again houses the City Hall and a library, and
invites visitors to step inside and ogle its stunning interior atrium,
with hand-painted details under colorful stained glass. In the basement, you'll find an exhibit on the history of the building and of

Sarajevo, as well as temporary exhibits. While Sarajevo has better history museums, this is worth a visit if you're an aficionado of opulent Habsburg-era architecture.

Cost and Hours: 10 KM, daily 10:00-18:00, www.sarajevo. ba.

▲City History Museum
(in Brusa Bezistan Covered Market)

Filling a big indoor silk bazaar just off old Sarajevo's main square, this good museum features a giant model of the city in 1878, at the apex of the Ottoman period and just before the new Austrian rulers renovated and expanded Sarajevo. The rest of the collection offers a fine historical overview of the city in English, with ample artifacts, traditional costumes, and a good video tracing Sarajevo's story (with English subtitles).

Cost and Hours: 3 KM, mid-April-mid-Oct Mon-Fri 10:00-18:00—off-season until 16:00, Sat 10:00-15:00, closed Sun; Abadžiluk 10, tel. 033/239-590, www.muzejsarajeva.ba.

Visiting the Museum: As you enter, you'll first circle clockwise around the ground floor for a quick look at prehistoric, Roman, and medieval Sarajevo. In the middle is a big Sarajevo model—handy for orientation to the Old Town. Near the end of this section (back near the entrance, in the corner), notice the two big **Bogomil tombstones** (from the medieval Bosnian Christian civilization)—an older, horizontal one and a later, vertical one. The vertical tomb is a transitional piece that demonstrates how Bogomil culture began to take on Turkish customs after the arrival of the Ottomans. The tomb has been rotated upright (in keeping with the Muslim tradition) and displays a Muslim-style crescent moon. A man with a bow and arrow is a common motif on Bogomil tombstones. Here, we see the bow and arrow (on the left side), but not the man—in keeping with the Muslim ban on depicting living things in art. But, in a sort of compromise, it does feature an animal. Nearby is an unusual wooden sarcophagus, which may have held the remains of an important person.

Upstairs, do another clockwise loop, beginning with the origins of the city of Sarajevo. One display case demonstrates the religious diversity of this city—from Orthodox Easter eggs, to a Torah and menorah, to a copy of the Old Testament. The traditional clothing exhibit shows how local styles were influenced by Venetian, Slavic, and Turkish trends, while the one on crafts and trade features items you may have found for sale in the bazaars. Under Ottoman rule, the city saw a flourishing of the arts (see the calligraphy) and education, but as that empire began to decline, illiteracy skyrocketed, and Bosnia's neighbors sensed weakness (exemplified by the case full of weapons). Ultimately Bosnia became part of the Austro-Hungarian Empire (see the new flag of Sarajevo up above), which changed local lifestyles and fashions. Notice the paintings of Bosnian Muslims of this era, who wore Austrian-style suits, but with fezzes and turbans. The remaining exhibits show architecture and decorative arts from the Habsburg period, when the very Ottoman-style Old Town was surrounded by a Viennese urban zone.

▲Old Serbian Orthodox Church

While fully Orthodox inside and out, this 16th-century church has features that resemble a synagogue or a mosque—hinting at

the mingling of faiths that has characterized Sarajevo for most of its history. Stepping inside, notice that the church (which was built on the site of an even earlier one) is set about three feet below street level. Because the Ottomans wouldn't allow churches to be taller than mosques, the builders went down instead of up. Also notice how—with its split-level design and upstairs gallery—it feels like a synagogue with an iconostasis. Upstairs in the gallery, you may see worshippers making a fuss over a small coffin, which contains the body of a child; this is believed to have healing power, especially for infertile women. Across the small courtyard is a museum with old icons, incense burners, vestments, and manuscripts in Cyrillic. Look for the document in squiggly Arabic script—a written confirmation from the Ottoman sultan permitting worshippers to practice the Orthodox Christian faith here. The wine shop keeps up the Bosnian tradition of Orthodox monks doubling as vintners.

Cost and Hours: 3 KM, includes church and museum, Mon-Sat 8:00-18:00, Sun until 16:00, Mula Mustafe Bašeskije 59.

▲▲Gazi Husrev-Bey Mosque
(Gazi Husrev-Begov Džamija)

Called "Begova Mosque" for short, this is Sarajevo's most important and most historic mosque.

Cost and Hours: Outer courtyard—free; mosque—3 KM (or 5-KM combo-ticket with Kuršumilja Madrasa courtyard across the street); buy ticket at little house to the right as you enter courtyard; opening times vary depending on prayer schedule and are posted at ticket office—generally May-Oct daily 9:00-12:00 & 14:00-15:00 & 16:15-17:45, Nov-April daily 9:00-11:00, shorter hours during Ramadan; Sarači, tel. 033/573-151, www.vakuf-gazi.ba.

Visiting the Mosque: Start in the outer courtyard. The **foun-**

tain in the middle (with water piped in from the mountains three miles away) is for washing before prayer. Around the left side, look for the two freestanding **mausoleums** (you can't enter them, but you can peek through the windows around the side). The larger one holds the remains of the mosque's founder and namesake, Gazi Husrev-Bey, a governor of Bosnia who donated vast sums in the 16th century to improve Sarajevo. The smaller mausoleum holds his assistant and secretary, a highly educated Croat named Tardić who had been captured in a battle. He accepted Gazi Husrev-Bey's offer of a job, a precondition of which was that he convert to Islam, and went on to become the governor's most trusted adviser. The **cemetery** behind the mausoleums has graves both old and new; one of the most recent holds the remains of the imam from the destroyed mosque in Banja Luka, a Serb stronghold in northern Bosnia.

Now, let's go inside. Buy a ticket at the office, noticing the long wooden shed nearby, which is used for ablution (washing before prayer). Then step into the mosque's **interior** (women must cover their heads, but visitors can keep their shoes on). You'll see many of the same elements found in other Bosnian mosques. Appreciate the remarkably spacious-feeling architecture. Many of the carpets are gifts from Muslim nations and date from the Tito era. As an anchor of the nonaligned world, which included many Muslim countries (in North Africa and the Middle East), Tito had particularly good relations with Islamic leaders. The elec-

tric lighting—the world's first in a mosque—was installed by the Habsburg rulers in 1898 (the same year they lit up Vienna's Schönbrunn Palace), suggesting how deeply the Habsburgs respected the local Islamic faith. The besieging Bosnian Serb forces in the 1990s didn't share this respect, and used the mosque's minaret for target practice. Looking through the windows, you can see the walls are six feet thick—which helped save it from utter destruction. The mosque was badly damaged, and renovated in 1996 using funds largely from Saudi Arabia; the interior—while covered in fine calligraphy—is still less ornately decorated than it once was.

Nearby: The **clock tower** across the narrow street is also part of the mosque complex; notice that its "noon" lines up with sunset—critical in establishing the five times each day that Muslims pray. Under the clock tower you'll find a free public WC and a little hole-in-the-wall bakery that's open late.

▲▲Sarajevo 1878-1918 Museum and Archduke Franz Ferdinand Assassination Site

Worth ▲▲▲ and ample goose bumps to historians with vivid imaginations, and interesting to anyone, this is the nondescript

street corner where the heir to the huge but declining Austro-Hungarian Empire met a bloody fate at the hands of a Bosnian Serb separatist, plunging Europe into the War to End All Wars (until the next war). The shots were fired as Franz Ferdinand and his wife Sophie sat, JFK-and-Jackie style, in an open-top car during a visit to the Bosnian capital (for the full story, see the sidebar). The street corner where it happened, across from the Latin Bridge (Latinska Ćuprija), is now home to a plaque

and a humble one-room museum, which shows a good video montage in its window that helps illustrate the story. The **Sarajevo 1878-1918 Museum** traces the four decades when this city was part of the Vienna-ruled Austro-Hungarian Empire, with a special emphasis on the assassination. Just inside the entrance, look for the symbolic footprints of the assassin, Gavrilo Princip. Beyond that, the museum holds one well-presented room featuring the trappings of the age, a map showing the sites relating to the assassination, life-size mannequins of Franz Ferdinand and Sophie, and clips from a 1970s-vintage Yugoslav film about the assassination, all with English labels.

Cost and Hours: 4 KM, Mon-Fri 10:00-18:00, Sat 10:00-15:00, closed Sun, Zelenih Beretki 1, tel. 033/533-288, www. muzejsarajeva.ba.

NEAR THE OLD TOWN (BAŠČARŠIJA)
Tomb of the Seven Brothers

This nondescript mosque, at the top of the parking lot across the Latin Bridge from the Old Town, is a favorite spot for Sarajevo

superstition. Along the right, outer wall of the mosque are a door and seven windows marking tombs of (according to legend) innocent people who were unjustly sentenced to death; a strange light was reported to be emanating from their graves at night. It's believed that if you put a coin of the same value in each of these eight slots, you can make a wish or a request. Then you are supposed to walk around the top of the mosque, turn left, and walk down the little lane. Listen carefully— the first words you hear as you walk along this street will help you divine the answer you seek. Interestingly—but not surprisingly for this ecumenical town—even non-Muslim Sarajevans come here when they are searching for enlightenment.

Cemeteries and Viewpoint just Above the Baščaršija

If you walk about 10 minutes up Kovači street from the Sebilj fountain, you'll come to a fine viewpoint over the Old Town, as well

as some large, thought-provoking cemeteries from the siege years. Looking even higher in the hills, you'll see more sprawling cemeteries blanketing the hillsides. People were buried in these places either at night or in heavy fog, when gravediggers could be safe from snipers.

At the top of Kovači street, the **Kovači Martyrs' Memorial Cemetery** is worth a pensive wander. The billboard near the entrance labels each grave. High on the hill is the ceremonial metallic-domed grave of wartime president Alija Izetbegović, surrounded by a crescent-shaped fountain that feeds a stream that trickles downhill between the other headstones. (Just uphill, inside an old tower from the city wall, is a small museum dedicated to Izetbegović.)

Just above this area is a neighborhood called **Vratnik** (roughly "Gateway"), the oldest part of town.

Svrzo's House (Svrzina Kuća)

If you'd like to tour a traditional home from the Ottoman period, hike five minutes uphill from the Old Town to see this well-preserved, sprawling estate, built in the 17th century by a wealthy local Bosniak family. It's similar to the "Turkish houses" you'll see in Mostar—except that it's made of wood, as is typical of Bosnia, while Herzegovinian homes (like those in Mostar) are made of stone. First, you'll head upstairs to see the men's sitting room *(halvat)*, the women's room (where the ladies of the house did their embroidery), and the dining room (where guests sat on the floor around the low table, or up on the long divans all around the room). The *kamarija* (balcony) overlooks the inner courtyard, with its garden and well. Then head downstairs to see the big kitchen and large *halvat*—for big family gatherings.

Cost and Hours: 3 KM, 5-KM guidebook, Mon-Fri 10:00-

The Shot Heard 'Round the World

On June 28, 1914, Archduke Franz Ferdinand—heir to the throne of the Habsburg Empire—and his wife, Sophie, visited Sarajevo. While they were in town, a local pan-Slavic movement to liberate Bosnia from the Austro-Hungarian Empire launched an assassination plot. Early in the day, the attempt failed when a bomb intended for the archduke's car instead wounded other members of his party. Believing the plot to be foiled, the archduke continued on his way, visiting the City Hall a few blocks up the river.

A 19-year-old Bosnian Serb named Gavrilo Princip, who was in on the plot, was waiting for Ferdinand's car along the river by the Latin Bridge (across the street from today's museum, by the tram stop). But when that area became too crowded, he crossed to the corner now marked by a plaque, and stepped into a nearby delicatessen. Meanwhile, after leaving the City Hall, Franz Ferdinand decided at the last moment to change his schedule and visit the people who had been wounded by the bomb. Confused by the last-minute change, the driver took a wrong turn up this street and paused directly in front of Princip. The assassin raised his gun and fired, killing both Franz Ferdinand and Sophie.

Princip and the other plotters were arrested. The Habsburgs wanted to send investigators into Serbia to root out the co-conspirators; Serbia's refusal to grant them access kicked off a chain reaction that brought all of Europe to war. While historians stress that Ferdinand's assassination was merely the event that ignited the tinderbox of World War I—not the "cause" of the war—its significance is undeniable.

Because Princip was too young to be executed, he was given a 20-year sentence at Theresienstadt prison outside of Prague (which the Nazis later converted into Terezín concentration camp), where he died at age 24. Much of the world considered him a monster, but by the end of World War I, the nascent nation of Yugoslavia—which emerged from the ashes of that war exactly as Princip and his accomplices had dreamed—celebrated him as a hero. They even gave his name to the bridge near the spot where his shot change history.

SARAJEVO

18:00—off-season until 16:00, Sat until 15:00, closed Sun, Glođina 8, tel. 033/535-264, www.muzejsarajeva.ba.

IN THE HABSBURG QUARTER

Immediately west of the Ottoman quarter is the more modern part of town, built at the end of the 19th century after Bosnia became part of the Austro-Hungarian Empire. While several of the sights scattered through this area are much older, most of the buildings here are evocative of those in Vienna, the capital at the time.

▲▲Old Synagogue (Stari Hram) and Bosnian Jewish Museum (Muzej Jevreja BiH)

Combining a classic old 16th-century synagogue (modeled after a synagogue in Toledo, Spain) with an excellent and insightful museum chronicling the Jewish faith in this country, this is one of the most interesting Jewish sites in southeastern Europe.

Cost and Hours: 3 KM, 5-KM guidebook, mid-April-mid-Oct Mon-Fri 10:00-18:00—off-season until 16:00, Sun until 13:00, closed Sat year-round, Josipa Štadlera 32, tel. 033/535-688, www.muzejsarajeva.ba.

Background: Soon after the Jews were expelled from Spain in the late 15th century, Sephardic Jews made their way to Bosnia, which they found to be an unusually tolerant place (typical of its entire history). Unlike many Central and Eastern European cities, Sarajevo did not relegate its Jews to a ghetto; they lived amid their non-Jewish neighbors. Local Sephardi used "Ladino," a unique language mixing Spanish and Hebrew (even today, rabbis greet each other not with *Shalom,* but with *Buenos días*).

Visiting the Synagogue and Museum: Buy your ticket and step into the **central hall,** with the *bema* (altar-like raised area) in the center and the wooden doors that hold the Torah. Women, who in accordance with Jewish tradition worship separately from men, stand up in the arcades ringing the hall. In the central hall, look for the replica of the important Sarajevo Haggadah book (see sidebar).

Near the stairs on the **ground floor,** you'll see a tombstone from a Jewish cemetery on the hill across the river, which is the second-biggest in Europe (after Prague's) and was tragically used as a sniper's nest during the siege; and a model of the original appearance of this synagogue.

Head **upstairs** to see exhibits of more Jewish religious items, and illustrations of how local Jews adopted local culture (for example, you'll see Jews wearing Muslim-style fezzes). The replica of an Ottoman-era "pharmacy" with herbal cures is a reminder that such businesses were typically run by Jewish Sarajevans.

The **top floor** focuses on the dark 20th century, including the Holocaust. Hanging from the ceiling is a giant book listing the 12,000 Jewish Sarajevans who were killed. The exhibit also profiles Bosnians who were designated as "Righteous Among the Nations"—an honorific for non-Jews who risk their own lives to save their Jewish neighbors. Among these is Derviš Korkut, the Muslim museum curator who saved the Sarajevo Haggadah from Nazi investigators. Some Jewish women were smuggled out of

The Sarajevo Haggadah

An ancient Jewish text telling the story of the Exodus—used as a sort of "order of service" for the Passover Seder—the Haggadah is considered the third most important book of the Jewish faith (after the Torah and Talmud). The Sarajevo Haggadah is filled with colorful illustrations as well as wine stains—indicating that it has been used at many Passover dinner tables. While the book's exact origins are unclear, it likely dates from around 1350 and was brought out of Spain by Sephardic transplants in the 16th century. No one knows exactly how or when it came to Bosnia.

Appropriately for a book about the Exodus, it has had quite an unlikely journey through a landscape of hardship. Bosnians—who, regardless of their ethnicity, consider the Sarajevo Haggadah a part of their national cultural heritage—proudly explain that the book has been protected time after time by people of a wide variety of faiths (not just Jews). During the WWII occupation, when an SS officer came here to claim the Haggadah, the Muslim curator of the museum lied about its whereabouts and carried it on horseback into the mountains to hide it away under the doorstop of a village mosque. Soon after the siege began in 1992, the room in the National Museum that held the Haggadah was almost entirely destroyed by mortar shells—but the book itself survived, secured in a steel box. The building was exposed to sniper fire, so under cover of darkness, Bosnian Army troops snuck to the museum, rescued the book, and stored it in the vault of the Bosnian Central Bank. Today, the National Museum still owns the book and displays it a few hours each month. See the museum's listing under "Near Sniper Alley," later.

Nazi-occupied areas by disguising themselves in Muslim veils. You'll also see Nazi-mandated armbands identifying Jews, photos of resistance fighters, and an exhibit on the odious Jasenovac concentration camp on today's Bosnian-Croatian border—where Jews, Serbs, Roma (Gypsies), antifascist Muslims and Croats, communists, and other enemies of the Ustaše-controlled state were savagely executed. Jasenovac lacked the "high-tech" gas chambers of other Nazi camps, so they resorted to more medieval methods, murdering their victims by knife, sword, or even a hammer to the skull. And yet, even through that dark history, Sarajevo remained a place where cultures coexist side-by-side.

▲War Childhood Museum (Muzej Ratnog Djetinstva)

On the hill behind the synagogue and Bosnian Jewish Museum, a few minutes' walk up Logavina street, you'll find this small, poignant museum documenting how children experience war. Though the memories here center on the Yugoslav Wars, you'll also find stories from children caught in other conflicts such as those in Syria, Afghanistan, and Palestine. It's a deeply touching place worth visiting for its personal, human perspective on the impact of mass violence.

Cost and Hours: 10 KM, daily July-Aug 10:00-20:00, Sept-June 11:00-19:00, Logavina 32, tel. 033/535-558, www.warchildhood.org.

Visiting the Museum: The museum holds items that people have donated from their own experiences growing up in war, all explained by the free audioguide or on panels with short English descriptions. The collection is constantly changing, so what you see might differ from what's described here. Heart-wrenching items include a mangled jungle gym, hit by a grenade that killed four children. You might also see a cookbook with Damir's reminiscence of how he would flip through the book, with all its luscious pictures, imagining how the dishes must taste as his family went hungry during the war. Elsewhere there's a wooden swing a grandfather built for his granddaughter, which brought her happiness in a very difficult time; a chalkboard pocked with a shrapnel hole; and a collection of humanitarian food aid. Filip recalled that humanitarian aid was something new to Yugoslavia, since they had thought of themselves as a rich country. He remembers people saying, "Come on, by Monday everything will be back to normal"—no one initially believed that neighbors would be killing neighbors.

Each child's story stands without naming the war from which it came, driving home the point that the experiences are sadly universal: Children everywhere have suffered from violence—and continue to do so today.

Catholic Cathedral

Dating from 1884-1889, this Historicist structure mingles different architectural styles typical of Viennese buildings of that age: a Neo-Gothic exterior and a Neo-Byzantine/Neo-Baroque interior. Notice the big gap across the street, offering a fine view of the adjacent hillside. During the siege, the church's front door was dangerously exposed—not only to snipers, but to antiaircraft machine guns, which were used to periodically spray bullets randomly over the town. Inside, the red-and-white-striped ribs—a Neo-Moorish style element—are rare in a Catholic church, but seem to fit here in ecumenical Sarajevo. Inside and on the left, look for the grave of the church's Croatian founder, Joseph Stadler, and a plaque commemorating St. John Paul II's 1997 visit.

Cost and Hours: Free, 2-KM guidebooklet, daily 9:00-16:00, no shorts, Trg Fra Grge Martića 2.

▲▲Srebrenica Exhibition (Memorijalna Galerija 11/07/95)

Worth ▲▲▲ for anyone who wants to better understand the atrocities in Bosnia's late-20th-century history, this important, emotionally exhausting exhibition uses photographs and video clips to tell the story of the remote Bosnian village that experienced the worst massacre on European soil since World War II.

Cost and Hours: 12 KM, daily July-Sept 9:00-22:00, May-June and Oct 10:00-20:00, Nov-April 10:00-18:00, Trg Fra Grge Matića 2/III, tel. 033/953-170, www.galerija110795.ba.

Tours: You can walk through the exhibition on your own, or pay 3 KM to rent a good 40-minute audioguide that explains the basics. Ask if any guided tours are scheduled when you visit.

Visiting the Exhibition: Because of the horrifying massacre that took place there (described in the sidebar), the name "Srebrenica" has become synonymous with some of the worst crimes against humanity in recent memory. The date you'll see everywhere—11/07/95—commemorates July 11, 1995, when Bosnian Serb forces invaded Srebrenica, beginning their genocidal attack. This exhibit, consisting mostly of haunting photographs by Tarik Samarah, documents the process of piecing together exactly what happened there. Photos show the faces of just 640 of the more than 8,000 victims; conditions in the refugee camps where survivors lived after the massacre; the process of exhuming, documenting, and investigating the many mass graves that have been discovered (mass funerals are held on July 11 each year to honor victims who were identified during that year); and some graphic and unsettling graffiti by UN troops from the Netherlands, which suggests that they felt more contempt than sympathy for the people they were assigned to protect.

Perhaps the most powerful parts of the exhibit are the wrenching movies that are shown at the far end of the exhibition hall. There are two screens—one with movies about Srebrenica, and another about the Siege of Sarajevo (on both, the movies alternate on a loop). Most powerful is *Srebrenica Massacre*, a 27-minute video that outlines (with English subtitles) the harrowing chain of events that led to the fall of Srebrenica and the ruthless murders of so many of its residents. Another good film is *Miss Sarajevo* (30 minutes), about life in Sarajevo during the siege.

Maps on the wall identify the locations of mass graves that have been found so far. Out in the hallway, a 50-foot-long wall lists the name and date of birth of each of the 8,372 victims who have

SARAJEVO

Srebrenica

Despite their hardships during the siege, many Sarajevans consider themselves fortunate not to have met the same fate as many of the Bosniaks living in eastern Bosnia during the war. These areas, bordering Serbia proper and intertwined with Serb-dominated parts of Bosnia, were aggressively targeted by the vicious military and paramilitary forces of Bosnian Serb President Radovan Karadžić. While many towns along the Foča River Valley were brutally besieged and overrun, the most notorious site of ethnic cleansing was in the town of Srebrenica.

Before the war, Srebrenica (SREB-reh-neet-seh, meaning "silver mine") was a mining center and spa town of about 36,000 people, which sat near the geographical center of Yugoslavia. While three-quarters of the population was Bosniak, it also had a large Serb community. There was nothing unique about Srebrenica that made it prime to become the poster child for ethnic cleansing—it simply got in the way of Karadžić's battle plans.

In 1993, as reports surfaced of Karadžić's forces using ethnic cleansing in multiple Bosniak villages in eastern Bosnia, the United Nations designated safe areas where civilian refugees could take shelter. Srebrenica was the first one. The UN dispatched a protection force (UNPROFOR) to these areas. But those UNPROFOR troops—including 400 Dutch soldiers sent to watch over Srebrenica—soon feared for their own lives as much as for those they were intended to guard. The UN demanded that their troops remain completely neutral, even when directly attacked—dooming them to an ultimately pointless mission.

Conditions in the "safe areas" swiftly deteriorated, and by 1995, Srebrenica had become a highly vulnerable refugee-crammed island in a tight bottleneck valley, entirely surrounded by Bosnian Serb forces. In July, the noose began to close around Srebrenica, as General Ratko Mladić invaded. On the afternoon of July 11, 1995, Mladić marched triumphantly through the town, claiming Srebrenica for the Serb people. Most of the estimated 50,000 to 60,000 people living in the town fled.

Approximately 25,000 refugees—mostly women, children, ill or injured people, and the elderly—showed up in desperation at the UN peacekeeping base at the nearby village of Potočari. The terrified Dutch troops there, unable to provide for either the safety or the basic nutritional needs of so many, took in only about 5,000 of the refugees (predominantly mothers with babies), leaving the rest to fend for themselves.

Both at Potočari and in Srebrenica, Bosnian Serb forces culled out any men between the ages of 12 and 77. In that moment, families were ripped apart forever, as husbands, fathers, and sons were taken away to be summarily executed. Many survivors still don't know exactly what happened to their relatives; they simply never came back. In some cases, troops walked through the throngs of refugees, murdering Bosniak men right out in the open, then tossing their bodies into a pile. Bosniak women were forcibly raped in front of dozens of witnesses. Crying children who couldn't be silenced were slaughtered. Two days later, the Dutch forces evicted the rest of the refugees from inside their camp, including more than 200 men, dooming them to certain death. (The Dutch role in Srebrenica remains a matter of deep guilt in the Netherlands.)

Late in the evening of July 11, approximately 12,000 Bosniak men—about half of them military, and half civilian—headed into the hills surrounding town, with the intention of hiking through the mountains to the free city of Tuzla, 35 miles away. A human chain eight miles long trudged slowly across the difficult terrain. Mladić shelled the hillsides, killing many. Others died of malnutrition or exhaustion from hiking through sweltering summer heat. Some committed suicide. The next day, the column was split in half, and one large group was surrounded by Bosnian Serb forces, bombarded with artillery (and, some allege, chemical weapons), and told to surrender. Thousands did...and were executed. After five days, survivors finally stumbled into safety in the town of Tuzla. Others wandered in the mountains for months.

While captured Bosniak men were sometimes killed on the spot, more typically they were taken to holding areas (typically schools, warehouses, or soccer fields) until they could be moved to remote areas for a systematic, mass execution—often by lining them up, blindfolding them, shooting them or slitting their throats, and then bulldozing them into mass graves.

All told, at least 8,000 people, mostly men, were murdered by the forces of Karadžić and Mladić over the course of just a

few days. Mass graves are still being discovered. The remains of people who once called Srebrenica home are dutifully pulled out of the ground, identified through DNA testing, and given a proper burial in a collective funeral each year on July 11.

There's no silver lining, no happy ending to the tale of Srebrenica. The best that victims' families can hope for is that their loved ones' remains will someday be identified so they can bury them properly. The World War II concentration camp memorials, museums, and documentation centers around Europe all share the same message: Never again. Srebrenica tells us that, despite the best efforts of civilized people, that message still falls on deaf ears. Appallingly, many people in the former Yugoslavia still try to deny or justify the events at Srebrenica. Visiting the Srebrenica Exhibition in Sarajevo helps deflect that bogus propaganda with facts. And various companies in Sarajevo (including Sarajevo Insider) run educational tours to Srebrenica.

been identified so far; the alphabetical list makes it clear that entire extended families were wiped out. Nearby, touchscreens with headphones let you view individual testimonials from survivors and victims' relatives (subtitled in English). For even more information, sit at one of the terminals in the first room, where you can click through more than four hours of video documentation. The quote on the wall reminds visitors of a lesson that, it seems, needs to be repeated again and again: "All that is necessary for the triumph of evil is that good men do nothing."

Nearby: Within a block or so of the Srebrenica Exhibition, you may see advertised the **Museum of Crimes Against Humanity and Genocide.** This private venture, cramped but packed with information, has its heart in the right place but isn't as thoughtfully presented as the Srebrenica Exhibition.

NEAR "SNIPER ALLEY"

For the most interesting approach to this area from the Old Town (Baščaršija), see my self-guided walk, earlier.

Historical Museum of Bosnia-Herzegovina (Historijski Muzej BiH)

Filling a still-bombed-out-feeling, Tito-era building next to the National Museum, this museum features a small and ramshackle but illuminating exhibit explaining the Siege of Sarajevo—worth ▲ if you're interested in that period or if you can get a local to come with you to explain the objects (English labels are sparse).

Cost and Hours: 7 KM, 5-KM guidebook, daily 9:00-19:00, until 21:00 in summer, Zmaja od Bosne 5, tel. 033/226-098, www.muzej.ba.

Visiting the Museum: Formerly the "Museum of the Revolution," the building's **stairwell** still features Socialist Realist mosaics from the communist period, and a statue of Tito stands in the inner courtyard. Head upstairs to see the exhibit.

The permanent exhibit—called **Sarajevo Surrounded**—is constantly in flux, but it always tells the story of the siege through photographs, news clippings, shells and weapons used in combat, and many actual items that show how Sarajevans improvised ways to carry on. You'll be inspired by the desperate ingenuity of the besieged Sarajevans.

As you explore, keep an eye out for these items:

The mockup of a typical siege-time **apartment** is packed with details. The TV, telephone, refrigerator, and other appliances were useless without electricity. (The power might come on sporadically, but never for very long.) Look around at the so-called "Sarajevo inventions," created by desperate and clever people to keep going.

A bag is made out of a plastic tarp donated by the international community.

In the apartment is a makeshift **stove,** and a collection of several other, smaller stoves is nearby. During the frigid Sarajevo winters, trees were cut down to fuel fires. When the trees were gone, firewood was in short supply (a bundle might cost the equivalent of $50), so residents burned their furniture, shoes, old toys—anything flammable. And they bundled up in as many clothes as possible.

The display of **cigarettes** explains how smokes were used as a sort of currency; even through the siege, the local cigarette factory kept working, though the product sometimes had to be packaged in makeshift wrappers.

Another display shows the various ways that people created **light,** including a candle made of pork fat with a wick made from carpet fibers. After 1994, natural gas was available in some areas; notice the recycled IV tube (still bloody inside) used to power the gas lamp.

Peruse the paltry **foodstuffs** that Sarajevans considered themselves lucky to find during wartime. Imagine picking over these meager offerings—rusty canned goods, military rations, plastic bags stuffed with grains—and trying to figure out how to use them to feed your family. Sarajevans learned how to stretch a "one-day ration" for up to two weeks. (Many nations sent old military rations—Sarajevans might find themselves eating leftover US rations from the Vietnam War.) Lawns were converted into makeshift produce gardens. Everyone came up with "siege recipes," replacing unavailable ingredients with whatever they could. For example, during a time when rice was relatively plentiful, they'd mix it with flour to make bread, or use it as filling for *burek* (savory pastries). Instead of spinach filling for a *burek,* they might use greens from buttercup flowers. And when they had a taste for coffee, they'd burn rice, grind it, and mix it with hot water; they swear the taste was similar...even if it was missing the caffeine kick.

The elaborate **satellite telephone** was, for a time, the only way that Bosnian President Alija Izetbegović could communicate with the outside world.

The **market kiosk** is stocked with a woefully sparse selection of items: humble woolens, a few grains, and pathetic twigs of firewood. There was very little to buy, and in order to buy it, you'd have to use a Monopoly-like money that was the city's ersatz legal tender during the siege.

Scattered throughout the displays are **children's items**—a heartbreaking reminder that not only "militants" were among the besieged in Sarajevo (though the Museum of War Childhood offers a better look at this aspect). Kids continued going to school, where many were injured by artillery attacks.

In other parts of the exhibition hall, you'll generally find temporary exhibits. But look for the well-done tables mapping the diplomacy that went into the Dayton peace process to end the conflict in Bosnia.

National Museum (Zemaljski Muzej)

This humble museum does a reasonable job of covering the colorful history of this fascinating nation. The dusty collections of archaeology, natural science, and ethnology are not hugely thrilling, but they are generally well described in English, and they're a good reminder that Bosnia is about more than just war. However, the main reason to visit is to peek at one of the world's most precious books, the Sarajevo Haggadah (see sidebar, earlier). The Haggadah is open just a few hours each month (see below), and can be unexpectedly in storage, so if you have your heart set on seeing it, time your visit to the book's display period, and call first to be sure it's on view.

Cost and Hours: 8 KM, Tue-Fri 10:00-19:00, Sat-Sun until 14:00, closed Mon, Zmaja od Bosne 7, tel. 033/262-710, www. zemaljskimuzej.ba. The Haggadah room is open Tue, Thu, and every first Sat of the month from 12:00 to 13:00. Outside those times, you can try to arrange a special viewing, which costs 150 KM.

Visiting the Museum: The large museum—filling four buildings surrounding a central garden—can be seen quickly. From the entrance, turn right into the **Archaeology** section. On the ground floor, look for third-century mosaics from Stolac. Then head upstairs, go through the left door, and look left (through the glass door with blue light); at limited times visitors can see the **Sarajevo Haggadah** in a display case. The rest of the upstairs has items from the Middle Ages.

Head out into the central botanical garden and turn left to find the **Ethnology** section, which is like an open-air Bosnian folk museum moved inside—with six authentic, mostly wooden interiors from buildings around the country. The rooms are arranged to emphasize how the various cultures that lived here influenced each other. You'll learn about traditional Bosnian lifestyles: how people would sit on the floor around a table to eat, sharing one very long napkin, and how backyards were often connected so that Muslim women could pass between houses without covering up. On the steps out front are *stećak*s, large engraved tombstones from the Bogomil times of the 12th to the 14th centuries (the best collection of these is on the outskirts of Stolac).

The **Natural History** section (in the building directly across the garden from the main building) displays vast collections of butterflies and bugs, plant life, birds, and rocks.

OUTER SARAJEVO
▲▲Sarajevo War Tunnel Museum (Sarajevski Ratni Tunel)
In the countryside on the southwestern outskirts of Sarajevo, near the airport, is a small but fascinating museum celebrating the ingenuity and determination of the besieged Sarajevans to continue supplying their city. Here you can walk through a small stretch of the actual half-mile supply tunnel they dug to stay alive during the siege. The still battle-scarred house that marks its entrance holds an exhibit displaying actual items used in the tunnel.

Cost and Hours: 10 KM, daily April-Oct 9:00-17:00, Nov-March until 16:00. Your ticket includes a free tour (usually lasting about 30 minutes)—though it's best to call ahead to arrange a time. Tuneli 1, tel. 033/778-670, mobile 061-213-760, www.tunelspasa.ba.

Getting There: The tunnel is a long detour from anyplace else in town. Therefore, the most convenient option is to take a guided tour that includes transportation from downtown and a clear explanation of what happened here. Various companies offer these tours, including Insider Tours (see "Tours in Sarajevo," earlier). By taxi, the fair metered rate from downtown is 20-25 KM one-way—just tell them *"tunel."* Alternatively, you can take tram #3 or bus #32 from the Old Town to the end of the line (Ilidža stop, about 40 minutes one-way), then walk 2.5 miles or pay 5-10 KM one-way for a taxi from there. If you're flying into or out of the city, the museum combines well with your trip to the airport. If you're driving from Mostar to Sarajevo, it makes sense to stop and tour the tunnel on your way into town (pay parking lot nearby).

Background: With the city almost entirely surrounded by the Bosnian Serb Army, the Sarajevans' lone connection to the outside world was a mountain pass. But between them and that pass was the city's airport—which couldn't be crossed by either side because it was controlled by the impartial UN. So, rather than go through the airport, they went beneath it—digging a half-mile-long tunnel under the runway. Coal-mine engineers spent four months and four days in 1993 digging a passageway that was about five feet tall and three feet wide. Once it was completed, Sarajevans could enter the basement of an apartment building, hunch over and hike through thickly humid air for 20 minutes, and emerge at a house on the other end. (After a heavy rain, the tunnel would fill with water, making the hike even more unpleasant.) From the house, they could hike over the mountains to get supplies. While money was scarce, people could trade cigarettes produced at Sarajevo's factory for what they needed, carrying their goods back over the mountains and through the tunnel. Eventually the tunnel was wired to also supply electricity and natural gas into the city, and was equipped with rails to more efficiently transport goods on wheeled carts. The tunnel was open to any Sarajevan—and people used it to shuttle back and forth, day and night—but it was carefully monitored for smugglers who might use it to profit from the tragedy inside the city. While the besieging enemy knew about the tunnel, its nonlinear course underground made it impossible for them to know exactly where it was—and even if they had known, to destroy it they'd have had to go through the UN-controlled airport. The best they could do was to relentlessly bombard the tunnel's entrances.

Visiting the Museum and Tunnel: After buying your ticket, you'll walk through a few rooms of museum exhibits, then crouch your way through the tunnel itself, and finally have the chance to watch a movie about this site's history.

In the museum's first room are tools used to dig and maintain the tunnel. Look for a model of the airport runway in relation to the tunnel, and a cross-section of the tunnel's structure. See the handwritten lists, used to keep track of who was coming and going. Video screens show the tunnel in active use.

In the next room is a reconstruction of the tunnel, which was used both by the military and by civilians. Notice the various types of carts used to transport food, weapons, and injured people. Notice the cables and pipes along the back wall—a reminder that the tunnel was used not only for people and supplies, but also for electricity and gas. To the right is the chair on wheels used to push the ailing President Izetbegović through the tunnel—hardly presidential transport, but the only way he could safely get in and out of the city for diplomatic meetings. In the display case in the corner, notice the makeshift canvas boots—roughly stitched together using material donated by the international community—which were pulled on over regular shoes to trudge through the sludge that collected on the tunnel floor.

Leaving the museum, you'll pass a guestbook with famous visitors (including actor "Stiv Bushemi"). Then walk down the steps and turn right to reach the tunnel itself. Before entering, you'll pass an artillery shell still embedded in the cement floor. Down a few more steps is another museum room, with two uniforms that show how the initially improvised Bosnian defense forces evolved as the war went on: At first, they wore jeans and tennis shoes, while later they had real uniforms and boots.

Now climb down the tight stairs and squeeze through an actual 80-foot-long stretch of the tunnel. Imagine yourself walking, crouched over, 30 times this far from one end to the other. If you'd like, you can hike through the tunnel wearing a backpack loaded with 65 pounds—roughly the amount that women typically carried through the tunnel (men would carry more than double that much).

Emerging at the far end, you'll peer into a mock-up of a siege-era apartment. Cigarettes (used for bartering) are stuffed into a wrapper made from an old newspaper. Lighting was often as simple as oil and water in a glass jar with a wick. The broken glass window illustrates the absurdity of trying to keep warm through a frigid winter when basic insulation was an impossibility. On the table are the contents of an aid package that was expected to last one person for 10 to 15 days (including the *ICAR* canned "mystery meat"). Tucked behind this mock apartment is an improvised generator, built from a car engine, used to provide intermittent electricity to Sarajevans.

The gift shop anchors a long building with three rooms showing the same, good 16-minute film that illustrates the construction and use of the tunnel. Posted around the site is a map of the besieged city—superimposed, not without irony, over a map from the 1984 Olympic Games.

Past the film-viewing rooms, you can walk through a field embedded with land mines, shells, and other artillery. While these have been defused, this area was bombarded with more than 300 grenades daily, with 3,777 being launched here in one day alone.

Finally you'll wind up in a quiet lawn where you can look out over the airport, on the horizon. (Locals say that when they saw a UN plane taking off—likely carrying international officials to safety—they knew trouble was brewing.) In 1993, for the first time, Bosnia-Herzegovina selected a band to represent the newly independent country at the Eurovision Song Contest (a Europe-wide TV extravaganza somewhat like the finale to *American Idol*). The band, Fazla, was trapped in Sarajevo by the siege. Determined to make it to the show in Ireland, they ran across the UN-controlled

SARAJEVO

airport runway with their instruments, which they then carried over the mountains to freedom. By the time the band returned, the siege tunnel under the airport was finished, and they were able to easily sneak back into the city. Even many people who managed to leave Sarajevo chose to return and remain under siege with their families and neighbors, rather than abandon their unique city and way of life.

▲▲City Views

This vertical city's gorgeous setting is best seen from high up. Fortunately, a cable car (described next) offers a sweeping view of Sarajevo, and a variety of other vistas are available.

One easy option is to walk from the Old Town up Kovači street—lined with characteristic bars and a mix of local and touristy artisans—for a decent (if not sky-high) view over town. Bus tours around Sarajevo include at least one panoramic viewpoint to enjoy one of Europe's most spectacularly set cities. You might also take a taxi up to the popular viewpoint called **White Bastion** (Bijela Tabija), at an old fortress (a taxi from the Old Town should cost about 10 KM round-trip). A bit lower on the hill is the **Yellow Bastion** (Žuta Tabija), which has fine views as well as a café. For this one, you'll actually hike steeply uphill from the Old Town (though a taxi can take you partway).

Closer to the modern downtown, the **Avaz Twist Tower** (next to the train station) has a sky-high café—just head inside and ride the elevator to floor 35 (cheap drinks, daily 8:00-22:30). You can drop a coin in the turnstile to walk up one more flight of stairs to an outdoor view terrace.

Two recommended restaurants—**Kibe Mahala** and **Park Prinčeva**—also offer great views over the Old Town area (see "Eating in Sarajevo," later).

▲▲Sarajevo Cable Car (Sarajevska Žičara)

The cable car provides the best views in town—and it's worth ▲▲▲ for outdoorsy types who'd like to hike back down rather than riding round-trip. You'll glide 15 minutes up the slopes of Mt. Trebević for a panorama of Sarajevo's mountain scenery—arguably best at sunset, but enjoyable any time of day. The valley station is located on the south side of the river, a little farther up the hillside behind the brewery. To reach it, walk toward the brewery, then look for the signs for *žičara*.

Cost and Hours: 15 KM one-way, 20 KM round-trip, daily

9:00-21:00, until 17:00 in winter, Hrvatin b.b., tel. 033/292-800, www.zicara.ba.

Visiting the Cable Car: On the ride up, gawk with abandon at the city growing smaller beneath you. You'll get a good overview of the Ottoman, Habsburg, and 20th-century neighborhoods, their little houses spreading up the slopes. The big, destroyed building on a hill overlooking the Old Town is the **Jajce Barracks.** Originally built in 1914 (toward the end of Habsburg rule), it was used by one military or another until the 1990s, when it was destroyed in the Yugoslav Wars. Higher above looms the older fortress known as the **White Bastion** (Bijela Tabija).

At the cable car's top station (about 3,800 feet above sea level), there's a little café and a few viewpoints. From here, it's a relatively easy walk downhill to see the ruined bobsled track from the 1984 Olympics. Follow the signs for *Bob staza* and you'll come to the crumbling, mossy, graffiti-covered track. Take a moment to imagine when this was a world-class venue, and Sarajevo was in the global spotlight for positive reasons.

From the bobsled track, you can either head back uphill to the cable car or hike down into town. The route down isn't well-signed, but it's not hard to figure out: Just go downhill. The path sticks to a road part of the way, diverts across some fields, and eventually ends up on steep city streets. Figure an hour or two to walk back to the city center, depending on your pace. One word of warning: Stay on the trodden paths, since bushwhacking can get you in trouble here. Sarajevo's mountainsides were mined during the war, and though the mines were subsequently cleared, it's better to be safe than sorry.

Sleeping in Sarajevo

The city enjoys a wide variety of good accommodations, ranging from budget hostels to cozy and warmly run little pensions to plush hotels. All of my listings are in or very near the Old Town (Baščaršija). Places that are actually in the Baščaršija come with some nighttime noise. And if you're near a mosque, you'll hear the (amplified) call to prayer in the wee hours.

$$$ Isa Begov Hamam Hotel is the place for those who want to be transported back to Ottoman times. With 15 plush rooms filling part of a classic bathhouse next to the modern mosque, it feels close to Istanbul. The bathhouse is fully functioning and open to guests—at a discount—and nonguests (air-con, across the river from the Old Town at Bistrik 1, tel. 033/570-050, www.isabegovhotel.com, info@isabegovhotel.com).

$$ Hotel Central is an affordable splurge right in the heart of the Old Town. The public areas and 32 rooms are done in a

Sarajevo Hotels & Restaurants

Accommodations

1. Isa Begov Hamam Hotel
2. Hotel Central
3. Hotel Story
4. Hotel Old Town
5. Hotel Latinski Most
6. Halvat Guest House
7. Ada Hotel
8. Hotel Michele
9. To Kandilj Pension
10. Vagabond Hostel

Eateries & Other

11. Prote Bakovića Eateries
12. Buregdžinica Sač
13. Mrkva
14. Petica
15. Galatasaray
16. Željo
17. ASDž Cafeteria
18. Aščinica "H.E.M"
19. Morića Han Café & Restaurant
20. Rahatlook

very snazzy style. Given the central location, request a quiet room (breakfast extra, air-con, elevator, pool/sauna, nearby pay parking, Ćumurija 8, tel. 033/561-800, www.hotelcentral.ba, info@hotelcentral.ba).

$$ Hotel Story, tucked down a traffic-free, pub-lined lane just off Ferhadija, has nine sleek, modern, stylish rooms (air-con, elevator, pay parking nearby, Saliha H. Muvekita 4, tel. 033/551-555, www.story-hotel.com, info@story-hotel.com).

$$ Hotel Old Town, tidy and businesslike, has 15 fresh,

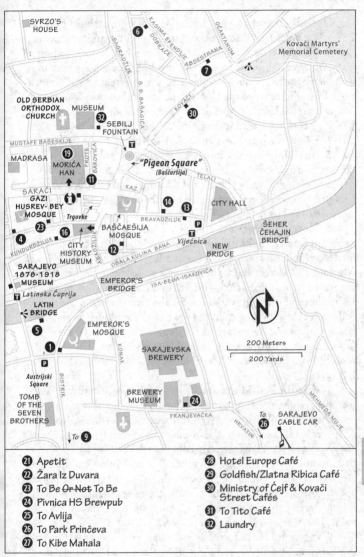

SARAJEVO

㉑ Apetit	㉘ Hotel Europe Café
㉒ Žara Iz Duvara	㉙ Goldfish/Zlatna Ribica Café
㉓ To Be Or Not To Be	㉚ Ministry of Ćejf & Kovači Street Cafés
㉔ Pivnica HS Brewpub	
㉕ To Avlija	㉛ To Tito Café
㉖ To Park Prinčeva	㉜ Laundry
㉗ To Kibe Mahala	

modern rooms that are a bit small for the price but right in the heart of the Old Town (cash only, air-con, elevator, free parking—but reserve ahead, Mali Čurčiluk 11A, tel. 033/574-200, www.hoteloldtown.ba, info@hoteloldtown.ba).

$ Hotel Latinski Most (Latin Bridge), in an 1880s villa overlooking the embankment where Archduke Franz Ferdinand was assassinated in 1914, retains a Habsburg theme in its 10 classy rooms at the top of this price range. It's just across the river from the Old Town in a pleasantly uncrowded neighborhood (air-con, free parking, Obala Isa Bega Isakovica 1, tel. 033/572-660, mobile 061-134-287, www.hotel-latinskimost.com, info@hotel-latinskimost.com).

$ Halvat Guest House is very tight but homey, offering six stylish-for-the-price rooms and one apartment squeezed into a modern shell. It's on a nondescript urban street that's a quick walk from the heart of the Old Town. The staff, led by Valida and Mumo, are welcoming (breakfast extra, cash only, air-con, free parking, Kasima Efendije Dobrače 13, tel. 033/237-714, mobile 061-248-098, www.halvat.com.ba, halvat@bih.net.ba).

$ Ada Hotel's eight rooms are basic and simple, but warm Aldina and her crew pride themselves on their hospitality. It's a five-minute uphill walk above the Old Town, near a large wartime cemetery (air-con, free parking, Abdesthana 8, tel. 033/475-870, www.adahotel.ba, adahotel@adahotel.ba).

$ Hotel Michele is a friendly, quirky guesthouse facing a school in a quiet, slightly dingy neighborhood. It's not as well-situated as my other listings, and is about a 10-minute uphill walk from Maršala Tita street. The 14 huge rooms and six gargantuan apartments are gaudy, decorated with antique furniture. This place has hosted several celebrities in town for the Sarajevo Film Festival... it doesn't take much prompting to get the receptionist to do some name-dropping. On my last visit, I slept in the Richard Gere room (air-con, ask about parking, Ivana Cankara 27, tel. 033/560-310, mobile 061-338-177, www.hotelmichele.ba, contact@hotelmichele.ba).

$ Kandilj Pension (Candle) has 10 simple, small yet comfortable rooms in a traditional Ottoman-style house with a snug breakfast cellar. With a cozy and pleasant old-fashioned feel, it's up a gentle hill and next to the Tomb of the Seven Brothers, across the river from the Old Town (air-con, Bistrik Potok 4, tel. 033/572-510, mobile 061-938-940, www.kandilj.com, info@kandilj.com, Adi). They also rent three modern, nicely equipped, well-priced apartments a steep five-minute walk above the pension (and 10 minutes above the river); if you don't mind the hike, these are a fine value (check-in and breakfast at pension).

¢ Vagabond Hostel, enthusiastically run by sisters Alvina and Aida, is fantastically located right along the main Ferhadija pedestrian street (so expect some noise). Unpretentious and youthful, its choices range from private rooms to 8-bunk dorms (breakfast, air-con in most rooms, shared kitchen, Ferhadija 21, tel. 033/238-811, www.vagabond.ba, hostel@vagabond.ba).

Eating in Sarajevo

Cosmopolitan Sarajevo boasts a wide array of good eateries, serving not only traditional Bosnian food (which is delicious), but also a wide range of international flavors, as well. I've focused my recommendations on the area in and near the Old Town (Baščaršija).

TRADITIONAL BOSNIAN FOOD

The Baščaršija is crowded with tourist-oriented eateries slinging good Bosnian fare. For a primer, see the "Balkan Flavors" sidebar on page 425.

Several obvious choices line the street called **Prote Bakovića,** which juts up from the main drag just a block over from Pigeon Square (across from the TI). Along here are a variety of crowd-pleasing eateries, including **$ Dveri** (with a cozy interior), **$ Dženita** (a straightforward, cheap option with lots of outdoor tables), and the slightly more upmarket **$$ Pod Lipom** (which loves to show off big photos of when Bill Clinton ate here). Comparison-shop menus and take your pick. But first read up on the cheaper options below.

Burek: These delicious "Bosnian pies," made with flaky phyllo dough and savory fillings, are available throughout the Balkans. While there are several choices in the Baščaršija, my favorite is **$ Buregdžinica Sač,** a hole-in-the-wall where they're made with fresh ingredients and baked the traditional way, under a metal lid that's covered with hot coals *(ispod sača).* Order at the counter, then take away or grab a table outside—this is Sarajevo's best quick meal. Choose between spinach, meat, tangy cheese, or potato—or ask for a mix of all four (Mon-Sat 8:30-20:00, closed Sun, in the alley off of Bravadžiluk street called Bravadžiluk Mali).

Ćevapčići: Around every corner in the Baščaršija, you'll run into a **$** *ćevabdžinica*—a cheap eatery selling tasty little sausage-shaped minced-meat patties. Bosnians agree that this is the best place in the country to get the local answer to hot dogs and hamburgers. While you can barely go wrong here, keep an eye out for these options: The highest concentration is along Bravadžiluk street, including **Mrkva** (Carrot), a slick and more modern-feeling option that's part of a local chain (Bravadžiluk 15); and the more traditional **Petica** (Five), run by the Ferhatović family (just off Bravadžiluk at Oprkanj 2). Other good Old Town choices are **Galatasaray** (Gazi Husrev-Begova 44), a few steps off of Sarači street near the mosque; and **Željo,** named for a local soccer team, which is a bit closer to the river (Kundurdžiluk 12).

Aščinica: An **$** *aščinica* is a Turkish-style cafeteria, where you survey your options at the display case and point to what you want. It's an efficient, affordable, and relatively untouristy way to get a taste of Bosnian cooking. The *aščinica* called **ASDž** is a good choice on a nondescript Old Town street (daily 9:00-19:00, Mali Čurčiluk 3, tel. 033/238-500). For a completely untouristy experience, head for **Aščinica "H.E.M,"** a remarkably cheap, country-cutesy lunch counter near the workaday Markale Market (limited English—point to what looks good, Mon-Sat 7:00-16:00, closed Sun, Bašeskije 21).

Bosnian Coffee *(Bosanska Kafa):* Known elsewhere as Turkish coffee, this thick, unfiltered, highly caffeinated sludge (which leaves a layer of "mud" at the bottom of your cup) is a Sarajevo staple. For tips on the proper ritual for drinking your Bosnian coffee—which is an integral part of Bosnian culture—see page 414. Choose any Baščaršija table with a view that you enjoy, or poke into the atmospheric **Morića Han** courtyard, a former caravanserai (which also has a restaurant). Or, for a more typically urban-Bosnian setting, head up the little lane toward the Old Synagogue to **Rahatlook,** with ample indoor and outdoor seating jammed with a mostly local clientele (Ferhadija 41). See more ideas under "Cafes," later.

OTHER OPTIONS

$$ Apetit features a small dining room with a busy chef who prepares Asian-European fusion cuisine with whatever he's found at today's market. As this is a popular place, reservations are recommended (Mon-Sat 12:00-22:00, closed Sun, Gazi Husrev-Begova 61, mobile 062-868-131, www.apetit.ba).

$$ Žara Iz Duvara (The Singing Nettle) is a cozy place with just a few tables, located behind Markale Market. On the diverse menu you'll find some traditional Bosnian specialties rarely seen elsewhere in Sarajevo; try the *sahan*—a platter with stuffed grape leaves, vegetables, and meatballs—or anything made with nettle. For those with special dietary requirements, everything is clearly labeled vegan, vegetarian, and lactose- or gluten-free (generally daily 14:00-23:00, Sun from 18:00; shorter hours and closed Sun in winter, Dženetića Čikma, mobile 062-147-300).

$$ To Be ~~Or Not~~ To Be, in the Old Town, is a popular, intimate little place (with six tables on two floors, plus some outdoor seating) where Alen serves up delicious comfort food from an eclectic international menu. The kitchen isn't much bigger than yours back home, but it's big enough to make an excellent meal. On the sign notice that "or not" is crossed out—during the siege, everyone here decided they definitely wanted to be (daily 11:00-23:00, Čizmedžiluk 5, tel. 033/233-265).

Sarajevska Brewery's **$ Pivnica HS** brewpub is a big, rollicking beer hall that also manages to feel cozy. Tucked in the back of the sprawling, spring-fed Sarajevska complex, this place has two levels of diners, a double-decker bar, and a long menu of pub grub. Although their regular Sarajevska lager is available anywhere, beer pilgrims come to the brewery to tap into the unfiltered wheat beer (sold only here) and the rare dark beer (daily 10:00-24:00, can be closed for special events—consider calling ahead, Franjevačka 15, tel. 033/239-740). Next door is the brewery's little **museum**—one well-presented room with old barrels, bottles, steins, photographs, and vintage ads (small entry fee, daily 10:00-18:00, www.pivnicahs.com).

$ Avlija sits in an unassuming, untouristy neighborhood a short walk above Maršala Tita street (and about 10-15 minutes from the Old Town). This very local-feeling hangout fills its namesake courtyard with bright, funky colors, rustic wooden tables, and happy drinkers and diners. The cuisine is a mix of Bosnian and international—affordable and very good (Mon-Sat 8:00-23:00, closed Sun, Sumbula Avde 2, tel. 033/444-483).

DINING HIGH ABOVE SARAJEVO, WITH PANORAMIC VIEWS

Two good options sit in the residential hills above the Old Town, overlooking a stunning sunset and the twinkling hillsides at twilight. In each case, it's a long and steep hike up from town—or a quick and cheap taxi ride (figure around 5-7 KM each way). One feels fancy, the other is more casual, but at either one you'll want to reserve before making the trip.

$$ Park Prinčeva feels like a big beer garden, with long picnic tables overlooking the city, roving musicians, traditionally dressed servers, and a menu of hearty Bosnian food. With point-blank views of City Hall and the Sarajevo hillsides, it's a memorable setting. It may not be high cuisine, but it's high-up cuisine (long hours daily, Iza Hrida 7, mobile 061-222-708, www.parkprinceva.ba).

$$ Kibe Mahala is elegant, with sleek decor, a Sinatra soundtrack, and a romantic, glassed-in terrace. While service can be uneven, it's affordable even though it feels like a splurge. Their specialty is lamb roasted on a spit; if you'd like to try this Balkan classic, order it when you reserve your table (Mon-Sat 11:00-23:00, closed Sun, Vrbanjuša 164, tel. 033/441-936, www.kibemahala.ba).

CAFÉS

Being at the intersection of two cultures famous for enjoying a cup of coffee (Viennese and Ottoman), Sarajevo has more than its share of cozy cafés. Explore the streets—both in the Old Town and in the modern areas—to find just the right spot. For Ottoman atmosphere in the Baščaršija, peruse your options along both Sarači (Leathermakers' Street) and Bravadžiluk (Locksmiths' Street)—or just cut to the chase and head for the **Morića Han** courtyard (see page 483). Bosnians prefer the more local-feeling **Rahatlook,** a few steps away, on the little lane leading to the Old Synagogue. For Viennese-style splendor, you'll stumble on many fine options, but likely none as impressive as the chandeliered café inside the **Hotel Europe.** Many modern cafés line lively Ferhadija street, which is great for people-watching. For a claustrophobic, cluttered old room that feels like the hipster version of *Antiques Roadshow,* head for the quirky, wildly decorated **Goldfish/Zlatna Ribica** (Kaptol 5). Several funky, tourist-oriented eateries line Kovači street, which angles steeply up into a residential zone from Pigeon Square; it's fun to comparison-shop here, but my favorite is the **Ministry of Ćejf** (at #26), with both Bosnian coffee and espresso drinks (for an explanation of *ćejf,* see page 416). And if you're nostalgic for the Red old days, it's obligatory to visit **Tito Café** behind the Historical Museum (see page 496).

Sarajevo Connections

From Sarajevo by Bus to: Mostar (nearly hourly, 3 hours), **Split** (3/day, 7.5-8 hours), **Dubrovnik** (3/day, 6 hours, leaves early in the morning; there's also a night bus in summer only), **Zagreb** (3/day, 8 hours, includes night bus), **Ljubljana** (1/day, sometimes overnight, 11 hours). Most (but not all) buses are operated by Centrotrans/ Eurolines (www.centrotrans.com); the general number for bus information at the main station is tel. 033/213-100. For information or tickets, you can also stop by the Centrotrans office in downtown Sarajevo (Ferhadija 16, closed Sun). A few additional buses depart from the predominantly Serb area of East Sarajevo (info tel. 057/317-377).

By Train: The bus is generally preferable, but a new train line from Sarajevo to **Mostar** is faster and cheaper (typically 2/day, 2 hours, www.zfbh.ba).

ROUTE TIPS FOR DRIVERS
From Mostar to Sarajevo

Whether you're driving or taking the bus, you're in for a scenic journey that also takes you past some interesting sights of historical note. The road is in excellent repair, and the glorious mountain views and intriguing villages will make you want to come back and stay longer in Bosnia. Even if you're not stopping along the way, keep track of these landmarks as you roll.

You'll begin by heading up the dramatically scenic **Neretva**

River Canyon, which surrounds a thrusting river that powers four hydroelectric dams. The scenery crescendos as you twist your way through the canyon.

The first major town you pass is **Jablanica,** famous among Bosnians as the best place to enjoy spit-grilled lamb. Look for a string of rustic restaurants lining the road; one good choice is **$$ Kovačević,** overlooking the river (on the right as you approach town).

Jablanica is also known as the site of the WWII **Battle of Neretva,** which demonstrated Tito's brilliance as a military tactician. Tito arrived here with his Partisan army, including some 4,000 injured troops and a squadron of desperate villagers and civilian refugees who had joined their ranks. Surrounded by his dual foes—Nazis and Četniks—Tito got clever: First, his troops destroyed five bridges across this river, leaving the clear impression that the Partisans planned to push away from the river. Then, as the Nazis redeployed their troops, Tito's men quickly repaired one of the bridges overnight. This allowed the Partisans—including all of their wounded and hangers-on—to cross the river, destroy the bridge again, and swing around to catch the Nazis off guard. Tito's victory at the Battle of the Neretva—and especially his pledge, "Wounded people we shall not leave"—still echoes in the collective memory of former Yugoslavs. In 1969, the victory was immortalized in the Oscar-nominated *Battle of Neretva,* which featured Yul Brynner, Orson Welles, and other big names lured by the Yugoslav government's generous funding.

To learn more about the battle, turn off at the brown *museum* sign in Jablanica (on the right—watch for this carefully) to reach the **Museum of the Battle for the Wounded at Neretva** (Muzej Bitka za Ranjenike na Neretvi). This huge, abandoned-seeming building was erected overlooking the gorge and the site of the famous bridge in 1978...and, it seems, hasn't been renovated since. In one grand hall, you'll see dusty old exhibits including original helmets and rifles; life-size dioramas of the wounded being evacuated; and a model showing how they used the wreckage of the original bridge to support their new, makeshift one. Huge windows look over the river gorge, where you can see a replica of the bridge that was built for the movie and kept here as a memorial. A second room features life-size models of Bosnian village life (2 KM, April-Oct Mon-Fri 8:00-16:00, Sat-Sun 9:00-16:00, July-Aug until 18:00; Nov-March closed Sat-Sun; tel. 036/752-705, www.muzej-jablanica.com).

Continuing along the main road, the next major town is **Konjic,** known for its traditional woodworking. The mountains above Konjic are a popular place for whitewater rafting. Also in those mountains, Tito had a failsafe bunker—one of many such complexes throughout Yugoslavia where he could retreat in case of invasion

SARAJEVO

or worse. This one has been opened as a museum, but it requires a reservation (call the Konjic TI at 036/728-123). Konjic's old bridge (which you'll see on the right as you drive over the modern bridge) dates from the same era as Mostar's Old Bridge. Both Jablanica and Konjic were held by Muslim forces during the Yugoslav Wars, which made them relatively safe havens, especially compared to Mostar or Sarajevo.

From Konjic, the road climbs up to **Ivan Planina** mountain, the geographical boundary between Herzegovina and Bosnia. Along this rugged road, you'll pass the deserted village of **Bradina;** soon after, just before the tunnel, is a huddle of abandoned homes. This is the birthplace of Ante Pavelić—the Bosnian Croat who led the ruthless Nazi-puppet Ustaše forces during World War II.

Passing through the **Ivan Tunnel** (nearly a half-mile long), you enter Kanton Sarajevo (*kanton,* based on the Swiss canton model, roughly means "county"). In addition to separating Herzegovina from Bosnia, this tunnel marks a dramatic weather divide—from the balmy, Mediterranean climate around Mostar to the cooler, continental climate of Sarajevo.

Winding down into the plain around **Sarajevo,** you'll enter the city limits. Just before the Hotel Radon Plaza (on the right) is a pink, destroyed student building—marking what was the front line of the besieged area of wartime Sarajevo. Everything you'll pass from here on out was under constant sniper fire for three and a half years (you're driving straight up what was called "Sniper Alley"). As you continue into town along the main drag, watch for these landmarks: on the left, the national TV headquarters (with a huge antenna array on the roof); on the right, a huge new mosque built with donations from Malaysia (one of 10 in town financed by wealthy investors from the Muslim world); on the left, the distinctive, blue, and aptly named Avaz Twist Tower, hosting the offices of Bosnia's main newspaper (*Dnevni Avaz,* "Daily Voice"—you can ride the elevator up for a grand view); also on the left, the US Embassy, followed by the famous Holiday Inn (built for the 1984 Olympics, and later a safe refuge for wartime journalists, now labeled *Hotel Holiday*); across the street from the Holiday Inn, the restored Bosnian Parliament building; and then the swanky Sarajevo City Center shopping mall. From here, keep following the river into the city center—going through the Austro-Hungarian part of town, passing the place where Archduke Franz Ferdinand was assassinated, and winding up at Sarajevo's Old Town, the Baščaršija.

It's important to find secure parking in Sarajevo. Most hotels have parking, and small public lots are scattered around the Old Town area; for a bigger, more secure garage, head for the BBI Centar shopping mall (on Maršala Tita street—see the "Sarajevo Hotels & Restaurants" map, earlier).

SLOVENIA

Slovenija

SLOVENIA

Tiny, overlooked Slovenia is one of Europe's most unexpectedly charming destinations. At the intersection of the Slavic, Germanic, and Italian worlds, Slovenia is an exciting mix of the best of each culture. Though it's just a quick trip away from the tourist throngs in Croatia, Venice, Munich, Salzburg, and Vienna, Slovenia has stayed mostly off the tourist track—making it a handy detour for in-the-know Back Door travelers. Be warned: Everyone I've met who has visited Slovenia wishes they'd allotted more time for this endearing, underrated land.

Today, it seems strange to think that Slovenia was ever part of Yugoslavia. Both in the personality of its people and in its landscape, Slovenia feels more like Austria.

Slovenes are more industrious, organized, and punctual than their fellow former Yugoslavs... yet still friendly, relaxed, and Mediterranean. Locals like the balance. And it's beautiful: Slovenia's rolling countryside is dotted with quaint alpine villages and the spires of miniature Baroque churches, against a backdrop of snowcapped peaks.

Only half as big as Switzerland, Slovenia is remarkably diverse for its size. Travelers can hike on alpine trails in the morning and explore some of the world's best caves in the afternoon, before relaxing with a glass of local wine and a seafood dinner while watching the sun set on the Adriatic.

Though not unaffected by the Great Recession, Slovenia enjoys a prosperity unusual for a formerly communist country. The Austro-Hungarian Empire left it with a strong work ethic and an impressive industrial infrastructure, which the Yugoslav government expanded. By 1980, 60 percent of all Yugoslav industry was in little Slovenia (which had only 8 percent of Yugoslavia's population and 8 percent of its territory). Of the 13 new nations that have joined the European Union since 2004, Slovenia was the only one

Slovenia

rich enough to enter as a net donor (with a higher per-capita income than the average), and the first one to join the euro currency zone (it adopted the euro in January 2007). Thanks to its longstanding ties to the West and its can-do spirit, Slovenia already feels more "Western" than any other destination in this book.

The country has a funny way of making people fall in love with it. Slovenes are laid-back, easygoing, stylish, and fun. They won't win any world wars (they're too well-adjusted to even try)... but they're exactly the type of people you'd love to chat with over a cup of coffee.

The Slovenian language is as mellow as the people. While Slovenes use Serb, German, and English curses in abundance, the worst they can say in their native tongue is, "May you be kicked by a hen." For "Darn it!" they say, "Three hundred hairy bears!" In bad traffic, they might mutter, "The street is white!" (If you want to get a local hopping mad—normally a difficult feat—all you have to do is mistake their beloved homeland for Slovakia.)

Coming from such a small country, locals are proud of the few things that are distinctly Slovenian, such as the roofed hayrack. Because of the

Slovenia Almanac

Official Name: Republika Slovenija, or simply Slovenija.

Size: At 7,800 square miles, it's about the size of New Jersey, but with one-fourth the population. Slovenia's two million people are 83 percent ethnic Slovenes who speak Slovene, plus a smattering of Serbs, Croats, and Muslim Bosniaks. Almost 60 percent of the country is Catholic.

Geography: Tiny Slovenia has four extremely different terrains and climates: the warm Mediterranean coastline (just 29 miles long—about one inch per inhabitant); the snowcapped, forested alpine mountains in the northwest (including 9,400-foot Mount Triglav); the moderate-climate, central limestone plateau that includes Ljubljana and the cave-filled Karst region; and to the east, a corner of the Great Hungarian Plain (the Prekmurje region, near Maribor and Ptuj). If you look at a map of Slovenia and squint your eyes a bit, it looks like a chicken running toward the east.

Latitude and Longitude: 46° N and 14° E (latitude similar to Lyon, France; Montreal, Canada; or Bismarck, North Dakota).

Biggest Cities: Nearly one in five Slovenes live in the two biggest cities: Ljubljana (the capital, pop. 280,000) and Maribor (in the east, pop. 158,000). Half the population lives in rural villages.

Snapshot History: After being dominated by the Germanic world for centuries, Slovenian culture proudly emerged in the 19th century. In the aftermath of World War I, Slovenia merged with its neighbors to become Yugoslavia, then broke away and achieved independence for the first time in 1991.

Economy: Slovenia has a gross domestic product of around $70 billion and a per-capita GDP of $34,500 (the highest, by far, of the former Yugoslavia). Slovenia's economy is based largely on manufactured metal products (trucks and machinery), which are traded with a diverse group of partners.

Currency: Slovenia uses the euro (€1 = about $1.20).

Government: The country is led by the prime minister (currently Marjan Šarec, a former comedian and founder of his own party), who heads the leading vote-getting coalition in legislative elections. He governs along with the figurehead president (Borut Pahor, a center-left former prime minister whose second and final term ends in 2022). Slovenia's relatively peaceful secession is credited largely to former president Milan Kučan, who remains a popular figure. The National Assembly consists of 90 elected legislators; there's also a second house of parliament, the National Council, which has much less power. Despite the country's small size, it is divided into some 200 municipalities—creating a lot of bureaucracy that locals enjoy complaining about.

Flag: Three horizontal bands of white (top), blue, and red. A shield in the upper left shows Mount Triglav, with a wavy-line sea below and three stars above.

The Average Slovene: The average Slovene skis in this largely alpine country, and is an avid fan of team handball (yes, handball). He or she lives in a 250-square-foot apartment, watches 16 hours of TV a week (much of it in English with Slovene subtitles), and enjoys a drink-and-a-half of alcohol every day.

Notable Slovenes: Even if you haven't heard of architect **Jože Plečnik** yet, you'll hear his name a hundred times while you're in Slovenia—especially in Ljubljana (see page 575). **Melanija Knavs** was born in the Slovenian city of Novo Mesto, emigrated to the US to pursue a modeling career, and eventually married a future president; today we know her as Melania Trump. In 1910, Cleveland had the biggest Slovenian population of any city in the world—just ahead of Trieste and Ljubljana; more recently, two half-Slovene Cleveland political figures—**Dennis Kucinich** and **George Voinovich**—became nationally known. And classical musicians might know composers **Giuseppe Tartini** and **Hugo Wolf.**

Sporty Slovenes: If you follow alpine sports or team handball, you'll surely know some world-class athletes from Slovenia. NBA fans might recognize basketball players **Goran Dragić, Primož Brezec, Boštjan Nachbar,** and 2018-19 Rookie of the Year **Luka Dončić.** Slovenian hockey player **Anže Kopitar** plays in the NHL, and skier **Tina Maze** won two gold medals at the 2014 Winter Olympics. The athletic Slovenes—perhaps trying to compensate for the minuscule size of their country—have accomplished astonishing feats: **Davo Karničar** has skied down from the "seven summits" (the highest points in each of the seven continents—that means the peaks of Everest, Kilimanjaro, McKinley, and so on). **Benka Pulko** became the first person ever to drive a motorcycle around the world—that is, all seven continents, including Antarctica, which is also the longest solo motorcycle journey by a woman (total trip: 111,856 miles in 2,000 days; for more, see www.benkapulko.com). **Dušan Mravlje** ran across all the continents. And Slovenian ultramarathon swimmer **Martin Strel** has swum thousands of miles, including the entire length of several major rivers such as the Danube, the Mississippi, the Yangtze, and the Amazon.

frequent rainfall in the mountainous northwest, the hayracks are covered by a roof that allows the hay to dry thoroughly. The most traditional kind is the *toplar*, consisting of two hayracks connected by one big roof. It looks like a skinny barn with open, fenced sides. Hay hangs on the sides to dry; firewood, carts, tractors, and other farm implements sit on the ground inside; and dried hay is stored in the loft above. But these wooden *toplarji* are firetraps, and a stray bolt of lightning can burn one down in a flash. So in recent years, more farmers have been moving to single hayracks *(enojni)*; these are still roofed, but have posts made of concrete rather than wood. You'll find postcards and miniature wooden models of both kinds of hayracks (a fun souvenir).

Another uniquely Slovenian memento is a creatively decorated front panel from a beehive *(panjske končnice)*. Slovenia has a

strong beekeeping tradition, and beekeepers believe that painting the fronts of the hives makes it easier for bees to find their way home. Replicas of these panels are available at gift shops all over the country. (For more on the panels and Slovenia's beekeeping heritage, see page 634.)

Slovenia is also the land of polka. Slovenes claim that polka music was invented here, and singer/accordionist Slavko Avsenik—from the village of Begunje near Bled—cranked out popular oompah songs that made him a superstar in Germany and other alpine lands. You'll see the Avsenik ensemble (now led by Slavko's grandson) and other oompah bands on Slovenian TV, where hokey Lawrence Welk-style shows remain an institution.

To really stretch your euros, try one of Slovenia's more than 400 farmhouse B&Bs, called "tourist farms" *(turistične kmetije)*—similar to *agriturismi* in Italy. These are actual working farms (often organic) that sell meals and/or rent rooms to tourists to help make ends meet. You can use a tourist farm as a home base to explore the entire country—remember, the farthest reaches of Slovenia are only a day trip away. A comfortable, hotelesque double with a private bathroom—plus a traditional Slovenian dinner and a hearty breakfast—costs as little as €50.

Most visitors to Slovenia are, in my experience, completely charmed by the place. The only problem is that the country is finally being discovered. Some of its biggest destinations (especially Lake Bled) can feel unpleasantly jammed in the summertime. And yet, it still feels untrampled compared to more famous stops, and there's plenty of Slovenia to go around. Visit soon, before the cat is fully out of the bag. And give yourself enough time to go beyond the big-name "whistle-stop" destinations, and dig a little deeper into this wonderful land.

HELPFUL HINTS

Telephones: Slovenian phone numbers beginning with 080 are toll-free while 090 and 089 denote expensive toll lines, but it's generally not possible to dial these from a US number (mobile or landline). Most Slovenian mobile-phone numbers begin with 03, 04, 05, or 07. For more details on how to dial to, from, and within Slovenia, see the Practicalities chapter.

Toll Sticker: To drive on Slovenia's expressways *(avtocesta)*, you'll need to display a toll sticker *(vinjeta,* veen-YEH-tah; €15/week, €30/month). If renting your car in Slovenia, it probably comes with a sticker (but make sure); if you're driving in from elsewhere, such as Croatia, you can buy one at a gas station, post office, or some newsstands (watch for *vinjeta* signs at gas stations as you approach the border). *Be warned:* This rule is taken very seriously. If you're found driving on expressways without the sticker, you'll immediately be fined €300 or more.

Cruise Port: The Slovenian town of **Koper** (see page 730) is becoming a popular port of call for Mediterranean cruises. Given the country's size, it's possible to see just about any of the Slovenia destinations covered in this book in a day in port (provided you use your time efficiently and have a private driver—I recommend Tina Hiti and Sašo Golub, listed on page 610).

SLOVENIAN HISTORY

Slovenia has a long and unexciting history as part of various larger empires. After Illyrian, Celtic, and Roman settlements came and went, this region became populated by Slavs—the ancestors of today's Slovenes—in the late sixth century. But Charlemagne's Franks conquered the tiny land in the eighth century, and, ever since, Slovenia has been a backwater of the Germanic world—first as a holding of the Holy Roman Empire and later, the Habsburg Empire. But even as the capital, Ljubljana, was populated by Austrians (who called the city Laibach), the Slovenian language and cultural traditions survived in the countryside.

Through the Middle Ages, much of Slovenia was ruled by the Counts of Celje (highly placed vassals of the Habsburgs). In this era before modern nations—when shifting allegiances and strategic marriages dictated the dynamics of power—the Counts of Celje rose to a position of significant influence in Central and Eastern Europe. Celje daughters intermarried with some of the most powerful dynasties in the region: the Polish Piasts, the Hungarian Anjous, and the Czech Přemysls. Before long, the Counts of Celje had emerged as the Habsburgs' main rivals. In the 15th century, Count Ulrich II of Celje married into Serbia's ruling family and managed to wrest control of Hungary's massive holdings. Had he not been assassinated in 1456, this obscure Slovenian line—rather than an obscure Austrian one—may have emerged as the dominant power in the eastern half of Europe. (Instead, the Habsburgs consolidated their vanquished foe's fiefdoms into their ever-growing empire.) In homage, the three yellow stars of the Counts of Celje's seal still adorn Slovenia's coat of arms.

Soon after, with Slovenia firmly entrenched in the Counter-Reformation holdings of the Habsburg Empire, the local Reformer Primož Trubar (1508-1586) strove both to put the Word of God into the people's hands, and to legitimize Slovene as a written language. This Slovenian answer to Martin Luther secretly translated the Bible into Slovene in Reformation-friendly Germany, then smuggled copies back into his homeland.

Over the next several centuries, much of Slovenia was wracked by Habsburg-Ottoman wars, as the Ottomans attempted to push north through this territory to reach Vienna. Slovenia also found itself caught in the crossfire between Austria and Venice. Seemingly exhausted by all of this warfare—and by their own sporadic, halfhearted, and unsuccessful uprisings against Habsburg rule—Slovenia languished as a sleepy backwater.

When the port city of Trieste (in Slovenian territory) was granted free status in 1718, it boosted the economy of Slovenian lands. The Enlightenment spurred a renewed interest in the Slovenian culture and language, which further flourished when Napoleon named Ljubljana the capital of his "Illyrian Provinces"—Slovenia's own mini empire, stretching from Austria's Tirol to Croatia's Dalmatian Coast. During this brief period (1809-1813), the long-suppressed Slovene language was used for the first time in schools and the government. This kicked off a full-throated national revival movement—asserting the worthiness of the Slovenian language and culture compared to the dominant Germanic worldview of the time. Inspired by the patriotic poetry of France Prešeren (1800-1849), Slovenian pride surged.

The last century saw the most interesting chapter of Slovenian history. Some of World War I's fiercest fighting occurred at the Soča (Isonzo) Front in northwest Slovenia—witnessed by young Ernest Hemingway, who drove an ambulance there. During World War II, Slovenia was divided among Nazi allies Austria, Italy, and Hungary—and an estimated 20,000 to 25,000 Slovenes perished in Nazi- and Italian-operated concentration camps.

As Yugoslavia entered its Golden Age under war hero Marshal Tito, Slovenia's prime location where Yugoslavia meets Western Europe (a short drive from Austria or Italy)—and the diligent national character of the Slovenian people—made it a prime candidate for industrialization.

After Tito's death in 1980, the various Yugoslav republics struggled to redefine their role in the union. While many factions reverted to age-old, pre-Tito nationalistic fervor, the Slovenes grew increasingly focused on their own future...and began to press for real reforms of the communist system. Slovenia had always been Yugoslavia's smallest, northernmost, most prosperous republic. Slovenes realized that Yugoslavia needed Slovenia much more than Slovenia needed Yugoslavia.

In 1988, the iconoclastic Slovenian magazine *Mladina* pushed the boundaries of Yugoslavia's nominally "free" press, publishing articles critical of the Yugoslav People's Army. Four young reporters (including Janez Janša, who would later become Slovenia's prime minister) were tried, convicted, and imprisoned, spurring outrage among Slovenes. A few months later, the Slovenian delegation defiantly walked out of the Yugoslav League of Communists Congress.

The first-ever free elections in Slovenia on April 8, 1990, ended communist rule and swept reformer Milan Kučan into the presidency. Kučan pursued a Swiss-style confederated relationship with his fellow Yugoslav republics, but he met with resistance from his counterparts, who were more focused on their own ethnic self-interests. Later that year, in a nationwide referendum, 88 percent of Slovenes voted for independence from Yugoslavia.

And so, concerned about the nationalistic politics of Serbian strongman Slobodan Milošević and seeking the opportunity for true democracy and capitalism, Slovenia seceded. Because more than 90 percent of the people here were ethnic Slovenes—and because Slovenia was careful to respect the rights of its minority populations—the break with Yugoslavia was simple and virtually uncontested. Its war for independence lasted just 10 days and claimed only a few dozen lives. (For more details, see page 743 in the Understanding Yugoslavia chapter.)

In May 2004 Slovenia became the first of the former Yugoslav republics to join the European Union. The Slovenes have been practical about this move, realizing it's essential for their survival as a tiny nation in a modern world. But there are tradeoffs, and "Euroskeptics" are down on EU bureaucracy. As borders disappear, Slovenes are experiencing more crime. Traditional farms are grappling with strict EU standards. Slovenian businesses are having difficulty competing with big German and other Western European firms. Before EU membership, only Slovenes could own Slovenian land, but now wealthy foreigners are buying property, driving up the cost of real estate. Still, overall, most Slovenes feel that EU membership was the right choice.

After independence, Slovenia impressed its European neighbors with its powerhouse economy and steady growth. However, the global financial crisis revealed that some of the affluence was deceptive: Many of Slovenia's biggest companies had been running up huge debts. As all of Europe's bubble burst in 2008, those corporate debts were assumed by Slovenia's big banks—devastating the economy and sparking financial worries.

In recent years, Slovenes have grown weary of a string of corrupt and incompetent politicians. Janez Janša, who became prime minister for the second time in 2011, was swept out of office amid a wave of protests and eventually sentenced to a prison term for corruption. His successor, Alenka Bratušek, resigned after just a year in office. One popular figure—at least in Ljubljana—is the visionary mayor Zoran Janković, who has reshaped the capital during his tenure (see page 561).

In the fall of 2015, Slovenia became the focal point of a Europe-wide debate when a flood of refugees from Syria and other nations showed up at its border. Like its neighbors Croatia and Hungary, Slovenia grappled with the challenge of caring for the new arrivals even as it facilitated their passage to wealthy northern European countries. News reports suggested that Slovenia responded to this humanitarian crisis with pragmatic compassion.

While many of the refugees expressed relief at what a friendly and competent place Slovenia was, those of us who already loved the country were hardly shocked. The Slovenes are adjusting to the 21st century with their characteristic sense of humor and easygoing attitude, just as they've done throughout their history.

SLOVENIAN FOOD

Slovenian cuisine offers more variety—and, often, better quality—than Croatian fare. Slovenes brag that their cuisine melds the best of Italian and German cooking—but they also embrace other international influences, especially French. Like Croatian food, Slovenian cuisine also features some pan-Balkan elements: The savory phyllo-dough pastry *burek* is the favorite fast food here, and when Slovenes host a backyard barbecue, they grill up *čevapčići* and *ražnjići*, topped off with the eggplant-and-red-bell-pepper condiment *ajvar* (see the "Balkan Flavors" sidebar on page 425). Slovenia enjoys Italian-style dishes, with a pizza or pasta restaurant on seemingly every corner. Hungarian food simmers in the northeast corner of the country (where many Mag-

Pršut

In Slovenia, Croatia, and Montenegro, *pršut* (purr-SHOOT) is one of the essential food groups. This air-cured ham (like Italian prosciutto) is soaked in salt and sometimes also smoked. Then it hangs in open-ended barns for up to a year and a half, to be dried and seasoned by the howling Bora wind. Each region produces a slightly different *pršut*. In Dalmatia, a layer of fat keeps the ham moist; in Istria, the fat is trimmed, and the *pršut* is drier.

Since Slovenia and Croatia joined the European Union, strict new standards have swept the land. Separate rooms must be used for the slaughter, preparation, and curing of the ham. While this seems fair enough for large producers, small family farms that want to produce just enough *pršut* for their own use—and maybe sell one or two ham hocks to neighbors—find they have to invest thousands of euros to be compliant.

yars reside). And in much of the country, particularly near the mountains, traditional Slovenian food has a distinctly Germanic vibe—including the "four S's": sausages, schnitzels, strudels, and sauerkraut.

Traditional Slovenian meals come with a hearty helping of groats—a grainy mush made with buckwheat, barley, or corn. Buckwheat, which thrives in this climate, often appears on Slovenian menus. You'll also see plenty of *štruklji*, a dumpling-like savory layer cake that can be stuffed with cheese, meat, or vegetables. *Repa* is turnip prepared like sauerkraut. Among the hearty soups in Slovenia is *jota*—a staple for Karst peasants, made from *repa*, beans, vegetables, and often sausage.

Slovenia also has some good pastas. In addition to the familiar Italian-style pastas you'd find anywhere (gnocchi, called *njoki* here, tend to be popular and good), you may see some regional variations. *Fuži*, from Istria in the southwest, are similar to penne. *Žlikrofi*, from Idrija, are ravioli-like filled dumplings.

The cuisine of Slovenia's Karst region (the arid limestone plain south of Ljubljana) is notable. The small farms and wineries of this region have been inspired by Italy's Slow Food movement—their owners believe that cuisine is meant to be gradually appreciated, not rushed. The Karst's tasty air-dried ham *(pršut)*, available throughout the country, is worth seeking out (see sidebar). Istria (the peninsula just to the south of the Karst, in southern Slovenia and Croatia) produces truffles that, locals boast, are as good as those from Italy's Piedmont region (see page 151). And in the hills just northwest of the Karst, the Goriška Brda wine region—surrounded on three sides by Italy—is becoming a magnet for in-the-know foodies seeking top-quality wines and affordable high cuisine.

Voda is water, and *kava* is coffee. Radenska, in the bottle with the three little hearts, is Slovenia's best-known brand of mineral water—good enough that the word *Radenska* is synonymous with bottled water all over Slovenia and throughout the former Yugoslavia. It's not common to ask for (or receive) tap water, but you can try requesting *voda iz pipe*.

Adventurous teetotalers should forgo the Coke and sample Cockta, a Slovenian cola with an unusual flavor (which supposedly comes from berry, lemon, orange, and 11 herbs). Originally called "Cockta-Cockta," the drink was introduced during the communist period, as an alternative to the difficult-to-get Coca-Cola. This local variation developed a loyal following...until the Iron Curtain fell, and the real Coke became readily available. Cockta sales plummeted. But in recent years—prodded by the slogan "The Taste of Your Youth"—nostalgic Slovenes are drinking Cockta once more.

The premier Slovenian brand of *pivo* (beer) is Union (OO-nee-ohn), but you'll also see a lot of Laško (LASH-koh), whose mascot is the Zlatorog (or "Golden Horn," a mythical chamois-like animal). For the full story on Slovenian wines, see the sidebar.

Regardless of what you're drinking, to toast, say, *"Na ZD-ROW-yeh!"*—if you can't remember it, think of "Nice driving!"

Slovenia's national dessert is *potica*, a rolled pastry with walnuts and sometimes also raisins. While traditionally eaten at Christmas, it's available year-round. Slovenes eat it from the hard outer crust in, saving the nutty center for last. For more tasty treats, see the "Bled Desserts" sidebar on page 624. Locals brag that Ljubljana has the finest gelato outside of Italy—which, after all, is just an hour down the road. And I agree.

SLOVENIAN LANGUAGE

While the casual tourist won't notice, Slovene is markedly different from the languages spoken in the other former Yugoslav republics. While Serbian and Croatian are mutually intelligible, Slovene is gibberish to Serbs and Croats. Most Slovenes, on the other hand, know Serbo-Croatian because, a generation ago, everybody in Yugoslavia had to learn it.

Linguists have identified some 46 official dialects of Slovene, and there are probably another 100 or so unofficial ones. Locals can instantly tell which city—or sometimes even which remote mountain valley—someone comes from by their accent.

Slovenian Wines

It should come as no surprise that Slovenia produces excellent *vino* (wine). After all, this little country abuts well-respected wine-growing neighbors Italy and Hungary. In fact, Slovenia's winemaking tradition originated with its pre-Roman Illyrian and Celtic inhabitants, meaning that wine has been grown much longer here than in most other European countries. As in Croatia, wine standards plummeted with Yugoslav-era collectivization, but in recent years ambitious vintner families have been determined to bring quality back to Slovenian wines— with impressive results.

Slovenia's three main wine-growing regions are Primorska, Posavje, and Podravje.

The best-known is the **Primorska** region, in the western hills. With a Mediterranean climate (hence its name: "by the sea"), Primorska is best known for its reds. Primorska's Goriška Brda ("Hillsides of Gorica") shares the terroir of Italy's Friuli/Venezia Giulia region (and its much-vaunted, DOC-classified Collio Goriziano wines). This area produces some of Slovenia's most respected wines, made mostly with internationally known grapes such as merlot and cabernet sauvignon. Goriška Brda also produces a good white using the *rebula* grape (also known by its Italian name, *ribolla gialla*). A bit farther south (and still within Primorska), the Karst grows lots of *refošk (refosco)* grapes, which thrive in iron-rich red soil *(terra rossa)*. The top product is the extremely full-bodied, "big" *teran*—infused with a high lactic acid content that supposedly gives the wine healing properties. Nearby coastal areas (around Koper) also grow *refošk,* along with the white *malvazija* grape that's also widely used in Croatian Istria.

To the northeast, near Hungary, is the **Podravje** region (the Drava River Valley), dominated by white grapes—especially *laški riesling* (known internationally as Welsh riesling) and *renski riesling* (what we'd call simply riesling). If you're visiting Ptuj or Maribor, you'll see local menus listing wines produced on the steeper right bank of the Drava River (Haloze) and the left bank (Slovenske Gorice, "Slovenian Hills").

And finally, a bit to the south of Podravje is the **Posavje** region (the Lower Sava River Valley, bordering Croatia). This area—which is still focused on quantity over quality—produces both white and red wines; it's known mostly for the light, russet-colored *cviček* wine (a blend of red and white grapes).

With any type of Slovenian wine, *vrhunsko* (premium) is a mark of quality, while *kakovostno* is a notch down, and *namizno* is a table wine. Other key terms are similar to Croatian: *suho* (dry), *sladko* (sweet), and *pol-* (half).

The tiny country of Slovenia borders Italy and Austria, with important historical and linguistic ties to both. For self-preservation, Slovenes have always been forced to function in many different languages. All of these factors make them excellent linguists. Most young Slovenes speak flawless English effortlessly—then admit that they've never set foot in the United States or Britain, but love watching American movies and TV shows (which are always subtitled, never dubbed).

Slovene pronunciation is very similar to Croatian (see page 783). Remember, *c* is pronounced "ts" (as in "cats"). The letter *j* is pronounced as "y"—making "Ljubljana" easier to say than it looks (lyoob-lyee-AH-nah). Slovene only has one diacritical mark: the *strešica*, or "little roof." This makes *č* sound like "ch," *š* sound like "sh," and *ž* sound like "zh" (as in "measure"). The letter *v* is pronounced like "u"—so the Slovenian word *avto* sounds like "auto," and the mountain Triglav is pronounced "TREE-glau" (rhymes with "cow").

The only trick: As in English, which syllable gets the emphasis is unpredictable. Slovenes use many of the same words as Croatians, but put the stress in much different places.

Learn some key Slovenian phrases (see the Slovenian survival phrases on the next page). You'll make more friends and your trip will go more smoothly.

Slovenian Survival Phrases

In the phonetics, ī sounds like the long i in "light," and bolded syllables are stressed. The vowel "eh" sometimes sounds closer to "ay" (depending on the speaker).

English	Slovenian	Pronunciation
Hello. (formal)	*Dober dan.*	**doh**-behr dahn
Hi. / Bye. (informal)	*Živjo.*	**zheev**-yoh
Do you speak English?	*Ali govorite angleško?*	ah-lee goh-voh-**ree**-teh ahn-**glehsh**-koh
Yes. / No.	*Ja. / Ne.*	yah / neh
I (don't) understand.	*(Ne) razumem.*	(neh) rah-**zoo**-mehm
Please. / You're welcome.	*Prosim.*	**proh**-seem
Thank you (very much).	*Hvala (lepa).*	**hvah**-lah (**leh**-pah)
Excuse me. / I'm sorry.	*Oprostite.*	oh-proh-**stee**-teh
problem	*problem*	proh-**blehm**
No problem.	*Ni problema.*	nee proh-**bleh**-mah
Good.	*Dobro.*	**doh**-broh
Goodbye.	*Na svidenje.*	nah **svee**-dehn-yeh
one / two	*ena / dve*	**eh**-nah / dveh
three / four	*tri / štiri*	tree / **shtee**-ree
five / six	*pet / šest*	peht / shehst
seven / eight	*sedem / osem*	**seh**-dehm / **oh**-sehm
nine / ten	*devet / deset*	deh-**veht** / deh-**seht**
hundred / thousand	*sto / tisoč*	stoh / **tee**-sohch
How much?	*Koliko?*	**koh**-lee-koh
local currency	*euro*	**ee**-oo-roh
Write it?	*Napišite?*	nah-**peesh**-ee-teh
Is it free?	*Ali je brezplačno?*	**ah**-lee yeh brehz-**plahch**-noh
Is it included?	*Ali je vključeno?*	**ah**-lee yeh vuk-**lyoo**-cheh-noh
Where can I find / buy...?	*Kje lahko najdem / kupim...?*	kyeh **lah**-koh nī-dehm / **koo**-peem
I'd / We'd like...	*Želel / Želeli bi...*	zheh-**lehl** / zheh-**leh**-lee bee
...a room.	*...sobo.*	**soh**-boh
...a ticket to ___.	*...vozovnico do ___.*	voh-**zohv**-neet-soh doh ___
Is it possible?	*Ali je možno?*	**ah**-lee yeh **mohzh**-noh
Where is...?	*Kje je...?*	kyeh yeh
...the train station	*...železniška postaja*	zheh-**lehz**-neesh-kah pohs-**tī**-yah
...the bus station	*...avtobusna postaja*	**ow**-toh-boos-nah pohs-**tī**-yah
...the tourist information office	*...turistično informacijski center*	too-**rees**-teech-noh een-for-maht-**see**-skee **tsehn**-tehr
...the toilet	*...vece (WC)*	**veht**-seh
men / women	*moški / ženski*	**mohsh**-kee / **zhehn**-skee
left / right / straight	*levo / desno / naravnost*	**leh**-voh / **dehs**-noh / nah-**rahv**-nohst
At what time...?	*Ob kateri uri...?*	ohb kah-**teh**-ree **oo**-ree
...does this open / close	*...se odpre / zapre*	seh ohd-**preh** / zah-**preh**
(Just) a moment.	*(Samo) trenutek.*	(sah-**moh**) treh-**noo**-tehk
now / soon / later	*zdaj / kmalu / pozneje*	zuh-**dī** / kuh-**mah**-loo / pohz-**neh**-yeh
today / tomorrow	*danes / jutri*	**dah**-nehs / **yoo**-tree

In a Slovenian Restaurant

English	Slovenian	Pronunciation
I'd like to reserve...	*Rezerviral bi...*	reh-zehr-**vee**-rahl bee
We'd like to reserve...	*Rezervirali bi...*	reh-zehr-**vee**-rah-lee bee
...a table for one / two.	*...mizo za enega / dva.*	**mee**-zoh zah **eh**-neh-gah / dvah
Is this table free?	*Ali je ta miza prosta?*	**ah**-lee yeh tah **mee**-zah proh-stah
Can I help you?	*Izvolite?*	eez-**voh**-lee-teh
The menu (in English), please.	*Jedilni list (v angleščini), prosim.*	yeh-**deel**-nee leest (vuh ahn-**glehsh**-chee-nee) **proh**-seem
service (not) included	*postrežba (ni) vključena*	post-**rehzh**-bah (nee) vuk-**lyoo**-cheh-nah
cover charge	*pogrinjek*	poh-**green**-yehk
"to go"	*za s sabo*	zah **sah**-boh
with / without	*z / brez*	zuh / brehz
and / or	*in / ali*	een / **ah**-lee
fixed-price meal (of the day)	*(dnevni) meni*	(duh-**new**-nee) meh-**nee**
specialty of the house	*specialiteta hiše*	speht-see-ah-lee-**teh**-tah **hee**-sheh
half portion	*polovična porcija*	poh-loh-**veech**-nah **port**-see-yah
daily special	*dnevna ponudba*	duh-**new**-nah poh-**nood**-bah
fixed-price meal for tourists	*turistični meni*	too-**rees**-teech-nee meh-**nee**
appetizers	*predjedi*	prehd-yeh-**dee**
bread	*kruh*	krooh
cheese	*sir*	seer
sandwich	*sendvič*	**send**-veech
soup	*juha*	**yoo**-hah
salad	*solata*	soh-**lah**-tah
meat / poultry	*meso / perutnina*	meh-**soh** / peh-root-**nee**-nah
fish / seafood	*riba / morska hrana*	**ree**-bah / **mor**-skah **hrah**-nah
fruit	*sadje*	**sahd**-yeh
vegetables	*zelenjava*	zeh-lehn-**yah**-vah
dessert	*sladica*	slah-**deet**-sah
(tap) water	*voda (iz pipe)*	**voh**-dah (eez **pee**-peh)
mineral water	*mineralna voda*	mee-neh-**rahl**-nah **voh**-dah
milk	*mleko*	**mleh**-koh
(orange) juice	*(pomarančni) sok*	(poh-mah-**rahnch**-nee) sohk
coffee	*kava*	**kah**-vah
tea	*čaj*	chī
wine	*vino*	**vee**-noh
red / white	*rdeče / belo*	ahr-**deh**-cheh / **beh**-loh
sweet / dry / semi-dry	*sladko / suho / polsuho*	**slahd**-koh / **soo**-hoh / **pohl**-soo-hoh
glass / bottle	*kozarec / steklenica*	koh-**zah**-rehts / stehk-leh-**neet**-sah
beer	*pivo*	**pee**-voh
Cheers!	*Na zdravje!*	nah **zdrow**-yeh
More. / Another.	*Še. / Še eno.*	sheh / sheh **eh**-noh
The same.	*Isto.*	**ees**-toh
Bill, please.	*Račun, prosim.*	rah-**choon** **proh**-seem
tip	*napitnina*	nah-peet-**nee**-nah
Delicious!	*Odlično!*	ohd-**leech**-noh

LJUBLJANA

Ljubljana (lyoob-lyee-AH-nah) is irresistible. With a lazy Old Town clustered around a castle-topped hill, Slovenia's capital is often likened to Salzburg. It's an apt comparison—but only if you inject a healthy dose of breezy Adriatic culture, add a Slavic accent, and replace favorite son Mozart with local architect Jože Plečnik.

Ljubljana feels smaller than its population of 280,000. With several clusters of good museums that try hard—but have only so much to say—it does its best to please sightseers. But ultimately, this town is all about ambience. The idyllic, cobbled core of Ljubljana is slathered with one-of-a-kind architecture. Festivals fill the summer, and people enjoy a Sunday stroll any day of the week. Fashion boutiques and al fresco cafés jockey for control of the Old Town, while the leafy riverside promenade crawls with stylishly dressed students sipping *kava* and polishing their near-perfect English. Laid-back Ljubljana is the kind of place where graffiti and crumbling buildings seem elegantly atmospheric instead of shoddy. But more and more of those buildings have been getting a facelift recently, as a spunky mayor has been spiffing up the place and creating gleaming traffic-free zones left and right—turning what was already an exceptionally livable city into a pedestrians' paradise.

Batted around by history, Ljubljana has seen cultural influences from all sides—most notably Prague, Vienna, and Venice. This has left the city a happy hodgepodge of cultures. Being the midpoint between the Slavic, Germanic, and Italian worlds gives Ljubljana a special spice.

The Story of Ljubljana

In ancient times, Ljubljana was on the trade route connecting the Mediterranean (just 60 miles away) to the Black Sea. (Toss a bottle off the bridge here, and it can float to the Danube and, eventually, all the way to Russia.) Legend has it that Jason and his Argonauts founded Ljubljana when they stopped here for the winter on their way home with the Golden Fleece. Some stories say Jason slayed a dragon here, while according to others, it was St. George; either way, the dragon remains the city mascot to this day.

Some of the area's earliest known inhabitants during the Neolithic and Bronze ages lived in rustic houses on tall wooden piles in the marshy lands surrounding today's city center. They poled around the shallow lagoons in dugout canoes. Sometimes called "crannog dwellers" (after similar homes in the Scottish Highlands), these earliest Ljubljanans left behind precious few artifacts, save for half of a wooden wheel and axle that's 5,200 years old (on display at the City Museum).

The area was later populated by the Illyrians and Celts, and was eventually Romanized (and called Emona) before being over-run by Huns, only to be resettled by Slavs—the ancestors of to-day's Slovenes.

In 1335, Ljubljana fell under the Habsburg emperors, who called it Laibach and steered its development for the next six centuries. Slovenian language and culture were considered back-wards, as most of Laibach's inhabitants spoke German and lived essentially Austrian lifestyles. This Austrian vibe persists today, thanks to abundant Austrian Baroque and Viennese Art Nouveau architecture.

Napoleon put Ljubljana on the map when he named it the capital of his Illyrian Provinces, a realm that stretched from the Danube to Dubrovnik, and from Austria to Albania (for just four short years, 1809-1813). For the first time, the Slovene language was taught in schools, awakening a newfound pride in Slovenian

PLANNING YOUR TIME

Ljubljana deserves at least a full day. Rather than checking off a list of museums, spend most of your time strolling the pleasant town center, exploring the many interesting squares and architectural gems, browsing the produce market, shopping at the boutiques, and sipping coffee at sidewalk cafés along the river.

Here's the best plan for a low-impact sightseeing day: Begin on Prešeren Square, the heart of the city, and follow my "Ljubljana Walk" through town—including a browse through the riverside market area. Then wander south through the Krakovo gardens to tour the Jože Plečnik House. In the afternoon, commit some quality time to people-watching at a riverside café, window-shop at cultural heritage. People still fondly recall this very brief era, which was the only time Ljubljana rose to prominence on the world stage. (Despite spending more than 600 years as part of the Habsburg Empire, Ljubljana has no "Habsburg Square"...but it does have a "French Revolution Square.")

In the mid-19th century, the railway connecting Vienna to the Adriatic (Trieste) was built through town—and Ljubljana boomed. An earthquake rocked the city in 1895, damaging many buildings. Locals cleverly exaggerated the impact (propping up buildings that were structurally sound, and even tearing down unwanted old houses that had been unharmed) in preparation for the visit of Emperor Franz Josef—who, just as they hoped, took pity on the city and invested generously in its reconstruction. Ljubljana was made over in the Art Nouveau style. A generation later, architect Jože Plečnik bathed the city in his distinctive, artsy-but-sensible, classical-meets-modern style.

In World War II, Slovenia was occupied first by the Italians, then by the Nazis. Ljubljana had a thriving resistance movement that the Nazis couldn't suppress—so they simply fenced off the entire city and made it a giant prison for three years, allowing in only basic food shipments. But the Slovenes—who knew their land far better than their oppressors did—continued to slip in and out of town undetected, allowing them to agitate through the end of the war.

In 1991, Ljubljana became the capital of one of Europe's youngest nations. Today the city is filled with university students, making it feel very youthful. Ljubljana is on the cutting edge when it comes to architecture, public art, fashion, and trendy pubs—a tendency embodied by its larger-than-life mayor, Zoran Janković (described in the sidebar on page 561). And yet, Ljubljana's scintillating avant-garde culture has soft edges—hip, but also non-threatening and user-friendly.

some colorful boutiques in the Old Town, or do more sightseeing (good options include the City Museum of Ljubljana; the Serbian Orthodox Church and Tivoli Park, with the Contemporary History Museum, west of downtown; or the Slovenian Ethnographic Museum and other sights in Metelkova, north of downtown).

Plenty of other worthwhile Slovenian destinations are a short distance from Ljubljana. With a second day, visit Lake Bled (see next chapter), or head for one of the two impressive caves (Škocjan or Postojna) and nearby sights in the Karst region south of the city (see the Karst chapter). If the weather's ideal, the five-hour Julian Alps driving loop is a long but very satisfying day out from Ljubljana.

Ljubljana is sleepy on Sundays (many shops are closed and the produce market is quiet, but museums are generally open, a modest flea market stretches along the riverfront, and the TI's walking tour still runs). The city is also relatively quiet in August, when the students are on break and many locals head to beach resorts. They say that in August, even homeless people go to the coast.

In summer, foodies should aim to be in Ljubljana on a Friday to enjoy the fun "Open Kitchen" street-food festival (see "Eating in Ljubljana," later).

Orientation to Ljubljana

Ljubljana's central zone is compact, and with a little wandering, you'll quickly get the hang of it. The Ljubljanica River—lined with cafés, restaurants, and a buzzing outdoor market—bisects the city, making a 90-degree turn around the base of a castle-topped hill. Most sights are either along or just a short walk from the river. Visitors enjoy the distinctive bridges that span the Ljubljanica, including the landmark Triple Bridge (Tromostovje) and pillared Cobblers' Bridge (Čevljarski Most)—both designed by Jože Plečnik. Between these two is a plain bridge (with great views) called Brv (roughly, "simple footbridge"). The center of Ljubljana is Prešeren Square, watched over by a big statue of Slovenia's national poet, France Prešeren.

I've organized the sights in this chapter based on which side of the river they're on: the east (castle) side of the river, which is where Ljubljana began and has more medieval charm; and the west (Prešeren Square) side of the river, which has a more Baroque/Art Nouveau feel and most of the urban sprawl. At the northern edge of the tourist's Ljubljana is the train station and Metelkova museum and nightlife zone; at the southern edge are the garden district of Krakovo and the Jože Plečnik House; and at the western edge is Tivoli Park.

Ljubljana's Two Big Ps: You'll hear the following two easy-to-confuse names constantly during your visit. Mind your Ps, and your visit to Ljubljana becomes more meaningful: **Jože Plečnik** (YOH-zheh PLAYCH-neek, 1872-1957) is the architect who shaped Ljubljana, designing virtually all the city's most important landmarks. **France Prešeren** (FRAHN-tseh preh-SHAY-rehn,

1800-1849) is Slovenia's greatest poet and the namesake of Ljubljana's main square.

TOURIST INFORMATION

Ljubljana's helpful, businesslike TI has a useful website (www. visitljubljana.com) and two branches: at the **Triple Bridge,** across from Prešeren Square (daily 8:00-21:00, Oct-May until 19:00, Stritarjeva 1, tel. 01/306-1215); and at the upper corner of the **market** (with bikes to rent and information about the rest of Slovenia; daily 8:00-21:00; Oct-May Mon-Fri 8:00-19:00, Sat-Sun 9:00-17:00; Krekov trg 10, tel. 01/306-4575). At either TI, pick up a pile of free resources, including the big city map, the *Tourist Guide,* and the monthly events guide.

The **Ljubljana Tourist Card,** which includes access to public transportation and covers entry to many city museums as well as the TIs' walking tours and boat trips, could save busy sightseers some money (€31/24 hours, €39/48 hours, €45/72 hours).

ARRIVAL IN LJUBLJANA

By Train: Ljubljana's train station (Železniška Postaja) is at the northern edge of the city center. Emerging from the passage up to track 1a, turn right and walk under the long canopy to find the yellow arrivals hall. Everything is well-signed in English, including the handy train-information office (with useful handouts outlining journeys to several domestic and international destinations), lockers, and—near the front of the station—a big ticket office with an ATM. Arrivals are *prihodi*, departures are *odhodi*, and track is *tir*.

You can **walk** to any of my recommended hotels within about 20 minutes (often less). To reach Prešeren Square at the city's center, exit the station to the right and walk a long block along the busy Trg Osvobodilne Fronte (or "Trg O.F." for short, with the bus station in the middle). After passing the bus stalls, turn left across Trg O.F. and go down Miklošičeva (look for the building with the round, red-brick columns). This takes you past some of Ljubljana's most appealing architecture to Prešeren Square.

Avoid unscrupulous **taxis** waiting to spring on unsuspecting tourists at the station—call one that charges fair rates instead (around €4-5 to any of my recommended hotels). Taking just a few more minutes to wait for your cab could easily save you €10 or more. See "Getting Around Ljubljana—By Taxi," later, for recommended taxi companies.

By Bus: Ljubljana's bus station (Autobusna Postaja) is a low-profile building (with ticket windows, a bakery, and newsstands) in the middle of Trg O.F., right in front of the train station. To get into the city center, see "By Train," earlier.

By Car: Ljubljana is not car-friendly; much of the central zone

Ljubljana

To Contemporary History Museum

Tivoli Park

SERBIAN ORTHODOX CHURCH

NATIONAL GALLERY

MODERN ART MUSEUM

NATIONAL THEATER

US EMBASSY

SLOVENIAN NATIONAL MUSEUM & NATURAL HISTORY MUSEUM

Trg Narodni Herojev

PARLIAMENT

MUSEUM ZONE & TIVOLI PARK WALK

Square of the Republic

LJUBLJANSKA BANKA

TIVOLSKA CESTA

CANKARJEVA CESTA

TOMŠIČEVA ULICA

ŠUBIČEVA ULICA

ŠTEFANOVA ULICA

GOSPOSVETSKA

KERSNIKOVA ULICA

SLOVENSKA CESTA

CIGALETOVA

Ajdovščina Park

DALMATINOVA ULICA

Miklošičev Park

THE SKYSCRAPER

NAZORJEVA ULICA

SLOVENSKA CESTA

ČOPOVA ULICA

POST

GRAND HOTEL UNION

FRANCISCAN CHURCH

MIKLOŠIČEVA

Prešeren Square

MEM. TO THE VICTIMS OF ALL WARS

ANCHOR

Congress Square

WOLFOVA

TRIPLE BRIDGE

BRV BRIDGE

Ribji Square

ERJAVČEVA CESTA

PREŠERNOVA

GREGORČIČEVA

IGRIŠKA ULICA

RIMSKA CESTA

AŠKERČEVA

SLOVENSKA CESTA

CESTA

VEGOVA

COBBLERS' BRIDGE

UNIVERSITY

FOUNTAIN

Novi Trg

NATIONAL & UNIVERSITY LIBRARY

French Revolution Square

N.U.K. #2

Courtyard

CITY MUSEUM

River

OLD

MESTNI TRG

Ljubljanica

BREG

GOSPOSKA

STARI TRG

REBER

HERCULES FOUNTAIN

LEVSTIKOV TRG

ZOISOVA CESTA

ST. JAMES BRIDGE

ROMAN CITY WALL

MIRJE

BARJANSKA CESTA

EMONSKA CESTA

KRAKOVO

REČNA UL.

GRADAŠKA ULICA

EIPPROVA ULICA

PLEČNIK HOUSE

FOOTBRIDGE

To Train & Bus Stations

METELKOVA CITY

KOLODVORSKA UL.

MUSEUM OF CONTEMPORARY ART

NATIONAL MUSEUM (METELK.)

SLOMŠKOVA

MALA ULICA

RESLJEVA CESTA

ČUFARJEVA

KOTNIKOVA ULICA

METELKOVA

VIDOVDANSKA CESTA

SLOVENIAN ETHNOGRAPHIC MUSEUM

Tabor

ROŽMANOVA ULICA

KOMENSKEGA ULICA

TABOR

ILIRSKA ULICA

See detail map

COOPERATIVE BANK

ZADRUŽNA ZVEZA

GALERIJA EMPORIUM

TRUBARJEVA CESTA

BUTCHERS' BRIDGE

GRAIN BRIDGE

DRAGON BRIDGE

RIVERSIDE MARKET

Kapitelj

PETKOVŠKOVO NABREŽJE

1st Mkt. Square

MARKET HALL

Main Market Square

VODNIK STATUE

POLJANSKI NASIP

CATHEDRAL

CIRIL - METODOV TRG

POLJANSKA TRG.

Krekov Square

FOUNTAIN

TOWN HALL

STUDENTOVSKA

STRELIŠKA ULICA

TOWN

FUNICULAR

TOWER

LJUBLJANA CASTLE

UL.

GORNJI TRG

KARLOVŠKA CESTA

N

100 Meters
100 Yards

along the river is entirely traffic-free. Even several blocks of the main thoroughfare, Slovenska cesta—north of Congress Square, between Šubičeva ulica and Gosposvetska cesta—are closed to all traffic except buses. To reach the southern part of the city when entering downtown from the north, you need to circumnavigate the core by looping east along Resljeva cesta, over the Dragon Bridge by the market, and through the tunnel beneath the castle; from here, Karlovška cesta cuts back west over the river to the southern stretch of Slovenska cesta.

Ask your hotel about parking—most have some available, usually for a price. Two particularly central (and expensive) parking lots are the one beneath **Congress Square** (€1.50/hour for first 3 hours, then €2.40/hour, or €1.80/hour overnight) and the one called **N.U.K. #2,** near the National and University Library (€1.20/hour 7:00-19:00, €1.80/hour overnight). Both of these lots are accessible on Slovenska cesta only from the south—if coming from the north, see directions above for looping around town. Another handy lot is **Kapitelj,** just southeast of the Dragon Bridge (€2/first hour, then €2.40/hour, or €1.50/hour 18:00-6:00).

Paid parking downtown is marked by blue lines (look for meters); these spaces are free Saturdays after 13:00 and all day Sunday. For cheaper parking and longer stays, you can park along the river just south of downtown (in zone 3, south of St. James Bridge—see the "Ljubljana" map). Along here, it's just €0.40-0.60 per hour, and free on weeknights between 17:00 and 7:00 and all day Sat-Sun.

There's a huge **gas station** on Tivolska cesta (just west of the train station, near the big Union brewery).

By Plane: See "Ljubljana Connections" at the end of this chapter.

HELPFUL HINTS

Pedestrian Safety: Many Ljubljana residents commute by bike—and they're not shy about whizzing past pedestrians, even in seemingly "pedestrian-only" areas. Stay out of the designated bike lanes on the sidewalks, and stay aware everywhere.

Closed Days: Most Ljubljana museums (except the castle and a few less-important museums) are closed on Mondays.

Markets: In addition to the regular **market** that sprawls along the riverfront (described in my "Ljubljana Walk," later), the wonderful **Open Kitchen** street-food festival runs Fridays from spring through fall (see "Eating in Ljubljana," later). A colorful **flea market** hops along the Ljubljanica River's Breg embankment (across the river from the castle) every Sun 8:00-14:00, and on summer Saturdays, there's also a lively and colorful **arts and handicrafts market** in the same place (Sat 8:00-14:00).

Laundry: For pricey full service, try **Tekstilexpress,** between the city center and Tivoli Park (takes 24 hours, Mon-Fri 7:00-19:00, Sat 9:00-13:00, closed Sun, Cankarjeva 10B, tel. 01/252-7354). **Hostel Celica** has self-service laundry—but hostel guests have priority (cheap but not very central at Metelkova 8).

Car Rental: Handy options include **Hertz** (Trdinova 9, tel. 01/434-0147, also at the airport, www.hertz.si), **Europcar** (in City Hotel at Dalmatinova 15, mobile 059-077-040, www.europcar.si), **Avis** and **Budget** (both in Grand Hotel Union at Miklošičeva 3, tel. for both 01/421-7340, www.avis.si, www.budget.si), and **Sixt** (facing the main platform at the train station, tel. 01/234-4650, www.sixt.si).

Best Views: The **Skyscraper's observation deck** offers the best views in town (see listing under "More Sights in Ljubljana," later). Views from the castle are nearly as good. At street level, my favorite views are from the bridge called Brv (between the Triple and Cobblers' bridges), especially at night, and from the river promenade.

GETTING AROUND LJUBLJANA

By Bus: Virtually all of Ljubljana's sights are easily accessible by foot. And using the buses is a bit of a headache: First, you have to buy a plastic Urbana card for €2, which you then load with credit to pay for rides (you can't pay the driver). A ride costs €1.30 (valid for up to 90 minutes, card shareable by multiple people). Buy the card at the TI, where you can return it to reclaim your €2 at the end of your trip. Transit info: www.lpp.si.

By Taxi: Always call for a cab, or you'll get ripped off. Legitimate taxis usually start at about €1.50, and then charge €1 per kilometer. But many unscrupulous cabbies legally charge far more, and tack on bogus additional "surcharges." (Because fares are unregulated, even if they use the meter you'll still pay way too much.) However, if you call a reputable taxi company, Ljubljana is a fantastic taxi town with very affordable rates—a ride within the city center (such as from the station to a hotel) should run less than €5. Good companies include **Laguna** (tel. 01/511-2314, mobile 031-492-299), **Metro Taxi** (tel. 080-1190, mobile 041-240-200), and **Intertours** (tel. 080-311-311, mobile 031-311-311). Dispatchers speak English, and your hotel, restaurant, or the TI can call a cab for you.

By Bike: Ljubljana is a cyclist's delight, with lots of well-marked bike lanes. It's easiest to rent bikes at the market square TI (€2/2 hours, €8/day; see "Tourist Information," earlier). Like many European cities, Ljubljana has a subsidized borrow-a-bike program (called BicikeLJ) with more than 60 locations around the city center. Once you register online with a credit card (€1 fee for a weekly subscription that doesn't require an Urbana public transit card), rides are free or very cheap (free for the first hour, €1 for the second, €2 for the third, and so on). If you're planning on doing lots of biking, it's worth the hassle to sign up (http://en.bicikelj.si).

By Shuttle Bus: A network of green electric carts, called **Kavalir,** are designed to get anyone (even tourists) around the traffic-free downtown pedestrian zone for free. Just wave one down and tell them where you want to go (or phone them—April-Oct call 031-666-331 or 031-666-332; Nov-March call 031-666-299).

Tours in Ljubljana

To help you appreciate Ljubljana, taking a walking tour—either through the TI or by hiring your own local guide—is worth ▲▲.

Walking Tour

The TI organizes excellent two-hour guided town walks of Ljubljana in English, led by knowledgeable guides. In summer, the walk also includes either a funicular ride up to the castle or a 30-minute boat ride on the river. From April through September, there are three tours daily (at 10:00, 14:00, and usually 16:00). From October through March, the walking tour goes daily at 11:00 (€17, meet at Town Hall around corner from Triple Bridge TI). They also offer a variety of other themed tours—get details at the TI.

Local Guides

Having an expert show you around his or her hometown for two hours for €100 has to be the best value in town (extra for more than 2 people). **Marijan Krišković,** who leads tours for me throughout Europe, is an outstanding guide (mobile 040-222-739, kriskovic@yahoo.com). **Barbara Jakopič,** thoughtful and extremely knowledgeable, also leads my tours (mobile 040-530-870, jakopic_b@yahoo.com). You can also book a guide through the TI (at least 24 hours in advance).

Boat Cruise

A boat trip on the Ljubljanica River is more romantic than thrilling. You'll see multiple companies hawking these €10, one-hour cruises all along the river in the center. But if you'd like some commentary en route, it's best to take the TI's version, which is narrated by a live guide (€12, 2/day in summer, get details at TI). Most other companies don't have commentary at all, though some may have recorded spiels (ask before you buy).

Excursions from Ljubljana

Many worthwhile sights near Ljubljana are tricky to reach by public transportation. To hit several efficiently in one day, join an ex-

Ljubljana at a Glance

▲▲▲People-Watching Ljubljana's single best activity is sitting at an outdoor café along the river and watching the vivacious, stylish, fun-loving Slovenes strut their stuff.

▲▲Riverside Market Lively market area in the Old Town with produce, clothing, and souvenirs. **Hours:** Best in the morning, especially Sat; market hall open Mon-Fri 7:00-16:00, Sat until 14:00, closed Sun. See page 559.

▲▲Serbian Orthodox Church of Sts. Cyril and Methodius Beautifully decorated house of worship giving insight into the Orthodox faith. **Hours:** Daily 8:00-19:00. See page 580.

▲▲National and University Library Jože Plečnik's pièce de résistance, with an intriguing facade, piles of books, and a bright reading room. **Hours:** Main staircase open Mon-Fri 10:00-18:00, Sat until 14:00, closed Sun except in summer; student reading room open to the public mid-July-mid-Aug Mon-Sat 10:00-18:00, Sun 11:00-19:00, rest of year Sat 14:30-18:00. See page 567.

▲▲Jože Plečnik House Final digs of the famed hometown architect who shaped so much of Ljubljana, explained by an enthusiastic guide. **Hours:** Tue-Sun 10:00-18:00, English tours begin at the top of each hour, last tour departs at 17:00, closed Mon. See page 574.

▲▲Slovenian Ethnographic Museum Engaging, well-presented collection celebrating Slovenian culture. **Hours:** Tue-Sun 10:00-18:00, closed Mon. See page 583.

▲Cathedral Italian Baroque interior and bronze doors with intricate, highly symbolic designs. **Hours:** Generally daily 11:00-18:00 but opens Tue at 14:00 and Sun at 13:30, on weekends closes for an hour around 15:30. See page 563.

▲Ljubljana Castle Tower with good views and so-so 3-D film. **Hours:** Grounds—daily 9:00-23:00, shorter hours Oct-May; castle—daily 9:00-21:00, shorter hours Oct-May. See page 572.

▲Contemporary History Museum Baroque mansion in Tivoli Park, with exhibit highlighting Slovenia's last 100 years. **Hours:** Tue-Sun 10:00-18:00, Thu until 20:00 June-Aug, closed Mon. See page 581.

▲City Museum of Ljubljana Modern, high-tech exhibit covering the city's history. **Hours:** Tue-Sun 10:00-18:00, Thu until 21:00, closed Mon. See page 569.

cursion. Three relatively well-established outfits are **Roundabout** (their one-day "Karst and Coast Mystery" tour takes you to Predjama Castle, Škocjan Caves, Lipica, and Piran for €60 plus admission to the caves and an optional wine tasting, their "off the beaten track" tours delve deeper into local culture www.travelroundabout. com), **Slovenia Explorer** (their ambitious "Slovenia in 1 Day" trip visits Lake Bled, Postojna Caves, and Predjama Castle for €140; www.slovenia-explorer.com), and **To Do in Slovenia** (www. todoinslovenia.com). **Nature Adventures** focuses on active trips including rafting, paragliding, skydiving, and horseback riding (www.adventures-nature.com).

Ljubljana Walk

This walk—which meanders in a big loop on both sides of the river—offers an orientation for your Ljubljana wanderings. The whole walk takes no longer than about an hour and a half (without entering sights). You'll end just a few steps from where you begin, but along the way I'll point out a few possible detours. (Ljubljana is so small and enjoyable to stroll, you'll be doing lots of circling back.)

• *Begin on the main square right in the center of Ljubljana, marked by the can't-miss-it pink church.*

PREŠEREN SQUARE AREA
▲▲Prešeren Square (Prešernov Trg)

This square is the heart of Ljubljana. The city's meeting point is the large **statue of France Prešeren,** Slovenia's greatest poet, whose works include the lyrics to the Slovenian national anthem (and whose silhouette adorns Slovenia's €2 coin). The statue shows Prešeren, an important catalyst of 19th-century Slovenian nationalism, being inspired from above by a Muse. This statue provoked a scandal and outraged the bishop when it went up a century ago—a naked woman sharing the square with a church! To ensure that nobody could be confused about the woman's intentions, she's conspicuously depicted with typical Muse accessories: a laurel branch and a cloak. Even so, for the first

few years citizens covered the scandalous statue with a tarp each night. And the model who posed for the Muse was so disgraced that no one in Slovenia would hire her—so she emigrated to South America and never returned.

LJUBLJANA

Stand at the base of the statue to get oriented. The bridge crossing the Ljubljanica River is one of Ljubljana's top landmarks, Jože Plečnik's **Triple Bridge** (Tromostovje). The middle (widest) part of this bridge already existed, but Plečnik added the two side spans to more efficiently funnel the six streets of traffic on this side of the bridge to the one street on the other side. The bridge's Venetian vibe is intentional: Plečnik recognized that Ljubljana, located midway between Venice and then-capital Vienna, is itself a bridge between the Italian and Germanic worlds. Across the bridge are the TI, WCs, ATMs, market and cathedral (to the left), and the Town Hall (straight ahead).

Now turn 90 degrees to the right, and look down the first street after the riverbank. Find the orange woman in the picture frame on the second floor of the first yellow house. This is **Julija,** the unrequited love of Prešeren's life. Tour guides spin romantic tales about how the couple met. But the truth is far less exciting: He was a teacher in her father's house when he was in his 30s and she was 4. Later in life, she inspired him from afar—as she does now, from across the square—but they never got together. She may have been his muse, but when it came to marriage, she opted for wealth and status.

When Ljubljana was hit by an earthquake in 1895, locals took the opportunity (using an ample rebuilding fund from the

Austro-Hungarian Empire) to remake their city in style. Today Ljubljana—especially the streets around this square—is an architecture-lover's paradise. The **Hauptmann House,** to the right of Julija, was the only building on the square to survive the quake. A few years later, the owner redecorated it in the then-trendy Viennese Art Nouveau style you see today, using bright colors (since his family sold dyes). All that remains of the original structure is the little Baroque balcony above the entrance.

Just to the right of the Hauptmann House is a car-sized **model** of the city center—helpful for orientation. The street next to it (with the McDonald's) is **Čopova,** once the route of Ljubljana's Sunday promenade. A century ago, locals would put on their Sun-

Ljubljana Center

NAZORJEVA ULICA

ČOPOVA ULICA

SLOVENSKA CESTA

POST

GRAND HOTEL UNION

COOPERATIVE BANK

MIKLOŠIČEVA

ZADRUŽNA ZVEZA

FRANCISCAN CHURCH

GALERIJA EMPORIUM

CITY MODEL

Prešeren Square

FRANCE PREŠEREN STATUE

To Tivoli Park

HAUPTMANN HOUSE

JULIJA RELIEF

WALK BEGINS

TRIPLE BRIDGE

CONE

MEM. TO THE VICTIMS OF ALL WARS

WC (IN TUNNEL)

ROMAN CITIZEN STATUE

ZVEZDA KAVARNA

ANCHOR

WOLFOVA

OLD

Ribji Square

FOUNTAIN OF 3 RIVERS

To Square of the Republic

P

WALK ENDS

Congress Square

BRV BRIDGE

Town Square

ROMANTIKA GELATO

River

BEST RIVERBANK CAFÉS

TOWN HALL

TOWN

GÜJŽINA GALERIJA IDRIJSKE ČIPKE

HONEY HOUSE

PIRANSKE SOLINE

DOBROTE DOLENJSKE

MESTNI

ULICA

COBBLERS' BRIDGE

CHA

CAFETINO

ZA POPEN'T

WOOL ART KNITWEAR

OSEM

ALTROKÈ

STARI TRG

UNIVERSITY

VEGOVA

GOSPOSKA

TURJAŠKA

Novi Trg

WC

NATIONAL & UNIVERSITY LIBRARY (N.U.K.)

BREG

REBER UL.

Ljubljanica

French Revolution Square

Križanke

CITY MUSEUM

HERCULES FOUNTAIN

GORNJI

EMONSKA

P

N.U.K. #2

To Plečnik House & Trnovo Church

STISKA ULICA

Levitskov Trg

LJUBLJANA

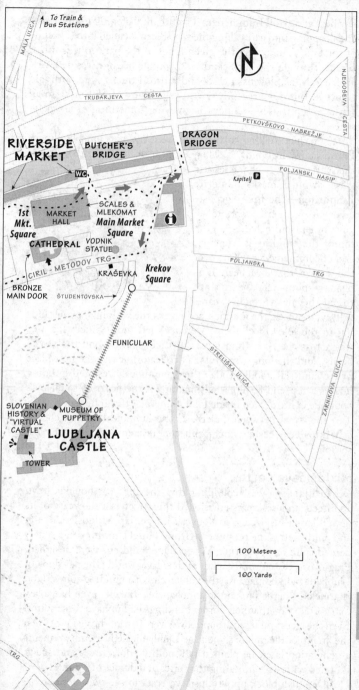

day best and stroll from here to Tivoli Park, listening to musicians and dropping into cafés along the way. Plečnik called it the "lifeline of the city," connecting the green lungs of the park to this urban center. Through the 20th century, this route became less pedestrian-friendly, as Slovenska cesta and railroad tracks were both laid across it. But more recently—with the closure of Slovenska to all traffic except buses—Čopova is enjoying something of a renaissance.

Continue looking to the right, past the big, pink landmark **Franciscan Church of St. Mary** (not much to see inside). Across the street, the characteristic glass awning marks **Galerija Emporium**—the first big post-quake department store, today government-protected. At the top of the building is Mercury, god of commerce, watching over the square that has been Ljubljana's commercial heart since the city began. (If you look care-

fully, you can see the mustachioed face of the building's owner hiding in the folds of cloth by Mercury's left foot.) Since this area was across the river from medieval Ljubljana (beyond the town's limits...and the long arm of its tax collector), it was the best place to buy and sell goods. Today this sumptuously restored building houses a top-end fashion mall, making it the heart of Ljubljana's boutique culture. Step inside for a glimpse of the grand staircase.

The street between Galerija Emporium and the pink church is **Miklošičeva cesta,** which connects Prešeren Square to the train station.

Miklošičeva cesta

When Ljubljana was rebuilding after the 1895 earthquake, town architects and designers envisioned this street as a showcase of its new, Vienna-inspired Art Nouveau image. Up Miklošičeva cesta and on the left is the prominent **Grand Hotel Union,** with a stately domed spire on the corner. When these buildings were designed, Prague was the cultural capital of the Slavic world. The new look of Ljubljana paid homage to "the golden city of a hundred spires" (and channeled Prague's romantic atmosphere). The city even had a law for several years that new corner buildings had to have these spires. Even the trees you'll see around town were part of the vision. When the architect Plečnik designed the Ljubljanica River embankments a generation later, he planted tall, pointy poplar trees and squat, rounded willows—imitating the spires and domes of Prague.

Detour a block up Miklošičeva cesta to see two more architectural gems of that era (across from the Grand Hotel Union): First is a Secessionist building—marked **Zadružna Zveza**—with classic red, blue, and white colors (for the Slovenian flag). Next is the noisy, pink, zigzagged **Cooperative Bank.** The bank was designed by Ivan Vurnik, an ambitious Slovenian architect who wanted to invent a distinctive national style after World War I, when the Habsburg Empire broke up and Eastern Europe's nations were proudly emerging for the first time.

• *Head back to Prešeren Square, then cross the Triple Bridge. The TI is straight ahead, and on your left is the first colonnade of Ljubljana's market.*

RIVERSIDE MARKET AREA

The east side of the river is the city's most colorful and historic quarter, packed with Old World ambience.

▲▲Riverside Market *(Tržnice)*

In Ljubljana's thriving Old Town market, big-city Slovenes enjoy buying directly from the producer. The market, worth an amble any time, is best on summer Fridays for its "Open Kitchen" street-food festival (see "Eating in Ljubljana," later); and on Saturday mornings any time of year, when the townspeople take their time wandering the stalls. Prices go down as the day gets late and as the week goes on. In this tiny capital of a tiny country, you may even see the president searching for the perfect melon.

The market area is slated for a "modernization" in the near future, so it may be torn up (or reorganized) when you visit.

The riverside **colonnade,** which echoes the long-gone medieval city wall, was designed by Jože Plečnik. This first stretch—nearest the Triple Bridge—is good for souvenirs: wood-carvings, replica painted frontboards from beehives, honey products (including honey brandy), and lots of colorful candles (bubbly Marta will gladly paint a special message on your candle for no extra charge).

LJUBLJANA

Farther in, the market is almost all local, and the colonnade is populated by butchers, bakers, fishermen, and lazy cafés. Peek down at the actual river and see how the architect wanted the town and river to connect. The lower arcade (which you can access directly from the Triple Bridge or by going down the spiral staircase by the beehive panels) has inviting cafés, a robust and stinky fish market *(ribarnica),* and public WCs. The recommended restaurant just below, **Ribca,** serves fun fishy plates, beer, and coffee with great riverside seating.

• *Across from the stairs that lead down into the fish market, about where the souvenir stands end, you reach Pogačarjev trg, the small...*

First Market Square

On your right, notice the 10-foot-tall concrete **cone.** Plečnik wanted to make Ljubljana the "Athens of the North" and imagined a huge cone-shaped national acropolis—a complex for government, museums, and culture. This ambitious plan didn't make it off the drawing board, but part of Plečnik's Greek idea came true: this marketplace, based on an ancient Greek agora. Plečnik's cone still captures the Slovenes' imaginations...and adorns Slovenia's €0.10 coin.

At the top of this square, you'll find the 18th-century **cathedral** standing on the site of a 13th-century Romanesque church. (We'll visit the cathedral from the other side later on this walk.)

The building at the end of the first market square is the seminary palace. In the basement is a **market hall** *(pokrita tržnica),* with vendors selling cheeses, meats, baked goods, dried fruits, nuts, and other goodies (Mon-Fri 7:00-16:00, Sat until 14:00, closed Sun). This place is worth a graze—walk all the way through. Most merchants are happy to give you a free sample (point to what you want, and say *probat, prosim*—"a taste, please").

• *Leaving the market hall at the opposite end, turn left to reach the modern...*

Butchers' Bridge and Main Market Square

Jože Plečnik designed a huge roofed bridge to be built here, but—like so many of his designs—the plans were scuttled. Decades later, Mayor Zoran Janković finally constructed this modern version of the bridge. While it looks nothing like Plečnik's original plans, the bridge kept the old name and has been embraced by the community (there's a handy public WC down below on the lower level). Almost as soon as it was built, the bridge's railings were covered with padlocks—part of the Europe-wide craze for young couples to commemorate their love. The bridge's sculptures—a mournful Adam and Eve being evicted from the Garden of Eden, and weird little lizards breaking out of their eggs along the railing—are by wild-

Mayor Zoran Janković

The latest chapter in Ljubljana's story has been written by its mayor, Zoran Janković. Sort of the Michael Bloomberg of Slovenia, this successful businessman transformed himself into a broadly supported mayor who is unafraid to pursue an ambitious civic agenda.

As chairman of the huge Mercator supermarket chain, Janković was famous for prowling around the front lines of his stores, micromanaging all day-to-day business. After corporate political shuffling forced him out, Janković turned his attention to the municipal realm—and, in 2006, was elected mayor of Ljubljana in a landslide.

The people of this city had grown accustomed to ineffectual leaders who would propose, then cancel, ambitious projects. But with Janković in office, project after project materialized, on time and under budget: the funicular to the castle, several new bridges (including the Butchers' Bridge at the market), the creation of quaintly cobbled traffic-free zones throughout almost the entire town center, the rejuvenation of miles of riverfront embankment for pedestrians, and closing a several-block stretch of one of Ljubljana's most heavily used downtown streets (Slovenska cesta) to all car traffic.

Ultimately, most Ljubljanans are thrilled with the transformation of their city—he was reelected in another landslide in 2012. Janković embodies the ideal of how a progressive electorate can trust a capable leader to wisely invest public funds in urban-beautification projects that benefit the common good.

eyed and wild-bearded local artist Jakov Brdar, who often hangs out near the bridge, asking passersby how they like his creations.

Sprawling up from the bridge is the **main market square** (Vodnikov trg), packed with produce and clothing stands. (The colorful flower market hides behind the market hall.) Wander this stretch of the market as you continue east. The vendors in the row nearest the colonnade sell fruit from all over, but the ones located deeper in the market sell only locally grown produce. Tell the vendor what you want—it's considered rude for customers to touch the fruits and vegetables before they're bought. Over time, shoppers develop friendships with their favorite producers. On busy days, you'll see a long line at one stand, while the other merchants stand bored. Your choice is simple: Get in line, or eat subpar produce.

Near the market hall, look for the little **scales** in the wooden kiosks marked *Kontrolna Tehtnica*—allowing buyers to immediately check whether the producer cheated them (not a common problem, but just in case). The Habsburg days left locals with the old German saying, "Trust is good; control is better." Nearby, look for the innovative "Nonstop Mlekomat" stand, a vending machine that lets you buy a plastic bottle, then fill it with a liter of raw, unskimmed, farm-fresh milk for €1.

• *At the far end of the colonnade, you'll find the...*

▲Dragon Bridge (Zmajski Most)

The dragon has been the symbol of Ljubljana for centuries, ever since Jason (of Argonauts and Golden Fleece fame) supposedly slew one in a nearby swamp.

This is one of the few notable bits of Ljubljana architecture *not* by Plečnik (but by Jurij Zaninović, a fellow student of Vienna architect Otto Wagner). While the dragon is the star of this very photogenic Art Nouveau bridge, the bridge itself was officially dedicated to the 40th anniversary of Habsburg Emperor Franz Josef's reign (see the dates on the side: 1848-1888). Tapping into the emp's vanity got new projects funded—vital as the city later rebuilt after the 1895 earthquake.

• *Turn around and continue browsing your way through the main market square. Wind up at the top-left (southeast) corner of the big square. Nearby on your left, you'll see the helpful TI; directly across the street from that, look for the funicular that trundles tourists up to Ljubljana Castle (see "More Sights in Ljubljana," later.)*

Facing the funicular, turn right and walk with the market on your right, passing the big statue of Slovene poet Valentin Vodnik and heading for the big dome. We're entering...

LJUBLJANA'S OLD TOWN

The historic center of Ljubljana stretches along one long street that curls around the base of its castle-topped hill, beginning near the market.

• *The first part is called...*

Cyril and Methodius Square (Ciril-Metodov Trg)

Named for the Greek-born missionaries who introduced Christianity to the Slavs (and invented the Cyrillic alphabet), this misnamed "square" is really just the first stretch of Ljubljana's Old Town drag. In the early 19th century, Ljubljana was little more than this solitary main street (plus a small "New Town" across the river).

Cyril and Methodius Square is great for a browse, with fun window-shopping. For example, on the left (directly across from the Vodnik statue), the recommended **Kraševka** boutique showcases products from the Karst region (see "Shopping in Ljubljana," later).

As you pass bollards that rise up from the street to block cars, you enter the mostly traffic-free cobbled zone. But it isn't "pedestrian-only." Here and throughout Ljubljana, be prepared for bikes to whiz past you constantly. Cyclists are accustomed to weaving between pedestrians; don't make any sudden movements, and listen for the insistent chime of bells.

Also keep an eye out for another vehicle: the green, enclosed golf carts (called Kavalir) that carry senior citizens (and sometimes tourists) around the downtown core. After Ljubljana pedestrianized much of its downtown core a few years back, local seniors complained about the hassle of getting around without a car. To mollify critics, the city subsidizes this free transportation service.

• *The big, yellow building on the right is Ljubljana's...*

▲Cathedral (Stolnica)

Ljubljana's cathedral is dedicated to St. Nicholas, protector against floods and patron saint of the fishermen and boatmen who have long

come to sell their catch at the market. While the interior is worth a peek, the intricately sculpted bronze doors—created for Pope John Paul II's visit here in 1996—are even more interesting.

Take a close look at the **door** about two-thirds of the way down the building, with of images of the six 20th-century bishops of Ljubljana. (If you're heading inside the cathedral, go through this door.) Another even more impressive bronze door is around the end of the building (hook right). You'll find it under the high arch (both described below).

Cost and Hours: €2, generally daily 11:00-18:00 but opens Tue at 14:00 and Sun at 13:30, on weekends closes for an hour around 15:30.

Visiting the Cathedral: Enter through the side door. In this Italian Baroque space, the transept is surrounded by sculptures of four bishops of Roman Ljubljana (when it was called Emona, or Aemon). Left of the main altar, notice the distinctive chair. This was designed by the very religious Jože Plečnik, whose brother was a priest here. Look up over the nave to enjoy the recently restored, gorgeous ceiling fresco. You'll exit through the main door (described next).

Bronze Main Door: Take a close look at this remarkable door, which fills Slovenes with pride. Buried deeply in the fecund soil of the nation's ancient and pagan history, the linden tree of life sprouts with the story of the Slovenes. The ceramic pots represent the original Roman settlement here. Just to the left, above the tree, are the Byzantine missionaries Cyril and Methodius, who came here to convert the Slavs to Christianity in the ninth century. Just above, Crusaders and Ottomans do battle. Near the top, see the Slovenes going into the cave—entering the dark 20th century (World War I, World War II, and communism). At the top is Pope John Paul II (the first Slavic pontiff, who also helped inspire the fall of communism). Below him are two men who are on track to becoming Slovenia's first saints; the one on the right is the Venerable Frederic Baraga, a 19th-century bishop who became a missionary in Michigan and codified Chippewa grammar (notice the Native American relief on the book he's holding). In the upper right-hand corner is a sun, which has been shining since Slovenia gained its independence in 1991.

• *Carry on past the cathedral on Cyril and Methodius Square, passing a lineup of tempting restaurant tables (including the recommended* **Klobasarna,** *one of the best places in town for a cheap, filling meal—look for the giant Carniolan sausage on the sign).*

Soon you'll run into the giant fountain that marks Ljubljana's...

▲Town Square (Mestni Trg)

The **Fountain of Three Carniolan Rivers** is inspired in style and theme by Rome's many fountains. The figures with vases repre-

sent this region's three main rivers: Ljubljanica, Sava, and Krka. This is one of many works in town by Francesco Robba, an Italian who came to Ljubljana for a job, fell in love with a Slovene, and stayed here the rest of his life—decorating the city's churches with beautiful Baroque altars. (This is a replica; Robba's

original fountain is at the National Gallery, described later.)

From the fountain, look down the wide gap between the buildings (and beyond the Triple Bridge) to see the giant pink church:

We've done a near-loop, and you're just a minute's walk (across the bridge) from Prešeren Square. We'll do another loop now, in the opposite direction.

Just beyond the fountain on the left is the **Town Hall** (Rotovž), highlighted by its clock tower and pillared loggia. Step inside the Renaissance courtyard to see paintings, artifacts, and (high on one wall of the atrium) a map of late-17th-century Ljubljana. Studying this map, notice how the river, hill, and wall worked together to fortify the town. Courtyards like this (but humbler) are hidden throughout the city. As rent in these old places is cheap, many such courtyards host funky and characteristic little businesses.

Back out on the square, turn with the Town Hall on your left. We'll continue down the Old Town's main drag, connecting to two other "squares"—Stari trg (Old Square) and Gornji trg (Upper Square)—which have long since grown together into one big, atmospheric promenade lined with quaint boutiques, great restaurants, and cafés. As you walk, keep your eyes open for Ljubljana's mascot dragon—it's everywhere.

• *Begin heading down the...*

▲Old Town Shopping Zone

Even for nonshoppers, this strip is a delight to browse, offering an ethnographic and culinary introduction to Slovenia. Several shops along this strip specialize in typical Slovenian products.

A block past the Town Hall on the left, at Mestni trg 7 (yellow sign), **Honey House** sells products harvested by beekeeper Luka. For tips on browsing your honey options, see page 634. Next door at #8, **Piranske Soline** sells products from the giant salt pans that sit just south of Piran on Slovenia's tiny coastline (see page 728). You can pick up some locally harvested sea salt, or peruse their salt-based beauty products (bath salts, body milk, and other exfoliants, www.soline.si). And across the street at #19, the recommended **Güjžina** specializes in the cuisine of Prekmurje in northeastern Slovenia, with strong influence from Hungary (the Pannonian Basin).

Farther along, on the right (at #17), **Galerija Idrijske Čipke** shows off handmade lace from the town of Idrija (www.idrija-lace.com). Next door, **Dobrote Dolenjske** sells a variety of flavored schnapps and gins, plus some handicrafts from the Dolenje region in the southeast (www.dobrote-dolenjske.si). Across the street at #10, notice the long passage that leads to one of Ljubljana's characteristic courtyards.

Continue along the street (which here changes names from Mestni trg to Stari trg—"Old Square"), passing more fun shops. On the left, at Stari trg 3, **Cha** tea shop sells over 100 varieties of tea, plus porcelain teapots and cups from all over. It's attached to the recommended **Čajna Hiša teahouse.** A few steps down on the left (at #5), **Cafetino** is one of the best places in town for coffee. They have more than 20 types available—espresso or Turkish-style, plus beans to take home. And just past that is the craft-beer bottle shop **Za Popen't Pivoteka.**

Now you'll wade through a stretch of enticing restaurants with wonderful outdoor tables (for my recommendations here, see the Old Town listings in "Eating in Ljubljana," later). Notice Julija and Romeo, facing each other wistfully across the street.

After the little "restaurant row," the lineup of shops resumes. On the left at Stari trg 11, look for **Wool Art Knitwear,** with unique (and very well-insulated) Serbian-style clothing. From here, you'll pass a few more funky shops, as well as some rare books and antique shops. If you smell something heavenly, watch on the left (at #17) for the recommended **Osem,** which bakes up fresh bread daily. Just past that (at #19) is **Altrokè,** with cuisine from Istria, in southern Slovenia—yet another subregion of this tiny yet wildly diverse land.

The cobbled charm culminates at the square called **Gornji trg.** Look uphill and notice the village charms of some of the oldest buildings in town: four medieval houses with rooflines slanted at the ends, different from the others on this street.

• *Just past the square's Hercules Fountain, turn right (on Stiška ulica) through the gap in the buildings to the...*

▲▲Ljubljanica Riverbank

Turn right and stroll for a couple of minutes along this beautiful promenade—worth ▲▲▲ on a sunny day, when the café tables are full. While this part of the embankment is sleepy, farther along it's a convivial people zone, packed with Slovenes out enjoying their capital. At some point in your visit, it's imperative to take a coffee break somewhere along here. (Why not now?)

Halfway to the first bridge, pause at the little notch and look down at the river and its **embankments**. Notice in particular the angled embankments across the river with seating carved out. These embankments were designed by (who else?) the great architect Jože Plečnik, who walked along this river every day on his way to the office.

• *While you could follow this promenade all the way back to the Triple Bridge and Prešeren Square—just a few minutes away—we're only going as far as the first bridge, with the tall pillars (Cobblers' Bridge). We'll cross the river here to explore some of Ljubljana's architectural masterpieces. And that means we're entering the world of Jože Plečnik. Walk halfway across the bridge and pause for a moment.*

JOŽE PLEČNIK'S LJUBLJANA

Jože Plečnik is to Ljubljana what Antoni Gaudí is to Barcelona: a homegrown, amazingly prolific genius who reshaped his town with a unique and beautiful vision. And Plečnik's mark on Ljubljana, much like Gaudí's on Barcelona, has a way of turning people who couldn't care less about architecture into fans. There's plenty to see. In addition to the Triple Bridge, riverside market and embankments, and the sights we're about to see, Plečnik designed the embankments along the Gradaščica River in the Trnovo neighborhood; the rebuilt Roman wall along Mirje street, south of the center; the Church of St. Francis, with its classicist bell tower; St. Michael's Church on the Marsh; Orel Stadium; Žale Cemetery; and many more buildings throughout Slovenia.

▲Cobblers' Bridge (Čevljarski Most)

Named for the cobblers (shoemakers) who set up shop along the river in olden times, the bridge encapsulates Plečnik's style per-

haps better than any other structure: simple, clean lines adorned with classical columns. Ideal for people-watching (with the castle hovering scenically overhead), this is one of Ljubljana's most appealing spots.

• *Cross Cobblers' Bridge, turn left, and walk one short block to the big fountain, which marks the bottom of a broad plaza called Novi trg. Turn right and head to the top of Novi trg, where you'll run into a red-brick building embedded with gray granite blocks in an irregular checkerboard pattern. This is the...*

▲▲National and University Library (Narodna in Univerzitetna Knjižnica, or NUK)

Widely regarded as Plečnik's masterpiece, this building is a bit underwhelming...until an understanding of its symbolism brings it to life. Aside from being a great work of architecture, the build-

ing also houses the most important library in Slovenia, with more than two million books (about one per Slovene). The library is supposed to receive a copy of each new book printed in the country. In a freaky bit of bad luck, this was the only building in town damaged in World War II, when a plane crashed into it. But the people didn't want to see their books go up in flames—so hundreds of locals formed a human chain, risking life and limb to save the books from the burning building.

On the surface, the red-and-gray color scheme of the **exterior** evokes the red soil and chunks of granite of the Karst region, south of Ljubljana. But on a deeper level, the library's design conveys the theme of overcoming obstacles to attain knowledge. In the facade, the blocks of irregular size and shape represent a complex numerological pattern that suggests barriers on the path to enlightenment. The sculpture on the river side (to the left) is Moses—known for leading his people through 40 years of hardship to the Promised Land. On the right side of the building, find the horse-head door-

knobs—representing the winged horse Pegasus (grab hold, and he'll whisk you away to new levels of enlightenment).

If you go inside, you'll notice the main staircase is dark and gloomy—modeled after an Egyptian tomb. But at the top, through the door marked *Velika Čitalnica*, is the bright, airy main reading room: the ultimate goal, a place of learning. The top-floor windows are shaped roughly like open books. Sadly, most of the time you can't actually enter the reading room; if it's closed, you'll just have to look at postcards in the shop, and imagine young Ljubljanans hunched studiously over their books, surrounded by Plečnik's bookshelves, railings, and high windows.

On your way back outside, duck through the little door on the right just inside the main door. This leads down to the build-

ing's basement, with more serene Plečnik design elements, and a wonderful little student **café** (also open to the public, described later, under "Eating in Ljubljana") filling a corridor.

Cost and Hours: The staircase is free to enter and open Mon-Fri 10:00-18:00, Sat until 14:00, closed Sun except in summer. The quiet main reading room is open to visitors (for €5) only during very brief windows: Most of the year, you can enter on Saturday afternoons (14:30-18:00), but hours are longer during the student break in the summer (mid-July-mid-Aug Mon-Sat 10:00-18:00, Sun 11:00-19:00).

• *Back outside, head back to the corner. As you face the building from the top of Novi trg, turn left and head one block down Gosposka street. On your left, you'll run into the...*

▲City Museum of Ljubljana (Mestni Muzej Ljubljana)

Though not a Plečnik sight, this thoughtfully presented, kid-friendly museum, located in the Auersperg Palace, offers a high-tech, in-depth look at the story of this city, using a wide range of well-described artifacts (all in English).

Cost and Hours: €6, more for temporary exhibits, Tue-Sun 10:00-18:00, Thu until 21:00, closed Mon, Gosposka 15, tel. 01/241-2510, www.mgml.si.

Visiting the Museum: In the **cellar** are Roman ruins (including remains of the original Roman road and sewer system, found right here) and layers of medieval artifacts. A model of the modern city—sitting upon footprints of the Roman (red) and medieval (blue) settlements—illustrates Ljubljana's many layers of history.

Upstairs on the second floor, walk through the excellent **permanent exhibit** (called "Ljubljana. History. City."). You're greeted by an artfully displayed collage of paintings and statues representing the pastiche of history in this crossroads city. Then head through the chronological exhibition, starting with prehistory—where you'll find the museum's prized possession, the world's oldest wooden wheel on an axle, dating from around 3200 BC and discovered in the Ljubljana marshlands. From there, you'll head through antiquity (Roman "Emona"), the Middle Ages (when "Laibach" was a market town), and the modern age (with Baroque architecture and the Slovenian national awakening). The detailed model of late-19th-century Ljubljana shows a city that looks much as it does today, minus the modern sprawl and Plečnik flourishes. The modern and contemporary section traces the city's tumultuous 20th and 21st centuries: becoming the capital of the modern state of Slovenia, Tito and the Partisans, Yugoslavia, and—finally—present-day independence. You'll see an actual Fiat Zastava 750 car, the classic "Fičko" car that everyone owned—or wanted to own—in communist Yugoslavia (sort of a proto-Yugo). Rounding out the collection is a range of temporary exhibits.

Nearby: Your ticket includes admission to two archaeological sites nearby (summer only)—pick up a map at the front desk.

• *With the museum at your back, you're facing yet another fine square. On the left side of the square, just past the big, boxy, orange building, step through the gate into the courtyard of...*

Križanke Theater

The Teutonic Knights of the Cross established this monastery around 1230, and it was redone in Baroque style in 1715. In 1945—after the Socialist Federal Republic of Yugoslavia came to power—the monastery complex was nationalized and closed. In 1952, city leaders decided to repurpose the space as an outdoor venue for the Ljubljana Summer Theatre (you'll still see the box office on this courtyard). Near the end of his life, Jože Plečnik drew up the designs for the theater, which turned out to be his last major work.

• *Exiting the Križanke, turn left and head a few more steps up to the top of the square, marked by the obelisk. This is...*

French Revolution Square (Trg Francoske Revolucije)

Plečnik designed the obelisk in the middle of the square to commemorate Napoleon's short-lived decision to make Ljubljana the capital of his Illyrian Provinces. It's rare to find anything honoring Napoleon outside of Paris, but he was good to Ljubljana. Under his rule, Slovenian culture flourished, the Slovene language became widely recognized and respected for the first time, schools were established, and roads and infrastructure were improved. The monument contains ashes of the unknown French soldiers who died in 1813, when the region went from French to Austrian control.

Detour to Jože Plečnik House: There's one more major Plečnik sight, and it's a big one: the house he lived in, now a museum. It's about a 10-minute walk away, and described later, under "More Sights in Ljubljana." If you're on a Plečnik roll, you can bail out of this walk and head there now: From the obelisk, turn left and walk down Emonska toward the twin-spired church. You'll pass (on the left) the delightful Krakovo district—a patch of green countryside in downtown Ljubljana. Many of the veggies you see in the riverside market come from these carefully tended gardens. When you reach the Gradaščica stream, head over the bridge (also designed by Plečnik) and go around the left side of the church to find the house.

• *To finish our walk and head back toward where we started, turn right at the obelisk (heading the way Napoleon is looking), and continue along the back of Plečnik's NUK. After one block, turn right down Turjaška and continue straight down Novi trg to the river. Turn left, pass the Cobblers' Bridge, and keep going (with the river on your right) for one more minute. When you reach the big staircase on your left (with the Gustav Mahler statue on the far side), head up it. At the top, you'll pass the highly recommended* **Romantica**—*with the best gelato in town.*

From the top of the stairs, bear right into the vast expanse of...

CONGRESS SQUARE (KONGRESNI TRG)

This grassy, tree-lined square hosts big events, from political rallies to music performances to celebrations. (When Slovenia defeated Serbia in the European basketball championship in 2017, this square was bedlam.) It's ringed by some of Ljubljana's most important buildings: the university headquarters, the Baroque Ursuline Church of the Holy Trinity, a classical mansion called the Kazina, and the Philharmonic Hall.

The green belt at the heart of the square, called Park Zvezda ("Star Park") for its radiating paths, is fronted by several inviting cafés and restaurants; the recommended **Zvezda Kavarna** is a top spot for its local cakes and ice cream.

Halfway up the square in the middle of the grassy section, the giant **anchor** celebrates the day in 1954 when Slovenia took possession of its tiny coastline, between Koper and Piran. (After World War I, even as the rest of what's now Slovenia joined Yugoslavia, that multicultural coastline became part of Italy.)

Just beyond that, notice the giant open space with two giant slabs, three trees, and six towering Slovenian flags. This is the **Monument to the Victims of All Wars,** erected in 2016, honoring—beyond generals and war heroes—the many lives lost to pointless conflict. The words along the base of the step are from 20th-century poet Oton Župančič: "One homeland is given to each one of us, and one life, and one death."

At the top end of the square, by the entry to a pedestrian underpass, a Roman sarcophagus sits under a gilded statue of a **Roman citizen**—a replica of a Roman tomb sculpture from 1,700 years ago, when this town was called Emona. The busy street above you has been the site of the main trading route through town since ancient Roman times. (Information boards tell you more.) More recently, this road has entered a new stage of evolution, as the main thoroughfare of a proudly green city: Most traffic has been banned from this city-center stretch, which is reserved only for buses and other authorized vehicles.

Take a few steps into the grubby underpass, and look left to find the easy-to-miss **Chopin Passage** (Chopinov Prehod), which displays exposed parts of the original Roman-era road and a model of Emona in ancient times.

• *Our walk ends where Ljubljana began. A variety of museums lie just west of Slovenska cesta (the big street at the end of this square), leading eventually to Tivoli Park. To visit these now, you can carry on under this underpass, pop out the other side, and turn to page 577.*

Otherwise, head toward the river to the bottom of Congress Square, turn left, and in about one minute you'll be back on Prešeren Square, where we began. Or, you could head to the water and nurse a coffee along Ljubljana's idyllic riverfront promenade.

More Sights in Ljubljana

Ljubljana is bursting with well-presented, we-try-harder museums celebrating Slovenian history and culture. These include the Slovenian History Exhibition at the castle, the City Museum of Ljubljana (described in my "Ljubljana Walk"), and the Contemporary History Museum in Tivoli Park. As these are similar and largely overlapping, if you get museumed out easily, just pick the one that's handiest to your sightseeing plan.

▲Ljubljana Castle (Ljubljanski Grad)

The castle above town offers enjoyable views over Ljubljana's rooftops, the surrounding countryside, and the Alps on the horizon.

There has probably been a settlement on this site since prehistoric times, though the first true fortress here was Roman. The 12th-century version was gradually added on to over the centuries, until it fell into disrepair in the 17th century. Today's castle—rebuilt in the 1940s and renovated in the 1970s—is a hollow-feeling replica, lacking any sense of real history. However, in recent years they've filled this shell with some worthwhile attractions and respectable restaurants. The castle is home to the Ljubljana Festival, with concerts throughout the summer (tel. 01/306-4293, www.ljubljanafestival.si).

Cost and Hours: The grounds are free to visit and open daily 9:00-23:00, shorter hours Oct-May. To enter the sights, you'll pay €10 (or €13 with the round-trip funicular) for the history exhibition, film, castle tower, and puppetry museum. The attractions are open daily 9:00-21:00, shorter hours Oct-May, tel. 01/232-9994, www.ljubljanskigrad.si.

Tours: For €2 extra, you can add either an audioguide or a guided tour—choose between the "Time Machine" tour (by guides dressed as historical figures) or the "Behind Bars" tour (with a medieval crime-and-punishment theme; tours depart from castle information center May-June 2/day, July-Sept 4/day, Oct-April 3/day Sat-Sun only). They also have an "Escape Castle" game, where you're set free to solve a series of puzzles around the castle grounds (add to any ticket for €2 extra).

Getting to the Castle: A slick **funicular** whisks visitors to the top in a jiff (€2.20 one-way, €4 round-trip, included in combo-tickets described earlier, runs every 10 minutes, 1-minute ride, runs during castle opening times noted above, catch it at Krekov trg—across the street from the main market-square TI). From the top, you'll find free WCs and a few easy flights of stairs up into the heart of the castle complex (or take the elevator). There are also two handy **trails** from town up to the castle. The steeper-but-faster route begins near the Dragon Bridge: Find Študentovska lane, facing the statue of Valentin Vodnik in the market. This lane dead-ends at a gravel path, which you'll follow up to a fork. Turn left to zigzag up the steepest and fastest route, which deposits you just below the castle wall; from here, turn left again and curl around the wall to reach the main drawbridge. Slower but a bit less steep is from a street called Reber, just off Stari trg, a few blocks south of the Town Hall: Walk up to the top of Reber, and, at the dead end, turn right and start climbing up the stairs. From here on out, keep bearing left, then go right when you're just under the castle (follow *Grad* signs).

Visiting the Castle: The castle's information office—where you can pick up your audioguide or meet a tour—is near the main gate (from the funicular, follow yellow *i* sign up the stairs). In the main castle courtyard, the sights cluster in two areas. The best sights are near the base of the tallest tower: The entrance to the history exhibit is to the left, while the "Virtual Castle" film, chapel, penitentiary, and tower climb are to the right. To the right of that is the rounded Erasmus Tower, with the Museum of Puppetry. The upper floors of the castle complex house two wedding halls—Ljubljana's most popular places to get married (free for locals).

The **Slovenian History Exhibition** offers a concise but engaging overview of this little country's story. As you enter, ask to borrow the free audioguide, then head downstairs and work your way up. Dark display cases light up when you approach, revealing artifacts, video clips, and touchscreens with more information. A unique feature of the museum is that you're invited to touch replicas of important historic items (in many cases, the originals are in other Ljubljana museums). Don't miss the top floor (go up the glassed-in staircase), which is the most interesting—covering the tumultuous 20th century. You'll learn about topics ranging from the battlefields of World War I, to the creation of Yugoslavia, to the fascist occupation and harrowing Italian-run concentration camps of World War II, to the cult of personality around Partisan war hero-turned-Yugoslav president Tito, to Slovenia's bid for independence.

Entering the door to the right of the tower, you'll first find the small **penitentiary** exhibit, recalling the post-Napoleonic era, when the castle was converted to a prison. It saw the most action during World War I, when it housed political prisoners (including the beloved Slovenian writer Ivan Cankar) and POWs. Modest

LJUBLJANA

exhibits inside actual former cells describe the history and list the names of past inmates.

If you head downstairs from the entrance, you'll find a Gothic **chapel** with Baroque paintings of St. George (Ljubljana's patron saint, the dragon-slayer) and coats of arms of the various aristocratic families that have called this castle home.

Heading up the stairs, you'll find the informative, entertaining, and nicely animated **"Virtual Castle" film,** in which Ljubljana's mascot dragon describes this hill's layers of history (12 minutes, plays on the half-hour; often in English, but otherwise borrow English headset).

Finally, climb the 92 spiral steps up to the **castle tower,** with one of the best views in town.

Don't miss the oddly fascinating **Museum of Puppetry** (ride up the elevator to the left as you face the round Erasmus Tower). This traces the history of puppetry as an art form, which flourished in the Modernist milieu of early-20th-century Ljubljana. You'll step into a surreal world of marionettes, shadow puppets, and other creations. This is not a goofy attraction for kids; in fact, some of the puppets are quite grotesque and disturbing. You'll see marionettes of Adolf Hitler and Partisan troops, watch grainy footage of famous puppet masters (including Milan Klemenčič, who pioneered the form here in 1910), then climb up to the mezzanine and put on a show of your own.

The castle also often has **temporary exhibits**—look for signs or ask at the information desk.

Eating: You can combine your visit to the castle with a meal at the recommended **$$$ Gostilna na Gradu,** with the best traditional Slovenian food in town, or the top-end **$$$$ Strelec** (both described later, under "Eating in Ljubljana"). **$ Gradska Kavana** ("Castle Café") serves only drinks and cakes, and **$ Gradska Vinoteka** ("Castle Winery") is a wine bar operated by Strelec.

▲▲Jože Plečnik House (Plečnikova Zbirka)

One of Ljubljana's most interesting sights is the house of the architect who redesigned much of the city. Today the house is decorated exactly as it was the day Plečnik died, containing much of his equipment, models, and plans. The house can be toured only with a guide, whose enthusiasm brings the place to life. Still furnished with unique, Plečnik-designed furniture, one-of-a-kind inventions, and favorite souvenirs from his travels, the

Jože Plečnik (1872-1957)

No other single architect has shaped one city as Jože Plečnik (YOH-zheh PLAYCH-neek) shaped Ljubljana. From libraries, cemeteries, and stadiums to riverside embankments and market halls, Plečnik left his mark everywhere.

Plečnik was born in Ljubljana to a cabinet maker. He dabbled as a self-trained architect, catching the eye of the great Secessionist architect Otto Wagner—who invited him to study in Vienna. Plečnik's first commissions, around the turn of the 20th century in Vienna, were pretty standard Art Nouveau. Then Tomáš Masaryk, president of the new nation of Czechoslovakia, decided that Prague Castle could use a new look by a Slavic architect. In 1921, Masaryk chose Jože Plečnik, who sprinkled the castle grounds with his distinctive touches. By now, Plečnik had perfected his simple, eye-pleasing style, which mixes modern and classical influences, with ample columns and pyramids—at once austere and playful.

By the time Plečnik finished in Prague, he had made a name for himself. His prime years were spent creating for the Kingdom of Yugoslavia (before the ideology-driven era of Tito). Plečnik returned home to Ljubljana and set to work redesigning the city, both as an architect and as an urban planner. He lived in a humble house (now a recommended museum) behind the Trnovo Church. On his daily walk to work, he pondered ways to make the city even more livable. As you wander through town, notice how thoughtfully he incorporated people, nature, the Slovenian heritage, town vistas, and symbolism into his works—it's feng shui on a grand urban scale.

For all of Plečnik's ideas that became reality, even more did not. After World War II, the very religious Plečnik fell out of favor with the communist government. (It's fun to imagine how this city might look if Plečnik had always gotten his way.) After his death in 1957, Plečnik was virtually forgotten by Slovenes and scholars alike.

But a 1986 exposition about Plečnik at Paris' Pompidou Center jump-started interest in the architect. Within a few years, Plečnik was back in vogue. Today, scholars laud him as a genius who was ahead of his time...while locals and tourists enjoy the elegant simplicity of his works.

LJUBLJANA

house paints an unusually intimate portrait of an artist. It's a ▲▲▲ pilgrimage for those who get caught up in Ljubljana's idiosyncratic sense of style.

Cost and Hours: €6, or €4 for just the modest museum and gardens, Tue-Sun 10:00-18:00—last tour departs at 17:00, closed Mon, 45-minute English tours begin at the top of each hour, Karunova 4, tel. 01/280-1604, www.mgml.si.

Getting Tickets: Tours are limited to seven people and can sell out, especially on summer weekends. Since you can only buy tickets in person (no reservations possible), it's smart to show up 15-20 minutes early at busy times.

Getting There: It's directly behind the twin steeples of the Trnovo Church, south of the town center. The 15-minute stroll from the center—the same one Plečnik took to work each day—is nearly as enjoyable as the house itself. You can either walk south along the river, then turn right onto Gradaška and stroll along the stream to the church; or, from French Revolution Square, head south on Emonska. If taking Emonska, you'll pass through the garden district of Krakovo, where pea patches and characteristic Old World buildings gracefully cohabitate.

Background: Ljubljana's favorite son lived here from 1921 until his death in 1957. He added on to an existing house, building a circular bedroom for himself and filling the place with bric-a-brac he designed, as well as artifacts, photos, and gifts from around the world that inspired him as he shaped Ljubljana. Living a simple, almost monastic lifestyle, Plečnik knew what he liked, and these tastes are mirrored in his home.

Visiting the House: While waiting for your tour to begin, explore the modest but engaging **museum,** offering biographical details about Plečnik along with his personal effects (such as notebooks, tools, and eyeglasses). Look for the small model of Ljubljana that locates the many structures he designed all around the city. You'll also see descriptions and photos of his greatest works, and large wooden models of two of his biggest "unrealized plans" that never made it off the drawing board: the cone-shaped "Cathedral of Freedom" and the roofed Butchers' Bridge at the market. One room features his redesign of Prague Castle, including a small model of his gardens and walkways. You can try sitting on chairs that Plečnik designed while you watch a video loop of short films about the architect.

The **tour** takes you through the actual rooms where Plečnik lived: kitchen, circular bedroom, sitting room, studio, and greenhouse. As you tour the place, appreciate the subtle details. Notice how reverently your guide (and other Slovenes) speaks of this man. Contrast the humbleness of Plečnik's home with the dynamic impact he had on the cityscape of Ljubljana and the cultural heritage of Slovenia. Wandering Plečnik's hallways, it's hard not to be tickled by this man's sheer creativity and by the unique world he forged for himself. As a visitor to his home, you're in good company. He invited only his closest friends here—except during World War II, when Ljubljana was occupied by Nazis and the university was closed, and Plečnik allowed his students to work with him here.

THE MUSEUM ZONE AND TIVOLI PARK

The west side of the river—beyond Prešeren Square and Congress Square—is the heart of modern Ljubljana, and home to several prominent squares and fine museums. These sights are listed roughly in order from Congress Square (described on my "Ljubljana Walk," earlier). The easiest way to get to this side of town is through the underpass (beneath Slovenska cesta) at the top of Congress Square. For the locations of these museums, see the "Ljubljana" map, earlier.

• *Emerging on the other side of the underpass, walk straight through the gap in the Maxi shopping center into the...*

▲Square of the Republic (Trg Republike)

This unusual plaza is ringed by an odd collection of buildings. While hardly quaint, the Square of the Republic gives you a good taste of a modern corner of Ljubljana. And it's historic—this is where Slovenia declared its independence in 1991.

The **twin office towers** (with the world's biggest digital watch, flashing the date, time, and temperature) were designed by Plečnik's protégé, Edvard Ravnikar. As harrowing as these structures seem, imagine if the builders had followed the original plans—the towers would be twice as tall as they are now and connected by a bridge, representing the gateway to Ljubljana. These buildings were originally designed as the Slovenian parliament, but they were scaled back when Tito didn't approve (since it would have made Slovenia's parliament bigger than the Yugoslav parliament in Belgrade).

Instead, the **Slovenian Parliament** is across the square, in the low-profile office building with the sculpted entryway. The carvings are in the Socialist Realist style, celebrating the noble Slovenian people conforming to communist ideals for the good of the entire society.

Completing the square are a huge conference center (Cankarjev Dom, the white building behind the skyscrapers), a shopping mall, and some public art.

• *Just a block north, across the street and through the grassy park (Trg Narodni Herojev), you'll find the...*

Slovenian National Museum (Narodni Muzej Slovenije) and Slovenian Museum of Natural History (Prirodoslovni Muzej Slovenije)

These two museums share a single historic building facing a park behind the Parliament. They're both average but worth considering if you have a special interest or if it's a rainy day.

The **National Museum** focuses on archaeological finds (their Metelkova branch—described later—features applied arts). On the ground floor are temporary exhibits and a lapidarium with carved-stone Roman monuments and exhibits on Egyptian mummies. Upstairs and to the right are more exhibits of the National Museum, with archaeological findings including the museum's two prized possessions: a fragment of a 45,000-year-old Neanderthal flute fashioned from a cave bear's femur—supposedly the world's oldest musical instrument; and the "figural situla," a beautifully decorated hammered-bronze bucket from the fifth century BC. Embossed with scenes of everyday Iron Age life, this object has been a gold mine of information for archaeologists.

Upstairs and to the left is the **Natural History** exhibit, featuring the flora and fauna of Slovenia. You'll see partial skeletons of a mammoth and a cave bear, plenty of stuffed reptiles, fish, and birds, and an exhibit on "human fish" (*Proteus anguinus*—long, skinny, pale-pink, sightless salamanders unique to caves in this part of Europe).

At the far end of the building is a glassed-in annex displaying Roman stone monuments (free).

Cost and Hours: €6 for National Museum, €4 for Natural History Museum, or €8.50 for both, some English descriptions, both open daily 10:00-18:00, Thu until 20:00 (National Museum open Thu until 22:00 June-Sept), Prešernova 20, tel. 01/241-4400, www.nms.si and www.pms-lj.si.

• *Turning left around the museum building and walking one block, you'll see the US Embassy. This pretty yellow chalet (with brown trim and a red roof, at Prešernova cesta 31) wins my vote for quaintest embassy building in the world. (Resist the urge to snap a photo...those guards are all business.) Just up Prešernova cesta from the embassy are two decent but skippable art museums.*

▲National Gallery (Narodna Galerija)

This fine museum presents a good, chronological exhibit of works by Slovenian and European artists, as well as temporary exhibits. While Slovenia doesn't have a particularly renowned artistic tradition, this well-presented collection nicely paints a picture of the nation's story and culture.

Cost and Hours: €7, more for special exhibits, permanent collection free first Sun of the month, open Tue-Sun 10:00-18:00, Thu until 20:00, closed Mon; two entrances: one at Cankarjeva 20 facing the National Museum, and another at the big glass box between two older buildings at Prešernova 24; tel. 01/241-5418, www.ng-slo.si.

Visiting the Museum: Enter through the main (historic) building. Downstairs is a skippable collection of medieval church art (carvings, altar paintings, and tapestries); upstairs are works from the 17th through 19th centuries. Spend some time with Marko Pernhart's Romantic views of the Slovenian countryside, including stunning panoramas of the Julian Alps (ringing the top of the stairwell).

Then you'll cross the modern skybridge (peeking down to see the original Fountain of Three Carniolan Rivers, from the Old Town's central square) to the 19th and 20th centuries. Find and savor the evocative portraits—bursting with personality—by Ivana Kobilca (1861-1926), a Slovenian painter working on the cusp of Impressionism. Art lovers enjoy her serene and lifelike *Summer* (1889-90), in which a young woman (Kobilca's self-portrait) plays with kids and flowers. Also look for pointillist works by Ivan Grohar (1867-1911), who painted Slovenian landscapes with a dash of Van Gogh and a dab of Seurat. You may also spot a few canvases by Vlaho Bukovac, the Dalmatian painter familiar to anyone who's visited Cavtat (see page 351).

On your way out, stop by the small room near the Cankarjeva entrance that displays small, faded, abstracted works by another beloved Slovenian artist, Zoran Mušič (1909-2005). His art focuses on a few key subjects: horses, mountainscapes, and still lifes. While his works can be challenging to appreciate, Mušič had a fascinating life: As a child, he was evacuated during World War I because of fighting along the Soča Front. As an adult, he was arrested by Nazis as a political dissident and imprisoned at Dachau Concentration Camp (1944-1945). And later in life, a turpentine allergy forced him to turn to media other than oil paints. Even so, he achieved notoriety outside of Slovenia, becoming widely respected in French and Italian art circles.

Museum of Modern Art (Moderna Galerija Ljubljana)

This museum has a permanent collection of modern and contemporary Slovenian artists, as well as temporary exhibits by both homegrown and international artists. To explore the "Continuities and Ruptures" permanent collection (aptly named for a place with such a fractured, up-and-down history), borrow the English floor plan and take a chronological spin through the 20th century. Unusual for a "modern" art museum is the room with Partisan art, with stiff, improvised, communist-style posters from the days when Tito and his crew were just a ragtag militia movement.

Cost and Hours: €5, ask about combo-ticket with contemporary branch at Metelkova—see page 584, Tue-Sun 10:00-18:00, Thu until 20:00 July-Aug, closed Mon, Cankarjeva 15, tel. 01/241-6800, www.mg-lj.si.

• *By the busy road near the art museums, look for the distinctive Neo-Byzantine design (tall domes with narrow slits) of the...*

▲▲Serbian Orthodox Church of Sts. Cyril and Methodius

Ljubljana's most striking church interior isn't Catholic, but Orthodox. This church was built in 1936, soon after the Slovenes joined a political union with the Serbs.

Wealthy Slovenia attracted its poorer neighbors from the south—so it built this church for that community. Since 1991, the Serb population has continued to grow, as people from the struggling corners of the former Yugoslavia flock to prosperous Slovenia. Its gorgeous interior—which feels closer to Moscow than to Rome—offers visitors a taste of this important faith.

Cost and Hours: Free, daily 8:00-19:00; divine liturgy Sun at 9:00, other days services at 8:30 and 18:00; Prešernova cesta 35, www.spc-ljubljana.si.

Visiting the Church: Step inside for the best glimpse of the Orthodox faith this side of Dubrovnik. The church is colorfully decorated without a hint of the 21st century, mirroring a very conservative religion. Much of the church's art consists of copies of famous frescoes that decorate medieval Serbian Orthodox monasteries throughout the Balkans. On the balcony (at the back of the nave), you'll see Cyrillic script that explains the history of the church. Notice that there are no pews, because worshippers stand throughout the service. On the left, find the little room with tubs of water, where the faithful light tall, skinny candles (purchased at the little window in the back corner). At the front of the church, the painted wooden screen, or iconostasis, is believed to separate our material world from the spiritual realm behind it. Ponder the fact that several centuries ago, before the Catholic Church began to adapt to a changing world, all Christians worshipped this way. For more on the Orthodox faith, see the sidebar on page 317.

• *On the other side of the busy street is...*

Tivoli Park (Park Tivoli)

This huge park, just west of the center, is where Slovenes relax on summer weekends. The easiest access is through the underpass from Cankarjeva cesta (between the Serbian Orthodox Church and the Museum of Modern Art). As you emerge, the Neoclassical pillars leading down the promenade make it clear that this part of the park was designed by Jože Plečnik. Along this "main boulevard" of the park, various changing photographic exhibitions are displayed.

• *Aside from taking a leisurely stroll, the best thing to do in the park is visit the...*

▲Contemporary History Museum (Muzej Novejše Zgodovine)

In a Baroque mansion (Cekinov Grad) in Tivoli Park, a well-done exhibit called "Slovenians in the 20th Century" traces the country's most eventful hundred years—from World War I, through the Yugoslav period, to independence in 1991 and EU membership today. Out front is a yellow Zastava car, which were ubiquitous during the Yugoslav years. Inside, the ground floor displays temporary exhibits, and upstairs you'll find several rooms using models, dioramas, light-and-sound effects, and English explanations to creatively tell the story of one of Europe's youngest nations. While it's a little difficult to fully appreciate, the creativity and the spunky spirit of the place are truly enjoyable.

Cost and Hours: €5, permanent exhibit free first Sun of the month, Tue-Sun 10:00-18:00, Thu until 20:00 June-Aug, closed Mon, guidebook-€5, in Tivoli Park at Celovška cesta 23, tel. 01/300-9610, www.muzej-nz.si.

Getting There: The museum is a 20-minute walk from the center, best combined with a wander through Tivoli Park. The fastest approach: As you emerge from the Cankarjeva cesta underpass into the park, climb up the stairs, then turn right and go straight ahead for five minutes. You'll continue up the ramp, then turn left after the tennis courts and look for the big pink-and-white mansion on the hill.

Visiting the Museum: The exhibit begins at the dawn of the 20th century, during Slovenia's waning days as part of the Austro-Hungarian Empire. Spiral stairs lead up to more exhibits about World War I. Back on the main floor, you'll walk through a simu-

LJUBLJANA

lated trench from the Soča Front, then learn about the creation of the post-World War I Kingdom of Serbs, Croats, and Slovenes (or, as this exhibit pointedly puts it, "Kingdom of Slovenes, Croats, and Serbs"). During this time, some of what had historically been Slovenian became part of Italy.

Your footfalls echo loudly as you enter the room describing Slovenia's WWII experience. You'll learn how during that war, Slovenia was divided between neighboring fascist powers Germany, Italy, and Hungary. Each one tried (but failed) to exert linguistic and cultural control over the people, hoping to eradicate the Slovenian national identity. Video screens show subtitled interviews with people who lived through those war years.

Passing through the ballroom, you reach the "Slovenia 1946-1960" exhibit, outlining both the good (modernization) and the bad (prison camps and secret police) of the early Tito years. Despite his ruthless early rule, Tito remains popular here; under his stern bust, page through the photo album of Tito's visits to Slovenia. Find the display of the country's former currencies. Examining the Yugoslav dinar, notice that the figureheads on that communist currency were generic, idealized workers, farmers, and other members of the proletariat...except for a few notable individuals (including Tito). Meanwhile, Slovenia's short-lived post-Yugoslav currency, the *tolar* (1991-2006, R.I.P.), featured artists and scientists rather than heads of state and generals.

The most evocative room (1991-2008) has artifacts from the Slovenes' brave declaration of independence from a hostile Yugoslavia in 1991. The well-organized Slovenes had only to weather a 10-day skirmish to gain their freedom. It's chilling to think that at one point, bombers were en route to level this gorgeous city. The planes were called back at the last minute by a Yugoslav People's Army officer with allegiances to Slovenia.

Nearby: As you exit, the giant, modern, blocky, light-blue building across the busy road is the **Pivovarna Union**—the brewery for Ljubljana's favorite industrial-produced beer, with a brewpub and the option of a brewery tour (www.union-experience.si).
• *On your way back to the center, you could stop by...*

▲The Skyscraper (Nebotičnik)

This 1933 building was the first skyscraper in Slovenia, for a time the tallest building in Central Europe, and one of the earliest European buildings that was clearly influenced by American architecture. Art Deco inside and out, it's a thrill for architecture fans and anyone who enjoys a great view—the top floor, which hosts a restaurant, café, and observation deck, offers the best panorama of Ljubljana's skyline. Zip up in the elevator just to take a peek, or stay for a drink or meal.

There are three levels: The best is floor #12, with a **$ café** where you can sit outside (or, in bad weather, head up the spiral stairs to the glassed-in terrace) and enjoy a drink or a light meal with unobstructed views over the city and castle. One floor below (#11) is the indoor club/lounge, with a similar menu. And on the next floor down (#10) is the **$$ restaurant,** with a full menu and less-impressive views. Good-value lunch deals are available in either place. I'd skip the restaurant and the club, and just grab a drink or snack up on the terrace.

Cost and Hours: Free to ride the elevator up for a peek, but you should buy at least a drink if you want to stick around; terrace and club open daily 9:00-late; restaurant open Mon-Sat 12:00-16:00 & 18:00-22:00, closed Sun; 2 blocks from Prešeren Square at Štefanova 1, tel. 040-601-787, www.neboticnik.si.

METELKOVA

Three museums face each other on a slick modern plaza next to the park called Tabor, about a 15-minute walk northeast of Prešeren Square in the dull but up-and-coming district of Metelkova. Nearby, you can explore the funky squatters' colony of Metelkova City (with Ljubljana's famous prison-turned-youth hostel). For locations, see the "Ljubljana" map, earlier.

▲▲Slovenian Ethnographic Museum (Slovenski Etnografski Muzej)

Housed in a state-of-the-art facility, this delightful museum is Ljubljana's most underrated attraction. With both permanent and temporary exhibits, the museum strives to explain what it is to be Slovene, with well-presented and well-described cultural artifacts from around the country. If you've caught the Slovenian folk-culture itch, this is the place to scratch it.

Cost and Hours: €6, free first Sun of month, Tue-Sun 10:00-18:00, closed Mon, great café, Metelkova 2, tel. 01/300-8745, www.etno-muzej.si.

Visiting the Museum: The ground and first floors have good temporary exhibits, while upstairs you'll find two permanent exhibits. (A third, much smaller permanent exhibit on the first floor displays old equipment for making gingerbread and candles, but has very little English.)

The best exhibit, filling the third floor, is called **"Between Nature and Culture."** As you exit the elevator, turn left and find the shrunken head, which comes with a refreshingly frank exhibit that acknowledges the shortsighted tendency for museum curators—including at this museum—to emphasize things that are foreign or different. Continue through "Reflections of Distant Worlds" (non-European cultures) to reach the core of the collection, which focuses on Slovenia. A good but slow-moving film visits the country's four major regions. Another exhibit ponders how people half a world away—in Slovenia and in North America—simultaneously invented a similar solution (snowshoes) for a common problem. One display deconstructs Slovenian clichés (including this country's odd fascination with its traditional hayracks). The arrangement of the collection emphasizes the evolution of an increasingly complicated civilization, from basic farming tools to ceramics to modern technology. You'll see exhibits on traditional Slovenian beekeeping, blacksmithing, weaving, shoemaking, costumes and customs, pottery, furniture, and religious objects. The children's "Ethnoalphabet" area features an A-to-Ž array of engaging, hands-on activities.

The other permanent exhibit, on the second floor (from the elevator, turn left to find the entrance), is called **"I, We, and Others."** A bit too conceptual for its own good, this heady exhibit ponders the notion of belonging. Designed for Slovenes more than foreigners (with very limited posted English information), it explores various aspects of how people define who they are, from individual and family to community and nation. Videos and sounds enhance the exhibits, and the curators neatly juxtapose well-known icons from different cultures (such as various national parliament buildings) in thought-provoking ways. While it's easy to get lost amid the navel-gazing, there is something particularly poignant about this topic here in the identity-obsessed Balkans.

Slovenian National Museum-Metelkova (Narodni Muzej Slovenije)

Next door to the Ethnographic Museum is this facility, where items (mostly applied arts) from the Slovenian National Museum that were formerly tucked away in storage are now displayed on two floors. The very pretty historical bric-a-brac is neatly presented without much context—it's just an excuse to get a bunch of interesting stuff out into public view. Each room has a different collection: furniture, pottery and ceramics, church vestments, weapons and armor, and more. The painting gallery is nicely organized by century and style. The museum also features temporary exhibits. Everything's labeled in English.

Cost and Hours: €6, Tue-Sun 10:00-18:00, closed Mon, Maistrova 1, tel. 01/230-7032.

Museum of Contemporary Art-Metelkova (Muzej Sodobne Umetnosti Metelkova, MSUM)

This cutting-edge branch of the Museum of Modern Art showcases changing exhibitions of present-day, mostly Slovenian and Eastern European artists. The modern space is at once sleek and playful, making this museum worth a visit for art lovers who appreciate works from the 1960s to the present.

Cost and Hours: €5, ask about combo-ticket with Museum of Modern Art, Tue-Sun 10:00-18:00, closed Mon, Maistrova 3, tel. 01/241-6825, www.mg-lj.si.

Metelkova City (Metelkova Mesto)

The heart of Slovenia's counterculture, this former military installation is now a funky, graffiti-slathered squatter's colony, billed as an "autonomous cultural center." Built by the Habsburgs in the 1880s, the complex—with barracks, warehouses, and a prison—was used by a laundry list of later occupiers, from Italian fascists to Nazis to the Yugoslav People's Army. After Yugoslavia pulled its troops out of Slovenia (following the Ten-Day War), the cluster of buildings sat derelict and abandoned. In 1993, transient artists moved in and set up galleries, theaters, bars, and nightclubs. While controversial at first, Meltelkova City has gradually become accepted by most Ljubljanans, and the city (which owns the property) not only tolerates but actively encourages this hotbed of youthful artistic expression. While edgy, this place is fascinating to explore and a great spot to ogle street art—it's sleepy by day and lively by night (www.metelkovamesto.org).

Anchoring the area is **Hostel Celica,** one of Europe's most notable youth hostels, which fills a former prison building. Twenty artists were invited to decorate cells that have been turned into accommodations, and the ground floor features vibrant public spaces, a good and affordable restaurant (a nice place for a lunch or a light dinner), and a shoes-off "Oriental café." You can drop by to see the building anytime, and ask to borrow a flashlight to explore the dank and gloomy basement solitary confinement cells, with a small but interesting exhibition on the history of the building (and the various prisoners who have called it home—including Janez Janša, who did time here during communism and later became Slovenia's prime minister). But if you visit, try to go at 14:00 for a free guided tour of the complex (tours run daily; you can also try calling to arrange a tour at other times, tel. 01/230-9700, www.hostelcelica.com).

Shopping in Ljubljana

Ljubljana, with its easygoing ambience and countless boutiques, is made to order for whiling away an afternoon shopping. It's also a fun place to stock up on souvenirs. Popular items include wood carvings and models (especially of the characteristic hayracks that dot the countryside), different flavors of schnapps (the kind with a whole pear inside—cultivated to actually grow right into the bottle—is a particularly fun gift), honey mead brandy (*medica*—sweet and smooth), bars of soap wrapped in wool (good for exfoliating), and those adorable painted panels from beehives (described on page 634). Rounding out the list of traditional Slovenian items are wrought-iron products from Kropa, crystal from Rogaska, lace from Idrija, and salt from Piran. The following neighborhoods are ideal places to browse.

AT CIRIL-METODOV TRG AND NEAR THE MARKET

The most atmospheric trinket-shopping is in the first stretch of the **market colonnade**, along the riverfront next to the Triple Bridge. See the "Ljubljana Hotels & Restaurants" map for locations.

If you're looking for serious handicrafts rather than trinkets, drop by the **Rustika** gallery, just over the Triple Bridge (on the castle side). In addition to beehive panels, they also have lace, painted chests and boxes, and other tasteful, local mementos (daily 9:00-20:00, Stritarjeva 9, mobile 031-459-509). A bigger but more downscale souvenir shop is **Dom Trgovina,** across from the TI on the main market square (Mon-Sat 9:00-21:00, Sun 10:00-20:30, Ciril-Metodov trg 5).

Kraševka sells high-quality artisanal products (mostly edible) from the Karst region, and also acts as a sort of information office for that area (Mon-Fri 9:00-19:00, Sat until 15:00, closed Sun, Vodnikov trg 4, tel. 01/232-1445).

Trgovina Ika, a small artisan boutique with its own hip and idiosyncratic sense of style, is a delightful place to browse for truly authentic Slovenian stuff that goes beyond souvenirs. Its unique items by local designers—jewelry, hats, scarves, shoes, and so on—are modern and fashionable (Mon-Fri 10:00-19:30, Sat 9:00-20:00, Sun 10:00-20:00, Ciril-Metodov trg 13, tel. 01/123-21743).

IN THE OLD TOWN

Ljubljana's main Old Town street—which changes names from Mestni trg to Stari trg, then Gornji trg—is also lined with several characteristic shops, selling a few of the unique gift items produced in this proud little country. Unless otherwise noted, all of these shops are open long hours on weekdays (often until 20:00); most close a bit earlier on Saturdays (around 17:00), and close in the early afternoon on Sundays (usually by 13:00 or 14:00).

This area is covered in my "Ljubljana Walk," earlier; see the "Ljubljana Center" map for locations. Make a point to seek out these goodies: honey (**Honey House,** Mestni trg 7); sea salt from Slovenia's tiny coastline (**Piranske Soline,** Mestni trg 8); hand-made lace from Idrija (**Galerija Idrijske Čipke,** at Mestni trg 17);

and brandies and handicrafts from the Dolenje region (**Dobrote Dolenjske,** also at Mestni trg 17).

Chocolate Shops: Three tempting, high-end (yet still afford-able) *čokoladnice* are within about a five-minute walk of each other, along Ljubljana's Old Town main drag. **Čokoladnica Cukrček** is the grande dame of this scene, best known for its foil-wrapped "Prešeren Balls" chocolates—a clever and civic-minded take on Salzburg's "Mozart Balls," replacing the composer with Slovenia's greatest poet (Ciril-Metodov trg, www.cukrcek.si). **La Chocolate** is slightly less expensive and feels a bit more modern (Mestni trg 8, www.lachocolate.si). And **Čokoladnica Ljubljana** attempts to compete with dragon-themed chocolates (Mestni trg 11, www. cokoladnica-lj.si).

Sleeping in Ljubljana

Ljubljana has good accommodations in all price ranges. I've fo-cused my listings in or within easy walking distance of the city center. To get the best value, book ahead and book directly with the hotel. The most expensive hotels raise their prices even more during conventions (Sept-Oct, and sometimes also June).

$$$$ Lesar Hotel Angel, on a cobbled square in the Old Town, feels plush and high-end. Its 15 rooms have crisp white decor, and the private garden is inviting (air-con, lots of stairs with no elevator, pay parking, Gornji trg 7, tel. 01/425-5089, www. angelhotel.si, info@angelhotel.si).

$$$$ Vander Urbani Resort is a novel concept: Nestled cen-tral as can be just off the in-love-with-life riverfront embankment, it really does feel like an intensely hip resort in the city center—right down to the minuscule rooftop swimming pool and sundeck. The hotel prides itself on the cutting-edge urban design of its 20 rooms—with lots of plain concrete—and tries to use Slovenian and organic products wherever possible (air-con, elevator, café, restau-rant, champagne bar, Krojaška ulica 6, tel. 01/200-9000, www. vanderhotel.com, info@vanderhotel.com).

$$$$ Cubo Hotel is a jolt of trendy minimalism on Lju-bljana's hotel scene. Its 26 large rooms are the best place in town for sleek, urban elegance. Choose between streetside rooms, which enjoy castle views but get some traffic noise, or quieter courtyard rooms (air-con, elevator, Slovenska cesta 15, tel. 01/425-6000, www.hotelcubo.com, reception@hotelcubo.com).

$$$ Hotel Mrak has 34 small but well-equipped rooms in a pleasant neighborhood near French Revolution Square. This trusty place—recently updated, with stylish business-class rooms—is my sentimental favorite in Ljubljana (RS%, air-con, elevator, restau-rant with terrace under "the oldest vine in Slovenia," pay parking,

Ljubljana Hotels & Restaurants

To Contemporary History Museum

Tivoli Park

SERBIAN ORTHODOX CHURCH

NATIONAL GALLERY

MODERN ART MUSEUM

NATIONAL THEATER

US EMBASSY

SLOVENIAN NATIONAL MUSEUM & NATURAL HISTORY MUSEUM

Trg Narodni Herojev

PARLIAMENT

Square of the Republic

LJUBLJANSKA BANKA

GOSPOSVETSKA CESTA

Ajdovscina Park

Miklošičev Park

THE SKYSCRAPER

GRAND HOTEL UNION

FRANCISCAN CHURCH

Prešeren Square

POST

MEM. TO THE VICTIMS OF ALL WARS

TRIPLE BRIDGE

Ribji Square

BRY BRIDGE

Congress Square

OLD

COBBLERS' BRIDGE

UNIVERSITY

FOUNTAIN

Novi Trg

NATIONAL & UNIVERSITY LIBRARY

French Revolution Square

CITY MUSEUM

Courtyard

N.U.K. #2

ROMAN CITY WALL

ST. JAMES BRIDGE

FOOTBRIDGE

KRAKOVO

PLEČNIK HOUSE

River

Ljubljanica

Accommodations

1 Lesar Hotel Angel
2 Vander Urbani Resort
3 Cubo Hotel
4 Hotel Mrak
5 Adora Hotel
6 Slamič B&B
7 Meščanka Rooms
8 Barbo Palace
9 Hotel Emonec
10 B&B Petra Varl
11 Penzion Pod Lipo
12 Hostel Celica

LJUBLJANA

Rimska 4, tel. 01/421-9650, www.hotelmrak.si, info@hotelmrak. si, Kuharič family).

$$$ Adora Hotel, tucked behind a church at the edge of the cobbled Old Town zone, has 10 rooms with a restrained rustic style. They also rent five apartments in the passage that runs over the busy street, which come with some noise (air-con, elevator, free loaner bikes, pay parking, Rožna ulica 7, mobile 082-057-240, www.adorahotel.si, info@adorahotel.si).

$$$ Slamič B&B has 17 modern rooms with hardwood floors, tasteful decor, and absentee management. It's over an appealing upscale café in a nondescript but central neighborhood (air-con, pay parking, reception open daily 7:30-23:00, Kersnikova 1, tel. 01/433-8233, www.slamic.si, info@slamic.si).

$$ Meščanka ("City Woman") rents seven cozy, well-equipped rooms and apartments in a fantastic location right along the bustling riverfront promenade. The decor is mod, funky, and colorful, and the good windows work hard to provide silence (breakfast extra at next-door restaurant, air-con, reception open 10:00-12:00 & 14:00-19:00—let them know if you're coming outside that time, Ključavničarska 4, mobile 051-880-044, www. mescanka.si, info@mescanka.si, Saša).

$$ Barbo Palace, in an excellent location a few steps from Congress Square and the river, is the best bet in town for a touch of history. Its 12 apartments and six rooms—all refurbished and very spacious—fill an antique building around a classic Old World atrium courtyard. With parquet floors and antique furnishings, but modern bathrooms and other amenities, this place offers the best of old and new (no breakfast but kitchenettes in the apartments, air-con, elevator, reception open 8:00-20:00—call ahead if arriving later, Gosposka 1, mobile 070-322-822, www.barbopalace.si, info@barbopalace.si).

$$ Hotel Emonec (eh-MOH-nets), with some of the most centrally located cheap beds in Ljubljana, hides just off Wolfova lane between Prešeren and Congress squares. Its 54 rooms—in three buildings across a courtyard from each other—feel like a cookie-cutter chain hotel, with tight bathrooms and a shoestring staff. But the price and ideal location make it worth considering (family rooms, air-con, self-service laundry, Wolfova 12, tel. 01/200-1520, www.hotel-emonec.com, hotelemonec@siol.net).

$ B&B Petra Varl offers five comfortable, affordable, nicely appointed rooms on a courtyard across from the bustling riverside market. As this place is Ljubljana's top budget option, book early (includes kitchenette with basic do-it-yourself breakfast, air-con, go into courtyard at Vodnikov trg 5 and look for *B&B* sign at 5A, mobile 031-851-842, bb@varl.si).

$ Penzion Pod Lipo has 10 rooms above a restaurant about a

12-minute walk from Prešeren Square. While the rooms are dated and simple, the place is affordable and thoughtfully run by jolly Marjan (breakfast extra, family room, sometimes unstaffed—let them know when you'll arrive, air-con, guest kitchen, putting green on terrace, Borstnikov trg 3, tel. 01/251-1683, mobile 031-809-893, www.penzion-podlipo.com, info@penzion-podlipo.com).

¢ **Hostel Celica,** a proud, innovative, and lively place, is owned by the city and run by a nonprofit student organization.

This former military prison's 20 cells *(celica)* have been converted into hostel rooms—each one unique and decorated by a different designer (free tours of the hostel daily at 14:00). The building also houses an art gallery, tourist information, self-service laundry, and a variety of eateries. For more on the history of this site, see the Metelkova section in "More Sights in Ljubljana" (private rooms available, offers active excursions around Slovenia, Metelkova 8, a dull 15-minute walk to Prešeren Square, 8 minutes to the train station, tel. 01/230-9700, www.hostelcelica.com, info@hostelcelica.com). The hostel hosts live-music events one night a week until around 24:00, but otherwise maintains "quiet time" after 23:00. However, the surrounding neighborhood—a bit run-down and remote, but safe—is a happening nightlife zone, which can make for noisy weekends.

Eating in Ljubljana

At this crossroads of cultures (and cuisines), Italian and French flavors are just as "local" as meat-and-starch Slovenian food. This cosmopolitan city also dabbles in other cuisines; you'll find Thai, Indian, Chinese, Mexican, and much more. Most places seem to offer a similar menu of Slovenian/Mediterranean fare with international flourishes. I've ranked these eateries from $ budget to $$$$ splurge. For more advice on eating in Slovenia, including ordering and tipping, see the "Eating" section of the Practicalities chapter. To locate these restaurants, see the "Ljubljana Hotels & Restaurants" map.

Lunch Deals: To stretch your budget, have your main meal at lunch, when most of Ljubljana's top eateries serve high-quality three-course meals (starter, main, dessert) at a very affordable price—usually around €10-12, not including drinks. You won't have much choice (they may only have one or two options each day), but the quality is high and the value is outstanding. I've noted "lunch special" where applicable. Some places offer these deals only on weekdays. After a big lunch, I'd recommend a light dinner—picnic, *burek*, pizza, sandwich...or just gelato.

Traditional Slovenian Food: Because Slovenes head into the countryside when they want traditional fare, Ljubljana isn't the best place to find authentic Slovenian grub. But if you'd like to try some, your best budget bets are **Klobasarna** or **Moji Štruklji Slovenije;** for a more formal sit-down meal, head for **Gostilna na Gradu** at the castle. Other places feature "regional" cuisines, such as Pannonian, from northeast Slovenia **(Güjžina),** or Istrian, from the Adriatic coast **(Altrokè).**

IN THE CITY CENTER

$$$$ Monstera Bistro is a magnet for foodies seeking top-quality, seasonal, international fare and an enticing wine list in a tight, cozy dining room. Owner/chef Bine Volčič, who prides himself on sustainability, is distinguishing himself as one of Slovenia's top chefs. The bistro is open most days for a more affordable lunch (Mon-Sat 11:30-16:00), and weekends only for a pricier, fixed-price dinner (Thu-Sat 19:00-23:00). Either way, the prices are a bargain for the quality, and it's essential to reserve—ideally several days ahead (Gosposka 9, tel. 040/431-123, www.monsterabistro.si).

$$$$ Gostilna As ("Ace"), tucked into a courtyard just off Prešeren Square, is a venerable mainstay that pleases fish lovers. It's dressy, pricey, and pretentious, with deliberate service. The dining room is old-fashioned and a bit stuffy, but in good weather, their rooftop terrace is gorgeous (mostly fish and Italian dishes, daily 12:00-24:00, reservations smart, Čopova 5A, or enter courtyard with *As* sign near relief of Julija on Wolfova, tel. 01/425-8822, www.gostilnaas.si). For cheaper food and drinks from the same kitchen, eat at the attached **$$$ As Aperitivo,** a much livelier and more casual spot. You'll sit in the leafy courtyard or the winter garden, with big windows that stay open in the summer (salads, sandwiches, pastas, and main courses, food served daily 12:00-24:00, longer hours for drinks, good gelato counter inside). The courtyard also has a couple of other fun eateries—and, in the summer, live music.

$ Ribca ("Fish") hides under the first stretch of market colonnade near the Triple Bridge. This is your best bet for a relatively quick and cheap riverside lunch. Choose between the two straight-

Ljubljana's "Open Kitchen" Friday Street-Food Festival

Ljubljana has one of the most appealing street-food markets anywhere: the Open Kitchen (Odprta Kuhna), which takes place on Fridays (in good weather) from spring through fall.

The event fills the first market square below the cathedral (across the Triple Bridge from Prešeren Square) with stalls fea-

turing noshes by Slovenian chefs. Only brick-and-mortar restaurants can have a stall, and they must create a street-food-type dish (or several). There's a dizzying and delicious variety of high-quality creations. You'll find delicately composed dishes from top-name, internationally recognized chefs; to giant, gut-busting portions of hearty Slovenian grub; to a wide variety of global cuisines (including Indian, Chinese, Iranian, South American, Thai, and so on). It's a melting pot of culinary Slovenia, all within a short walk.

While the specific lineup can change, on a recent visit I saw vegan burgers, huge simmering pans of paella, Argentinian steaks, ribs and pulled pork, Belgian waffles, poke bowls, hearty sausages and *čevapčiči* (a kebab-like grilled meat), delicate macarons, and an entire roast pig on a spit. Most places have big plates for around €6-8; you'll run out of stomach space well before you run out of money. Happy eaters fill long, shared tables in the shade of the cathedral, or sit on the nearby steps (at little tables). Mellow music plays, and everyone has a great time.

For the people of Ljubljana, the Open Kitchen is both a culinary event and a social one. Visiting foodies make it a priority. The festival's massive success has put it in the global spotlight and has expanded to "popup" events in other cities around Slovenia—check the website for details (festival runs mid-March-late Oct Fri 10:00-22:00; can be cancelled when it rains; at Pogačarjev trg, www.odprtakuhna.si).

forward menus: grilled fillets or fried small fish. They also serve fish-topped pizzas. With the fragrant fish market right next door, you know it's fresh. If you just want to enjoy sitting along the river below the bustling market, this is also a fine spot for a coffee or beer (Mon 8:00-16:00, Tue-Sat 8:00-21:00, Sun 11:30-18:00, tel. 01/425-1544).

Fast and Cheap

$ Klobasarna is a budget foodie option specializing in *kranjska klobasa*—traditional Carniolan sausage, from the Slovenian uplands. The menu is simple—one wiener or two, extra for seasonal soup—and delicious. The soups are hearty and filling, often either *jota* (turnip stew) or *ričet* (barley stew). They also serve the Slovenian dumplings called *štruklji* (Mon-Sat 10:00-23:00, Sun until 15:00, Ciril-Metodov trg 15, mobile 051-605-017).

$ Moji Štruklji Slovenije ("My Slovenian Dumplings"), the second store in the market colonnade after Ribca, is an ideal spot to sample the traditional Slovenian rolled dumplings called *štruklji*. They have over 20 varieties, both sweet and savory, which are fun to peruse in the display case. The interior seating is tight, so grab an outdoor table tucked under Plečnik's colonnade. Next door, they also have a counter selling hearty Slovenian stews and soups (Mon-Thu and Sat 7:00-20:00, Fri until 22:00, Sun 10:00-16:00, Adamič-Lundrovo nabrežje 1, mobile 059-042-190).

$ Hood Burger, part of a locally beloved chain, is Slovenia's answer to In-N-Out. The owners pride themselves on using locally sourced ingredients ("100 percent Slovenian beef!"), and cultivate a personal relationship with their producers. The result is tasty, authentic burgers (daily 11:00-24:00, handiest location is just off Prešeren Square at Nazorjeva 4).

$ Kavarna NUK, in the basement of Jože Plečnik's masterpiece library building, is a central and affordable place for a good meal. While designed mostly for students—with low prices (hearty meals for €5)—it's open to the public. Entering NUK, immediately turn left and head down to the basement to find the café. Order at the counter, then find a table in the harmonious Plečnik-designed corridor. The short but good menu includes big salads (with a salad bar), pastas, and more (Mon-Fri 8:00-20:00, Sat 9:00-18:00, closed Sun, Turjaška ulica 1, tel. 01/320-6066).

$ Paninoteka, with wonderful outdoor seating overlooking Cobblers' Bridge and fine indoor seating, has affordable and tasty sandwiches; their full menu is good, but more expensive (daily 9:00-22:00, Jurčičev trg 3, mobile 040-349-329).

Pizzerias: $ Pizzeria Foculus, tucked in a boring alleyway a few blocks up from the river, has a loyal local following, a happening atmosphere, an inviting interior, a few outdoor tables, and Ljubljana's best pizza (over 50 types, daily 11:00-24:00, just off French Revolution Square across the street from Plečnik's National and University Library at Gregorčičeva 3, tel. 01/251-5643). **$ Ljubljanski Dvor** enjoys the most convenient and scenic location of any pizzeria in town. On a sunny summer day, the outdoor riverside terrace is unbeatable; I'd skip the dull interior and the pricier pasta restaurant higher up (Mon-Sat 10:00-24:00, Sun from 12:00,

50 yards from Cobblers' Bridge at Dvorni trg 1, tel. 01/251-6555). Ljubljanski Dvor also has a handy **$ takeout window** (go around back to the walk-up window on Congress Square). Enjoy a cheap slice at one of their outdoor tables facing Congress Square, or get it to go and munch it along the river.

In the Old Town

The main drag through the Old Town (which starts at the Town Hall and changes names as it goes: Mestni trg, then Stari trg, then Gornji trg) is lined with inviting eateries. Tables clutter the cobbled pedestrian street. If you're at a loss for where to eat in town, stroll here to survey your options, then pick your favorite menu and ambience. As many restaurants along here are uniformly good, no one place really has the edge.

Several popular options cluster in one particularly atmospheric stretch; all except Romeo offer a similar menu of Mediterranean-Slovenian cuisine and wonderful outdoor seating: **$$$$ Valvas'or,** the upscale option, has a dressy dining room and a posh gold color scheme (weekday lunch deal, Mon-Sat 12:00-23:00, closed Sun, Stari trg 7, tel. 01/425-0455). **$$$ Julija** features homey country-Slovenian decor inside (lunch deals, daily 12:00-22:00, Stari trg 9, tel. 01/425-6463). **$ Romeo,** across the street, is a lowbrow bar serving unexceptional Mexican food...but the name sure is clever (get it? "Romeo and Julija"). And **$$ Marley & Me** comes with a warm welcome from Matej (weekday lunch specials, daily 11:00-23:00, Stari trg 9, tel. 08/380-6610). I've also enjoyed a great salad lunch at the nearby **$ Čajna Hiša** teahouse (described later, under "Drinks and Treats.") Additional options are just a few steps away:

$$$ Güjžina highlights food and wine from the Hungarian-influenced region of Slovenia called Prekmurje. The tight but cozy dining room offers a menu of rich, flavorful dishes (including *bograč*—a spicy, goulash-like stew served in its own kettle—and the roasted dumplings called *dödöle*) and a chance to sample the products of one of Slovenia's top wine-growing regions. This is a fine place to try *gibanica* poppyseed layer cake—originating in Prekmurje, and beloved throughout Slovenia (daily 8:00-24:00, Mestni trg 19, mobile 083-806-446).

$$$ Altrokè highlights cuisine from Istria—the region shared by southern Slovenia and northern Croatia. That means Adriatic seafood, *pršut,* and lots of truffles, served in a cozy stone-walled dining room right along the Old Town's main drag (daily 12:00-23:00, Stari trg 19, mobile 082-055-282).

AT THE CASTLE

Ljubljana's castle complex has some basic eateries, and two high-end splurges—one traditional, the other pretentious and modern. For either of these, reserve ahead before making the trip.

$$$ Gostilna na Gradu offers Slovenian cuisine in the castle courtyard high above town—if you don't mind going up to the castle to get it (the handy funicular costs €4 round-trip). Run by a team of well-respected chefs (including Ana Roš of the world-famous Hiša Franko—see "The Julian Alps" chapter), it serves up a seasonal menu of traditional flavors with modern flair, at fairly high prices. Choose between the dull vaulted interior, the glassed-in arcade, or the outdoor tables (Mon-Sat 10:00-24:00—food served until 22:00, Sun 9:00-18:00—food served until 17:00, Grajska Planota 1, mobile 031-301-777, www.nagradu.si).

$$$$ Strelec (STREH-lets) is a heavily themed, full-of-itself splurge with a big-name chef, elaborately described menu items that are based on real historical recipes, and a growing reputation (Mon-Sat 12:00-22:00, closed Sun, tel. 031/687-648, www.kaval-group.si).

DRINKS AND TREATS

Riverfront Cafés: Enjoying a coffee, beer, or ice-cream cone along the breezy Ljubljanica River embankment (between the Triple and Cobblers' bridges) is Ljubljana's single best experience—worth ▲▲▲. Tables spill into the street, and some of the best-dressed, best-looking students on the planet happily fill them day and night. (A common question from first-time visitors to Ljubljana: "Doesn't anybody here have a job?") This is some

of the top people-watching in Europe. When ordering, the easiest choice is a *bela kava* (white coffee)—a caffe latte.

Quality Coffee: While the riverfront strip has good coffee and amazing ambience, coffee snobs may want something more serious. **Črno Zrno,** tucked on historic Gornji trg at the end of the Old Town drag, is owned by Alexander Nino, who sources beans from his native Colombia and serves a wide variety of coffee drinks in a tiny, colorfully tiled, hole-in-the-wall interior (Mon-Fri 10:30-14:00 & 15:00-18:30, Sat 10:00-17:00, Sun 11:00-17:00, Gornji trg 17, mobile 031-446-398).

Bakery: $ Osem ("Eight"), along the Old Town's main drag, is a simple space that bakes breads from scratch each morning.

You'll smell it before you see it (Mon-Fri 8:00-18:00, Sat until 13:00, closed Sun, Stari trg 17, mobile 040-562-699).

Teahouse: If coffee's not your cup of tea, go a block inland to the teahouse **$ Čajna Hiša.** They serve about 50 types of tea, light food (including great salads and sandwiches), and desserts (Mon-Fri 8:00-22:00, Sat until 15:00, closed Sun, on the atmospheric main drag in the Old Town a few steps from Cobblers' Bridge at Stari trg 3, tel. 01/421-2444). They also have an attached tea shop, **Cha** (described on my "Ljubljana Walk," earlier).

Microbrews: Sir William's Pub is where beer aficionados go to get a taste of Slovenia's burgeoning craft-beer scene. It has a few outdoor tables and a classic British pub interior, and a thoughtfully curated menu of both domestic and international microbrews on tap and by the bottle (no food, Mon-Fri 8:00-24:00, Sat from 10:00, Sun from 17:00, Tavčarjeva ulica 8A, mobile 059-944-825). The city also has a few well-stocked bottle shops, including **Za Popen't Pivoteka,** tucked just off of the Old Town's main drag (passage at Stari trg 5). They sell 200 kinds of beer in individual bottles. While they stock a few Slovenian beers, they focus on international microbrews—including several American brands. The name is a play on words, loosely meaning "foamy goodness" (tel. 01/256-5916, www.zapopent.si).

Cakes: Zvezda Kavarna, a trendy, central place at the bottom of Congress Square, is a local favorite for cakes, pastries, and ice cream. A nostalgic specialty here—once popular in communist times, and recently reintroduced to great acclaim—is the *emona kocka* (Emona cube), a layer cake with nuts, cake, and chocolate (Mon-Sat 7:00-23:00, Sun 10:00-20:00, a block from Prešeren Square at Wolfova 14, tel. 01/421-9090). Their **deli,** one door toward Prešeren Square, has takeaway coffee and smoothies, a wide variety of cakes to go, and some of the most decadent ice cream in town (same hours).

Ice Cream: Ljubljana is known for its Italian gelato-style ice cream. You'll see fine options all along the Ljubljanica River embankment, but many places serve ice cream only in summer. **Romantica,** just up the steps from the river, is the foodies' choice, with creative and delicious artisanal flavors (just uphill from Ljubljanksi Dvor pizzeria at Dvorni trg 1). **Fétiche Patisserie,** along the riverfront café embankment, is another good choice, with some unusual, pungent, Asian-themed flavors.

ELSEWHERE IN LJUBLJANA

In Krakovo: The Krakovo district—just south of the city center, where garden patches nearly outnumber houses—is home to **$$$ Pri Škofu** ("By the Bishop"), a laid-back, leafy place with appealing outdoor seating, a nondescript modern interior, and a focus on freshness, serving international cuisine with a Slovenian flair. This hidden gem is deliciously memorable; reserve ahead (creative soups, lunch specials, homemade desserts, Tue-Fri 17:00-23:00, Sat-Sun from 13:00, closed Mon, Rečna 8, tel. 01/426-4508).

Funky Student Zone on Trubarjeva Cesta: For something cheaper, grungier, and less touristy, join the students wandering the graffiti-slathered Trubarjeva cesta, just north of Butchers' Bridge and Dragon Bridge. Here you'll find a variety of cheap global fare, from falafel to Asian noodles to pizza by the slice, mixed in among home decor galleries, vape shops, and erotic boutiques. A few blocks east, detour a short block to the riverfront to find **$ EK Bistro,** a brunch/lunch spot with a big foodie reputation. Grab an outdoor table facing an untouristy stretch of river, or squeeze into the rustic, cave-like brick-and-stone interior to peruse the short menu of egg dishes, sandwiches, and other brunch options (Mon-Fri 11:00-16:00, Sat-Sun from 8:00, Petkovškovo nabrežje 65, mobile 051-624-061).

Ljubljana Connections

As Slovenia's transportation hub, Ljubljana is well-connected to both domestic and international destinations. When checking schedules, be aware of city name variations: In Slovene, Vienna is "Dunaj," Budapest is "Budimpešta," and Venice is "Benétke."

Local Alternative: When considering bus and train connections, don't overlook the very handy **GoOpti** shared transfer service, which is often more convenient, faster, and not much more expensive. Locals swear by this service for airport transfers and reaching otherwise tricky-to-connect places like Venice and Istria (for details, see "By Shared Shuttle Service," later).

BY TRAIN
From Ljubljana by Train to: Lesce-Bled (roughly hourly, 40-60 minutes—but bus is better because it goes right to Bled town center), **Postojna** (nearly hourly, 1 hour), **Divača** (close to Škocjan Caves—free shuttle bus meets some connections, nearly hourly, 2 hours), **Sežana** (close to Lipica, nearly hourly, 2 hours), **Piran** (direct bus is better—see later; otherwise allow 4 hours, train to Koper, 4/day, 2.5 hours; then bus to Piran, 7/day, 30 minutes), **Maribor** (hourly, 2-3 hours, most with a transfer in Zidani Most), **Ptuj** (3/day direct, 2.5 hours, more with transfer in Pragersko or Maribor), **Zagreb** (4/day direct, 2.5 hours), **Rijeka** (2/day direct in summer, 1/day off-season, 3 hours), **Pula** (1/day with change at Divaca, likely in summer only, 4 hours), **Split** (2/day, including 1 night train, 9 hours on the train, plus layover time in Zagreb), **Vienna** (that's **Dunaj** in Slovene, 1/day direct, 6 hours; otherwise 4/day with transfer in

Villach or Maribor, 6 hours), **Budapest** (that's **Budimpešta** in Slovene; 1/day direct, 8.5 hours, other connections possible with 1-2
changes but complicated, no convenient night train), **Venice** (called
Benétke in Slovene; fastest by bus or GoOpti—see later; otherwise
2/day with transfer in Trieste, 5.5 hours), **Salzburg** (2/day direct,
4.5 hours, including 1 night train, an additional 2/day possible with
transfer in Villach), **Munich** (2/day direct, 6.5 hours, including 1
night train; also possible 2/day with transfer in Villach). If heading
to **Italy,** you can ride the train to **Trieste** (2/day, 2.5 hours) and
connect to high-speed Italian trains from there. Train info: Toll-
free tel. 080-81-11, www.slo-zeleznice.si.

BY BUS

The bus station is a low-profile building in front of the train station.
Most buses depart from the numbered stalls in the middle of the
street. (Buses run by Flixbus have their own departure point and
tickets—see later.) For any of these buses, buy tickets at the bus
station ticket windows or at the automated e-kart kiosk (pay with
credit card or cash), not from the driver. For bus information, pick
up one of the blue phones inside the station to be connected to a
helpful English-speaking operator. Most timetables can be found
at www.ap-ljubljana.si or www.getbybus.com. However, buses operated by Flixbus have their own website (www.flixbus.com).

By Bus to: Bled (Mon-Sat hourly—usually at the top of each
hour, fewer on Sun, 1.5 hours), **Postojna Caves** (3/day, 1 hour; or
ride an hourly bus to Postojna town and walk or taxi from there),
Divača (close to Škocjan Caves, about every 2-3 hours, 1.5 hours),
Piran (5/day Mon-Fri, 2/day Sat, 4/day Sun, 2.5 hours, more with
change in Portorož), to **Bovec** in the Julian Alps (scenic mountain
connections 2/day July-Aug: 15:00 departure goes over **Vršič Pass,**
7:30 Mon-Sat departure uses Predel Pass via Italy; also possible
May-June and Sept 2/day with change in Kranjska Gora; otherwise
1-2/day via Idrija; either way it's about 4-4.5 hours to Bovec), **Kobarid** (2/day in July-Aug via Bovec, described above, 5 hours; otherwise faster but less scenic via Idrija, 1-2/day, 3.5 hours), **Rijeka**
(2/day, fewer off-season, 2.5 hours), **Zagreb** (10/day, less on weekends, 2.5 hours). To reach Croatia's Istria—specifically **Rovinj**—
the bus is your best option (usually at least 2/day direct, 4-5 hours).

In addition to the connections above, **Flixbus** offers frequent,
direct, long-distance buses to cities including **Rijeka** (2.5 hours),
Rovinj (3 hours), **Venice** (4 hours), **Zagreb** (2.5 hours), **Vienna**
(5.5 hours), **Munich** (5.5 hours), and **Budapest** (6.5 hours)—often
faster and cheaper than by train. These buses depart from platform/
peron 29/30, and tickets are not sold at the main bus ticket office—
buy them online (www.flixbus.com) or on board.

Nomago, a newer company, is also expanding its coverage

of buses to destinations near and far; it may be worth checking their website for additional or better routes than those listed above (www.nomago.eu).

BY SHARED SHUTTLE SERVICE

If bus and train schedules don't quite serve your needs, **GoOpti**—a company with an innovative business model for shared minibus transfers—can be a convenient and inexpensive alternative. Slovenes love it. First, go to www.goopti.com and select your destination, date, and preferred arrival or departure time. Then, 24 hours before your trip, you'll get an update of the specific pickup time, based on the needs of other passengers. Prices can flex dramatically, but it's quite affordable (for example, an advance nonrefundable purchase from Ljubljana could be €15 to Piran, or €20 to Venice or Zagreb). They also offer airport transfers to or from downtown Ljubljana for €10 (see "By Plane," next). For a few euros extra, they can pick you up at your hotel rather than the train or bus station; to lock in a specific time, you can pay even more for a "VIP" transfer.

GoOpti reaches destinations throughout Slovenia (including Ljubljana, the airport, Lake Bled, towns in the Karst such as Postojna and Sežana, and Piran and other Slovenian coastal destinations), but it's also handy for farther-flung international destinations—such as Venice or its airport, Trieste, various Austrian cities (Vienna, Salzburg, Klagenfurt, etc.), and Croatian cities such as Zagreb and Pula.

BY PLANE

Slovenia's only **airport** (airport code: LJU) is 14 miles north of Ljubljana, about halfway to Bled. Confusingly, the airport goes by three names: Ljubljana Airport (the international version); Brnik (for the town that it's near); and Jože Pučnik Airport (a politician for whom it was controversially renamed in 2007). The airport is small and manageable. If you're on an early-morning flight, don't bother showing up before 5:00, when the airport opens. Airport info: tel. 04/206-1000, www.fraport-slovenija.si.

Getting to Downtown Ljubljana: Exiting the baggage-claim area, you'll see three desks lined up offering €10/person shared **shuttle** rides into Ljubljana that take about 30 minutes (GoOpti, www.goopti.com; Nomago, www.nomago.eu; and Ride2, www.ride2.com). While it's better to book these ahead—as they can fill up—they often have space for those who just show up. They'll take you to the bus/train station area, though you may be able to pay €5 extra for door-to-door service. These companies also go from downtown *to* the airport; book online in advance.

Otherwise, you could take **public bus** #28 (labeled *Ljubljana-Brnik,* to the right as you exit the airport; Mon-Fri 2/hour until

20:00—faster departures at :30 past the hour for €5.60, otherwise 45 minutes, €4.10; 7/day Sat-Sun). Most expensive is a **taxi;** the fair rate is around €30, but the rip-off cabbies who wait at the airport charge much more; it's best to call for a taxi (or ask the information desk to call one for you).

To Lake Bled: For tips on going from the airport directly to Lake Bled, see "Lake Bled Connections" in the next chapter.

Airport Alternatives: Ljubljana's airport—the only one in the country—charges high taxes and fees, and has limited connections to some European destinations. To save money (or to avoid a layover), many Slovenes fly in and out of relatively nearby airports in neighboring countries: **Zagreb** (2-hour drive from Ljubljana); **Venice** (3-hour drive from Ljubljana); **Trieste** (2-hour drive from Ljubljana); and **Klagenfurt/Kärnten** (especially for those going to Lake Bled, from which it's a 2-hour drive). To get between these airports and your Slovenian destination, GoOpti, described earlier, is typically cheaper than a taxi and more convenient than a bus or train connection. Nomago also runs buses to the Venice and Trieste airports (www.nomago.eu).

LAKE BLED

Lake Bled—Slovenia's leading mountain re-sort—comes complete with a sweeping alpine panorama, a fairy-tale island, a cliff-hanging medieval castle, a lazy lakeside promenade, and the country's most sought-after desserts. And the charms of its glorious mountain scen-ery and traditional folk life only crescendo as you explore the surrounding areas. Taken together, there are few more-enjoyable places to simply be on vacation.

Since the Habsburg days, Lake Bled (locals pronounce it like "blade") has been *the* place where Slovenes wow visiting diplomats. In the late 19th century, local aristocrats surrounded the humble lakefront village with classy villas. Tito also had one of his vaca-tion homes here (today's Hotel Vila Bled), where he entertained illustrious guests.

Lake Bled has plenty of ways to idle away an afternoon. While the lake's main town, also called Bled, is more functional than quaint, it offers postcard views of the lake and handy access to the region. Hike up to Bled Castle for intoxicating vistas. Ride a tra-ditional *pletna* boat out to the island, climb up to the church, ring the bell, and make a wish. Wander or bike the dreamy path around the lake. Sit on a dock, dip your feet in the water, and watch the lake's resident swans. Then dive into some of Bled's famous cakes while you take in the view of Triglav, Slovenia's favorite mountain. Bled quiets down at night—there's no nightlife beyond a hand-ful of pubs—giving hikers and other holiday makers a chance to recharge.

Bled is also a great jumping-off point for a car trip through the Julian Alps (see next chapter), and a wide variety of other worthwhile side-trips begin right at its doorstep. These include the less-developed lake named Bohinj, even deeper in the mountains; a spectacular (yet easy) hike in the nearby mountain gorge of Vintgar; the pleasant Old Town of Radovljica, with its fascinating little beekeeping museum; and the ironworking town of Kropa.

PLANNING YOUR TIME

Bled and its neighboring mountains deserve at least two days. With one day, spend it in and around Bled (or, spend a quick morning in Bled and an afternoon day-tripping). With a second day and a car, drive through the Julian Alps using the self-guided tour in the next chapter. The circular route takes you up and over the stunning Vršič Pass, then down the scenic and historic Soča River Valley. Without a car, skip the second day, or spend it doing nearby day trips: Bus or bike to Radovljica and its bee museum, hike Vintgar Gorge, or visit Lake Bohinj (all described under "Near Lake Bled," at the end of this chapter).

Orientation to Lake Bled

The town of Bled is on the east end of 1.5-mile-long Lake Bled. The lakefront is lined with soothing parks and boxy resort hotels. A 3.5-mile path meanders around the lake. As no motorized boats are allowed, Lake Bled is particularly peaceful.

The tourists' center of Bled has two parts, which melt into each other: a simple village and a cluster of giant hotels. The main thoroughfare, called **Ljubljanska cesta,** leads out of Bled town toward Ljubljana and most other destinations. Just up from the lakefront is the modern **commercial center** (Trgovski Center Bled), with a supermarket, ATM, shops, and a smattering of lively cafés. Nicknamed "Gaddafi," the commercial center was designed for a city in Libya, but the deal fell through—so the frugal Slovenes built it here instead.

Bled's Old Town, under the castle, has a web of tight streets and big-but-humble old houses surrounding the pointy spire of St. Martin's Church. In this area, you'll find the bus station, some good restaurants, a few hostels, and more locals than tourists.

The mountains poking above the ridge at the far end of the lake are the Julian Alps, crowned by the three peaks of Mount Triglav. The big mountain behind the town of Bled is Stol ("Chair"), part of the Karavanke range that defines the Austrian border.

Lake Bled

P Pletna Boat Dock
R Rowboat Rental

To Podhom &
Vintgar Gorge

634

To
Zasip

CESTA VINTGAR

Rečica River

KOLODVORSKA CESTA

REČIŠKA CESTA

See Bled Town detail map

PREŠERNOVA CESTA

BLED TOWN

CASTLE   CHURCH

To Lesce
(Train Station),
Radovljica &
Ljubljana

BLED JEZERO
STATION

ROWING
CENTER

R

SWIMMING
POOL

LJUBLJANSKA CESTA

COMMERCIAL
CENTER

Lake   Bled

Bled
Island

CHURCH
OF THE
ASSUMPTION

99
STEPS

R

P

CAMP-
GROUND

R

P

R

P

SUMMER
LUGE

ALP
PENZION &
ESSENSE SPA

▲ Mt. Straža

VILA
BLED

CESTA SVOBODE

ADVENTURE
PARK

1 Kilometer

MLINO

GARDEN VILLAGE
GLAMPGROUND

To Selo,
Tourist Farm Mulej &
Kralov Med Beehive

1/2 Mile

To Lake Bohinj   209

TOURIST INFORMATION

Bled's most central TI is in the long, lakefront casino building across the street from the big, white Hotel Park (as you face the lake, the TI is hiding around the front at the far left end, overlooking the lake). Pick up the map with the lake on one side and the whole region on the other and the free, up-to-date Bled information booklet. Get advice on hikes and day trips, and if you're doing any serious hiking, spring for a good regional map. They also rent cars and bikes (July-Aug Mon-Sat 8:00-21:00, Sun 9:00-17:00; mid-April-June and Sept-mid-Oct Mon-Sat 8:00-19:00, Sun 9:00-17:00; off-season Mon-Sat 8:00-18:00, Sun 9:00-16:00; Cesta Svobode 10, tel. 04/574-1122, www.bled.si).

The TI's other branch—handy for drivers, on the main road out of town—conveniently shares an office with the **Triglav National Park Information Center,** which offers advice for those heading into the mountains. The center, with free parking, is called "Triglavska Roža" (bike rentals, maps and guidebooks for sale, daily 8:00-18:00, off-season until 16:00, Ljubljanska cesta 27, tel. 04/578-0205, www.tnp.si).

ARRIVAL IN BLED

By Train: Two train stations have the name "Bled." The **Bled Jezero** (Bled Lake) station is across the lake from Bled town and is used only by infrequent, slow, tourist-oriented trains into the mountains. You're much more likely to use the **Lesce-Bled** station in the nearby village of Lesce (pronounced lest-SEH). The Lesce-Bled station is on the main line and has far better connections to Ljubljana and international destinations. When buying a train ticket or checking schedules, request "Lesce-Bled" rather than just "Bled." (This is so important, I'll remind you again later.)

The small **Lesce-Bled station** is in Lesce, about 2.5 miles from Bled. From the station in Lesce, you can take the bus into Bled town (2-3/hour, 10 minutes, catch it across the street from the train station); or pay about €15 for a taxi. If taking the train out of Lesce-Bled, buy tickets at this station or on the train—nobody in Bled town sells tickets.

By Bus: Bled's main bus station is just up from the lake in the Old Town; to reach the lake, walk straight downhill on Cesta Svobode. Note that many buses also stop on the way into town, along Ljubljanska cesta, which is handier for walking to many of my recommended accommodations (for details, see "Sleeping in Bled," later)—be sure to ask your driver.

By Car: Coming from Ljubljana, you'll wind your way into Bled on Ljubljanska cesta, which rumbles through the middle of town before swinging left at the lake. Parking can be challenging on busy days in peak season. Most accommodations have a line on free parking nearby—ask when you book. But if you're here for a quick visit, you can try to find a spot in the short-term parking lot just above the commercial center (free for 1 hour, €2/2 hours, 2-hour limit). To stretch your visit, there are two parking lots between Hotel Krim and the ice rink (both €2/hour); the paved lot has a four-hour limit, but the gravel lot has no time limit. If doing the luge ride, you can pay €3 to park all day at that lot (described on page 617). A bit farther up from the lake, the town primary school *(osnovna šola)* has cheap parking with no time limit (€1/hour; see locations on map). Additional spaces are closer to the main road, along Seliška cesta, across from the big Spar and Mercator supermarkets.

For more driving tips, see "Route Tips for Drivers" under "Lake Bled Connections," later.

By Plane: For details on getting from Ljubljana's airport to Bled, see "Lake Bled Connections," later.

HELPFUL HINTS

Money: Bled town's handiest ATMs are at **SKB Banka** (upstairs in round building at commercial center), at far end of

LAKE BLED

Bled Town

To Podhom &
Vintgar Gorge

To Zasip

POLJSKA POT

REČIŠKA CESTA

CESTA

PARTIZANSKA CES.

GRAJSKA CESTA

24

15

8

7

5

GRAJSKA

23

13

14

16

22

OLD TOWN

21

ST. MARTIN'S

P

CASTLE

12

P

To Rowing
Center &
Campground

SWIMMING
POOLS &
BOAT RENTALS

Lake
Bled

To Island & Church

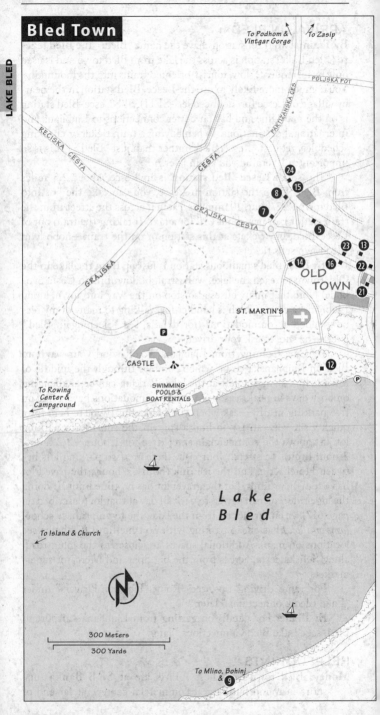

300 Meters

300 Yards

To Mlino, Bohinj
& 9

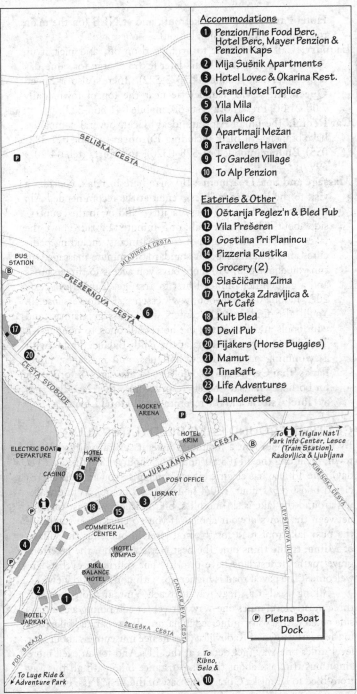

Accommodations

1. Penzion/Fine Food Berc, Hotel Berc, Mayer Penzion & Penzion Kaps
2. Mija Sušnik Apartments
3. Hotel Lovec & Okarina Rest.
4. Grand Hotel Toplice
5. Vila Mila
6. Vila Alice
7. Apartmaji Mežan
8. Travellers Haven
9. To Garden Village
10. To Alp Penzion

Eateries & Other

11. Oštarija Peglez'n & Bled Pub
12. Vila Prešeren
13. Gostilna Pri Planincu
14. Pizzeria Rustika
15. Grocery (2)
16. Slaščičarna Zima
17. Vinoteka Zdravljica & Art Café
18. Kult Bled
19. Devil Pub
20. Fijakers (Horse Buggies)
21. Mamut
22. TinaRaft
23. Life Adventures
24. Launderette

SELIŠKA CESTA

MLADINSKA CESTA

BUS STATION

PREŠERNOVA CESTA

CESTA SVOBODE

HOCKEY ARENA

HOTEL KRIM

LJUBLJANSKA CESTA

To Triglav Nat'l Park Info Center, Lesce (Train Station), Radovljica & Ljubljana

ELECTRIC BOAT DEPARTURE

CASINO

HOTEL PARK

POST OFFICE

LIBRARY

RIBENSKA CESTA

LEVŠTIKOVA ULICA

COMMERCIAL CENTER

HOTEL KOMPAS

RIKLI BALANCE HOTEL

CANKARJEVA CESTA

HOTEL JADRAN

POD STRAŽO

To Luge Ride & Adventure Park

ŽELEŠKA CESTA

To Ribno, Selo &

Ⓟ Pletna Boat Dock

Hotel Park (facing the lakefront), and at **NLB** (on the main road into town, at Pension Union).

Laundry: Call **Anže Štalc** to arrange drop-off, and pick it up cleaned and folded 24 hours later (extra charge for same-day express service, mobile 041-575-522). There's also a **Speed Queen** self-service launderette near the top of town (daily 7:00-21:00, Prešernova cesta 50, mobile 041-366-323).

Car Rental: The Julian Alps are ideal by car. Several companies have branches in Bled, including **Europcar** (mobile 031-382-055), **Budget** (mobile 041-578-0320), and **Hertz** (tel. 04/201-6999).

Massage and Spa Treatments: If you're here to relax, consider a visit to the **Essense** wellness center at the recommended Alp Penzion. This modern, classy facility—hiding in the country-side about a 20-minute walk or 5-minute taxi ride above the lake—offers a wide range of spa treatments, including pedi-cures and Thai massage. A standard 50-minute massage will run you about €50; €10 more buys you access to three saunas and a garden hot tub (call first to arrange, Cankarjeva cesta 20A, mobile 040-996-666, www.essense.si, info@essense.si). You'll also find wellness centers with massage, saunas, and whirlpools at a few of the big hotels (all open to nonguests). The biggest is the **Živa** spa at the Rikli Balance Hotel, with a swimming pool, lakeview hot tubs, and massages; Hotel Park's **Thai Center** spa also does good massages (information for both at www.sava-hotels-resorts.com). There are also spas at **Hotel Astoria** and the recommended **Hotel Lovec**.

GETTING AROUND LAKE BLED (LITERALLY)

By Bike: You can rent a mountain bike at several points around town, including the TI (€3.50/hour, €6/3 hours, €8/half-day, €11/day). The TI also has electric bikes, which give you a much-appre-ciated boost (€5/1 hour, €10/4 hours, €15/8 hours). While walk-ing around the lake is slo-mo bliss, biking it lets you fast-forward between the views of your choice. If you go clockwise, you'll use the busy lakefront road for the first stretch, but after the village of Mlino, traffic thins out. The best views are from the lakefront gravel path; pedestrians have priority, but courteous cyclists are welcome. (The paved road is higher up, with not-as-good views.)

Biking is also a great way to reach Vintgar Gorge—about three mostly level miles one-way, perfect for combining a country-side pedal with a walk immersed in nature. The separated bike path to the nearby town of Radovljica (and its bee museum) is about four level miles one-way (get details at the TI). And for an even more ambitious trip, ask about the long-distance bike path all the way from Bled to Kranjska Gora, at the base of the Vršič Pass. For other ideas, ask for the TI's excellent biking map, with various bike trips clearly marked and described.

By Horse and Buggy: Buggies called *fijaker*s are the romantic, expensive, and easy way to get around the lake. Hire one along the lakefront between Hotel Park and the castle (see the "Bled Town" map for location; around the lake-€50, one-way up to castle-€50, round-trip to castle with 30-minute wait time-€60, mobile 041-710-970, www.fijaker-bled.si).

By Tourist Train: A little train makes a circuit around the lake every 40 minutes in summer (€5, look for it near the TI, weather-dependent, mobile 051-337-478).

By Shuttle Bus to the Castle and Vintgar Gorge: These two destinations—both walkable—are much easier with wheels. In the summer, a handy shuttle bus starts from the main bus station, then goes up to the castle and on to the Vintgar Gorge entrance (€1/ride, 6/day mid-June–mid-Sept, get schedule at TI). Various private companies offer a similar service for €5 each way; while more expensive, these are worth considering in spring and fall: Maya runs a shuttle from near the TI, departing at :00 and :30 past each hour, while Mamut departs from the bus station at :45 past the hour (for details, check at each office). Each of these stops both at Vintgar Gorge and the castle (same price)—take your pick.

By Hop-On, Hop-Off Bus to Outlying Towns: In summer (July-Aug only), a hop-on, hop-off bus service is designed to reach villages to the east that are otherwise poorly served by public transportation, including Kropa (ironwork museum) and the musical village of Begunje, along with some larger towns such as Radovljica. The bus runs only a few days a week, with a different route each day (€8, ask for schedule at TI).

By Taxi: Your hotel can call a taxi for you. Or contact **Bled Tours,** run by Sandi and Cvetka, and their team of English-speaking drivers (prices for up to 3 people: €12 to the castle, €15 to Vintgar Gorge, €50 to Ljubljana airport, €130 to Klagenfurt airport in Austria). They also offer self-guided excursions that include admission, such as Bled Castle and Vintgar Gorge for €45/person, or €36/person for a few hours in Radovljica (mobile 031-205-611 or 031-321-122, www.bledtours.si, info@bledtours.si).

By Boat: For information on renting your own boat or riding the characteristic *pletna* boats, see "Sights at Lake Bled," later.

By Private Plane: If you have perfect weather, there's no more thrilling way to experience Slovenia's high-mountain scenery than from a small propeller plane soaring over the peaks. Private flights depart from a grass airstrip near the village of Lesce, a 10-minute drive or taxi ride from Bled. It's expensive...but unforgettable (€100 for 15-minute hop over Lake Bled only, €170 for 30-minute flight that also buzzes Lake Bohinj, €240 for deluxe 45-minute version around the summit of Triglav, price covers up to 3 passengers, arrange at least a day in advance, tel. 04/532-0100, www.alc-lesce.si, info@alc-lesce.si).

Tours at Lake Bled

Local Guides

Tina Hiti and **Sašo Golub,** an energetic couple, are both excellent guides who enjoy sharing the town and region they love with American visitors. Hiring one of them can add immeasurably to your enjoyment and understanding of Bled and the surrounding area (€50 for 2-hour tour of Bled, arrange several days in advance, www.pg-slovenia.com, info@pg-slovenia.com, Tina's mobile 040-166-554, Sašo's mobile 040-524-774). Tina and Sašo are especially handy for side-tripping into the countryside if you don't want to drive yourself. I've spent great days with both of them and was thankful they were behind the wheel. Their most popular trip is a day in the Julian Alps (€230 round-trip from Bled, €40 extra to pick up or drop off in Ljubljana, extra charge for 5 or more people, €10 extra per person for picnic lunch). They also offer many other options, including all-day shore excursions from the cruise port in Koper (€450 for a day visiting Ljubljana and Bled, up to 3 people, more for bigger van), food tours, airport transfers, and trips in the Slovenian countryside to research your roots. As Tina and Sašo both lead tours for me in Europe, they may send you off with a well-trained substitute—perhaps Tina's father **Gorazd,** a former Yugoslav Olympian in ice hockey who brings the older generation's perspective to the trip; **Ervin,** who provides a younger view; and others (**Nejc** or **Grega**).

Excursions

To hit several far-flung day-trip destinations in one go, consider a package tour from Bled. Destinations range from Ljubljana and the Karst region to the Austrian Lakes to Venice. For example, an all-day Julian Alps trip to the Vršič Pass and Soča Valley runs about €80 per person (sold by various agencies around town—ask the TI). This tour is handy, but two people can rent a car for the day for less and do it at their own pace using the self-guided driving tour in the next chapter.

Adventure Trips

Various Bled-based companies specialize in taking tourists on active, outdoorsy excursions into the surrounding countryside and mountains. One popular choice is an all-day white-water rafting trip on the Soča River (around €125/person). Other options include canyoning, river tubing, mountain biking, paragliding, rock climbing, and more.

Three well-established companies have offices near Bled's bus station: **Mamut** (mobile 040-121-900, www.slovenija.eu.com), **TinaRaft** (mobile 041-646-255, www.tinaraft.si), and **Life Adventures** (mobile 040-508-853, www.lifeadventures.si). Note that these companies tend to attract a young, sometimes rowdy crowd that enjoys lubricating their adventures with alcohol. Another option, **Zipline Dolinka,** offers a 2.5-hour zipline course (with five runs) that zigzags over an alpine river near Bled (mobile 031-845-900, www.zipline-dolinka.si).

Sights at Lake Bled

Bled doesn't have many sights, but there are plenty of rewarding and pleasant activities.

▲▲▲Walk Around the Lake

Strolling the 3.5-mile lake perimeter is enjoyable, peaceful, and scenic. At a leisurely pace, it takes about an hour and a half...not

counting stops to snap photos of the ever-changing view. On the way, you'll pass some beautiful villas, mostly from the early 19th century. The most significant one was a former residence of Marshal Tito—today the Hotel Vila Bled—where the dictator entertained international big shots, from Indira Gandhi to Nikita Khrushchev to Kim Il-Sung to Raúl Castro (you'll pass the base of the stairs on the lakeside path; its café terrace is open for visitors, but there's not much to see). For the more adventurous, hiking paths lead up into the hills surrounding the lake (ask TI for details and maps; or hike to—and

through—Vintgar Gorge, described in the "Near Lake Bled" section, later).

▲▲The Island (Blejski Otok)

Bled's little island—capped by a super-cute church—nudges the lake's quaintness level over the top. Locals call it simply "The Island" *(Otok)*. While it's pretty to look at from afar, it's also fun to visit.

The island has long been a sacred site with a romantic twist. On summer Saturdays, a steady procession of brides and grooms, cheered on by their entourages, heads for the island. Ninety-nine steps lead from the island's dock up to the Church of the Assumption on top. It's tradition for the groom to carry—or *try* to carry—his bride up all of these steps. About four out of five are successful (proving themselves "fit for marriage"). During the communist era, the church was closed and weddings were outlawed here. But the tradition reemerged—illegally—even before the regime ended, with a clandestine ceremony in 1989.

Cost and Hours: Free to visit island, church—€6, ticket includes tower climb, daily 9:00-19:00, April and Oct until 18:00, Nov-March until 16:00.

Getting There: The most romantic route to the island is to cruise on one of the distinctive *pletna* boats (€15/person round-trip, trip takes 20-25 minutes each way, includes 30-minute stay on the island—allow about 1.5 hours for the full experience; might have to wait for more passengers to fill the boat; boats generally run from dawn, last boat leaves one hour before church closes; replaced by enclosed electric boats in winter—unless the lake freezes, in which case you can rent ice skates; mobile 031-316-575). Look for *pletna* boats at various spots around the lake. If you're in town, the handiest options are directly below the TI, or in front of Grand Hotel Toplice. Farther around the lake, you can also catch a *pletna* in the village of Mlino; at the bottom of the grand staircase leading up to Vila Bled (it's a shorter trip from here, but the same cost); and at the campground. For more on these characteristic little vessels, see the "*Pletna* Boats" sidebar. Note that *pletna* boatmen stick close to the 30-minute waiting time on the island—which can go very fast. Another option—cheaper but far less romantic—is to take an **electric boat** (€12 round-trip, departs about hourly from the lakefront below the TI). You could also **rent your own boat** and row to the island (see "Boating" listing, later).

Visiting the Island: At the top of the stairs, the **Potičnica café** sells *potica*, the Slovenian nut-roll cake that's traditional at Christmastime but delicious any day of the year. The attached **souvenir shop** is the best in Bled, well-stocked with a variety of high-quality Slovenian gifts, trinkets, and keepsakes. Upstairs in the same building is an easy-to-miss **art gallery,** which displays changing exhibits.

The island's main attraction is the **church.** An eighth-century Slavic pagan temple dedicated to the goddess of love and fertility once stood here; the current Baroque version (with Venetian flair—the bell tower is separate from the main church) is the fifth to occupy this spot. Go inside and find the rope for the church bell, hanging in the middle of the aisle just before the altar. A local superstition claims that if you can get this bell to ring three times with one big pull of the rope, your dreams will come true. Worth a try—but be careful if you're slight of build, as the rope can take you for a ride.

If you're waiting for a herd of tourists to ring out their wishes, pass the time looking around the area in front of the altar. When the church was being renovated in the 1970s, workers dug up several medieval graves (you can see one through the glass under the bell rope). They also discovered Gothic frescoes on either side of the altar, including, above the door on the right, an unusual ecclesiastical theme: the *bris* (Jewish circumcision ritual) of Christ.

Your ticket also includes the **bell tower.** At 91 steps, it's a shorter climb than the one up from the boat dock. Up top, you'll find a restored pendulum mechanism from 1890 and fine lake views that are marred by a mesh covering that makes it impossible to snap a clear picture.

To descend by a different route, walk down the trail behind the church (around the right side), then follow the path around the island's perimeter back to where your *pletna* boat awaits.

▲▲Bled Castle (Blejski Grad)

Bled's cliff-hanging castle, dating in one form or another from 1,000 years ago, was the seat of the Austrian bishops of Brixen, who controlled Bled in the Middle Ages. Today it's a fine tourist attraction with a little history and lots of big views. The various sights at the castle—a decent history museum, a frescoed chapel, an old-fashioned printing press, and a wine cellar—are more cute than interesting, but the real reason to come up here is to bask in the sweeping panoramas over Lake Bled and the surrounding mountainscapes.

Cost and Hours: €11, daily 8:00-20:00, June-Aug until 21:00, Nov-March until 18:00, printing press and wine cellar close one hour earlier; tel. 04/572-9782, www.blejski-grad.si.

Getting There: To really earn those views, you can **hike** up the steep hill (about 20 minutes if you're in decent shape). The handiest trails are behind big St. Martin's Church: Walk past the front door of the church with the lake at your back, and look left after the first set of houses for the *Grad* signs marking the steepest

Pletna Boats

The *pletna* is an important symbol of Lake Bled. In addition to providing a pleasant way to reach the island, these boats also carry on a tradition dating back for generations. In the 17th century, Habsburg Empress Maria Theresa granted the villagers from Mlino—the little town along the lakefront just beyond Bled—special permission to ferry visitors to the island. (This provided a much-

needed source of income for Mlino residents, who had very limited access to farmland.) They built their *pletna*s by hand, using a special design passed down from father to son for centuries—like the equally iconic gondolas of Venice. Eventually, this imperial decree and family tradition evolved into a modern union of *pletna* oarsmen, which continues to this day.

Today *pletna* boats are still hand-built according to that same centuries-old design. There's no keel, so the skilled oarsmen work hard to steer the flat-bottomed boat with each stroke—boats piloted by an inexperienced oarsman can slide around on very windy days. There are 21 official *pletna*s on Lake Bled, all belonging to the same union. The gondoliers dump all their earnings into one fund, give a cut to the tourist board, and divide the rest evenly amongst themselves. Occasionally a new family tries to break into the cartel, underselling his competitors with a "black market" boat that looks the same as the official ones. While some see this as a violation of a centuries-old tradition, others view it as good old capitalism. Either way, competition is fierce.

route (follow the wooden stakes all the way up the steep switchback steps); or, for a longer but less steep route, continue past the church on the same street about five minutes, bearing uphill (left) at the fork, and find the *Blejski Grad - Castle - 10 Min* sign just after the Penzion Bledec hostel on the left. Once you're on this second trail, don't take the sharp-left uphill turn at the fork (instead, continue straight up, around the back of the hill).

If you'd rather skip the hike, you have other options. If you have a **car,** simply drive up (€3 for parking up to 2 hours). Otherwise, consider a **shuttle bus** (€1 for the official TI bus that runs mid-June–mid-Sept only, otherwise €5 for a private shuttle; see "Getting Around Lake Bled," earlier). A **taxi** runs about €12. Or— if you're wealthy and romantic—consider a **horse and buggy** (€50, €10 extra for driver to wait 30 minutes and bring you back down). Note: All of these options take you only to the parking lot, from which it's still a steep and slippery-when-wet five-minute hike up to the castle itself.

Eating: The **$$$$ restaurant** at the castle is pricey, but worth the splurge for the views and excellent, rotating menu featuring regional cuisine. Come for dinner while it's still light out and savor the setting. The sleek, woody interior is often jammed with tour groups; in good weather, I'd rather dine on the outside terrace. Call far ahead to book a view table—they fill up quickly. If you have a reservation to dine here, it's free to enter the castle grounds (daily in summer 11:00-22:00, shorter hours off-season, tel. 04/620-3444, www.jezersek.si). Paupers can grab a basic sandwich at the simple **$ café** by the round tower, or bring their own **picnic** to munch along the wall with million-dollar views over Lake Bled (buy sandwiches at the Mercator grocery store in the commercial center before you ascend; see "Eating in Bled," later).

Summer Performances: From late June through mid-September, the castle hosts a weekly, kid-pleasing, knights'-tournament-themed show called "Sir Lambergar's Adventure" (likely Tue and Thu at 17:00; details on castle website).

Visiting the Castle: After buying your ticket, go through the gate and huff the rest of the way up to the outer courtyard. We'll tour the castle clockwise, starting from here. As the castle is continually being spruced up, some details may be different than described.

Turning left at the entrance, you'll pass WCs, then the door to Mojster Janez's working replica of a **printing press** (grajska tiskarna/manufaktura) from Gutenberg's time. You can buy your own custom-made souvenir certificate using this very old technology. While this may seem like a tourist gimmick, there's actually some interesting history here. As in many lands, the printing press was a critical tool in the evolution of Slovenia's culture. Look above the press for a life-size mannequin of Primož Trubar (1508-1586), a Slovenian cross between Martin Luther and Johannes Gutenberg. In Trubar's time, Slovene was considered a crude peasants' language—not just unworthy of print, but actually illegal to print. So this Reformer went to Germany and, in 1550—using presses like this one—wrote and printed the first two books in the Slovene language: *Abecedarium* (an alphabet primer to teach illiterate

Slovenes how to read) and *Catechismus* (a simplified version of the New Testament). Trubar smuggled his printed books back to Slovenia (hidden in barrels of playing cards) and, en route to Ljubljana, was briefly given refuge in this castle. (Trubar is still much-revered today, appearing on the Slovenian €1 coin.) Up the stairs is an exhibition in English about early printing methods and the importance of moveable type for advancing the Protestant Reformation, whose goal was to get the Word of God more easily into the hands of everyday people. You'll also see one of those first Trubar books—notice it was printed in Tübingen, Germany, an early enclave of the Reformation. There's also a small painting gallery showcasing local artists.

Just past the printing press is the castle's oldest tower, from the 11th century, which is filled with a **"Beehouse"** selling various honey products under a hive-like dome. Nearby is a **café terrace** offering reasonably priced drinks and cakes with grand views.

Begin climbing the stairs up to grander and grander **views** over the lake. Reaching the terrace at the very top, you'll find the best vistas; the restaurant; a tiny chapel with 3-D frescoes that make it seem much bigger than it is (next to the museum entrance); a small shop selling iron items that are still forged the traditional way; and the well-presented castle **museum,** which strains to make the story of Bled, the castle, and the surrounding region of Carniola interesting. The ground floor has exhibits about geology, prehistoric artifacts, ironworking, and the seasonal life cycle of the region, while the upstairs has a cool 3-D model of the surrounding mountains, smaller models illustrating the growth of the castle structure, information about early inhabitants, and exhibits on the development of tourism at Lake Bled (including its many fine vacation villas). While video screens and some English information are helpful, there's only so much to say.

When you're done up here, head down the stairs between the museum and restaurant (passing WCs). Coming back down into the lower courtyard, turn left down the ramp to find the **wine cellar,** where you can bottle and cork your own souvenir bottle of wine (you're paying for the experience more than the wine). Slovenian wines are well-explained by attendants who dress as monks, since winemaking was a monastic responsibility in the Middle Ages.

Before leaving the castle, climb the stairs (just past the wine cellar) up to the wooden **defensive gallery** for the best views in town of the mountains east of Bled. The biggest one is called Stol (Chair). In the foreground, you can see the steeple marking the town of Podhom; just to the left, the folds in the hills hide the dramatic Vintgar Gorge (described later).

Boating

Bled is the rowing center of Slovenia, and it has hosted multiple world championships, including one in 2020. Town officials even lengthened the lake a bit so it would perfectly fit the standard two-kilometer laps, with 100 meters more for the turn (on maps, you can see the little divot taken out of the far end). The town has produced many Olympic medalists, who've won gold in Sydney, silver in Athens, and bronze in London. You'll likely see crews practicing out on the water, and young rowers jogging around the lake.

If you want to get into the action, you'll find **rental rowboats** at various points around the lake (€10-20/hour). Look for them at Pension Pletna in the lakeside village of Mlino (a scenic 15-minute walk around the lake from Bled); at the swimming pool under the castle (the closest but priciest option); under Grand Hotel Toplice; and in the modern building just before the campground on the far end of the lake. You can also rent **stand-up paddleboards** at various points around the lake, including from Mamut near the bus station (€30/6 hours).

Swimming

Lake Bled has several suitable spots for a swim. The swimming pool complex under the castle uses lake water and routinely earns the "blue flag," meaning the water is top-quality. There's also a waterslide and an inviting cluster of sunning beds (€9 to swim all day, less for afternoon only, daily 9:00-19:00, closed Oct-mid-June and in bad weather, tel. 04/578-0528). Lake Bled's

main beach is at the campground at the far end of the lake, though you can also swim near the village of Mlino.

▲Luge Ride (Poletno Sankanje)

Bled's "summer toboggan" luge ride, atop Mount Straža overlooking the lake, allows you to scream down a steep, curvy metal rail track on a little plastic sled. This is a really scary one—speedy, with lots of tight turns, and with great views over the lake—but it's quite pricey. A chairlift takes you to the top of the track, where you'll sit on your sled, take a deep breath, and remind yourself: Pull back on the stick to slow down, push forward on the stick to go faster. You'll drop 480 feet in altitude on the 570-yard-long track, speeding up to about 25 miles per hour as you race toward the lake.

Cost and Hours: €10/ride, cheaper for multiple rides, weather-dependent—if it rains, you can't go. In summer, it's open daily

(July-Aug 10:00-20:00, June 11:00-19:00, shoulder season generally 11:00-18:00, weekends only in April and Oct, closed late Oct-early April; tel. 04/578-0534, www.straza-bled.si).

Getting There: The base of the chairlift is on the hillside just south of town; to get there, head up to the neighborhood just above Grand Hotel Toplice, and follow *Straža* signs with the lake on your right (by car or by foot).

Nearby: Near the base of the chairlift are other attractions, including an airbag jump and a tubing hill (each covered by its own ticket). Up near the top of the chairlift is Adventure Park (Pustolovski Park): a series of five high-ropes courses designed for everyone age five and up. You'll get rigged up in a safety harness and go through a training course, then be set loose on your choice of courses (€22 for adults, €18 for kids 7-14, €10 for kids under 7, similar hours to luge ride, last entry two hours before closing, mobile 031-761-661, www.pustolovski-park-bled.si).

▲Kralov Med Beehive Demonstration

Tucked in Selo village, a long walk or short drive from Bled, this fascinating countryside sight is worth ▲▲▲ (or zzz) for fans of
the apicultural arts. (Read the "Slovenian Beekeeping" sidebar, later in this chapter, before your visit.) Local beekeepers Blaž and Danijela Ambrožič have built an apiary (freestanding house of beehives) and teach visitors all about this very Slovenian form of agriculture. First you'll see the painted panels, with bees buzz-

ing in and out. Their prized possession is a gigantic Winnie-the-Pooh-style hive that they transplanted from a tree trunk. They'll demonstrate how you can hold your hand within inches of the buzzing hive without getting stung, thanks to the peaceful nature of the indigenous Carniolan bee. Inside, you can watch through a big (and safe) window as they pull out the honeycomb frames from the hive and work with the bees. You'll see the centrifuge-like device they use to safely extract honey from the comb. In another hut is an "api-therapy" room, where a specially designed bunk lets you watch and listen to the mesmerizing bees without any danger of being stung. You can also sample (and buy) different types of honey and pollen, along with other bee-related gifts. Outside is a perennial garden that demonstrates when various plants blossom, providing much-needed pollen for the bees.

Cost and Hours: €8/person and up, call or email a few days ahead to arrange a time and establish the price, demonstrations usually last an hour or more and may even run for just two people, apiary and parking are next to the house at Selo pri Bledu 42—once parked there, call Danijela at 041-227-407 or Blaž at 041-657-120 and they'll come meet you, www.kralov-med.si, ambrozicdanijela@gmail.com.

Getting There: Blaž's beehives are in the village of Selo, a five-minute drive or taxi ride or 30-minute walk from Bled town. Head out of town along the lake (past Grand Hotel Toplice), then turn left (inland) at the Mercator grocery store in the village of Mlino. In the next village, Selo, look for the two colorful beehive apiaries below the main road, just above the recommended Tourist Farm Mulej.

Nightlife in Bled

Bled is quiet after hours. However, the town does have a few fun bars that are lively with a young crowd (all open nightly until late). Since many young people in Bled are students at the local tourism school, they're likely to speak English...and eager to practice with a native speaker. Try a Smile, a Corona-type Slovenian lager. *Šnops* (schnapps) is a local specialty—popular flavors are plum *(slivovka)*, honey *(medica)*, blueberry *(borovničevec)*, and pear *(hruškovec)*.

Kick things off with the fun-loving local gang at **Gostilna Pri Planincu** near the bus station (described later, under "Eating in Bled"). Then head down Cesta Svobode toward the lake. On the left, you'll see the mellow **Vinoteka Zdravljica,** with Slovenian wines by the glass for less than €3. Just after that is **Art Café,** with a trendy ambience. Around the lake near the commercial center, **Bled Pub** (a.k.a. The Cocktail Bar or Troha—for the family that owns it) is a trendy late-night spot where bartenders sling a dizzying array of mixed drinks to an appreciative, youthful crowd (between the commercial center and the lake, above the recommended Oštarija Peglez'n restaurant). If you're still standing, several other bars and cafés percolate in the commercial center, including **Kult Bled,** facing the main road at the base of the round tower. Slathered with iconic film images and neon colors, it attracts a thirty-something crowd and occasionally hosts live music. **Devil** is open even later (on the lower level of Hotel Park, facing the lake).

Sleeping in Bled

Bled has more hotel beds per capita than anywhere in Slovenia—and most of them are in big convention hotels. I prefer staying in smaller, more characteristic, pension-type accommodations on the town's fringe, most of them an easy walk from the lake. These places book up early; reserve well ahead.

PENSIONS ABOVE THE LAKE

These friendly, cozy, characteristic accommodations are Bled's best values. But it's important to **book direct**—you'll typically save around 15-20 percent compared to booking through a third-party website. These places are perched on a hilltop a 5- to 10-minute climb up from the lake (easier than it sounds). There are two ways to get here from the town center: Walk around the lake to Grand Hotel Toplice, then cross the street and go up the stairs around the right side of the Hotel Jadran. Or, from the main road into town (Ljubljanska cesta), take the small service road just above the commercial center (in front of Hotel Lovec), and loop up around the big Kompas and Rikli Balance hotels. If arriving by bus, ask nicely if your driver will let you disembark along Ljubljanska cesta (just above the traffic light) to avoid the long walk from the bus station. From this bus stop, you can walk down Ljubljanska cesta and take the road just above the post office, which leads up to this area.

$$$$ Penzion Berc (pronounced "berts") is the priciest option in this area, with 11 sharp, comfortable, woody rooms—all with balconies—filling a tidy chalet. It's well-run by Miha, who charges more because he includes thoughtful touches like free loaner electric bikes and minifridges stocked with free drinks. He also runs the recommended Fine Food Berc restaurant and arranges excursions (air-con, Želeška cesta 15, tel. 04/574-1838, www.penzion-berc.si, info@penzion-berc.si).

$$$ Hotel Berc, across the street and run by Miha's brother Luka, has 17 nearly-as-nice rooms with balconies, loaner bikes, and lower rates (cash only, air-con, Pod Stražo 13, tel. 04/576-5658, www.berc-sp.si, hotel@berc-sp.si).

$$$ Mayer Penzion, next door and thoughtfully run by the Trseglav family (relatives of the Berc brothers), comes with 13 rooms (family rooms, elevator, Želeška cesta 7, tel. 04/576-5740, www.mayer-sp.si, penzion@mayer-sp.si).

$$ Penzion Kaps, conscientiously run by Peter (whose father, Anton, is a great craftsman) and Darija, has 13 comfortable rooms with balconies, modern bathrooms, and classic old wood carvings. The inviting breakfast room in the basement clusters around a giant ceramic stove (cash only, family rooms, air-con, laundry service, free loaner bikes, Želeška cesta 22, mobile 041-618-513, www.penzion-kaps.si, info@penzion-kaps.si).

$ Friendly Mija Sušnik rents out two comfortable two-bedroom apartments. Modern, tidy, and equipped with kitchens, these are a good budget choice for families (cash only, no breakfast, laundry service, free parking, Želeška cesta 3, tel. 04/574-1731, mobile 040-971-278, susnik@bled-holiday.com). It's just toward the lake from the bigger pensions, with a big crucifix out front. Her sister Ivanka also rents apartments, but they're farther from the lake.

ON OR NEAR THE LAKE
You'll pay a premium to be closer to the lake—but it's hard to argue with the convenience.

$$$$ Hotel Lovec (LOH-vets) sits in a convenient (but not lakefront) location along the main road just above the commercial center. Gorgeously appointed inside and out, and run by a helpful staff, it's professional yet welcoming and cheery. Its 61 plush, well-designed rooms come with all the comforts and a respected restaurant (family rooms, great breakfast, air-con, elevator, free parking, Ljubljanska cesta 6, tel. 04/620-4100, www.lovechotel.com, reservations@kompas-lovec.com).

$$$$ Grand Hotel Toplice (TOHP-leet-seh) is the grande dame of Bled, with 87 high-ceilinged rooms, parquet floors, a genteel lakeview café/lounge, posh decor, all the amenities, and a long list of high-profile guests—from Madeleine Albright to Jordan's King Hussein to Slovene-by-marriage Donald Trump (ask to see their "wall of fame"...or is it "shame"?). Once elegant, this place is a bit faded these days, but it's still a classic. Rooms in the back are cheaper, but have no lake views and overlook a noisy street—try to get one as high up as possible (air-con, elevator, free parking, Cesta Svobode 12, tel. 04/579-1000, www.hotel-toplice.com, ghtoplice@hotelibled.com). The hotel's name—*toplice*—means "spa"; guests are free to use the hotel's swanky, natural-spring-fed indoor swimming pool (a chilly 72 degrees Fahrenheit).

NEAR THE OLD TOWN
$$$ Vila Mila rents seven rooms in a handsome, beautifully renovated house at the top of the Old Town. It comes with a pleasant terraced garden and an eco-friendly focus (air-con, Grajska cesta 20, mobile 051-501-909, www.vilamila.si).

$$$ Vila Alice, a beautifully appointed option along the main road through the sleepy upper part of town, offers seven rooms in a classy villa with elegant public spaces, a private garden, and a sauna (no breakfast, air-con, free parking, Prešernova cesta 26, mobile 059-958-780, www.vila-alice.com, info@vila-alice.com).

$$ Apartmaji Mežan, run by welcoming Janez and Saša, has four family-friendly apartments in a modern home buried in the middle of town, just uphill from the church. As it's next to an old barn, it's technically a tourist farm (cash only, no breakfast,

Riklijeva 6, mobile 041-210-290, www.apartmaji-mezan.si, sasa.
mezan@gmail.com).

¢ **Travellers Haven** is a low-key hostel run with a smile by
Mirjam. The beds fill eight rooms in a nicely renovated hundred-
year-old villa in the Old Town. The lodgings are well-maintained
and the hangout areas are inviting, though the tight bathrooms
offer little privacy (reception open 8:00-13:00 & 16:00-23:00,
laundry machines, rental bikes, Riklijeva cesta 1, mobile 041-396-
545, thbled1@gmail.com).

OUTSIDE OF TOWN

The following listings are a bit farther out: Alp Penzion is a
20-minute walk from the lakefront, but still doable for nondrivers,
while the tourist farm and "glampground" are best for drivers. See
the "Lake Bled" map for locations.

$$$$ Garden Village is pricey...but very cool. Alternately
billed as a "glampground" and a "green resort," this splurge combines the closeness to nature of camping with the amenities of a
hip resort. From the main lodge, restaurant, and rustic pond/pool,
the complex tumbles down a ravine toward a gushing river, connected by slippery plank walks. You can choose between the tree
house (with a loft and netted hammock area up top for kids); the
glamping tents, with canvas walls and nestled in an abundant produce garden; or the simpler pier tents on stilts over the river. All of
these include breakfast, Wi-Fi, and other amenities, but additional
charges for cleaning and shorter stays can add up (on the road toward Lake Bohinj, turn off on the left just before Vila Bled, Cesta
Gorenjskega odreda 16, tel. 08/389-9220, www.gardenvillagebled.
com, reservations@gardenvillagebled.com).

$$$ Alp Penzion makes the most of a peaceful countryside
setting amid hayfields, within a 20-minute, partly uphill walk of
the lake (better for drivers or for those who don't mind the walk).
With 12 rooms (some with balconies), this kid-friendly place is en-
thusiastically run by the Sršen family (family rooms, dinner pos-
sible in summer—ask when you book, air-con, free loaner bikes,
Cankarjeva cesta 20A, tel. 04/574-1614, www.alp-penzion.com,
bled@alp-penzion.com). Just next door is the relaxing Essense spa
(described earlier, under "Helpful Hints").

$$ Tourist Farm Mulej, possible for hardy walkers but much
better for drivers, is a new but traditional farmhouse in a tranquil
valley about a half-mile from the lake (1.5 miles from Bled town).
Damjana and Jože, who run this working farm (with 100 milk
cows...and their smells), also rent out eight modern rooms and two
apartments—all with balconies—and serve breakfasts and dinners
made with food they produce. Be sure to see the udderly fascinating, fully automated cow-milking machine called Lely, who's prac-

tically a member of the family (cash only, family rooms, air-con, free loaner bikes, Selo pri Bledu 42a, tel. 04/574-4617 or 04/022-4888, www.mulej-bled.si, info.mulej@gmail.com). It's in the farm village of Selo—drive along the lakeside road south from Bled, then turn off in Mlino toward Selo, and look for the signs (to the right) once in the village.

Eating in Bled

With a finite number of restaurants in town, places can fill up at dinnertime—it's always best to book ahead. In addition to the places recommended here, consider the high-quality (and expensive) restaurant up at the castle, described in its sight listing earlier.

$$$$ Fine Food Berc—just up the hill from the lakefront, at the recommended Penzion Berc—is a dreamy splurge restaurant. You'll dine at white-tablecloth tables positioned just so on the lush lawn, or in the country-cozy interior. The menu is tempting and high-end, a mix of traditional Slovenian and international dishes (daily 18:00-23:00, Želeška cesta 15, tel. 04/574-1838).

$$$$ Okarina serves a diverse array of cuisines, all of them well-executed: international fare, traditional Slovenian specialties (with an emphasis on game), and Indian (Himalayan) dishes. Creative cooking, fine presentation, and an atmosphere as tastefully eclectic as the food make this place a great splurge. As they're under new management in 2020, some details may be different (Mon-Fri 12:00-15:00 & 18:00-23:00, Sat-Sun 12:00-23:00, closed Nov-mid-April, next to recommended Hotel Lovec at Ljubljanska cesta 8, tel. 04/574-1458).

$$$ Oštarija Peglez'n (The Old Iron), conveniently located on the main road between the commercial center and the lake, cooks up tasty Slovenian and Mediterranean meals, with an emphasis on fish and fun family-style shareable plates. Choose between the delightful Slovenian cottage interior or the shady streetside terrace (daily 12:00-23:00, Cesta Svobode 19A, tel. 04/574-4218).

$$$ Vila Prešeren is a handy lakeside choice, featuring international cuisine (as well as some traditional Slovenian dishes) at tables on a giant terrace reaching down to the lakefront. I'd come here only in good weather, when you can linger on the terrace over a meal, a drink, or a classic Lake Bled dessert; otherwise, skip it (daily 7:00-23:00, Veslaška promenada 14, tel. 04/575-2510).

$$ Gostilna Pri Planincu (By the Mountaineers) is a homey, informal bar coated with license plates and packed with fun-loving and sometimes rowdy natives. A big, dull dining area sprawls behind the small, local-feeling pub, and there's outdoor seating out front and on the side patio. The menu features huge portions of stick-to-your-ribs Slovenian pub grub, plus Balkan grilled-meat

Bled Desserts

While you're in Bled, be sure to enjoy the town's specialty, a cream cake called **kremna rezina** (KRAYM-nah ray-ZEE-nah; often referred to by its German-derived name, **kremšnita,** KRAYM-shnee-tah). It's a layer of cream and a thick layer of vanilla custard artfully sandwiched between sheets of delicate, crispy crust. Heavenly. Slovenes travel from all over the country to sample this famous dessert. You may also see some newfangled strawberry and chocolate *kremšnita* variations, but purists swear by the original.

Slightly less renowned—but just as tasty—is **grmada** (gur-MAH-dah, "bonfire"). This dessert was developed by Hotel Jelovica as a way to get rid of their day-old leftovers. They take yesterday's cake, add rum, milk, custard, and raisins, and top it off with whipped cream and chocolate syrup.

There's also *prekmurska gibanica*—or just **gibanica** (gee-bah-NEET-seh) for short. Originating in the Hungarian corner of the country, *gibanica* is an earthy pastry filled with poppy seeds, walnuts, apples, and cheese, and drizzled with rum.

Yet another dessert is the very traditional **potica** (poh-TEET-seh), a walnut roll that's usually eaten at Christmastime. While it's rare to find this in bakeries, the café on the island in the lake sells several varieties.

Desserts are typically enjoyed with a lake-and-mountains view—the best spots are the terrace at Vila Prešeren, the Panorama restaurant by Grand Hotel Toplice, and the terrace across from Hotel Park (figure around €5 for cake and coffee at any of these places). For a more local place—but lacking a lakeview setting—consider the recommended Slaščičarna Zima (only slightly cheaper).

specialties. Look for their huge, home-style traditional daily specials. Service is playfully opinionated and not always efficient—don't come here if you're in a rush (daily 9:00-23:00, Grajska cesta 8, tel. 04/574-1613, www.pri-planincu.com). Upstairs is a timbered **$ pizzeria** dishing up wood-fired pies (opens at 11:00). The cartoon mural along the outside of the restaurant shows different types of mountaineers (from left to right): thief, normal, mooch ("gopher"), climber, and naked (...well, almost).

$ Pizzeria Rustika, a cozy and convivial spot tucked deep in the Old Town, offers good wood-fired pizzas and salads. Its upstairs terrace is relaxing on a balmy evening (daily 12:00-23:00, Riklijeva cesta 13, tel. 04/576-8900).

Supermarket: The **$ Mercator** grocery store, in the commercial center, has the makings for a bang-up picnic. They sell sandwiches to go for about €3 or will make you one to order (point to what you want). This is a great option for hikers and budget travelers (Mon-Fri 7:30-20:00, Sat until 21:00, Sun 8:00-15:00). There's another location closer to the Old Town and castle (Mon-Sat 7:00-21:00, Sun 8:00-17:00).

Dessert: While tourists generally gulp down their cream cakes on a hotel restaurant's lakefront terrace, residents favor the desserts at **Slaščičarna Zima** (a.k.a. the Brown Bear, for the bear on the sign). It's nicely untouristy, but lacks the atmosphere of the lakeside spots (daily 7:30-21:00, near bus station at Grajska cesta 3, tel. 04/574-1616).

Splurge Restaurant Near Bled

$$$$ Vila Podvin, in the village of Mošnje (about a 15-minute drive from Lake Bled, just past Radovljica), has gained a big culinary reputation in recent years. The talented celebrity chef, Uroš Štefelin (who has been featured on some popular Slovenian cooking shows), prides himself on melding traditional Slovenian recipes with modern techniques and flavors. The dressy but inviting interior and fine garden are equally enjoyable places to dine. Their traditional Slovenian lunch special—available until 15:00—is a nice way to affordably sample their menu. Reservations are smart (Tue-Sat 12:00-22:00, Sun until 17:00, closed Mon, Mošnje 1, tel. 08/384-3470, www.vilapodvin.si). They also rent very sharp rooms and offer cooking classes (explained on their website).

Lake Bled Connections

The most convenient train connections to Bled leave from the Lesce-Bled station, about 2.5 miles away (see details under "Arrival in Bled," earlier). Remember, when buying a train ticket to Lake Bled, make it clear that you want to go to the **Lesce-Bled station** (not the Bled Jezero station, which is poorly connected to the main line). No one in the town of Bled sells train tickets. Buy them at the station just before your train departs; if the ticket window there is closed, buy your ticket on board from the conductor.

Note that if you're going to **Ljubljana,** it's better to take the bus (which leaves from Bled town itself) rather than the train (which leaves from the Lesce-Bled train station).

From Lesce-Bled by Train to: Ljubljana (roughly hourly, 40-60 minutes), **Salzburg** (3/day, 4 hours, some change in Villach, Austria), **Munich** (3/day, 5.5 hours, some change in Villach), **Vienna** (that's **Dunaj** in Slovene, 3/day, 5.5-6 hours, transfer in Villach), **Venice** (2/day with transfer in Villach, 5 hours; instead consider a GoOpti minibus—see below), **Zagreb** (4/day direct, 3-3.5 hours).

By Bus to: Ljubljana (Mon-Sat hourly—usually at :30 past the hour, fewer on Sun, 1.25 hours), **Radovljica** (Mon-Fri 2-3/ hour, Sat hourly, Sun almost hourly, 15 minutes), **Lesce-Bled train station** (2-3/hour, 10 minutes), **Lake Bohinj** (hourly at :20 past the hour, 40 minutes to Bohinj Jezero stop, 50 minutes to Bohinj Vogel or Bohinj Zlatorog stop, 1/day in summer continues all the way to Savica Waterfall trailhead), **Vintgar Gorge** (direct tourist bus mid-June-mid-Sept, private shuttle buses at other times; also possible to take a public bus to Podhom or Spodnje Gorje and walk 15 minutes; for details, see "Vintgar Gorge," later). Confirm times at the TI or by using the schedules posted at the Bled bus station. Buy tickets on the bus.

By Shared Minivan Shuttle: GoOpti can also be an efficient and affordable way to link Lake Bled to various destinations near and far, including the airport. When figuring out a long journey, be sure to compare GoOpti to your other options (www.goopti.com).

By Plane: Ljubljana Airport (airport code: LJU) is between Lake Bled and Ljubljana, about a 45-minute drive from Bled. The best compromise of cost and speed is to book a shared minivan transfer with **GoOpti,** which usually runs around €13 (see description on page 600). A variety of other Bled-based shuttle buses also make the trip for around €15; to see what best matches your schedule, check with **Mamut** (www.slovenija.eu.com), **Maya** (www. bledtransfers.si), and **Zup Prevozi** (www.zup-prevozi.eu). Because these run somewhat irregularly, it's always best to book ahead. A taxi costs around €50-60 (set price up front—since it's outside of town, they don't use the meter; I'd book ahead with **Bled Tours** for the same price, see page 609). For details on the Ljubljana airport, see page 600.

Route Tips for Drivers: Bled is less than an hour north of Ljubljana on the slick A-2 expressway. The exit is marked for *Lesce,* but you'll also see signs for *Bled,* which will lead you directly to the lake (where the road becomes Ljubljanska cesta).

To reach **Radovljica** (bee museum) or **Lesce** (train station), drive out of Bled on Ljubljanska cesta toward the expressway. Watch for the turnoff to *Lesce* on the right. They're on the same road: Lesce first (to reach train station, divert right when entering town), then Radovljica. (Signs to *Radovljica* will divert you out to the main road that parallels the expressway, then back down into Radovljica; instead, follow signs to *Lesce,* and drive through that town for the more direct route.) Also along this road, between Lesce and Radovljica, is the well-marked turnoff to the road to **Kropa** (with its Iron Forging Museum).

Near Lake Bled

The countryside around Bled offers several day trips that can be done easily without a car (bus connection information is described in each section). The four trips listed here are the best (two small-town/museum experiences, two hiking/back-to-nature options). They're more convenient than can't-miss, but each is worthwhile on a longer visit, and all give a good taste of the Julian Alps. For a self-guided driving tour through farther-flung (and even more striking) parts of the Julian Alps, see the next chapter.

Vintgar Gorge

For those seeking an easy yet spectacular walk, Vintgar (VEENT-gar), worth ▲▲, is one of my favorite low-impact hikes in Slovenia or Croatia. Just north of Bled, the River Radovna has carved this mile-long, picturesque gorge into the mountain-side. Boardwalks and bridges put you right in the middle of the magic in this "poor man's Plitvice." Shaded and relatively cool, this is a refreshing place for a walk on a hot day (and extra cold on a cool day—bundle up).

The gorge—easily reachable from Bled by bus or foot—works well for those who are itching for a hike but don't have a car. From the entrance, allow about 1.5 hours for a round-trip hike, including time for photos (and there will be photos). On sunny days, the gorge can be crowded (and less idyllic) after about 11:00—if you anticipate crowds, get an early start.

Cost and Hours: €10 to enter gorge, daily July-Aug 7:00-

Near Lake Bled

20:00, June until 19:00, April-May and Sept 8:00-18:00, Oct-Nov 9:00-16:00, closed Dec-March, tel. 04/572-5266.

Getting to Vintgar Gorge: The gorge is 2.5 miles north of Bled. To reach the gorge entrance, you can drive (10 minutes), walk (takes at least one hour one-way), pedal a rental bike (about 30 minutes, easiest with an electric bike), take a shuttle bus (about 10 minutes), or take a public bus (15-minute ride plus 15-minute walk).

Walkers and **cyclists** leave Bled on the road between the castle and St. Martin's Church and take the uphill (left) road at the fork. Just after the little yellow chapel, turn right on the road with the big tree, then immediately left at the Mercator grocery store. When the road swings left, continue straight onto Partizanska (marked for *Podhom* and *Zasip;* ignore the bus sign for *Vintgar* pointing left). At the fork just after the little bridge, go left for Podhom, then simply follow signs for *Vintgar.*

Drivers follow signs to *Podhom*, then *Vintgar* (see walking/cycling instructions, above), and park for free right at the gorge entrance.

The easiest option for a quick visit is to take a **shuttle bus** to the gorge entrance. The cheap option (€1 one-way) is the official shuttle bus that departs only in the summer (mid-June-mid-Sept); at other times, you can pay €5 one-way for a bus operated by a private agency (see "Getting Around Lake Bled (Literally)," earlier).

Finally, there are **public bus** connections that get you close: Take the bus either to Podhom (Mon-Fri hourly, none Sat-Sun, 15 minutes) or Spodnje Gorje (take bus in direction of Krnica, hourly, 15 minutes); from either of these bus stops, it's a 15-minute walk to the gorge (follow signs for *Vintgar*).

Gorge Hike: After buying your ticket, you'll hit the board-walk trail (sometimes a bit slippery) and crisscross over the most dramatic and narrow stretch, tiptoeing over several waterfalls and marveling at the clarity of the water. Then the gorge—and the trail—flattens out and passes under a high stone footbridge and over a scenic dam. Finally, at the end of the gorge, you'll reach a footbridge over a plunging waterfall (next to a snack stand and WCs). For more views, continue on five minutes downhill (follow-ing the *Pod Slap* signs), then circle over the river again to reach a knoll where you can peer up at the waterfall and bridge you just crossed.

When finished, you can simply go back the way you came, or take a prettier return to Bled (described next).

Scenic Hike Back to Bled: If you still have energy once you reach the end of the gorge, consider this longer hike back with pan-oramic views. Behind the snack stand deep in the gorge, find the trail marked *Pod Katarina*. You'll go uphill for 25 strenuous min-utes (following the red-and-white circles and arrows) before crest-ing the hill and enjoying beautiful views over Bled town and the region. Continue straight down the road 15 minutes to the typical, narrow old village of Zasip, then walk (about 30 minutes) or take the bus back to Bled.

Radovljica

The town of Radovljica (rah-DOH-vleet-suh, "Radol'ca" for short), perched on a plateau above the Sava River, has the charming Old Town that Bled lacks (re-freshingly, it also lacks much of Bled's summer crowds). The traffic-free core of the town, once hemmed in by a stout wall (still faintly visible in some areas), is jammed with historic buildings that surround the long, skinny

main square called Linhartov trg. While Radovljica's Old Town is a pleasant place to stroll or nurse a coffee, you can see it all in a few minutes. The main reason to visit here is to tour its small but strangely fascinating beekeeping museum—despite having only a few rooms, it still ranks as one of Europe's biggest on the apiarian arts. Skip the town on Mondays, when the museum is closed (and be aware that the museum has shorter hours off-season).

Tourist Information: The enthusiastic TI loves to help visitors appreciate the town (daily 9:00-19:00; Oct-April Mon-Fri until 16:00, Sat-Sun until 18:00; Linhartov trg 1, tel. 04/531-5112, www.radolca.si).

GETTING TO RADOVLJICA

Buses to Radovljica generally leave Bled at least every half-hour (fewer on weekends, buy ticket from driver, trip takes about 15 minutes). To reach the town center and the bee museum from the bus station, leave the station going straight ahead, cross the bus parking lot and the next street, then turn left down the far street (following brown sign for *Staro Mesto*). In five minutes, you'll reach the start of the pedestrianized Linhartov trg (with the TI—on the right—and the start of my Old Town Stroll).

Drivers leave Bled on Ljubljanska cesta and follow the directions under "Route Tips for Drivers" under "Lake Bled Connections," earlier. The road dead-ends at Radovljica's pedestrian zone, where you'll find a parking lot (on the right), the TI, and the start of my Old Town Stroll.

A handy **bike** path scenically and peacefully connects Bled with Radovljica (about 4 miles, get details at TI).

Sights in Radovljica

Old Town Stroll

Whether arriving by bus or by car, you'll enter the Old Town next to the TI. If you curl around below the main road (that is, the downhill road by the TI), you'll find the scant remains of the city's original **defensive trench**—the only surviving one in Slovenia.

On the left, just as you enter the Old Town, you'll see **Vinoteka Sodček,** a wine bar and shop that offers a handy opportunity to learn about and sample Slovenian wines. Their €15 tasting includes five wines, plus cheese and *pršut* (air-dried ham)—it's best to call ahead to arrange this. You can also buy bottles of wine here for €10-15. Owner Aleš and his well-trained staff know their stuff; this is an easygoing, low-pressure place for learning and stocking up (Mon-Sat 9:00-22:00, closed Sun, Linhartov trg 8, tel. 04/531-5071).

Continuing into the Old Town, after a half-block you'll pass a fun little **secondhand shop** on the right—crammed with everything from basic kitchenware to genuine Slovenian antiques.

Beyond that, the street opens up into **Linhartov trg,** a charming square fronted by historic buildings. On the left, look for the

LAKE BLED

Keramika sign marking the **Magušarjeva Hiša,** a fine old Gothic house where potter Urban Magušar lives, and where he displays rural pottery from the local region. In the workshop *(manufaktura)* across the street, he has a studio and exhibition space and teaches pottery classes (Mon-Fri 10:00-13:00 & 14:00-16:00, Wed until 19:00, closed Sat-Sun—except first Sat morning each month, Linhartov trg 12, mobile 041-734-808).

Just beyond, the **Vidičeva Hiša** café serves great ice cream and cakes. Farther along is the traditional, recommended **Lectar** restaurant, with a living museum in the basement where you can watch bakers making traditional gingerbread ornaments (€2 entry).

Across the street is a monument with a student holding a big medallion image of **Josipina Hočevar,** a Radovljica native who later helped fund the town's water system (see the old well nearby) and a school and many important buildings in Krško, near Zagreb. Next to that is the **Šivičeva Hiša,** an atmospheric late-Gothic house with a gallery that's open to the public (closed Mon). If you go a block down any street to the right, you'll come to a fine valley **viewpoint** emphasizing Radovljica's dramatic position on a long promontory (the best view is at the far end of the main square).

Dominating the main part of the square is the big, yellow town **"castle"** (actually a mansion); upstairs you'll find the **Apicultural Museum** (described next), the Linhart Museum, and the Baroque Hall.

Beyond the mansion (and connected to it by a gallery) is **St. Peter's Church;** to its right is its rectory, where you can dip into the pretty courtyard.

Circle all the way around the church, then go through the gate to the edge of the ravine. Burrowed into the hillside is a **WWII-era bunker** left behind by the Nazis. Peeking into the window of the bunker, you'll see it's been turned into a chapel dedicated to Edith Stein, a 20th-century Polish Jew who became a Carmelite nun but was arrested by the Nazis and executed at Auschwitz. She was later sainted by Pope John Paul II (notice the menorah and Star of David inside the chapel, on the right). While she has no official ties to Radovljica, locals are inspired by Edith's example.

▲▲Apicultural Museum (Čebelarski Muzej)

This museum celebrates Slovenia's long and very proud beekeeping heritage. While the exhibits about the history of beekeeping are oddly fascinating, the highlight is the extensive collection of colorfully painted frontboard panels (used on the front of hives)—one of Slovenia's most cherished folk arts. Replicas of these panels are sold in souvenir shops nationwide, but these are the real deal.

Cost and Hours: €4, good English descriptions, small English guidebook is a nice souvenir; Tue-Sun 10:00-18:00, closed Mon, shorter hours Nov-April, Jan-Feb closed Sat-Mon; clean and easy WCs, upstairs at Linhartov trg 1, tel. 04/532-0520, www.mro.si.

Visiting the Museum: Everything is well-described in English, but this commentary will help you locate the highlights. Note that a renovation set to be complete by mid-2020 may mean some changes.

The **first room** of the museum traces the history of beekeeping, from the time when bees were kept in hollowed-out trees to the present day. The bust celebrates beekeeper extraordinaire Anton Janša. On the nearby wall, you'll see excerpts from his first-ever textbook on beekeeping, as well as documents from other VIBs (very important beekeepers).

In the **second room** are old-fashioned tools. When a new queen bee is born, the old queen takes half the hive's bees to a new location. Experienced beekeepers used the long, skinny instrument (a beehive stethoscope) to figure out when the swarm was working up a steady buzz, indicating they were ready to fly the coop. Then, once the bees had moved to a nearby tree, the beekeeper used the big spoons to retrieve the queen—surrounded by an angry ball of her subjects—from her new home before she could get settled in. The beekeeper transferred the furious gang into a man-made hive designed for easier, more sanitary collection of honey. You can also see the tools beekeepers used to create smoke, which makes bees less aggressive. Even today, some of Slovenia's old-fashioned beekeepers simply light up a cigarette and blow smoke on any bees that get ornery. The life-size model of a man carrying a box on his back illustrates how dedicated beekeepers would trudge uphill with their hives to help them reach higher and higher blossoms as the summer wore on. You'll also see a variety of old beehives (and a press used to squeeze every last drop of honey out of that comb), as well as photos of apiaries—large, freestanding buildings that house multiple hives. The map on the wall shows how the Carniolan bee—favored by beekeepers for its relatively mellow personality and fast growth in springtime—has been exported far and wide throughout the world, thanks to its adaptability to new climates.

The **third room** features the museum's highlight: whimsically painted beehive frontboards (called *panjske končnice*). Beekeepers, believing these paintings would help the bees find their way home, developed a tradition of decorating their hives with religious, historical, and satirical folk themes. It was also a creative way to mark their own hives. The oldest panel dates from 1758, but the practice really took off in the 19th century. Take your time perusing these delightful illustrations. The depiction of a hunter's funeral shows all the animals happy...except his dog. In another panel, animals shave the hunter—evoking an old Slovenian saying about "shaving the fool." Panels also reveal professional stereotypes of the time: One popular panel shows two farmers fighting over a cow, while a lawyer milks it. Another features a giant snail running over very slow-moving tailors (who were considered extremely lethargic in sewing new clothes). Historical panels include a bloody beheading during a local battle and several scenes of troublesome Turks. There's everything from portraits of Habsburg emperors, to a "true crime" sequence of a man murdering his family as they sleep, to proto-"Lockhorns" cartoons of marital strife, to awkward depictions of foreign lands (based on likely incomplete or faulty descriptions of the day), to 18th-century erotica (one with a woman showing some leg and another with a flip-up, peek-a-boo panel). A few panels blur the line between humorous and misogynistic: Look for the devil sharpening a woman's tongue on a wheel; the mill where old women are put in and young women are pulled out; or the man carrying a cross—and his wife—on his back. (Equal-opportunity offenders, beekeepers also painted scenes of drunk men being yanked out of bars and away from card games by their wives.) The life-size wooden statues were used to "guard" the beehives—and designed to look like fearsome Ottoman and Napoleonic soldiers.

The **fourth room** examines the biology of bees. In the summer only, look for the actual, functioning beehive. Try to find the queen—she's usually marked with a dot on her back. The surround-sound hive nearby lets you step inside to hear the noise of a buzzing queen. You'll also see bee-related products, including wax items, ornaments, and pastries. Another exhibit shows how bees—so respected here in Slovenia, and around the world—are a popular decorative motif, adorning everything from coins to buildings (in many cultures, diligent bees, who store their honey, are symbolic of banks).

The **fifth room** features a modern beekeeper's house, special exhibits, and a good but dry, detailed 14-minute film about the Carniolan bee. Just beyond is another room of antique beekeeping equipment.

Back at the entrance, the ticket desk sells a few choice souvenirs, including hand-painted replicas of frontboards, honey brandy, candles, ornaments, and other bee products.

Slovenian Beekeeping

Since the days before Europeans had sugar, Slovenia has been a big honey producer. Slovenian farmer Anton Janša (1734-1773) is considered the father of modern beekeeping. Habsburg Empress Maria Theresa brought him to Vienna to become Europe's first official teacher of this art. And even today, beekeeping is considered a crucial part of Slovenian culture. The area around Lake Bled (Carniola) has about 6,000 inhabitants, including 65 beekeepers who manage 5,000 hives—the most bees per capita of any place in Europe.

Most Slovenian beekeepers maintain large buildings called apiaries, which hold banks of smaller hives (as opposed to beekeepers in North America, who tend to have a few separate large hives). This innovation—one of many by Janša— allows beekeepers to maximize efficiency. Hives always face southeast, to enjoy sun in the morning and shade in the afternoon. The front panel of each individual hive is painted

in bright colors, often depicting creative folk scenes. This originally was designed to help both the bees and the beekeepers (who were often illiterate) distinguish the hives from each other. (While bees may not be able to tell a painting of a bear from one of a flower, they can distinguish enough patterns and colors to keep themselves from accidentally going to the wrong hive, where they'd be attacked as an outsider.)

Replicas of those characteristic **beehive panels** are available at shops in Bled and Ljubljana and make for appealing souvenirs. Basic reproductions of the beehive panels cost around €12-15, while better-quality, hand-painted ones run €20-30 or more. When perusing your options, it helps to know the stories behind each one (see the Apicultural Museum listing for a rundown on some of the designs).

Nearby: Sharing a ticket desk with the bee museum, the skippable **Linhart Museum** celebrates one of Slovenia's leading Enlightenment thinkers: Radovljica-born Anton Linhart, the 18th-century politician and historian who wrote some of the first plays in the Slovenian language, setting the stage for patriotic poet France Prešeren (€5 combo-ticket with Apicultural Museum, same hours).

The other apian souvenir is **honey.** In 2013, Slovenian honey was designated as a unique product by the European Union—a certification that means only honey produced in a certain place and manner can carry that name. Taste can differ tremendously from hive to hive, and is determined by the specific flowers and blossoms a hive's bees gather pollen from. Ideally find a shop that will let you sample several. In general, honeys made from mixed flowers and linden blossoms (which tend to be cloudy from a natural crystallization process) have the sweetest, mildest flavor; those made from chestnut or pine trees can have a bitter aftertaste. The honeys that appear creamy are infused with flavors and are most often eaten on bread or pancakes; plain honey is more versatile.

Besides honey, beekeepers also make money by raising new queen bees. Each hive has one, and they can't be bred—one of the larvae is simply fed special "royal jelly" that encourages her to become a leader. In the springtime, when bees are born, the beekeeper keeps a close eye on the hive to figure out whether there are any potential queens. If he finds one, he'll move the old queen—who brings half the hive with her—to a new home (before she can find one on her own).

Slovenes still reserve an importance and affection for bees that's rare in modern times. For example, the Slovene language has different words for "to give birth" and "to die": One they use exclusively for humans and bees, and a different one for all other animals. If a beekeeper dies, it's believed (with some pretty incontrovertible evidence) that the new beekeeper must formally "introduce" himself to the hive by going there and explaining to the bees what has happened; otherwise, they become confused and agitated, and often die themselves.

To learn more about Slovenian beekeeping, visit the insightful Apicultural Museum in Radovljica. For an even more vivid, practical experience, call Blaž at Kralov Med near Bled for a demonstration (see "Sights at Lake Bled," earlier). At either place, you'll get a sense for just how proud Slovenes are of their bees.

Eating in Radovljica

Several Radovljica restaurants near the bee museum have view terraces overlooking the surrounding mountains and valleys.

$$$ Lectar offers pricey, hearty Slovenian fare in a rural-feeling setting with a user-friendly, super-traditional menu. Its several heavily decorated rooms are often filled with tour groups, but in good weather, don't miss the terrace out back. Come here if you want to linger over rustic Slovenian specialties. The restaurant is known for its heart-shaped gingerbread cookies (called *lect*), inscribed with messages of love. In the cellar is a living museum where you can pay €2 to watch costumed bakers make and decorate these hearts according to the traditional recipe (daily 12:00-22:00, family-friendly, Linhartov trg 2, tel. 04/537-4800).

$$ Gostilna Avguštin, across the street, is the simpler local alternative for a nice variety of unpretentious, stick-to-your-ribs Slovenian fare, including hearty pastas, meal-sized salads, and vegetarian options. Their terrace in back enjoys an even better view than Lectar's (daily 10:00-21:00, Linhartov trg 15, tel. 04/531-4163).

Kropa

Tucked in a narrow gully below the Jelovica Plateau, the modest metalworking village of Kropa has a big history as one of the earliest and most prolific industrial centers of Europe. Kropa thrills engineers—for whom it merits ▲▲—but may leave others cold.

GETTING TO KROPA

Kropa is poorly connected by bus, other than a weekly summer-time bus from Bled—see the hop-on, hop-off bus listing in "Getting Around Lake Bled (Literally)," earlier—and sporadic weekday connections to Radovljica; skip Kropa unless you have a car. Drivers can find the well-marked road to Kropa off the road that runs between Lesce and Radovljica.

BACKGROUND

Beginning in the 15th century, the people of Kropa harnessed their substantial natural resources: iron ore from nearby mines; plenty of wood to keep the furnaces burning; and water from their rushing river, which they diverted into channels to power waterwheels. By the 16th century, Kropa was already known as one of the most important blacksmithing towns in Europe, and was granted a prized semiautonomous status by the Habsburg Empire. Blacksmiths here specialized in spikes and nails, producing 127 types—from small tacks for shoes, to bigger nails for horseshoes, to huge spikes used for major construction projects all over Europe. The romantic wooden pilings in the Venice lagoon are held together with Kropa spikes.

By the 18th century—still well before the dawn of the Industrial Age—Kropa was one of the most industrially developed places in Europe. Its 70 houses were packed with 1,400 men, women, and children, who all worked in the foundries. But by the late 18th century, local iron ore deposits were depleted, the industry collapsed, and some 800 local residents died of disease and other poverty-related causes. The 19th century saw another boost, as Kropa spikes were in demand to build the Vienna-Trieste railway. By modern times, the nail and spike industry had been replaced by decorative blacksmithing (especially at the big Uko factory across from the museum), which included items such as fancy gates and mailboxes. Today, Kropa's 90 houses hold a more reasonable population of 200.

Sights in Kropa

▲Iron Forging Museum (Kovaški Muzej)

This modest but engaging exhibit traces the history of this metalworking burg. Filling two floors of a typical old Kropa house, the displays have little English explanation but capture the blacksmithing spirit of Kropa.

Cost and Hours: €3, Tue-Sun 10:00-18:00, closed Mon, shorter hours Nov-April, Kropa 10, tel. 04/533-7200, www.mro.si.

Visiting the Museum: When you buy your ticket, ask the attendant if she's willing to show you around the museum—this really helps bring the (otherwise poorly explained) exhibits to life. If she's busy, the following describes some things to look for on your own.

Go up to the first floor and enter the room with the big town model of Kropa as it was in the 19th century. Notice just how ingeniously the town channeled its water supply to use its raw power for its foundries. The next room shows big chunks of iron ore, and the buckets used to gather and carry it. (Many workers here farmed during the summer and were miners in the winter.) Although the big model of a blast furnace seems fairly sophisticated and modern, it was used in Kropa all the way back in the mid-15th century. A waterwheel pumped bellows onto a wood fire, superheating it to melt down the raw iron ore to create impure "pig iron." The second, smaller chimney was a furnace that further refined the iron. Look at the blacksmiths' tools and pass through the room with several huge bellows, then enter the room with ornamental iron gratings and other decorations. These date from Kropa's later era of blacksmithing, between the two World Wars. Near the base of the stairs is a big music box with a piano, drums, and cymbals (ask the ticket seller to start it for you).

Climb the stairs to the top floor, where you'll see a model of a typical family home, as well as mannequins of the family in period dress. The next room displays the vast range of nails and spikes that were produced here. A worker was expected to produce 2,000 of these spikes in one day.

Strolling the Town

Walk from the museum up through this hardworking yet charming village. Notice the **canals** that have been split off from the main river to channel water to turn waterwheels (you'll see a replica waterwheel by the Uko factory).

The main **bridge** through town offers a good view up and down the thundering river—making it clear why this was an attractive place for early industry. The blocky, boldly communist-era **monument** next to the bridge honors the Partisans who died during World War II while evicting the Nazis from Yugoslavia. Although its aesthetic is off-putting Socialist Realism, its content—with locally made iron decorations—is unique to Kropa. Notice the Kropa resident handing over his hammer in exchange for a rifle. Locals have long enjoyed military exemption because their metalworking prowess was so valuable to the war effort. The communist Yugoslav government—always eager to celebrate industry's role in advancing the cause of the proletariat—made Kropa Slovenia's first town to be protected as a cultural monument, in 1953.

Crossing the bridge and continuing up the road, near the top of town on the left you'll pass a traditional **spike forge** with firewood stacked out front. This working facility—which still merges the power of wood, water, and a blacksmith's arm to create spikes—is part of the Iron Forging Museum, but unfortunately, it's rarely open to individual visitors (may be possible July-Aug on Tue, or you can call the museum a few days ahead to book a private demonstration for €20). For most of its history, Kropa had 15 such forges.

Lake Bohinj

The pristine alpine Lake Bohinj (BOH-heen), 16 miles southwest of Bled, enjoys a quieter scene and (in clear weather) even better vistas of Triglav and the surrounding mountains. This is a real back-to-nature experience, with just a smattering of hotels and campgrounds, rather than the well-oiled resort machine of Bled. Some people adore Bohinj; others are bored by it. While

spectacular in clear, sunny weather, it's disappointing in the clouds (and, because of its position deep in the mountains, it can be socked-in here even when it's clear in Bled). But if the weather is great and you're finding Bled too touristy to allow you to really enjoy nature, go to Bohinj.

GETTING TO LAKE BOHINJ

From Bled, hourly **buses** depart at :20 past each hour for Bohinj, stopping at three destinations: Bohinj Jezero (the village of Ribčev Laz, 40 minutes), then Bohinj Vogel (a 10-minute walk from the base of the Vogel Mountain cable car, 50 minutes), and finally a few hundred yards more to Bohinj Zlatorog (Hotel Zlatorog and the one-hour hike to the Savica Waterfall trailhead, 50 minutes). In summer (July-Aug), one daily bus continues all the way to the Savica Waterfall trailhead (see details under "Savica Waterfall," later). Off-season, there are fewer buses—confirm times before you depart.

Drivers leave Bled going south along the lakefront road, Cesta Svobode; in the village of Mlino, you'll peel off from the lake and follow signs to *Boh Bistrica* (a midsize town near Lake Bohinj). Once in the town of Bohinjska Bistrica, turn right, following *Boh Jezero* signs. The road takes you to the village of Ribčev Laz and along the lakefront road with all the attractions—the drive from Bled to the lake takes about 30 minutes. You can follow this road all the way to the Vogel cable-car parking lot; at the Vogel turnoff, you can continue straight ahead to reach the Savica Waterfall trailhead, or turn right and cross the bridge to curl around the far end of the lake and see the pristine river that feeds the lake (which flows out of the pool at the base of the Savica Waterfall).

Sights at Lake Bohinj

A visit to Bohinj has three main options: a village (offering boat trips on the lake), a cable car (and nearby cemetery), and a waterfall hike. I've listed them as you'll reach them along the main road from Bled, which runs along the south side of the lake. The lake's website is helpful: www.bohinj.si.

Ribčev Laz Village

Coming from Bled, your first views of Bohinj will be from the little village called Ribčev Laz (loosely translated as "Good Fishin' Hole") at the southeast corner of the lake. Here you'll find a TI, a handful of hotels and ice-cream stands, and the Bohinj Jezero bus stop.

On the way into town, on a small hill to the right, is a **monument** to the four Bohinj-area mountaineers who first summited Mount Triglav on August 26, 1778.

The town's main landmark is its picturesque lakefront church, **St. John the Baptist** (to your right as you face the lake, past the stone bridge; not open to visitors).

A five-minute stroll down the main lakefront road is a dock where you can catch an electric **tourist boat** to make a silent circuit around the lake (€10.50 round-trip, €9 one-way, 5/day April-Oct). The boat stops at the far end of the lake, at Camp Zlatorog—a 10-minute walk from the Vogel cable car (described next).

Across from the Ribčev Laz dock is a fun concrete 3-D model of Triglav. Finally, a few more steps down the road, just beyond a boat-rental dock, is a statue of **Zlatorog,** the Golden Horn—a mythical chamois-like creature native to the Julian Alps.

▲Vogel Mountain Cable Car

For a mountain perch without the sweat, take the cable car up to the top of Vogel Mountain, offering impressive panoramic views of Mount Triglav and the Julian Alps. On a clear day, this is the best mountain panorama you can get without wings (the light is best in the morning).

Cost and Hours: €20 round-trip, daily 8:00-18:00, runs every 30 minutes in summer and continuously in winter, closed Nov, www.vogel.si.

Getting There: To reach the cable-car station, drivers follow signs to *Vogel* (to the left off the main lakefront road, marked *1915* and *1917*); by bus, get off at the Bohinj Vogel stop (request this stop from driver) and hike about 10 minutes up the steep road on the left (away from the lake).

Visiting the Summit: After you arrive at the top, savor the views from the metal platform where you exit the cable car...just don't look down. Walking up through the cable-car station (past the Viharnik snack bar, with basic food and far-from-basic views), you'll pop out at the summit, a ski-in-winter, hike-in-summer area with a pasture filled with grazing cows and smaller chairlifts to various recreation areas.

The first chairlift is designed for skiers and doesn't run in summer, but if you hike down into the little valley, you can take the second chairlift up the adjacent summit (Orlove Glave) for views into another valley on the other side. Then, from Orlove Glave, you can hike or ride the chairlift back to where you started. With plenty of time and very strong knees, you could even hike from Orlove Glave all the way back down to Lake Bohinj.

If you need a break near the cable-car station, the alpine hut Merjasec (Wild Boar) offers tasty strudel and a wide variety of local brandies (including the notorious "Boar's Blood"—a concoction of several flavors guaranteed to get you snorting).

World War I Cemetery

Back down below the cable car, on the main road just beyond the Bohinj Vogel bus stop, look for the metal gate on the left marking the final resting place for some WWI Soča Front soldiers (see sidebar on page 668). While no fighting occurred here (it was mostly on the other side of these mountains), injured soldiers were brought to a nearby hospital, and those who didn't recover ended up here. Notice that many of the names are not Slovenian, but Hungarian, Polish, Czech, and so on—a reminder that the entire multiethnic Austro-Hungarian Empire was involved in the fighting. If you're walking down from the cable-car station, the cemetery makes for a poignant detour on your way to the main road (look for it through the trees).

Savica Waterfall (Slap Savica)

Up the valley beyond the end of the lake is Bohinj's final treat, a waterfall called Slap Savica (sah-VEET-seh). Hardy hikers enjoy following the moderate-to-strenuous uphill trail (including 553 stairs) to see the cascade, which dumps into a remarkably pure pool of aquamarine snowmelt.

Cost and Hours: €3, daily in summer from 8:00 until dusk, allow up to 1.5 hours for the round-trip hike.

Getting There: Drivers follow the lakefront road to where it ends, right at the trailhead. Without a car, getting to the trailhead is a hassle. Boats on the lake, as well as most public buses from Bled, take you only as far as the Bohinj Zlatorog stop—still a one-hour hike from the trailhead. However, in summer (July-Aug), one bus a day goes from Bled all the way to the Savica trailhead (likely departing Bled at 10:00, returning at 12:20). Otherwise, you can change to a local bus in the Bohinj area to reach the falls. Frankly, if the connections don't fit your itinerary, it's not worth the fuss.

Sleeping at Lake Bohinj

If you'd like to get away from it all and settle in at Bohinj, consider **$$ Hotel Stare** (STAH-reh). Well-run by mild-mannered Jože, it has 10 older, rustic but well-maintained rooms (five with balconies) in a pristine setting at the far end of the lake (Ukanc 128, mobile 040-558-669, www.bohinj-hotel.com, info@bohinj-hotel.com). They also rent an eight-person villa for longer stays.

THE JULIAN ALPS

Vršič Pass • Soča River Valley • Bovec • Kobarid

The countryside around Lake Bled is plenty beautiful. But to max out your Slovenian mountain experience, head for the cut-glass peaks of the Julian Alps. The northwestern corner of Slovenia—within yodeling distance of Austria and Italy—is where mountain culture has a Slavic accent.

The Slovenian mountainsides are laced with hiking paths, blanketed in deep forests, gurgling with intensely colorful rivers, and speckled with ski resorts and vacation chalets. Beyond every ridge is a peaceful alpine village nestled around a quaint Baroque steeple. And in the center of it all is Mount Triglav—ol' "Three Heads"—Slovenia's national symbol and, at 9,396 feet, its tallest mountain.

The single best day in the Julian Alps is spent driving up and over the 50 hairpin turns of breathtaking Vršič Pass (vur-SHEECH) and back down via the Soča (SOH-chah) River Valley, lined with offbeat nooks and Hemingway-haunted crannies. As you curl between the peaks, you'll enjoy stunning high-mountain scenery, whitewater rivers with superb fishing, rustic rest stops, thought-provoking WWI sights, and charming hamlets.

A pair of Soča Valley towns watches over the region. Centrally situated Bovec is all about good times (it's the whitewater-adventure sports hub), while Kobarid has Old World charm and attends to more serious matters (WWI history). Though neither is a destination in itself, both Bovec and Kobarid are pleasant, functional, and convenient home bases for lingering in this gloriously beautiful region. I've also recommended a handful of countryside hotels and tourist farms.

PLANNING YOUR TIME

Most visitors do this area as a surgical strike on a full-day side-trip from Lake Bled or Ljubljana—and even that fleeting glimpse is very satisfying. But there's plenty here to make it worth slowing down and spending a night (or even longer). If you'd like to take advantage of the Soča Valley's hiking trails, evocative WWI historical sites, and many adventure sports (especially river rafting on the Soča)—and have some flexibility for the ever-changing weather—give yourself multiple nights.

GETTING AROUND THE JULIAN ALPS

The Julian Alps are best by **car.** Even if you're doing the rest of your trip by train, consider renting a car here, if only for the day, to achieve maximum mountain thrills. I've included a self-guided drive that incorporates the best of the Julian Alps: Vršič Pass (usually open May-Oct) and the Soča Valley.

If you're without your own wheels, hiring a **local guide with a car** can be a great value, maximizing not only what you see, but also what you learn. Or you can choose a cheaper but less personalized day-trip **excursion** from Bled. (Both options are explained under "Tours at Lake Bled," page 610.)

In the summer, a **public bus** more or less follows my driving-tour route, described next, over the Vršič Pass (departs Ljubljana daily July-Aug at 15:00, 4.5 hours to Bovec, 5 hours to Kobarid; and another bus departs Ljubljana Mon-Sat at 7:30 and uses the Predel Pass via Italy, 4 hours to Bovec). Additional Vršič Pass buses leave from Kranjska Gora at the foot of the mountains, which is also connected by bus to Ljubljana and Bled—some departures are coordinated to do the full trip with an easy change (6/day June-Sept, 2 hours from Kranjska Gora to Bovec). Bovec is well-connected to Ljubljana any time of year via Idrija; while you'll miss the high-mountain scenery of the Vršič Pass, this gives you more options for linking the Soča Valley to the rest of Slovenia (1-2/day, about 4 hours total). To confirm schedules, see www.ap-ljubljana.si or www.getbybus.com.

Julian Alps Drive

VRŠIČ PASS LOOP

This all-day, self-guided drive—rated ▲▲▲—takes you over the highest mountain pass in Slovenia, with stunning scenery and a few quirky sights along the way. From waterfalls to hiking trails, WWI history to queasy suspension bridges, this trip has something for everyone.

Most of the Julian Alps are encompassed by Triglav National Park (Triglavski Narodni Park). This drive starts and ends in either Bled or Ljubljana, going over the Vršič Pass and through the Soča River Valley. While not for stick-shift novices, all but the most timid drivers will agree that the scenery is worth the many hairpin turns. Frequent pullouts offer plenty of opportunities to relax, stretch your legs, and enjoy the vistas.

Planning Your Drive: This drive can be done in a day (about five hours of driving), but consider spending the night along the way for a more leisurely pace. You can return to your starting point, or do this trip one-way as a very scenic detour between Bled and Ljubljana. These rough estimates do not include stops: Bled to the top of Vršič Pass—1 hour (30 minutes more from Ljubljana; add about 30 minutes round-trip for Planica ski-jump detour); Vršič Pass to Trenta (start of Soča Valley)—30 minutes; Trenta to Bovec—30 minutes; Bovec to Kobarid—30 minutes; Kobarid to Ljubljana or Bled—2 hours.

The best sources of information are the Bled TI (see the Lake Bled chapter), the Triglav National Park Information Center in Trenta, and the TIs in Bovec and Kobarid (all described later in this chapter). Local TIs hand out good, free maps covering this area, or you can invest in a more detailed one. If the pass is closed, you can still access the Soča Valley by looping around through Italy and taking the **Predel Pass**—a route nearly as scenic as this main option. Just reverse the Predel Pass route described on page 657.

From Bled or Ljubljana to Vršič Pass

From Bled or Ljubljana, take the A-2 expressway north, enjoying views of Mount Triglav on the left as you drive. About 10 minutes past Bled, you'll approach the industrial city of **Jesenice,** whose iron- and steelworks once filled this valley with multicolored smoke. (It was nicknamed the "Detroit of Yugoslavia.") Many of these old factories closed in the 1980s, and the air is much cleaner now.

Just after the giant smokestack with the billboards, the little gaggle of colorful houses on the right (just next to the freeway) is **Kurja Vas**

JULIAN ALPS

("Chicken Village"). This unassuming place is locally famous for producing hockey players: 18 of the 20 players on the 1971 Yugoslav hockey team—which went to the World Championships—were from this tiny hamlet.

As you zip past Jesenice, keep your eye out for the exit marked *Jesenice-zahod*, *Trbiž/Tarvisio*, *Kr. Gora*, and *Hrušica* (it's after the gas station, just before the tunnel to Austria). When you exit, turn left toward *Kranjska Gora* and *Trbiž/Tarvisio* (yellow sign).

Just after the exit, the big turquoise building surrounded by tall lights was the former border station (the overpass you'll go under leads into Austria). Locals have fond memories of visiting Aus-

The Julian Alps &
Northwest Slovenia

1 Pristava Lepena Resort
2 Tourist Farm Pri Plajerju
3 Tourist Farm Kranjc
4 Hiša Franko Restaurant

tria during the Yugoslav days, when they smuggled back forbidden Western goods. Some items weren't available at home (VCRs, Coca-Cola, designer clothes), while other goods were simply better in Austria (chocolate, coffee, dishwasher soap).

Just after the exit, you'll cross the Sava River. The main river of the former Yugoslavia, this 600-mile-long waterway begins in these mountains, flows past Ljubljana and Zagreb, defines the Croatian-Bosnian border, and finally joins the Danube in Belgrade. According to some geologists, the Balkans begin on the south bank of the Sava.

Slovenes brag that their country—"with 56 percent of the land covered in forest"—is Europe's second-greenest. As you drive toward Kranjska Gora, take in all this greenery...and the characteristic Slovenian hayracks (recognized as part of the national heritage and now preserved). The Vrata Valley (on the left) is a popular starting point for climbing Mount Triglav. Paralleling the road on the left is a "rails-to-trails" bike path—converted from an old railway bed—that loops from here through Italy and Austria, allowing bikers to connect three countries in one day.

About two miles from the highway turnoff, at the intersection in Dovje, watch on the right for the statue of Jakob Aljaž, who actually bought Triglav—back when such a thing was possible (he's pointing at his purchase). About five miles later, in Gozd Martuljek, you'll cross a bridge and enjoy a great head-on view of Špik Mountain.

From here, it's about three miles to Kranjska Gora—a leading winter resort particularly popular with Croatian skiers. As every Slovene and Croatian wants a ski bungalow here, this area has some of the highest property values in the country.

Entering Kranjska Gora, you'll see a turnoff to the left marked for *Bovec* and *Vršič*, which leads up to the pass. But winter sports fa-

natics (or anyone, on a clear day) may first want to take a 30-minute detour to see the biggest ski jump in the world, a few miles ahead at Planica: Stay straight through Kranjska Gora, then turn left at signs for *Planica.* You'll drive in along a row of eight dizzyingly high ski jumps to the modern, wood-clad Nor-

dic Center (pay parking), with 360-degree views of alpine scenery. Every few years, tens of thousands of sports fans flock to this little valley to watch the ski-flying world championships. This is where a local boy was the first human to fly more than 100 meters on skis. Today's competitors routinely set new world records (currently 832 feet) on the outrageously steep ski-flying jump directly across from the Nordic Center. Thrill seekers who'd like to get a small taste of that experience can invest €25 (or €40 for a tandem run) in the adrenaline-pumping zipline that runs parallel to the jump. For something lower-impact, explore the Nordic Center, which has an information desk, WCs in the basement, a café with a sunny terrace, a small alpine-sports museum (overpriced and skippable for nonenthusiasts), and a wind-tunnel skydiving simulator (free entry to Nordic Center, daily July-Sept 9:00-18:00, March-June and Oct until 17:00, winter until 16:00, www.nc-planica.si). In the lower stairwell, peek through the window into the parking garage—

where, in summer, they pump in artificial snow for cross-country ski practice.

Before leaving Planica, ponder this: From this spot, you're a few minutes' walk from both Italy and Austria. This region spanning three nations lobbied unsuccessfully under the name Senza Confini (Italian for "without borders") to host the 2006 Winter Olympics. This philosophy is in tune with the European Union's vision for a Europe of regions, rather than nations.

Back in Kranjska Gora, follow the signs for *Vršič*. You'll pass (on the right) a lovely alpine lake called **Jasna,** created by damming the runoff-fed Pišnica streams that flow down the mountain toward the Sava. This is a popular place for fly-fishing and swimming (look for the tall, wooden diving structure). On the lakeshore, watch for the bronze Golden Horn statue (similar to one at Lake Bohnj)—a popular photo op. The touristy restaurants and cafés here are some of the last you'll see for a while.

Before long, you'll officially enter **Triglav National Park** and come to the first of this road's 50 hairpin turns (24 up, then 26 down)—each one numbered and labeled with the altitude in meters. Notice that the turns are cobbled to provide better traction. If the drive seems daunting, remember that 50-seat tour buses routinely conquer this pass...if they can do it, so can you. Better yet, imagine—and watch for—the bicyclists who regularly pedal to the top. The best can do it in less than 30 minutes—faster than driving.

After switchback #8, with the cute waterfall, park your car on the right and hike up the stairs on the left to the little **Russian Orthodox chapel.** This road was built during World War I by at least 10,000 Russian POWs of the Austro-Hungarian Empire to supply the Soča Front. The POWs lived and worked in terrible conditions, and several hundred died of illness and exposure. On March 8, 1916, an avalanche thundered down the mountains, killing hundreds more workers. This chapel was built where the final casualty was found. Take a minute to

pay your respects to those who built the road you're enjoying today.

Back on the road, continue up, up, up the switchbacks. As you smell the clutch burn, be glad it's a rental. After #16, keep an eye out (on the left) for **Tonkina Koča**—one of many mountain huts situated partway up the road, where hikers can pause for a break, a

JULIAN ALPS

Mount Triglav

Mount Triglav ("Three Heads") stands watch over the Julian Alps, and all of Slovenia. Slovenes say that its three peaks are the guardians of the water, air, and earth. This mountain defines Slovenes, even adorning the nation's flag: You'll often see the national seal, with three peaks (the two squiggly lines under it represent the Adriatic). Or take a look at Slovenia's €0.50 coin.

From the town of Bled, you'll see Triglav peeking up over the ridge on a clear day. (You'll get an even better view from nearby Lake Bohinj.)

It's said that you're not a true Slovene until you've climbed Triglav. One native took these words very seriously and climbed the mountain 853 times...in one year. Climbing to the summit—at 9,396 feet—is an attainable goal for any hiker in good shape. If you're here for a while and want to become an honorary Slovene, befriend a local and ask if he or she will take you to the top. Or join a tour; several local companies specialize in summiting visitors.

If mountain climbing isn't your style, relax at an outdoor café with a piece of cream cake and a view of Triglav. It won't make you a Slovene...but it's close enough on a quick visit.

rustic meal, or even an overnight (its deck is a nice place to nurse a drink; open mid-June-mid-Sept, mobile 041-396-645).

Just beyond, after #17, look up as high as you can on the cliff face to see sunlight streaming through a **"window"** in the rock. This natural formation, a popular destination for intrepid hikers, is big enough for the Statue of Liberty to crawl through.

After #22, at the pullout for Erjavčeva Koča restaurant, you may see tour-bus groups making a fuss about the mountain vista. They're looking for a ghostly face in the cliff wall, supposedly belonging to the mythical figure **Ajda.** This village girl was cursed by the townspeople after correctly predicting the death of the Zlatorog (Golden Horn), a magical, beloved, chamois-like animal. Her tiny image is just above the tree line, a little to the right—try to get someone to point her out to you (you can see her best if you stand at the signpost near the road). The picnic tables here are one of the best places along this drive for a do-it-yourself feast.

After #24, you reach the **summit** (5,285 feet). Consider getting out of the car to enjoy the views (in peak season, you'll pay an attendant a €3 "ecological tax" to park here). Hike up to the Tičarjev Dom hut for a snack or drink on the grand view terrace. On the right, a long gravel chute gives hikers a thrilling glissade. (From the pull-out just beyond #26, it's easy to view hikers "ski-

ing" down.) If you have time and energy to burn, from the summit consider hiking about 20 minutes uphill to the Poštarski Dom ("Postman's Lodge," with good food). Along the way, you'll see the ruins of a cable-car line, which ran supplies between here and the valley floor during World War I.

As you begin the descent, keep an eye out for old WWI debris. A lonely guard tunnel stands after #28, followed by a tunnel marked *1916* (on the left) that was part of the road's original path. A bit later, watch for the turnoff at the right, at a little gravel parking lot with a picnic table (labeled *Viewpoint Šupca*). From the platform viewpoint, you can see mountain valleys formed in two different ways: To the left, the jagged V-shaped Soča Valley, carved by a raging river; and on the right, the gentle U-shaped Trenta Valley, gouged by a glacier.

Continuing down, you'll see abandoned checkpoints from when this was the border between Italy and the Austro-Hungarian Empire. At #48 is a statue of **Julius Kugy,** an Italian botanist who explored the alpine flora of this region.

At #49, the road to the right (marked *Izvir Soče*) leads to the **source of the Soča River.** If you feel like stretching your legs, drive about five minutes down this road to a restaurant parking lot. From here, you can take a challenging 20-minute uphill hike (which includes some stretches where you'll cling to guide wires) to the Soča source. This is also the starting point for the well-explained, 12-mile Soča Trail (Soška Pot), which leads all the way to the town of Bovec.

Nearing the end of the switchbacks, follow signs for *Bovec*. Crossing the Soča River, you begin the second half of this trip.

From Vršič Pass to Soča River Valley

During World War I, the terrain between here and the Adriatic made up the Soča (Isonzo) Front. As you follow the Soča River south, down what's nicknamed the "Valley of the Cemeteries," the scenic mountainsides tell the tale of this terrible warfare. Imagine a young Ernest Hemingway driving his ambulance through these same hills (see sidebar).

Hemingway in the Julian Alps

It was against the scenic backdrop of the Slovenian Alps that a young man from Oak Park, Illinois, first came to Europe—the continent with which he would forever be identified. After graduating from high school in 1917 and working briefly as a newspaper reporter, young Ernest Hemingway wanted to join the war effort in Europe. Bad vision kept him out of the army, but he craved combat experience—so he joined the Red Cross Ambulance Corps instead.

After a short detour through Paris, Hemingway was sent to the Italian Front. On his first day, he was given the job of retrieving human remains—gruesomely disfigured body parts—after the explosion of a munitions factory. Later he came to the Lower Piave Valley, not far from the Soča Front. In July 1918, his ambulance was hit by a mortar shell. Despite his injuries, he saved an Italian soldier who was also wounded. According to legend, Hemingway packed his own wound with cigarette butts to stop the flow of blood.

Sent to Milan to recuperate, Hemingway fell in love with a nurse, but she later left him for an Italian military officer. A decade later, Hemingway wrote about Kobarid (using its Italian name, Caporetto), the war, and his case of youthful heartbreak in *A Farewell to Arms*.

But it's not all so gloomy. There are plenty of other diversions—interesting villages and churches, waterfalls and suspension bridges, and more. Perhaps most impressive is the remarkable clarity and milky-blue color of the Soča itself, which Slovenes proudly call their "emerald river."

After switchback #49, you'll cross a bridge, then pass a church and a botanical garden of alpine plants (Alpinum Juliana, summer only).

At long last—well after you think you're done with the pass—you finally reach the last Vršič switchback (#50), which sends you into the village of **Trenta.** As you get to the cluster of buildings in Trenta's "downtown," look on the left for the **Triglav National Park Information Center,** which also serves as a regional TI (daily July-Aug 9:00-19:00, May-June and Sept-Oct 10:00-18:00, Dec-April 10:00-14:00, closed Nov, tel. 05/388-9330, www.tnp.si). The €6 museum here provides a look (with English explanations) at the park's flora, fauna, traditional culture, and mountaineering history. An AV show celebrates the region's forests, and a poetic 15-minute slideshow explains the wonders and fragility of the park (included in museum entry, ask for English version as you enter).

After Trenta, you'll pass through a tunnel; then, on the left, look for a classic **suspension footbridge.** Pull over to walk out for a bounce, enjoying the river's crystal-clear water and the spectacular mountain panorama. Or you can take your pick among many such bridges for the next several miles; the best is coming up soon (I'll point it out).

About five miles beyond Trenta, in the town of Soča, is the **Church of St. Joseph** (with reddish-brown steeple, tucked behind the big tree on the right). Step inside to see some fascinating art. During World War II, an artist hiding out in the mountains filled this church with patriotic symbolism. The interior is bathed in Yugoslav red, white, and blue—a brave statement made when such nationalistic sentiments were dangerous. On the ceiling is St. Michael (clad in Yugoslav colors) with Yugoslavia's three WWII enemies at his feet: the eagle (Germany), the wolf (Italy), and the serpent (Japan). The tops of the walls along the nave are lined with Slavic saints. Finally, look carefully at the Stations of the Cross and find the faces of hated Yugoslav enemies: a lederhosen-clad Hitler (pulling a rope to lift up the cross; fourth from altar on left) and Mussolini (seated, as Herod; first from altar on right).

Behind the church, above the lovingly tended town graveyard, the stylized cross on the hill marks a **WWI cemetery**—the final resting place of some 1,400 Austro-Hungarian soldiers who were killed in action. Notice one small corner of the main cemetery (just before the WWI section) that's marked with a red star and labeled *Padli Borci Nov* (Our Fallen Fighters). These are

the graves of local Partisans who—two generations later—fought alongside Tito to force out the Nazis (notice the death dates: 1943, 1944, 1945).

For another good example of how the Soča River cuts like God's band saw into the land, stop about two minutes past the church at the small gravel lot (on the left) marked *Velika Korita Soče* **(Grand Canyon of Soča).** While the entire Soča Valley is dramatic, this half-mile stretch, 30 to 50 feet deep, is considered the most impressive. Venture out onto the suspension bridge over the gorge.

If the water's high, notice the many side streams pouring into the churning river in a series of mini waterfalls. For more views, cross over the bridge and hike down along the treacherously uneven and narrow rocky path downstream to another bridge.

Just beyond the suspension bridge is the turnoff (on the left) to the Lepena Valley, home of the recommended Pristava Lepena ranch, with accommodations, a restaurant, and Lipizzaner horses (see "Sleeping in Bovec," later). If you head up this valley, you'll find a big gravel pullout on the right (marked *Velika Korita*) that lets you cross another springy bridge over a particularly wide stretch of the river. This is a popular place for those who enjoy hiking up alongside the "Grand Canyon" we passed earlier (about 5 miles round-trip, uneven terrain).

A few miles after the Lepena Valley turnoff, watch on the left for the large **barn** (marked *Žičnica Golobar*). Pull over here if you'd like a close look at one of the stations for a primitive, industrial cable-car line, which was used mostly for logging.

Soon you'll exit the national park, pass a WWI graveyard (on the left), and come to a fork in the road. The main route leads to the left, through Bovec. But first, take a two-mile detour to the right (marked *Trbiž/Tarvisio* and *Predel/Kluže*), where the WWI **Kluže Fortress** keeps a close watch over the narrowest part of a valley leading to Italy (free to enter main courtyard, €3 to tour exhibit about local history and nature; July-Aug daily

9:00-20:00; June and Sept daily 9:00-17:00, Sat until 20:00; May and Oct open Sat-Sun only 10:00-17:00; closed Nov-April). In the 15th century, the Italians had a fort here to defend against the Ottomans. Five hundred years later, during World War I, Austrians used it to keep Italians out of their territory. Notice the ladder rungs fixed to the cliff face across the road from the fort—allowing soldiers to quickly get up to the mountaintop.

Back on the main road, immediately after the Kluže turnoff, watch for the gravel pullout on the left with the little wooden hut (look for the green sign with old photos; a newer house has also been built here). To see some original **WWI-era fortifications,** pull over here and hike on the gravel path 10 minutes through the woods to reach the Ravelnik Outdoor Museum. Here you can see trenches dug into the dirt and rocks, abandoned pillboxes, rusty sheds, and other features of an evocative wartime landscape. While not entirely typical of Soča Front embattlements—which were mostly high on the mountaintops—Ravelnik offers a more accessible taste of those times. (For a more authentic, mountaintop outdoor museum, drive 30 minutes beyond Kobarid and up to Kolovrat—described on page 670.)

Continue following the main road to **Bovec,** which saw some of the most vicious fighting of the Soča Front. The town was hit hard by earthquakes in 1994, 1998, and 2004, but today it's been rebuilt and remains the adventure-sports capital of the Soča River Valley, famous for its whitewater activities. (The Soča's water, which comes from high-mountain runoff, never goes above 68 degrees Fahrenheit.) For good lunch stops in Bovec, turn right at the roundabout as you first reach the town; you'll pass Martinov Hram's inviting restaurant terrace on the right, and soon after, the outdoor tables for Thirsty River brewery, with tempting food stands nearby (for details on these, see "Eating in Bovec," later). But if you're not eating or spending the night in Bovec, you could skip the town entirely and not miss much (continue along the main road to bypass the town center).

About three miles past Bovec, as you cross the bridge (with the yellow *Boka* sign), look high up on the rock wall in the gorge to your right to spot the **Boka waterfall,** which carves a deep gutter into the cliff as it tumbles into the valley. (Hardy hikers can climb up for a better view of this fall—the trailhead is just after the bridge on the right—but it's a strenuous hike.)

Head south along the spectacularly turquoise river. When you pass the intersection at the humble village of **Žaga,** you're just four miles from Italy. Continuing south, you'll pass a pullout (just before Srpenica) that is a popular put-in point for kayaking trips along the river. Keep an eye out for happy kayakers.

After Srpenica, you'll pass the huge **TKK** factory complex, which produces a wide range of chemicals.

Soon you'll see signs for **Kobarid,** home to a sleepy main square and some fascinating WWI sights. Don't blink or you'll miss the Kobarid turnoff on the right—it lets you head into town past the highly recommended Kobarid Museum, which tells the tale of the WWI-era Soča Front. Farther along, you'll reach the tidy main square. Driving up to the Italian mausoleum hovering over the town is a must. (These sights are described later, under "Sights in Kobarid.")

Leaving Kobarid, continue south along the Soča to **Tolmin.** (For a steep, scenic detour to some poignant WWI sites, you can turn off in Idrsko to reach the Kolovrat Outdoor Museum—described on page 670.) Notice the architecture transitioning from a woodsy Austrian vibe to more stony Italian (this area was historically Italian).

Before you reach Tolmin, decide on your preferred route back to civilization...

JULIAN ALPS

From Soča River Valley to Ljubljana

There are two ways to complete a loop-trip back to Ljubljana through more varied scenery. The first route is faster and more scenic, while the longer second route is a bit smoother. Either option brings you back to the A-1 expressway south of Ljubljana, and will get you to the city in about two hours. To reach Bled, you could follow either of these routes, then carry on northward for another hour. Or for more direct routes to Bled, see the next section.

Idrija Route: This ruggedly scenic approach takes you along ever-narrower valleys and through the charming town of Idrija. Begin by driving through Tolmin on the main road, following the Soča River to Most na Soči. Enjoy the valley scenery as you twist through the hills, following the Idrijca River. About 40 minutes after Most na Soči, you'll reach the outer limits of the town of **Idrija** (EE-dree-yah), known to all Slovenes for three things: its tourable mercury mine (www.muzej-idrija-cerkno.si), delicate lace *(čipko)*, and tasty *žlikrofi* (filled dumplings, like ravioli). Idrija (pop. 6,000) feels like a once-gloomy post-industrial city that's enjoying renewed life today (www.visit-idrija.si). If you're ready for a bite, several restaurants in town offer a chance to sample *žlikrofi;* I ate well at **$ Gostilna Mlinar,** a guesthouse high above town (try their sampler plate of three types of *žlikrofi;* closed Mon-Tue; turn left at the bridge just before you enter Idrija, then twist up the narrow road, watching for the guesthouse on the right at the very top of town, tel. 05/377-6316). From Idrija, it's another 30 minutes to the expressway (at Logatec); from there, you can head north to Ljubljana in less than 30 minutes.

Nova Gorica Route: This route—which swings to the southwest—starts at the roundabout before you reach Tolmin (head to the right, toward *Nova Gorica*). Along this road, you'll pass a hydroelectric dam and go under a 1906 rail viaduct that once connected this area to the port of Trieste. In the charming town of **Kanal,** you'll cross over the Soča on a picturesque bridge that's faintly reminiscent of Mostar's (as in that Bosnian city, young people stage a competition that involves jumping off this bridge into the raging river below). Farther along, the striking **Solkan Bridge** (another link in the Trieste rail line) is the longest single-span stone arch bridge in the world. About 40 minutes from the Tolmin area, you arrive in **Nova Gorica.** This fairly dull city is divided in half by the Italian border (the Italian side is called "Gorizia"). Because Italians aren't allowed to gamble in their hometowns, Nova Gorica is packed with casinos—including Europe's biggest. Rocks spell out the words *NAŠ TITO* ("Our Tito") on a hillside above town—a strange relic of an earlier age. From Nova Gorica, you can hop on the H-4 expressway, which links easily to the main A-1 expressway (from here, it's about an hour to Ljubljana, and 30 minutes farther to Bled). The road from Nova Gorica to Ljubljana takes you through the heart of the Karst region—if you have time and daylight to spare, you could tour a cave, castle, or Lipizzaner stud farm on your way back up to Ljubljana (see the Karst chapter).

From Soča River Valley to Bled

Car Train Option: The fastest route from Tolmin to Bled is to load your car onto a "Car Train" (Autovlak, a.k.a. "Motorail") that cuts directly through the mountains. The train departs from Most na Soči (just south of Tolmin, along the Idrija route described above) and arrives at Bohinjska Bistrica, near Lake Bohinj, about 45 minutes later (€14 for the car; afternoon departures—14:45 and 18:45—run late April-late Sept only, also departs year-round at 7:45 and 10:38—confirm schedule at the Bled TI before making the trip, www.slo-zeleznice.si). No reservations are necessary, but arrive at the train station about 30 minutes before the scheduled departure to allow time to load the car. Note: The train can be quite jerky and bumpy, and you have to stay inside your car the entire time. If you're claustrophobic, prone to motion sickness, or both, consider giving this train a miss. For others, it's a hoot.

To get to the car train, drive through Tolmin to Most na Soči. About a mile past Most na Soči, watch on the right for the big bridge over the river, marked for *Čepovan* and *železniška postaja* (train station). Crossing the bridge, turn right to find the train station; once there, go around the far-left side of the long station building and drive up the ramp to wait your turn to load. Taking off, you'll cross a scenic viaduct, then twist through the mountains, going through multiple tunnels, including a final 10-minute passage from Podbrdo beneath the mountains to Bohinjska Bistrica, where you'll unload your car. From there, it's less than a half-hour drive back to Bled, or a 10-minute drive (in the opposite direction) to Lake Bohinj.

Through Italy via Predel Pass: Although this route requires some backtracking, it also includes a fun detour through Italy—and some different scenery. From Kobarid, drive back the way you came (through Bovec), then turn off for the Kluže Fort, marked for *Predel* and *Italy*. In a few miles, after passing the fort, the road curves up through two small villages (first Log pod Mangartom, then Strmec na Predelu). Continue past the ruined fortress and cross the Italian border (there's generally no need to stop). Then curl down a few hairpin turns past the end of tranquil, scenic Lake Predel, and continue straight through the industrial city of Cave del Predil (overhead are the five rounded peaks of the Cinque Punte formation) and along the valley road, following signs for Slovenia. Approaching Tarvisio, turn right (continuing to follow signs for *Kranjska Gora* and Slovenia); from here, it's about a half-hour (10 miles) back across the Slovenian border to Kranjska Gora. This is where you first began your ascent of the Vršič Pass—just retrace your steps back to Bled.

Other Driving Routes: The fastest route (about 2 hours) essentially follows the car-train route, but goes over rather than through the mountains. This route is partially on a twisty, rough, poor-quality road (go through Tolmin, turn off just after the train station at Bača pri Modreju to Podbrdo, then from Petrovo Brdo take a very curvy road through the mountains into Bohinjska Bistrica and on to Bled). For timid drivers, start out on the Idrija route toward Ljubljana (described earlier), but turn off in Straža (before Idrija—watch for turnoff to *Cerkno*) toward Gorenja Vas, Škofja Loka, and Kranj, then continue on to Bled.

Bovec

The biggest town in the area, with about 1,600 people, Bovec (BOH-vets) has a happening main square and all the tourist amenities. It's best known as a hub for whitewater adventure sports. While not exactly quaint, Bovec is pleasant enough to qualify as a good lunch stop or overnight home base. If nothing else, it's a nice jolt of civilization wedged between the skyscraping alpine cliffs.

Orientation to Bovec

TOURIST INFORMATION
The helpful TI is on the main square (June-Aug Mon-Fri 8:00-20:00, Sat 9:00-20:00, Sun 9:00-17:00; May and Sept Mon-Fri 8:30-17:00, Sat 9:00-18:00, Sun until 13:00; off-season shorter hours and closed Sat-Sun—except during ski season; Trg Golobarskih Žrtev 8, tel. 05/302-9647, www.soca-valley. com).

ARRIVAL IN BOVEC
The main road skirts Bovec, but you can turn off (watch for signs on the right) to go through the heart of town, then rejoin the main road farther along. The turnoff road goes right past the main square, Trg Golobarskih Žrtev, with the TI, various tour companies, and eateries.

Parking is tight in high season (May-Sept). Your best bet is to drive into town, and then—when you reach the main square—turn right (uphill) sharply, then turn right again just before the church (following the *P 80 m* sign). This leads to a big, free gravel parking lot a five-minute walk downhill to town. To park a bit closer, you can leave your car at the big parking lot behind the Mercator supermarket (on the left just before the main square; park here for up to one hour free with a clock on your dashboard—but confirm locally).

Activities near Bovec

As the de facto capital of Slovenia's "Adrenaline Valley," Bovec offers many opportunities to enjoy the nature all around it. For great mountain views of the surrounding terrain, simply hike five minutes up (or drive) to the church at the top of town.

Adventure Sports

The Soča Valley offers abundant opportunities to get out on the rushing, crystal-clear waters of the river. The main options are rafting, kayaking, and hydrospeeding (a masochistic variation on boogie boarding—lying face-down on a short surfboard and shooting headfirst toward the rapids). The official season is March 15 until October 31, but from an adrenaline perspective, these activities are best in spring—when the water is highest. The river is tamer in summer, and by fall, water levels are even lower.

When conditions are ideal, most **rafting** companies put in near the Boka waterfall (just downriver from Bovec), and pick up at the village of Trnovo ob Soči. (When water levels are low, companies put in near Sprenica instead.) Most rafting trips last about 2.5-3 hours, with about 1.5 hours actually on the river and extra time to swim.

Kayaking is available at various points along the river, with a dramatic range in level of difficulty; the TI's free river map outlines your options and notes areas that are unsafe. To get a glimpse of kayakers, hang out at Napoleon Bridge, just outside Kobarid.

The most popular place for **canyoning**—a risky activity that involves wading and rappelling in rushing rivers, always with a guide—is in Canyon Sušec, about halfway between Bovec and Kobarid.

While it's less adventurous, the Soča River is popular for fishing, predominantly for the endemic marble trout. Only **fly fishing** is allowed; some areas are catch-and-release, and all areas require a permit.

Other popular activities include skydiving and paragliding; biking (including electric mountain bikes); ziplines (there's a course above Bovec and another high in the Učja Valley); and even—*gasp!*—golf (Bovec has a 9-hole course, www.golfbovec.si). All of these activities come with some degree of risk (except, perhaps, golf); use common sense and investigate the company's safety record. The Bovec TI is a good source of information, and an ever-changing roster of local adventure-travel companies run a variety of tours. At last count, the town had seven different companies; well-established outfits include Bovec Šport Centar (www.bovec-sc.si) and Soča Rafting (www.socarafting.si), but it's also a good idea to consult recent online reviews.

Sightseeing Flights and Skydiving

Bovec's little airport is used mainly for skydiving flights (see www.skydivebovec.com). But **Janez Let** runs scenic sightseeing flights (€90/20-minute "introductory" flight for up to 3 people, longer itineraries available, mobile 041-262-726, www.janezlet.si).

Knin Cable Car

A cable car slo-o-owly trundles visitors 7,200 feet above sea level to near the summit of Mount Knin, which overlooks Bovec and a scenic swath of the Soča Valley. On a clear day, you can see all the way to the Adriatic. Up top, you can walk around an irregular limestone landscape (but watch your step—there are some extremely deep hidden crevasses) and pay extra to try out a fixed-anchor (a.k.a. *via ferrata*) climbing course.

Cost and Hours: €20 round-trip, 35 minutes each way, hours sporadic and weather-dependent but typically June-mid-Sept daily 8:00-16:00, Sat-Sun only in shoulder season, bottom station is just outside Bovec near the road to Kobarid, www.kanin.si.

Sleeping in Bovec

Dobra Vila and Hotel Sanje ob Soči are situated near the turnoff from the main road into central Bovec (about a 10-minute walk into town). Martinov Hram and Stari Kovač are closer to the main square, in the town center.

$$$$ Dobra Vila, run with class by Juri, has 11 boldly stylish yet classic rooms and a large back terrace. You'll stay in a gorgeously restored former telephone office that feels like a sophisticated whisper of ages past (air-con, Mala vas 112, tel. 05/389-6400, www.dobra-vila-bovec.si, welcome@dobra-vila-bovec.si). They also have the most elegant restaurant in town (see "Eating in Bovec," later).

$$ Hotel Sanje ob Soči means "Dreams by the Soča"—which

describes both what you'll do here and the vision that entrepreneurial owners Boštjan and Valentina have for their sleek, modern, spa-like lodgings. The 10 rooms and nine apartments fill a pine-clad, Scandinavian-feeling shell on the edge of Bovec. The rooms—all with terraces, and each one named for the mountain that dominates its view—are fairly simple and Ikea-furnished (breakfast extra, air-con, children's play area, Mala vas 105a, tel. 05/389-6000, mobile 031-331-690, www.sanjeobsoci.com, info@sanjeobsoci.com).

$ Martinov Hram has 12 nice, modern rooms over a popular restaurant a few steps from Bovec's main square. While the rooms are an afterthought to the busy restaurant (reception at the bar), they're comfortable (rooms on sunny side have air-con, Trg Golobarskih Žrtev 27, tel. 05/388-6214, www.martinov-hram.si, martinov-hram@siol.net).

$ Stari Kovač B&B is your basic budget option, with eight apartments in an old-feeling guesthouse with woody charm, a steep block downhill from the main square (breakfast extra, cash only, Rupa 3, tel. 05/388-6699, mobile 041-646-427, www.starikovac.com, info@starikovac.com).

NEAR BOVEC

$$$$ Pristava Lepena is a relaxing oasis hiding out in the Lepena Valley just north of Bovec. This place is its own little village, with a series of rustic-looking but comfy cabins, a restaurant, exercise room, kids' play area, tennis court, outdoor swimming pool, sauna/whirlpool, and resident Lipizzaner horses and mountain goats, plus a children's farm with chickens and rabbits. The 13 cozy rooms have wood-burning stoves and all the amenities (closed mid-Oct–March except around Christmas and New Year, multinight stays preferred, lunch and dinner available for extra; just south of the village of Soča, exit the main road at the sign for *Lepena,* and follow the signs to Lepena 2; tel. 05/388-9900, mobile 041-671-981, www.pristava-lepena.com, info@pristavalepena.com).

$ Tourist Farm Pri Plajerju is on a picturesque plateau at the edge of Trenta (at the bottom of the Vršič Pass road). Run by the Pretner family (gregarious Marko is a park ranger, shy Stanka is "the boss"), this organic farm raises sheep and rents five apartments in three buildings separate from the main house. The location, deeper in the mountains, makes it a bit less convenient for side-tripping—it's 30 minutes to Bovec and an hour to Kobarid (breakfast and dinner extra; watch for signs to the left after coming over the pass and going through Trenta, Trenta 16a; tel. 05/388-9209, mobile 041-600-590, www.eko-plajer.com, info@eko-plajer.com).

Eating in Bovec

In addition to the predictable fare, Bovec specializes in mountain food, including trout, lamb, foraged wild mushrooms, and the stick-to-your-ribs potato-and-cheese omelet called *frika*. The local dessert is *bovški krafi*—dumplings stuffed with dried and chopped-up miniature pears that grow locally (Martinov Hram is a good place to try this dish).

$$$ Martinov Hram, run by the Berginc family (sisters Sara and Suzi), has an inviting outdoor terrace under a grape trellis. Inside, the nicely traditional decor pairs well with regional specialties and homemade bread (Tue-Sun 12:00-22:00, closed Mon; on the main road through Bovec, just before the main square on the right at Trg Golobarskih Žrtev 27; tel. 05/388-6214).

$$$$ Dobra Vila, also a recommended hotel, is the only place in town for an elegant, upscale meal of well-presented international cuisine with local flair. Book ahead (€50 four-course meals only, daily 19:00-22:00, see contact information earlier).

Brewpub and Alpine Street Food: $ Thirsty River is an inviting microbrew tasting room with a wonderful location right on Bovec's main square. The basic interior is rustic and cozy, but in good weather, the outdoor tables will kill your momentum (as will the excellent beers). They also sell sandwiches and meat-and-cheese platters (daily 8:00-23:00). In summer, a row of little **wooden sheds** is set up nearby, serving up appealing street food. The best of these is **$ Cuisine of Local Treats** (Kuhnjca Lokanik Dobrot), where Bojan and daughter Anja serve up delicious, filling portions of hearty mountain foods, with lots of mushrooms and melted cheese, plus local trout and lamb (roughly May-Sept daily 16:00-20:00, closed off-season, mobile 041-695-744). When closed, the sign reads *Sem šel po gobe* ("I went mushroom hunting").

Near Bovec: $$$$ Pristava Lepena—a recommended hotel listed earlier—is also open to nonguests for meals in their big, rustic dining room. While it's pricey, a meal here comes with a beautiful 15-minute drive and a peek at the lovely Lepena Valley (daily 12:00-22:00).

Bovec Connections

From Bovec by Bus to: Kobarid (6/day Mon-Fri, 2-3/day Sat-Sun, 30 minutes), **Ljubljana** (see "Getting Around the Julian Alps," earlier, for connections via the Vršič Pass or via Idrija).

Kobarid

Kobarid (KOH-bah-reed) feels older, a bit smaller (pop. 1,090), and a bit more appealing than its big brother Bovec. This humble settlement was immortalized by Ernest Hemingway, who drove an ambulance in these mountains during World War I. He described Kobarid as "a little white town with a campanile in a valley. It was a clean little town and there was a fine fountain in the square." Sounds about right. Even though Kobarid loves to tout its Hemingway connection, historians believe that Papa did not actually visit Kobarid until he came back after the war to research his book.

Aside from its brush with literary greatness, Kobarid is known as a hub of information about the Soča Front (with an excellent WWI museum, a hilltop Italian mausoleum, and walks that connect to surrounding sites). You won't find the fountain Hemingway wrote about—it's since been covered up by houses. You will find a modern statue of Simon Gregorčič (overlooking the main intersection), the beloved Slovenian priest-poet who came from and wrote about the Soča Valley.

Orientation to Kobarid

The main road, Gregorčičeva, cuts right through the heart of little Kobarid, bisecting its main square (Trg Svobode).

TOURIST INFORMATION

The TI has good information on the entire area (July-Aug 9:00-20:00; May-June and Sept 9:00-13:00 & 14:00-19:00—from 15:00 Sat-Sun; off-season shorter hours and closed Sun; on the main square at Trg Svobode 16—follow the white footprints behind the statue of Gregorčič, tel. 05/380-0490, www.soca-valley.com).

ARRIVAL IN KOBARID

Driving into town from Bovec, watch carefully on the right for the poorly marked first turnoff into Kobarid (if you miss the turnoff, just carry on a bit longer, then turn right later to reach the main square). Turning into town, you could make a sharp left to reach the cheese factory (marked by the big modern tower) and Great Kozjak Waterfall trail, or continue straight ahead to pass the Kobarid Museum, then the main square. You'll find pay parking on

JULIAN ALPS

Kobarid

MILANOVA

MARKOVA

KRILANOVA

To Italy & ⑨

STREŠOVA

MUČENIŠKA

MATELIČEVA

Trg Svobode ①

⑥

⑦

WALK OF PEACE VISITORS CENTER

GREGORČIČEVA

ITALIAN MAUSOLEUM

To Bovec & Vršič Pass

To Great Kozjak Waterfall Hike, Drežnica & ⑤

NAPOLEON BRIDGE

Soča River

JANKA URSIČA

VOLARIČEVA

⑧

P

④

KOBARID MUSEUM

To City Center

ALPINE CHEESE MUSEUM

To Great Kozjak Waterfall Hike & Drežnica

③

GORIŠKA CESTA

②

200 Meters

200 Yards

To Tolmin, Most na Soči (Car Train), Idrija & Ljubljana

N

Accommodations
1. Hotel Hvala
2. Apartmaji Pri Nas
3. Hiša Sonca Rooms
4. Apartments Mašera
5. To Tourist Farm Kranjc

Eateries
6. Hiša Polonka
7. Kotlar Restaurant
8. Picerija Fedrig
9. To Hiša Franko Rest. & Rooms

the main square, from which it's an easy five-minute stroll back to the museum. Another parking lot is behind the museum, next to a playing field.

Sights in Kobarid

▲▲Kobarid Museum (Kobariški Muzej)

This old-school but world-class museum—worth ▲▲▲ for history buffs—offers a haunting look at the tragedy of the Soča Front. The tasteful exhibits, with fine English descriptions and a pacifist tone, take an even-handed approach to the fighting—without getting hung up on identifying the "good guys" and the "bad guys." The museum's focus is not on the guns and heroes, but on the big picture of the front and the stories of the common people who fought and died here.

Cost and Hours: €7, daily 9:00-18:00, July-Aug until 20:00, Oct-March

10:00-17:00, Gregorčičeva 10, tel. 05/389-0000, www.kobariski-muzej.si.

Tours: History buffs can call ahead to arrange a private tour of the collection (€20/hour) or the sights outside (€30/hour). You can also arrange a guide through the Walk of Peace Visitors Center, listed later.

Visiting the Museum: The entry is lined with hastily made cement and barbed-wire gravestones, flags representing all the nationalities involved in the fighting, and pictures of soldiers and nurses from diverse backgrounds who were brought together at the Soča Front. The rooms in this front part of the museum typically show good temporary exhibits about the war.

Buy your ticket and ask to watch the English version of the 20-minute film on the history of the Soča Front (informative but dry, focused on military history).

The first floor up is divided into several rooms, which you'll tour counterclockwise. The White Room—filled with rusty crampons, wire-cutters, pickaxes, and shovels—explains wintertime conditions at the front. What looks like a bear trap was actually used to trap enemy soldiers. The Room of the Rear shows the day-to-day activities away from the front line, from supplying troops to more mundane activities (milking cows, washing clothes, getting a shave, lifting weights, playing with a dog). Peruse the case of personal effects that troops carried to the front line. The somber and heartbreaking Black Room commemorates the more than one million casualties of the Soča Front. Horrific images of war injuries juxtaposed with medals earned prompts the question, was it worth it? Nearby is a display case of artificial limbs. The little altar was purchased by schoolchildren, who sent it to the front to offer the troops some solace. The door—etched with personal messages from troops—was relocated here from a military prison near Kobarid.

Through the door marked *The Krn Range Room* (also on the first floor up), pass the small model of the mountaintop war zone and find your way to the Kobarid Rooms, which trace the history of this region from antiquity to today. High on the wall, look for the timelines explaining the area's turbulent past. In the second room, a timeline shows wave after wave of invaders (including Ottomans, Habsburgs, and Napoleon). In the next room, above a display case with military uniforms, another timeline shows the many flags that flew over Kobarid's main square during the 20th century alone.

On the top floor, you'll see a giant model of the surrounding mountains, painstakingly tracing the successful Austrian-German *Blitzkrieg* attack during the Battle of Kobarid. Crawl into the small cave and press the button to hear a patriotic song about a soldier, who reads a letter he's written to his family.

▲▲Italian Mausoleum (Kostnica)

The 55 miles between Kobarid and the Adriatic are dotted with more than 75 cemeteries, reminders of the countless casualties on the Soča Front. One of the most dramatic is this mausoleum, overlooking Kobarid. The access road, across Kobarid's main square from the side of the church, is marked by stone gate towers with the word *Kostnica*— one tower is topped with a cross and the other with a star for the Italian army.

Take the road up Gradič Hill—passing Stations of the Cross—to the mausoleum. Built in 1938 (when this was still part of Italy) around the existing Church of St. Anthony, this octagonal pyramid holds the remains of 7,014 Italian soldiers. The stark, cold Neoclassical architecture is pure Mussolini. Names are listed alphabetically, along with mass graves for more than 1,700 unknown soldiers *(militi ignoti)*.

Walk behind the church and enjoy the **view.** Scan the WWI battlements high on the mountain's rock face. Incredibly, troops fought on these treacherous ridges; civilians in the valleys only heard the distant battles. Looking up and down the valley, notice the "signal churches" evenly spaced on hilltops, each barely within view of the next—an ancient method for quickly spreading messages or warnings across long distances.

If the **church** is open, go inside and look above the door to see a brave soldier standing over the body of a fallen comrade, fending off enemies with nothing but rocks.

When Mussolini came to dedicate the mausoleum, local revolutionaries plotted an assassination attempt that they believed couldn't fail. A young man planned to suicide-bomb Mussolini as the leader came back into town from this hilltop. But as Mussolini's car drove past, the would-be assassin looked at his fellow townspeople around him, realized the innocent blood he would also spill, and had a last-minute change of heart. Mussolini's trip was uneventful, and fascism continued to thrive in Italy.

Near the mausoleum, you'll see a small, skippable **museum** displaying items from WWI that have been discovered in the area.

Alpine Cheese Museum

This humble exhibit, at the big Planika ("Edelweiss") dairy at the edge of town, examines the history of cheesemaking in this area since ancient times. It's part of a larger facility that also includes a big supermarket (stocked with ample local dairy products) and a very local-feeling café. The museum is inside the big barn across the parking lot.

Cost and Hours: €3, Mon-Sat 10:00-12:00 & 16:00-18:00, mornings only in Oct, closed Sun and Nov-April, Gregorčičeva 32, tel. 05/384-1013, www.mlekarna-planika.si. To get here, turn right into Kobarid, then take the sharp left that leads you down beneath the underpass to the cheese factory (marked by the tall modern tower).

▲Great Kozjak Waterfall (Veliki Kozjak) Hike

For a rewarding, fairly easy hike in the Kobarid area, consider trekking to the Great Kozjak Waterfall—a dramatic cascade that plunges 50 feet through a narrow cavern into a beautiful pool. While the walk from the trailhead suggests 30 minutes one-way from the parking lot, allow 1.5 hours round-trip to linger and explore. You'll head across a meadow to the Soča River, then follow the trail through the woods. Along the way, you'll pass the ruins of a World War I bunker and trenches, and a suspension bridge. The riverbank is a popular swimming and sunbathing area. When you reach a smaller waterfall, you'll have to buy tickets and head onward for the big one (€4, daily 8:00-20:00). While you could walk all the way to the waterfall from Kobarid (add about 15-20 minutes each way), it's more rewarding to start at the official trailhead parking lot. Far from undiscovered, Great Kozjak can be crowded during peak season—in summer, time your visit early or late.

Getting There: The trailhead is across the river from Kobarid's town center. Follow brown signs for *Slap Kozjak* under the main road, over the Napoleon Bridge, and then left at the fork. After Kamp Koren, watch on the left for the turnoff to the big waterfall parking lot (payment required). You'll carry on along the gravel road by foot the rest of the way.

WWI Sights near Kobarid

For those fascinated by this region's WWI history, there's much to see beyond the excellent museum and mausoleum in Kobarid. Several outdoor museums in the area let you get close to the places where the fighting actually occurred. Some are reachable by car, while others require a challenging mountain hike. Along the main road, you can see a stirring WWI cemetery behind the town church in Soča, or hike through scant fortifications at the Ravelnik Outdoor Museum just outside Bovec (both described on the self-guided drive, earlier). For those interested in seeing more, consider these options.

The Soča (Isonzo) Front

The valley in Slovenia's northwest corner—called Soča in Slovene and Isonzo in Italian—saw some of World War I's fiercest fighting. While the Western Front gets more press, this eastern border between the Central Powers and the Allies was just as significant. In a series of 12 battles involving 22 different nationalities along a 60-mile-long front, 300,000 soldiers died, 700,000 were wounded, and 100,000 were declared MIA. In addition, tens of thousands of civilians died. A young Ernest Hemingway, who drove an ambulance for the Italian army in nearby fighting, would later write the novel *A Farewell to Arms* about the battles here (see the "Hemingway in the Julian Alps" sidebar, earlier).

On April 26, 1915, Italy joined the Allies. A month later, it declared war on the Austro-Hungarian Empire (which included Slovenia). Italy unexpectedly invaded the Soča Valley, quickly taking the tiny town of Kobarid, which it planned to use as a home base for attacks deeper into Austro-Hungarian territory. For the next 29 months, Italy launched 10 more offensives against the Austro-Hungarian army, which was encamped on higher ground on the mountaintops. None of the Italian offensives was successful, even though the Italians outnumbered their opponents three to one. This was unimaginably difficult warfare—Italy had to

attack uphill, waging war high in the mountains, in the harshest of conditions. Trenches had to be carved into rock instead of mud. The fighting coincided with the most brutal winter in a century; many unprepared conscripts—brought here from faraway lands and unaccustomed to the harsh winter conditions atop the Alps—froze to death. Some 60,000 soldiers were killed by avalanches.

Visitors take a look at this tight valley, hemmed in by seemingly impassible mountains, and wonder: Why would people fight

▲Walk of Peace (Pot Miru)

This walking route—which extends more than 140 miles from these mountains all the way to the Adriatic—is designed to link museums, cemeteries, churches, and other sites related to the warfare of the Soča Front. But it also introduces visitors to all aspects of the region's culture and natural sites. To learn more about shorter hikes along its route, and the many outdoor museums and cemeteries in this region, visit the **Walk of Peace Foundation Visitors Center,** across the street from the Kobarid Museum. They hand out good, so fiercely over such inhospitable terrain? At the time, Slovenia was the natural route from Italy to the Austro-Hungarian capitals at Vienna and Budapest. The Italians believed that if they could hold this valley and push over the mountains, Vienna—and victory—would be theirs. Once committed, they couldn't turn back, and the war devolved into one of attrition: Who would fall first?

In the fall of 1917, Austro-Hungarian Emperor Karl appealed to his ally Germany, and the Germans agreed to assemble an army for a new attack to retake Kobarid and the Soča Valley. In an incredible logistical accomplishment, they spent just six weeks building and supplying this new army by transporting troops and equipment high across the mountaintops under cover of darkness...above the heads of their oblivious Italian foes dozing in the valley below.

On October 24, Austria-Hungary and Germany launched an attack that sent 600,000 soldiers down into the town of Kobarid. This crucial twelfth battle of the Soča Front, better known as the Battle of Kobarid, was the turning point—and saw the introduction of innovations that are commonplace in the military today. German field commanders were empowered to act independently on the battlefield, reacting immediately to developments rather than waiting for approval. For the first time ever, the Austrian-German army used elements of a new surprise-attack *Blitzkrieg* technique. (German officer Erwin Rommel made great strides in the fighting here, later becoming Hitler's "Desert Fox" in North Africa.)

The attack caught the Italian forces off guard and quickly broke through three lines of defense. Within three days, the Italians were forced to retreat. The Austrians called their victory the "Miracle at Kobarid." But Italy felt differently. The Italians see the battle of Caporetto (the Italian name for Kobarid) as their Alamo. To this day, when an Italian finds himself in a mess, he might say, "At least it's not a Caporetto."

A year later, Italy came back—this time with the aid of British, French, and US forces—and easily retook this area. On November 4, 1918, Austria-Hungary conceded defeat. After more than a million casualties, the fighting at Soča was finally over.

free maps and booklets, and sell a fine guidebook to WWI sights in the area. Tour their engaging, state-of-the-art exhibition, with additional temporary exhibits upstairs (free, July-Aug Mon-Fri 9:00-19:00, Sat-Sun 10:00-13:00 & 14:00-19:00, shorter hours spring and fall, and closed Nov-March—but you can try knocking on weekdays, Gregorčičeva 8, tel. 05/389-0167, www.potmiru. si). They can arrange **guides** to join you for part of the walk (€30/hour). Contact them at least one day ahead to check their schedule and/or arrange a tour.

Kobarid Historical Walk

This shorter walk to WWI sights around Kobarid is well-explained by the free brochure available at the TI, museum, and information center (3 miles, mostly uphill, allow 3-5 hours; or you can just do a shorter, easier stretch along the river, 1-2 hours).

▲Kolovrat Outdoor Museum

For drivers (especially those headed to points south) who want to get a vivid, high-altitude look at what life was like along the Soča Front, this is perhaps the area's best outdoor museum (worth the detour and ▲▲ for anyone interested in the Soča Front). It's located high on a ridge—straddling Slovenia and Italy—about 30 minutes from Kobarid, manageable on the way to the Karst, Goriška Brda, Venice, or Croatia.

This area—an Italian-built mountaintop fortification—is free and always open. The gentle pasture sprawling away from the parking area is scattered with half-ruined concrete bunkers; if you walk through this area, and keep going, you'll be in Italy in five minutes. Most interesting is the hilltop above, where trenches carved into the rock have been excavated and restored. You can clamber around inside a fortified labyrinth sculpted into the mountaintop and reinforced with wood and sandbags. Peer out through strategically placed viewpoint slits, and imagine the impossibly difficult life of the soldiers stationed along the Soča Front.

Getting There: Leave Kobarid on the main road toward Tolmin. Just a mile out of town, in the village of Idrsko, turn right toward *Livek* and twist up, up, up the hillside. At the far end of the village of Livek, watch for brown *Kolovrat* signs to the left. Following this road, you'll drive along a mountain spine for about five miles, watching for the small parking area and information boards for Kolovrat. When you're ready to leave the

museum, carry on along the same road, then turn left at the fork to wind back down into Tolmin.

Sleeping in Kobarid

My first listing is right on the main square. The others hide on side streets about a block off the main road through town.

$$$ Hotel Hvala is the only real hotel in town. Run by the Hvala family, its 32 contemporary rooms are faded but central; the cheaper "mansard" rooms are on the top floor. The mural on the wall in the elevator shaft tells the story of the Soča Valley as you go up toward the top floor (some rooms with air-con, elevator, Trg Svobode 1, tel. 05/389-9300, www.hotelhvala.si, info@hotelhvala.si).

$$$ Apartmaji Pri Nas ("Our Place") has six stylish apartments in a pleasant suburban home along the main road that skirts the town center of Kobarid (no breakfast but kitchens in each unit, air-con, Goriška cesta 5, mobile 031-377-585, www.pri-nas.si, prinas.kobarid@gmail.com).

$ Hiša Sonca ("House of the Sun"), in a cheery, yellow family home along the main road, has two comfortable, air-conditioned rooms (sharing a well-equipped kitchen, a "salt spa," and lots of stairs) and one big apartment that sleeps up to eight. My favorite place in Kobarid is well-run by Natalija, who also has another apartment a block closer to the town center (breakfast extra, cash only, laundry service, 2 blocks from main square at Mučeniška 1, mobile 031-664-253, www.apartmakobarid.com, info@www.apartmakobarid.com).

$ Apartments Mašera has six big rooms and four apartments (all with kitchens and a balcony or terrace) in a big, sprawling building tucked behind the Kobarid Museum (breakfast extra, air-con, Gregorčičeva 10, tel. 05/389-1210, www.apartments-masera-si.book.direct, apamasera@gmail.com, Martin and Petra).

IN THE MOUNTAINS HIGH ABOVE KOBARID

One of my favorite Soča Valley accommodations hides in a tiny village a twisty 10-minute drive up from Kobarid's main square. **$ Tourist Farm Kranjc** is a remote but scenic working sheep farm with eight comfortable rooms, organic meals prepared with home-grown produce, and a huge view terrace. While this farm—which feels traditional, but has modern style—is a bit less convenient to the sights, it's ideal if you want to huddle high in the mountains (dinner extra, air-con, also ask about their "glamping" cots with private bathroom, Koseč 7, tel. 05/384-8562, mobile 041-946-088, www.turizem-kranjc.si, info@turizem-kranjc.si, Urška and the Kranjc family). It's in the village of Koseč. From Kobarid, leave town by crossing the Napoleon Bridge (toward Kamp Koren and Great Kozjak Waterfall). Just after that bridge, turn left and twist up to Drežnica, where you'll turn right to reach Koseč; once in the village, look for signs directing you up the steep road to the left.

Eating in and near Kobarid

While Kobarid has a handful of good eateries, foodies make a pilgrimage for Hiša Franko—just outside town.

$$ Hiša Polonka ("Blue House"), a side project of the people who run the esteemed Hiša Franko (see below), is my favorite lunch stop in town. Conveniently located on the road between Kobarid's main square and the museum, this is the place for well-prepared traditional, local fare (including microbrews) at reasonable prices. The vibe is pubby and casual; the service is relaxed (Thu-Mon 12:00-23:00, closed Tue-Wed, Gregorčičeva 1, tel. 05/995-8194).

$$$ **Kotlar Restaurant,** on the main square, has a classy interior that sprawls around the prow of a faux sailboat. The emphasis is on seafood and locally sourced meats (daily 12:00-23:00, Trg Svobode 11, tel. 05/389-1110, www.kotlarkobarid.com).

$ **Picerija Fedrig** serves up basic but good pizzas (flexible hours but usually Mon-Tue 17:00-21:30, Wed-Sun from 12:00, shorter hours and closed Mon-Tue off-season, Volaričeva 11, tel. 05/389-0115).

FINE DINING NEAR KOBARID

$$$$ **Hiša Franko,** less than a five-minute drive outside of Kobarid, is becoming internationally known as one of Slovenia's finest restaurants. Chef Ana Roš (profiled on *Chef's Table* and named World's Best Female Chef 2017) has a deep respect for locally sourced ingredients and Slovenian alpine culinary tradition. But she's also experimental, injecting international touches into her cooking. Sommelier Valter Kramar (Ana's husband) elegantly pairs Slovenian wines with each course. The place is welcoming and unpretentious—you'll want to book far ahead for modern Slovenian cuisine at its very best (fixed-price meals only, Wed-Fri 19:00-23:00, Sat-Sun 12:00-16:00 & 19:00-23:00, closed Mon-Tue, Staro Selo 1, they also rent rooms, tel. 05/389-4120, www.hisafranko.com, info@hisafranko.com). To reach Hiša Franko, leave Kobarid following signs for *Italija* and *Robič,* and look for the restaurant's sign on the right.

Kobarid Connections

From Kobarid by Bus to: Bovec (6/day Mon-Fri, 2-3/day Sat-Sun, 30 minutes), **Ljubljana** (see "Getting Around the Julian Alps," earlier, for connecting to Ljubljana via the Vršič Pass, or faster via Idrija).

LOGARSKA DOLINA & THE NORTHERN VALLEYS

The Julian Alps around Lake Bled are Slovenia's most accessible and most famous pincushion of peaks. But the high-mountain thrills don't end there. Stretching to the east, along the border with Austria, is the Kamniško-Savinjske range—home to several remote valleys. One particularly inviting nook between the cut-glass peaks is the time-passed valley called Logarska Dolina. To get way, way, way off the beaten track—with gravel roads, unpasteurized milk, and the few Slovenes who still don't speak English—head to Logarska Dolina, its surrounding valleys, and the breathtaking Panoramic Road above them all.

Logarska Dolina—very loosely translated as "Woodsman's Valley"—thrills adventurous drivers, true back-to-nature nuts, and those intrigued by old-fashioned farming lifestyles...or, better yet, travelers who are all of the above. Most of all, Logarska Dolina is the ideal excuse for a long drive on high-mountain roads to one of Slovenia's most traditional corners.

Traveling here, you come to appreciate the vibrant culture and history that pervades even this remote and rugged corner of a tiny country. Some 25,000 years ago, hardy Ice Age people already lived in Logarska Dolina. Archaeologists have uncovered some remarkable remains from these prehistoric times—mostly tools made from bone, among them a flute and the oldest needle ever discovered. Today's residents focus on sheep, and locally made products—from cheese to thick felt hats, vests, and slippers—are a proud Logarska Dolina symbol. Other treasured aspects of the local culture include woodcarving, marble carving, rollicking zither sing-alongs, and huge ceramic stoves that work hard to keep mountain folk warm through the frigid winter.

Logarska Dolina

Kamniško

Road
Path

Not to scale:
Solčava to Entry Kiosk
is a 7-Minute Drive.

Cable Car to
Velika Planina

To Ljubljana

Luče

Ojstrica
7,710'

Raduha
6,765'

Robanov Kot

SAVINJA

Solčava

RIVER
CENTER
RINKA

PANORAMIC
ROAD

1 Hotel/Restaurant Plesnik
2 Vila Palenk
3 Na Razpotju Guesthouse &
   Fairytale Forest
4 Lenar Tourist Farm
5 Ojstrica Country House & Rest.
6 Tourist Farm Govc-Vršnik
7 Firšt Gostišče Rooms,
   Rest. & Museum
8 Tourist Farm Žibovt
9 Tourist Farm Klemenšek
10 Orlovo Gnezdo Mountain Hut

With some effort and a bit of extra time, you can enjoy two other interesting sights in this part of Slovenia. Between Ljubljana and Logarska Dolina is the rugged, above-it-all herders' settlement of Velika Planina—which feels even more trapped-in-time than Logarska Dolina. And to the east, Velenje Castle has a fine little museum.

If you want to dig deep into the Slovenian mountains—like the glaciers that carved Logarska Dolina during the last Ice Age—these northern mountains are the place. Slovenes like to keep this getaway a secret; it's one of their favorite escapes from the daily grind (and, along with Lake Bled, one of the country's most popular places to get married). Travelers who find Lake Bled too touristy prefer Lake Bohinj (see page 639). But travelers who think Bohinj is too touristy...*love* Logarska Dolina.

PLANNING YOUR TIME

A trip to Logarska Dolina can be done as a long, full-day circular drive from either Bled or Ljubljana. But to really escape to the mountains, spend the night. If you're heading between Ljubljana/Bled and Ptuj/Maribor on the A-1 expressway, Logarska Dolina is roughly on the way (though it's still an hour off the expressway).

Savinjske Mountains

Skuta
8,310'

NOTE:
THIS VIEW
LOOKS SOUTH

Rinka
Waterfall

⑩

Matkov Kot

Logarska Dolina

P

③
④ ⑤
① ℹ
P
②

Pavličevo
Sedlo

ENTRY
KIOSK

ROAD

⑦
⑨

⑧

AUSTRIA

CHURCH OF THE
HOLY SPIRIT

DCH

LOGARSKA DOLINA

Velika Planina combines conveniently with Logarska Dolina, but makes for a very long day.

GETTING TO LOGARSKA DOLINA

I'd skip this region without a car. Public transportation to the northern valleys is extremely time-consuming. An infrequent bus runs from the city of Celje to Solčava, then on to Logarska Dolina (1/day June-Sept, weekdays only May and Oct, none off-season). But once you're there, many of the region's best attractions (such as the Panoramic Road) are unreachable by public bus.

On the other hand, Logarska Dolina is made to order by car. The valley is nearly due north from Ljubljana. But because of the mountains that lie between them, you'll need to boomerang substantially to the east to get there. From Ljubljana, take the A-1 expressway east (toward Celje) to the Šentrupert exit. From here, most of the route is well-marked with brown *Log Dolina* signs. Head north on road 225 along the Savinja River, past Mozirje and Nazarje, then continue northwest on road 428 through Ljubno, Luče, and Solčava. (For details on getting around the valleys once you're in Solčava, see "Route Tips for Drivers," later.) Figure about an hour from Ljubljana to the Šentrupert exit, then another hour to Solčava.

A good, detailed map is essential (such as the 1:50,000 *Zgornja Savinjska Dolina* map, available locally).

The route I've described above is the most straightforward. Detailed maps will show some seeming "shortcuts" that appear to take you more directly between Ljubljana and Logarska Dolina. These are scenic...but slow. Two variations are the road through Kamnik, then over the mountains via Gornji Grad to pick up the main road into Solčava (near Ljubno); and the even more dramatic version of this route, cutting the corner from Krivčevo north through Podvolovljek to Luče, which lets you tie in a detour to Velika Planina. Another seeming shortcut via Kranj—dipping into Austria on the impossibly twisty Jezersko-Pavličevo Sedlo road, through Villach—is also possible, and also time-consuming.

Orientation to Logarska Dolina

This area—also called Solčavsko—is tucked in the northern corner of Slovenia, just a few miles from Austria. Although vast (about 40 square miles), the area has only 580 inhabitants. This chapter's core sights branch off from an east-west axis formed by the valley of the Savinja River. The main attraction here is the valley called **Logarska Dolina,** which cuts through the mountainscape south from the Savinja River Valley. Roughly parallel to Logarska Dolina are two smaller valleys: gentle **Robanov Kot** to the east and rugged **Matkov Kot** to the west. (*Dolina* means "valley;" *kot*—literally "corner"—is a short valley.) Running along the top of the Podolševa ridge above the Savinja River is the rough, gravelly **Panoramic Road** (Panoramska Cesta)—with spectacular views over the entire region.

TOURIST INFORMATION

The region's best source of information is in Solčava, at the **Center Rinka,** which hands out maps and brochures, has a good exhibit about the region, can help you find a room or plan a hike, and can arrange activities such as guided hikes, bike rental, horseback riding, rock climbing, archery, and paragliding (daily June-Aug 8:00-20:00, April-May and Sept until 18:00, Oct-March until 17:00, Solčava 29, tel. 03/839-0710, www.solcavsko.info, info@solcavsko.info). For more on the Center Rinka, see "Sights in Logarska Dolina," later.

Within **Logarska Dolina,** there's a modest **TI kiosk** across the parking lot from Hotel Plesnik (very flexible hours but generally July-Aug daily 9:00-17:00, Sept until 14:00, likely closed at other times and in bad weather, take left fork to hotel after you enter Logarska Dolina to Logarska Dolina 9, tel. 03/838-9004, www.logarska-dolina.si). If it's closed, the nearby Hotel Plesnik

Farming in (and Above) the Northern Valleys

It's fascinating to observe the ingenious ways that intrepid lo-

cals eke out a living in such an inhospitable land. In Logarska Dolina, farmers don't just cultivate the valleys—they also use the land at the very tops of the hills. Especially from the Panoramic Road, you can see that the highest points of various ridges are shaved bare—like bald heads in a crowd. Cows graze even on this sharply angled land. Locals joke that these farms are so steep that cows' front legs are shorter than their rear legs to make it easier for them to climb uphill—and dogs have to hang on to the grass with their teeth and bark through their rear ends.

This region's abundant traditional homes have wooden roofs and siding. These shingles are generally made of hard, durable larch wood, split by hand. In the fall, you'll see endless stacks of neatly arranged firewood, ready to warm the family through the winter. Each house has a tiled stove for heat.

It's a rough lifestyle. A farming family's primary source of income is mostly cows (milk and meat), but also pigs and goats. Some of the farms in the Savinja River Valley raise yaks imported from Scotland, which are bred for their meat. A second source of income is forestry: The trees on a farm's property can be harvested and sold. Finally, farmers make a living from travelers, in the form of overnights or meals eaten at their farms.

The many tourist farms *(turistična kmetija)* in this region are a recent phenomenon. During the Yugoslav era, people who lived here stopped farming and moved or commuted into nearby towns in the valley for factory work. But Slovenia's industry was designed to work as a cog in the Yugoslav machine: Other regions provided raw materials, and a large, ready-made market to buy the finished product. After the Slovenes declared independence, many of the factories closed, and the farmers-turned-workers returned to their ancestral farming ways. To supplement their income, many families have converted their working farms into tourist farms, inviting guests to visit, stay, and dine with them, and appreciate their unique lifestyles. Even though many of the farms in Logarska Dolina seem generations old, some date from only the mid-1990s.

also provides basic tourist information. There's also a **TI** along the main road in **Luče** (tel. 03/839-3555).

Sights in Logarska Dolina

The road running along the Savinja River and the Panoramic Road running above it are connected at both ends—forming a handy loop that allows drivers to see everything efficiently. I suggest driving the Panoramic Road first, to get a good overview of the region, then winding down along the Savinja River to dig into the valleys. (If you have bad morning weather that may clear in the afternoon, do the opposite.)

Route Tips for Drivers: The village of Solčava is the gateway to the region and has the handy and interesting Center Rinka. From Solčava, you can twist up to the Panoramic Road (follow signs to *Podolševa*). At the far (west) end of this sky-high road, you'll come to a fork: Going left drops you directly down into Logarska Dolina. But for a longer detour (and more scenery), going right takes you toward the Austrian border at Pavličevo Sedlo, and a very rugged, gravelly loop around the top, then bottom, of Matkov Kot (easy to miss—follow signs for tourist farms).

After visiting Logarska Dolina, take the Savinja River road back to Solčava. If you have time, you can detour into the valley of Robanov Kot when you head south from Solčava.

▲▲▲Panoramic Road (Panoramska Cesta)

The Logarska Dolina valley itself (described later) is beautiful. But the region's spectacular highlight is the Panoramic Road, twisting along the top of the cliff above it. At an altitude of around 4,000 feet (compared to about 2,500 feet in Logarska Dolina), this road offers one thrilling drive. For a sneak preview, see www.solcavska-panoramska-cesta.si.

As you rattle along the rough road, all around you are vast swaths of mountain forests, broken only by hilltops covered with patches of green grass. Each of these hills is its own farm that raises grass to feed livestock (see sidebar). You're just an avalanche's tumble from the Austrian border. Several stretches of the Panoramic Road are what Slovenes poetically call "white roads"—that is, unpaved gravel.

About halfway along the Panoramic Road, the late-19th-century **Church of the Holy Spirit** (Sveti Duh) hovers on a hilltop above the hamlet of Podolševa. Climb up to the church for sweeping views over Logarska Dolina. If the church is open, duck inside and find a very unusual relief of three men representing the Holy Trinity. God is in the cen-

ter, Jesus is on the left, and on the right is the Holy Spirit, depicted not as a dove but as a balding man.

Watch for pullouts offering stunning views all along the Panoramic Road; the best stretch is between the Klemenšek and Žibovt tourist farms. Pack along a picnic, or consider stopping off at a tourist farm for a meal (Tourist Farm Klemenšek owns some of the best views in the region—listed under "Eating in Logarska Dolina," later). Some farms serve *kislo mleko,* or "soured milk"...which is exactly what it sounds like. Fresh, unpasteurized milk is set out in the open air, usually in a darkened room. The fat rises to the top and forms a skin on top. The bottom of the milk is like yogurt, white and relatively flavorless. But the yellowish top layer comes with a kick: a pungent barnyard aftertaste. I tried it—once—and enjoyed it...the experience, if not the flavor.

▲▲Logarska Dolina

This valley, 4.5 miles long and about a quarter-mile wide, is the region's main draw. A flat, broad meadow surrounded on all sides

by sheer alpine cliffs, it's an idyllic place for a drive, hike, or bike ride. Various sights—caves, waterfalls, old log cabins, and so on— surround the valley, but it's most appealing simply as a place to commune with gorgeous Slovenian na-ture.

Though you can enter the valley year-round, you'll pay a €7 entry fee per car from April through October (at other times, or if there's bad weather and the entry kiosk is closed, it's free). After the valley entrance, the road forks. Take the left fork to reach the TI kiosk (see "Tourist Infor-mation," earlier) and hotels; or take the right fork to bypass them (the two forks eventually rejoin).

At the far end of the valley, you'll find a parking lot with some snack stands. From here, you can follow the *Slap Rinka—10 min* signs up the moderately strenuous path to the **Rinka Waterfall.** This is where mountain runoff tumbles into the valley, feeding the Savinja River, which courses through the valley and region. Relax at the little mountain hut called **Orlovo Gnezdo** ("Eagle's Nest") and enjoy a drink with a view of the falls, which plunge 300 feet down from the adjacent cliffs.

With more time, Logarska Dolina is an inviting, mostly level place to go for a longer **hike,** surrounded by cow-filled meadows and towering peaks. The "Nature-Ethnographic Trail" is a two-hour, four-mile (one-way) hike that starts near the entrance of the valley and leads to the end of the valley. A brochure that describes the route is available at the Logarska Dolina TI kiosk and at the Center Rinka, along with information about more adventurous hikes up into the region's mountains.

▲Center Rinka

This sleek building sits along the main road in the village of Solčava, just 50 yards from the twisty route up to the Panoramic Road. Named for the big waterfall that feeds the Savinja River (which carved out this region's beauty), it's a state-of-the-art visitors center that celebrates the local landscape and culture. A small but endearing—and free—exhibition on the natural area includes displays about area caves and the prehistoric findings unearthed in them, local handicrafts (felt and woodworking), trees, wildflowers, and animals. It provides a good foundation for exploring the region, and the 15-minute film makes you wish you had more time here. The center also offers free Wi-Fi, a café/bar selling locally made products (meats, cheeses, and cookies), a shop with local handicrafts, and a children's play area. A visit here is smart both in good weather (to plan your high-mountain fun) and in bad weather (to learn about the region without getting wet).

Cost and Hours: Free, daily June-Aug 8:00-20:00, April-May and Sept until 18:00, Oct-March until 17:00, Solčava 29, tel. 03/839-0710, www.solcavsko.info.

Nearby: The village of **Solčava** itself is a pleasant place, hemmed in tightly by alpine cliffs and capped by the picturesque Church of Christ the King.

Robanov Kot and Matkov Kot

These smaller, sleepier valleys, dotted with traditional farm buildings, flank Logarska Dolina. They offer the same surrounded-by-mountains feeling, but they're less cultivated and less crowded than Logarska during the peak season. With extra time, poke into one or both of these mini valleys simply to enjoy the peaceful views.

Robanov Kot, near Solčava, is more gentle and accessible, with better and more level roads. This valley is well-marked with a brown sign just south of Solčava; it's home to the recommended Tourist Farm Govc-Vršnik.

The **Matkov Kot** road is more rugged, with cliff-hanging gravel portions that can feel like little more than tractor ruts. But the valley scenery is breathtaking (sometimes literally)—and arguably rivals the Panoramic Road. Adventurous drivers who enjoy mountain vistas will find it worth the grinding gears. It's easy to miss this poorly marked valley—look for signs to the tourist farms (the recommended Tourist Farm Perk is on this road) and for *Matkov Škaf.*

Other Sights

If you have ample time here, you can consider some other offbeat attractions that are more charming than thrilling.

The **First Gostišče**—which has a restaurant and rents rooms on the road between Solčava and Logarska Dolina—has a cave on their property called Fidova Zijalka, the residence of a 19th-century hermit and medicine man named Fida. Much higher on the hill is another cave called Potočka Zijalka, where prehistoric findings have helped advance our modern understanding of life during the last Ice Age. Honoring this heritage, the First family operates their own modest, two-room museum of prehistoric cave findings and folk medicine (small entrance fee, same hours as restaurant—see page 682). They also have an "ethnographic park": Pay a few euros and pick up the essential English guidebooklet at the main building, then hike steeply up into the hills behind for a one-hour loop that takes you to the cave, with commentary en route about local flora, fauna, and farming lifestyles.

If you're traveling with kids, consider paying a visit to the **Fairytale Forest,** next to and run by the recommended Na Razpotju Guesthouse in the middle of Logarska Dolina. Speckled through a gentle wood are 35 woodcarvings illustrating local fairy tales, all explained in English (small entrance fee, April-Nov daily 10:00-18:00; listed under "Sleeping in Logarska Dolina," next).

Sleeping in Logarska Dolina

All of my listings are in Logarska Dolina or within about a 15-minute drive. Many accommodations in this region have their own restaurants, and it's common (and typically a good value) to take "half-board" at your accommodation—dinner for a fixed additional price. There are no restaurants in this area that are worth going out of your way for, so eating where you sleep makes sense.

IN LOGARSKA DOLINA

These options sit in the valley of Logarska Dolina itself. They're listed in the order you'll reach them as you drive down the valley.

Hotel Plesnik and **Vila Palenk,** both part of the only big hotel outfit in the area, sit proudly in the middle of Logarska Dolina. **$$$$** Hotel Plesnik, with lively public spaces and 30 modern rooms with traditional farmhouse furnishings, is a big, classy, overpriced splurge (elevator). The nearby, smaller **$$$** Vila Palenk has 11 additional, slightly cheaper rooms (family room, no elevator, breakfast at the main hotel). Reservations for both are handled through the same office (dinner available at hotel restaurant, indoor swimming pool, Logarska Dolina 10, tel. 03/839-2300, www.plesnik.si, info@plesnik.si). After entering Logarska Dolina, you'll come to a fork; bear left to reach the hotel.

$$ Lenar Tourist Farm rents six rooms and three apartments with cozy farmhouse decor in two adjacent homes. This place has nice views over a small orchard and the grand valley of Logarska Dolina (apartment for up to 6 people, breakfast extra, cash only, Logarska Dolina 11, mobile 041-851-829, www.lenar.si).

$$ Na Razpotju Guesthouse ("At the Crossroads") is good for families, with 10 pastel rooms named for mountain herbs and a small theme park of carved fairy tales (dinner available, family rooms, a quarter-mile from Hotel Plesnik toward the far end of the valley, Logarska Dolina 14, mobile 031-249-441, www.logarska-narazpotju.si).

$$ Ojstrica Country House has nine simple rooms and a restaurant halfway along Logarska Dolina (dinner available, Logarska Dolina 13a, tel. 03/838-9051, mobile 041-664-455, www.logarska-ojstrica.si, info@logarska-ojstrica.si).

NEAR LOGARSKA DOLINA

In Robanov Kot: $$ Tourist Farm Govc-Vršnik (pronounced "goats vurshnick")—in this smaller, relaxing valley (a scenic 15-minute drive from Logarska Dolina)—is my favorite option in the region, and the most modern and accessible of my touristfarm listings. English-speaking Marjana and the Vršnik family run this farm with a soft-spoken, warmhearted hospitality. They have cows, a traditional beehive, and 10 cozy rooms with bright, woody decor (dinner available, cash only, Robanov Kot 34, tel. 03/839-5016, www.govc-vrsnik.com). As you enter the valley of Robanov Kot (just south of Solčava), watch for signs (it's the second tourist farm on the left).

Between Solčava and Logarska Dolina: $ Firšt Gostišče, situated along the picturesque riverside road just outside Logarska Dolina, feels like a rural rest stop, with a popular restaurant, six straightforward rooms, and a small museum about local prehistoric finds (dinner available, Logarska Dolina 1a, tel. 03/839-4678, www.first-logarska.si).

On the Panoramic Road: $ Tourist Farm Žibovt is dramatically situated at the far end of the Panoramic Road, within sight of the Austrian border. It perches on a ledge with fine views of a tranquil meadow that ends at a sheer cliff plunging to the bottom of Logarska Dolina. In addition to renting six basic but cheery rooms, the Poličnik family serves meals and turns out a wide range of dairy products—including the unforgettable *kislo mleko* ("soured milk"). They also make traditional wooden games and have beehives that produce homemade honey; a small marble quarry is nearby (cash only, closed mid-Oct-mid-April, Logarska Dolina 24, tel. 03/584-7118, www.nad1000m.si/zibovt, kmetija.zibovt@gmail.com, Žarko and Martina Poličnik). The farm is well-marked at the far end of the Panoramic Road (near the Austrian border crossing at Pavličevo Sedlo).

Eating in Logarska Dolina

Many of the region's tourist farms serve full meals to passersby in summer and light meals and snacks at other times. The food here is traditional and heavy, and no place is worth a long drive for a meal. Base your decision on convenience.

Picnics: The best option is to bring a picnic with you and eat whenever you find the scenic perch you like best. If you wait to buy your picnic until you reach the valley, you're too late. Instead, shop at one of the small grocery stores along the main road in Luče or Solčava. Also in Solčava, the Center Rinka's café/bar sells locally produced meats and cheeses to supplement your picnic. Spectacularly located picnic benches punctuate the Panoramic Road, including ones a few hundred yards on either side of the recommended Tourist Farm Klemenšek.

In Logarska Dolina: Several of my recommended accommodations also have food, including **$$$ Hotel Plesnik** (big restaurant with pricey food, daily) and **$$ Ojstrica Country House** (woody, convivial space with a bar frequented by locals, daily). On the road between Logarska Dolina and Solčava, **$$$ First Gostišče** serves up small bites and pricier main courses (Tue-Sun 12:00-21:00, closed Mon).

On the Panoramic Road: $$ Tourist Farm Klemenšek, set on a grassy ridge with spectacular views, has the classic Logarska Dolina setting, home cooking, and indoor or outdoor tables (July-Aug daily; May-June and Sept-mid-Oct Sat-Sun only; closed mid-Oct-April; halfway between Sveti Duh and the end of the Panoramic Road, tel. 03/838-9024, www.nad1000m.si/klemensek).

Velika Planina

This extremely remote and rustic herdsmen's settlement sits on a mile-high island, surrounded by 360 degrees of cut glass. Accessible only by a cable-car ride, chairlift, and short hike—or by driving a very rough road and taking a longer hike—Velika Planina is an alpine wonderland, offering an insightful look at farming lifestyles. While it takes some effort to reach, it's worth the trip in perfect summer weather for those lingering in the mountains. Velika Planina is also very loosely on the way between Ljubljana (or Lake Bled) and Logarska Dolina (the cable car is a five-mile detour from the Kamnik-Luče road, described earlier, under "Getting to Logarska Dolina").

Orientation: A large meadow with houses (the literal meaning of its name), Velika Planina feels like you're at the end of the world—and yet, on a clear day you can see Ljubljana on the horizon. The focal point for tourists is Pastirsko Naselje (Pastors' Settlement), also known as Veliki Stan (Big Town) and Tiha Dolina (Silent Valley). This is where about 35 farmers—who live most of the year in a dozen different villages scattered

throughout the valley below—bring their 400 cows for high-altitude grazing each summer (early June-mid-Sept). At other times, it's scenic but very desolate—I'd skip it if the cows aren't up, or if the weather is bad. For more information, and to confirm cable-car timetables, see www.velikaplanina.si.

Getting There: North of Ljubljana is the city of Kamnik, and north of that is the village of Kaminška Bistrica, where a **cable car** heads up into the mountains (€17 round-trip, runs at the top of each hour mid-June-mid-Sept 8:00-20:00—more frequently with demand, shorter hours off-season, tel. 031/680-862; buses connect Kamnik to the cable car 3/day in summer, 15 minutes). From the top of the cable car (4,655 feet), you have various ways to get to the Pastirsko Naselje village. One option is a long 40-minute hike. But most visitors prefer to continue on to a chairlift (€2 extra, coordinated to meet arriving cable cars). From the chairlift's first station (Zeleni rob), it's a level 20-minute hike to the village, and from the second/top station (Gradišče, 5,472 feet), it's a downhill 20-minute hike.

It's also possible to **drive** most of the way to Velika Planina, but it requires negotiating a confusing maze of steep and unpaved roads; because locals don't want cars anywhere near the village (which would ruin the rustic ambience), you'll have to park a long hike away. If you'd like to try, from the Kamnik-Luče road, near Podvoljovek, watch for the turnoff to *Tiha Dolina*. Once on this maze of roads, carefully track signs to *Veliki Stan* until you see the *do not enter sign*—from here, you'll have to hike in.

Visiting Velika Planina: Here in the "big village," farmers reside in unique traditional houses: tiny residential quarters in the center, surrounded by stables for the animals (which helps heat the living area), all covered by a unique oval roof. The homes are made of larch wood, which helps provide natural weatherproofing. One of the huts, the **Preskar Hut,** hosts a small museum of 19th-century farming lifestyles; others, including the **Pri Gradišekovih** (near the top of town), may be open to sell cheese and other food. Perched on a ridge just above the settlement, just enjoying the view, is the rustic, wooden **Chapel of St. Mary of Snows** (which was destroyed during WWII and rebuilt in 1988). A priest still comes up each Sunday throughout the summer to say Mass for this tiny community.

Velika Planina has its own very distinctive and proud culture. The farmers' traditional costume is a cloak made of overlapping corn stalks (which resembles a giant hula skirt) and a floppy hat—both of which provide protection from the elements. While here, they produce a unique, pear-shaped cheese called *trnič*, which tastes like a very young Swiss cheese—mild and semicrumbly. It's often served with a buckwheat mush called *žganci* and eaten with a wooden spoon that's another one of this area's local traditions. The soured milk *(kislo mleko)* from Logarska Dolina is also produced here.

Herdsmen gather and socialize in a common hut called "The Parliament." They are keeping up with modern times: They only wear the traditional costume as a photo op for tourists, and many of the huts have been modernized (solar panels are the only source of electricity). But old-timers are concerned that the next generation isn't eager about carrying on the tradition. High-maintenance cows require 24/7 attention, and most young people have other jobs now. Visit now, while this last vestige of traditional herding still survives.

Velenje Castle

This scenic, 700-year-old, hill-capping castle seems out of place over the modern industrial town of Velenje (which was once named "Titovo Velenje" for the Yugoslav dictator, Tito). Even more unusual is the eclectic, extensive, and endearing museum it houses. While it's not worth going far out of your way to see, a trip to the castle makes a good rainy-day activity or a fine diversion if you've got extra time at the end of your Logarska Dolina day.

Cost and Hours: €2.50, Tue-Sun 10:00-18:00, Nov-March until 17:00, closed Mon, Ljubljanska cesta 54, tel. 03/898-2630, www.muzej-velenje.si.

Getting There: Velenje Castle is easy to visit en route to or from Logarska Dolina, especially if you're headed east on the expressway. From the road connecting Logarska Dolina to the expressway, you can detour east just south of Mozirje (via Gorenje) into Velenje, where you'll look for easy-to-miss brown signs to turn off for the castle. From Velenje, you can head south straight to the expressway.

Visiting the Castle: You'll find a surprising diversity of exhibits surrounding the tranquil castle courtyard: replicas of a circa-1930s general store and pub; a Czech professor's three-room collection of African art and everyday items; a survey of regional history through the Middle Ages, including a replica of a countryside home; a city history overview (the town was founded only after World War II, so much of its story dates from Tito's Yugoslav era); an exhibit on the WWII experience in the local area; various Slovenian paintings and sculptures; a movie about the city's postwar development; and temporary exhibits. Separate buildings house a collection of Baroque church art and an exhibit on mastodons (the remains of two of these extinct tusked mammals were found near here in 1964).

PTUJ & MARIBOR

The vast majority of Slovenia's attractions are concentrated in the western third of the country: the mountains, the sea, the capital, and the Karst. East of Ljubljana, the mountains gradually fade into cornfields, the towns and cities become less colorful, and "Oh, wow!" turns into "So what?" But there's hope, in the form of Slovenia's oldest town (and winner of the "funniest name" award): Ptuj (puh-TOOey—the "P" is almost silent; and yes, it really does sound like someone spitting). This small, sleepy, pleasant town boasts a creaky Old Town and a hilltop castle packed with museum exhibits. For a big-city complement to Ptuj, drop into Maribor—the country's second city and the de facto capital of eastern Slovenia. Expect some contrasts from the more touristed parts of Slovenia. Even in this tiny country, rivalry rages between cities—and people here in the "02 Zone" (the area code-derived nickname that Slovenes use for this region) have their own dialect and identity.

PLANNING YOUR TIME

With a week or more in Slovenia and a desire to delve into the less-visited areas of the country, Ptuj deserves a look. A few hours are enough to feel you've mastered the town; if you're a restless sightseer, it's tough to fill an entire day here. Begin by touring the castle, then enjoy a wander through the Old Town and consider Ptuj's other museums, or relax at the thermal baths across the river. If you can't sit still that long, consider spending a few more hours on a side trip into Maribor.

Ptuj and Maribor are conveniently located on the train network and are easy to reach from Ljubljana, as well as from international destinations like Zagreb, Vienna, and Budapest.

Ptuj

With a storied past, a much-vaunted castle, and easygoing locals who act like they've never met a tourist, Ptuj is charming. Populated since the early Stone Age, Ptuj has a long and colorful history that reads like a Who's Who of Central Europe: Celts and Romans, Dominican friars and Habsburg counts, Nazis and Yugoslavs...not to mention a fuzzy monster named Kurent. The people of Ptuj are particularly proud of their Roman era, when "Poetovio" was a bustling metropolis of 40,000 people (nearly quadruple today's size). But even as it clings to its noble past, today's Ptuj is refreshingly real, with a sleepy small-town ambience and an interesting castle/ museum.

While it hosts plenty of visitors (mostly Germans and Austrians, who call it "Pettau"), Ptuj is hardly a tourist town. Real people, not nightclubs or souvenir shops, populate the Old Town. If this makes Ptuj feel a bit less polished than the big-name sights in western Slovenia, so much the better—think of it as a diamond in the rough.

Orientation to Ptuj

Ptuj is squeezed between its historic castle and the wide Drava River. With just 11,000 people (23,000 in greater Ptuj), it still ranks as Slovenia's eighth-largest town. The Old Town is shaped roughly like a triangle, with the castle and two monasteries as its three points. You can walk from one end of the Old Town to the other in about 10 minutes. The town slopes gradually uphill from the river to the castle.

TOURIST INFORMATION

Ptuj's TI shares the square called Slovenski trg with its landmark City Tower (daily 9:00-18:00, off-season until 17:00, Slovenski trg 5, tel. 02/779-6011, www.ptuj.info). The TI has a line on local guides and runs occasional town walks in English, including one led by a guide clad in a Roman toga.

ARRIVAL IN PTUJ

The humble **train station** is about a 10-minute walk from the center. Exit the station to the left, then cross the busy road to the **bus station.** From the bus station, the Old Town is just on the other

Ptuj

Accommodations
1 Hotel Mitra
2 Vladimir Šilak Rooms
3 muziKafe B&B

Eateries
4 Gostilna Ribič
5 Gostilna Amadeus

side of the big commercial center. If you're **driving** in from the expressway, cross the big bridge into town and then watch for *P* signs to the left. Street parking in town is abundant and affordable—look for blue lines—but it's limited to two hours. To visit the castle, follow brown *Grad* signs to twist up the road and park just below it.

Sights in Ptuj

PTUJ CASTLE (PTUJSKI GRAD)

Overlooking the town from its perch over the Drava River, Ptuj's castle is less than thrilling from afar. But the horseshoe-shaped castle complex hosts a series of surprisingly rich and engaging exhibits, making a visit here worth ▲▲. The core of the collection shows off the lifestyles of the castle's historic residents, while other exhibits display weapons, musical instruments, and traditional costumes used for the annual Kurentovanje festival.

Cost and Hours: €6; daily 9:00-18:00 (Sat-Sun until 20:00 in July-Aug), mid-Oct-April until 17:00; tel. 02/748-0360, www.pmpo.si.

Getting There: The castle is about a 10-minute cobbled hike above the Old Town. Several trails lead up from the Old Town, all well marked with *Grad* signs (easiest to find is the lane called Grajska ulica, near the TI).

❍ Self-Guided Tour: While good English descriptions are posted in most rooms, this tour links up the highlights. You'll follow a one-way route. The entrances to each exhibit are not all well-marked, but attendants are always around to direct you to what you want to see. Touring the whole shebang takes about two hours.

• *Buy your ticket in the long building just below the main part of the castle. This same building also has the castle's highlight, the...*

Collection of Traditional Carnival Masks: Ptuj's Mardi Gras celebration, called Kurentovanje, is well-known for its processions of fanciful masked characters (see sidebar). This exhibit—colorful as an episode of *Sesame Street*—offers an entertaining look at the complete Kurentovanje experience. The various costumes are all lined up in one long hall, as if reenacting the procession that stomps through Ptuj's streets each spring. First come the spearmen, dressed more or less like normal folks. Soon after, the plow is used to symbolically "wake up the soil" and set the stage for a season of bountiful crops. Then you'll see a group of striking Kurent costumes—from old homemade ones (turn an old coat inside-out to reveal the fur lining) to today's store-bought versions (they run about €500). After the giant hen comes the bear, a reminder of times when Roma entertainers actually did bring trained bears to town. The horse (called Rusa) is taken by a farmer from house to house, trying to "sell" it to neighbors. But the horse is unruly and obnoxious—supposedly good luck for the health and fertility of livestock. The costume of the old woman carrying the old man on her back seems whimsical, but it represents a powerful theme: We carry the memory of the deceased with us always. Near the end are Jürek (swaddled in greenery, representing spring) and Rabolj (a Kurent-like monster, representing winter); these two do battle—and, of course, the spring always wins.

• *Now head up into the main part of the castle, climbing the cobbled road into the courtyard. Show your ticket to go through the gate, and then climb the main stairs (on the left side of the courtyard) one floor up.*

Courtyard: Look over the courtyard for this quick history lesson: In the 11th century, the archbishops of Salzburg built a fortress here. In the 12th century, the Lords of Ptuj, who watched over the

Salzburgers' land, moved in. The lords died out in the mid-15th century, and from then on, the castle changed hands frequently. Over the next several centuries, Ptuj Castle gradually acquired its current appearance: a Romanesque core (14th century, barely visible now) with a

Renaissance arcaded courtyard (designed by Italian experts who came to fortify the castle against the Ottomans), accentuated by an austere Baroque addition (the outermost wing, with the decorated stone window frames). Most of what you'll see in today's exhibit dates from the time of the Counts of Herberstein (1873-1945).

Now look over the door at the end of the arcade to see the **castle seal**, a hodgepodge of symbols representing previous owners. What's an English phrase (in the banner at the top) doing on a seal for a castle in Slovenia? It's because of a Hungarian princess, of course. In the Middle Ages, when a princess of Hungary moved to Scotland to be with her new husband, she took with her a particularly protective chamberlain. When the chamberlain buckled the princess to her horse for a treacherous river crossing, he'd fasten her on with three belts instead of just one, and shout "Grip fast!" when they came to any rough patches. That chamberlain's descendants took the name Leslie and eventually bought this castle in 1656. The family crest became those three buckles the chamberlain had used to protect his princess (in the left shield). You'll spot this insignia throughout the castle.

• *Going through the door, you enter the...*

Feudal Dwelling Culture Collection: This exhibit displays artifacts belonging to the castle's previous owners. The route takes you more or less clockwise in a roughly chronological order, from the 16th to the 19th century. In the first few reception halls are 17th-century tapestries from Brussels depicting the travels of Ulysses. Nearly every big room has its own ceramic stove (fed from behind the wall by servants). Look up: While some of the rooms have exposed wooden-beam ceilings, others are adorned with cake-frosting stucco work—it's original, and nearly 300 years old. At the end of the first hall is a gallery of portraits of the Herbersteins, who furnished this wing and were eager to establish their legitimacy as a ruling family.

• *Looping back to where you began, head down the hallway into the residential part of the castle (in the hall, notice the yellowed, 700-year-old Herberstein family tree on your right). The first big room is the...*

Kurentovanje

Ptuj is famous for its distinctive Mardi Gras celebration, called Kurentovanje (koo-rent-oh-VAWN-yeh). Locals dress up in elaborate costumes and parade through the streets, celebrating the end of winter and heralding the arrival of spring. Nearby villages have similar, smaller and more traditional processions.

It seems quaint today, but in the Middle Ages, Kurentovanje was deadly serious. The winter is particularly harsh here, so when spring began to approach, the peasants wanted to offer encouragement. They'd put on frightening masks and costumes and parade around making as much noise as possible to scare off the winter.

Kurentovanje's most notable character is Kurent, a fun-loving Slavic pagan god of hedonism—sort of the Slovenian Bacchus. A Kurent is covered with fur and has a long, red tongue, horns, a snout, whiskers, red-ringed eyes, a wooden club with a spiny hedgehog skin wrapped around one end, and red or green socks. It wears a chain of five bells around its waist, and jumps around and swings its hips to get them clanging as loudly as possible. Kurents travel together in packs, so the combined noise can be deafening.

Traditionally the role of Kurent was played by young men of the village, who used it as an opportunity to catch the eye of a potential wife. (Young women still toss handkerchiefs to the Kurents as they pass by.) Each young man makes his own costume in secret—making the big reveal all the more frightening. Traditionally, they'd use the stinkiest animal hides they could find, to make the beast smell as hideous as it looked and sounded.

These processions have evolved into modern extravaganzas. Nowadays, men and women of any age buy their Kurent costumes in a store, and Kurentovanje's daytime parades are followed by evenings of music, celebration, and general debauchery. In recent years, in a sort of "creature exchange" program, characters from Mardi Gras celebrations in other countries have come to take part in Kurentovanje.

Imagine about 350 of these hairy beasts, each one with five huge bells clanging at top volume, stomping down Prešernova street. Or come the Sunday before Ash Wednesday, and see for yourself. For details on all the festivities, check out www.kurentovanje.net. Or, to watch a segment from my TV show about the spectacle, search for "Rick Steves Woolly Beasts" on YouTube.

Kurentovanje ends at midnight on Shrove Tuesday (before Ash Wednesday), when people move into the more pensive season of Lent...confident that spring will soon return.

Countess' Salon: Also called the "Chinese Salon," this room reveals the fascination many 17th- and 18th-century Europeans had for foreign cultures. But the European artists who created these works never actually visited China, instead basing their visions on stories, often specious, that they heard from travelers. The results are highly inaccurate at best and flights of pure fantasy at worst (look around for animals and instruments that never existed). This European interest in Chinese culture is known as *chinoiserie*. We'll see a similar fixation on Turkish culture soon.

• *Head through the next few rooms (countess' bedroom, countess' dressing room, old chapel, chambermaid's room). Before entering the 14th-century core—and oldest part—of the castle, keep your head up to see a very unusual chandelier: an anatomically correct (or surgically enhanced?) female dragon. Continue into the...*

Bedrooms: The first shows off what prim and proper 17th-century Europeans considered to be "erotic" art (with a mythical creature trying to woo a woman), while the second is decorated in Napoleonic-era Empire-style furniture. In this room, notice the stove: Scented water was poured into the top, and fragrant steam emerged at the bottom. Fancy. The third bedroom brings the survey of furniture up to date: 19th-century Biedermeier...simple, practical, and comfortable.

• *Going into the arcade, turn left to find the...*

Festival Hall: Decorating the walls is Europe's biggest collection of *turqueries*. Like the faux-Chinese stuff we saw earlier, this is a (usually highly inaccurate) European vision of Turkish culture. After the Habsburg armies defeated the Ottomans and forced them out of Central Europe, the two powers began a diplomatic relationship. In the late 17th century, many Austrian officers went to Turkey—returning with souvenirs and tall tales, which were patched together to form the idiosyncratic vision of the Ottoman Empire you see here.

The left wall shows Ottoman politicians of the day, many with generic European features (presumably painted by artists who'd never laid eyes on a Turkish person). Along the back wall are portraits of four sultans' wives. Imagine how astonishing the notion of a harem must have been in the buttoned-down Habsburg days. And yet, even these unmistakably titillating paintings are appropriately repressed. The first woman (on left) wears two different layers of semitransparent clothing (what's the point?). And the fourth woman (on right) reaches for some fruit (symbolic of...well, you know) and teasingly pulls open her dress so we can see what's underneath, which is...more clothes.

Finally, look on the right wall, with 17th-century Eurofied visions of people from other cultures: Africans, Native Americans, and Asians, all with exaggerated features. At the far end of the Festival Hall, you can poke into the castle's chapel.

• *Exiting the Festival Hall, go straight ahead along the arcade to its end, where you'll take the tight, medieval spiral staircase up one level. At the top, the row of sandstone dwarves leads to two skippable rooms of paintings. Instead, turn left into...*

Medieval Knights, Founders, and Patrons of the Arts: This exhibit tells you more than you ever wanted to know about the Lords of Ptuj. Touring its several rooms, you'll see family trees and crests, artifacts from lords gone by, models of local buildings, and a fine 1380 statue of St. George (Ptuj's patron saint) slaying the dragon. The darkened rooms highlight the Middle Ages, with some precious statues by the greatest local masters of the day.

• *Exit to the right, and walk to the end of the arcade.*

Castle Gallery: This painting gallery features aristocratic portraits, mythological scenes, and varied landscapes from the late 16th to late 18th century. As most of these are lesser painters' copies of famous works by great masters, you likely won't recognize many names in here. One name in particular you won't recognize is Johann Christian Schröder (1655-1702), a Prague court painter whose depictions of biblical scenes constitute the majority of the collection.

• *Head back down to the courtyard. Ask one of the attendants to direct you (across the courtyard from the main staircase) to the...*

Collection of Musical Instruments: This fun, well-presented exhibit groups instruments by type of music, which you'll hear as you enter each room. The first section celebrates Ptuj's civic marching band, a prized local tradition. The next section displays ancient Roman instruments. The tibia (in the display case), dating from the second century AD, is the only one ever found; it had two pipes made of bone leading to a single mouthpiece (illustrated on the wall). The next section features woodwinds and strings, including a rare, preserved lute. And the last section shows off a Bösendorfer piano and other keyboard instruments.

• *As you exit, you can ask to be directed to the anticlimactic finale (to the right), the...*

Collection of Arms: Squeezed into one corner of a huge, vaulted room is an armory collection spanning several centuries, from the 1400s through World War I. They're displayed on racks, as they would have been in a real armory. Also in this hall, look for models of the castle as it appeared in 1657 and in 1812.

• *Your castle visit is over. Enjoy the views, then head back down into town.*

OLD TOWN

The sights in Ptuj's Old Town are simple and quick to see.

▲Slovenski Trg

Once Ptuj's main square, and now its most atmospheric, Slovenski trg is fronted by the TI, Hotel Mitra, and the City Tower. Around this square are several reminders of Ptuj's Roman past.

The white marble slab in the middle of the square, known as the **Orpheus Monument,** was commissioned by a Roman mayor in the second century AD to honor an esteemed figure: himself. Notice the musician playing the lyre (near the top, center of slab, below the naked woman). Since the lyre is commonly associated with Orpheus, the monument's nickname stuck. But when Rome fell, so did many of its structures, including this one. It finally reappeared in the 16th century as the town pillory, where criminals were punished (secured by chains that were embedded in the holes you still see in the slab). In the Middle Ages, the town judge would come out onto the balcony over the door of his white house, at the top of the square (at #6), to witness justice being served.

The **City Tower** was built in the late 16th century to defend against Ottoman invaders (who passed by here on their way to lay siege to Vienna). After a fire, the rebuilt tower was capped with this jaunty Baroque steeple.

Embedded in the staircase at the back of the tower are more fragments from Ptuj's Roman era. This so-called **"open-air museum"** is just a taste of the vast Roman material unearthed in Ptuj. In the middle of the staircase, make out the letters: POET-OVIONA—a longer version of Ptuj's Roman name, Poetovio.

Just behind the City Tower is **St. George's Parish Church** (Cerkev Svetega Jurija, open daily 7:00-11:00 & 18:00-18:30), which dates back before any other building in Slovenia. The current Gothic version is packed with diverse ecclesiastical art. Inside, notice (on your left) the gorgeous circa-1380 statue of St. George, Ptuj's patron saint, slaying the dragon. Then go to the first big pillar on the right, where you'll see a glass-covered relief depicting throngs of admirers adoring the Baby Jes...wait—where's Jesus? (Not to mention Mary's hands?) Several years ago, Jesus was stolen from this pillar. To help prevent further vandalism, the priests reduced the opening times (notice the seven-hour midday break).

Prešernova Street (Prešernova Ulica)

Stretching away from the City Tower is Ptuj's main drag and oldest street. Wider than most streets in town, it led to what was once the medieval market square (now Slovenski trg)—so merchants set up market stalls all along the street. Many of the houses here have long since been renovated in Renaissance or Baroque style, making it Ptuj's most picturesque thoroughfare.

Town Square (Mestni Trg)

Today Ptuj's main square, this lively people zone (just down Murkova street from Slovenski trg) is a hub of activity. Major events and festivals—including the Kurentovanje Mardi Gras festival—take place here.

The square is watched over by the distinctive **Town Hall,** built by a visionary mayor a century ago. Over the left door (on the corner) are two statues commemorating Ptuj's Roman history: on the right, Emperor Trajan, who granted Ptuj city status in the early second century AD; and on the left, St. Viktorin, a third-century Ptuj bishop and scholar who was martyred by Emperor Diocletian.

Facing the Town Hall in the middle of the square is a statue of **St. Florian,** who traditionally protects towns against fire. Ptuj was devastated by four fires in the late 17th and early 18th centuries. This statue is a 1993 replica of one that was built here after the fourth and final fire, in 1744 (after which they finally wised up and rebuilt with stone instead of wood). Largely as a result of Ptuj's frequent fires, its rival Maribor (to the north) gradually supplanted it as the region's main center of commerce and winemaking. Ptuj's fate was sealed a century later, when the rail line between Vienna and Trieste was routed through Maribor. Today Maribor has 10 times as many people as Ptuj—and 10 times the industry, congestion, and urban gloominess.

Ptuj Cellar (Ptujska Klet)

Ptuj's wines are well-respected, and this is the main facility for the dominant producer, Pullus. Over the centuries, Celts, Romans, and Minorite monks all made wine in this area. Today this enormous cellar, branching out under the Old Town, continues this proud tradition—and holds a staggering 1.3 million gallons of wine (about 85 percent of it white). The cellar is also home to a "wine archive" with bottles dating back to 1917. The vintners are proudest of their award-winning sauvignon blanc, but their best seller—at a million bottles a year—is a local wine called Haložan (a semidry blend of four whites).

Tours and Tastings: Cellar tours and wine tastings are possible if you call ahead (€15, Mon-Sat 9:00-17:00, closed Sun, mobile 041-394-896, www.pullus.si). While these are often available in English, you may wind up joining a German- or Slovene-language tour.

Shop: If you just want to pick up a bottle, stop by their wine shop, around the corner from the cellar (Mon-Fri 9:00-12:00 & 13:00-17:00, Sat 8:00-12:00, closed Sun, Vinarski trg 1, tel. 02/787-9810).

Minorite Church and Monastery (Minoritski Samostan)

This church, dedicated to Saints Peter and Paul, was one of the only buildings in town destroyed in World War II. (The Allies believed that the occupying Nazis were storing munitions here.) Only the foundation at the back end of the church survived, and it was left in ruins for decades. In 1989, friars celebrated their 750th anniversary in Ptuj by rebuilding the back part of the church. About a decade later, the front half was also reconstructed, and the statues in the niches above the door were replaced a few years after that. Step into the contemporary, minimalist interior, with its modern stained-glass windows and stations of the cross. At the altar are the original statues that once adorned the church facade. Go through the door on the right into the peaceful cloister. A handful of friars can still be seen roaming these tranquil halls, and you're welcome to stroll here, too.

Cost and Hours: Free, daily 7:30-18:30, Minoritski trg.

Ptuj Thermal Baths (Terme Ptuj)

This gigantic bath complex, a 15-minute walk across the river from Ptuj's Old Town, is a fun place to splash around. The "Thermal Park" has multiple swimming pools and whirlpools—all naturally fed by thermal springs—and slides, including the "longest slide in Slovenia." The complex also offers indoor pools, saunas, and various spa treatments. Additional indoor pools are available at the hotel across the street.

Cost and Hours: €15/all day, more on weekends but cheaper for shorter visits; Mon-Fri 8:00-22:00, Sat-Sun from 7:00, outdoor pools have shorter hours; towel rental available, Pot v Toplice 9, tel. 02/749-4530, www.terme-ptuj.si.

PTUJ & MARIBOR

Sleeping in Ptuj

Central Ptuj has only a few hotels and a handful of *sobe*/guest-houses. While the options seem limited, the rooms are generally a good value compared to the western part of the country.

$$ Hotel Mitra offers Ptuj's nicest rooms and best location: right on its most appealing street, a few steps from the landmark City Tower. It's the closest thing in town to a business-class hotel. Each of the 29 rooms—well-appointed, with cushy decor—has its own historical theme (air-con, elevator, limited free parking, Prešernova 6, tel. 02/787-7455, www.hotel-mitra.si, info@hotel-mitra.si).

$ Vladimir Šilak rents 16 comfortable rooms around a charming courtyard in his gorgeously renovated Old Town home. The building dates from sometime between the 12th and 15th centuries, and Vladimir has lovingly restored it using quality materials. If you want to sleep in a centuries-old house with huge medieval vaults and three-foot-thick walls, this is the place (family rooms, apartments with kitchenettes also available, breakfast extra in apartments, air-con, free parking, bike rental, Dravska 13, tel. 02/787-7447, mobile 031-597-361, www.rooms-silak.com, info@rooms-silak.com).

$ muziKafe B&B rents seven fun, colorful, funky (in a good way) rooms above a lively café in the heart of the atmospheric Old Town. After traveling around the world for a year, the owners decided to open a place where fellow globetrotters feel at home (breakfast extra, Vrazov trg 1, tel. 02/787-8860, www.muzikafe.si, info@muzikafe.si).

Eating in Ptuj

Little Ptuj isn't known for its high cuisine. You'll spot several breezy cafés and packed pizzerias, but high-quality eateries are in short supply.

$$$ Gostilna Ribič ("Fisherman's Inn") is every local's first recommendation for a splurge dinner. One of the most popular (and expensive) places in town, it has a short menu that's focused on fresh, local dishes, with an emphasis on fish. Sit in the classy interior or outside on the relaxing riverside terrace (Tue-Thu 11:00-22:00, Fri-Sun until 23:00, closed Mon, Dravska ulica 9, tel. 02/749-0635). If you're ready for a break from Slovenian cuisine, the **$ Chinese restaurant** (Kitajski Vrt) across the street is quite good.

$$ Gostilna Amadeus serves up traditional Slovenian cuisine to tour groups, individual tourists, and a few locals. They're especially proud of their *štruklji* (traditional Slovenian rolled dumplings). The bar, with outdoor seating and drinks only, is downstairs; to eat a meal, head upstairs to their nicely appointed dining room (Mon and Wed-Sat 12:00-22:00, Sun until 16:00, closed Tue, Prešernova 36, tel. 02/771-7051).

$ muziKafe, which also rents rooms (see earlier), is a cool hangout with an artistic spirit right in the center of the creaky Old Town. They serve drinks, light food, snacks, and cakes in a colorful, convivial atmosphere. Their vaulted cellar also hosts musical performances a few nights each week (Mon-Sat 8:00-23:00, Sun 10:00-22:00, Vrazov trg 1, tel. 02/787-8860, www.muzikafe.si).

Ptuj Connections

From Ptuj by Train to: Maribor (8/day, 1 hour, additional connections possible with transfer in Pragersko), **Ljubljana** (3/day direct, 2.5 hours; more with transfer in Pragersko or Maribor), **Zagreb** (4/day, 3 hours, transfer in Pragersko and sometimes also Zidani Most), **Budapest** (that's **Budimpešta** in Slovene, 1/day direct, 6 hours; other connections take longer and require more changes), **Vienna** (that's **Dunaj** in Slovene, 1/day with transfer in Pragersko, 4.5 hours; 1/day with transfer in Maribor, 6.5 hours; additional connections require more changes, 5-6 hours). For destinations in western Slovenia, first go to Ljubljana.

Maribor

The second-biggest city in Slovenia (with 158,000 people), Maribor lives forever in the shadow of its much glitzier big sister, Ljubljana. Maribor is too small to offer an exciting big-city experience and too big to be charming. But this home of industry, business, and one of Slovenia's three universities is worth a quick look if you want to round out your Slovenian experience.

The lazy provincial town of Maribor woke up fast in 1846, when the Habsburgs built the train line from Vienna to the coast through here. It quickly modernized, losing some of its quaintness but gaining an urban, industrial flavor. However, Maribor was devastated in World War II (unlike other Slovenian cities), when it served as a headquarters for occupying Nazi forces. Since the city's factories also produced plane engines and other war supplies, it became a "secondary target," where Allied warplanes—mostly American—would drop their bombs if unable to hit their primary targets in Germany or Austria.

Today, rebuilt Maribor feels mellow for its size. Nestled up against a gentle vineyard-covered hill, it's almost cozy. From a tourist's perspective, the town is pleasant enough but pretty dull—there's little to do other than wander its pedestrian-only streets. The city doesn't merit a detour, but it's worth a couple of hours for a stroll if you're passing through or have run out of diversions in Ptuj.

The countryside surrounding Maribor—called Mariborsko Pohorje—is an inviting recreational area, with vine-strewn hills lively with hikers and bicyclists in summer and with skiers in winter. Maribor is also the center of a thriving wine-growing region—especially popular among Austrians, who flow over the border to sample wines here, then stumble home. If you have time to spare, ask the TI for details about either of these outlying activities.

Orientation to Maribor

Maribor lines up along the bank of the Drava River. At the center of its concrete sprawl is the mostly traffic-free Old Town, with a variety of fine squares.

TOURIST INFORMATION

The main TI is at the northeast corner of the Old Town (Mon-Fri 9:00-19:00, Sat-Sun until 17:00, shorter hours Nov-March, Partizanska 6a—on the far side of the Franciscan Church from Trg Svobode, tel. 02/234-6611, www.visitmaribor.si).

ARRIVAL IN MARIBOR

The train station (which has big lockers) is a 10-minute walk east of the Old Town. Exit the station to the left and head up busy Partizanska cesta. Follow Partizanska as it swings right at the bus station, then continue three more blocks toward the Franciscan church, with its twin red-brick spires. The main TI is in front of the church, and the Old Town is immediately behind the church.

Maribor Walk

Maribor's Austrian-feeling Old Town lacks big-league sights, but its squares and lanes are worth a wander. This lightly narrated self-guided walk gives you the lay of the land. You could do it in less than a half-hour, not including stops.

Entering the Old Town from the train station (on Partizanska, passing the Franciscan church with its two red-brick spires—see

"Arrival in Maribor," earlier), you find yourself on **Trg Svobode.** The oddly bulbous monument honors local Partisans (Yugoslav freedom-fighters) who were executed by Nazis during World War II. Wine cellars honeycomb the earth under this square.

At the end of the square, with the tall tower, is the town's **castle** (Mestni Grad), which houses a good regional museum.

Adjoining Trg Svobode is a second square, **Grajski trg**— Maribor's liveliest, bustling with cafés and restaurants. At the top of the square is the venerable **Café Astoria,** a local landmark.

Recent-history buffs may want to take a detour from here to Maribor's most interesting museum: the **Maribor National Liberation Museum** (Muzej Narodne Osvoboditve Maribor), about a five-minute walk up the street that's at the top of Grajski trg (between Café Astoria and the castle). The ground floor features generally good temporary exhibits. Upstairs, the permanent collection holds a hodgepodge of items from the city's history, mostly focusing on Slovenia's turbulent 20th century (€3, Mon-Fri 8:00-17:00, Sat 9:00-12:00, closed Sun, Ulica Heroja Tomšiča 5, tel. 02/235-2600, www.mnom.si).

Back on Grajski trg, follow lively **Slovenska ulica,** lined with characteristic cafés, sweet shops, and happy al fresco diners. Take a left at Tyrševa/Gosposka, passing some fun student-oriented boutiques. Then turn right on 10 Oktobra to find the big parking-lot square called Slomškov trg, with the city **cathedral** (skip the tower climb—the view is nothing special).

From the cathedral, walk straight down toward the river, cutting through Rotovški trg. You'll wind up on the long, narrow **Glavni trg,** surrounded by historic buildings (including the City Hall) and presided over by an impressive 18th-century plague column.

If you continue down to the riverbank, you'll find yourself in the district called **Lent,** where vintners traditionally offer tastings of their wines. While it's usually pretty quiet, this area hops each summer when Maribor hosts its Lent Festival (late June-early July, www.festival-lent.si). Along this embankment, look for the locally revered "old vine" stretching along a railing—it's supposedly 400 years old and still produces wine-worthy grapes.

Maribor Connections

From Maribor by Train to: Ptuj (8/day, 1 hour, more with transfer in Pragersko), **Ljubljana** (hourly, 2-3 hours, most with transfer in Zidani Most), **Vienna** (that's **Dunaj** in Slovene, 2/day direct, 4 hours, additional connections require changes in Spielfeld-Strass and Graz).

THE KARST

Caves, Castles, and Horses

In Slovenia's Karst region, about an hour south of Ljubljana on the A-1 expressway, you'll find some of the most impressive cave systems on the planet, have a chance to get to know the famous Lipizzaner stallions up close and personal (and for a fraction of what you'd pay in Vienna), and see one of Europe's most dramatically situated castles—burrowed into the face of a mountain.

The word "karst" is used worldwide to refer to an arid limestone plateau, but Slovenia's is the original. In fact, that term comes from the Slovenian *Kras*—the name of a specific region near the Italian border. Since this limestone terrain is easily dissolved by water, karstic regions are punctuated by remarkable networks of caves and underground rivers.

Your top Karst priority is a cave visit. Choose between Slovenia's two best caves, Škocjan or Postojna—each with a handy side trip nearby (to help you pick, see the sidebar later in this chapter). In the neighborhood of Škocjan is Lipica, where the Lipizzaner stallions strut their stuff. Just up the road from Postojna is Predjama Castle, picturesquely nestled into the side of a cliff.

I've listed public-transit possibilities, but most recommended destinations are challenging to reach without a car. To efficiently hit several in one day, consider taking a guided excursion from Ljubljana (see page 552).

Sleeping and Eating in the Karst

Majerija is the region's most enticing splurge, filling an 18th-century farmhouse in the Vipava Valley, about a 30-minute drive from either cave. They have both a fine **$$$$** restaurant focusing on top-quality updated Slovenian fare (Thu-Sat 12:00-15:00 & 18:00-22:00, Sun 12:00-17:00, closed Mon-Wed year-round and Thu in off-season) and 10 modern, stylish, comfortable **$$** rooms (breakfast extra, Slap 18, in Vipava,

tel. 05/368-5010, mobile 041-405-903, www.majerija.si, info@majerija.si).

$ Tourist Farm Hudičevec (hoo-DEE-cheh-vets), midway between Škocjan and Postojna (15 minutes from either), is a simpler option. This kid-friendly complex, with seven rooms and five apartments, is run by the farming Simčič family (dinner available, ask about larger apartments, tel. 05/703-0300, www.hudicevec.si, info@hudicevec.si). Idyllic and remote as this place sounds, it's actually right next to the expressway (which makes it easy to reach, but also comes with some road noise, and large tour groups may show up for dinner). Take the Razdrto exit from the expressway, turn right toward Postojna, then start looking right away for the low-profile sign directing you back under the road.

Škocjan Caves and Lipica Stud Farm

Drivers can easily combine these two attractions, which are just a short distance from each other. By public transportation, it's more challenging (see "Getting to Škocjan" and "Getting to Lipica," below).

▲▲▲Škocjan Caves (Škocjanske Jame)

Škocjan (SHKOHTS-yahn) offers fantastical cave formations and a spectacularly vast canyon with a raging underground river. The main attraction is a guided hike through the caves; this hike is about two miles long, goes up and down more than 400 steps, and is mostly underground. For a few euros more, you can extend your hike through two adjacent valleys and the less remarkable Mahorčič Cave, just above river level.

While anyone in good shape can enjoy Škocjan, those who have trouble walking or tire easily are better off touring the Postojna Caves instead (described later).

Cost and Hours: Most visitors take the two-hour **tourist path 1**—billed as the "classic tour" or "Through the Underground Canyon"—with English commentary (€16-20 depending on the time of year; June-Sept tours daily at the top of each hour 10:00-17:00; April-May and Oct tours daily at 10:00, 12:00, 13:00, and 15:30;

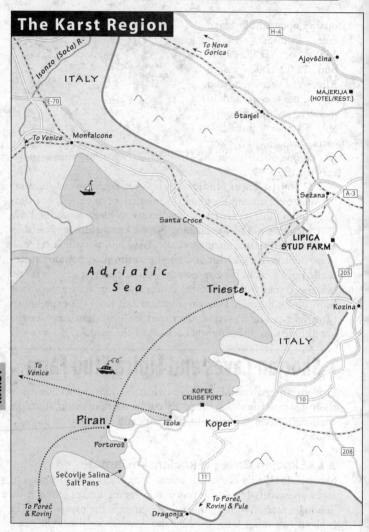

The Karst Region

off-season tours daily at 10:00 and 13:00, plus Sunday at 15:00). Call or pick up the current brochure—which you'll find everywhere in Slovenia—to confirm schedule before making the trip; tel. 05/708-2104, www.park-skocjanske-jame.si.

To extend the hike, you can buy the €24 ticket for **tourist path 2**—called "Following the Reka River Underground"—which gives you access to more valleys and the Mahorčič Cave and takes 1-1.5 additional hours. This can be done on your own June-Sept (10:00-15:00), but for safety reasons, you must go with a guide in April-May and Oct (at 11:00 and 14:00), and it's closed Nov-March.

You'll need to decide whether you want to pay for the extension before buying your ticket. Consider this: Path 1 alone provides enough hiking (and plenty of caves) to exhaust most visitors. But those with abundant stamina and time, a love of caves, and a spirit of exploration will feel that the extension is a few extra euros well spent.

Getting to Škocjan: By car, take the A-1 expressway south from Ljubljana about an hour and get off at the Divača exit (also marked with brown signs for *Lipica* and *Škocjanske jame*) and follow signs for *Škocjanske jame*. (Before or after Škocjan, drivers can easily visit the Lipica Stud Farm, described next.) The caves have free and easy parking.

By public transportation, take the train or bus to Divača (see "Ljubljana Connections," on page 598), which is about three miles from the caves. To get from the Divača train station to the caves, you can either take the free local shuttle bus (5/day May-Oct, none Nov-April, 10 minutes, coordinated to meet some trains—check schedules at Ljubljana TI); walk about 45 minutes; or take a taxi (around €10-15, try calling Taxi Šeki, tel. 041/621-347).

Services: You'll find WCs at the ticket office and at the starting point for tourist path 1, but none in the caves themselves. The ticket office has free lockers—ask for the key.

Eating: A **$** snack bar at the cave ticket office sells basic, over-priced sandwiches and other snacks.

Visiting the Caves: Upon arrival, get a ticket for the next tour. You'll pass waiting time at a covered terrace with an info kiosk, gift shop, café, and interactive educational center with exhibits about the caves.

Tourist Path 1: At tour time, your guide (toting an industrial-strength flashlight) calls everyone together, and you march silently for 10 minutes to the cave entrance. There you split into language groups and enter the cave.

The first half of the experience is the **"Silent Caves"** (so called for the lack of running water), with a wide array of wondrous for-mations and what seem like large caverns. The experience builds and builds as you go into ever-more-impressive grottoes, and you think you've seen the best.

But then you get to the truly colossal final cavern—the **"Murmuring Water Cave"**— with a mighty river crashing through the bottom. You feel like a bit player in a sci-fi thriller. It's a world where a thousand evil *Wizard of Oz* monkeys could comfortably fly in formation. You hike high above the river for about a mile, crossing a breathtak-ing (but stable-feeling) footbridge 150 feet above the torrent. Far below, the scant remains of century-old trails from the early days of tourism are evocative. The cave finally widens, sunlight pours in, and you emerge—like lost creatures seeking daylight—into a lush canyon. This is the **Big Collapsed Valley,** which used to be part of the Škocjan network until its roof fell in.

After Your Tour: Exiting the cave, your options are a bit con-fusing, but guides are generally standing by to advise you. The basic choice is a speedy return, or a slow and scenic one (which may include tourist path 2). Regardless of your route, *P* and *i* signs direct you back to the ticket office.

To **return to the surface** as quickly as possible, turn right and follow signs steeply uphill to the small funicular, which lifts you back to the ticket office. (From the top of the funicular, you can also head straight and walk gently uphill 10 minutes to the museums, which are included in your ticket and described later.)

For a **longer, more strenuous, and more scenic return,** turn left and loop around the perimeter of the Big Collapsed Valley. After passing a fountain (marking the entrance of the off-limits Tominc Cave), you'll come to a fork: The tunnel on the left is a round-trip detour (returning to this point) that takes you to the thundering waterfall at the bottom of the canyon, illustrating how the Reka River grinds like God's band saw into the land. The stairs in the middle lead to the upper part of the canyon; from here, more stairs on the left lead up to the ticket booth. If you head straight past these stairs, you'll cross a modern bridge and reach the entrance to the tour extension, described next.

Tourist Path 2 (Mahorčič Cave and Small Collapsed Valley): Following the directions above, you'll wind up along the rim of the Big Collapsed Valley across from the Škocjan exit (at a modern bridge). After showing your ticket, hike along a "natural bridge" (actually a short stretch of cave) from the Big Collapsed Valley to the Small Collapsed Valley; you'll wind down to the entrance to Mahorčič Cave, where you'll walk just above the Reka River. Compared to the main cave on tourist path 1, Mahorčič is smaller, but very atmospheric, as it's short enough to let in evocative rays of natural light— and you're much closer to the river. Exiting this cave, you'll hike uphill about a half-mile, across farm fields, to get back to the ticket office.

Museums: Two small, skippable museums sit high on the hill in the village of Škocjan, a 15-minute, mostly uphill walk from the Škocjan Caves ticket office or a 10-minute uphill walk on a gravel path straight ahead from the top of the funicular—just follow the church icon and *Muzej* signs. First, in the thatched stone house, is an **ethnological collection**—one small, rustic room with primitive local farming tools and a video re-creating hand scythes (pick up the English flier). Second, in the white house across the way, is an exhibit on the **biology, geology, and archaeology** of the caves (admission to both parts covered by cave ticket, open June-Sept daily 9:00-18:00, shorter hours off-season). A bit higher is the humble

Škocjan village church, boldly perched on a bulb of land that over-looks cliffs in all directions.

Back in the entrance building, you can also explore the free museum about the **history of cave exploration.** You'll see a model of the valleys and villages of the region, along with a cutaway model of the caves, plus lots of old photographs.

▲▲Lipica Stud Farm (Kobilarna Lipica)

The Lipica (LEE-peet-suh) Stud Farm, a 10-minute drive from the Škocjan Caves, was founded in 1580 to provide horses for the Habsburg court in Vienna. Today you can tour the Lipizzaner stables to visit these mag-nificent animals, whose stalls are labeled with their purebred bloodlines. While the stuffy Viennese cousins of Slovenia's Lipizzaners perform under chandeliers, a visit to Lipica is a more intimate experience: You can get nose to nose with the stallions, learn how they're raised and trained, and—on most days—watch them train or perform. The Lipizzaners' clever

routine—stutter-stepping sideways to the classical beat—thrills visitors. Horse lovers will be in heaven here; even those who don't know a mare from a gelding will find it interesting.

Getting to Lipica: The Lipica Stud Farm is in Slovenia's southwest corner (a stone's throw from Trieste, Italy). By car, exit the A-1 expressway at Divača and follow brown *Lipi* signs. As you drive into the farm, you'll go through pastures where the stallions often roam. Park in front of the hotel/casino, then walk through the trees, following signs to the ticket office.

It's a hassle by public transportation. You can take the train or bus from Ljubljana to Divača (about six miles from Lipica) or to Sežana (about four miles from Lipica). From those places, you can hire a taxi (€15 from Divača, €10 from Sežana).

Visiting the Stud Farm: There are three activities at Lipica—you can tour the farm for a look at the horses, watch a training session, and, on some days, see a more elaborate performance of the prancing stallions. No matter when you come, the tour is a must to really understand the horses. Whether you view a training session or a performance depends on the day of the week; plan your day carefully to ensure that you get to see one or the other. Note that in summer, Monday is the only day you can't see the horses training or performing (but the tour still runs).

Cost: Stud farm tour only—€16, tour plus training ses-sion—€21, tour plus performance—€23, cheaper off-season, tel. 05/739-1580, www.lipica.org.

Tours: The essential 50-minute guided tour gives you a firm

KARST

The Lipizzaner Stallions

In 1580, horse-loving Habsburg archduke Charles II wanted to create the perfect animal: He imported Andalusian horses from his homeland of Spain, then bred them with a local line of Karst horses to produce an extremely intelligent and easily trainable breed. Italian and Arabian bloodlines were later added to tweak various characteristics. Charles' creation, the Lipizzaner stallions—known for their noble gait and Baroque shape—were made famous by Vienna's Spanish Riding School.

These regal horses have changed shape with the tenor of the times: They were bred strong and stout during wars, frilly and slender in more cultured eras. But they're always born black, fade to gray, and turn a distinctive white in adulthood. Until World War I, Lipica bred horses for Austria's needs. (Each time a horse was sent to Vienna, trainers here honored it by planting three linden trees; *lipica* means "small linden.") Now Austria breeds its own line, and these horses prance for Slovenia—a treasured part of its cultural heritage (and featured on Slovenia's €0.20 coin). While many other Lipizzaner lines have their own stud farms around the world, this is the original one, and still has about 360 horses.

What's so special about these horses? Aside from their obvious physical majesty, they're trained to "dance" in remarkable ways—prancing sideways, sashaying diagonally, or joining another horse in a synchronous pas de deux. Even when they're simply trotting, they keep their heads angled steeply down, oh so genteelly. The three most difficult moves involve first getting the horse to rear up on its hind legs; then, the horse might take a step (called *larada*), spring upward (*kapriola*), or jump as high as possible three times (*kurbetta*).

To achieve this mastery, the stallions follow a very specific lifetime regimen: After being weaned at age one, they roam in pastures for three years. At age four, they enroll in "school," where they "study" for five years; only the best move up to the next grade. Finally, at age nine, the valedictorians begin performing, which they do until around age 25; after that, they retire and are put out to pasture (typically living until about 30). Even those who flunk out are highly valuable as sires; the cream of the crop can fetch upwards of €200,000 on the private market.

While the stallions are studying, the Lipizzaner mares freely roam the pastures; they're trained to return to their stables with a single whistle at the end of each day. But they have an important job as well. Mares are pregnant continuously: After the 11 months and one week of gestation, they give birth, are given eight days off, and are impregnated again on the ninth day.

background to help you understand just how special these beasts are. You'll learn about the breed's history, walk through some of the gelding and mare stables, enjoy a brief guided tour of the museum (described later), and then—as a grand finale—see the very best stallions, who live in luxurious, spacious stables. In the stables, you'll notice that each stallion has three names: its own name (created by combining its father's line with its mother's) followed by the names of its father and mother. Males have only six bloodlines (and females 17), so many names are recycled—which is why many horses have numbers after their names. English tours run daily April-Oct on the hour 10:00-17:00; Nov-March at 10:00, 11:00, 13:00, 15:00, and sometimes also 14:00.

Training Sessions: These 45-minute sessions provide your best chance to see the horses in action. Sessions run at 11:00 on Tue-Thu (April), Wed-Thu (May-June), Wed-Thu and Sat (July-Oct), and Sat only (Nov-Dec; none Jan-March). Time your visit to do the training session and tour back-to-back. These are not performances—they are true training sessions, with young, gray-mottled stallions (and red-shirted jockeys) mixing in with more mature, pure-white stallions, whose jockeys wear black vests. While you likely won't see a complete routine, the sessions are narrated in English by an expert, so they're more educational than performances. For maximum information, get close to the expert and don't be afraid to ask questions.

Performances: The choreographed performances take place several afternoons a week—at 15:00—in high season: Tue, Fri, and Sun (May-Oct), also on Sat (July-Sept), Sun only in April, none Nov-March. If you're nearby on one of those days, they're worth planning your day around. As with the training sessions, it's smart to precede a performance with the 14:00 tour, which gives you background information to better appreciate the horses' moves.

Lipikum Museum: Included in your tour ticket is this small, state-of-the-art museum. Succinct, insightful, and all in English, the museum uses informative panels, video screens, and interactive components to illustrate all aspects of the Lipizzaner. Notice that—like the horses themselves—the museum rooms begin black, then turn gray, and end white as you proceed through the exhibit. A Lipizzaner skeleton shows anatomy, and 18th-century paintings illustrate how the breed used to vary in color (until a mutation crept into the bloodline, turning all of them white). The guided tour dips into the museum briefly, but it's worth coming back afterward to linger over the exhibits.

Eating: There's a small self-service **$ café** just above the ticket booth, and a **$$$ restaurant** inside the hotel.

Postojna Caves and Predjama Castle

These two sights are easy for drivers to connect, since they're along the same road. If you're using public transportation, it's not too difficult to reach the caves, and in summer there's a shuttle between the caves and the castle included in the combo-ticket for both sights.

▲▲Postojna Caves (Postojnska Jama)

Postojna (poh-STOY-nah) is the most accessible—and most touristy—cave experience in the region. It's the biggest cave system in Slovenia, with more than 12 miles of explored caves (three of which you'll see on the tour). It's also the easiest to visit, since much of the tour is on a fast-moving train and the rest is well-paved, well-lit, and not too steep. All of this makes it Slovenia's single most popular tourist attraction.

Cost and Hours: €28, €39 combo-ticket covers caves, castle, and summer-only shuttle between them; for a few euros more, you can add the Expo and Vivarium exhibits described later; tours leave daily at the top of each hour May-Sept 9:00-17:00, July-Aug until 18:00, fewer tours off-season—check website for times; tours last 1.5 hours, confirm schedule ahead, Jamska cesta 30, tel. 05/700-0100, www.postojnska-jama.eu.

Crowd Control: From mid-May through mid-September, try to show up 30 to 40 minutes early for the morning tours (popular with tour buses); at other times, aim for 15 minutes ahead. During very busy times (especially in the summer), it's best to book your ticket a day ahead on their website.

Adventure Tours: If you'd like to do some more adrenaline-fueled spelunking in Postojna, check their website for details on booking one of the more adventurous routes through the caves.

Getting to Postojna: The caves are just outside the town of Postojna, about 45 minutes south of Ljubljana on the A-1 expressway. By **car,** take the expressway south from Ljubljana and get off at the Postojna exit. Leaving the expressway, turn right and follow the *jama/grotte/cave* signs through town until you see the tour buses. Drivers pay to park a third of a mile from the cave entry. There are direct **buses** from Ljubljana to the caves (3/day). By **train,** you'll arrive at the train station in the town of Postojna; from here, you can walk to the caves in about 30 minutes or pay for a taxi (tel. 041-959-037).

Visiting the Caves: A visit here is basically an easy, lightly guided stroll through an amazing underground cavern. The optional audioguide offers more information than the official tour guide spiel. Whether you arrive by car, tour bus, or on foot, you'll walk past a paved outdoor souvenir mall to the gaping hole in the moun-

Postojna vs. Škocjan: Which Caves to Visit?

The recipe for creating a cave is simple: Begin with limestone. Then, just add water and wait two million years. (Serves half a million tourists each year.)

The Karst has two big cave systems: Postojna and Škocjan. Each one is massive. Stalagmites and stalactites—in a slow-motion love story—silently work their way toward each other, a third of an inch per century, until that last drip never drops. Minerals picked up by the water as it seeps through various rocks create the different colors (iron makes red, limestone makes white, and so on). Both caves were excavated and explored in the mid-19th century.

However, what you'll see inside each cave system—and how you'll see it—is quite different. Slovenes debate long and hard about which cave system is better. The formations at Postojna are slightly more abundant, varied, and colorful, with stalagmites and stalactites as tall as 100 feet. Postojna is easier to reach by public transportation and far less strenuous to visit than Škocjan—of the three-mile route, you'll walk only about a mile (the rest of the time, you're on a speedy underground train). But Postojna is also more expensive and much more touristy (they get a half-million visitors each year, five times as many as Škocjan)—you'll wade through tour buses and tacky souvenir stands on your way to the entrance, and be pushed to add on mediocre exhibits for more money. Most importantly, Postojna lacks Škocjan's spectacular, massive-cavern finale. Škocjan also comes with a fairly strenuous hike, leaving you feeling like you really did something adventurous. Finally, the choice of a likely side trip might help you decide: Near Postojna is the cliff-hanging Predjama Castle, while Škocjan is closer to the Lipica Stud Farm.

No matter which cave you visit, you'll find it chilly but not really cold (a light sweater is fine). Both caves technically forbid photography (a laughable rule that nobody takes seriously).

These caves are also home to a unique cave-dwelling creature—the so-called "human fish" (a.k.a. olm or *Proteus anguinus*), which is a long, skinny, pale-pink salamander-like creature with fingers and toes. The world's biggest cave-dwelling animal, these amphibians can grow up to a foot long, live for about a century, and survive up to a decade without eating (the live specimens on display in Postojna are never fed during the four months they're on view). As they're endemic to Slovenia, the "human fish" are celebrated as a sort of national mascot.

tain. Buy your ticket, then climb up the stairs and wait with the mob to board the little open-air train, which slings you deep into the mountain, whizzing past wonderful formations. (The ride alone is exhilarating.) Then you get out, assemble into language groups, and follow a guide on a well-lit, circular, paved path through more formations.

First you'll hike uphill into the "Big Mountain"—the highest point inside the caves, and (surprisingly) actually higher than where you entered. You're surrounded by a sea of fairy-chimney stalagmites and stalactites, some of them a hundred feet tall. Then you'll hike downhill and cross a bridge over a canyon into "Spaghetti Hall," named for the long, skinny stalactites that seem to be dripping from the ceiling. Also in this area are some amazing, translucent "curtains" of rock. Circling down beneath the bridge you just crossed, you'll come to some huge, white, melting-ice-cream formations (including one called "The Organ," for obvious reasons). You'll

wind up in the impressively vast cavern called the "Concert Hall," peering into an aquarium with the strange "human fish." Then you'll load back onto the train and return to the bright daylight. Exiting the train, notice that the ceiling of this part of the cavern is charred black. The only coloring in the cave caused by humans, this is residue from a huge WWII explosion; the Partisan Army blew up a fuel and ammo depot the Nazis kept here.

Add-On Exhibits: While the caves are the main attraction, a few euros apiece buys you admission to a couple of optional add-ons—which are basically an attempt to wring a little more cash out of gullible tourists. But if you have time and money to spare, you could consider splurging on one or both of them. The high-tech **Expo Cave Karst,** in the adjacent hotel complex, explains the geology of the Karst and of Postojna Caves, with several exhibits specifically designed for kids. The **Vivarium Proteus,** which fills a smaller cave next to the ticket booth, promises to educate you more about speleobiology (the study of cave-dwelling animal life). You'll be given a flashlight and sent to look for 17 different species of animals—but since the cave dwellers (naturally) hide from view, you just wind up squinting into empty aquariums most of the time. One interesting feature is a wall with graffiti signatures from past visitors—some dating all the way back to the 13th century. Either of these also includes the Butterflies of the World collection—two dozen frames filled with samples of butterflies.

KARST

▲Predjama Castle (Predjamski Grad)

Burrowed into the side of a mountain close to Postojna is dramatic Predjama Castle (prehd-YAH-mah), one of Europe's most scenic castles (despite its dull interior). Predjama is a hit with tourists for its striking setting, exciting exterior, and romantic legend.

Notice as you approach that you don't even see Predjama—crouching magnificently in its cave—until the last moment. The first castle here was actually a tiny ninth-century fortress embedded deep in the cave behind the present castle. Over the centuries, different castles were built here, and they gradually moved out to the mouth of the cave. While the original was called "the castle in the cave," the current one is *pred jama*—"in front of the cave."

While enjoying the view, ponder this legend: In the 15th century, a noble-man named Erasmus killed the emperor's cousin in a duel. He was imprisoned under Ljubljana Castle and spent years nursing a grudge. When he was finally released, he used his castle—buried deep inside the cave above this current version—as a home base for a series of Robin Hood-style raids on the local nobility and merchants. (Actually, Erasmus stole from the rich and kept for himself—but that was good enough to make him a hero to the peasants, who hated the nobles.)

Soldiers from Trieste were brought in to put an end to Erasmus' raids, laying siege to the castle for over a year. Back then, the only way into the castle was through the cave in the valley below—then up, through an extensive labyrinth of caves, to the top. While the soldiers down below froze and starved, Erasmus' men sneaked out through the caves to bring in supplies. (They liked to drop their leftovers on the soldiers below to taunt them, letting them know that the siege wasn't working.)

Eventually, the soldiers came up with a plan. They waited for Erasmus to visit the latrine—which, by design, had to be on the thin-walled outer edge of the castle—and then, on seeing a signal by a secret agent, blew Erasmus off his throne with a cannonball. Erasmus is supposedly buried under the huge linden tree in the parking lot.

As the legend of Erasmus faded, the function of the castle changed. By the 16th century, Predjama had become a castle for hunting more than for defense—explaining its current pictur-esque-but-impractical design.

After driving all the way here, it seems a shame not to visit the interior—but it's truly skippable. The management (which also

KARST

runs the nearby Postojna Caves) is very strict about keeping the interior 16th-century in style, so there's virtually nothing inside except 20th-century fakes of 16th-century furniture, plus a few forgettable paintings and cheesy folk displays. English descriptions are sparse, and the free English history flier is not much help. But for most, the views of the place alone are worth the drive. Also skip the "cave under Predjama Castle"—it's redundant if you're going to Postojna or Škocjan.

Cost and Hours: €14 to go inside; daily May-Sept 9:00-18:00, July-Aug until 19:00, shorter hours off-season; tel. 05/751-6015, www.postojnska-jama.eu.

Getting to Predjama: Predjama Castle is on a twisty rural road 5.5 miles beyond Postojna Caves. By car, just continue on the winding road past Postojna, following signs for *Predjama* and *Predjamski Grad* (coming back, follow signs to *Postojna*). If using public transportation, you can take the train to the town of Postojna; in the summer, you can buy a €39 combo-ticket that includes the caves, the castle, and a shuttle-bus trip between them (departs about hourly). If you're in a pinch, consider paying for a taxi (figure €30 for the trip there and back, including some wait time) or hitching a ride with a friendly tour bus or tourist's car, as most visitors do both sights.

KARST

PIRAN

Croatia's 3,600-mile-long coast gets all the acclaim, but don't overlook Slovenia's own 29 miles of Adriatic coastline. The Slovenian coast has only a handful of towns: big, industrial Koper; lived-in and crumbling Izola; and the swanky but soulless resort of Portorož. But the gem of the Slovenian Adriatic is Piran (pee-RAHN). Most Adriatic towns are all tourists and concrete, but Piran has kept itself charming and shipshape while holding the tourist sprawl at bay. Its glassy square feels tugged at the top by a stout Venetian-style bell tower—as if without this anchor, the whole thing might just slide off into the tidy, picturesque harbor. Even though the town can be crowded with a United Nations of vacationers (especially Italians) in peak season, as you get to know it, Piran becomes one of the most pleasant and user-friendly seaside towns this side of Dubrovnik.

PLANNING YOUR TIME

You can see everything in Piran (including a pop into the Maritime Museum and a hike up the bell tower) in just a couple of hours. Then simply bask in the town's ambience. Enjoy a gelato or a *kava* (coffee) on the sleek, marbled Tartini Square, surrounded by Neoclassical buildings and watched over by the bell tower. Go for a swim at one of its rocky beaches. Wander Piran's piers and catch its glow at sunset.

Piran also works as a base for visiting the caves, horses, and castles of the nearby Karst region (see previous chapter). Notice, too, that it's conveniently on the way between Ljubljana/the Karst and Croatia's Istria (see "Route Tips for Drivers," described later in "Piran Connections").

Orientation to Piran

Piran is small; everything is within a few minutes' walk. Crowded onto the tip of its peninsula, the town can't grow. Its population—7,500 a century ago—has dropped to about half that today, as many young people find more opportunity in bigger cities.

Piran clusters around its boat-speckled harbor and showpiece piazza, Tartini Square (Tartinijev trg). Up the hill behind Tartini Square is the landmark bell tower of the Cathedral of St. George. A few blocks toward the end of the peninsula from Tartini Square is the heart of the Old Town, May 1 Square (Trg 1 Maja).

From Tartini Square and the nearby marina, a concrete promenade—lined with rocks to break the storm waves, and with expensive tourist restaurants to break your budget—stretches along the town's waterfront, inviting you to stroll.

TOURIST INFORMATION

The helpful TI is inside the grand Venetian-style Town Hall on Tartini Square (daily July-Aug 9:00-21:00, May-June and Sept until 19:00, Oct-April until 17:00, at #2, tel. 05/673-4440, www.portoroz.si).

ARRIVAL IN PIRAN

By Car: Driving and parking in Piran is a headache; park your car as quickly as possible and forget about it. Fortunately, the city makes this easy by offering a free shuttle bus connecting the main parking garage with downtown (4/hour).

If you're overnighting in town and don't want to haul your bags from the garage, take a ticket at the parking barrier, drive into the Old Town, drop off your bags, and pick up a voucher from your hotel; if you leave within 15 minutes, the voucher gets you out free. Then park at the big garage described next. If you're day-tripping to Piran, simply park at the garage when you arrive.

As you drive into town, you'll pass the big **parking garage** as you come down the hill (€1.90/hour, €19/day, typically discounted with a voucher from your hotel). From the garage, ride the elevator down to floor 1, exit, and walk about 50 yards to the waterfront parking lot for locals (called Fornače), where you'll see a stop for the free shuttle bus that zips you right to Tartini Square. (Or, if

PIRAN

Piran

Accommodations
1. Hotel Piran
2. Art Hotel Tartini
3. PachaMama Pleasant Stay
4. Bevk Apartments (2)

Eateries & Other
5. Restaurant Neptun
6. Pri Mari Restaurant
7. Fritolin pri Cantini
8. Pizzeria Petica
9. Sarajevo '84
10. Bakery & Grocery
11. Café Teater
12. Launderette
13. Bike Rental

you've packed light, you can walk to Tartini Square in about 15 minutes—just follow the water.)

A second garage, called **Arze** (higher up, near the town cemetery), is slightly cheaper (€1.20/hour, €12/day)—but the shuttle bus into town only runs 4/day (though you could use the "electric car" shuttle service—see below). Park here only if you want to save money and don't mind a longer walk.

By Bus: Piran has two bus stops. Shuttle buses from the parking garage and nearby towns (such as Portorož) stop right at Tartini Square; intercity buses (such as those to Ljubljana) use the low-profile main bus station along the water, near the entrance to town—an easy walk to the center.

HELPFUL HINTS

Getting Around: The city provides a free **"electric car"** shuttle service in summer (May-Oct); just call Maestro (mobile 031-288-574) and tell them where you want to go, ideally an hour before you need them. This is handy for reaching the cheaper Arze garage.

Laundry: The **Speed Queen** self-service launderette is conveniently located right on May 1 Square (daily May-Sept 7:00-23:00, Oct-April 8:00-21:00, mobile 040-771-773).

Walking Tour: In summer, a 1.5-hour walking tour of town departs three mornings each week from the statue of Tartini (€9, July-Sept Mon, Wed, and Fri at 11:00). They also do a sunset food-and-wine tour each evening (€14, July-Aug at 19:00, Sept at 18:00; mobile 051-727-602, www.piranwalkingtour.com).

Bike Rental: The **TI** rents city bikes that are good enough for a quick spin along the coast. For a more serious adventure on two wheels, rent a pricier trekking bike from **Luma Šport,** across the street from the intercity bus station (daily June-Aug 9:00-12:00 & 17:00-21:00, shoulder season 9:00-18:00 in good weather, shorter hours off-season, Dantejeva 3, mobile 041-781-414, www.lumasport.com, Magda). The TI hands out a free map illustrating ambitious rides in the region.

Sights in Piran

▲▲Tartini Square (Tartinijev trg)

Tartini Square was once part of a protected harbor. In 1894, the harbor smelled so bad that they decided to fill it in. And today,

rather than fishing boats, it's filled with skateboarding kids. While traffic used to clog this square, it has now been pedestrianized. The "square"—a shiny marble oval surrounded by a tidy geographical grid pattern—is one of Slovenia's most appealing public spaces. Be sure to nurse a coffee while you're here. Survey the many café vantage points and take your pick.

The dynamic statue in the middle honors **Giuseppe Tartini**

(1692-1770), a composer and violinist once known throughout Europe. Behind Tartini, the Neo-Renaissance **Town Hall** (housing the TI) dates from the 1870s.

The fine little sand-colored palace in the corner (at #4, where Tartini's left hand is gesturing) is the **"Venetian House"** (c. 1450), the oldest preserved house on the square. Classic Venetian Gothic, it comes with a legend: A wealthy Venetian merchant fell in love with a simple local girl when visiting on business, became her sugar daddy, and eventually built her this flat. When the townsfolk began to gossip about the relationship, he answered them with the relief you see today (with the Venetian lion, between the two top windows): *Lassa pur dir* ("Let them talk").

Today the Venetian House's ground floor hosts a branch of the enticing **Piranske Soline shop,** selling a classy range of culinary and health aids produced using the salt that's gathered just around the bay from here. While those salt pans are worth a visit (Sečovlje Salina Nature Park, described later), this shop offers a chance to get a feel for that age-old local industry with minimal effort (open long hours daily, ulica IX Korpusa 2, tel. 05/673-3110, www.soline.si).

▲Cathedral and Bell Tower of St. George (Stolna Cerkev Sv. Jurija)

Piran is proud of its many churches, which number more than 20. While none is of any real historic or artistic importance, the Cathedral of St. George—dominating the town from the hilltop just above Tartini Square—is worth a visit for its fine interior, its striking crucifix, and its climbable bell tower. This cathedral dates from the 14th century and was decorated in the Baroque style by Venetian artists in the 17th century. It dominates the

Old Town with its bell tower *(campanile),* a miniature version of the more famous one on St. Mark's Square in Venice. Why such a big church for such a little town? So that would-be invaders, surveying Piran from the sea, would spot a huge church and assume it marked a big city...not worth the risk to plunder.

Cost and Hours: Church and museum—€2, changeable hours—likely July-Aug daily 10:00-13:00 & 17:00-20:00, May-June and Sept-Oct Wed-Mon 10:00-16:00, closed Tue and closed Nov-April; bell tower—€1 to go up and "€0 to go down," July-Aug daily 9:00-20:00, May-June and Sept-Oct daily 10:00-18:00, closed Nov-April.

Church and Museum: While you can peek into the church

through a grate at the far end, you'll need to enter through the door on the side (facing town) and buy a ticket for the church museum.

The modest **museum** contains treasury items (including an elaborately decorated silver-and-gold statue of the church's namesake, St. George, slaying a dragon) and a little crypt displaying some early foundations of the church building along with archaeological finds.

Head up the stairs into the **church interior,** which is serenely decorated in Venetian Renaissance and Baroque style. You'll see several dynamic interpretations of George and his dragon-slaying (including a giant statue along the left side of the nave, and a painting on the ceiling).

But the church's prized possession hides in the presbytery: Stand behind the main altar, facing the wall behind it, and look right. This *Piran Crucifixion*, dating from the 14th century, is powerful and emotive. Nailed to a Y-shaped cross, Christ is at once expressionistic (with gnarled toes, awkwardly disjointed shoulders, and an elongated frame that exaggerates his agony) and gruesomely medieval. When the crucifix was restored recently, historians found countless layers of additions and modifications (including 10 layers of paint), suggesting how its appearance has flexed with the tenor of the times. Now protected in its glass box from the fickle seaside air, the crucifix is explained in detail by a free brochure available in the museum.

Bell Tower: The tower (with bells dating from the 15th century) welcomes tourists willing to climb 146 steps for the best view in town.

View Terrace: Even if you don't ascend the tower, head to the grassy terrace behind the cathedral for sweeping views of the bays that flank Piran. First, looking over the rooftops of Piran, you'll see a long peninsula jutting out. This is the northern edge of Croatia's Istria.

Then, looking in the opposite direction, you'll see a huge port city in the distance: Trieste, Italy. Until 1920, this metropolis (the main port of the Austro-Hungarian Empire) had close ties to Slovenia—much of its population spoke Slovene. After it was annexed by Italy, many Slovenes moved closer to their compatriots in Yugoslavia, but a large Slovene-speaking minority still lives here (mostly in the rural areas on the city's outskirts).

Ponder how tiny Slovenia's coastline is—wedged between Italy and Croatia (two nations with some of the longest coastlines in all of Europe). For years, Croatia maintained that, in accordance with the letter of international maritime law, a country with such a short coastline should not be allowed to operate a port—and yet, Slovenia does (its busy port town, Koper, is tucked just behind the peninsula in front of Trieste). Croatia said "the law's the law!"—but

Piran History

Piran was named for the fires (*pyr* in Greek) that were lit at the tip of its peninsula to assist passing ships. Known as "Pirano" in *Italiano*, the town is home to a long-standing Italian community (about 1,500 today)—so it's legally bilingual, with signs in two languages. As with most towns on the eastern Adriatic, it has a Venetian flavor. Piran wisely signed on with Venice as part of its trading empire in 933, and because of its valuable salt industry and strong trade, managed to enjoy some autonomy in later centuries. After plagues killed most of Piran's population in the 15th century, local Italians let Slavs fleeing the Ottomans repopulate the town. Piran's impressive walls were built to counter the growing Ottoman threat. Too much rain ruined the town's valuable salt basins, but in the 19th century, the Austrian Habsburg rulers rebuilt the salt industry. (These salt fields are still open for tourist visits—see "Sečovlje Salina Nature Park," later.) With that change came a new economic boom, and Piran grew in importance once again. After World War I, this part of the Habsburg Empire was assigned to Italy, but fascism never sat well with the locals. After World War II, the region was made neutral, then became part of Yugoslavia in 1956. In 1991, with the creation of Slovenia, the Slovenes of Piran were finally independent.

Slovenes, along with many international observers, perceived it as bullying. After years of wrangling, in 2009, when Croatia needed Slovenia's support to join the EU, the Slovenes said, "Not so fast..." and vetoed Croatia's EU bid for 10 months. Eventually cooler heads prevailed—Croatia is in the EU, and Slovenia's port is still busy.

Looking farther right, to the base of Piran's peninsula, you'll get a good view of the hill-capping, crenellated castle that protected this strategic location.

Sergej Mašera Maritime Museum (Pomorski Muzej Sergej Mašera)

This humble museum—worth considering only on a rainy day—faces the harbor and the square, filling three floors of an elegant old building with faintly endearing exhibits. The first floor contains a darkened room of "underwater finds," including a collection of amphorae from antiquity that are visible through a glass floor. The second floor is a series of dusty rooms on the history of seafaring, with a wide assortment of model ships, and a town model that illustrates how today's Tartini Square was once an enclosed and fortified harbor. And the top floor hosts a modern exhibit honoring illustrious Slovenian seamen, with historical documents and uniforms. The exhibits are described only in Slovene and Italian, but you can borrow a handy iPad at the entrance with both written and audio explanations in English.

Cost and Hours: €4; July-Aug Tue-Sun 9:00-12:00 & 17:00-21:00, Sept-June Tue-Sun 9:00-17:00, closed Mon year-round; Cankarjevo nabrežje 3, tel. 05/671-0040, www.pomorskimuzej.si.

Aquarium

Piran's small, modern aquarium is well-presented, convenient (right off Tartini Square), and another decent rainy-day activity. You'll stroll through a few rooms with tanks clearly labeled in English and filled with Adriatic sea life.

Cost and Hours: €5, mid-June-Aug Tue-Sun 9:00-21:00, shorter hours off-season, closed Mon year-round, Kidričevo nabrežje 4, tel. 05/673-2572, www.aquariumpiran.si.

May 1 Square (Trg 1 Maja)

This square, deep in a warren of cobbled lanes in the middle of the Old Town's peninsula, marks the center of medieval Piran, where its main streets converged. Once the administrative center of town, today it's the domain of local kids and ringed by a few humble eateries (including the recommended Fritolin pri Cantini). The stone rainwater cistern dominating the square's center was built in 1775 after a severe drought. Rainwater was captured here with the help of drains from roofs and channeled by hardworking statues into the system. The water was filtered through sand and stored in the well, clean and ready for townspeople to draw—or, later, pump—for drinking.

Harborfront Stroll

Wandering along the harborfront, with its chunky breakwater, is a delight: almost no pesky mopeds or cars, and virtually no American tourists—mostly Slovenes and Italians. Children sell seashells on cardboard boxes. Husky sunbathers lie like large limpets on the rocks. Walk around the lighthouse at the tip of the town and around the corner, checking out the cafés and fish restaurants along the way.

Swimming

Piran has clear, warm, enticing water. And, while the town is too small and skinny to have a conventional "beach," tourists find plenty of ways to go for a swim. Here are a few ideas, listed in geographical order from Tartini Square:

The big concrete pad in front of **Hotel Piran,** with a half-dozen ladders descending directly into the deep, may be the easiest choice. Coin-op showers, two nearby cafés (one in the hotel itself, and the adjacent Teater Café), and rentable beach chairs (€15 buys you two chairs and an umbrella) make this spot especially handy.

It's a public beach, so you can spread out a towel on the concrete and lounge for free.

If you continue past Hotel Piran along the embankment **promenade** (lined with restaurants), you'll see plenty of swimmers and sunbathers trying to get comfortable on the big breakwater; try to find a flat rock to spread out on. (A few sunbathers scramble for space along the walkway, but this can get crowded.) Along here, several ladders provide easy access to the sea. While there's no shower on the promenade, it's a quick walk to the others noted here.

If you continue to the end of the promenade and hook around the lighthouse at the tip of town, you'll soon come to an even bigger **concrete pad.** A bit less inviting than the one in front of Hotel Piran, it's quite large, making this a good choice if the first two options are crowded. Cafés and free showers are nearby.

Other options are a bit farther afield. Right near the traffic gate and parking lot at the **entrance to town,** you'll find a small pebbly beach (with free showers); beyond that is a long stretch—basically the entire length of the Fornače parking lot—of concrete pad with ladders providing easy access into the sea. While not exactly serene, it's uncrowded. To get to this area quickly, just hop on the free shuttle bus from Tartini Square.

If you walk about 10 minutes past the Fornače parking lot and garage, you'll reach a public beach in front of the **Bernardin** hotel complex.

With a car, you can drive to the **town center of Portorož,** which has a pleasant boardwalk and a sandy beach that's arguably more appealing than anything in Piran itself.

Sleeping in Piran

Piran's accommodations options are limited, but I've listed the best in each price range. Many accommodations offer discounted rates at the town parking garage—ask.

$$$$ Art Hotel Tartini faces Piran's gorgeous main square. Recently refurbished, its 46 rooms are bright white, minimalist, artsy, and a bit pretentious. If it's not closed for a special event, be sure to head up to the rooftop terrace, with great views over Tartini Square (air-con, elevator, Tartinijev trg 15, tel. 05/671-1000, www. arthoteltartini.com, info@arthoteltartini.com).

$$$ Hotel Piran, the waterfront grande dame of Piran, owns the best sea views in town and 92 upscale rooms. The nonview rooms face a gloomy street; all of the seaview rooms come with a little balcony—worth paying extra for (air-con, elevator, rooftop terrace, Stijenkova 1, tel. 05/666-7100, www.hotel-piran.si, info@ hotel-piran.si).

$$ PachaMama Pleasant Stay is a vibrant guesthouse run with a youth-hostel mentality by well-traveled Mitja (who named the place for "Mother Earth" in an Incan language). The 12 rooms, just a block off Tartini Square, are modern, woody, sleek, small, straightforward, and well-priced. They share a multilevel terrace out back, in the shadow of the town bell tower (shared kitchen, air-con, lots of stairs, Trubarjeva 8, tel. 05/918-3495, mobile 051-214-518, www.pachamama.si, info@pachamama.si).

$ Bogdan and Jana Bevk rent six good apartments in two different buildings with roof terraces; both are buried in a quiet part of the Old Town. They also have a bigger, pricier apartment right on Tartini Square. As they live elsewhere, call when you arrive so Bogdan can meet you and take you to the apartment (no breakfast, air-con, lots of stairs, Marxova 13 and Prežihova 4, mobile 051-623-682, tel. 05/902-2111, www.bevk.si, info@bevk.si).

Eating in Piran

Pricey tourist bars and restaurants face the sea (figure about €20/main course), while the laid-back, funky, and colorful local joints seem to seek an escape from both the tourists and the sun in the back lanes. Get off the beaten track to find one of my recommended restaurants, and you'll enjoy a seafood-and-pasta feast for half what you'd pay in Venice (just across the sea).

$$$ Restaurant Neptun, with fresh seafood and pastas served in a fishnet-strewn dining room, is my longtime favorite. I find it far classier than the tacky tourist fish joints. The Grilj family works hard to please six tables of diners (plus two more outside in the nondescript alley in good weather). Everything's made to order with fish straight out of the Adriatic—nothing's frozen. I can't resist their gnocchi with scampi. Consider splurging on a whole fish, grilled to perfection (Wed-Mon 12:00-16:00 & 18:00-22:00, closed Tue except in Aug, Župančičeva 7, tel. 05/673-4111). Don't confuse this with Neptun Café, at the waterfront bus station.

$$$ Pri Mari Restaurant is about a 10-minute walk from Tartini Square, near the entrance to town. Gregarious Mara and Tomaž will welcome you into their cheery dining room like an old friend, then treat you to tasty Venetian-style cooking. It's smart to reserve ahead in summer (mid-June-Aug Tue-Fri 18:00-23:00, Sat-Sun 12:00-16:00 & 18:00-22:00; off-season Tue-Sat 12:00-16:00 & 18:00-22:00, Sun 12:00-18:00; closed Mon year-round; Dantejeva 17, tel. 05/673-4735, www.primari-piran.com).

$$ Fritolin pri Cantini is a popular spot for simple but tasty fried and grilled fish dishes on the atmospheric May 1 Square. Order at the counter, then watch for the fish with your number to be posted on the wall—meaning it's time to go reel in your catch.

The same people own the next-door Cantina Klet bar, with table service for drinks, plus ham-and-cheese nibble plates; if ordering a drink, you're welcome to use their table as a home base for the fish window (daily 11:00-23:00, Prvomajski trg 10, mobile 041-873-872).

$$ Pizzeria Petica ("Five"), buried deep in town, is atmospheric and tasty. Dine in the cozy interior, or sit outside on a nondescript lane, and choose from a wide menu of pizzas and seafood dishes (cash only, unpredictable hours but typically daily 11:00-22:00, Župančičeva 6, tel. 080-3588).

$ Sarajevo '84, part of a small Slovenian chain, oozes Yugo-nostalgia for the year that the Bosnian capital hosted the Olympics. This is the spot for a break from fish and pasta—the menu features gigantic, splittable portions of inexpensive, stick-to-your-ribs Bosnian grilled meats. Sit in the Bosnian-themed interior, or out on the terrace, overlooking a busy street and the sailboat harbor (daily 10:00-22:00, Tomšičeva 43, tel. 05/923-5044).

Quick Bites and Picnics: For food on the go, duck behind the Town Hall (which houses the TI). You'll find an outdoor market (Mon-Sat 7:00-13:00); the **Naša Pekarna** bakery selling pizza slices, sandwiches, and *burek* to go (daily 6:30-20:00); a Mercator supermarket (Mon-Fri 7:00-19:00, Sat 7:00-13:00, Sun 8:00-12:00); and a pay WC.

Drinks: Café Teater is *the* place for drinks with Adriatic views and a characteristic old interior. Catching the sunset here is a fine way to kick off your Piran evening (pricey cocktails, open long hours daily, Stjenkova 1). If you prefer to sit out on Tartini Square, you can take your pick of cafés.

Piran Connections

BY BUS

Piran has a small, unstaffed bus station, right along the water near the entrance to town. The ticket machine is only for local tickets. For long-distance connections, you can usually buy your ticket from the driver. But for buses operated by Flixbus or Fils, you'll need to buy your ticket in advance online (see below).

Sorting through schedules is a headache. Specific routings change frequently—both with the season, and year to year—and there's no unified schedule website; you'll want to check several websites to understand all of your options. For starters, check www.ap-ljubljana.si, which catches most, but not all, buses. But also check www.getbybus.com, www.flixbus.com, and www.fils.hr. Fortunately, the TI generally has a handle on your options at any given time. And if you're in a pinch, consider the GoOpti shared transfer service described on page 600—which can be easier and not much more expensive.

To Ljubljana: The best connection is by **bus** (5-7/day Mon-Fri, 2/day Sat, 4/day Sun, 2.5 hours). By **train,** the trip takes four hours (bus between Piran and Koper, then train between Koper and Ljubljana).

To Croatia's Istria by Bus: Buses to Croatian Istria—including **Rovinj, Poreč,** and **Pula**—are sparse, and can change from year to year. There is usually not a direct bus to any of these, but you can typically reach them with a change in Portorož (Flixbus often serves this route, www.flixbus.com). There is typically also a bus to Rovinj from Koper, the big port city a bit farther away (operated by Črnja Tours, check schedules at www.crnja-tours.hr or www.getbybus.com).

BY BOAT

Liberty Lines runs boats from Trieste (Italy) to Piran, Poreč, and Rovinj—potentially handy for connecting Piran to those Istrian destinations (www.libertylines.it).

A boat called the *San Frangisk*—designed for day-trippers, but also convenient for one-way transport—sails from Piran once or twice weekly to Venice (operated by Top Line, www.benetke.com).

ROUTE TIPS FOR DRIVERS

Piran is a natural stopover between Ljubljana and Croatia's Istria. You can do the Karst sights on the way down (lined up conveniently along the A-1 expressway), sleep in Piran, then continue to Istria; or simply make a beeline to Piran and see the town before moving on to sleep in Istria.

From Ljubljana to Piran: Piran is about 1.5 hours from Ljubljana, barring traffic. From Ljubljana, take the A-1 expressway south to Koper; when the expressway ends at the outskirts of Koper, follow *Portorož/Portorose* signs—enjoying grand views over the bay to Trieste on your right, and passing the charming old town of Izola—then *Piran/Pirano* signs. For arrival and parking instructions, see "Arrival in Piran," earlier.

From Piran to Croatia's Istria: Leaving Piran, go through Portorož, then Lucija, then follow signs to *Pula.* Just after you enter Seča, signs on the right point to the salt pans of Sečovlje Salina Nature Park (described below). The border is just a few minutes straight ahead. (If you want to see the salt museum, remember that it's between the Slovenian and Croatian border posts—just after leaving Slovenia, keep an eye on the right for the very easy-to-miss gravel road.) Once in Croatia, follow *Pula* signs to get on the *ipsilon* highway that zips you down through the middle of Istria.

Near Piran

While Piran is easily the most worthwhile destination on Slovenia's coast, the historic and well-presented salt pans at **Sečovlje Salina Nature Park**—a short drive or boat ride to the south—are interesting and convenient, especially if you're heading to Croatia. The big city of **Koper** is skippable, but unavoidable if you're visiting this region by cruise ship. Fortunately, if you do come to Koper on a ship, it's easy to get to Piran, and possible to reach other attractions in Slovenia.

Sečovlje Salina Nature Park

A few miles south of Piran, a literal stone's throw from the Croatian border, the Sečovlje Salina Nature Park (Krajinski Park Sečoveljske Soline) features enormous salt pans, which have been used since the Middle Ages for harvesting this precious mineral. Back in the days before refrigeration, salt's preservative powers made it more valuable than gold. As you drive by on the way to Croatia, you'll wonder what this massive complex is...so why not stop for a visit?

The "nature park" has two parts: Lera, to the north, harvests salt using 700-year-old techniques, and has a fine visitors center and a saltwater spa; Fontanigge, to the south (closer to Croatia), has a good museum to explain traditional salt-harvesting methods. I never thought salt could be so interesting. The only catch is that, in order to preserve the unique landscape around the salt pans, visitors aren't allowed to drive all the way to the attractions; you'll have to walk (20 minutes to Lera; at Fontanigge, it's a 2-mile walk or bike ride on a gravel road).

Cost and Hours: €7, €6 Nov-March; covers entry to the entire salt fields complex, including the visitors center at Lera (daily June-Aug 8:00-21:00, April-May and Sept until 19:00, Oct-March until 17:00) and the museum at Fontanigge (daily June-Aug 9:00-18:00, April-May and Sept until 17:00, Oct-March until 16:00). Tel. 05/672-1350, www.kpss.si.

Getting There: The nature park is between Piran and the Croatian border. For **drivers** heading south toward Croatia (see "Route Tips for Drivers," earlier), you'll pass the entrance to the Lera salt field on your right, just after entering the town of Seča (watch for *Sečoveljske soline* signs). To visit Lera, go down a steep cobbled stretch, then cross a bridge over a channel to reach the ticket booth (from here, it's a 20-minute walk—described later). For Fontanigge—farther along the main road—it's more complicated: You'll actually have to cross the Slovenian border, then a few feet later, just before you reach the Croatian border post, you'll see a poorly marked gravel road on the right, leading to the salt field. It's a five-minute drive to the gate, where you'll park and walk about 30-40 minutes to the museum (or borrow a bike to ride there).

Fit cyclists can **bike** from Piran all the way to the salt fields in about an hour (for bike-rental information, see "Helpful Hints," earlier).

If you don't have your own wheels, the only possibility is to take the very sporadic *Solinarka* **boat** from Piran (goes right to the museum, typically runs once a week in July-Aug only, ask for schedule at the Piran TI).

Visiting the Park: Remember, there are two parts to the nature park, which are a drive, bike ride, or long hike away from each other. If you're choosing just one, make it Lera, which is easier to reach (since it's a shorter walk). Fontanigge is for die-hards.

Lera: The Lera section has a multimedia visitors center, small café, and salt-products shop, and gives you a good look at the salt pans themselves.

Buy your ticket at the small wooden kiosk near the parking lot (with WCs). From here, it's just over a mile (20-minute walk) to the attractions, passing a shop selling products made with the salt harvested here. If it's not too hot, it's actually enjoyable to walk through the neat patchwork of vast, wood-framed **salt pans,** connected by a series of canals with little doors. Keep an eye out for workers harvesting salt just as it was done from medieval times up until the Austrians arrived in 1904. Museum docents do it the way their ancestors did: First, they fill up the shallow pans with seawater, then they seal them off and allow the water to naturally evaporate, leaving behind those precious deposits. Once most of the water is gone, they use large rake-like tools to sweep the salt into big piles. You'll most likely see salt gatherers at work during the peak of summer (July-Aug), when the hot sun speeds evaporation. (Be warned that the walk can be blazing hot, with nearly no shade—perfect conditions for harvesting salt.)

The **multimedia center** shows a mesmerizing 30-minute film (with English subtitles) of modern-day locals harvesting salt the same way their ancestors did. "In 700 years," the movie notes, "only the clothing has changed." Traditional tools decorate the walls. In the adjoining hall, you can see a model of the entire area of the salt pans; learn more about the history and ecology of salt-gathering; and watch short video clips about local birds (which thrive in this salty ecosystem). Everything is nicely presented and well-described in English.

Next to the multimedia center is a small **$ café** (selling afford-able meals and drinks—not surprisingly, all those piles of salt just seem to make people thirsty). Climbing the spiral staircase on the adjacent building, you'll reach a **rooftop viewpoint** offering pan-oramic views over the entire area. Also nearby are WCs.

To get the most out of your visit, consider booking an afford-able **guided tour** (€40 for a small group plus entrance tickets, 1.5-hour guided walk through the salt fields, reserve 3 days ahead at www.kpss.si).

In a different part of Lera (about a mile from the ticket booth) is the **Thalasso Lepa Vida Spa,** where you can soak in salty water and order a range of other treatments, such as salt-pan mud wraps and other salty exfoliations (€20/up to 2 hours, includes museum ticket and free golf-cart ride from ticket booth to the spa, other treatments cost extra, June-Aug daily 9:00-20:00, Sept daily 10:00-19:00, weather-dependent and closed off-season, tel. 05/672-1360, www.thalasso-lepavida.si).

Fontanigge: This part of the park—within a few feet of the Croatian border, which is just over the little river—is home to the Salt-Making Museum. From the parking lot, it's nearly two miles along a bumpy gravel road to the museum. You can walk, or you can borrow a bicycle to pedal yourself out to the exhibit. Well-explained by posted English information and a knowledgeable do-cent, the museum demonstrates tools and methods, illustrating the lifestyles of the people who eked out a hard living on these salty marshes (for example, since they all shared a communal oven, each family had their own stamp for marking their loaves of bread).

PIRAN

Koper Cruise Port

The big city a half-hour to the north of Piran, Koper, is a gloomy industrial burg (pop. 25,000) that is emerging as a popular cruise port. I wouldn't bother coming here unless you're arriving by cruise ship—in which case, you can follow my instructions below.

Ships put in right in front of the Old Town. You'll exit the terminal building into a tidy collection of tourist stalls and a small TI kiosk (TI tel. 05/664-6403, www.koper.si). Across the street, you'll see fragments of Koper's stout town wall. The bus stop di-rectly in front of the port gate serves a hop-on, hop-off tourist train that does a pointless loop around the Old Town perimeter. Free Wi-Fi is available in the port area.

While **Koper** itself is worth a quick stroll, most cruisers will want to move on to more enticing destinations farther afield. The easiest (and probably best) choice is **Piran,** well-connected by bus;

also consider riding a bus to **Trieste,** or hiring a guide for a busy day driving all over Slovenia (**Ljubljana, Lake Bled,** the famous **caves,** and more). Each option is described next.

Koper: While this big city lacks charm, its main square is worth a quick peek, and it has a fine harborfront promenade. To explore, turn right as you exit the port, then turn left at the speed bump just past the big, blocky wall. Climbing up the stairs and turning left, you can walk to the view terrace overlooking the cruise port. From here, do a 180 and follow brown *Center/Centro* signs directly away from the port. After a long block, you'll pop out in Koper's main square, **Titov trg.** On this square, you'll find a climbable, 204-step bell tower; a TI (inside the crenellated castle, Praetorian Palace/Pretorska Palača); a loggia with café tables; and a Mercator supermarket with an ATM by the front door. After exploring here, head to the most scenic stretch of Koper's waterfront: Facing the palace with the TI, turn right down Kuričeva ulica. You'll head through the atmospheric Old Town until you reach a little square with a loggia. Just beyond this is the waterfront; if you follow it to the left, you'll find a broad and nicely manicured promenade.

To Piran: Slovenia's most charming coastal town is easily reached by bus (2-3/hour Mon-Fri, fewer Sat-Sun, 45 minutes). To reach the bus stop, exit your ship to the right, walking with the sea on your right-hand side. Just follow the road as it curves to the right. After about 10 minutes, you'll reach the big market hall *(tržnica)*, surrounded by a giant parking lot. At the roundabout, turn right and head for the Koper Tržnica bus stop on the right side of the street (next to the parking lot), where you can catch the Piran-bound bus.

To Trieste or Ljubljana: While the bus to Piran leaves from Koper's town center, other connections depart from Koper's adjacent train and bus stations, which sit beyond the far end of the Old Town. To avoid the long walk, you can hop on any public bus, all of which head for this station. From the main bus station, you can ride the bus into the nearby Italian port city of **Trieste** (6/day, none on Sun, 45-60 minutes)—the historic port of the Austro-Hungarian Empire, with a fine Old Town and a romantic harbor. To go farther afield, you can head north to **Ljubljana.** Reaching the capital takes about 2.5 hours by bus or by train, but connections are sparse (about 4/day on either, though the only times convenient for cruisers are the 10:03 train, which runs daily, or the 10:50 bus, which runs Mon-Fri only).

To Elsewhere in Slovenia: As the drive to Ljubljana takes an hour less (about 1.5 hours each way), hiring your own **guide/driver** is a smart splurge to efficiently link together several worthwhile Slovenian stopovers. A popular round-trip from Koper is to visit both Ljubljana and Lake Bled before returning to your ship; if you skip Bled, you'll have time to tour one of the great caves (Škocjan or Postojna) or other sights (such as the Lipica Stud Farm) between the coast and Ljubljana. Bled-based guides Tina Hiti and Sašo Golub can take you on an all-day excursion to see Ljubljana and Bled for €450 (price for up to 3 people, €550 in a larger van; for details, see page 610).

PIRAN

UNDERSTANDING YUGOSLAVIA

While "Yugoslavia" may feel like a distant memory to today's visitors, the sprawling country that once contained all of the destinations in this book—and many more—still looms large in the region's history and consciousness. Many visitors have only a few impressions of Yugoslavia (1918-1992): A charismatic strong-arm leader. A cheery communist heritage. And a gruesome breakup marred by sectarian conflict and ethnic cleansing, which filled our nightly news with painful and poignant images. Now you're visiting in person...and you're struggling to make sense of that complicated recent history.

You can learn a lot from talking to locals, of course. However, everyone seems to have a slightly different version of events, and conspiracy theories still run rampant. A very wise Bosniak once told me, "Listen to all three sides—Muslim, Serb, and Croat. Then decide for yourself what you think." A Serb told me a similar local saying: "You have to look at the apple from all sides."

To provide some context for these interactions, here's an admittedly oversimplified, as-impartial-as-possible summary of how Yugoslavia was formed, what it was like, and how—and why—it broke apart.

BALKAN PENINSULA 101

For starters, it helps to have a handle on the different groups who've lived in the Balkans—the southeastern European peninsula between the Adriatic and the Black Sea, stretching roughly from Hungary to Greece. Despite its current, somewhat sinister connotations, the word "Balkan" probably comes from a Turkish term meaning, simply, "wooded mountains."

The Balkan Peninsula has always been a crossroads of cultures. The Illyrians, Greeks, Celts, and Romans had settlements here before the Slavs moved into the region from the north around the seventh century. During the next millennium and a half, the western part of the peninsula—which would become Yugoslavia—was divided by a series of cultural, ethnic, and religious fault lines.

The most important religious influences were **Western Christianity** (i.e., Roman Catholicism, first brought to the western part of the region by Charlemagne and later reinforced by the Austrian Habsburgs), **Eastern Orthodox Christianity** (brought to the east from the Byzantine Empire), and **Islam** (brought to the south by the Ottomans).

Two major historical factors made the Balkans what they are today: The first was the **split of the Roman Empire** in the fourth century AD, dividing the Balkans down the middle into Roman Catholic (west) and Byzantine Orthodox (east)—roughly along today's Bosnian-Serbian border. The second was the **invasion of the Islamic Ottomans** in the 14th century. The Ottoman victory at the Battle of Kosovo Polje (1389) opened the door to the region and kicked off five centuries of Islamic influence in Bosnia-Herzegovina and Serbia, further dividing the Balkans into Christian (north) and Muslim (south).

Because of these and other events, several distinct ethnic identities emerged. The major ethnicities of Yugoslavia—Croat, Slovene, Serb, and Bosniak—are all considered South Slavs. The huge Slav ethnic and linguistic family—some 400 million strong—is divided into three groups: South (the peoples of Yugoslavia, explained next, plus Bulgarians), West (Poles, Czechs, and Slovaks), and East (Russians, Ukrainians, and Belarusians).

The South Slavs, who are all descended from the same ancestors and speak closely related languages, are distinguished by their religious practices. Roman Catholic **Croats** or **Slovenes** are found mostly west of the Dinaric Mountains (Croats along the Adriatic coast and Slovenes farther north, in the Alps); Orthodox Christian **Serbs** live mostly east of the Dinaric range; and Muslim **Bosniaks** (whose ancestors converted to Islam under the Ottomans) live mostly in the Dinaric Mountains. Two other, smaller Orthodox ethnicities have been influenced by other large groups: the **Montenegrins** (shaped by centuries of Croatian and Venetian Catholicism on the coast, while remaining more traditional and Orthodox in the interior) and the **Macedonians** (with ties to Bulgarians and Greeks). To complicate matters, the region is also home to several non-Slavic minority groups, including **Hungarians** (in the northern province of Vojvodina) and **Albanians,** concentrated in Kosovo (descended from the Illyrians, who lived here long before the Greeks and Romans).

Of course, these geographic divisions are extremely general. The groups overlapped a lot—which is exactly why the breakup

Who's Who in Yugoslavia

Yugoslavia was made up of six republics, which were inhabited by eight major ethnicities (not counting small minorities such as Jews, Germans, and Roma). This chart shows each ethnicity and the republic(s) in which they were most concentrated. Not coincidentally, the more ethnically diverse a region was, the more conflict it experienced.

	Serbia*	Croatia	Bosnia-Herz.	Slovenia	Montenegro	Macedonia
Serbs (Orthodox)	X	X	X		X	
Croats (Catholic)		X	X			
Bosniaks (Muslims)			X			
Slovenes (Catholic)				X		
Macedonians (like Bulgarians)						X
Montenegrins (like Serbs)					X	
Albanians	X		X			X
Hungarians	X	X		X		

*Within Serbia were two "autonomous provinces," each of which was dominated by a non-Slavic ethnic group: Hungarians in Vojvodina and Albanians in Kosovo.

of Yugoslavia was so contentious. One of the biggest causes of this ethnic mixing came in the 16th century. The Ottomans were threatening to overrun Europe, and the Austrian Habsburgs wanted a buffer zone. The Habsburgs encouraged Serbs who were fleeing from Ottoman invasions to settle as a "human shield" along today's Croatian-Bosnian border (known as *Vojna Krajina*, or "Military Frontier").

Imagine being a simple Croat farmer in a remote village. One day your new neighbors move in: big, tough Serb refugees with chips on their shoulders after having been kicked out of their ancestral homeland. And imagine being one of those Serbs: angry, frightened, and struggling to make a new life far from home. The cultural clash between these two groups reverberated for centuries.

Another legacy of the Ottomans—which directly resulted in

The Balkans c. 1800

Vienna
Buda • Pest
Zagreb
Venice
Adriatic Sea
Sarajevo
Belgrade
BALKAN
Black Sea
PENINSULA
Dubrovnik
REPUBLIC OF RAGUSA (DUBROVNIK)
Istanbul
300 Kilometers
300 Miles
Aegean Sea
Mediterranean Sea

▪ Habsburg Empire	⌇ Former Yugoslavia Border (1945-1989)
▪ Ottoman Empire	⌇ Former Yugoslav Republic Borders (1945-1989)
▪ Venetian Empire	⌇ Current National Borders

the strife of the 1990s and continued tension today—was their occupation of Kosovo. This southern province is considered the ancestral homeland of the Serbs, whose civilization began here before
they moved their capital north to Belgrade, fleeing the Ottomans
after the Battle of Kosovo Polje. Under Ottoman rule, Kosovo was
opened up to settlement by (Muslim) Albanians, who quickly came
to represent a majority of the population. Centuries later, Kosovo—
today 95 percent Albanian—looms large in the Serb consciousness,
and their loss of this land still deeply offends many.

After the Ottoman threat subsided in the late 17th century,
some of the Balkan states (basically today's Slovenia and Croatia)
became part of the Austrian Habsburg Empire. The Ottomans
stayed longer in the south and east (today's Bosnia-Herzegovina
and Serbia)—making the cultures in these regions even more different. By the mid-19th century, the Ottoman Empire had become

the dysfunctional "Sick Man of Europe," allowing Serbia to regain its independence through diplomatic means. Meanwhile, Bosnia-Herzegovina was taken into the Habsburg fold (frustrating the Serbs, who already had visions of uniting the South Slav peoples).

But before long, World War I erupted, after a disgruntled Bosnian Serb nationalist—with the aim of uniting the South Slavs—killed the Austrian archduke and heir to the Habsburg throne during a visit to Sarajevo (see page 503). This famously kicked off a chain of events that caused Europe, and the world, to descend into a Great War. During the war, the Serbs fought valiantly (alongside England, France, and the US) with the Allies, while their Slovene and Croat cousins—citizens of the multiethnic Austro-Hungarian Empire—were compelled to take up arms against them.

SOUTH SLAVS UNITE

When the Austro-Hungarian Empire fell at the end of World War I, the map of Europe was redrawn for the 20th century. After centuries of being governed by foreign powers, the South Slavs began to see their shared history as more important than their differences. The Serbs pushed for the creation of an independent South Slav state, recognizing that a tiny country of a few million Croats or Slovenes couldn't survive on its own. And so, rather than be absorbed by a non-Slavic power, the South Slavs decided that there was safety in numbers, and banded together to form the Kingdom of the Serbs, Croats, and Slovenes (1918), later known as the Kingdom of Yugoslavia (Land of the South Slavs—*yugo* means "south"). "Yugoslav unity" was in the air. But this new union was fragile and ultimately bound to fail (not unlike the partnership between the Czechs and Slovaks, formed at the same time and for similar reasons).

From the very beginning, the various ethnicities struggled for power within the new Yugoslavia. The largest group was the Serbs (about 45 percent), followed by the Croats (about 25 percent). Croats often felt they were treated as lesser partners under the Serbs. For example, many Croats objected to naming the country's official language "Serbo-Croatian"—why not "Croato-Serbian"? Serbia already had a very strong king, Alexander Karađorđević, who assumed that his nation would have a leading role in the federation. A nationalistic Croat politician named Stjepan Radić, pushing for a more equitable division of powers, was shot by a Serb during a parliamentary session in 1928. Karađorđević abolished the parliament and became dictator. Six years later, infuriated Croat separatists killed him. By the time World War II came to Yugoslavia, the kingdom was already on the verge of collapse. The conflicts between the various Yugoslav groups had set the stage for a particularly complex and gruesome wartime experience.

YUGOSLAVIA

WORLD WAR II

Observers struggle to comprehend how it was possible for inter-ethnic conflict to escalate so quickly here in the early 1990s. Most of the answers can be found in the war that shook Europe 50 years earlier. In the minds of many combatants, the Yugoslav Wars of the 1990s were a continuation of unresolved conflicts from World War II.

Capitalizing on a power struggle surrounding Yugoslavia's too-young-to-rule king, and angered by a popular uprising against the tenuous deals that Yugoslavia had struck with Nazi Germany, Hitler sent the Luftwaffe to air-bomb Belgrade on April 6, 1941. This classic blitzkrieg maneuver was followed by a ground invasion, and within 11 days, Yugoslavia had surrendered. The geographic core of the nation (much of today's Croatia and Bosnia-Herzegovina) became the misnamed Independent State of Croatia, which was run by a Nazi puppet government called the Ustaše. Much of today's Serbia was occupied by Nazi Germany, Slovenia had a Quisling-like puppet dictator, and Montenegro was folded into Mussolini's Italy.

Many Croat nationalists supported the Ustaše in the hopes that it would be their ticket to long-term independence from Serbia. Emboldened by their genocide-minded Nazi overlords, Ustaše leaders used death camps to exterminate their enemies—specifically, the Serbs who, they felt, had wronged them in the days of the Kingdom of Yugoslavia. Not only were Jews, Roma, and other Nazi-decreed "undesirables" murdered in Ustaše concentration camps, but also hundreds of thousands of Serbs living in Croatia and Bosnia. (Estimates range from 800,000—the highball figure taught to Yugoslav schoolkids—to the offensively low 40,000 posited by nationalistic Croatian leaders in the 1990s.) Other Serbs were forced to flee the country or convert to Catholicism. Most historians consider the Ustaše camps to be the first instance of ethnic cleansing in the Balkans. (Half a century later, the Serbs justified their ruthless treatment of Croats and Bosniaks as retribution for these WWII atrocities.)

In the chaos of war, two distinct resistance movements arose, with the shared aim of reclaiming an independent Yugoslavia—but starkly different ideas of what that nation would look like.

First, in the eastern mountains of Yugoslavia rose the Četniks—a fearsome paramilitary band of mostly Serbian men fighting to reestablish a Serb-dominated monarchy. Wearing long beards and traditional mountain garb, and embracing a skull-and-crossbones logo adorned with the motto "Freedom or Death" in Cyrillic, the Četniks were every bit as brutal as their Ustaše enemies. In pursuit of their goal to create a purely Serb state, the Četniks expelled or massacred Croats and Muslims living in the territory they held. (To this day, if a Croat wants to deeply insult a Serb, he'll call him a "Četnik." And a Serb might use "Ustaše" to really hit a Croat where it hurts.)

The second resistance group—fighting against both the Četniks and the Ustaše—was the ragtag Partisan Army, led by Josip Broz, who was better known by his code name, Tito. The clever and determined Partisans had dual aims: to liberate Yugoslavia as a free nation on its own terms, and to make that new state a communist one. Even while the war was still underway, the Partisan leadership met at the second convention of the Anti-Fascist Council of National Liberation of Yugoslavia in Jajce, Bosnia, to lay the foundations for what would become a postwar, communist Yugoslavia.

After years of largely guerrilla fighting among these three groups, the Partisans emerged victorious. And so, as the rest of Eastern Europe was being "liberated" by the Soviets, the Yugoslavs regained their independence on their own. Soviet troops passed through, in pursuit of the Nazis, but were not allowed to stay.

After the short but rocky Yugoslav union between the World Wars, it seemed that no one could hold the southern Slavs together in a single nation. But one man could, and did: Tito.

TITO'S YUGOSLAVIA

Communist Party president and war hero Tito emerged as a political leader after World War II. With a Slovene for a mother, a Croat for a father, a Serb for a wife, and a home in Belgrade, Tito was a true Yugoslav. Tito had a compelling vision that this fractured union of the South Slavs could function.

But Tito's new Yugoslavia could not be forged without force. In the first several years of his rule, Tito sometimes resorted to ruthless strong-arm tactics to forcibly persuade his subjects. Many soldiers who had fought against the Partisans were executed to create an intimidating example. To this day, Croatians—many of whose grandparents fought proudly with the Ustaše, furthering their ideal of an independent Croatian state—feel that they were disproportionately targeted by Tito, and in some cases, denied development funding in retaliation for their prior support of Partisan enemies. In particular, Croats resented Tito's treatment of Cardinal Alojzije Stepinac, the spiritual leader who (like many Croats) had supported the Ustaše. Stepinac was arrested, sham-tried, and convicted, and died under house arrest. (Today, Croatia is the Yugoslav successor state where you'll find the least Tito nostalgia.) Similarly, the Četniks—who had also fought Tito's Partisans in the war—felt bruised as they gave up on their dreams of reinstalling the Serbian king.

Ultimately Tito prevailed, and while many Yugoslavs weren't

Tito (1892-1980)

The Republic of Yugoslavia became synonymous with one man, who led the fight to make it a reality. Josip Broz—better known as Marshal Tito—presided over the most peaceful and prosperous era in this region's long and troubled history. Three decades after his death, Tito is beloved by many of his former subjects...and yet, he was a communist dictator who dealt brutally with his political enemies. This love-him-and-hate-him autocrat is one of the most complex figures in the history of this very complicated land.

Josip Broz was born in 1892 to a Slovenian mother and a Croatian father in the northern part of today's Croatia (then part of the Austro-Hungarian Empire). After growing up in the rural countryside, he was trained as a metalworker. He was drafted into the Austro-Hungarian army, went to fight on the Eastern Front during World War I, and was captured and sent to Russia as a prisoner of war. Freed by Bolsheviks, Broz fell in with the Communist Revolution...and never looked back.

At war's end, Broz returned home to the newly independent Yugoslavia, where he worked alongside the Soviets to build a national Communist Party. As a clandestine communist operative, he adopted the code name he kept for the rest of his life: Tito. Some believe this was a Spanish name he picked up while participating in that country's civil war, while others half-joke that the name came from Tito's authoritarian style: *"Ti, to!"* means "You, do this!" But one thing's clear: In this land where a person's name instantly identifies his ethnicity, "Tito" is ethnically neutral.

When the Nazis occupied Yugoslavia, Tito raised and commanded a homegrown, communist Partisan Army. Through guerilla tactics, Tito's clever maneuvering, and sheer determination, the Partisans liberated their country. And because they did so mostly without support from the USSR, Yugoslavia was able to set its own postwar course.

The war hero Tito quickly became the "president for life" of postwar Yugoslavia. But even as he introduced communism to his country, he retained some elements of a free-market economy—firmly declining to become a satellite of Moscow. He also pioneered the worldwide Non-Aligned Movement, joining with nations in Africa, the Middle East, Asia, and Latin America in refusing to ally with the US or USSR (see page 139). Stubborn but suitably cautious, Tito expertly walked a tightrope between East and West.

There was a dark side to Tito. In the early years of his regime, Tito resorted to brutal, Stalin-esque tactics to assert his control. Immediately following World War II, the Partisan Army massacred tens of thousands of soldiers who had supported the Nazis. Then Tito systematically arrested, tried, tortured, or executed those who did not accept his new regime. Survivors whose lives were ruined during this reign of terror will never forgive Tito for what he did.

But once he gained full control, Tito moved away from strong-arm tactics and into a warm-and-fuzzy era of Yugoslav brotherhood. Tito believed that the disparate peoples of Yugoslavia could live in harmony. For example, every Yugoslav male had to serve in the People's Army, and Tito made sure that each unit was a microcosm of the complete Yugoslavia—with equal representation from each ethnic group. Yugoslavs from diverse backgrounds were forced to work together and socialize, and as a result, they became friends. He also worked toward economic diversification: Yugoslav tanks, some of the best in the world, were made of parts assembled in five different republics.

Tito's reign is a case study in the power of the cult of personality. Rocks on hillsides throughout Yugoslavia were rearranged to spell "TITO," and his portrait hung over every family's dinner table. Each of the six republics renamed one of its cities for their dictator. The main street and square in virtually every town were renamed for Tito. Each year, young people would embark on a months-long, Olympics-style relay, from each corner of Yugoslavia, to present a ceremonial baton to Tito on his official birthday (May 25). Tito also had vacation villas in all of Yugoslavia's most beautiful areas, including Lake Bled, the Brijuni Islands, and the Montenegrin coast. People sang patriotic anthems to their Drug (Comrade) Tito: "Comrade Tito, we pledge an oath to you."

Tito died in 1980 in a Slovenian hospital. His body went on a grand tour of the Yugoslav capitals: Ljubljana, Zagreb, Sarajevo, and Belgrade, where he was buried before hundreds of thousands of mourners, including more heads of state than at any other funeral in history. At his request, his tomb was placed in the greenhouse where he enjoyed spending time.

The genuine outpouring of grief at Tito's death might seem unusual for a man who was, on paper, an authoritarian communist dictator. But even today, many former Yugoslavs—especially Slovenes and Bosniaks—believe that his iron-fisted government was a necessary evil that kept the country strong and united. The eventual balance Tito struck between communism and capitalism, and between the competing interests of his ethnically diverse nation, led to this region's most stable and prosperous era. In a recent poll in Slovenia, Tito had a higher approval rating than any present-day politician, and 80 percent of Slovenes said they had a positive impression of him.

And yet, the Yugoslavs' respect for their former leader was not enough to keep them together. Tito's death began a long, slow chain reaction that led to the end of Yugoslavia. As the decades pass, the old joke seems more and more appropriate: Yugoslavia had eight distinct peoples in six republics, with five languages, three religions (Orthodox Christian, Catholic, and Muslim), and two alphabets (Roman and Cyrillic), but only one Yugoslav—Tito.

entirely convinced of his vision, they went along with it...for the time being.

Tito's new incarnation of Yugoslavia aimed for a more equitable division of powers. It was made up of six republics, each with its own parliament and president: **Croatia** (mostly Catholic Croats), **Slovenia** (mostly Catholic Slovenes), **Serbia** (mostly Orthodox Serbs), **Bosnia-Herzegovina** (the most diverse—mostly Muslim Bosniaks, but with very large Croat and Serb populations), **Montenegro** (mostly Orthodox—sort of a Serb/Croat hybrid), and **Macedonia** (with about 25 percent Muslim Albanians and 75 percent Orthodox Macedonians). Within Serbia, Tito set up two autonomous provinces, each dominated by an ethnicity that was a minority in greater Yugoslavia: Albanians in **Kosovo** (to the south) and Hungarians in **Vojvodina** (to the north). By allowing these two provinces some degree of independence—including voting rights—Tito hoped they would balance the political clout of Serbia, preventing a single republic from dominating the union.

Each republic managed its own affairs, but always under the watchful eye of president-for-life Tito, who said that the borders between the republics should be "like white lines in a marble column." "Brotherhood and unity" was Tito's motto, nationalism was strongly discouraged, and Tito's tight—often oppressive—control kept the country from unraveling.

Tito's Yugoslavia was communist, but it wasn't Soviet communism; you'll find no statues of Lenin or Stalin here. Despite strong pressure from Moscow, Tito broke away from Stalin in 1948 and refused to ally himself with the Soviets—and therefore received good will (and $2 billion) from the United States. He ingeniously played the East and the West against each other. He'd say to both Washington and Moscow, "If you don't pay me off, I'll let the other guy build a base here." Everyone paid up.

Economically, Tito's vision was for a "third way," in which Yugoslavia could work with both East and West without being dominated by either. Yugoslavia was the most free of the communist states. While large industry was nationalized, Tito's system allowed for small businesses. Though Yugoslavs could not become really rich, through hard work it was possible to attain modest wealth to buy a snazzy car, a vacation home, Western imports, and other niceties. By some GDP and other economic measures, Yugoslavia was at times more prosperous than poorer capitalist European countries like Italy or Greece. This experience with a market economy benefited Yugoslavs when Eastern Europe's communist regimes eventually fell.

Even during the communist era, Yugoslavia remained a popular tourist destination for visitors from both East and West, keeping its standards more in line with Western Europe than the Soviet states. Meanwhile, Yugoslavs, uniquely among communist citizens, were allowed to travel to the West. In fact, because Yugoslavs could travel relatively hassle-free in both East and West, their "red passports" were worth even more on the black market than American ones.

THINGS FALL APART

With Tito's death in 1980, Yugoslavia's six constituent republics gained more autonomy, with a rotating presidency. But before long, the fragile union Tito had held together started to unravel.

The breakup began in the late 1980s, with squabbles in the autonomous province of Kosovo between the Serb minority and the ethnic-Albanian majority. Remember that the Serbs consider Kosovo the cradle of their civilization—the medieval homeland of their most important monasteries and historic sites. Most significantly, it was the location of the Battle of Kosovo Polje ("Field of Blackbirds"), an epic 14th-century battle that formed the foundation of Serbian cultural identity...even though the Serbs lost to the Ottoman invaders (sort of the Serb Alamo). One Serb told me, "Kosovo is the Mecca and Medina of the Serb people." But by the 1980s, 9 of every 10 Kosovans were Albanian, and the few Serbs still living there felt oppressed and abused by the Albanian leadership. To many Serbs, this was the most offensive of the many ways in which they felt they'd been victimized by their neighbors for centuries.

Serbian politician Slobodan Milošević saw how the conflict could be used to Serbia's (and his own) advantage. In April of 1987,

Milošević delivered a rabble-rousing speech to aggrieved Serbs in Kosovo, pledging that Serbia would come to the aid of its brothers (famously asserting, "No one has the right to beat you"). He returned two years later for the 600th anniversary of the Battle of Kosovo Polje, arriving by helicopter to evoke old prophecies of a winged savior coming to unite the Serb people. Once there, he delivered another inflammatory speech. ("Six centuries later, now, we are being again engaged in battles...they are not armed battles, although such things cannot be excluded yet.") With these visits, Milošević upset the delicate balance that Tito had so carefully sought, while setting the stage for his own rise to the Serbian presidency.

When Milošević-led Serbia annexed Kosovo soon after, other republics (especially Slovenia and Croatia) were concerned. The Croats and Slovenes had always had reservations about Yugoslav unity, and with the sea change signaled by Milošević's rhetoric, they decided it was time to secede. Some of the leaders—most notably Milan Kučan of Slovenia—tried to avoid warfare by suggesting a plan for a loosely united Yugoslavia, based on the Swiss model of independent yet confederated cantons. But other parties, who wanted complete autonomy, refused. Over the next decade, Yugoslavia broke apart, with much bloodshed.

The Slovene Secession

Slovenia was the first Yugoslav republic to hold free elections, in the spring of 1990. Voters wanted the communists out, and they wanted their own independent nation. The most ethnically homogeneous of the Yugoslav nations, Slovenia was also the most Western-oriented, prosperous, and geographically isolated—so secession just made sense. But that didn't mean it would be achieved without violence.

After months of stockpiling weapons, Slovenia closed its borders and declared independence from Yugoslavia on June 25, 1991. Belgrade sent in the Yugoslav People's Army to take control of Slovenia's borders with Italy and Austria, figuring that whoever controlled the borders had a legitimate claim on sovereignty. Fighting broke out around these borders. Because the Yugoslav People's Army was made up of soldiers from all republics, many Slovenian troops found themselves fighting their own countrymen. (The army had cut off communication between these conscripts and the home front, so they didn't know what was going on—and often didn't realize they were fighting their friends and neighbors until they were close enough to see them.)

Slovenian civilians bravely entered the fray, blockading the Yugoslav barracks with their own cars and trucks. Most of the Yugoslav soldiers—now trapped—were young and inexperienced, and were terrified of the improvised (but relentless) Slovenian militia, even though their own resources were far superior.

After 10 days of fighting and fewer than a hundred deaths, Belgrade relented. The Slovenes stepped aside and allowed the Yugoslav People's Army to leave with their weapons and to destroy all remaining military installations as they went. When the Yugoslav People's Army cleared out, they left the Slovenes with their freedom.

The Croatian Conflict

In April of 1990, a retired general and historian named Franjo Tuđman—and his highly nationalistic, right-wing party, the HDZ (Croatian Democratic Union)—won Croatia's first free elections (for more on Tuđman, see page 26). Like the Slovenian reformers, Tuđman and the HDZ wanted more autonomy from Yugoslavia. But Tuđman's methods were more extreme than those of the gently progressive Slovenes. Tuđman invoked the spirit of the Ustaše, who had ruthlessly run Croatia's puppet government under the Nazis. He removed mention of the Serbs as equal citizens of the new nation. He reintroduced symbols that had been embraced by the Ustaše, including the red-and-white checkerboard flag and the kuna currency. (While many of these symbols predated the Ustaše by centuries, they had become irrevocably tainted by their association with the Ustaše.) The 600,000 Serbs living in Croatia were mindful that their grandparents had been massacred by the Ustaše. And so, extremists within this community began to rise up.

The first conflicts were in the Serb-dominated Croatian city of Knin. Tuđman had decreed that Croatia's policemen must wear a new uniform, which was strikingly similar to Nazi-era Ustaše garb. Infuriated by this slap in the face, and prodded by Slobodan Milošević's rhetoric, Serb police officers in Knin refused. Over the next few months, tense negotiations ensued. Serbs from Knin and elsewhere began the so-called "tree trunk revolution"—blocking important Croatian tourist roads to the coast with logs and other barriers. Meanwhile, the Croatian government—after being denied support from the United States—illegally purchased truckloads of guns from Hungary. (A UN weapons embargo, which was designed to prevent the outbreak of violence, had little effect on the Serb-dominated Yugoslav People's Army, which already had its own arsenal. But it was devastating to separatist Croatian and—later—Bosnian forces, which were just beginning to build their armies.) Croatian policemen and Serb irregulars from Knin fired the first shots of the conflict on Easter Sunday 1991 at Plitvice Lakes National Park.

By the time Croatia declared its independence (on June 25, 1991—the same day as Slovenia), it was already embroiled in the beginnings of a bloody war. The Yugoslav People's Army (always dominated by Serbs, and now without the many Croats and Slovenes who defected) swept in, ostensibly to put down the Croat rebellion and keep the nation together. The ill-prepared Croatian resistance, made up mostly of policemen and a few soldiers who defected from the People's Army, were quickly overwhelmed. The Serbs gained control over the parts of inland Croatia where they were in the majority: a large swath around the Bosnian border (including Plitvice) and part of Croatia's inland panhandle (the region of Slavonia). They declared their own independence from Croatia, and called this territory—about a quarter of Croatia—the **Republic of Serbian Krajina** (*krajina* means "border"). This new "country" (hardly recognized by any other nations) minted its own money and raised its own army, much to the consternation of Croatia—which was now worried about the safety of Croats living in Krajina.

As the Serbs advanced, more than 200,000 Croats fled to the coast, where they would live as refugees in resort hotels. The Serbs began a campaign of ethnic cleansing, systematically removing

Croats from contested territory—often by murdering them. (Many thousands of Croat civilians were killed.) The bloodiest siege was at the town of **Vukovar,** which the Yugoslav People's Army surrounded and shelled relentlessly for three months. By the end of the siege, thousands of Croat soldiers and civilians had disappeared. Many were later discovered in mass graves; hundreds remain missing, and bodies are still being found.

In a surprise move, Yugoslav forces also laid siege to the tourist resort of **Dubrovnik**—which resisted and eventually repelled the invaders (see page 298). By early 1992, both Croatia and the Republic of Serbian Krajina had established their borders, and a tense ceasefire fell over the region.

The standoff lasted until 1995, when the now well-equipped Croatian army retook the Serb-occupied areas in a series of two offensives—**"Lightning"** *(Blijesak)*, in the northern part of the country, and **"Storm"** *(Oluja)*, farther south. Some Croats retaliated for earlier ethnic cleansing by doing much of the same to Serbs—torturing and murdering them, and dynamiting their homes. Croatia quickly established the borders that exist today, and the Erdut Agreement brought peace to the region. But the country's demographics are forever changed: Of the 600,000 Serbs who had once lived in Croatia, approximately half were forced out, and more than 6,000 died in the war. Today, fewer than 200,000 Serbs—one-third of the original number—live in Croatia.

The War in Bosnia-Herzegovina

As violence erupted in Croatia and Slovenia, Bosnia-Herzegovina was suspiciously quiet. Even optimists knew it couldn't last. At the crossroads of Balkan culture, Bosnia-Herzegovina was even more diverse than Croatia; it was populated predominantly by Muslim Bosniaks (43 percent of the population), but also by large numbers of Serbs (31 percent) and Croats (17 percent). Bos-niaks tended to live in the cities, while Serbs and Croats were more often farmers.

In the fall of 1991, Bosnia-Herzegovina's president, Alija Izetbegović, began to pursue independence. While most Bosnian Croats and virtually all Bosniaks supported this move, Bosnia's substantial Serb minority resisted it. Bosnian Serbs preferred to remain part of an increasingly dominant ethnic group in a big country (Yugoslavia) rather than become second fiddle in a new, small country (Bosnia-Herzegovina). And so the Serbs within Bosnia-Herzegovina—whether they agreed or not—united into their own "state," called the **Republic of the Serb People of Bosnia-Herzegovina.** Its president, Radovan Karadžić, enjoyed the semisecret military support of Slobodan Milošević and the Yugoslav People's Army. The stage was set for a bloody secession.

In the spring of 1992, as a referendum on Bosnian independence loomed, the Serbs made their move. To legitimize their territorial claims, the Serbs began a campaign of ethnic cleansing against Bosniaks and Croats residing in Bosnia. Initially Karadžić's forces moved to take control of a strip of Muslim-majority towns (including Foča, Goražde, Višegrad, and Zvornik) along the Drina River, between Serbia proper and Serb-controlled areas closer to Sarajevo. They reasoned that their claim on this territory was legitimate, because the Ustaše had decimated the Serb population there during World War II. The well-orchestrated Karadžić forces secretly notified Serb residents to evacuate before they invaded each mixed-ethnicity town. Then troops would encircle the remaining Bosniaks and Croats with heavy artillery and sniper fire in an almost medieval-style siege. Many people were executed on the spot, while others were arrested and taken to concentration camps. Survivors were forced to leave the towns their families had lived in for centuries.

It was during this initial wave of Bosnian Serb ethnic cleansing—orchestrated by Radovan Karadžić and his generals—that the world began to hear tales as horrifying as anything you can imagine. Militia units would enter a town and indiscriminately kill anyone they saw—civilian men, women, and children. Pregnant women mortally wounded by gunfire were left to die in the street. Fleeing residents crawled on their stomachs for hours to reach cover, even as their family and friends were shot and blown up right next to them. Soldiers rounded up families, then forced parents to watch as they slit the throats of their children—and then the parents were killed, too. Dozens of people would be lined up along a bridge to have their throats slit, one at a time, so that their lifeless bodies would plunge into the river below. (Villagers downstream would see corpses float past, and know their time was coming.) While in past conflicts houses of worship had been considered off-limits, now Karadžić's forces actively targeted mosques and Catholic churches. Perhaps most despicable was the establishment of so-called "rape camps"—concentration camps where mostly Bosniak women were imprisoned and systematically raped by Serb soldiers. Many were intentionally impregnated and held captive until they had come to term, when they were released to bear and raise a child forced upon them by their hated enemy. These are the stories that turned "Balkans" into a dirty word.

The Bosnian Serb aggressors were intentionally gruesome and violent. First, leaders roused their foot soldiers with hate-filled propaganda (claiming, for example, that the Bosniaks were intent on creating a fundamentalist Islamic state that would do even worse to its Serb residents). Then, once the troops were furious and motivated, they were ordered to carry out unthinkable atrocities. For some people who perpetrated these attacks, the war represented a cathartic opportunity to exact vengeance for decades-old perceived injustices. Everyday Serbs—who for centuries have been steeped in a national identity of victimhood—saw this as an opportunity to finally make a stand. But their superiors had even more dastardly motives. They sought not only to remove people from "their" land, but to do so in such a heinous way as to ensure that the various groups could never again tolerate living together.

Bosnia-Herzegovina was torn apart. Even the many mixed families were forced to choose sides. If you had a Serb mother and a Croat father, you were expected to pick one ethnicity or the other—and your brother might choose the opposite. The majority of people, who did not want this war and couldn't comprehend why it was happening, now faced the excruciating realization that their neighbors and friends were responsible for looting and burning their houses, and shooting at their loved ones. As families and former neighbors trained their guns on each other, proud and beautiful cities such as Mostar were turned to rubble.

Even as the Serbs and Croats fought brutally in the streets, their leaders—Slobodan Milošević and Franjo Tuđman, respectively—were secretly meeting to carve up Bosnia into Serb and Croat sectors, at the Bosniaks' expense (the so-called Karađorđevo Agreement). Bosniak President Alija Izetbegović—who was left out of the conversation—desperately pleaded with the international community to support the peaceful secession of a free Bosnian state. Motivated more by fear than by nationalism, Izetbegović insisted that the creation of an independent Bosnia-Herzegovina was the only way to protect the lives of the Bosniak people.

At first, the Bosniaks and Croats teamed up to fend off the Serbs. But even before the first wave of fighting had subsided, Croats and Bosniaks turned their guns on each other. The Croats split off their own mini-state, the **Croatian Republic of Herzeg-Bosnia.** A bloody war raged for years among the three groups: the Serbs (with support from Serbia proper), the Croats (with support from Croatia proper), and—squeezed between them—the internationally recognized Bosniak government, with little support from anybody.

The United Nations Protection Force (UNPROFOR)—dubbed "Smurfs" both for their light-blue helmets and for their ineffectiveness—exercised their very limited authority to provide humanitarian aid. Their charge allowed them only to feed civilians caught in the crossfire—an absurd notion in places like Sarajevo, where civilians were forced to live like soldiers. (A political cartoon from the time shows a Bosnian Serb preparing to murder a Bosniak with a knife. A UN soldier appears and says, "Not so fast!" He proceeds to feed the Bosniak...then walks away, mission accomplished, while the Serb butchers his victim.) Later, the UN tried to designate "safe areas" where civilians were protected, but because the UNPROFOR troops were forbidden to use force—even in self-defense—they became helpless witnesses to atrocities.

For three and a half years, the capital of Sarajevo—still inhabited by a united community of Sarajevans (which included Bosniaks, Croats, and Serbs)—was surrounded by Karadžić's Bosnian Serb army (for more on the "Siege of Sarajevo," see page 492). Other Bosniak cities were also besieged, most notoriously Srebrenica in July of 1995. While a Dutch unit of UNPROFOR troops sat impotently by, General Ratko Mladić invaded Srebrenica and oversaw the murder of at least 8,000 of its residents, mostly men. Additionally, 35,000 to 40,000 Bosniak women and children were forcibly removed from the city; many of them (including babies) died en route. For more on this particularly dark chapter, see the "Srebrenica" sidebar on page 508.

After four long years, the mounting atrocities—including the siege of Srebrenica and the bombing of innocent civilians at a market in Sarajevo—finally persuaded the international community to act. In the late summer of 1995, NATO began bombing Bosnian Serb positions, forcing them to relax their siege and come to the negotiating table. The Dayton Peace Accords—brokered by US diplomats including Richard Holbrooke at Wright-Patterson Air Force Base near Dayton, Ohio—finally brought an end to the wars of Yugoslav succession.

The Dayton Peace Accords carefully divided Bosnia-Herzegovina into three different units: the Federation of Bosnia and Herzegovina (Bosniaks and Croats), the Serb-dominated Republika Srpska, and the mixed-ethnicity Brčko District. While this compromise helped bring the war to an end, it also created a nation with four independent and redundant governments—further crippling this war-torn and impoverished region.

The Fall of Milošević

After years of bloody conflicts, Serbian public opinion had decisively swung against their president. The transition began gradually in early 2000, spearheaded by Otpor, a nonviolent, grassroots, student-based opposition movement, and aided by similar groups. Using clever PR strategies, these organizations convinced Serbians that real change was possible. As anti-Milošević sentiments gained momentum, opposing political parties banded together behind one candidate, Vojislav Koštunica. Public support for Koštunica mounted, and when the arrogant Milošević called an early election in September 2000, he was soundly defeated. Though Milošević tried to claim that the election results were invalid, determined Serbs streamed into their capital, marched on their parliament, and—like the Czechs and Slovaks a decade before—peacefully took back their nation.

In 2001, Milošević was arrested and sent to The Hague, in the Netherlands, to stand trial before the International Criminal Tribunal for the Former Yugoslavia (ICTY). Milošević served as his own attorney as his trial wore on for five years, frequently delayed due to his health problems. Then, on March 11, 2006—as his trial was coming to a close—Milošević was found dead in his cell. Ruled a heart attack, Milošević's death, like his life, was controversial. His supporters alleged that Milošević had been denied suitable medical care, some speculated that he'd been poisoned, and others suspected that he'd intentionally worsened his heart condition to avoid the completion of his trial. Whatever the cause, in the end Milošević escaped justice—he was never found guilty of a single war crime.

More War Leaders on Trial

On July 18, 2008, Serbian police announced that they had captured Radovan Karadžić, the former leader of the Bosnian Serb state who is considered one of the worst culprits in the brutal ethnic cleansing.

Karadžić, who went into hiding shortly after the war (in 1996), had been living for part of that time in a residential neighborhood of Belgrade, posing as an alternative-medicine healer named Dr. Dragan David Dabić. (Karadžić had previously received training as a psychiatrist.) This expert on what he called "Human Quantum Energy" had his own website and even presented at conferences.

How did one of the world's most wanted men effectively disappear in plain sight for 12 years? He had grown a very full beard and wore thick glasses as a disguise, and frequented a neighborhood bar where a photo of him, in his earlier life, hung proudly on the wall...and yet, he was undetected even by those who saw him every day. It's alleged that at least some Serb authorities knew of his whereabouts, but, considering him a hero, refused to identify or arrest him. In 2016, the court in The Hague convicted Karadžić; an appeal was rejected in 2019, and Karadžić will spend the rest of his life in prison.

In May of 2011, the last "most wanted" criminal of the conflict—Karadžić's military leader, General Ratko Mladić—was found and arrested. In 2017, Mladić was convicted as responsible for both the Siege of Sarajevo and the Srebrenica massacre, and sentenced to life in prison.

But the trials and the appeals continued. In November of 2017, The Hague was again in the news, when Bosnian Croat military leader and convicted war criminal Slobodan Praljak—who was responsible for the bombing of Mostar's Old Bridge—lost an appeal. In protest, he drank cyanide in the courtroom, dying shortly thereafter.

Montenegro and Kosovo: Europe's Newest Nations

After the departures of Croatia, Slovenia, Bosnia-Herzegovina, and Macedonia (which peacefully seceded in 1991 and is now called North Macedonia), by the late 1990s only two of the original six republics of Yugoslavia remained united: Serbia (which still included the provinces of Kosovo and Vojvodina) and Montenegro. But in 2003, Montenegro began a gradual secession process that ended when it peacefully tiptoed its way to independence in 2006. (For all the details, see "Montenegro: Birth of a Nation" on page 393.)

The Yugoslav crisis concluded in the place where it began: the Serbian province of Kosovo. Kosovo's majority Albanians rebelled against Serbian rule in 1998, only to become victims of Milošević's ethnic cleansing (until US General Wesley Clark's NATO warplanes forced the Serbian army out). For nearly a decade, Kosovo remained a UN protectorate within Serbia—still nominally part of Serbia, but for all practical purposes separate and self-governing (under the watchful eye of the UN). Reading between the lines, Serbs point out that independent Kosovo quickly became a very close ally of the US, allowing one of Europe's biggest military bases—Camp Bondsteel—to be built in their territory.

On Sunday, February 17, 2008, Kosovo's provisional government unilaterally declared its independence as the "Republic of Kosovo." The new Kosovo government carefully stated that it would protect the rights of its minorities, including Serbs. But the Serbs deeply believed that losing Kosovo would also mean losing their grip on their own history and culture. They also feared for the safety of the Serb minority there (and potential retribution from Albanians who had for so long been oppressed themselves). But Kosovo's independence appears to be holding—representing, perhaps, the final chapter of a long and ugly Yugoslav succession. Kosovo is the seventh country to emerge from the breakup of Yugoslavia.

FINDING THEIR WAY:
THE FORMER YUGOSLAV REPUBLICS

Today, Slovenia and Croatia are as stable as many Western European nations, Bosnia-Herzegovina has made strides in putting itself back together, North Macedonia feels closer to Bulgaria than to Belgrade, and the sixth and seventh countries to emerge from "Yugoslavia"—Montenegro and Kosovo—are fledgling democracies.

And yet, nagging questions remain. Making the wars even more difficult to grasp is the uncomfortable reality that there were no clear-cut "good guys" and "bad guys"—just a lot of ugliness on all sides. In the war between the Croats and the Serbs, it's tempting for Americans to take Croatia's "side" because we saw them in the role of victims first; because they're Catholic, so they seem more "like us" than the Orthodox Serbs; and because we admire their striving for independence. But in the streets and the trenches, it was never that straightforward. The Serbs believe that *they* were the victims first—back in World War II, when their grandparents were executed in Croat-run Ustaše concentration camps. And when Croats retook the Serb-occupied areas in 1995, they were every bit as brutal as the Serbs had been a few years before. Both sides resorted to genocide, both sides had victims, and both sides had victimizers.

Even so, many can't help but look for victims and villains. During the conflict in Bosnia-Herzegovina, several prominent and respected reporters began to show things from one "side" more than the others—specifically, depicting the Bosniaks (Muslims) as victims. This reawakened an old debate in the journalism community: Should reporters above all remain impartial, even if "showing all sides" might make them feel complicit in ongoing atrocities?

As for villains, it's easy to point fingers at Slobodan Milošević, Radovan Karadžić, Ratko Mladić, and other political or military leaders who have been arrested and tried at The Hague. Others condemn the late Croatian President Franjo Tuđman, who, it's now known, secretly conspired with Milošević to redraw the maps of their respective territories. And of course, the foot soldiers of those monstrous men—who followed their immoral orders—cannot be excused.

And yet, you can't paint an entire group with one brush. While some Bosnian Serbs did horrifying things, only a small fraction of all Bosnian Serbs participated in the atrocities. Travelers to this region quickly realize that the vast majority of people they meet here never wanted these wars. And so finally comes the inevitable question: Why did any of it happen in the first place?

Explanations tend to gravitate to two extremes. Some observers consider this part of the world to be inherently warlike—a place where deep-seated hatreds and age-old ethnic passions unavoidably flare up. This point of view sees an air of inevitability about the recent wars...and the potential for future conflict. And it's hard to deny that the residents of the region tend to obsess about exacting vengeance for wrongdoings (real or imagined) that happened many decades or even centuries in the past.

For others, however, this theory is an insulting oversimplification. Sure, animosity has long simmered in the Balkans—as it has in many other parts of Europe (the centuries of French-English or Russian-German warfare, for example). And for many centuries leading up to World War II, the various groups had lived more or less in harmony. The critical component of these wars—what made them escalate so quickly and so appallingly—was the single-minded, self-serving actions of a few selfish leaders who shamelessly and aggressively exploited existing resentments to advance their own interests. It wasn't until Milošević, Karadžić, Tuđman, and others expertly manipulated the people's grudges that the region fell into war. By vigorously fanning the embers of ethnic discord, polluting the airwaves with hate-filled propaganda, and carefully controlling media coverage of the escalating violence, these leaders turned what could have been a healthy political debate into a holocaust.

Tension still exists throughout the former Yugoslavia—especially in the areas that were most war-torn. Croatians and Slovenes continue to split hairs over silly border disputes, Bosnia-Herzegovina groans under the crippling inefficiency of four autonomous governments, and Serbs ominously warn that they'll take up arms to reclaim Kosovo. Observers can't deny the painful possibility that, just as grudges held over from World War II were quickly ignited in the 1990s, holdover tensions from the recent wars could someday ignite a new wave of conflict. When people from a certain generation encounter other former Yugoslavs in their travels, they instantly evaluate each other's accent to determine: Are they one of us, or one of them?

For the visitor, it's tricky to get an impartial take on the current situation, or even sometimes to pin down historical "facts." As the people you meet tell you their stories, sometimes it's just as important to listen to the tone and subtext of their tale as it is to try to judge its veracity. Are they preaching a message of reconciliation or one of provocation?

With time, hard feelings are fading. The appealing prospect of European Union membership is a powerful motivator for groups to set aside their differences and cooperate. The younger generations don't look back—teenaged Slovenes no longer learn Serbo-Croatian, have only known life in an independent little country, and get bored (and a little irritated) when their old-fashioned parents wax nostalgic about the days of a united Yugoslavia.

A middle-aged Slovene friend of mine thinks fondly of his

months of compulsory service in the Yugoslav People's Army, when his unit was made up of Slovenes, Croats, Serbs, Bosniaks, Albanians, Macedonians, and Montenegrins—all of them compatriots, and all good friends. To the young Yugoslavs, ethnic differences didn't matter. My friend still often visits with an army buddy from Dubrovnik—600 miles away, not long ago part of the same nation—and wishes there had been a way to keep the country all together. But he says, optimistically, "I look forward to the day when the other former Yugoslav republics also join the European Union. Then, in a way, we will all be united once again." While this may not be a universally held opinion...at least it's a start.

PRACTICALITIES

This chapter covers the practical skills of European travel: how to get tourist information, pay for things, sightsee efficiently, find good-value accommodations, eat affordably but well, use technology wisely, and get between destinations smoothly. For more information on these topics, see www.ricksteves.com/travel-tips.

Tourist Information

National tourist offices are a wealth of information. Before your trip, visit each country's website for events, activities, and attractions by region. Explore information on Croatia's islands and active tourism (tel. 212/279-8672, http://us.croatia.hr), Slovenia's outdoor activities and tourist farms (www.slovenia.info), Montenegro's scenic coastline and rugged interior (http://montenegro.travel), and Bosnia-Herzegovina's hiking opportunities and well-preserved historical sites (www.bhtourism.ba).

A good first stop in every town is generally the tourist information office—abbreviated **TI** in this book (though locally, you may see them marked *TZ*, for *turistička zajednica*). Throughout

Croatia and Slovenia, you'll find TIs are usually well-organized and always have an English-speaking staff; in Bosnia and Montenegro, TIs can be more hit-or-miss.

TIs are in business to help you enjoy spending money in their town, but even so, I still make a point to swing by to pick up a city map and get information on public transit, walking tours, special events, and nightlife. Anticipating a harried front-line staffer, prepare a list of questions and a proposed plan to double-check. Some TIs have information on the entire country or at least the region, so try to pick up maps and printed information for destinations you'll be visiting later in your trip.

Travel Tips

Emergency and Medical Help: For any emergency service—ambulance, police, or fire—call **112** from a mobile phone or landline. Operators, who in most countries speak English, will deal with your request or route you to the right emergency service. If you get sick, do as the locals do and go to a pharmacist for advice. Or ask at your hotel for help—they'll know of the nearest medical and emergency services.

ETIAS Registration: Beginning in 2021, US and Canadian citizens may be required to register online with the European Travel Information and Authorization System (ETIAS) before entering certain European countries (quick and easy process, $8 fee, valid 3 years). A useful private website with more details is www.schengenvisainfo.com/etias.

Theft or Loss: To replace a passport, you'll need to go in person to an embassy or consulate (see next). If your credit and debit cards disappear, cancel and replace them (see "Damage Control for Lost Cards," later). File a police report, either on the spot or within a day or two; you'll need it to submit an insurance claim for lost or stolen rail passes or electronics, and it can help with replacing your passport or credit and debit cards. For more information, see www.ricksteves.com/help.

US Embassies: In **Croatia**—Ulica Thomasa Jeffersona 2, Zagreb, tel. 01/661-2200, consular services tel. 01/661-2345, https://hr.usembassy.gov; in **Slovenia**—Prešernova 31, Ljubljana, passport services available Mon-Fri 9:00-11:30 & 14:00-16:00, tel. 01/200-5500, https://si.usembassy.gov; in **Montenegro**—Džona Džeksona 2, Podgorica, must call for appointment, tel. 020/410-500, https://me.usembassy.gov; and in **Bosnia-Herzegovina**—Ulica Robert C. Frasure 1, Sarajevo, Mon-Thu mornings, must call for appointment, tel. 033/704-000, https://ba.usembassy.gov.

Canadian Embassies: In **Croatia**—Prilaz Đure Deželića 4, Zagreb, Mon-Thu 10:00-12:00 & 13:00-15:00, Fri 10:00-12:00, tel. 01/488-1200, after-hours emergencies call collect Canadian tel. 613/996-8885, www.canadainternational.gc.ca/croatia-croatie; in **Slovenia**—Linhartova cesta 49a, Ljubljana, Mon, Wed, Fri 8:00-12:00, tel. 01/252-4444, after-hours emergencies call collect Canadian tel. 613/996-8885, some services provided through Canadian Embassy in Budapest, Hungary, www.canadainternational. gc.ca/hungary-hongrie; in **Montenegro**—contact the Canadian Embassy in Belgrade, Serbia; from Montenegro dial 00-381-11-306-3000, after-hours emergencies call collect Canadian tel. 613/996-8885, www.canadainternational.gc.ca/serbia-serbie; and in **Bosnia-Herzegovina**—contact the Canadian Embassy in Budapest, Hungary; from Bosnia-Herzegovina dial 00-36-1-392-3360, for after-hours emergencies call collect Canadian tel. 613/996-8885, www.canadainternational.gc.ca/hungary-hongrie.

Borders: Even though Croatia and Slovenia are both in the EU, you'll still have to stop and show your passport when you cross the border between them (or when crossing into Bosnia-Herzegovina or Montenegro). But whether by car, train, or bus, you'll find that border crossings are generally a nonevent: Flash your passport, maybe wait a few minutes, and move on. Drivers may be asked to show proof of car insurance ("green card"), so be sure you have it when you pick up your rental car. Because Slovenia belongs to the Schengen open-borders agreement, you don't have to stop or show a passport when crossing between Slovenia and Austria, Italy, or Hungary. (Croatia is in talks to join Schengen in the near future.) Crossing from Croatia into Bosnia-Herzegovina or Montenegro is fairly straightforward, if occasionally a bit slow. If you encounter delays crossing borders, it's usually because of heavy traffic—particularly when traversing the Croatian coast during the popular summer months—rather than bureaucracy. If you plan to cross a border when it's busy, ask locally about the best time of day to arrive to avoid the longest lines (I've also offered some tips throughout this book). When you change countries, you change phone cards, postage stamps, and, in most cases, money.

Time Zones: Croatia, Slovenia, Bosnia-Herzegovina, and Montenegro, like most of continental Europe, are generally six/nine hours ahead of the East/West Coasts of the US. The exceptions are the beginning and end of Daylight Saving Time: Europe "springs forward" the last Sunday in March (two weeks after most of North America) and "falls back" the last Sunday in October (one week before North America). For a handy time converter, use the world clock app on your mobile phone or download one (see www.timeanddate.com).

Business Hours: Particularly in seasonal resort areas along the coast, business hours can be very unpredictable—dictated entirely by demand. A shop may be open daily from 9:00 to 24:00

in August, with its hours becoming progressively shorter in the shoulder season until it closes entirely in mid-October. In larger, less touristy cities and towns—and in most of Slovenia—hours are a bit more predictable (typically Mon-Fri from around 8:00 or 9:00 until 17:00, Sat mornings from 8:00 or 9:00 until 12:00 or 13:00, and closed Sun). In both Croatia and Slovenia, you will find a few businesses open on Sundays, but generally only in touristy areas or in large cities (especially near bus or train stations). Friday and Saturday evenings are rowdy; Sunday evenings are quiet.

Watt's Up? Europe's electrical system is 220 volts, instead of North America's 110 volts. Most electronics (laptops, smartphones, cameras) and newer hair dryers convert automatically, so you won't need a converter, but you will need an adapter plug with two round prongs, sold inexpensively at travel stores in the US. Avoid bringing older appliances that don't automatically convert voltage; instead, buy a cheap replacement in Europe.

Discounts: Discounts for sights are generally not listed in this book. However, seniors (age 65 and over), youths under 18, and students and teachers with proper identification cards (obtain from www.isic.org) can get discounts at many sights—always ask. Some discounts are available only to European citizens.

Online Translation Tips: Google's Chrome browser instantly translates websites; Translate.google.com is also handy. The Google Translate app converts spoken or typed English into most European languages (and vice versa) and can also translate text it "reads" with your smartphone's camera.

Smoking Bans: Both Croatia and Slovenia have enacted smoking bans in most public places, though patrons at outdoor tables can still smoke. Montenegro recently passed a similar ban, but the jury is still out on enforcement. Bosnia-Herzegovina has no such ban, so be ready for lots of smoke, indoors and out.

Money

Here's my basic strategy for using money in Europe:
- Upon arrival, head for a cash machine (ATM) at the airport and withdraw some local currency, using a debit card with low international transaction fees.
- In general, pay for bigger expenses with a credit card and use cash for smaller purchases. Use a debit card only for cash withdrawals.
- Keep your cards and cash safe in a money belt.

PLASTIC VERSUS CASH

Although credit cards are widely accepted in Europe, cash is sometimes the only way to pay for cheap food, bus fare, taxis, tips, and local guides. Some businesses (especially smaller ones, such as B&Bs and mom-and-pop cafés and shops) may charge you extra for using a credit card—or might not accept credit cards at all. Having cash on hand helps you out of a jam if your card randomly doesn't work.

I use my credit card to book and pay for hotel reservations, to buy advance tickets for events or sights, and to cover most other expenses. It can also be smart to use plastic near the end of your trip to avoid another visit to the ATM.

WHAT TO BRING

I pack the following and keep it all safe in my money belt.

Debit Card: Use this at ATMs to withdraw local cash.

Credit Card: Handy for bigger transactions (at hotels, shops, restaurants, travel agencies, car-rental agencies, and so on), payment machines, and online purchases.

Backup Card: Some travelers carry a third card (debit or credit; ideally from a different bank) in case one gets lost, demagnetized, eaten by a temperamental machine, or simply doesn't work.

A Stash of Cash: I carry $100-200 in US dollars as a cash backup, which comes in handy in an emergency (such as when banks go on strike or your ATM card gets eaten by the machine).

What NOT to Bring: Resist the urge to buy local currencies before your trip or you'll pay the price in bad stateside exchange rates. Wait until you arrive to withdraw money. I've yet to see a European airport that didn't have plenty of ATMs.

BEFORE YOU GO

Use this pre-trip checklist.

Know your cards. Debit cards from any major US bank will work in any standard European bank's ATM (ideally, use a debit card with a Visa or MasterCard logo). As for credit cards, Visa and MasterCard are universal, American Express is less common, and Discover is unknown in Europe.

Know your PIN. Make sure you know the numeric, four-digit PIN for all of your cards, both debit and credit. Request it if you don't have one, as it may be required for some purchases in Europe (see "Using Credit Cards," later), and allow time to receive the information by mail.

Report your travel dates. Let your bank know that you'll be using your debit and credit cards in Europe, and when and where you're headed.

Adjust your ATM withdrawal limit. Find out how much you can take out daily and ask for a higher daily withdrawal limit if you want to get more cash at once. Note that European ATMs will

Exchange Rates

Slovenia and Montenegro both use the euro, while Croatia and Bosnia-Herzegovina have different currencies. (Check www.oanda.com for the latest exchange rates.)

Croatia
Croatia's currency is called the kuna (abbreviated kn locally, HRK internationally):

6 Croatian kunas (kn) = about $1

To roughly convert Croatian kunas into dollars, divide by six (e.g., 6 kn = about $1; 60 kn = about $10; 200 kn = about $33).

A kuna is broken into 100 smaller units, called lipas. There are coins of 1, 2, 5, 10, 20, and 50 lipas; and 1, 2, and 5 kunas.

Croatia doesn't officially use the euro, and many vendors there (frustrated by thousands of cruise passengers who don't want to visit an ATM) flat-out refuse to take euros. If you try to spend euros in Croatia, don't be surprised if you're turned away. Confusingly, most hotels quote prices in euros for the convenience of their international guests. But they'll convert the bill to kunas to determine your final payment.

Slovenia and Montenegro
Slovenia and Montenegro use the euro currency:

1 euro (€) = about $1.20

To convert prices in euros to dollars, add about 20 percent: €20 is about $24, €60 is about $72. Just like the dollar, one euro (€) is broken down into 100 cents. Coins range from €0.01 to €2, and bills from €5 to €200 (bills over €50 are rarely used; €500 bills are being phased out).

Bosnia-Herzegovina
In this country, you'll use the Bosnian convertible mark (abbreviated KM locally, BAM internationally):

1.50 Bosnian convertible mark (KM) = about $1

To very roughly determine prices in US dollars, subtract about 25 percent (for example, 10 KM is about $7, and 50 KM is about $35). A convertible mark is broken down into 100 feninga. There are bills of 1, 5, 10, 20, 50, 100, and 200 marks, and coins of 1, 2, and 5 marks and 5, 10, 20, and 50 feninga. Most Bosnian merchants are willing to take euros, and some (especially in Mostar) will also accept Croatian kunas.

So, that 50-kn bottle of Croatian wine is about $8, the €25 Slovenian feast is about $30, the 60-KM Bosnian coffee set is around $45, and the 300-kn taxi ride through Zagreb is... uh-oh.

withdraw funds only from checking accounts; you're unlikely to have access to your savings account.

Ask about fees. For any purchase or withdrawal made with a card, you may be charged a currency conversion fee (1-3 percent) and/or a Visa or MasterCard international transaction fee (less than 1 percent). If you're getting a bad deal, consider getting a new debit or credit card. Reputable no-fee cards include those from Capital One, as well as Charles Schwab debit cards. Most credit unions and some airline loyalty cards have low or no international transaction fees.

IN EUROPE
Using Cash Machines

European cash machines have English-language instructions and work just like they do at home—except they spit out local currency instead of dollars, calculated at the day's standard bank-to-bank rate.

In most places, ATMs are easy to locate—in Croatia and Slovenia ask for a *Bankomat*. When possible, withdraw cash from a bank-run ATM located just outside that bank. Ideally, use the machine during the bank's opening hours, so you can go inside for help if your card is munched.

If your debit card doesn't work, try a lower amount—your request may have exceeded your withdrawal limit or the ATM's limit. If you still have a problem, try a different ATM or come back later—your bank's network may be temporarily down.

Avoid "independent" ATMs, such as Travelex, Euronet, Moneybox, Your Cash, Cardpoint, and Cashzone. These have high fees, can be less secure than a bank ATM, and may try to trick users with "dynamic currency conversion" (see next page).

Exchanging Cash

In general, avoid exchanging money in Europe; it's a big rip-off. But because the countries in this region have different currencies, you may wind up with leftover cash. Coins can't be exchanged once you leave the country, so spend them before you cross the border. Bills are easy to convert to the "new" country's currency, but remember that regular banks have the best rates for the conversion. Post offices and train stations usually change money if you can't get to a bank.

Using Credit Cards

Despite some differences between European and US cards, there's little to worry about: US credit cards generally work fine in Europe. I've been inconvenienced a few times by self-service payment machines that wouldn't accept my card, but it's never caused me serious trouble (I carry cash just in case).

European cards use chip-and-PIN technology; most chip cards issued in the US instead have a signature option. Some card readers will accept your card as-is while others may generate a receipt for you to sign or prompt you to enter your PIN (so it's important to know the code for each of your cards). If a cashier is present, you should have no problems.

At self-service payment machines (transit-ticket kiosks, parking, etc.), results are mixed, as US cards may not work in some unattended transactions. If your card won't work, look for a cashier who can process your card manually—or pay in cash.

Drivers Beware: Be aware of potential problems using a US credit card to fill up at an unattended gas station, enter a parking garage, or exit a toll road. Always carry cash as a backup and be prepared to move on to the next gas station if necessary. When approaching a toll plaza, use the "cash" lane.

Dynamic Currency Conversion

If merchants offer to convert your purchase price into dollars (called dynamic currency conversion, or DCC), refuse this "service." You'll pay extra for the expensive convenience of seeing your charge in dollars. If an ATM offers to "lock in" or "guarantee" your conversion rate, choose "proceed without conversion." Other prompts might state, "You can be charged in dollars: Press YES for dollars, NO for euros (or kunas)." Always choose the local currency.

Security Tips

Pickpockets target tourists. Keep your cash, credit cards, and passport secure in your money belt, and carry only a day's spending money in your front pocket or wallet.

Before inserting your card into an ATM, inspect the front. If anything looks crooked, loose, or damaged, it could be a sign of a card-skimming device. When entering your PIN, carefully block other people's view of the keypad.

Don't use a debit card for purchases. Because a debit card pulls funds directly from your bank account, potential charges incurred by a thief will stay on your account while your bank investigates the fraudulent use.

To access your accounts online while traveling, be sure to use a secure connection (see the "Tips on Internet Security" sidebar, later).

Damage Control for Lost Cards

If you lose your credit or debit card, report the loss immediately to the respective global customer-assistance centers. With a mobile phone, call these 24-hour US numbers: Visa (tel. +1 303/967-1096), MasterCard (tel. +1 636/722-7111), and American Express (tel. +1 336/393-1111). From a landline, you can call these US numbers collect by going through a local operator. European toll-free numbers can be found at the websites for Visa and MasterCard.

You'll need to provide the primary cardholder's identification-verification details (such as birth date, mother's maiden name, or Social Security number). You can generally receive a temporary card within two or three business days in Europe (see www.ricksteves.com/help for more).

If you report your loss within two days, you typically won't be responsible for unauthorized transactions on your account, although many banks charge a liability fee.

TIPPING

Tipping is a fairly recent innovation, imported to Croatia and Slovenia by tourists. Many locals still don't tip at all, so any tip is appreciated—and a generous, Yankee-sized tip is extravagant. As in the US, the proper amount depends on your resources, tipping philosophy, and the circumstances, but some general guidelines apply.

Restaurants: You don't need to tip if you order your food at a counter. At restaurants that have a waitstaff, round up the bill 5-10 percent after a good meal. For details on tipping in restaurants, see page 781.

Taxis: For a typical ride, round up your fare a bit (for instance, if the fare is 71 kn, pay 75 kn). If the cabbie hauls your bags and zips you to the airport to help you catch your flight, you might want to toss in a little more. But if you feel like you're being driven in circles or otherwise ripped off, skip the tip.

Services: In general, if someone in the service industry does a super job for you, a small tip of a euro (or the local equivalent) is appropriate...but not required. If you're not sure whether (or how much) to tip, ask a local for advice.

GETTING A VAT REFUND

Wrapped into the purchase price of your souvenirs is a Value-Added Tax (VAT) of 25 percent in Croatia, 22 percent in Slovenia, 17 percent in Bosnia, and 19 percent in Montenegro ("VAT" is called "PDV" in this part of the world). You're entitled to get most of that tax back if you purchase more than a certain amount (for example, 740 kn in Croatia, €50.01 in Slovenia) of goods at a store that participates in the VAT refund scheme. Typically, you must ring up the minimum at a single retailer—you can't add up your purchases from various shops to reach the required amount. (If the store ships the goods to your US home, VAT is not assessed on your purchase.)

Getting your refund is usually straightforward...and worthwhile if you spend a significant amount on souvenirs.

Get the paperwork. Have the merchant completely fill out the necessary refund document. You'll have to present your passport. Get the paperwork done before you leave the store to ensure you'll have everything you need (including your original sales receipt).

Get your stamp at the border or airport. Process your VAT document at your last stop in the country in which you made your purchase (or, if you bought it in the European Union, at your last stop in the European Union), such as at the airport. Arrive an additional hour before you need to check in to allow time to find the customs office—and wait. Some customs desks are positioned before airport security; confirm the location before going through security.

It's best to keep your purchases in your carry-on. If your item (such as a knife) isn't allowed as carry-on, pack it in your checked bag and alert the check-in agent. You'll be sent (with your tagged bag) to a customs desk outside security; someone will examine your bag, stamp your paperwork, and put your bag on the belt. You're not supposed to use your purchased goods before you leave. If you show up at customs wearing your brand-new Slovenian shoes, officials might look the other way—or deny you a refund.

Collect your refund. You can claim your VAT refund from refund companies, such as Global Blue or Planet, with offices at major airports, ports, or border crossings (either before or after security, probably strategically located near a duty-free shop). These services (which extract a 4 percent fee) can refund your money in cash immediately or credit your card. Otherwise, mail the stamped refund documents to the address given by the shop where you made your purchase.

CUSTOMS FOR AMERICAN SHOPPERS

You can take home $800 worth of items per person duty-free, once every 31 days. Many processed and packaged foods are allowed, including vacuum-packed cheeses, dried herbs, jams, baked goods, candy, chocolate, oil, vinegar, mustard, and honey. Fresh fruits and vegetables and most meats are not allowed, with exceptions for some canned items. As for alcohol, you can bring in one liter duty-free (it can be packed securely in your checked luggage, along with any other liquid-containing items).

To bring alcohol (or liquid-packed foods) in your carry-on bag on your flight home, buy it at a duty-free shop at the airport. You'll increase your odds of getting it onto a connecting flight if it's packaged in a "STEB"—a secure, tamper-evident bag. But stay away

PRACTICALITIES

from liquids in opaque, ceramic, or metallic containers, which usually cannot be successfully screened (STEB or no STEB).

For details on allowable goods, customs rules, and duty rates, visit http://help.cbp.gov.

Sightseeing

Sightseeing can be hard work. Use these tips to make your visits to Croatia's and Slovenia's finest sights meaningful, fun, efficient, and painless.

MAPS AND NAVIGATION TOOLS

A good map is essential for efficient navigation while sightseeing. The maps in this book are concise and simple, designed to help you locate recommended destinations, sights, and local TIs, where you can pick up more in-depth maps.

You can also use a mapping app on your mobile device. Be aware that pulling up maps or looking up turn-by-turn walking directions on the fly requires a data connection: To use this feature, it's smart to get an international data plan. With Google Maps or City Maps 2Go, it's possible to download a map while online, then go offline and navigate without incurring data-roaming charges, though you can't search for an address or get real-time walking directions. A handful of other apps—including Apple Maps and Navmii—also allow you to use maps offline.

PLAN AHEAD

Set up an itinerary that allows you to fit in all your must-see sights. For a one-stop look at opening hours, see this book's "At a Glance" sidebars for major cities and regions (Istria, Dubrovnik, and Ljubljana). The hours at sights tend to fluctuate with demand from season to season (especially in coastal towns), but you can easily confirm the latest by checking with the TI or visiting museum websites.

Don't put off visiting a must-see sight—you never know when a place will close unexpectedly for a holiday, strike, or restoration. Many museums are closed or have reduced hours at least a few days a year, especially on holidays such as Christmas, New Year's, and Labor Day (May 1). A list of holidays is in the appendix; check for possible closures during your trip. In summer, some sights may stay open late. In the off-season, hours may be shorter.

Going at the right time helps avoid crowds. This book offers tips on the best times to see specific sights. Try visiting popular sights very early or very late. Evening visits (when possible) are usually peaceful, with fewer crowds. Mid-morning is usually the worst time to visit a popular sight.

Study up. To avoid redundancy, many cultural or historical details are explained for one sight in this book and not repeated for another; to get the full picture, read the entire chapter for each destination before you visit.

RESERVATIONS, ADVANCE TICKETS, AND PASSES

Given how precious your vacation time is, I recommend getting reservations for any must-see sight that offers them (see page 11).

To deal with lines, many popular sights sell advance tickets that guarantee admission at a certain time of day, or that allow you to skip entry lines. Either way, it's worth giving up some spontaneity to book in advance. While hundreds of tourists sweat in long ticket-buying lines, those who've booked ahead are assured of getting in. In some cases, getting a ticket in advance simply means buying your ticket earlier on the same day. But for other sights, you may need to book weeks or even months in advance. As soon as you're ready to commit to a certain date, book it.

The advance-purchase price is often less expensive than what you would pay on-site (my listings include the online price, if available). And many museums offer convenient mobile ticketing. Simply buy your ticket online and send it to your phone, eliminating the need for a paper ticket.

AT SIGHTS

Here's what you can typically expect:

Entering: You may not be allowed to enter if you arrive too close to closing time. And guards start ushering people out well before the actual closing time, so don't save the best for last.

Photography: If the museum's photo policy isn't clearly posted, ask a guard. Generally, taking photos without a flash or tripod is allowed. Some sights ban selfie sticks; others ban photos altogether.

Audioguides and Apps: Many sights rent audioguides with recorded descriptions in English. If you bring your own earbuds, you can often enjoy better sound. If you don't mind being tethered to your travel partner, you'll save money by bringing a Y-jack and sharing. Museums and sights often offer free apps that you can download to your mobile device (check their websites).

Temporary Exhibits: Museums may show special exhibits in addition to their permanent collection. Some exhibits are included in the entry price, while others come at an extra cost (which you may have to pay even if you don't want to see the exhibit).

Expect Changes: Artwork can be on tour, on loan, out sick, or shifted at the whim of the curator. Pick up a floor plan as you enter, and ask museum staff if you can't find a particular item.

PRACTICALITIES

Services: Important sights usually have a reasonably priced on-site café or cafeteria (handy places to rejuvenate during a long visit). The WCs at sights are free and generally clean.

Before Leaving: At the gift shop, scan the postcard rack or thumb through a guidebook to be sure you haven't overlooked something that you'd like to see. Every sight or museum offers more than what is covered in this book. Use the information I provide as an introduction—not the final word.

Sleeping

Extensive and opinionated listings of good-value rooms are a major feature of this book's Sleeping sections. The accommodations scene in Croatia and Slovenia is quirky and complicated. In most Croatian destinations, you have two basic choices: either a big hotel or what locals call "private accommodations"—a rented apartment (*apartman*, plural *apartmani*) or a room in a private home (*soba*, pronounced SOH-bah; plural *sobe*, SOH-bay). I've explained the ins and outs of each in this section. Rather than list accommodations scattered throughout a town, I choose places that are convenient to your sightseeing.

My recommendations run the gamut, from dorm beds to fancy rooms with all the comforts. I look for places that are clean, central, relatively quiet at night, reasonably priced, friendly, small enough to have a hands-on owner or manager, and run with a respect for local traditions. My favorites are small, family-run hotels (which are rare) and friendly local people who rent "hotelesque" private rooms without a reception desk (which are, thankfully, abundant). I'm more impressed by a handy location and a fun-loving philosophy than flat-screen TVs and a fancy gym. Most of my recommendations fall short of perfection. But if I can find a place with most of these features, it's a keeper.

Book your accommodations as soon as your itinerary is set, especially if you want to stay at one of my top listings or if you'll be traveling during busy times. See the appendix for a list of major holidays and festivals.

Some people make reservations as they travel, calling or emailing ahead a few days to a week before their arrival. If you're trying for a same-day reservation, it's best to call hotels at about 9:00 or 10:00, when the receptionist knows which rooms will be

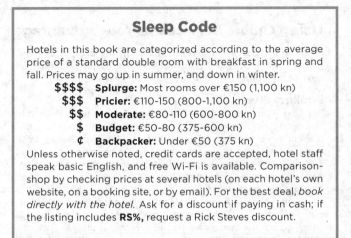

Sleep Code

Hotels in this book are categorized according to the average price of a standard double room with breakfast in spring and fall. Prices may go up in summer, and down in winter.

$$$$	**Splurge:**	Most rooms over €150 (1,100 kn)
$$$	**Pricier:**	€110-150 (800-1,100 kn)
$$	**Moderate:**	€80-110 (600-800 kn)
$	**Budget:**	€50-80 (375-600 kn)
¢	**Backpacker:**	Under €50 (375 kn)

Unless otherwise noted, credit cards are accepted, hotel staff speak basic English, and free Wi-Fi is available. Comparison-shop by checking prices at several hotels (on each hotel's own website, on a booking site, or by email). For the best deal, *book directly with the hotel*. Ask for a discount if paying in cash; if the listing includes **RS%**, request a Rick Steves discount.

available. If you encounter a language barrier, ask the fluent receptionist at your current hotel to call for you. Some apps—such as HotelTonight.com—specialize in last-minute rooms, often at boutique or business-class hotels in big cities.

RATES AND DEALS

In Croatia, most hotels are outrageously expensive, but private accommodations are an excellent value. My recommendations range from $15 bunks to $500-plus splurges, but most cluster somewhere in between: For a well-located standard double room in peak season on the Croatian coast, plan on spending $150-300 in a big resort hotel; $80-130 in a small hotel or a hotelesque private room or apartment (with your own bathroom, TV, and other amenities); or $50-80 for a more basic private room with a shared bathroom. While most Croatian accommodations quote their rates in euros, when you check out, payment is expected in kunas (or by credit card). Bosnian accommodations also quote their rates in euros.

Slovenia has a wider range of affordable small hotels (about $90-130 in Ljubljana and Lake Bled, and $70-90 in small towns and the countryside), which makes private accommodations a lesser value there.

I've categorized my recommended accommodations based on price, indicated with a dollar-sign rating (see sidebar). The price ranges suggest an estimated cost for a one-night stay in spring and fall in a standard double room with a private toilet and shower, including breakfast, and assume you're booking directly with the hotel (not through a booking site, which extracts a commission). Notice that my price ranges are intentionally *not* based on peak-of-peak season—July and August—when rates skyrocket and fewer

Using Online Services to Your Advantage

From booking services to user reviews, online businesses play a greater role in travelers' planning than ever before. Take advantage of their pluses—and be wise to their downsides.

Booking Sites

Booking websites such as Booking.com and Hotels.com offer one-stop shopping for hotels. While convenient for travelers, they present a real problem for independent, family-run hotels. Without a presence on these sites, small hotels become almost invisible. But to be listed, a hotel must pay a sizeable commission... and promise that its own website won't undercut the price on the booking-service site.

Here's the work-around: Use the big sites to research what's out there, then book directly with the hotel by email or phone, in which case hotel owners are free to give you whatever price they like. Ask for a room without the commission mark-up (or ask for a free breakfast if not included, or a free upgrade). If you do book online, be sure to use the hotel's website. The price will likely be the same as via a booking site, but your money goes to the hotel, not agency commissions.

As a savvy consumer, remember: When you book with an online booking service, you're adding a middleman who takes roughly 20 percent. To support small, family-run hotels whose world is more difficult than ever, book direct.

Short-Term Rental Sites

Rental juggernaut Airbnb (along with other short-term rental sites) allows travelers to rent rooms and apartments directly from locals, often providing more value than a cookie-cutter hotel. Airbnb fans appreciate feeling part of a real neighborhood and getting into a daily routine as "temporary Europeans." Depending on the host, Airbnb can provide an opportunity to get to know a local person, while keeping the money spent on your accommo-

of my readers are traveling. Room prices can fluctuate wildly with demand and amenities (size, views, room class, and so on), but relative price categories remain constant. Short stays (of less than three nights) are discouraged, especially in peak season. Expect to pay 20-50 percent extra if you're staying just one or two nights, and don't be surprised if some places have a minimum-stay requirement in summer. But if you can fill a gap in their reservations schedule, they might waive this surcharge.

Three or four people can save money by requesting one big room. Traveling alone can be expensive: A single room is often only 20 percent cheaper than a double.

Room rates are especially volatile at hotels—especially big Croatian resorts—that use "dynamic pricing" to set rates. Prices dations in the community.

Critics view Airbnb as a threat to "traditional Europe," saying it creates unfair, unqualified competition for established guesthouse owners. In some places, the lucrative Airbnb market has forced traditional guesthouses out of business and is driving property values out of range for locals. Some cities have cracked down, requiring owners to occupy rental properties part of the year (and staging disruptive "inspections" that inconvenience guests).

As a lover of Europe, I share the worry of those who see residents nudged aside by tourists. But as an advocate for travelers, I appreciate the value and cultural intimacy Airbnb provides.

User Reviews

User-generated review sites and apps such as Yelp and TripAdvisor can give you a consensus of opinions about everything from hotels and restaurants to sights and nightlife. If you scan reviews of a restaurant or hotel and see several complaints about noise or a rotten location, you've gained insight that can help in your decision-making.

But as a guidebook writer, my sense is that there is a big difference between the uncurated information on a review site and the vetted listings in a guidebook. A user-generated review is based on the limited experience of one person, who stayed at just one hotel in a given city and ate at a few restaurants there. A guidebook is the work of a trained researcher who forms a well-developed basis for comparison by visiting many restaurants and hotels year after year.

Both types of information have their place, and in many ways, they're complementary. If something is well reviewed in a guidebook and it also gets good online reviews, it's likely a winner.

can skyrocket during festivals and conventions, while business hotels can have deep discounts on weekends when demand plummets. Of the many hotels I recommend, it's difficult to say which will be the best value on a given day—until you do your homework.

Booking Direct: Once your dates are set, compare prices at several hotels. You can do this by checking Hotels.com, Booking.com, and hotel websites. After you've zeroed in on your choice, book directly with the hotel itself. Contact small family-run hotels directly by phone or email. When you go direct, the owner avoids the commission paid to booking sites, thereby leaving enough wiggle room to offer you a discount, a nicer room, or a free breakfast (if it's not already included). If you prefer to book online or are considering a hotel chain, it's to your advantage to use the hotel's website.

Booking directly also increases the chances that the hotelier will be able to accommodate any special needs or requests (such as shifting your reservation). Going through a middleman makes it more difficult for the hotel to adjust your booking.

Getting a Discount: Some hotels extend a discount to those who pay cash or stay longer than three nights. And some accommodations offer a special discount for Rick Steves readers, indicated in this guidebook by the abbreviation **"RS%."** Discounts vary: Ask for details when you reserve. Generally, to qualify for this discount, you must book direct (not through a booking site), mention this book when you reserve, show this book upon arrival, and sometimes pay cash or stay a certain number of nights. In some cases, you may need to enter a discount code (which I've provided in the listing) in the booking form on the hotel's website. Rick Steves discounts apply to readers with either print or digital books. Understandably, discounts do not apply to promotional rates.

HELPFUL HINTS

Get help finding your accommodations. On the Croatian coast, most of my recommendations are small family homes with just a few rooms, often tucked up narrow lanes from the main square or main drag. As these can be tricky to find, use the maps in this book, get careful directions from your host, and ask anyone you pass as you're looking. If they offer to come meet you at the ferry... accept! Even if the *soba* owner is not there to meet you, someone at the bar next door can track him or her down for you.

B.Y.O.B. (bring—or buy—your own breakfast). Many of my accommodations don't provide breakfast. In each town, I've recommended some places to buy your own. But if you'd like a simple "picnic breakfast" in your room, bring along or buy some individual instant coffee pouches (like Nescafé or Starbucks Via), and grab some goodies at the bakery the evening before.

Bring earplugs. Bars and nightclubs fill the old town centers of many cities in this book—including Dubrovnik, Split, and Ljubljana. I've noted the specific hotels that suffer the worst noise. If you're a light sleeper, make a point of requesting a quiet room.

Expect odors. Croatia and Slovenia both have a smoking ban for most accommodations (though larger hotels may have some designated smoking rooms). However, guests can still smoke on balconies and other outdoor areas, so it may not be possible to completely escape a somewhat smoky room.

Throughout this region, some buildings have Yugoslav-era septic-tank systems that aren't properly vented. On rainy days, a faint sewage smell may drift into rooms. This isn't harmful, but it's impossible to predict and can be unpleasant. Nothing can be done about it, so don't bother complaining (unless you want to try to switch to a less-smelly room).

Perhaps because of poor ventilation—or because they tend to be located in musty old stone buildings—some hotels and *sobe* in Croatia use heavily perfumed air fresheners in their rooms. It's usually easy to locate and unplug these, but if you are very sensitive to fragrances, try asking your *soba* host to remove them before you arrive.

Bring bug spray. Window screens are rare in this area, so in warm weather be prepared to share your room with mosquitoes and other bugs.

Shower smartly. If there seems to be no hot water, try flipping the switch with a picture of a water tank, usually next to the light switch. (Ideally, discover this switch long before you need to shower, and keep it on—otherwise you'll have to wait 20-30 minutes for the water to heat up.) In many *sobe,* the hot-water tank is tiny—barely big enough for one American-length shower. So two people traveling together may want to practice the "navy shower" method (douse yourself, turn off water, soap up, then turn water back on for a quick rinse)...or the second person may be in for a chilly surprise. The incredibly high water pressure in most Croatian showers makes the hot water go that much faster (turn the faucet on only partway to help stretch the precious hot water).

TYPES OF ACCOMMODATIONS
Private Accommodations (*Sobe* and Apartments)

Private accommodations offer travelers a characteristic and money-saving alternative for a fraction of the price of a hotel. You have two options: *sobe* (rooms) or *apartmani* (apartments). Often, a house renting both types is called a *vila* or *villa*—like a small guesthouse or pension.

Often run by empty-nesters, private accommodations are similar to British bed-and-breakfasts...minus the breakfast (ask your host about the best nearby breakfast spot). Generally the more you pay, the more privacy and amenities you get: private bathroom, TV, air-conditioning, kitchenette, and so on. The simplest *sobe* allow you to experience Croatia on the cheap, at nearly youth-hostel prices, while giving you a great opportunity to connect with a local family. The fanciest *sobe* are downright swanky and offer near-hotel anonymity.

Apartments are typically bigger and cost slightly more than *sobe,* but they're still far cheaper than hotels. At many places, the only real difference between a *soba* and an apartment is that the apartment comes with a kitchenette. If you make good use of the kitchen, this can be a good investment to help stretch your meal budget. Apartments are also more likely to have laundry facilities.

Making Hotel Reservations

It's possible to travel most of the year without reservations, especially if you arrive early in the day (although popular tourist towns can be completely full in late July and August). But given the good value of the accommodations I've found for this book, I'd recommend that you reserve your rooms as soon as you've pinned down your travel dates. For busy national holidays, it's wise to reserve far in advance (see the appendix).

Because my favorite accommodations tend to be small-time entrepreneurs renting only a few rooms, they book up fast with my readers. I've tried to list several good options, so if your first choice is full, you can simply try others on the list. Sometimes one of my listings might offer to find you somewhere else to stay. This can be convenient, but don't feel obligated—you'll have more control over your options if you book direct, using my recommendations.

Requesting a Reservation: For *sobe* and family-run hotels, it's generally best to book your room directly via email or phone. For business-class and chain hotels, or if you'd rather book online, reserve directly through the hotel's official website (not a booking website). Almost all of my recommended hotels take reservations in English.

Here's what the hotelier or *soba* host wants to know:

- Type(s) of rooms you want and size of your party
- Number of nights you'll stay
- Your arrival and departure dates, written European-style as day/month/year (for example, 18/06/21 or 18 June 2021)
- Special requests (en suite bathroom, cheapest room, twin beds vs. double bed, quiet room)
- Applicable discounts (such as a Rick Steves reader discount,

Registered *sobe* are rated by the government using a system that assigns stars based on amenities. Three or more stars means that you'll have your own bathroom, while two stars puts the bathroom down the hall. (Apartments always have private bathrooms.) Many *sobe* and apartments also have air-conditioning, and sometimes TV (but usually no telephone). The prices for private accommodations fluctuate dramatically with the seasons, and remember that stays of fewer than three nights often come with a 20-50 percent surcharge (though this can be waived outside peak season).

There are typically two kinds of *soba* hosts: those who want

From:	rick@ricksteves.com
Sent:	Today
To:	info@hotelcentral.com
Subject:	Reservation request for 19-22 July

Dear Hotel Central,

I would like to stay at your hotel. Please let me know if you have a room available and the price for:
- 2 people
- Double bed and en suite bathroom in a quiet room
- Arriving 19 July, departing 22 July (3 nights)

Thank you!
Rick Steves

cash discount, or promotional rate)

Confirming a Reservation: Most places will request a credit-card number to hold your room. If you're using an online reservation form, make sure it's secure by looking for the *https* or a lock icon at the top of your browser. If the hotel's website doesn't have a secure form where you can enter the number directly, it's best to share that confidential info via a phone call.

Canceling a Reservation: If you must cancel, it's courteous—and smart—to do so with as much notice as possible, especially for smaller family-run places and *sobe.* Cancellation policies can be strict; read the fine print before you book. Many discount deals may require prepayment, with no cancellation refunds.

Reconfirming a Reservation: Always call or email to reconfirm your room reservation a few days in advance. For smaller hotels and *sobe,* I call again on my day of arrival to tell my host what time to expect me (especially important if arriving late—after 17:00).

Phoning: For tips on calling hotels overseas, see page 784.

minimal interaction with their guests, and hosts who are friendly and may want to get to know you. Think about the kind of experience you want: Just a key and an affordable bed...or a chance to get to know a Croatian? Some *soba* hosts rent rooms scattered around town, in which case you probably won't see much of the hosts. In other cases, they have one or two rooms in their own home, making it easier to strike up a friendship. Read my descriptions and online reviews to help shape your decision.

Before you commit, be clear on the location. I like to virtually "explore" the neighborhood using the Street View feature on

PRACTICALITIES

Google Maps. Also consider the proximity to the bus station or boat dock, and how near or far the property is from the charming Old Town where you'll be spending most of your time. Ask about amenities (elevator, air-conditioning, laundry, Wi-Fi, parking, etc.). Reviews from previous guests can help identify trouble spots.

Since the best-value *sobe* deservedly book up early, reservations are highly recommended. It's important to **book directly** with your host. The importance of this can't be overstated. Several *soba* hosts I list in this book told me that some of my readers have emailed them to check availability and then proceeded to book through a third party. This frustrates them because it costs everybody more money—except the middleman. Making your

reservation directly with the host often results in a better price (see the sidebar). Any special prices or discounts I've negotiated for this book are invalidated if you use a middleman.

After you've reserved, keep in mind that your host loses money if you don't show up. For this reason, some hosts may request your credit-card number to secure the reservation. (They'll generally ask for payment in cash when you're there; your credit card won't be charged.) A few hosts might ask you to wire or mail money as a deposit. Because wiring money can come with substantial fees—which you (rather than the *soba* host) will incur—it usually works better to mail them a check or travelers check, or pay them through PayPal. Ask your *soba* host which options they accept.

Soba hucksters who accost you on the street can be very persuasive about luring travelers away from their reserved rooms. But if you've already booked a room at a particular place, you owe it to them to show up.

If you like to travel spontaneously, during most of the year you'll have no problem finding *sobe* as you go (late July and August are the exceptions). Locals hawking rooms meet each arriving boat, bus, and train. The quality can be hit or miss, but many of these are good options. In fact, I've found some of my favorite *sobe* in this book this way. The person generally shows photos of her place, you haggle for a price, then she escorts you to your new home. Be sure you understand exactly where it's located (i.e., within easy walking distance of the attractions) before you accept. Because Europeans tend to dramatically lowball walking estimates, ask to see the location on a map.

Finding Private Accommodations: Websites such as Airbnb, FlipKey, Booking.com, and the HomeAway family of sites (HomeAway, VRBO, and VacationRentals) let you browse a wide range of properties. Many of my handpicked recommendations also rent their rooms on one or more of these sites. Because of the quirky nature of Croatian accommodations, similar places may be shuffled, somewhat arbitrarily, between multiple classifications ("Hotels," "B&Bs and Inns," "Specialty Lodging," and "Vacation Rentals")—making it difficult to compare apples to apples.

While these sites are a useful resource for finding a bed, they lack the personal vetting you'll enjoy at the places I recommend in this book. And, at times, I've found even some "top-ranked" places on TripAdvisor or Booking.com to be mysteriously lackluster in person. At the end of the day, it makes sense to use both my advice and these sites in a complementary way to find the best fit for your trip.

As a last resort, you can also keep an eye out for rooms as you walk or drive through town—you'll see blue *sobe* and *apart-mani* signs everywhere. While it takes nerve to just show up without a room, this is standard operating procedure for many backpackers. If you're in a pinch, you can enlist the help of a travel agency on the ground to find you a room—but you'll pay 10-30 percent extra.

Note that *sobe* aren't as common or as good a value in Slovenia as they are in Croatia, but the Slovenes have their own cheap option: tourist farms *(turistične kmetije).* At these working farms, you can get a hotelesque room, plus breakfast and dinner, for a surprisingly low cost. For more on tourist farms, see page 677.

Other Options: Swapping homes with a local works for people with an appealing place to offer and who can live with the idea of having strangers in their home (don't assume where you live is not interesting to Europeans). A good place to start is HomeExchange. To sleep for free, Couchsurfing.com is a vagabond's alternative to Airbnb. It lists millions of outgoing members who host fellow "surfers" in their homes.

Hotels

For most travelers, Croatian hotels are a bad value—they tend to be big, impersonal, and overpriced. While most hotels have been renovated, they still carry on the old Yugoslav aesthetic of mass tourism. That means crowded "beach" access (often on a concrete pad), less-than-enthusiastic staff, a travel-agency desk selling excursions

PRACTICALITIES

in the lobby, corny live music in the lounge a few nights each week, and a seaview apéritif bar. More money buys you a friendlier, more polished staff and newer decor.

The hotel situation is more straightforward in Slovenia and Bosnia, which have a wider range of small, reasonably priced hotels. While you will find a few communist-era holdover hotels in resorty parts of these countries, they don't dominate the scene as they do in Croatia.

Some hotels can add an extra bed (for a small charge) to turn a double into a triple; some offer larger rooms for four or more people (I call these "family rooms" in the listings). If there's space for an extra cot, they'll cram it in for you. In general, a triple room is cheaper than the cost of a double and a single. Three or four people can economize by requesting one big room.

Arrival and Check-In: Hotel elevators are common, though some older buildings still lack them. You may have to climb a flight of stairs to reach the elevator (if so, you can ask the front desk for help carrying your bags up). Elevators can be very small—you may need to send your bags up without you.

The EU requires that hotels collect your name, nationality, and ID number. When you check in, the receptionist will normally ask for your passport and may keep it for anywhere from a couple of minutes to a couple of hours. If you're not comfortable leaving your passport at the desk for a long time, ask when you can pick it up. Or, if you packed a color copy of your passport, you can generally leave that rather than the original.

If you're arriving in the morning, your room probably won't be ready. Check your bag safely at the hotel and dive right into sightseeing.

In Your Room: In private accommodations and some hotels, towels aren't replaced. The cord that dangles over the tub or shower in big resort hotels is not a clothesline—you pull it if you've fallen and can't get up. More pillows and blankets are usually in the closet or available on request.

Checking Out: While it's customary to pay for your room upon departure, it can be a good idea to settle your bill the day before, when you're not in a hurry and while the manager's in.

Hotelier Help: Hoteliers and *soba* hosts can be a great help and source of advice. Most know their city well, and can assist you with everything from public transit and airport connections to finding a good restaurant, the nearest launderette, or a late-night pharmacy. English works in all but the cheapest places. Many of my recommended hoteliers (as well as local guides and business owners) love interacting with my readers. But lengthy email exchanges can be exhausting and time-consuming. When corresponding with these

Keep Cool

If you're visiting Croatia and Slovenia in the summer, you'll want an air-conditioned room. Most hotel air-conditioners come with a control stick that generally has similar symbols and features: fan icon (click to toggle through wind power, from light to gale); temperature control (20 degrees Celsius is comfortable); louver icon (choose steady airflow or waves); snowflake and sunshine icons (cold air or heat, depending on season); and clock ("O" setting: run X hours before turning off; "I" setting: wait X hours to start). When you leave your room for the day, turning off the air-conditioning is good form.

people, try to keep major trip-planning questions and follow-ups to a minimum. Be careful not to take advantage of their good nature.

Hotel Hassles: Even at the best places, mechanical break-downs occur: Sinks leak, hot water turns cold, toilets may gurgle or smell, the Wi-Fi goes out, or the air-conditioning dies when you need it most. Report your concerns clearly and calmly.

If you find that night noise is a problem (if, for instance, your room is over a nightclub or facing a busy street), ask for a quieter room in the back or on an upper floor. To guard against theft in your room, keep valuables out of sight. Some rooms come with a safe, and other hotels have safes at the front desk. I've never bothered using one and in a lifetime of travel, I've never had anything stolen from my room.

For more complicated problems, don't expect instant results. Above all, keep a positive attitude. Remember, you're on vacation. If your hotel is a disappointment, spend more time out enjoying the place you came to see.

Hostels

A hostel provides cheap dorm beds where you sleep alongside strangers for about $25-35 per night. Travelers of any age are welcome if they don't mind dorm-style accommodations and meeting other travelers. Most hostels offer kitchen facilities, guest computers, Wi-Fi, and a self-service laundry. Hostels almost always provide bedding, but the towel's up to you (though you can usually rent one for a small fee). Family and private rooms are often available.

Hostels are a relatively new concept in Croatia. Official Hostelling International (IYHF) hostels are usually poorly located and institutional, while independent hostels are loosely run, tend to attract a youthful party crowd, and are grungier than the European norm. If you need a cheap bed and aren't into the party scene, you'll probably do better for only a little more money by sleeping in basic private accommodations (rooms in private homes with shared bathrooms, described earlier).

Slovenia has a more appealing range of hostels. For example, one of Europe's most innovative hostels is Ljubljana's Celica, a renovated former prison (see page 585).

In each town, I've tried to list the best-established, most reputable hostel options, both independent and official. But this scene is evolving so fast that avid hostelers will do better getting tips from fellow travelers and searching sites such as www.hostels.com, www.hostelworld.com, and www.hostelz.com.

At any hostel, cheap meals are sometimes available, and kitchen facilities are usually provided for do-it-yourselfers. Expect crowds in the summer, snoring, and lots of noisy backpacker bonding in the common room while you're trying to sleep. Hosteling is ideal for those traveling solo: Prices are per bed, not per room, and you'll have an instant circle of friends. At most hostels, you can reserve online or by phoning ahead (usually with a credit card).

Eating

For listings in this guidebook, I look for restaurants that are convenient to your hotel and sightseeing. In Croatia and Slovenia, restaurants offer good food for reasonable prices—especially if you get off the main tourist trail. When restaurant-hunting, choose a spot filled with locals, not the place with the big neon signs boasting, "We Speak English and Accept Credit Cards." Venturing even a block or two off the main drag leads to higher-quality food for a better price.

RESTAURANT PRICING

I've categorized my recommended eateries based on the average price of a typical main course, indicated with a dollar-sign rating (see sidebar). Obviously, expensive specialties, fine wine, appetizers, and dessert can significantly increase your final bill.

The categories also indicate the personality of a place: **Budget** eateries include street food, takeaway, order-at-the-counter shops, basic cafeterias, and bakeries selling sandwiches. **Moderate** eateries are nice (but not fancy) sit-down restaurants, ideal for a straightforward, fill-the-tank meal. Most of my listings fall in this category—great for getting a good taste of the local cuisine at a reasonable price.

PRACTICALITIES

Restaurant Code

Eateries in this book are categorized according to the average cost of a typical main course. Drinks, desserts, and splurge items can raise the price considerably.

 $$$$ **Splurge:** Most main courses over €17 (125 kn)
  $$$ **Pricier:** €13-17 (100-125 kn)
   $$ **Moderate:** €10-13 (75-100 kn)
    $ **Budget:** Under €10 (75 kn)

In Croatia and Slovenia, a takeout spot is **$**; a basic sit-down *konoba* or pizzeria is **$$**; a casual but more upscale restaurant is **$$$**; and a swanky splurge is **$$$$**. In Bosnia, eateries are cheap—almost all are **$**, a few are **$$**, and virtually none are more expensive.

Pricier eateries are a notch up, with more attention paid to the setting, presentation, and (often inventive) cuisine. **Splurge** eateries are dress-up-for-a-special-occasion swanky—typically with an elegant setting, polished service, and pricey and intricate cuisine.

While not quite high cuisine, the food of this region is surprisingly diverse. Choosing between strudel and baklava on the same menu, you're constantly reminded that this is a land where East meets West. I've listed the specific specialties in the introduction to each country in this book, but throughout Croatia and Slovenia you'll sink your teeth into lots of tasty Italian-style food (pizzas and pastas), as well as seafood and impressive, underrated local wines. You'll also find some pan-Balkan elements such as grilled meats and phyllo dough, which distinguish the cuisine throughout the former Yugoslavia (see the "Balkan Flavors" sidebar on page 425).

At fish restaurants, seafood is often priced by weight—either by kilogram (just over two pounds) or by hectogram (about 3.5 ounces). A one-kilogram portion feeds two hungry people or three light eaters. For tips on ordering seafood, see "Croatian Food" on page 28.

While bread, cover, and service charges haven't traditionally been applied in these countries, a few tourist-oriented restaurants have started to pad their bills with these extra fees. If you're concerned about this, ask up front.

When you're in the mood for something halfway between a restaurant and a picnic meal, look for bakeries selling *burek* (the savory phyllo-dough pastry) and other goodies, or shops advertising "pizza cut" (pizza by the slice). Many grocery stores sell premade sandwiches, and others might be willing to make one for you from what's in the deli case.

Tipping: You only need to tip at restaurants that have table service. If you order your food at a counter, don't tip. At restaurants that have a waitstaff, it's common to tip after a good meal by rounding up the bill 5-10 percent. My rule of thumb is to estimate about 10 percent, then round down slightly to reach a convenient total. For a 165-kn meal, I pay 180 kn—a tip of 15 kn, or about 9 percent. That's plenty. A 15 percent tip is overly generous, verging on extravagant. At some tourist-oriented restaurants, a 10 or 15 percent "service charge" may be added to your bill, in which case an additional tip is not necessary.

Staying Connected

One of the most common questions I hear from travelers is, "How can I stay connected in Europe?" The short answer is: more easily and cheaply than you might think.

The simplest solution is to bring your own device—mobile phone, tablet, or laptop—and use it just as you would at home (following the money-saving tips below, such as getting an international plan or connecting to free Wi-Fi whenever possible). Another option is to buy a European SIM card for your US mobile phone. Or you can use European landlines and computers to connect. Each of these options is described next, and more details are at www.ricksteves.com/phoning. For a very practical one-hour talk covering tech issues for travelers, see www.ricksteves.com/mobile-travel-skills.

USING A MOBILE PHONE IN EUROPE
Here are some budget tips and options.

Sign up for an international plan. To stay connected at a lower cost, sign up for an international service plan through your carrier. Most providers offer a simple bundle that includes calling, messaging, and data. Your normal plan may already include international coverage (T-Mobile's does).

Before your trip, call your provider or check online to confirm that your phone will work in Europe, and research your provider's international rates. Activate the plan a day or two before you leave, then remember to cancel it when your trip's over.

Use free Wi-Fi whenever possible. Unless you have an unlimited-data plan, you're best off saving most of your online tasks for Wi-Fi. You can access the internet, send texts, and even make voice calls over Wi-Fi.

Most accommodations in Europe offer free Wi-Fi, but some—especially expensive hotels—charge a fee. Many cafés (including Starbucks and McDonald's) have free hotspots for customers; look for signs offering it and ask for the Wi-Fi password when you buy something. You'll also often find Wi-Fi at TIs, city squares, major

Hurdling the Language Barrier

Croatia and Slovenia have one of the smallest language barriers in Europe. You'll find that most people in the tourist industry—and virtually all young people—speak excellent English. When only a few million people on the planet speak your language, you learn English early and well. (In Croatia, all schoolchildren start learning English in the third grade.) And since TV is subtitled rather than dubbed, people get plenty of exposure to American English. Of course, not *everyone* speaks English. Be reasonable in your expectations, especially when trying to communicate with clerks or service workers. (Throughout the region, German and Italian often work where English fails.)

Even when dealing with an English-speaker, it's polite to know a few words of the local language. "Hello" is *dobar dan* in Croatian, and *dober dan* in Slovene. *Hvala* means "thank you" in both languages. I've listed the essential phrases in each country introduction (Croatian on page 33, and Slovene on page 538).

Croatians and Slovenes pronounce a few letters differently than in English, and they add a few diacritics (little pronunciation markings). Here are a few rules of thumb:

J / j sounds like "y" as in "yellow"
C / c sounds like "ts" as in "bats"
Č / č and **Ć / ć** sound like "ch" as in "chicken"
Š / š sounds like "sh" as in "shrimp"
Ž / ž sounds like "zh" as in "leisure"
Đ / đ (only in Croatian) is like the "dj" sound in "jeans"

Croatian and Slovene are notorious for their seemingly unpronounceable consonant combinations. Most difficult are hv (as in *hvala,* "thank you") and nj (as in Bohinj, a lake in Slovenia). Don't over-pronounce these. In **hv,** the h is nearly silent; to approximate it, simply turn the hv into an f (for *hvala,* just say "FAH-lah"). When you see **nj,** the j has a very slight "y" sound that can be omitted: for Bohinj, just say BOH-heen. Listen to locals and imitate.

A few key words are helpful for navigation: *trg* (pronounced "turg," square), *ulica* (OO-leet-sah, road), *cesta* (TSEH-stah, avenue), *autocesta* (OW-toh-tseh-stah, expressway), *most* (mohst, bridge), *otok* (OH-tohk, island), *trajekt* (TRAH-yehkt, ferry), and *Jadran* (YAH-drahs, Adriatic).

Note that Bosnia and Montenegro each have their own languages, but both are very closely related to Croatian—using virtually all of the same letters and words listed above. English is common in those countries, as well.

Don't be afraid to interact with locals—give it your best shot, and they'll appreciate your efforts.

How to Dial

International Calls

Whether phoning from a US landline or mobile phone, or from a number in another European country, here's how to make an international call. I've used one of my recommended Dubrovnik hotels as an example (tel. 385-20/453-834).

Initial Zero: Drop the initial zero from international phone numbers—except when calling Italy.

Mobile Tip: If using a mobile phone, the "+" sign can replace the international access code (for a "+" sign, press and hold "0").

US/Canada to Europe

Dial 011 (US/Canada international access code), country code (385 for Croatia), and phone number.

▶ To call the Dubrovnik hotel from home, dial 011-385-20/453-834.

Country to Country Within Europe

Dial 00 (Europe international access code), country code, and phone number.

▶ To call the Dubrovnik hotel from Slovenia, dial 00-385-20/453-834.

Europe to the US/Canada

Dial 00, country code (1 for US/Canada), and phone number.

▶ To call from Europe to my office in Edmonds, Washington, dial 00-1-425-771-8303.

Domestic Calls

In Croatia and Slovenia, to call within the same country, (such as from one Croatian landline or mobile phone to another), simply dial the phone number, including the initial 0 if there is one.

▶ To call a recommended Dubrovnik hotel from within Dubrovnik, dial 453-834.

museums, public-transit hubs, airports, and aboard trains and buses.

Minimize the use of your cellular network. The best way to make sure you're not accidentally burning through data is to put your device in "airplane" mode (which also disables phone calls and texts), turn your Wi-Fi back on, and connect to networks as needed. When you need to get online but can't find Wi-Fi, simply turn on your cellular network (or turn off airplane mode) just long enough for the task at hand.

Even with an international-data plan, wait until you're on Wi-Fi to Skype, download apps, stream videos, or do other mega-byte-greedy tasks. Using a navigation app such as Google Maps

PRACTICALITIES

More Dialing Tips

Toll and Toll-Free Numbers: It's generally not possible to dial European toll or toll-free numbers from a US mobile or land-line (although you can sometimes get through using Skype). Look for a direct-dial number instead.

More Phoning Help: See www.howtocallabroad.com.

European Country Codes		Ireland & N. Ireland	353 / 44
Austria	43	Italy	39
Belgium	32	Latvia	371
Bosnia-Herzegovina	387	Montenegro	382
Croatia	385	Morocco	212
Czech Republic	420	Netherlands	31
Denmark	45	Norway	47
Estonia	372	Poland	48
Finland	358	Portugal	351
France	33	Russia	7
Germany	49	Slovakia	421
Gibraltar	350	Slovenia	386
Great Britain	44	Spain	34
Greece	30	Sweden	46
Hungary	36	Switzerland	41
Iceland	354	Turkey	90

over a cellular network can take lots of data, so do this sparingly or offline.

Limit automatic updates. By default, your device constantly checks for a data connection and updates apps. It's smart to disable these features so your apps will only update when you're on Wi-Fi. Also change your device's email settings from "auto-retrieve" to "manual" (or from "push" to "fetch").

Use Wi-Fi calling and messaging apps. Skype, WhatsApp, FaceTime, and Google Hangouts are great for making free or low-cost calls or sending texts over Wi-Fi worldwide. Just log on to a Wi-Fi network, then connect with any of your friends or family members who use the same service. If you buy credit in advance,

PRACTICALITIES

Tips on Internet Security

Make sure that your device is running the latest versions of its operating system, security software, and apps. Next, ensure that your device and key programs (like email) are password-protected. On the road, use only secure, password-protected Wi-Fi hotspots. Ask the hotel or café staff for the specific name of their Wi-Fi network, and make sure you log on to that exact one.

If you must access your financial info online, use a banking app rather than accessing your account via a browser. A cellular connection is more secure than Wi-Fi. Avoid logging onto personal-finance sites on a public computer.

Never share your credit-card number (or any other sensitive information) online unless you know that the site is secure. A secure site displays a little padlock icon, and the URL begins with *https* (instead of the usual *http*).

with some of these services you can call or text anywhere for just pennies.

Some apps, such as Apple's iMessage, will use the cellular network for texts if Wi-Fi isn't available: To avoid this possibility, turn off the "Send as SMS" feature.

Buy a European SIM card. If you anticipate making a lot of local calls or need a local phone number, or your provider's international-data rates are expensive, consider buying a SIM card in Europe to replace the one in your (unlocked) US phone or tablet.

SIM cards are sold at department-store electronics counters, some newsstands, and vending machines. If you need help setting it up, buy one at a mobile-phone shop (you may need to show your passport).

There are no roaming charges when using a European SIM card in other EU countries, though to be sure you get this "roam-like-at-home" pricing, buy your SIM card at a mobile-phone shop and ask if this feature is included. Be aware that Bosnia and Montenegro are not in the EU, so roaming charges could be much higher.

WITHOUT A MOBILE PHONE

It's less convenient but possible to travel in Europe without a mobile device. You can make calls from your hotel and check email or get online using public computers.

Most **hotels** charge a fee for placing calls—ask for rates before you dial. You can use a prepaid international phone card (relatively rare in Croatia and Slovenia; usually available at newsstands, tobacco shops, and train stations) to call out from your hotel. Dial the toll-free access number, enter the card's PIN code, then dial the number.

You'll only see **public pay phones** in a few post offices and train stations. Most don't take coins but instead require insertable phone cards, which you can buy at a newsstand, convenience store, or post office. Except for emergencies, they're not worth the hassle.

Some hotels have **public computers** in their lobbies for guests to use; otherwise you may find them at public libraries (ask your hotelier or the TI for the nearest location). On a European keyboard, use the "Alt Gr" key to the right of the space bar to insert the extra symbol that appears on some keys. If you can't locate a special character (such as @), simply copy and paste it from a web page.

MAIL

You can mail one package per day to yourself worth up to $200 duty-free from Europe to the US (mark it "personal purchases"). If you're sending a gift to someone, mark it "unsolicited gift." For details, visit www.cbp.gov, select "Travel," and search for "Know Before You Visit." The Croatian and Slovenian postal services work fine, but for quick transatlantic delivery (in either direction), consider services such as DHL (www.dhl.com).

Transportation

Figuring out how to get around in Croatia and Slovenia is one of your biggest trip decisions. **Cars** work well for two or more traveling together (especially families with small kids), those packing heavy, and those delving into the countryside. **Trains, buses,** and **boats** are best for solo travelers, blitz tourists, city-to-city travelers, and those who want to leave the driving to others. Smart travelers can use short-hop **flights** within Europe to creatively connect the dots on their itineraries (especially to skip the long overland journeys between places like Dubrovnik, Sarajevo, and Zagreb). Just be aware of the potential downside of each option: A car is an expensive headache in any major city; with trains and buses you're at the mercy of a timetable; and flying entails a trek to and from a usually distant airport.

Cars are a worthless headache in places like Ljubljana and Dubrovnik. But in some parts of Croatia and Slovenia, a car is helpful, if not essential: Istria (especially the hill towns), the Julian Alps, Logarska Dolina, the Karst, and Montenegro's Bay of Kotor. A trip into Mostar (and on to Sarajevo) is best by car—allowing you to stop off at interesting places en route—but doable by public transportation. In other areas, a car is unnecessary: Ljubljana, Zagreb, and most of the Dalmatian Coast (Dubrovnik, Split, Hvar, and Korčula). For most trips, the best plan is a combination: Use pub-

PRACTICALITIES

Public Transportation Routes in Croatia and Slovenia

lic transportation in some areas, then strategically rent a car for a day or two in a region that merits it. (I've noted which areas are best by car, and offered route tips and arrival instructions in most chapters.)

PUBLIC TRANSPORTATION

Throughout this book, I've suggested whether trains, buses, or boats are better for a particular destination (in the "Connections" section at the end of each chapter). When checking timetables *(vozni red)*, arrivals are *prihodi* and departures are *odhodi* in Slovenian. (In Croatian, arrivals are *dolasci* and departures are *polasci*.) *Svaki dan* means "daily," but some transit doesn't run on Sundays *(nedjeljom)* or holidays *(praznikom)*. You'll notice that many posted schedules list departure times, but not the duration of the trip; try asking for this information at the ticket window.

Trains

Trains are ideal for certain routes in Croatia and Slovenia (such as between Ljubljana and Zagreb) and for connecting to some other countries. But their usefulness is limited, and you'll find buses, boats, and flights better for most journeys.

Schedules and Tickets: Pick up train schedules from stations as you go. To study ahead on the Web, check www.bahn.com (Germany's excellent Europe-wide timetable). You can also check www.slo-zeleznice.si for Slovenia, and www.hzpp.hr for Croatia. Buy tickets at the train station (or on board, if the station is unattended)—you rarely need a reservation.

Rail Passes: While rail passes can be a good deal in some parts of Europe, they usually aren't as useful in Croatia or Slovenia. Point-to-point tickets are affordable and often the better option. Each country has its own Eurail pass, covering 3 to 8 days of travel within a month, or is covered by the Eurail Global Pass for most of Europe. Again, none of these passes is likely to save you much money, but if a pass matches your itinerary, give it a look and crunch the numbers. For options and prices on pertinent Eurail passes, see www.ricksteves.com/rail.

Buses

Buses often take you where trains don't. For example, train tracks run only as far south as Split; for destinations on the Dalmatian Coast farther south, you'll rely on buses (or boats). Even on some routes that are served by trains, buses can be a better option. For instance, Ljubljana and Lake Bled are connected by both train and bus—but the bus station is right in the town center of Bled, while the train station is a few miles away. Buses can even be convenient for connecting to islands (via ferry, of course). For example, if heading from the island of Korčula to Dubrovnik, the bus connection runs more frequently than the comparable boat connection, and takes about the same amount of time.

Confusingly, a single bus route can be operated by a variety of different companies, making it difficult to find comprehensive schedules. Your first stop is www.getbybus.com, which includes many (but not necessarily all) bus connections in Croatia, and many in neighboring countries, and lets you book tickets online (for a small fee). In addition, these online-timetable sites are helpful: www.autobusni-kolodvor.com for Croatia and www.ap-ljubljana.si for Slovenia. And a separate company, called Flixbus, runs additional buses in some areas—especially connecting Slovenia and northern Croatia to international destinations—that won't show up on any other site (www.flixbus.com). For smaller towns, the TI can also help you sort through your options.

Get creative with checking schedules: If you're going from a small town to Split, and that town doesn't have its own online timetable, try checking the "arrivals" schedules on the Split website (www.ak-split.hr). If your trip involves a connection at an intermediate station, don't be surprised if it's difficult to get the schedule details for your onward journey. Be patient, and try calling that town's TI (or the TI or bus station at your final destination) for details.

Prices vary slightly among companies, even for identical journeys. For popular routes during peak season, either book ahead online or drop by the station to buy your ticket a few hours in advance—or even the day before—to ensure getting a seat (ask the bus station ticket office or the local TI how far ahead you should arrive). Buses have some overhead bag storage on board, but you'll likely check your big bag under the bus (for the extra cost of about $2 per bag).

If you're headed south along the coast, sitting on the right side comes with substantially better scenery (sit on the left for northbound buses). When choosing a seat, also take the direction of the sun into consideration.

Bus routes that cross borders can be subject to significant delays during peak times. The most notable example is Neum—a short stretch of Bosnia that sits between Dubrovnik in the south and Mostar or Split in the north. If traveling on a summer weekend, don't expect the estimated trip durations to be exactly right (or

PRACTICALITIES

ask around for advice about which departures might be less affected by border lines).

Shared Transfers

As an alternative to buses in Slovenia and northern Croatia, consider the Ljubljana-based **GoOpti** shared transfer service. You'll sign up on their website for an intercity transfer, and they'll try to find other travelers with similar plans, then tell you the time of departure. You'll all load into the same van and split the cost (and carbon footprint) of the ride. It's affordable, efficient, and very convenient (www.goopti.com; for all of the details, see page 600).

Boats

All along the Croatian coast, slow car ferries and speedy catamarans inexpensively shuttle tourists between major coastal cities and quiet island towns. Boats run often in summer (June-Sept), but frequency drops sharply off-season.

A **ferry** *(trajekt)* takes both passengers and cars; while pokey, it can run in almost any weather. The number of cars is limited, but there's virtually unlimited deck space for walk-on passengers. Watching the ferry crew scurrying around to load and unload cars and trucks onto their boat—especially if it's a small one—is a ▲▲▲ Croatian experience.

Popular tourist destinations in Croatia are increasingly more connected by much faster, passenger-only **catamarans.** These are efficient, but they have to slow down (or sometimes can't run at all) in bad weather. Catamarans are smaller, with limited seats, so they tend to sell out quickly. Because of the high speeds, you'll generally have to stay inside the boat while en route, rather than being outside on the deck.

If you're island-hopping in Dalmatia, you'll choose between boats operated by three companies. Most of Croatia's boats—big and small—are operated by the state-run company called **Jadrolinija** (yah-droh-LEE-nee-yah, www.jadrolinija.hr, tel. 051/666-111). Jadrolinija has a virtual monopoly on the big car-ferry routes, and also runs some handy high-speed cata-marans. Two other privately run catamarans—which often have more tourist-friendly schedules than Jadrolinija—are **Krilo** (www.krilo.hr) and **Nona Ana** (www.gv-line.hr). Because schedules can change dramatically from season to season, and no single website can show you all of your options, carefully review each of these three sites when making your island-hopping plans. Local TIs are the best source of information for how their town is connected to the rest of the coast.

You'll be competing with lots of other travelers for a few precious seats on the most convenient catamarans. It's possible to book tickets on each of these companies' websites. Ideally book at least a day or two ahead—or even earlier for popular routes in peak times. (Jadrolinija only lets you book online up until the day before; if you wait until the day of, you have to go in person to the ticket office.)

Because all boats have open seating, it's smart to show up 30-60 minutes before departure time to get a good seat. Advance reservations are not necessary for walk-on passengers on car ferries; you can almost always find a seat on the deck or in the onboard café.

Boat rides are cheap for foot passengers. A short hop, such as from Split to the island of Hvar or Korčula, costs around $10-20 on a catamaran or a ferry. For a longer trip, such as from Split to Dubrovnik, figure $30.

Drivers cannot reserve a car space in advance on most routes (though Jadrolinija may be adding this feature soon—check their

website). This means that drivers will want to arrive at the dock up to a few hours early, especially in peak season. Because volumes flex with the season, the local TI is your best resource for advice on how early to get in line. Notice that on some islands, the car-ferry port is a long drive from the main tourist town (for example, Vela Luka on Korčula Island is a 1-hour drive from Korčula town; Stari Grad on Hvar Island is a 20-minute drive from Hvar town).

You can buy overpriced, low-quality food and drinks on board most boats. Bring your own snacks or a picnic instead.

TAXIS AND RIDE-BOOKING SERVICES

Most European taxis are reliable and cheap. In many cities, two people can travel short distances by cab for little more than the cost of bus or subway tickets. If you like ride-booking services such as Uber, their apps usually work in Croatia just like they do in the US: Request a car on your mobile phone (connected to Wi-Fi or data), and the fare is automatically charged to your credit card. Uber is not active in Slovenia.

RENTING A CAR

It's cheaper to arrange most car rentals from the US, so research and compare rates before you go. Most of the major US rental agencies (including Avis, Budget, Enterprise, Hertz, and Thrifty) have offices throughout Europe. Also consider the two major Europe-based agencies, Europcar and Sixt. Consolidators such as Auto Europe (www.autoeurope.com—or the sometimes cheaper www.autoeurope.eu) compare rates at several companies to get you the best deal.

In this region, I prefer to connect long distances by train or bus, then rent cars for a day or two where they're most useful. But be aware that some companies have a minimum rental period (generally three days); you can keep the car for a shorter time, but you'll pay for the minimum period anyway. If you want the car for just a day or two, try to find a company that allows short rentals.

Wherever you book, always read the fine print. Check for add-on charges—such as one-way drop-off fees, airport surcharges, or mandatory insurance policies—that aren't included in the "total price."

Rental Costs and Considerations

Figure on paying roughly $250 for a one-week rental for a basic compact car. Allow extra for supplemental insurance, fuel, tolls, and parking. To save money on fuel, request a diesel car.

Manual vs. Automatic: Almost all rental cars in Europe are manual by default—and cars with a stick shift are generally cheaper. If you need an automatic, request one in advance. When selecting a car, don't be tempted by a larger model, as it won't be as maneuverable on narrow, winding roads or when squeezing into tight parking lots.

Age Restrictions: Some rental companies impose minimum and maximum age limits. Young drivers (25 and under) and seniors (69 and up) should check the rental policies and rules section of car-rental websites.

Choosing Pick-up/Drop-off Locations: Always check the hours of the locations you choose: Many rental offices close from midday Saturday until Monday morning and, in smaller towns, at lunchtime.

When selecting an office, plug the address into a mapping website to confirm the location. A downtown site is generally cheaper—and might seem more convenient than the airport. But pedestrianized and one-way streets can make navigation tricky when returning a car at a big-city office or urban train station. Wherever you select, get precise details on the location and allow ample time to find it.

Have the Right License: If you're renting a car, bring your driver's license. In Slovenia, Croatia, and Bosnia, you're also technically required to have an International Driving Permit—an official translation of your license (sold at AAA offices for about $20 plus the cost of two passport-type photos; see www.aaa.com). While that's the letter of the law, I generally rent cars without having this permit. How this is enforced varies from country to country: Get advice from your car-rental company.

Crossing Borders in a Rental Car: Be warned that international trips—say, picking up in Ljubljana and dropping in Dubrovnik—while efficient, can be expensive (see the "Rental-Car Conundrum" sidebar for ways around this).

Always tell your car-rental company up front exactly which countries you'll be entering. Some companies levy extra insurance fees for trips taken in certain countries with certain cars (such as BMWs, Mercedes, and convertibles). Or the company may prohibit driving the car in off-the-beaten-track destinations, such as Bosnia-Herzegovina. As you cross borders, you may need to show the proper paperwork, such as proof of insurance (called a "green card"). Double-check with your rental agent that you have all the documentation you need before you drive off.

Picking Up Your Car: Before driving off in your rental car, check it thoroughly and make sure any damage is noted on your rental agreement. Rental agencies in Europe tend to charge for even minor damage, so be sure to mark everything. Find out how your car's gearshift, lights, turn signals, wipers, radio, and fuel cap function, and know what kind of fuel the car takes (diesel vs. unleaded). When you return the car, make sure the agent verifies its condition with you. Some drivers take pictures of the returned vehicle as proof of its condition.

Car Insurance Options

When you rent a car in Europe, the price typically includes liability insurance, which covers harm to other cars or motorists—but not the rental car itself. To limit your financial risk in case of damage to the rental, choose one of these options: Buy a Collision Damage Waiver (CDW) coverage with a low or zero deductible from the car-rental company (roughly 30-40 percent extra), get coverage through your credit card (free, but more complicated), or get collision insurance as part of a larger travel-insurance policy.

Basic **CDW** costs $15-30 a day and typically comes with a

The Rental-Car Conundrum

Virtually everyone planning a trip by car to this region runs into the same problem: International drop-off fees for rental cars are astronomical (usually several hundred dollars). Generally there's no extra charge for picking up and dropping off a car in different towns within the same country (for example, the long 9-hour drive between Zagreb and Dubrovnik), but you'll pay through the nose to drop off across the border (including the quick 2-hour drive from Zagreb to Ljubljana). This is especially frustrating when connecting some car-friendly parts of southern Slovenia (such as the Karst) with similar areas in nearby northern Croatia (such as Istria or Plitvice Lakes National Park).

First, compare rates at various rental companies to see if one happens to offer a lower drop-off charge. In recent years, Sixt has allowed you drop off internationally for only around $100 extra (www.sixt.com). But if there's no way around the high fee, think creatively to avoid this huge and unnecessary expense.

Let's say you want to pick up a car in Ljubljana, drive through Slovenia's Karst to Istria, then continue to Split and drop your car...but the drop-off fee is $400. Here are two possible alternatives: First, you could do a circuit around the sights of southern Slovenia, then head back up to Ljubljana (fast and easy, thanks to the short distances and speedy expressways), drop your Slovenian car there, and take public transit to northern Croatia (such as the bus to Rovinj, or the train to Zagreb, Rijeka, or Pula). After sightseeing there, you could pick up a second car for your Croatian driving (for example, take the bus from Rovinj—which doesn't generally have handy car-rental offices—to a nearby city that does, such as Pula or Poreč). Another option is to begin your trip in Croatia, pick up your rental car there, then loop up into Slovenia with the Croatian car before returning to Croatia.

There's no doubt that these solutions add some hassle to your itinerary, but they could save you hundreds of dollars.

$1,000-2,000 deductible, reducing but not eliminating your financial responsibility. When you reserve or pick up the car, you'll be offered the chance to "buy down" the basic deductible to zero (for an additional $10-30/day; this is sometimes called "super CDW" or "zero-deductible coverage").

If you opt for **credit-card coverage,** you must decline all coverage offered by the car-rental company—which means they can place a hold on your card for up to the full value of the car. In case of damage, it can be time-consuming to resolve the charges. Before relying on this option, quiz your credit-card company about how it works.

If you're already purchasing a **travel-insurance policy** for your trip, adding collision coverage can be an economical option. For example, Travel Guard (www.travelguard.com) sells affordable renter's collision insurance as an add-on to its other policies; it's valid everywhere in Europe except the Republic of Ireland, and some Italian car-rental companies refuse to honor it, as it doesn't cover you in case of theft.

For more on car-rental insurance, see www.ricksteves.com/cdw.

Navigation Options

If you'll be navigating using your phone or a GPS unit from home, remember to bring a car charger and device mount.

Your Mobile Phone: The mapping app on your phone works fine for navigating Europe's roads, but for real-time turn-by-turn directions and traffic updates, you'll need mobile-data access. And driving all day can burn through a lot of very expensive data. The economical workaround is to use map apps that work offline. By downloading in advance from Google Maps, City Maps 2Go, Apple Maps, Here WeGo, or Navmii, you can still have turn-by-turn voice directions and maps that recalibrate even though they're offline.

You must download your maps before you go offline—and it's smart to select large regions. Then turn off your data connection so you're not charged for roaming. Call up the map, enter your destination, and you're on your way. Even if you don't have to pay extra for data roaming, this option is great for navigating in areas with poor connectivity.

GPS Devices: If you want the convenience of a dedicated GPS unit, consider renting one with your car ($10-30/day). These units offer real-time turn-by-turn directions and traffic without the data requirements of an app. The unit may come loaded only with maps for its home country; if you need additional maps, ask. Also make sure your device's language is set to English before you drive off.

A less-expensive option is to bring a GPS device from home. Be sure to buy and install the maps you'll need before your trip.

Paper Maps and Atlases: Even when navigating primarily with a mobile app or GPS, I always make it a point to have a paper map, ideally a big, detailed regional road map. It's invaluable for getting the big picture, understanding alternate routes, and filling in if my phone runs out of juice. The free maps you get from your car-rental company usually don't have enough detail. It's smart to buy a better map before you go, or pick one up at a local gas station, bookshop, newsstand, or tourist shop.

Driving in Croatia and Slovenia

To Salzburg · 145m · 2.5h

To Vienna · 250m · 4h

To Vienna · 260m · 4.5h

300m · 6h

AUSTRIA

Ptuj

35m · 1h   Velenje

Logarska Dolina   45m · 1.25h   20m · 5h   55m · 1h

Bled   Ljubljana   40m · 75h   Šentrupert exit

Kobarid   60m · 2.5h

30m · 1h

70m · 2h   90m · 2h   220m · 5h

ITALY   70m · 1.75h   SLOVENIA   Zagreb

155m · 3h   50m · 1h   100m · 2h

To Venice   125m · 3h   Škocjan Caves   75m 2h   165m · 3h (via expressway)

35m · 1h   140m · 4h

Piran   85m · 2h

25m 1h   45m · 1.25h   110m · 2.5h (via expressway)

Motovun   40m 1.25h   Rijeka/Opatija

45m 1.5h   45m · 1.5h   85m · 1.75h

30m 1h

Rovinj   55m · 1.5h   65m · 2.5h   Plitvice Lakes Nat'l Park

30m .75h   Pula   Rab (town)

Senj

110m · 3h

Adriatic   Zadar   100m · 2h (via expressway)

CROATIA

Sea

ITALY

m = miles
h = hours
······ = car ferry

Note: Your times may vary based on traffic, construction, and road conditions.

DRIVING

Drivers should be prepared for twisty seaside and mountain roads, wonderful views, and plenty of tempting stopovers.

Road Rules: Seat belts are required, and two beers under those belts are enough to land you in jail. Be aware of typical European road rules; for example, many countries—including all those in this book—require headlights to be turned on at all times, and nearly all forbid handheld mobile-phone use. In Europe, you're not allowed to turn right on a red light, unless a sign or signal specifically authorizes it, and on expressways it's illegal to

pass drivers on the right. Ask your car-rental company about these rules or check the "International Travel" section of the US State Department website (www.travel.state.gov, search for your country in the "Learn About Your Destination" box, then click "Travel and Transportation").

Fuel: Gas is expensive—often about $5 per gallon. Diesel cars are more common in Europe than back home, so be sure you know what type of fuel your car takes before you fill up (diesel is *dizel* in both languages). Fuel pumps are color-coded for unleaded gasoline (green) or diesel (black).

Tolls: Croatia and Slovenia are crisscrossed by an impressive network of expressways (*autocesta* in Croatian, *avtocesta* in Slovene). I don't call them "freeways" because they're not—you'll pay to use them.

In Croatia, you'll pay about 0.50 kunas per kilometer—so a 100-kilometer trip (60 miles), which lasts about an hour, costs 50 kunas (about $8). You'll take a toll-ticket when you enter the expressway, then submit it when you get off (but don't lose your ticket, or you'll pay the maximum).

Slovenia has done away with its tollbooth system. Instead, drivers who use Slovenia's expressways are required to buy a toll sticker, called a vignette (Slovene: *vinjeta,* veen-YEH-tah; €15/week, €30/month). Vignettes are sold at gas stations, post offices, and some newsstands. Your rental car might already come with one—ask. A few of my readers have reported waiting too long to buy one, and getting slapped with a €150 fine, plus €15 for the sticker. If you're coming into Slovenia on an expressway, watch for *vinjeta* signs at gas stations as you approach the border, and purchase the sticker before you cross.

Bosnia-Herzegovina and Montenegro don't levy tolls—in fact, they don't even have expressways.

Road Conditions: Croatian, Slovenian, and even Bosnian roads are extremely well-engineered and typically in excellent repair. (The less said about Montenegrin roads, the better.) Croatia is still working on finishing its speedy A-1 expressway from Zagreb all the way south to Dubrovnik; currently it ends about 70 miles south of Split, where you'll have to transfer to the winding coastal road. For the latest on new expressways in Croatia, see www.hac.hr and www.hak.hr; for Slovenia, see www.dars.si. Secondary roads can be very twisty—especially along the coast or through the mountains. If you get way off the beaten track, you might find gravel. Locals poetically describe these as "white roads." (Get it? No asphalt.) Keep a close eye out for bikers. You'll see scads of them on mountain roads, struggling to earn a thrilling downhill run.

Maps and Signage: A good map is essential. While most roads are numbered, the numbers rarely appear on signs. Instead, do as the Croatians and Slovenes do, and navigate by town name—at every major intersection, directional signs point to nearby towns and cities. The color of the sign tells you what type of road you're approaching: yellow is a normal road, while blue (in Croatia) or green (in Slovenia) indicates that the route is via expressway. Brown indicates a cultural or natural attraction (such as a castle or a cave). On expressways, each tunnel and bridge is identified and labeled with its length in meters. Learn the universal road signs. As you approach any town, follow the *Centar* signs (usually also signed with a bull's-eye symbol).

STOP · **AND LEARN THESE ROAD SIGNS**

Speed Limit (km/hr) · Yield · No Passing · End of No Passing Zone

One Way · Intersection · Main Road · Expressway

Danger · No Entry · Cars Prohibited · All Vehicles Prohibited

No Through Road · Restrictions No Longer Apply · Yield to Oncoming Traffic · No Stopping

Parking · No Parking · Customs or Toll Road · Peace

Bosnian Detour: If you'll be driving along the Dalmatian Coast, notice that between Split and Dubrovnik, you'll actually pass through Bosnia-Herzegovina for a few miles (through the town of Neum). Don't stress about this international detour—it lasts about 20 minutes, and the borders are a breezy formality (you may need to show your passport, and it's usually pretty quick, but it can get backed up on very busy days; for details, see page 360).

Parking: Get parking advice from your hotel, or look for the blue-and-white *P* signs. Street parking marked with blue lines must be paid for (look for pay-and-display parking meters, or ask at a nearby newsstand if you can pay for parking there). Parking is a costly headache in big cities. You'll pay about $15-25 a day to park safely. Rental-car theft can happen in cities, so ask at your hotel for advice. Many coastal towns—such as Rovinj and Piran—are off-limits to cars...unless you're sleeping in the city center, in which case you may be granted permission to drive in just long enough to drop off your bags, then return to the parking lot outside of town. Ask your hotelier about this in advance.

FLIGHTS

Croatia is a little country with long distances (for example, it's at least a seven-hour drive from Zagreb to Dubrovnik), so flying can save you a lot of time. Flying also makes sense if you're going to Sarajevo, which is relatively far from other destinations in this book, but easily connected to Zagreb by two daily flights on Croatia Airlines.

Croatia's national carrier, **Croatia Airlines** (www. croatiaairlines.com), offers both domestic flights and flights to most major European capitals. Many of these seats are sold at discounted promotional rates—provided you book far enough ahead.

To compare flight costs and times, begin with an online travel search engine: Kayak is the top site for flights to and within Europe, easy-to-use Google Flights has price alerts, and Skyscanner includes many inexpensive flights within Europe.

Flights to Europe: Start looking for international flights about four to six months before your trip, especially for peak-season travel. Depending on your itinerary, it can be efficient and no more expensive to fly into one city and out of another. If your flight requires a connection in Europe, see our hints on navigating Europe's top hub airports at www.ricksteves.com/hub-airports.

Flights Within Europe: Flying between European cities is surprisingly affordable. Before buying a long-distance train or bus ticket, check the cost of a flight on one of Europe's airlines, whether a major carrier or a no-frills outfit like EasyJet or Ryanair. If you're not sure who flies to your destination, check its airport's website for a list of carriers. Be aware that flying with a discount airline can have drawbacks, such as minimal customer service and time-consuming treks to secondary airports.

Flying to the US and Canada: Because security is extra tight for flights to the US, be sure to give yourself plenty of time at the airport. Charge your electronic devices before you board in case security checks require you to turn them on (see www.tsa.gov for the latest rules).

Resources from Rick Steves

Begin Your Trip at RickSteves.com

My mobile-friendly **website** is *the* place to explore Europe in preparation for your trip. You'll find thousands of fun articles, videos, and radio interviews; a wealth of money-saving tips for planning your dream trip; travel news dispatches; a video library of my travel talks; my travel blog; my latest guidebook updates (www.ricksteves.com/update); and my free Rick Steves Audio Europe app. You can also follow me on Facebook, Instagram, and Twitter.

Our **Travel Forum** is a well-groomed collection of message boards where our travel-savvy community answers questions and shares their personal travel experiences—and our well-traveled staff chime in when they can be helpful (www.ricksteves.com/forums).

Our **online Travel Store** offers travel bags and accessories that I've designed to help you travel smarter and lighter. These include my popular carry-on bags (which I live out of four months a year), money belts, totes, toiletries kits, adapters, guidebooks, and planning maps (www.ricksteves.com/shop).

Our website can also help you find the perfect **rail pass** for your itinerary and your budget, with easy, one-stop shopping for rail passes, seat reservations, and point-to-point tickets (www.ricksteves.com/rail).

Rick Steves' Tours, Guidebooks, TV Shows, and More

Small Group Tours: Want to travel with greater efficiency and less stress? We offer more than 40 itineraries reaching the best destinations in this book...and beyond. Each year about 30,000 travelers join us on about 1,000 Rick Steves bus tours. You'll enjoy great guides and a fun bunch of travel partners (with small groups of 24 to 28 travelers). You'll find European adventures to fit every vacation length. For all the details, and to get our tour catalog, visit www.ricksteves.com/tours or call us at 425/608-4217.

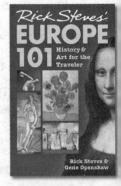

Books: *Rick Steves Croatia & Slovenia* is just one of many books in my series on European travel, which includes country and city guidebooks, Snapshots (excerpted chapters from bigger guides), Pocket guides (full-color little books on big cities), "Best Of" guidebooks (condensed, full-color country guides), and my budget-travel skills handbook, *Rick Steves Europe Through the Back Door.* A complete list of my titles—including phrase books; cruising guides; and travelogues on European art, history, and culture; and more—appears near the end of this book.

TV Shows and Travel Talks: My public television series, *Rick Steves' Europe,* covers Europe from top to bottom with over 100 half-hour episodes—and we're working on new shows every year (watch full episodes at my website for free). My free online video library, Rick Steves Classroom Europe, offers a searchable database of short video clips on European history, culture, and geography (classroom.ricksteves.com). And to raise your travel I.Q., check out the video versions of our popular classes (covering most European countries as well as travel skills, packing smart, cruising, tech for travelers, European art, and travel as a political act—www.ricksteves.com/travel-talks.

Radio: My weekly public radio show, *Travel with Rick Steves,* features interviews with travel experts from around the world. It airs on 400 public radio stations across the US, or you can hear it as a podcast. A complete archive of programs is available at www.ricksteves.com/radio.

Audio Tours on My Free App: I've produced dozens of free, self-guided audio tours of the top sights in Europe. For those tours and other audio content, get my free **Rick Steves Audio Europe app,** an extensive online library organized by destination. For more on my app, see page 11.

APPENDIX

Holidays and Festivals

This list includes selected festivals in this region, plus national holidays. Many sights and banks close on national holidays. As both Croatia and Slovenia are predominantly Catholic, religious holidays—Easter, Ascension Day, Whitsunday, and Whitmonday—are a big deal, and frequent. In the Muslim areas of Bosnia (including Mostar and Sarajevo), locals observe the month of Ramadan. Before planning a trip around a festival, verify its dates by checking the festival's website or contacting the national tourist office in Croatia (http://us.croatia.hr) or Slovenia (www.slovenia.info). Unless stated otherwise, all holidays listed here apply to both Croatia and Slovenia.

Jan 1	New Year's Day
Jan 6	Epiphany
Jan 7	Orthodox Christmas, Bosnia-Herzegovina
Feb	Kurentovanje Carnival, Ptuj, Slovenia (11 days leading up to Ash Wednesday, www.kurentovanje.net)
Feb 8	National Day of Culture, Slovenia (celebrates Slovenian culture and national poet France Prešeren)

March 1	Independence Day, Bosnia-Herzegovina (non-Serbian areas only; closures)
Late March	Ski Flying World Championships, Planica, Slovenia (3 days, www.planica.si)
March/April	Easter and Easter Monday: April 12-13, 2020; April 4-5, 2021
April 27	National Resistance Day, Slovenia
April/May	Orthodox Easter: April 19-20, 2020; May 2-3, 2021; Bosnia-Herzegovina
April/May	Ramadan (Muslim holy month): April 24-May 23, 2020; April 13-May 12, 2021; Bosnia-Herzegovina
May 1	Labor Day, Croatia and Slovenia
May 2	Second Labor Day, Croatia and Slovenia (some closures)
May 9	Victory Day, Bosnia-Herzegovina (Serbian areas only; closures)
May	Ascension: May 21, 2020; May 13, 2021
May/June	Pentecost and Whitmonday: May 31-June 1, 2020; May 23-24, 2021
May/June	Corpus Christi: June 11, 2020; June 3, 2021
Early June	Dance Week Festival, Zagreb, Croatia (www.danceweekfestival.com)
June 22	Antifascist Struggle Day, Croatia
June 25	National Day, Slovenia; Statehood Day, Croatia
Early July	Ultra Europe Music Festival, Split, Croatia (www.ultraeurope.com)
July 10-Aug 25	Dubrovnik Summer Festival, Croatia (www.dubrovnik-festival.hr)
Early July-Sept	Ljubljana Festival, Slovenia (www.ljubljanafestival.si)
Late July	International Folklore Festival, Zagreb, Croatia (5 days, costumes, songs, dances from all over Croatia; www.msf.hr)
Late July	Motovun Film Festival, Istria, Croatia (www.motovunfilmfestival.com)
Aug 5	National Thanksgiving Day, Croatia
Aug 15	Assumption of Mary
Late Aug	Diocletian Days, Split, Croatia (toga-clad celebrations)
October	White Truffle Days, Livade, Croatia (Istrian truffle festival, weekends only)

Oct 8	Independence Day, Croatia
Oct 31	Reformation Day, Slovenia
Nov 1	Day of the Dead/Remembrance Day (religious festival, decorated cemeteries, some closures)
Nov 2	All Souls' Day (religious festival, some closures)
Nov 11	St. Martin's Day (official first day of wine season)
Dec 24-25	Christmas Eve and Christmas Day
Dec 26	Boxing Day/St. Stephen's Day; Independence and Unity Day, Slovenia

Books and Films

To learn about Croatia and Slovenia past and present, check out a few of these books and films.

Books: Lonnie Johnson's *Central Europe: Enemies, Neighbors, Friends* is the best historical overview of Croatia, Slovenia, and their neighboring countries. The most readable history of Croatia itself is Benjamin Curtis' *A Traveller's History of Croatia*. Rebecca West's classic, bricklike *Black Lamb and Grey Falcon* is the definitive travelogue of the Yugoslav lands (written during a journey between the two World Wars). For a more recent take, Croatian journalist Slavenka Drakulić has written a quartet of insightful essay collections from a feminist angle: *Café Europa: Life After Communism; The Balkan Express; How We Survived Communism and Even Laughed;* and *A Guided Tour Through the Museum of Communism*. Drakulić's *They Would Never Hurt a Fly* profiles Yugoslav war criminals. For a thorough explanation of how and why Yugoslavia broke apart, read *Yugoslavia: Death of a Nation* (by Laura Silber and Allan Little). Joe Sacco's powerful graphic novel, *Safe Area Goražde,* describes the author's actual experience living in a mostly Muslim town in Bosnia-Herzegovina while it was surrounded by Serb forces during the wars of the 1990s. Sacco's follow-up, *The Fixer and Other Stories,* focuses on real-life characters he met in siege-time Sarajevo.

Films: To grasp the Yugoslav Wars that shook this region in the early 1990s, there's no better film than the Slovene-produced *No Man's Land,* which won the 2002 Oscar for Best Foreign Film. The BBC produced a remarkable five-hour documentary series called *The Death of Yugoslavia,* featuring actual interviews with all of the key players (it's difficult to find on home video, but try searching for "Death of Yugoslavia" on YouTube; the book *Yugoslavia: Death of a Nation,* noted earlier, was a companion piece to this film). BBC also produced a harrowing documentary about the infamous Bosnian massacre, *Srebrenica: A Cry From the Grave* (also available on YouTube). *In the Land of Blood and Honey*—Angelina

Jolie's intense, difficult-to-watch directorial debut—tells the story of the Bosnian conflict through the eyes of a civilian woman held in a "rape camp." And *The Diplomat* is a documentary about Richard Holbrooke, the American who negotiated the peace to end the Yugoslav Wars.

On a lighter note, a classic from Tito-era Yugoslavia, *The Battle of Neretva* (1969), imported Hollywood talent in the form of Yul Brynner and Orson Welles to tell the story of a pivotal and inspiring battle in the fight against the Nazis. More recent Croatian films worth watching include *Border Post* (*Karaula,* 2006), about various Yugoslav soldiers working together just before the war broke out, and *When Father Was Away on Business* (1985), about a prisoner on the Tito-era gulag island of Goli Otok, near Rab. Other local movies include *Armin* (2007), *How the War Started on My Island* (1996), *Underground* (1995), and *Tito and Me* (1992).

Fans of HBO's *Game of Thrones* may recognize locations in Dubrovnik and other Croatian coastal towns, where much of the series was filmed (for details, see page 286).

Conversions and Climate

Numbers and Stumblers

- Europeans write a few of their numbers differently than we do. 1 = 1, 4 = 4, 7 = 7.
- In Europe, dates appear as day/month/year, so Christmas 2021 is 25/12/2021.
- Commas are decimal points and decimals are commas. A dollar and a half is 1,50, one thousand is 1.000, and there are 5.280 feet in a mile.
- When counting with fingers, start with your thumb. If you hold up your first finger to request one item, you'll probably get two.
- What Americans call the second floor of a building is the first floor in Europe.
- On escalators and moving sidewalks, Europeans keep the left "lane" open for passing. Keep to the right.

Metric Conversions

A **kilogram** equals 1,000 grams (about 2.2 pounds). One hundred **grams** (a common unit at markets) is about a quarter-pound. One **liter** is about a quart, or almost four to a gallon.

A **kilometer** is six-tenths of a mile. To convert kilometers to miles, cut the kilometers in half and add back 10 percent of the original (120 km: 60 + 12 = 72 miles). One **meter** is 39 inches—just over a yard.

1 foot = 0.3 meter	1 square yard = 0.8 square meter
1 yard = 0.9 meter	1 square mile = 2.6 square kilometers
1 mile = 1.6 kilometers	1 ounce = 28 grams
1 centimeter = 0.4 inch	1 quart = 0.95 liter
1 meter = 39.4 inches	1 kilogram = 2.2 pounds
1 kilometer = 0.62 mile	32°F = 0°C

Clothing Sizes

When shopping for clothing, use these US-to-European compari-sons as general guidelines (but note that no conversion is perfect).

Women: For pants and dresses, add 32 in Croatia and Slove-nia (US 10 = Croatian 42). For blouses and sweaters, add 8 for most of Europe (US 32 = European 40). For shoes, add 30-31 (US 7 = European 37/38).

Men: For shirts, multiply by 2 and add about 8 (US 15 = Euro-pean 38). For jackets and suits, add 10. For shoes, add 32-34.

Children: Clothing is sized by height—in centimeters (2.5 cm = 1 inch), so a US size 8 roughly equates to 132-140. For shoes up to size 13, add 16-18, and for sizes 1 and up, add 30-32.

Climate

First line is the average daily high; second line, average daily low; third line, average days with rain. For more detailed weather statis-tics for destinations in this book (as well as the rest of the world), check www.wunderground.com.

	J	F	M	A	M	J	J	A	S	O	N	D
CROATIA • Dubrovnik												
	53°	55°	58°	63°	70°	78°	83°	82°	77°	69°	62°	56°
	42°	43°	57°	52°	58°	65°	69°	69°	64°	57°	51°	46°
	12	12	11	11	10	6	5	4	7	11	14	14
SLOVENIA • Ljubljana												
	36°	41°	50°	60°	68°	75°	80°	78°	71°	59°	47°	39°
	25°	25°	32°	40°	48°	54°	57°	57°	51°	43°	36°	30°
	7	7	7	9	10	9	6	6	6	7	9	9
BOSNIA-HERZEGOVINA • Sarajevo												
	36°	42°	52°	59°	68°	75°	79°	80°	73°	62°	48°	39°
	23°	25°	32°	38°	45°	51°	53°	53°	48°	41°	33°	27°
	9	9	12	15	15	13	11	11	12	12	12	11

Fahrenheit and Celsius Conversion

Europe takes its temperature using the Celsius scale, while we opt for Fahrenheit. For a rough conversion from Celsius to Fahrenheit, double the number and add 30. For weather, remember that 28°C is 82°F—perfect. For health, 37°C is just right. At a launderette, 30°C is cold, 40°C is warm (usually the default setting), 60°C is hot, and 95°C is boiling. Your air-conditioner should be set at about 20°C.

Packing Checklist

Whether you're traveling for five days or five weeks, you won't need more than this. Pack light to enjoy the sweet freedom of true mobility.

Clothing

☐ 5 shirts: long- & short-sleeve
☐ 2 pairs pants (or skirts/capris)
☐ 1 pair shorts
☐ 5 pairs underwear & socks
☐ 1 pair walking shoes
☐ Sweater or warm layer
☐ Rainproof jacket with hood
☐ Tie, scarf, belt, and/or hat
☐ Swimsuit
☐ Sleepwear/loungewear

Money

☐ Debit card(s)
☐ Credit card(s)
☐ Hard cash (US $100-200)
☐ Money belt

Documents

☐ Passport
☐ Tickets & confirmations: flights, hotels, trains, rail pass, car rental, sight entries
☐ Driver's license
☐ Student ID, hostel card, etc.
☐ Photocopies of important documents
☐ Insurance details
☐ Guidebooks & maps

Toiletries Kit

☐ Basics: soap, shampoo, toothbrush, toothpaste, floss, deodorant, sunscreen, brush/comb, etc.
☐ Medicines & vitamins
☐ First-aid kit
☐ Glasses/contacts/sunglasses
☐ Sewing kit
☐ Packet of tissues (for WC)
☐ Earplugs

Electronics

☐ Mobile phone
☐ Camera & related gear
☐ Tablet/ebook reader/laptop
☐ Headphones/earbuds
☐ Chargers & batteries
☐ Phone car charger & mount (or GPS device)
☐ Plug adapters

Miscellaneous

☐ Daypack
☐ Sealable plastic baggies
☐ Laundry supplies: soap, laundry bag, clothesline, spot remover
☐ Small umbrella
☐ Travel alarm/watch
☐ Notepad & pen
☐ Journal

Optional Extras

☐ Second pair of shoes (flip-flops, sandals, tennis shoes, boots)
☐ Travel hairdryer
☐ Picnic supplies
☐ Water bottle
☐ Fold-up tote bag
☐ Small flashlight
☐ Mini binoculars
☐ Small towel or washcloth
☐ Inflatable pillow/neck rest
☐ Tiny lock
☐ Address list (to mail postcards)
☐ Extra passport photos

Pronouncing Place Names

Remember that j is pronounced as "y," and c is pronounced "ts." For the special characters, č is "ch," š is "sh," ž is "zh," and đ is similar to "j."

Name	Pronounced
Bohinj	BOH-heen
Bovec	BOH-vets
Brijuni (Islands)	bree-YOO-nee
Brtonigla	bur-toh-NEEG-lah
Cavtat	TSAV-taht
Cetinje	TSEH-teen-yeh
Dubrovnik	doo-BROHV-nik
Grožnjan	grohzh-NYAHN
Herzegovina	hert-seh-GOH-vee-nah
Hum	hoom
Hvar	hvahr (or simply "far")
Istria	EE-stree-ah
Jadrolinija (Ferry Company)	yah-droh-LEE-nee-yah
Kobarid	KOH-bah-reed
Korčula	KOHR-choo-lah
Krka	KUR-kuh
Lipica (Lipizzaner Stud Farm)	LEE-peet-suh
Ljubljana	lyoob-lyee-AH-nah
Međugorje	medge-oo-gor-yeh
Mljet (National Park)	muhl-YET
Mostar	MOH-star
Motovun	moh-toh-VOON
Njeguši	NYEH-goo-shee
Opatija	oh-PAH-tee-yah
Otočac	OH-toh-chawts
Pelješac	PEHL-yeh-shahts
Piran	pee-RAHN
Plitvice (National Park)	PLEET-veet-seh
Polače	POH-lah-cheh
Pomena	POH-meh-nah

(continued on next page)

Pronouncing Place Names

(continued from previous page)

Name	Pronounced
Poreč	poh-RETCH
Postojna (Caves)	poh-STOY-nah
Predjama (Castle)	prehd-YAH-mah
Ptuj	puh-TOO-ey
Pula	POO-lah
Rab	Rob
Radovljica	rah-DOH-vleet-suh
Rijeka	ree-YAY-kah
Rovinj	roh-VEEN
Sarajevo	sah-rah-YEH-voh
Senj	sehn
Škocjan (Caves)	SHKOHTS-yahn
Soča (River Valley)	SOH-chah
Vršič (Pass)	vur-SHEECH
Zagreb	ZAH-grehb

INDEX

INDEX

MAP INDEX